THE WORLDS OF THOMAS JEFFERSON AT MONTICELLO

THE WORLDS OF
THOMAS JEFFERSON
AT MONTICELLO

Susan R. Stein

HARRY N. ABRAMS, INC., PUBLISHERS
in association with the
THOMAS JEFFERSON MEMORIAL FOUNDATION, INC.

For my family

Editor: Mark Greenberg
Designer: Dana Sloan

The exhibition and catalogue have been supported in part by the
National Endowment for the Humanities and the Pew Charitable Trusts.

Library of Congress Cataloging-in-Publication Data
Stein, Susan, 1949–
The worlds of Thomas Jefferson at Monticello / Susan R. Stein.
p.   cm.
Includes bibliographical references and index.
ISBN 0-8109-3967-3
1. Jefferson, Thomas, 1743–1826—Collectibles—Exhibitions.
2. Monticello (Va.)—Exhibitions.
I. Thomas Jefferson Memorial Foundation, Inc.
II. Title.
E332.2.S84 1993
973.4'6'092—dc20   92-27218
CIP

Published in 1993 by Harry N. Abrams, Incorporated, New York
A Times Mirror Company

Printed in Japan

PAGE 1:
Thomas Jefferson
Charles Fevret de Saint-Mémin (1770–1852)
engraving, D: 5.4 (2⅛ in.)
Thomas Jefferson Memorial Foundation

PAGES 2–3:
Monticello, the West Front
Photo: Robert Lautman

PAGE 5:
Mantle Clock
c. 1784–89
Gille l'Aine (active 1760–90), Paris
marble, gilt, and ormolu
73 × 32.4 × 17.1
(28¾ × 12¾ × 6¾ in.)

◆ Contents ◆

ADVISORY PANEL

Noble Cunningham

Daniel P. Jordan

Jean Lee

Jan Lewis

Frederick D. Nichols

Merrill D. Peterson

Kym S. Rice

Dell Upton

MONTICELLO STAFF MEMBERS
WHO CONTRIBUTED TO THE CATALOGUE:

William L. Beiswanger,
an architectural historian,
is director of restoration.

Ann Moore Lucas,
an architectural historian, is research fellow.

Susanne M. Olson,
an historian, is assistant curator.

M. Drake Patten,
an archaeologist, is archaeological lab supervisor.

Lucia C. Stanton,
an historian, is director of research.

Susan R. Stein,
an art historian, is curator.

◆ Acknowledgments ◆

Many people have contributed generously to the advancement of this project throughout its many months of preparation.

Several Monticello staff members, and especially the contributors to the catalogue, participated in many different ways. Ann Moore Lucas, research fellow, was unfailingly helpful. She managed to turn up new information and ideas regularly. Lucia C. Stanton, director of research, consulted often with Ann and me, fixing our mistakes and freely sharing her far greater knowledge of Jefferson and the Monticello plantation. Susanne M. Olson, assistant curator, worked particularly hard and made an exciting discovery about the maker of Jefferson's silver goblets. William L. Beiswanger, who has studied Monticello's architecture for a long time, was always willing to discuss any hypothesis.

Louise M. Lowe handled the intricacies of securing photographs with patience and efficiency. Robert Lautman made new photographs of Monticello, and Edward Owen shot most of the objects. George Sexton Associates designed the exhibition installation.

A corps of talented and energetic research assistants helped along the way: Elizabeth O'Leary, Ann Macon Smith, and Maurie D. McInnis deserve special mention. Kathleen Placidi, Anne B. Jamieson, Stacey Sell, and Joyce Robinson, graduate students in art history at the University of Virginia, completed research projects that proved useful. Elizabeth O'Halloran made it a practice to be indispensable.

Professors Merrill D. Peterson and Noble Cunningham, the eminent historians and biographers of Jefferson, S. Allen Chambers, Jan Lewis, Kym S. Rice, and Lucia C. Stanton, read the manuscript and did everything they could to correct my errors. What mistakes remain are my own.

Many colleagues and friends have graciously provided assistance: Ted Daeschler, The Academy of Natural Sciences of Philadelphia; Alan Stahl, American Numismatic Society; Silvio Bedini; Michael Wentworth, Boston Athenaeum; Graham Hood, Ronald Hurst, and Margaret Pritchard, Colonial Williamsburg Foundation, Inc.; David Cassidy and Janice Dockery, The Historical Society of Pennsylvania; Karen Jefferson and Dr. Thomas C. Battle, Moorland-Spingarn Research Center, Howard University; Heinrich-Th. Schulze Altcappenberg, Kunstmuseum Düsseldorf; Kenneth Finkel, The Library Company of Philadelphia; Ronald E. Grim, Katherine Engstrom, and C. Ford Peatross, Library of Congress; Lisa Royce, The Mariners' Museum; Anne Bentley and Chris Steele, Massachusetts Historical Society; Morrison H. Heckscher, The Metropolitan Museum of Art; Christine Meadows, Mount Vernon Ladies' Association; Martha Rowe and Whaley Batson, Museum of Early Southern Decorative Arts; Keith Melder and Cory Gillilland, National Museum of American History; Michael T. Wright, National Museum of Science and Industry, London; Dr. Ellen G. Miles and Wendy Wick Reaves, National Portrait Gallery; Wendy Shadwell, The New-York Historical Society; Roberta Waddell, The New York Public Library; Nancy Davis and Linnea Hamer, The Octagon Museum; Paul Lawrence Farber, Oregon State University; Genevieve Fisher, Kathleen Skelly, and Stephen Williams, Peabody Museum of Archaeology and Ethnology, Harvard University; Robert L. Self; Virginius R. Shackelford, Jr.; Michael Plunkett, Gregory Johnson, and William Runge, Alderman Library, University of Virginia; Dr. Jack A. Cranford, Virginia Museum of Natural History, Virginia Polytechnic Institute; Rosalind Savill, Wallace Collection; David Meschutt, West Point Museum; Bert Denker, Nancy Goyne Evans, Donald Fennimore, and Robert Trent, Winterthur Museum.

The Virginia Foundation for the Humanities, its director, Robert C. Vaughan, staff, and fellows, provided a congenial and supportive sanctuary for the preparation of the manuscript. The book reflects the serious concentration of an accomplished editor, Mark Greenberg, and a talented designer, Dana Sloan.

Two individuals not only genially tolerated my absence from other obligations but also encouraged me at every step: Daniel P. Jordan, executive director of the Thomas Jefferson Memorial Foundation, and Kenneth S. Abraham, my husband.

Susan R. Stein

✦ Foreword ✦

At the age of sixteen, in the first letter to have survived in his own hand, Jefferson argued for permission to enter the College of William and Mary on the basis of his desire to "get a more universal Acquaintance, which may hereafter be serviceable to me." The goal of "a more universal acquaintance" became a lifelong pursuit for the man sometimes called the American Leonardo. Monticello, his mountaintop home in Virginia, perhaps best personifies that quest in its reflection of the many elements of his genius.

The architecture of Monticello has long received serious attention, but only with this exhibition and catalogue have its *contents* received equal billing. The idea for the exhibition originated with Monticello's curator, Susan R. Stein, who wanted to return Jefferson's dispersed belongings to their original locations to honor the 250th anniversary of his birth. Hundreds of descendants and repositories worldwide were contacted by Ms. Stein and research fellow Ann Moore Lucas to locate works of art and artifacts. Their efforts were rewarded in a grand style, and Monticello has temporarily become more like the home Jefferson and his family knew than at any time since his death on July 4, 1826.

The exhibition could not have been possible without the outstanding generosity of the many lenders—institutions and individuals—who demonstrated a powerful sense of civic responsibility by sharing their treasures with us. The positive responses to Monticello's requests has been astonishing. Our gratitude to each lender cannot be measured, but two colleagues deserve special recognition. Roger Kennedy, director of the National Museum of American History, gave a gratifying word of early endorsement and agreed to lend America's most significant political icon, the lap desk upon which Jefferson wrote the Declaration of Independence. Louis L. Tucker, director of the Massachusetts Historical Society, graciously promised several key works from its collection, including portraits of Washington, Lafayette, Columbus, and Vespucci that originally hung in the Parlor. *The Worlds of Thomas Jefferson at Monticello* also benefitted from the support of the National Endowment for the Humanities.

Building upon the important *Eye of Thomas Jefferson*, the National Gallery of Art's 1976 exhibition and book, *The Worlds of Thomas Jefferson at Monticello* provides a definitive assessment of Jefferson as a collector and consumer, and reveals fresh angles of vision on his private, public, and universal worlds at Monticello. The book explains what Jefferson acquired and why, as well as how it all fits into the larger cultural history of the early Republic.

The catalogue and exhibition are part of an international commemoration of the anniversary of Jefferson's birth. The Thomas Jefferson Memorial Foundation, which has owned and operated Monticello since 1923, hopes that the commemoration will become a way for people the world over to gain "a more universal acquaintance" with the historical Thomas Jefferson as well as with his enduring interests, values, ideals, and political principles—a legacy well captured in *The Worlds of Thomas Jefferson at Monticello*.

Daniel P. Jordan
Executive Director
Thomas Jefferson Memorial Foundation

THE WORLDS OF
THOMAS JEFFERSON AT MONTICELLO

In the years between 1769 and 1809, Thomas Jefferson (1743–1826) created an extraordinary house and plantation near Charlottesville, in central Virginia. The house, which he named "Monticello" (Italian for "little mountain"), still stands on the pastoral mountaintop where it was ornamented by elaborate gardens and surrounded by working farms. Jefferson's far-reaching intellect and nearly limitless curiosity were reflected in the worlds he forged there. As early as 1782 the uniqueness of the man and of the place were readily apparent to a visitor to Monticello, the marquis de Chastellux, a French nobleman who had fought in the American Revolutionary War:

Mr. Jefferson is the first American who has consulted the Fine Arts to know how he should shelter himself from the weather . . . an American who, without ever having quitted his own country, is Musician, Draftsman, Surveyor, Astronomer, Natural Philosopher, Jurist, and Statesman . . .[1]

Monticello's extremely crowded interior eventually became as remarkable as its columned, Neoclassical exterior and the man who occupied it. Soon after Chastellux visited, Jefferson went abroad, and while there as American minister to the court of Louis XVI he shopped for a lifetime. When he returned from France in 1789, he brought back an abundance of furniture, china, silverware, fabrics, portraits, and many other examples of French decorative art. Virtually all made its way to Monticello, where it became part of the eclectic collection of copies of Old Master paintings, sculpture, musical and scientific instruments, North American Indian artifacts, portraits, furnishings, and decorative arts acquired over a period of fifty years. Monticello, even in Jefferson's time, was a museum and laboratory as well as a home. Its contents reflected the diversity of his interests and his experiences on both sides of the Atlantic.

After Jefferson died on July 4, 1826—the fiftieth anniversary of the Declaration of Independence—his daughter and heir, Martha Jefferson Randolph (1772–1836), was compelled to sell Monticello and much of its contents, the surrounding farms, and most of its slaves to pay her father's debts. A Dispersal Sale, held in January 1827, scattered Jefferson's possessions among numerous buyers, chiefly from Albemarle and neighboring counties, and the members of his family. A great many of the objects that formed the contents of Jefferson's Monticello, however, still survive. Since the Thomas Jefferson Memorial Foundation took title to Monticello in 1923, it has acquired a large number of these objects. Many that are now privately owned or in museum collections have been

Thomas Jefferson (1743–1826)
*1856 copy by Sully after 1821
original life portrait
Thomas Sully (1783–1872)
oil on canvas, 87.6 × 69.9
(34½ × 27½ in.)
Thomas Jefferson Memorial
Foundation*

The United States Military
Academy at West Point
commissioned a portrait from
Thomas Sully in 1821.
Jefferson thought the trouble
of Sully's journey to Monticello
"illy bestowed on an ottamy
[skeleton] of 78."

East Front
Margaret Bayard Smith, 1809:

"The principal front looks to
the east, on an open country,
and is adorned with a noble
portico . . ."

Marquis de Chastellux
(1734–1788)

1782
Charles Willson Peale
(1741–1827)
oil on canvas, 57.6×51
(22¹¹/₁₆×20 in.)
Independence National
Historical Park Collection,
Philadelphia

The marquis de Chastellux
arrived at Monticello in 1782
on Jefferson's thirty-ninth
birthday. He published his
impressions of his visit in
Travels in North-America in the
Years 1780, 1781, and 1782,
published in Paris in 1786.

returned to Monticello for the exhibition "The Worlds of Thomas Jefferson at Monticello," which celebrates the 250th anniversary of Jefferson's birth. Of the objects that have not survived, a large number are known through the rich accounts of a seemingly endless flow of visitors to Monticello during Jefferson's time, as well as through several drawings, letters to and from Jefferson, and the records of purchases that he faithfully noted in his copiously detailed Memorandum Books.[2]

This essay describes and interprets the worlds that Jefferson built at Monticello through the design of his house and his enduring effort to furnish and decorate it. Jefferson's Monticello is woven out of both American self-confidence and an absorption with the arts of eighteenth-century France; of both untutored innocence of taste and remarkable sophistication. It is, in short, not the story of a single world but of the series of worlds that Jefferson made at Monticello for himself and for so many who have come after him.

◆ Setting the Stage ◆

Jefferson was influenced by both the ideal rural villas of antiquity and by eighteenth-century French Neoclassical and Anglo-Palladian architecture. He was widely read in the traditional, classical literature of architecture and shared the earlier vision of Richard Boyle, the third earl of Burlington, of an "architectural mission to revive and perpetuate a body of inherited wisdom from Vitruvian antiquity."[1] Jefferson's interest in classical architecture was but a part of his wider classical education, which itself was the product of the Age of Enlightenment, the period of intellectual excitement and optimism dominated by faith in rational thought and in the ability and intelligence of man. The eminent scholar and Jefferson biographer Merrill Peterson wrote:

The controlling assumptions of enlightened thought were so thoroughly assimilated in Jefferson's mind that he cannot possibly be understood apart from them. First, untrammeled free inquiry in the pursuit of knowledge. Nothing was to be taken for granted; everything was to be questioned, taken apart, traced back to its origins, and reconstructed in the light of intelligence.[2]

Jefferson developed a special appreciation for Epicurus, the fourth-century B.C. Athenian whose doctrines held "everything rational in moral philosophy which Greece and Rome have left us."[3]

Jefferson's library was one of the largest in America, and in 1815 it became the nucleus of the Library of Congress. The very organization of that library reflected Jefferson's classical education, the breadth of his interests, and his passion for order. It was organized into three "classes"—History, Philosophy, and the Fine Arts—which reflected the faculties of the mind—Memory, Reason, and Imagination.[4] As one of the Fine Arts, architecture was grouped with gardening, painting, sculpture, music, poetry, oratory, and criticism.

Jefferson had begun to collect architectural books as early as 1772.[5] His first purchase was James Gibbs's *Book of Architecture* (1728), which he bought in Williamsburg while a student at the College of William and Mary. Gibbs (1682–1754) was a decided Palladian, "the first British architect to publish a book devoted entirely to his own designs (independent of the orders) . . ."[6] His book was specifically directed at gentlemen and builders located in distant places where trained architects were unavailable. It was known in Virginia, where one of his designs was the source for John Tayloe's Mount Airy (1758–62) in tidewater Virginia. Jefferson's earliest designs for Monticello show Gibbs's influence.

Jefferson's architectural collection included five editions— three in English and two in French—of Palladio's *Quattro Libri*. He was reported to have referred to it simply as "the Bible."[7] Andrea Palladio, the sixteenth-century Italian who rekindled the classical architectural tradition, undoubtedly shaped what Jefferson knew of architecture. However, Jefferson proved to be no slavish copyist of Palladio. He was innovative and eager to combine a variety of architectural ideas and sources and merge them with his own notions. His lifelong experimentation with architecture, with Monticello as his laboratory, reveals two facets of his complex character: the influence of the larger world upon him and his determination to influence that world.

Jefferson spent most of his adult life designing and redesigning Monticello. He wrote, "Architecture is my delight, and putting up, and pulling down, one of my favorite amusements."[8] From his father, Peter Jefferson (1707/08–1757)—one of the surveyors who first mapped the complete Virginia–North Carolina dividing line with Joshua Fry in 1749— Jefferson inherited sizable property in Albemarle County when he came of age in 1764. He selected a parcel, which he named "Monticello," for the site of his new home. In May 1768, at the age of twenty-five, he began to level the already gentle top of the 987-foot-high mountain. A fire destroyed the Jefferson family home at Shadwell and left only a few books and bedsteads untouched. Following that, Jefferson moved to a small one-room mountain-top dwelling, which may have been what is now Monticello's south pavilion. He wrote to his friend James Ogilvie in 1771:

I have lately removed to the mountain . . . I have here but one room which, like the coblers,' serves me for parlour, for kitchen and hall. I may add, for bed chamber and study too. My friends sometimes take a temperate dinner with me and then retire to look for beds elsewhere. I have hope, however, of getting more elbow room this summer.[9]

But when he returned to Monticello after his marriage to Martha Wayles Skelton in 1772, only the same small dwelling was habitable. Martha, the beloved wife of ten years who bore him six children, was never to know the completed structure.

The first Monticello, an ambitious and sophisticated enterprise by any American standard, was much the product of the architecture that Jefferson had studied in his books. Its front has been likened to Palladio's Villa Pisani, which Jefferson knew through Leoni's edition of Palladio's *Quattro Libri*.[10] Sources for the final design of the first Monticello have also been cited as a combination of the "two level central porticos of the Villa Cornaro at

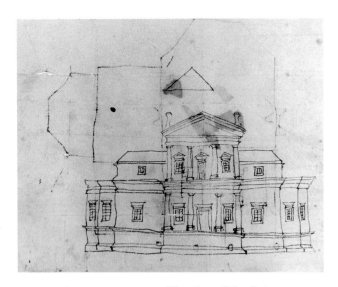

Elevation of the first Monticello

1769–70
Thomas Jefferson
ink on paper, 11.4 × 14
(4½ × 5½ in.)
Thomas Jefferson Memorial Foundation

Jefferson's design for the first Monticello was heavily influenced by architectural books, in particular Andrea Palladio's *Quattro Libri*.

Piombinio Dese with the flanking elevations of the Villa Saraceno at Finale from Palladio's *Quattro libri*, [and] the Doric details are derived from another of Gibbs's books, *Rules for drawing the several Parts of Architecture* (1732)."[11]

Several plans of Robert Morris (c. 1702–1754), illustrated in his *Select Architecture* (1755) and acquired by Jefferson in 1770 or 1771, also served as sources for the first Monticello. Morris, the author of at least four architectural books, also contributed to the popular *Modern Builder's Assistant* (1757) by William and John Halfpenny. Modern scholars call Morris the "outstanding theoretical writer of the first half of the eighteenth century."[12] Jefferson seems to have been inspired by two of Morris's schemes: Plate 37, "A Little Building intended for Retirement," which shows a cruciform plan with a two-story main axis and single-story wings, and Plate 2, which shows a projecting octagonal room at the rear.[13]

The resulting highly imaginative design, which called upon Jefferson's knowledge of ancient, Renaissance, and contemporary architecture, was a far cry from the predictable Georgian and vernacular architecture of the colonies. Baron von Closen, a visitor, remarked:

The house was built quite recently, in the latest Italian *style. There is a colonnade around the structure and the frieze is very charmingly decorated with all kinds of sculptures drawn from mythology.*[14]

The most revealing comment of this early period was that of the marquis de Chastellux. He seemed to write as much about what Monticello was intended to become as about how it actually appeared at the time.

The ground floor consists chiefly of a large and lofty salon, *or drawing room, which is to be decorated entirely in the antique style; above the* salon *is a library of the same form.*[15]

Comparatively little is known about the works of art and objects that furnished Monticello before Jefferson departed for France in 1784. Few of these objects have survived, and the small number of visitors who compiled descriptions commented mainly about the ambitious architectural scheme and the accomplishments of their host rather than about the works of art or furnishings. Yet the very first known description of Monticello by someone other than Jefferson—an account by a German officer incarcerated in the barracks outside Charlottesville—mentions books, music, and architecture.[16] Jacob Rubsamen, a Virginian, translated the account and sent it to Jefferson in December 1780. Rubsamen wrote that Jefferson had "a Copious and well chosen Library . . . an elegant building . . . an Elegant harpsichord piano forte and some Violins."[17]

Whatever the precise contents of Monticello before 1785, it seems fairly clear that the beginnings of its special character were there: the library, musical instruments, and the remarkably designed structure that would house them and their owner. Although it was unrealized at that moment, Jefferson also had an art collection in mind, based on the great works of the ancient world.

◆ Loss and Change ◆

The art of life is the art of avoiding pain: and he is the best pilot who
steers clearest of the rocks and shoals with which it is beset. Pleasure is
always before us; but misfortune is at our side: while running after that,
this arrests us. The most effectual means of being secure against pain is
to retire within ourselves, and to suffice for our own happiness.

—Thomas Jefferson
to Maria Cosway, October 12, 1786

After Martha Jefferson died on September 6, 1782, Jefferson was inconsolable. She
had borne him six children in ten years but died before she had reached her thirty-fourth
birthday. For three weeks Jefferson kept to his own room, with his young daughter Martha,
who was then ten, at his side. He wrote two months later to the marquis de Chastellux that
his recent letter had

*found me a little emerging from that stupor of mind which had rendered me as dead to the world as
she was whose loss occasioned it. . . . Before that event my scheme of life had been determined. I
had folded myself in the arms of retirement, and rested all prospects of future happiness on
domestic and literary objects. A single event wiped away all my plans and left me a blank which I
had not the spirits to fill up.*[1]

Of Martha, relatively little is known; no portraits of her survive. Family accounts
report that she was gentle, attractive, played the harpsichord and pianoforte, shared a love
of Laurence Sterne's *Tristam Shandy* with Jefferson, and helped manage a busy plantation.
Isaac, the slave whose graphic memories of Monticello were recorded after Jefferson's
death, said that "Mrs. Jefferson was small . . . Polly [Maria] low like her mother and
longways the handsomest, pretty lady just like her mother."[2] When Jefferson met her,

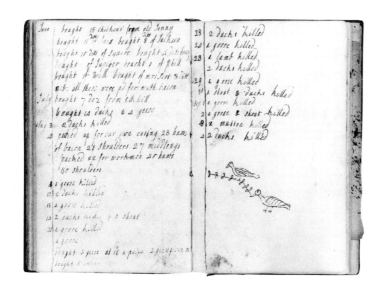

Martha Wayles Jefferson's
Account Book

*February 10, 1772 to April 25,
1782*
*Martha Wayles Jefferson
(1748–1782)*
Library of Congress

In her account book Jefferson's
wife, Martha, recorded
plantation transactions such as
slaughtering ducks, preserving
pork, and trading bacon to the
slave "old Jenny" for
chickens.

Bell used by Martha
Wayles Jefferson

*wood, bronze?, 8.9 × 6.4
(3½ × 2½ in.)
Moorland-Spingarn Research
Center, Howard University*

According to Hemings family
tradition, Martha Wayles
Jefferson kept this bell by her
bedside during her last illness
and used it to summon her
servants. After her death the
bell was given to nine-year-old
Sally Hemings, who had
assisted her mother, Betty, in
Mrs. Jefferson's care.

probably in Williamsburg in the fall of 1770, she was the widow of Bathurst Skelton and the mother of a young son. She was then living at The Forest, her father John Wayles's plantation in Charles City County, west of Williamsburg. The summer before her wedding to Jefferson on January 1, 1772, her son died at just under four years old.

Much of her life, like those of many women of her time, was devoted to loss, bereavement, and the attempt to repress the powerful emotions associated with death.[3] Her mother, of the influential Eppes family, died just after her birth, and her father was widowed twice more. She gave birth to seven children, but only three were alive at her death and only two would live to adulthood. Few reminders survive to recall Mrs. Jefferson's life: several silver spoons bearing the initials $\frac{S}{BM}$ several locks of hair, and a layette pincushion sewn while she was expecting her daughter Martha.

Like many other plantation mistresses, Mrs. Jefferson played an important role in supervising the estate's diverse operations and activities. It was essential for her to be generally informed about sewing, spinning, weaving, cooking, brewing, raising fowl, dairying, preserving many kinds of food, educating children, and caring for the sick. She apparently tried to be as fastidious a record keeper as her spouse and kept an account of her farm-related ventures for ten years—nearly the duration of her marriage—between February 1772 and April 1782. Her notes reveal the breadth and variety of her participation in the management of the Monticello plantation. She noted the important undertakings associated with her responsibilities, which ranged from the opening of a barrel of flour to the slaughter of pullets, turkeys, hogs, sheep, and lambs; soap and candle making; purchasing coffee, butter, and loaves of sugar; recording the dates on which the Muscovy ducks began to lay eggs and when the first patch of peas came to table in 1774.

Mrs. Jefferson was probably also responsible for the slaves (Jefferson called them "household servants") assigned to the house and for the work that they accomplished: cleaning, laundry, cooking, serving, and many other household tasks. The valuable ceramics and silver at most plantations were stored in locked closets, cupboards, butler's secretaries, or sideboards and would have required the plantation mistress's key before and after meals. It also would have been typical for a mistress such as Mrs. Jefferson to confer with the cook to discuss available food supplies and menus, and she was often in the company of her own maid, as well as the slaves who tended to poultry, dairy, smokehouse, and laundry.

In every sense Jefferson's loss of his wife and his profound unhappiness after her death paved the way for his participation in public life over the next twenty-seven years. His willingness to leave Albemarle County for long periods would not have been fathomable had she been alive. In 1784, Jefferson was appointed a minister plenipotentiary, joining John Adams and Benjamin Franklin, to negotiate treaties of amity and commerce with Louis XVI. When Jefferson arrived in Paris later that year, his world changed dramatically. Ultimately, that change would not only influence Jefferson but would transform Monticello as well.

Before Jefferson's journey to Europe, his firsthand knowledge of the larger world was confined to America. He had briefly toured Philadelphia in 1766 and lived there intermittently in 1775 and 1776 while a delegate to the Continental Congress. As a representative to the Confederation Congress, he resided in Annapolis in 1783 and 1784. Otherwise, Jefferson had largely remained in Virginia until he was just past forty. When he was appointed minister plenipotentiary to France by Congress on May 7, 1784, he did not return home from Annapolis.[4] Rather, he made arrangements for his two youngest daughters, Mary and Lucy Elizabeth, then six and two, to remain with their aunt Elizabeth Wayles Eppes (Martha Wayles Jefferson's half-sister) and her husband, Francis, at Eppington, in Chesterfield County. He then met his oldest daughter, Martha, in Philadelphia and departed for New York and Boston. They were joined by James Hemings, a mulatto slave, whom Jefferson referred to as a "servant."

En route to Boston, Jefferson stopped in New Haven to meet Ezra Stiles, the president of Yale College, who described him as "a most ingenious Naturalist and Philosopher, a truly scientific and learned Man, and every way excellent."[5] Their conversation, which covered topics ranging from Jefferson's new role as minister plenipotentiary with Adams and Franklin, to the salaries of professors, largely focused on "the great Bones dug up on the Ohio."[6] Obviously in preparation for refuting the arguments of the comte de Buffon— "the celebrated Physiologist of the present age, who has advanced a theory in general very degrading to America"—Jefferson asked Stiles about the "Animal Incognitum" or what the Russians called the "mammoth."[7] Stiles replied, citing numerous examples of bones and teeth of extinct large creatures found throughout Europe, Asia, and New York State. The discussion with Stiles indicated how important the study of mastodon bones was to Jefferson's defense of the North American continent and its species.

Jefferson took his new role as a commercial envoy seriously. Jefferson, "Patsy" (as Martha was called), and Hemings journeyed through Hartford, New London, Newport, and Providence before arriving in Boston. The days in New England were well spent. Jefferson assembled dossiers on Connecticut, Rhode Island, Massachusetts, and New Hampshire, recording facts about the price of labor, shipbuilding, navigation, exports, imports, manufactures, and the amount of debt to Great Britain before setting sail on the *Ceres.* There followed a peaceful crossing, an arduous landing on the British coast (instead of Brest in France), and a rough trip across the English Channel.

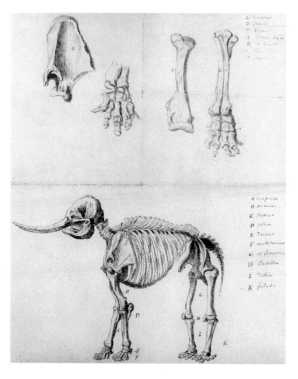

Mastodon Skeleton

1801
Rembrandt Peale (1778–1860)
ink on paper, 38.7 × 32.1
(15¼ × 12⅝ in.)
The American Philosophical Society

Charles Willson Peale mounted the first mastodon skeleton in his Philadelphia Museum in 1801. His son Rembrandt's drawing was used as a guide for the difficult task of arranging the bones.

◆ A New Horizon: Jefferson in Paris ◆

When Jefferson arrived in Paris on August 6, 1784, his world was transformed.[1] He had left behind a rural Virginia landscape punctuated by what he considered unmistakably crude buildings, described in *Notes on the State of Virginia* (Paris 1785; London 1787) as ugly, uncomfortable, and perishable.[2] The fire at Shadwell had certainly demonstrated to him the vulnerability of buildings constructed in wood. The architecture of London, which Jefferson thought "the most wretched stile I ever saw, not meaning to except America where it is bad, nor even Virginia where it is worse than in any other part of America," could compare to what he knew at home.[3] In Williamsburg, then the capital of Virginia, he remarked:

The College and Hospital are rude, mis-shapen piles, which, but that they have roofs, would be taken for brick-kilns. . . . The genius of architecture seems to have shed its maledictions over this land.[4]

But in Paris he found a cityscape of grandeur and excitement.[5] He first stayed in lodgings near the Palais Royal, recently remodeled by the duc d'Orléans, or "Philippe-Egalité," and the focus of Parisian life. Jefferson became a frequent visitor to the Palais

Construction of the Hôtel de Salm

c. 1786
oil on canvas, 56.5 × 101
(22¼ × 39¾ in.)
Musée Carnavalet, Paris

Jefferson observed the completion of the Hôtel de Salm, designed by Pierre Rousseau, during his time in Paris. He recommended its two fronts as models for new buildings in the United States.

Royal, an architectural arena containing six restaurants, shops selling all sorts of choice goods, a theater and theatrical company, a waxworks, a chess parlor, and galleries containing Old Masters, medals, and natural-history specimens. Always motivated by what might benefit America, Jefferson thought that the idea of the Palais Royal, ". . . which has greatly enriched the owner of the ground, has added one of the principal ornaments to the city and increased the convenience of the inhabitants," might serve as a model for Shockoe Hill in Richmond.[6]

The contrast between Paris and the young cities of the New World must have been striking, and nothing conveyed the contrast more dramatically than Parisian architecture. Paris, in fact, was undergoing a series of important changes that would continue to transform it during Jefferson's stay there. A new wall around the city, called the Wall of the Farmers-General, punctuated by elegant tollhouses designed by the visionary architect Claude-Nicolas Ledoux, was begun in the 1780s. Although these Neoclassical gatehouses were imaginative interpretations of Palladio's designs and were seen as emblems of the new architecture, they were also notoriously unpopular symbols of the country's oppressive taxation and financial problems that were to cause the political unrest that lay ahead. Major changes had also occurred to the bridges crossing the Seine, especially the tearing down of the dwellings that lined the Pont au Change and the Pont Notre-Dame, thus providing an unobstructed view. Jefferson thought much of the advancements and wrote:

I will observe to you that wonderful improvements are making here in various lines. In architecture the wall of circumvallation round Paris and the palaces by which we are to be let in and let out are nearly compleated, 4 hospitals are to be built instead of the old hotel-dieu, one of the old bridges has all it's houses demolished and a second nearly so, a new bridge is begun at the Place Louis XV.[7]

Jefferson was especially interested in the new architecture that surrounded him. New buildings included not only the remodeled Palais Royal but also the Halle aux Bleds (the grain market) with its stunning dome; various churches, including the Madeleine and Soufflot's Sainte-Geneviève (now the Panthéon); and an astonishing number of residences in the Chaussée d'Antin and Faubourg du Roule as well as substantial building in other, generally older quarters. Among the new residences was the Hôtel de Salm, located facing the Seine, whose dome thoroughly captured Jefferson's imagination and which was to influence his later design for Monticello. He wrote to Madame de Tessé (Adrienne-Catherine de Noailles), the aunt of Lafayette's wife and his dear friend:

While at Paris, I was violently smitten with the hotel de Salm, and used to go to the Thuileries almost daily to look at it. The loueuse des chaises, inattentive to my passion, never had the complaisance to place a chair there; so that, sitting on the parapet, and twisting my neck round to see the object of my admiration, I generally left it with a torticollis.[8]

Paris was not alone in stimulating his architectural imagination. On a trip through France in 1787, he at last saw for himself the first-century A.D. Roman temple, the Maison Carrée, at Nîmes. He called it "the best morsel of antient architecture now remaining" two years after he had used what he knew of it from afar as the basis for his design of the Virginia

The Maison Carrée, the Arena and the Tour Magne at Nîmes

1787
Hubert Robert (1733–1808)
oil on canvas, 243 × 244
(95¹¹⁄₁₆ × 96¹⁄₁₆ in.)
Musée du Louvre, Paris

Jefferson admired the Maison Carrée on his journey through southern France in the spring of 1787. Later that year he saw Robert's series of Roman monuments in France, which included the Maison Carrée, in the Salon at the Louvre.

State Capitol.[9] Jefferson had hired the architect Charles-Louis Clérisseau to make measured drawings of the Maison Carrée, although there is some debate about the degree of Clérisseau's involvement in the Capitol project.[10] At the very least he had drafted an extensive series of drawings for Jefferson in 1786 and may have played an even larger role. In any case, Jefferson thought very highly of Clérisseau and thought carefully about selecting an appropriate gift for him. His first choice, which he later had made for himself, was a copy of a Roman pouring vessel called an "askos" that had been excavated at Nîmes (Cat. 185); but he finally decided on a coffee urn made from his own design (Cat. 182).

The treatment of light was one of the features of French architecture of the eighteenth century that diverged most from the New World norm. Many Virginia buildings were dark and ill lighted, causing Jefferson to comment that "The only public buildings worthy [of] mention are the Capitol, the Palace, the College, and the Hospital for Lunatics, all of them in Williamsburg, heretofore the seat of our government."[11] The Capitol was the only one that qualified as "a light and airy structure."[12] In contrast, both French palaces and private dwellings boasted large, tall windows such as those found at the Hôtel de Villeroy where Madame de Tessé lived on the rue de Varenne.[13]

Late-eighteenth-century French architects, like those everywhere in Europe, were employing several devices to increase available light within buildings. Mirrors, as well as white or light-colored painting or decorative gilding on wall surfaces, heightened the amount of interior light. The great Hall of Mirrors at Versailles epitomized the ideal. American residences and public buildings, however, characteristically had smaller windows, fewer and more modestly sized mirrors, and wall surfaces without gilding. The end result, even in the most impressive American structures, was darker and more spare.

Jefferson's frequent visits to the Hôtel de Villeroy and to the homes of many other friends and colleagues afforded him ample opportunity to observe not only the way people lived but also how architecture served their needs. Among the dwellings that Jefferson knew well was the less-imposing house, "where all is beautiful," of his close friends the Cornys, who lived in the Chaussée d'Antin.[14] He often visited the Hôtel de La Rochefoucauld and its garden in the rue de Seine, home of the duc de La Rochefoucauld-Liancourt, who had translated the *Constitutions des Treize Etats-Unis de l'Amérique*. Jefferson also traveled to Benjamin Franklin's expansive residence in Passy, the Hôtel de Valentinois, which had been lent to Franklin by Le Ray de Chaumont. Franklin occupied a wing or pavilion that faced the Seine with uncommon views of the Ecole Militaire and the church of Sainte-Geneviève.[15] Not very far away in Auteuil was the Hôtel de Rouhault, John and Abigail Adams's residence for about a year, distant from what Adams called the "putrid streets of Paris."[16]

The Paris of the late eighteenth century was a far cry from the wide-boulevarded city created by Baron Haussmann in the nineteenth century. It was a curious composite of what remained of medieval Paris—narrow dwellings, twisting streets—and the modernization characterized by varying forms of Neoclassicism from the seventeenth century onward. What John Adams said about the streets of Paris undoubtedly was true. The largely unpaved roads, crowded with people, animals, carts, and carriages, were notoriously difficult to traverse after a rain. Sanitation, without proper sewage and water systems, left much to be desired, as it did in all cities of the day. Jefferson merely said that ". . . our streets are somewhat dirty."[17]

What transpired on these streets, at least at the outset of his stay, made more of an impression on the high-minded Jefferson. Although his later high opinion of Parisian life and the French differed substantially from what he penned in November 1784, just a few months after his arrival, his remarks indicate disdain and disapproval of the prostitutes he saw on street corners:

It is difficult for young men to refuse it where beauty is a begging in every street. Indeed from what I have seen here I know not one good purpose on earth which can be effected by a young gentleman's coming here. He may learn indeed to speak the language, but put this in the scale against the other things he will learn and evils he is sure to acquire and it will be found too light. I have always disapproved of a European education for our youth from theory: I now do it from inspection.[18]

The English painter and satirist William Hogarth, whose *Harlot's Progress* (1731) and *Rake's Progress* (1735) were well known in America, had no doubt already familiarized Jefferson with the seamier side of urban life.

Jefferson's success in establishing himself—personally and diplomatically—soon overshadowed the sentiments he had earlier expressed about life in Paris. A circle of friends that included Americans, British, and French stimulated him: Benjamin Franklin; the marquis de Lafayette; John and Abigail Adams; John Trumbull, the American artist; Angelica Schuyler Church, the sister-in-law of Alexander Hamilton; William Short, Jefferson's private secretary and protégé; Richard and Maria Cosway, the British artists; Monsieur and Madame Ethis de Corny; Madame de Tessé; Madame Sophie-Ernestine de Tott, an aspiring artist and the daughter of the baron de Tott.

Many of these new friends encouraged Jefferson's interest in the arts. In Madame de Tessé, he found agreeable, clever companionship. Her niece said that she was in every respect a remarkable person, with "an imposing air, grace and dignity in all her movements, and above all, [she was] infinitely witty."

She was one of those ladies of the Old Regime, captivated by the philosophical ideas of the century, and intoxicated by the seductive innovations which were to bring about, in their eyes, the regeneration and happiness of our country. In a word, she was a liberal and a philosopher. In philosophy, Voltaire, with whom she was closely connected, was her master; in politics, M. de La Fayette, her nephew, was her hero.[19]

She shared Jefferson's passion for the fine arts, politics, and horticulture. The stylish gardens at her country estate, called Chaville (also a Crown property, like the Hôtel de Villeroy on the rue de Varenne), on the road to Versailles, were renowned. In fact, in 1786

Jefferson placed a huge order for thirty-four kinds of seeds and seventeen different plants, including four types of magnolia, with John Bartram in Philadelphia for the garden at Chaville. In 1792, after the Revolution had forced the de Tessés to vacate their property, André Thouin, chief gardener of the Jardin National, collected 148 species for the state; among these were many American specimens given to the de Tessés by Jefferson.[20]

The villa itself at Chaville had been designed by Etienne-Louis Boullée in 1764. Here Madame de Tessé frequently held salons where she entertained Jefferson and other friends. These included Madame de Tott, Lafayette, Gouverneur Morris, and others. But it was Madame de Tessé who was closest to Jefferson; together they shared a love of the ancient past. On his visit to Nîmes in 1787, Jefferson wrote her:

From Lyons to Nismes I have been nourished with the remains of Roman grandeur. They have always brought you to mind, because I know your affection for whatever is Roman and noble . . . I thought of you again, and I was then in great good humour, at the Pont du Gard, a sublime antiquity, and [well] preserved . . . Loving, as you do Madam, the precious remains of antiquity, loving architecture, gardening, a warm sun, and a clear sky, I wonder you have never thought of moving Chaville to Nismes.[21]

Madame de Tessé presented Jefferson, prior to his return to America in 1789, with a remarkable broken green-marble column decorated with the ten lost tribes of Israel and the twelve signs of the zodiac and bearing a Latin inscription that, loosely translated, reads:

To the Supreme Ruler of the Universe, under whose watchful care the liberties of N. America were finally achieved, and under whose tutelage the name of Thomas Jefferson will descend forever blessed to posterity.[22]

The column, later placed in Monticello's Entrance Hall, held a bust of Jefferson by Giuseppe Ceracchi.

Hôtel de Langeac

Jefferson's own house in Paris was the superb Hôtel de Langeac, where he resided from the autumn of 1785 until his return to America in 1789.[23] Demolished in 1842, the house was located at the corner of the Champs-Elysées and the rue de Berri, adjoining the Grille de Chaillot, just inside the city gates. Jefferson was fortunate to secure such splendid accommodations. The hôtel, which was virtually new, had been designed by the architect Jean-F. T. Chalgrin in 1768 for the marquise de Langeac, the mistress of the comte de Saint-Florentin. After she was banished from Paris when Louis XVI ascended to the throne in 1774, work on the hôtel was suspended. The property was conveyed to the comte d'Artois in 1777, but the marquise's son, the comte de Langeac, recovered it one year later and construction continued. Finances forced him to sell part of the estate in 1780, and to lease the remainder to Jefferson for an annual rent of 7,500 livres.

Although Jefferson described it to Abigail Adams without

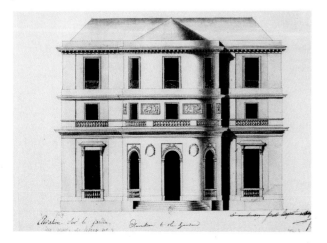

Hôtel de Langeac, Elevation

c. 1780

ink on paper, 33.7 × 27.5 (13¼ × 10⅞ in.)

Bibliothèque Nationale, Paris

The garden front of Jefferson's residence in Paris from 1785 until 1789.

great enthusiasm except for the "clever garden," the Hôtel de Langeac was unquestionably grand.[24] Chalgrin, a popular architect, had also designed the church of Saint-Philippe-du-Roule with its Roman basilica plan, only a short distance from the Hôtel de Langeac; the Hôtel de La Vrillière; the north tower of Saint-Sulpice; and the Arc de Triomphe. Drawings of the Hôtel de Langeac still survive at the Bibliothèque Nationale in Paris. They reveal an interesting plan for the main floor that shows a circular room with a skylight, an oval salon with three bays projecting toward an ornamental garden, and a dining room and *petit salon* facing the Champs-Elysées. A large courtyard with an entrance on the rue de Berri led to the house on one side and an extensive compound of servant's quarters, stables, and outbuildings on the other. Both house and service wing were embraced on one side by ornamental gardens in the fashionable, meandering "English" style; the site also contained a sizable kitchen garden.

The interior treatment of the Hôtel de Langeac was quite splendid, undoubtedly enhanced by light, painted finishes ornamented with gilding, and many mirrors. Jefferson brought seven of these mirrors back to America in 1790. The artist Jean-Simon Berthélemy decorated the ceiling of the oval salon with a painting of the rising sun that even was mentioned in Thiery's *Guide des amateurs et des étrangers vagageurs à Paris* (1787).[25]

Jefferson felt compelled to make certain that his accommodations at least minimally befitted his ministerial rank. The expenses, nonetheless, were surprisingly high. He thought it more economical to purchase furniture rather than pay 40 percent a year to lease it, and wrote, "Perhaps it may be thought reasonable to allow me an outfit [household furnishings]. The usage of every other nation has established this, and reason really pleads for it. I do not wish to make a shilling, but only to be defrayed and in a moderate style."[26]

Shopping for a Lifetime

Although Jefferson did get off to a slow start, his numerous purchases during his years in France, which he termed "moderate," ultimately were anything but that. As he initially put together his household, he assembled, for the most part, only the necessary accoutrements. These purchases, noted in his Memorandum Books, included linen for sheets and tablecloths, many pairs of candlesticks, andirons, wood, a coal grate, mattresses, blankets, stoves, carpets, kitchen utensils, lanterns, a coffee mill, teapots, and other necessities.

A close examination of all of Jefferson's French household acquisitions, from kitchen equipment to bedding to furniture, reveals that he bought well but not opulently. In August 1784, several weeks after he arrived in Paris, and still situated only in temporary quarters, he bought only a little china—one dozen coffee cups, saucers, and teacups. However, he purchased considerably more silver flatware: two dozen forks, two ragout spoons, a ladle, a dozen teaspoons, and twenty-four tablespoons (Cat. 177–179).[27]

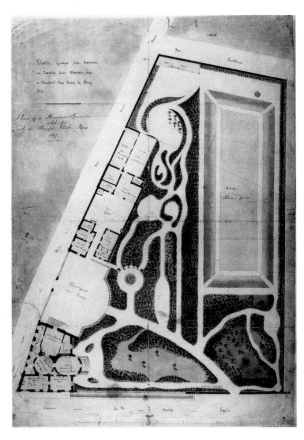

Hôtel de Langeac, Plan of the House and Gardens

c. 1780 with later additions
ink on paper
Bibliothèque Nationale, Paris

Grevin's Packing List

July 17, 1790
William Short Papers, Library
of Congress

Grevin's list of Jefferson's belongings sent from Paris to the United States begins with fifteen cases of books.

A more complete picture of the variety of objects that embellished the Hôtel de Langeac can be found by scrutinizing the enormous shipment of goods that Jefferson eventually brought back from France. When he set off for America on August 23, 1789, he did not know that President Washington would invite him to serve as secretary of state, and he fully intended to return to Paris. When he accepted Washington's offer, Jefferson wrote his secretary, William Short, requesting him to terminate the lease on the Hôtel de Langeac, oversee the packing and shipping of his belongings, and make some additional essential purchases.

The result was a large shipment packed nearly a year after Jefferson's departure by a master packer (*emballeur*) called Grevin, whose sixteen-page invoice, dated July 17, 1790, described eighty-six crates of goods.[28] Jefferson by then was living in Philadelphia as secretary of state, and in a characteristically efficient fashion he wanted to make sure that the invoice might also serve as a customs declaration. The packing list itemizes much of the contents of the Hôtel de Langeac and also lists objects purchased by William Short for Jefferson after his departure.

Judging from the packing list, the Hôtel de Langeac contained abundant seating furniture: two day beds (*lits de repos*) and forty-eight chairs. These, packed in various numbered crates, included twenty-two armchairs, twenty-two side chairs, and four bergères (easy chairs). It seems likely that the chairs were en suite, which was typical of the period, and consisted of four or five suites: (1) twelve crimson chairs, presumably silk damask, described as six large armchairs, four armchairs, and two bergères with removable cushions; (2) eighteen blue silk chairs listed as six large armchairs, ten side chairs, and two bergères; (3) six armchairs of red Morocco (goatskin); (4) six chairs covered in crimson *velours d'Utrecht* (velvet with a pressed design); and (5) six chairs also upholstered in *velours d'Utrecht* but with no color mentioned. Examples of four types of chairs appear in the exhibition.

As many as fourteen of the eighteen chairs of the blue silk suite were placed in the dining room of the Hôtel de Langeac, where large blue silk damask draperies, later transported to Monticello, hung on all three of the windows facing the Champs-Elysées. Six of these large blue window coverings appeared on Grevin's packing list and must have hung on the first floor in two of the three public rooms (where the windows were the largest), each containing three windows. Because the description of the chairs on the Grevin list indicates that the blue chairs were *chaises* (side chairs), they would very probably have been dining chairs. The dining table (or tables) was quite long, at least compared to English ones, and Jefferson expected to host as many as twenty—an uncommonly large number for an English party—and asked Abigail Adams to purchase for him in London twenty napkins and a tablecloth that measured four aunes long (approximately fifteen and a half feet). Mrs. Adams found that the largest available English size was somewhat smaller: "four yds. and three quarters are the largest size ever used here which will cover a table for 18 persons . . . it is only upon extraordinary occasions that you meet with that number at the tables here."[29] For Jefferson, the standard was different.

The *petit salon*, which communicated with the dining room and the grand oval salon, had extended views of the Champs-Elysées and the garden of the Hôtel de Langeac. Two to six of the remaining blue silk damask chairs, two of which were bergères, and a blue damask ottoman were probably placed here; the chairs could then have been taken into the dining room if needed. The *petit salon* may also have held several of the six chairs without an identified color on Grevin's packing list. The three windows of the *petit salon* were also draped with the remaining blue silk damask to match the seating furniture.

The exquisite damasks woven in Lyons and elsewhere in France were highly prized, and as was typical of the time, Jefferson spent more on upholstery fabrics than he did on standing furniture. He made purchases of damask from the silk merchants Barbier and Tetard on March 1 and May 20, 1785, and September 1, 1786. Although only a few tiny threads of the textiles survive, Jefferson must have been fascinated with the richness of their decorative schemes. These characteristically elaborate patterns, handwoven in widths of approximately twenty-two inches, had repeats ranging from eighteen inches to as much as twelve feet. The damasks were replete with classical motifs such as urns, musical instruments, or buildings, carefully arranged within a diamond-shaped border draped with pearls, flowers, or vegetal patterns. The most deluxe examples, suitable for the grandest royal residences, were iconographically elaborate and thus had the longest repeats. The palace at Versailles, for example, had draperies illustrating the continents.

Jefferson probably had at least two different damask patterns, one crimson and one blue, and these were placed on his seating furniture. Examples of four of the four or five suites of chairs survive in Monticello's collection, and they reveal much about Jefferson's taste. Three of the designs, all by unidentified cabinetmakers, referred to as *ébénistes* or *menusiers*, are highly characteristic of the period (Cat. 158, 160, 162). Two sets were patinated, and recent research on the surviving examples has not found any evidence of gilding on the frames.

The fourth chair, attributed to the most famous of Parisian *ébénistes*, was the work of Georges Jacob. Jacob, whose sons first joined his shop and later succeeded him, founded a dynasty of cabinetmakers. The Jacobs, especially Georges, were trend-setting designers who sensed the preferences of their powerful patrons. He had the uncommon ability both to follow prevailing style and to create it. To what extent Jefferson was familiar with the individual characteristics of particular cabinetmakers is unknown, but he made a wise choice in his selection of a suite of mahogany chairs by Jacob. Unusually simple in design and with little carved ornament, these large armchairs, called *fauteuils à la reine*, with flat rectangular backs are elegant, sinuous precursors of the later Directoire and Empire periods. In contrast to the feminine patinated suites, these mahogany chairs are generously proportioned and, without unnecessary bulk, decidedly masculine.

Jefferson acquired many tables for different purposes in France, including three gaming tables (now missing) called *tables à trois fins*. Given that he bought marble for them, they probably were *tables à combination* or *tables bouillottes* for various kinds of games such as *jeu de nain jaune, jeu de toton à lettres*, or cards. Typically, a table like this was marble topped and had an additional removable top with baize on one side and a game on the other. On the packing list, Grevin described them as "trois tables à jouer adessu de Marbre et une Couverture de bois garni de toffe verte."

For drawing, Jefferson acquired what Grevin called a *table à pupitre*, an architect's table with a movable top, properly named a *table à la tronchin* (Cat. 166). He also acquired four marble tabletops with gilded brass bands and galleries, but it is not known if the bases for them were made in France or in America upon his return. The simplicity of the unembellished design of an almost square marble tilt-top table resembles the spare approach of the mahogany chairs attributed to Georges Jacob (Cat. 162). The table, which resembles the French *table redressable*, is supported by a modest tripod with snake feet.[30] A related rectangular *table redressable* is supported by a trestle with two pairs of snake feet (Cat. 165). The third marble top was later made into a table, echoing the trestle design, in Monticello's joinery (Cat. 165). A round Brescia marble table, the only table with its gilded gallery and band intact, consists of a mahogany skirt, like a drum, on four square, tapering legs (Cat. 167). The largest of the tables was a round *guéridon* with both marble top and pedestal (Cat. 163).

Of the seven movable mirrors that adorned the walls of the Hôtel de Langeac, the details of three are known. Each, although gilded, has a comparatively simple profile without elaborate, deep carving. A pair of rectangular mirrors over nine feet tall were two of four full-length mirrors shipped in Crate No. 48; the surviving pair was installed in Monticello's Parlor. The third extant French pier mirror (purchased after Jefferson's death at the Dispersal Sale and now in a private collection) was probably one of a round-headed pair. It was later installed opposite the window in Jefferson's bedroom in Monticello.

The Hôtel de Langeac dining room, with its table (or tables) seating twenty, was ornamented by silverware and biscuit (unglazed, high-fired porcelain) figurines. Jefferson owned several *plateaux*—flat ornamental plaques of mirrored glass surrounded by a gallery for use on a dining table or sideboard. Typically, these *plateaux* held decorative ornaments in addition to branched candelabra to magnify the amount of light. He paid 422 livres for some purchased from Bazin in 1786.[31] Although none of the French candelabra are known, one of four pairs of Sheffield silver-plate examples, purchased by Trumbull, survive (Cat. 264). With their columnar design, they are strikingly Neoclassical.

The French silverware echoed Jefferson's straightforward Neoclassical taste. He purchased flatware, four covered vegetable dishes, or casseroles, that became family treasures, and plates. Jefferson also designed coffee urns and a pair of unusually elegant Neoclassical footed goblets and found a fine silversmith to carry out his ideas.

At least seven figurines made of biscuit decorated the *plateaux* or were placed in other rooms as mantel decorations. Only *Hope with Cupid* and *Venus with Cupid* survive; the identities of the others are not known. One might have been a copy of the Farnese Hercules.[32] In any case, Jefferson certainly understood their symbolism and iconography. For Abigail Adams, then residing in London, he procured "three plateaux de dessert with a silvered balustrade round them, and four figures of Biscuit."[33] Jefferson wrote Mrs. Adams:

With respect to the figures I could only find three of those you named, matched in size. These were Minerva, Diana, and Apollo. I was obliged to add a fourth, unguided by your choice. They offered me a fine Venus; but I thought it out of taste to have two at table at the same time. . . . At length a fine Mars was offered, calm, bold, his faulchion not drawn, but ready to be drawn. This will do, thinks I, for the table of the American Minister in London, where those whom it may concern may look and learn that though Wisdom is our guide, and the Song and Chase our supreme delight, yet we offer adoration to that tutelar god also who rocked the cradle of our birth, who has accepted our infant offerings, and has shewn himself the patron of our rights and avenger of our wrongs.[34]

Not satisfied with this only slightly veiled Anglophobic allusion, Jefferson continued, "I fancy it must be the quantity of animal food eaten by the English which renders their character insusceptible of civilisation. I suspect it is in their kitchens and not in their churches that their reformation must be worked."[35]

Before Jefferson was able to travel in France in 1787, where he was soon enamored with "the remains of Roman grandeur," he enjoyed a garden tour of English country estates with John Adams in the early spring of 1786. The real reason for Jefferson's visit to England, however, was to finalize a treaty with Portugal. When Jefferson and Adams were introduced to the king and queen, they did nothing to ameliorate Jefferson's opinion of the haughty English. Jefferson later recalled that "On my presentation as usual to the King and Queen at their levees, it was impossible for anything to be more ungracious than their notice of Mr. Adams & myself."[36]

Before departing on March 6, 1786, Jefferson anticipated some purchases that he wished to make and requested the approval of the French government of the English-made articles with which he expected to return: "A set of table furniture consisting in China, silver & plated ware . . . small tools for wooden & iron work, for my own amusement . . . a box of books . . . riding horse, saddle etc."[37] On his trip he did not fail to recognize the abundant consumer goods available in London, as in Paris, and a year later told Madame de Corny that the ". . . splendor of their shops, . . . is all that is worth seeing in London."[38] Jefferson, who later told Lafayette that he was not much disposed to English-made goods, purchased gloves, a hat, maps, a walking stick, knives, cotton stockings, a thermometer, protractor, globe, theodolite (Cat. 214), telescope, hydrometer, three plated reading lamps (Cat. 268), books, and more in London—more than enough English goods to arouse Lafayette's criticism.[39] Jefferson responded that he only bought English goods when French ones were not available, and he wrote Lafayette, "It is not from a love of the English but a love of myself that I sometimes find myself obliged to buy their manufactures."[40] Jefferson particularly admired English-made scientific instruments, and he acquired telescopes, money scales, and drafting instruments from London merchants for years to come.

On his trip with John Adams to explore English country-house gardens, guided by Thomas Whately's *Observations on Modern Gardening* (1770), Jefferson made only some rather clipped notes about what he investigated. His preoccupation with the gardens, which were integrally connected with the ambitious schemes of the great country houses, over-shadowed his interest in the houses themselves. He made astonishingly little mention of the architecture that he saw. He dismissed Chiswick, Lord Burlington's domed adaptation of Palladio's Villa Rotonda, with the simple comment, "The Octagonal dome has an ill effect, both within and without."[41]

The major stopping points on Jefferson and Adam's tour were Chiswick; the Renaissance Hampton Court, which Jefferson labeled "old fashioned"; Twickenham, with Alexander Pope's famous garden; Esher Place; Paynshill, with what Jefferson thought was an ill-situated dwelling house; Woburn; Caversham; Wotton; Stowe; Blenheim; Kew; and Leas-owes, about whose owner, Jefferson remarked, "It is said . . . [he] died of the heartaches which his debts occasioned him."[42] The pair also visited Shakespeare's birthplace, where they were shown the chair in which he sat. Adams reported in his diary that "We cut off a chip according to custom."[43] At Blenheim, the great estate of the duke and duchess of Marlborough (designed by Sir John Vanbrugh), if Adams and Jefferson had got inside, they might have seen a fine collection of paintings, including works by Titian, Carracci, Raphael, Holbein, Poussin, and others.[44]

In 1788 Jefferson prepared "Hints to Americans Travelling in Europe." He advised obtaining the map of the country in advance, buying the plan of the town and a book "noting it's curiousities," and avoiding "all the little details . . . which will load the memory with trifles, fatigue the attention . . ."[45] Jefferson also made a list of eight "objects of attention for an American," including agriculture, mechanical arts, lighter mechanical arts and manufactures, gardens, architecture, politics, and painting and statuary.[46] He particularly valued the study of architecture, writing, "It is among the most important arts: and it is desireable to introduce taste into an art which shews so much."[47] Surprisingly, given the works of art that he already owned, he wrote that painting was

too expensive for the state of wealth among us. It would be useless therefore and preposterous for us to endeavor to make ourselves connoisseurs in those arts. They are worth seeing, but not studying.[48]

Collecting Art in France

In all, Jefferson shipped sixty-three paintings back to America. Of these, forty-nine found their way to the four public rooms at Monticello and were identified by Jefferson in the Catalogue of Paintings &c. at Monticello, believed to have been compiled sometime after 1809 (see Appendix II). The other paintings were hung in Monticello's private rooms.

Jefferson's purpose in collecting art in Paris was entirely didactic, but the selections were notably different from the desiderata that he had compiled about 1771 for a projected art gallery at Monticello. The "first" Monticello even included two niches for sculpture in the Parlor. The earlier list, heavily weighted toward classical subjects, was influenced chiefly by Joseph Spence's *Polymetis: Or, An Enquiry concerning the Agreement between the Works of the Roman Poets, and the Remains of the Antient Artists. Being an Attempt to illustrate them mutually from one another.*[49] Reverend Spence, an Oxford professor of poetry and later Regis Professor of history, read "Roman writers only, or such of the Greeks as were quite Romanized," and using a fictional character Polymetis, established a list of the great works of the ancient artists and illustrated them with engravings drawn by Louis-Philippe Boitard.[50]

Jefferson's *desiderata* named nineteen works in an undated building notebook of around 1771, fourteen of which were sculptures: the Medici *Venus* from the Uffizi Gallery, Florence; *Apollo Belvedere; Farnese Hercules; Antinous; Dancing Faun; Messenger pulling out a thorn [Spinario]; Roman slave whetting his knife; Gladiator at Montalto [Cincinnatus]; Myrmillo expiring [Dying Gladiator]; Gladiator reposing himself after the engagement; Hercules and Antaeus; The Wrestlers; Rape of the Sabines;* and *Diana Venatrix.* Jefferson apparently was serious about acquiring sculpture. The five paintings on the list were: *St. Paul Preaching at Athens, St. Ignatius at Prayer; Jephtha Meeting His Daughter, Sacrifice of Iphigenia,* and the *History of Selencus Giving His Beloved Wife Stratonice to His Only Son Selencus Who Languished for Her.* Only three of Jefferson's nineteen desired works were biblical subjects; none were modern historical subjects. Of the subjects Jefferson wanted in 1771, he was only to acquire *Jephtha Meeting His Daughter* and small versions of *Hercules* and *Diana Venatrix.*

If Jefferson obtained an awareness of classical works of art from Spence, he apparently gained knowledge about the informative, didactic qualities that art possessed from reading Jonathan Richardson's *The Theory of Painting* (1773). In it, Richardson maintained that "Painting is . . . of great use, as being one of the means whereby we convey our ideas to each other, and which, in some respects, has the advantage of all the rest."[51] Painting, Richardson contended, could reveal an entire scene at once and thus was capable of circumventing the imperfection and ambiguity of language.

A third author who was immensely influential in shaping Jefferson's ideas about art was Daniel Webb, who wrote *An Inquiry into the Beauties of Painting; and into the Merits of the most celebrated painters, ancient and modern* (1760). Webb argued for the superiority of history painting because it was capable of revealing so much.

He that paints a history well, must be able to write; he must be thoroughly informed of all things related to it . . . A painter, therefore, of this class must possess all the good qualities requisite to an historian . . . he must moreover know the forms of arts, the habits, customs, buildings &c. of the age, and country, in which the thing was transacted . . . And as his business is not to write the History of a few years, or of one age, or country, but of all ages, and all nations, as occasion offers, he must have a proportionable fund of ancient and modern learning of all kinds.[52]

Webb's influence on Jefferson appears to have been significant. His encouraging the artist John Trumbull to paint American history and his later essentially history-based collection at Monticello underscored his acceptance of Webb's point of view.

The works that Jefferson read prepared him well for the fertile artistic environment in Paris. The focus of the visual arts were the biennial Salons, held for about one month beginning on August 25, the king's feast day, in the Salon Carré of the Louvre. There the latest works of the members or candidates for membership in the Académie Royale de Peinture et Sculpture were displayed.[53] While Jefferson was in Paris, three Salons were held—in 1785, 1787, and 1789. Although it is likely that he attended the Salons of 1785 and 1789, it is only known for certain that he viewed the Salon of 1787. Jefferson wrote about it to John Trumbull in London:

The Salon has been open four or five days. I inclose you a list of it's treasures. The best thing is the Death of Socrates by David, and a superb one it is. A crucifixion by Roland in imitation of Relief is as perfect as it can be. Five pieces of antiquities by Robert are also among the foremost. Many portraits of Madme. Le Brun are exhibited and much approved. There are abundance of things in the stile of mediocrity. Upon the whole it is well worth your coming to see . . . The whole will be an affair of 12. or 14. days only and as many guineas; and as it happens but once in two years, you should not miss it.[54]

LAUDA-CONATUM
EXPOSITION au SALON du LOUVRE En 1787.

With his letter Jefferson enclosed a copy of *Explication des peintures, sculptures et gravures, de Messieurs de l'Académie Royale* (1787). Trumbull, however, was too busy to come, as he had just begun the *The Sortie Made by the Garrison of Gibraltar* (Cat. 32).[55]

About 330 paintings were packed onto the walls of the Salon Carré in 1787, hung by a *tapisseur*, who had the thankless task of deciding where each work would be placed. These works were either landscapes, still lifes, genre scenes, portraits, or history paintings (including religious subjects), representing each of the five classes of painting. History painting, of course, was ranked the highest in the hierarchy. In a room crammed with paintings hung frame-to-frame, Jefferson's immediate recognition and high praise of the *Death of Socrates*, one of the great works of Jacques-Louis David, was brilliant and perceptive. Jefferson's appreciation for David's talent even before he was fully admired by the critics was a strong signal not only of his growing sophistication but also of his preference for Neoclassicism.

David's historical canvases completed before the French Revolution appealed powerfully to Jefferson. He venerated David, whose masterpieces *Belisarius* (first exhibited in the Salon of 1781 with a reduced replica displayed in 1785) and *The Oath of the Horatii* (shown the same year), dealt so closely with the role of the citizen and the state. In 1789 Jefferson wrote Madame de Bréhan, who was in America, about recent developments in the political and artistic scene in Paris and reported, "We have nothing new and excellent in your charming art of painting. In fact I do not feel an interest in any pencil but that of David."[56]

Perhaps Jefferson had visited David's studio and seen *The Return of the Sons of Brutus*, which was then under way. Surprisingly, he purchased no works by David during his stay in France, and only one picture by David was to be incorporated into the Monticello collection, an engraved portrait of Napoleon, which probably was given to him.

Although Jefferson's purchases of works of art suggest a dominant interest in the Old Masters, a good deal of what he wrote about art, chiefly in letters to the mesdames de Tessé, de Tott, and de Bréhan, reveals not only his predictable penchant for the Neoclassicism of the period but also the way in which he responded to painting. In 1787 he was smitten by Jean Germain Drouais's *Marius at Minturnes* and described his experience of this painting to Madame de Tott:

Have you been, Madam, to see the superb picture now exhibiting in the rue Ste. Nicaise, No. 9. chez Mde. Drouay? It is that of Marius in the moment when the soldier [ente]rs to assassinate him. It is made by her son, a student at Rome under the care of David, and is much in David's manner. All Paris is running to see it, and really it appears to me to have extraordinary merit. It fixed me like a statue a quarter of an hour, or half an hour, I do [not] know which, for I lost all ideas of time, "even the consciousness of my existence."[57]

Two points about the passage are important. First, Jefferson was highly aware of the quintessence of Neoclassical painting, which characteristically captures the moment just before the critical action takes place. Second, he could be absorbed by a painting as much

Seven Men in Conversation before the Bust of Brutus

French (attributed to a follower of David)
ink on paper
30.4 × 36.8 (12 × 14.5 in.)
Department of Drawings and Prints, Uffizi, Florence

From left: Thomas Jefferson, unidentified, John Adams, unidentified, Jacques-Louis David, Philip Mazzei, and William Short.

as he was by architecture. The final line is the revealing one: The art historian Michael Fried states that at that time "the persuasive representation of absorption began to emerge in both criticism and painting as a conscious and explicit desideratum."[58]

Although Jefferson's time in France postdates the analytical reviews of the Salons (the last was the Salon of 1781) by the art critic and famous encyclopedist Denis Diderot (there is no evidence suggesting that Jefferson read any of them), Jefferson seems to have viewed at least some works of art in precisely the way that Diderot described and that was intentionally demanded by eighteenth-century beholders. The parallels between some of Jefferson's comments and those of Diderot are strikingly similar. In Diderot's acclaimed commentary on the painter Joseph Vernet in the *Salon de 1767*, he wrote:

I was motionless, my eyes wandered without fixing themselves on any objects, my arms fell to my sides, my mouth opened. . . . The immobility of beings, the solitude of a place, its profound silence, all suspend time; time no longer exists, nothing measures it, man becomes as if eternal.[59]

Without question, Jefferson, like Diderot, was capable of being absorbed and transformed by painting.[60] It is no surprise, therefore, that this experience led to his purchase and transportation of over five dozen paintings to Monticello and that the parlor of his Virginia house became nearly as crowded as the 1787 Salon Carré.

The other works in the Salon of 1787 that Jefferson mentioned to Trumbull were "five pieces of antiquities by Robert." Hubert Robert, who had studied in Rome and was a friend of Piranesi, was acknowledged by the Académie as a painter of ruins. In 1787, a total of nine canvases were shown by Robert—five with ruins as their subjects and four others set in classical settings. The pictures that Jefferson singled out were *The Interior of the Temple of Diana* (Nîmes), *The Maison Carrée* (Nîmes), *The Triumphal Arch and Amphitheater* (Orange), *The Pont du Gard* (Nîmes), and *The Temple of Jupiter* (Rome).

David was not alone in painting history paintings of classical subjects; he was merely the best. The Salon showed Vien's *The Farewell of Hector and Andromache*, Doyen's *Priam Demanding the Body of Hector from Achilles*, Sauvage's *Anacreon and Lycoris*, Taillasson's *Virgil Reading the Aeneid to Augustus and Octavia*, and Regault's *The Reunion of Orestes and Iphigenia*. Other painters, like Hué and even the amateur marquis de Turpin with his *Villa Madama near Rome*, featured architectural ruins in their pictures. Jefferson also saw seven marble busts by Houdon (for whom he would sit in 1789), including Louis XVI, Prince Henry of Prussia, the marquis de Lafayette, and the plaster that Washington sat for at Mount Vernon.

Aside from copies of five portraits obtained from the Uffizi Gallery in Florence and five from collections in England, Jefferson acquired most of the remainder of his collection between November 1784 and May 1785. He attended the De Billy sale on November 16–19, 1784, "in the salle de vente of M. Paillet in the former Hôtel Bullion, Rue Platrière."[61] Several months later, he purchased at least five paintings from the sale of the collection of the late Dupille de Saint-Séverin in the Marais in February 1785. The entries in his Memorandum Book reveal that he was buying more than one picture at a time, perhaps suggesting that his sources were shops or dealers. Of a total of twenty-one purchases, only three sources were named—Valade, Mlle. Guyard (Adélaïde Labille-Guiard), and Corneillon, from whom Jefferson also bought engravings. Corneillon also attended the Saint-Séverin sale, and it is possible that he was a dealer who procured paintings for Jefferson.

The paintings cost surprisingly little. The average cost per picture was 29 livres (equivalent to five dollars today), although Jefferson paid as little as 6 livres and as much as 240 livres for an unlocated work by Mlle. Labille-Guiard, the portrait artist. At the time of purchase his descriptions typically conveyed no information about their subjects. Only once did he mention a title—"Ecce Homo."[62] He once wrote, "5 ptgs (heads) 11F [livres] 16," but more often simply noted "pictures."[63]

Although his Memorandum Book entries suggest otherwise, Jefferson was greatly concerned both with the artist and subject of his pictures. In 1789 he prepared an inventory of the works that he owned, in which each painting was identified by title and artist. Once he had retired from the presidency, Jefferson took time to prepare the carefully researched and annotated Catalogue of Paintings &c. at Monticello (Appendix II). He included descriptive details and literary sources.

Jefferson's collection favored Baroque artists, although he obtained several copies of Italian Renaissance paintings by Raphael (*Transfiguration* and *Holy Family*), Leonardo (*John the Baptist*), Pordenone (*Christ before Pilate*), and Titian (*Danäe*). Northern Renaissance paintings were clearly in the minority with only three artists represented—Jan Gossaert (*Jesus in the Praetorium*); Hendrick Goltzius (*Saint Jerome in Meditation*); and from Frans Floris, an original, *Descent from the Cross*. Baroque artists were better illustrated: Gerard Seghers, Antoine Coypel, Anthony van Dyck, Peter Paul Rubens, Francisco Solimena, José de Ribera, Jean Valentin de Bologne, Guido Reni, Eustache Le Sueur, and Domenichino Zampieri. The artist that Jefferson positively favored was Reni, as he had copies of six of his works—*David with the Head of Goliath, Ecce Homo, John the Baptist, Herodias Bearing the Head of Saint John, Head of a Monk,* and *Christ.*

The subjects of the paintings Jefferson acquired during his tenure in France fell into three categories: biblical (twenty-six works), classical (seven), and biographical (sixteen). Of the biblical subjects, only three were Old Testament stories: *The Sacrifice of Isaac, David with the Head of Goliath,* and *Jephtha Leading His Daughter Seila to be Sacrificed.* In addition to *The Prodigal Son* (Luke 15:11–32), the New Testament subjects fully treated the principal events of the life of Jesus and included a portrait of Saint Joseph, a baptism, accusation, flagellation, crucifixion, transfiguration, descent, and ascension, as well as scenes of Jesus in the Praetorium, bearing the cross, driving out the money changers from the temple, and an *Ecce Homo.* Portraits of St. Jerome, St. Peter, John the Baptist, Herodias with the head of John the Baptist, Mary Magdalene, and St. Susanna augmented the story of the life of Jesus.

Jefferson acquired a total of twenty-three portraits between 1784 and 1789, including seven terra-cotta patinated plaster busts sculpted by Jean-Antoine Houdon, the greatest sculptor of the age. All of the portraits depicted men whom Jefferson admired; they can be divided into three groups: three Enlightenment figures who provided the underpinnings of Jefferson's values (Francis Bacon, Isaac Newton, and John Locke); discoverers and explorers of America (Columbus, Vespucci, Magellan, Cortez, Raleigh); and contemporaries (Franklin, Lafayette, Madison, Washington, Paine, John Paul Jones, Turgot, Voltaire, and

Jefferson himself). Also included were two Italians who fit none of the categories: Andrea Doria (1466–1560), a Genoese admiral who liberated his city from the French, and Castruccio Castracani (1281–1328), the ferocious duke of Lucca who defeated the Florentines and later captured Pisa.

Unlike the biblical and biographical works of art, the six works with classical subjects do not share similar themes and seem to bear no connection with one another. They are *Democritus and Heraclitus*, the laughing and weeping philosophers; *Daphne Transformed into a Laurel*; *Cyclops Forging Thunderbolts*; *The Sacrifice of Lyustra*; and two scenes from the life of Diogenes.

John Trumbull: American History Painter in Paris

While in Paris and inspired by David, whose works embodied the spirit of the incipient French Revolution, Jefferson encouraged the ambition of a young American painter to portray American history. Jefferson saw a great opportunity for John Trumbull to become a history painter and thus to convey the experience of the American Revolution. Although their relationship subsequently chilled, Jefferson was an important mentor to Trumbull during his years in Paris. The son of the governor of Connecticut, he had graduated from Harvard College in 1773 and had served in the Revolutionary War as an aide to generals Washington and Gates. He had then studied painting with the thriving Benjamin West in London, as did so many other young American painters.

Introduced to the young painter by Abigail Adams, Jefferson, in turn, acquainted him with the artists of his own social circle, as well as with the marquis de Lafayette, Count Rochambeau, and the marquis de Chastellux. After their first meeting, Jefferson reported to Francis Hopkinson: "Our countryman Trumbul [*sic*] brought with him his Battle of Bunker's hill [completed in March 1786] and Death of Montgomery to have them engraved here . . ."[64] He informed Ezra Stiles that "His natural talents for this art seem almost unparalleled."[65] In his *Autobiography*, written much later, Trumbull said of Jefferson that "He had a taste for the fine arts, and highly approved my intention of preparing myself for the accomplishment of a national work."[66] It was Benjamin West, however, who helped launch Trumbull's Revolutionary War series by sharing materials that West himself had gathered for his own *Death of General Montgomery in the Attack on Quebec*.[67]

While it is not known with any certainty whether the idea for Trumbull's masterpiece, *The Declaration of Independence*, was indeed Jefferson's, he may well have proposed the subject. No mention of it is known until the painter's 1786 visit to the Hôtel de Langeac.[68] Trumbull's own outline for his series on the American Revolution, prepared the previous year, referred only to the surrenders at Saratoga and Yorktown and the principal battles. In his *Autobiography*, Trumbull credited Jefferson's help with the configuration: "I began the composition of the Declaration of Independence, with the assistance of his information and advice."[69] Jefferson encouraged Trumbull's effort in every way—by sketching the plan of the Assembly Room at Independence Hall, describing the positions of those present, as well as the appearance of the absent members of the Congress, and even by housing him at the Hôtel de Langeac while he worked on the painting.

In May 1789 Jefferson invited Trumbull, who was then in London, to assume the

Self-Portrait

1777
John Trumbull (1756–1843)
oil on canvas, 75.5 × 60.3
(29¾ × 23¾ in.)
Bequest of George Nixon Black,
Courtesy Museum of Fine Arts,
Boston

duties of his private secretary, a post that would have afforded Trumbull the opportunity to remain in Europe and paint. Trumbull replied that he was occupied "commemorating the great events of our country's revolution" and could not be persuaded to abandon his plan to return to America to pursue his artistic profession.[70] Trumbull did not yet fully appreciate the difficulty that American artists faced if they wished to be anything other than portrait painters. Although Trumbull stated then that he wanted his paintings engraved and sold by subscription, it was not until 1797 that *Bunker's Hill, The Sortie Made by the Garrison of Gibraltar,* and *The Death of Montgomery* were engraved.

Trumbull's artistic career proceeded fitfully, without the substantial public success achieved by West and Copley in London. Unable to support himself, he deserted his American history series in 1793 and accepted a post in 1794 as Chief Justice John Jay's secretary on the Treaty Commission in London, ultimately staying away from painting for a long time. To keep himself going, he bought and sold Old Master paintings in Paris and speculated in the English and German brandy and tobacco trade.[71]

The situation seemed to brighten for Trumbull in America in the patriotic aftermath of the War of 1812. The construction of the new Capitol in Washington accorded Trumbull an opportunity to decorate it with accurate depictions of the Revolution. He wrote to the then-retired President Jefferson in 1816 to seek his support for the project. On Trumbull's behalf Jefferson wrote to Senator James Barbour of Virginia:

I pretended not to be a connoisseur in the art myself, but comparing him with others of that day I thought him superior to any historical painter of the time except David: it is in the historical line only that I am acquainted with his painting . . . The subjects on which Col. Trumbull has

The Declaration of Independence

1787–1820
John Trumbull (1756–1843)
oil on canvas, 53.7 × 79.1
(21⅛ × 31⅛ in.)
Yale University Art Gallery

employed his pencil are honorable to us, and it would be extremely desirable that they should be retained in this country as monuments of the taste as of the great revolutionary scenes of our country."[72]

Only ten days later, Congress voted a resolution to hire Trumbull to paint *The Surrender of General Burgoyne at Saratoga, The Surrender of Lord Cornwallis at Yorktown, The Declaration of Independence,* and *The Resignation of General Washington.*

Jefferson knew other artists in Paris in addition to Trumbull: Jean-Antoine Houdon, the virtuoso sculptor whose selection as the artist for the Virginia legislature's full-length portrait of General Washington that Jefferson had urged in 1785; Madame de Bréhan, a writer and amateur artist and the sister-in-law of the comte de Moustier, a diplomat who was named minister plenipotentiary from the French court to the United States in 1787; and the talented English couple, Richard and Maria Cosway. Jefferson found Madame de Bréhan "Simple beyond example in her dress, tho neat, hating parade and etiquette, affable, engaging, placid, and withal beautiful," but it was Maria Cosway who captured his heart and his head.[73]

Maria Cosway

John Trumbull introduced Maria Cecilia Hadfield Cosway (1759–1838) to Jefferson at the Halle aux Bleds in August 1786.[74] Jefferson had gone there to inspect the dome but instead was enchanted by the charming and talented twenty-seven-year-old Mrs. Cosway. Born to an English innkeeper in Leghorn, Italy, she was a musician, composer, engraver, and painter in her own right, and was the sister of the émigré architect George Hadfield, who later completed plans (as did Jefferson) for the United States Capitol. She spoke English, French, and Italian.

Maria was the wife of the English artist Richard Cosway (1742–1821), whom the Prince of Wales had appointed his principal painter in 1785. He generally was known as a portrait miniaturist but also was an inspired collector and connoisseur. In London the Cosways then lived in the middle portion at Schomberg House in Pall Mall where Thomas Gainsborough was their neighbor. The vast Cosway collection there consisted of Old Master pictures, primarily sixteenth- and seventeenth-century Italian and seventeenth-century Flemish works.[75] Accompanied by his wife, Cosway was in Paris to paint the portraits of the family of Philippe-Egalité, the duc d'Orléans.[76]

Maria Cosway captivated Jefferson. Upon leaving her when she was to depart for London in 1786, he composed one of the most celebrated love letters in the English language, in which he imagined a "dialogue between my Head and my Heart."[77] Her interest in art sparked Jefferson's own, and with her he explored the environs of Paris and wrote about what he saw and thought about art. Often alone, though sometimes accompanied by other friends, they visited the "port de Neuilly, the hills along the Seine, the rainbows of the machine of Marly, the terras of St. Germains, the chateaux, the gardens, the [statues] of Marly, the pavillon of Lucienne . . . Madrid, the King's garden, the Dessert."[78]

In the remarkable "Dialogue" written to Mrs. Cosway, Jefferson communicated an idea about the representation of the American landscape that was to become one of the cornerstones of his future art collection at Monticello. With the hope that she would visit America, Jefferson asked:

Where could they find such objects as in America for the exercise of their enchanting art? especially the lady, who paints landscape so inimitably. She wants only subjects worthy of immortality to render her pencil immortal. The Falling spring, the Cascade of Niagara, the Passage of the Potowmac thro the Blue mountains, the Natural bridge. It is worth a voiage across the Atlantic to see these objects; much more to paint, and make them, and thereby ourselves, known to all ages.[79]

At a time in America when artists were primarily portraitists and no tradition of landscape painting yet existed (very few views of the Virginia countryside are known before the 1790s), Jefferson believed that the natural wonders of America should be documented for posterity. Years later, he acquired two engraved views of Niagara Falls by John Vanderlyn (Cat. 57, 58) and two paintings by William Roberts—*The Junction of the Potomac and Shenandoah, Virginia* (Harpers Ferry) (Cat. 60) and of the incredible Natural Bridge (Cat. 59) in Rockbridge County, Virginia—as well as two engravings after the paintings. Jefferson, who had owned Natural Bridge since 1774, considered it one of the wonders of the world.

For Jefferson, the experience of the landscape was described in terms that refer to nature's ability to purify and elevate. When it came to art and nature, his writings suggest that his usually classical self was poised closer to the romantic. In a description of Monticello to Maria Cosway, in which he felt free to speak of his emotions, he said:

And our own dear Monticello, where has nature spread so rich a mantle under the eye? mountains, forests, rocks, rivers. With what majesty do we there ride above the storms! How sublime to look down into the workhouse of nature, to see her clouds, hail, snow, rain, thunder, all fabricated at our feet![80]

Nature was capable of supplying a degree of comfort to Jefferson, whose emotional life had been shattered by the loss of his wife. In the same passage recounting the wonders of nature, Jefferson concluded by referring to his own misery, "the human heart knows no joy which I have not lost, no sorrow of which I have not drank! Fortune can present no grief of unknown form to me!"[81] The workhouse of nature, by overwhelming him with its variety and force, could supply a curative, and he said that he would go to "the remotest sources of the Missouri" to find a drop of balm. Thus he saw nature not only as the place or context of history but also as a powerful healing force that could purify one's own condition.

A trip to Germany in 1788, which included a stop at Elector Johann Wilhelm von der Pfalz's Düsseldorf Gallery, where he saw works by Veronese, Poussin, and del Sarto, prompted Jefferson to write Mrs. Cosway and tell her of his exceptional passion for two painters, Adriaen van der Werff (1659–1722) and Carlo Dolci (1616–1688), who were then about as popular as they are today. He saw Van der Werff's *Sarah Delivering Hagar to Abraham* and four pictures by Dolci, *Saint Mary Magdalen, Saint Agnes, The Virgin and the Infant Jesus*, and *Christ Bearing His Cross*.[82] Perhaps recalling Jonathan Richardson's advice to look at paintings for their content rather than the celebrity of their artists, Jefferson was enthralled with them both.

Sarah Delivering Hagar
to Abraham

*Adriaen van der Werff
(1659–1722)
oil on canvas, 76.5 × 61
(30⅛ × 24 in.)
Bayerische Staatsgemälde-
sammlungen, Munich*

I surely never saw so precious a collection of paintings. Above all things those of Van der Werff affected me the most. His picture of Sarah delivering Agar to Abraham is delicious. I would have agreed to have been Abraham though the consequences would have been that I should have been dead five or six thousand years. Carlo Dolce became also a violent favorite. I am so little of a connoisseur that I preferred the works of these two authors to the old faded red things of Rubens.[83]

Dolci, a Florentine, is known for his gentle portraits. Jefferson saw four of his works, but he wrote little of them.[84] Van der Werff's painting *Sarah Delivering Hagar to Abraham* intrigued Jefferson, and the vocabulary he applied to it is uncharacteristic of his writings. What did he mean, for example, by the word "delicious"? In the eighteenth century, the word not only meant "highly pleasing or enjoyable to the bodily senses" but also could connote "sensuous indulgence and voluptuousness."[85] The painting shows Sarah, Abraham's wife, bringing back Hagar, Abraham's concubine, to Abraham. Jefferson's word choice indicates that, at the very least, the painting gave him great pleasure in the sense of being a delightful work. What is unclear, however, is the object of the word "delicious"; is Jefferson referring to Hagar alone or to the narrative subject of the painting?

Jefferson revealed to Maria Cosway, as he did to Madame de Tott, that he could abandon reason. He wrote, "I am but a son of nature, loving what I see and feel, without being able to give a reason, nor caring much whether there be one."[86] Painting, for Jefferson, was a mighty medium indeed, for it was capable of loosening the confines of his rational self. Nature could supersede reason, if only briefly.

The special friendship between Jefferson and Cosway was renewed through correspondence near the end of their lives, and their last years were surprisingly similar. They both faced impoverishment in their old age but were gratified by founding educational institutions. As Jefferson founded the University of Virginia late in his life, in 1812 Cosway established the Collegio della Grazie in Lodi, Italy, a school for girls and young women. She left her Edgware Road house permanently after she was widowed in 1821, and could no longer afford to live in London. She wrote Jefferson, "Accept of the best wishes from one, who, ever retains with the deepest sense of gratitude your kindness to her."[87] Jefferson's affection for Cosway remained strong. Expecting that a letter in December 1820 to her might be his last, Jefferson said:

Mine is the next turn, and I shall meet it with good will; . . . May these my dear friend, be as many as you yourself wish, and all of them filled with health and happiness, will be among the last and warmest wishes of an unchangeable friend.[88]

In fact, he was to hear from her several more times. In her last letter to him in September 1824, she remarked that her salon in Lodi was painted with representations of the four parts of the world with a blank spot reserved for Monticello and the University of Virginia, awaiting his description of them.

The Family Divided and Reunited

Jefferson took his daughter Martha, then twelve years old, with him to Paris and enrolled and boarded her in a convent school, the Abbaye Royale de Panthemont, which still stands at the rue de Grenelle and the rue de Bellechasse in the Faubourg Saint-Germain, a short walk from the Hôtel de Salm. Although she had studied French in Philadelphia in 1783, Martha wrote to a friend:

I did not speak a word of French. . . . There are fifty or sixty pensioners in the house, so that speaking as much as I could with them I learnt the language very soon. At present I am charmed with my situation.[89]

Martha Jefferson (1772–1836)
1789
Joseph Boze (1745–1826)
oil on ivory, 8.9 × 6.4
(3½ × 2½ in.)
Diplomatic Reception Rooms, United States Department of State

She studied painting—she drew flowers and "landskips"—and learned to play the harpsichord. Martha also took lessons in needlework, dancing, history, geography, reading, and of course, Latin, of which she said, "*Titus Livius* puts me out of my wits."[90] She made many friends among the students and saw her father once a week. Her attachment to him was great; she missed him terribly whenever he traveled outside Paris, reminding him, "Pray write often and long letters."[91]

During this period, Jefferson was a remote but devoted parent. He was at once affectionate, demanding, accessible, and moralistic—and never missed an occasion to remind Martha of her obligations.

You know what have been my fears for some time past; that you do not employ yourself so closely as I could wish. . . . Consider therefore the conquering your Livy as an exercise in the habit of surmounting difficulties, a habit which will be necessary to you. . . . My expectations from you are high: yet not higher than you may attain. . . . To your sister and yourself I look to render the evening of my life serene and contented. It's morning has been clouded by loss after loss till I have nothing left but you.[92]

Martha's two younger sisters had been left behind at Eppington with Aunt Eppes, their mother's half sister, and her husband, Francis. Lucy Elizabeth (b. 1782), the youngest, died at the age of two, barely a month after her father's arrival in Paris. Her aunt wrote Jefferson, "Its impossible to paint the anguish of my heart on this melancholy occasion. A most unfortunate Hooping cough has deprived you, and us of two sweet Lucys [Lucy Eppes, the young daughter of Elizabeth and Francis Eppes], within a week."[93]

Within months Jefferson campaigned to bring Mary (1778–1804), or "Polly," to Paris. After the loss of her mother at the age of four, Polly was much attached to Aunt Eppes and was not inclined to journey to a distant place. When told about her father's intentions, she responded, "I should be happy to see you, but I can not go to France, and hope that you and sister Patsy are well."[94] Jefferson was resolute that she should come, even after Mrs. Eppes reported that Polly "is more averse to it than I could have supposed."[95] Polly sailed to London, arriving at the home of John and Abigail Adams on June 26, 1787, with a slave named Sally Hemings (b. 1773) who, Mrs. Adams said, was "quite a child, and Captain

Ramsey [the captain of the ship on which they traveled] is of opinion [that she] will be of so little Service that he had better carry her back with him."[96] In a little more than two weeks, the young pair had safely arrived in Paris. The delicate Polly was soon matriculated at the Abbaye with her sister, where she would stay for only two years.

◆ Return to America ◆

When Jefferson's request for a leave of absence from his post in Paris was granted on August 26, 1789, he waited nearly a month to depart. He planned to return and put William Short in charge of his house and American concerns while he was away. The principal object of his journey was to restore his daughters, Martha and Maria, to their country. John Trumbull made arrangements for Jefferson, his daughters, and Sally and James Hemings to sail on the *Clermont*, bound for Norfolk, Virginia, from Cowes on the English side of the Channel. Adrien Petit, Jefferson's maître d'hôtel, came along to escort them to Le Havre and the packet *Anna* departing for Cowes. On October 23, they sailed for America.

Even while aboard the *Clermont*, Jefferson's acquisitive streak remained unchecked. He was highly impressed with a table aboard the ship and asked the captain, Nathaniel Colley, to obtain two for him in London. The table is similar to what Thomas Sheraton in *The Cabinet-Maker and Upholsterer's Drawing Book* (1791) called a "Universal" table, which contained two sliding leaves that could nearly double the table's surface area (Cat. 126). Jefferson specified "The fitness of the mahogany to be more attended to than the price. The French spotted mahogany is the handsomest to be had."[1]

Just after Jefferson and his party landed at Norfolk on November 23, a fire broke out on the ship. Miraculously unscathed were the numerous parcels containing dozens of bottles of wine (Meursaults, Sauternes, Rochegudes, and Frontignans), Parmesan cheese, raisins, vinegar, oil, macaroni, kitchen furniture, books, a bust of Lafayette and a pedestal for it, mattresses and two bedsteads, a guitar, pictures, a clock, servants' clothes, chariot, phaeton, models of various machines, a harpsichord made by Jacob Kirckman, and plaster busts of John Paul Jones destined for various American patriots.

The fire was not the only surprise in Norfolk. There Jefferson learned that George Washington had invited him to serve as the first secretary of state, writing him:

In the selection of Characters to fill the important offices of Government in the United States I was naturally led to contemplate the talents and disposition which I knew you to possess. . . . I was determined, as well by motives of private regard as a conviction of public propriety, to nominate you for the Department of State, . . .[2]

The Senate had already confirmed his appointment by the time he landed in Norfolk. In a somewhat equivocal acceptance, Jefferson wrote President Washington that his preference was to remain in his post as minister plenipotentiary, "But it is not for an individual to choose his post. . . . You are to marshal us as may best be for the public good."[3]

Jefferson and his family made their way slowly to Monticello, arriving one month later. They had gone by ferry to Hampton and traveled from Williamsburg to Richmond, where Jefferson inspected the construction of the new Capitol that he had worked on with the French architect Clérisseau. To William Short he wrote:

Our new Capitol when the corrections are made of which it is susceptible will be an edifice of first rate dignity. . . . it will be worthy of being exhibited along side the most celebrated remains of antiquity."[4]

Jefferson described the Capitol as

the model of the Temples of Erectheus at Athens, of Balbec, and of the Maison quarrée of Nismes. All of which are nearly of the same form and proportions, and are considered as the most perfect examples of cubic architecture, as the Pantheon of Rome is of the spherical.[5]

It must have been gratifying for Jefferson to see the Capitol under way. When the Virginia legislature wanted to pursue another design in 1785, he had fought, albeit from a distance, for adopting the Maison Carrée as a model; he called it "one of the most beautiful, if not the most beautiful and precious morsel of architecture left to us by antiquity."[6] Moreover, Jefferson was intensely committed to edifying Americans and believed that each public building presented an opportunity to educate the population. He wrote James Madison:

You see I am an enthusiast on the subject of the arts. But it is an enthusiasm of which I am not ashamed, as its object is to improve the taste of my countrymen, to increase their reputation, to reconcile to them the respect of the world and procure them its praise.[7]

Given Jefferson's low opinion of the prevailing American building style, he was resolute that the young country should have exemplary public architecture to serve as a model for the future.

Before reaching Monticello on December 23, Jefferson and his daughters stopped at Eppington to see the Eppeses and Skipwiths in Chesterfield County, all of whom were relatives of his late wife. Young Martha's account of the family's return to Monticello and the emotional reception that they received from the slave community is memorable. When the carriage at last reached the top of the little mountain, Jefferson was carried to the house by his slaves, some of whom were reported to have cried, laughed, and kissed the ground.[8]

Not long after arriving in Albemarle County, Jefferson addressed his fellow citizens and commented:

It rests now with ourselves alone to enjoy in peace and concord the blessings of self-government, so long denied to mankind: to shew by example the sufficiency of human reason for the care of human affairs and that the will of the majority, the Natural law of every society, is the only sure guardian of the rights of man.[9]

In spite of the tumultuous greeting and the deteriorating condition of his farms, Jefferson did not stay long at Monticello. Exactly two months after their return Martha was wed there, presumably in the Parlor, on February 23, 1790, to Thomas Mann Randolph, Jr., the son of Thomas Mann Randolph of Tuckahoe, whom Jefferson had known all his life. Less than a week later, on March 1, Jefferson left for New York, then the temporary capital of the United States.

New York

After stops in Alexandria and what turned out to be a final visit to the ailing Benjamin Franklin in Philadelphia, Jefferson reached New York on March 21. The brouhaha over the proposed form of address for the president as "His Highness the President of the United States and Protector of Their Liberties"—not sought by Washington—had died down. Eight months earlier from Paris he had written Madison:

The president's title as proposed by the senate was the most superlatively ridiculous thing that I ever heard of. It is a proof the more of the justice of the character given by Doctr. Franklin of my friend [John Adams]: 'Always an honest man, often a great one, but sometimes absolutely mad.'[10]

New York, which had yet to become a great city, had a population of just over 33,000, and was quickly expanding north of the settlement in lower Manhattan. Jefferson wanted a house on Broadway conveniently located near his department. Instead, he found a small house not too far away at 57 Maiden Lane, which he rented for one year. He moved to it on June 2 and left it for good on September 1. In spite of the temporary location of the federal government in New York, Jefferson carried out some considerable renovations to the dwelling before occupying it, insisting to his landlord that a gallery be added to the back of the house.

Once settled in his house and without his French belongings, Jefferson furnished his residence. A look at his Memorandum Book for the summer of 1790 suggests that he outfitted his lodgings without any hope that his possessions would arrive soon. He bought looking glasses, plated spoons, and a ladle from William Grigg, a hardware and jewelry merchant on William Street; plated candlesticks from William Buckle, a jeweler and ironmonger on Water Street; thirty green, presumably Windsor, chairs (soon shipped to Monticello) from one of several Andersons (these inexpensive chairs would suffice until his French ones arrived); several bedsteads, one of which was made by Samuel Prince; a teaboard; china and glassware from William Williams on William Street and Maiden Lane; and assorted furniture from Thomas Burling, the prominent cabinetmaker at 36 Beekman Street who had been trained by Prince. The works purchased from Burling included a revolving high-backed chair (Cat. 129), a sofa (Cat. 130), and may also have included a sideboard, now missing. Although only the sofa and revolving chair survive, the amount of Jefferson's bill suggests that he made many purchases from Burling, possibly including shield-back chairs (Cat. 133). Like Jefferson, President Washington also had many furnishings made by New York cabinetmakers.

After Jefferson had lived in New York for scarcely three months, the government recessed for that same amount of time and would resume operation in Philadelphia. Before getting situated there, Jefferson was off to Virginia with James Madison. They stopped briefly in Philadelphia, staying with their former landlady, Mrs. House. The pair then traveled south through the eastern shore of Maryland, traversed the Chesapeake Bay to reach Annapolis, rested at Georgetown, traveled by boat up the Potomac to see the Great Falls, and then went to Mount Vernon. On September 19, following a night at Madison's Montpelier in Orange County, Jefferson arrived at Monticello. There he saw his daughter Martha, who was expecting her first child in February, and her husband. On this trip Jefferson tried to strike a deal with the senior Randolph at Tuckahoe to buy Edgehill, Randolph's Albemarle County property, for the young couple. But Randolph drove a hard bargain; no agreement was reached at this meeting.

Philadelphia

Before very long it was time for Jefferson to head north to Philadelphia to rejoin the government. During his earliest stay there, in 1766, he had met Dr. John Morgan, a physician, who had just returned from a trip abroad with a group of plates, drawings, and copies after Poussin, Titian, Domenichino, Carracci, Le Brun, and others that Jefferson no doubt inspected at Morgan's home. This collection, the best in Philadelphia, also included a portrait of Dr. Morgan by Angelica Kauffmann.[11]

The Philadelphia of the early 1790s was a much more sophisticated place than it had been formerly; it was increasingly style conscious and consumer oriented. Jefferson was regarded as a cosmopolitan and artistic pacesetter in what was then the largest city in America. The French style was widely known and popularized not only by Jefferson, but also by Robert Morris, who had numerous imported French furnishings in his home. Morris had hired Pierre L'Enfant to design his house and even engaged French chefs.[12] Jefferson's service in France was widely known, if not envied, and it was recorded that he "had resided at the Court of France, and at first appeared in somewhat of its costume and wore an elegant Topaz ring."[13] (Later, he adopted a plainer appearance.)

English influence, however, was more prevalent than French, not only in the homogeneous brick architecture that comprised the cityscape but also in the stylistic sources for furniture designs. George Hepplewhite's *Cabinet-Maker and Upholsterer's Guide* of 1788 was readily available. The stylish Philadelphians William and Anne Bingham, who had traveled to London and the West Indies, erected the first Regency-style town house upon the plan of an English architect. The decorated façade concealed lavish interiors with wallpaper, bright silk curtains, fine furniture, and works of art. Painting and sculpture had become increasingly accessible since Jefferson's initial visit, as the number of artisans grew. The painter Charles Willson Peale had a studio there and was busy painting portraits of Philadelphians of means. The ranks of silversmiths, cabinetmakers and other artisans included Philadelphia-trained craftsmen as well as a surprising number of French émigrés such as Simon Chaudron, the watchmaker patronized by Jefferson. In addition to the latest English designs of Sheraton and Hepplewhite, Philadelphia cabinetmakers were also influenced by French styles.

The house that Jefferson rented in Philadelphia from Thomas Leiper was at 274 Market, or High, Street, just a few blocks away from the American Philosophical Society,

HIGH STREET, from Ninth Street. PHILADELPHIA.

President Washington's house, the State House, and Jefferson's own offices at Eighth and Market streets. William Temple Franklin, the grandson of Benjamin Franklin, who recognized Jefferson's penchant for things French, described the houses to be constructed by Thomas Leiper:

Each House is 25 Feet front and 44 Feet deep, besides which the Part containing the Stairs is 18 by 11. And the Kitchen 18 Feet in length on the Yard, with two stories of Chambers over it. The Drawing Rooms are 23. Ft. 9 by 20. in the Clear, the Back Chambers 20. by 17 . . . The Front parlours are 20 Ft. 9 in. by 14 Ft. 3 . . . On the first Floor, by means of a Door of Communication you would have four good Rooms.—The two largest for your Dining and Drawing Rooms and the others for your Bed Chamber and Study. As they all communicate they would make a handsome suite, and constitute what the french call <u>un Appartment complet</u>.[14]

The entrepreneurial Leiper, a director of the Bank of Pennsylvania who also owned snuff mills and quarries, had spared little expense in completing the house. The interior was expensively finished with stucco cornices, doweled floors, oversize window panes, and mahogany balusters and handrails. It was "among the most heavily insured properties carried by the Mutual Assurance Company prior to 1800."[15]

Jefferson again undertook significant alterations to his rented dwelling. In addition to making changes to the interior plan, he added a book room, stable, and garden house. He sketched the plan for the house as he remodeled it, showing eight large rooms. In the Market Street house, for the first time, Jefferson installed a bed alcove like the ones he had seen in France. A few years later, these would become one of Monticello's most distinctive features. The garden house apparently was meant to be a secluded study, but it was never finished to his satisfaction and was used only as a storeroom or closet. He wanted the room to be illuminated by skylights only, without lateral windows. What he got instead was "a window-door at each end, no sky-light, and a set of joists which were in the way."[16]

Jefferson's stay in Philadelphia did not have an auspicious beginning; his house was not ready to occupy for six weeks after his arrival on November 20, 1790, and the delay certainly complicated his move. He wrote his daughter Maria:

The workmen are so slow in finishing the house I have rented here that I know not when I shall have it ready except one room which they promise this week, and which will be my bedroom, study, dining room and parlour.[17]

To further upset the transition to Philadelphia, Jefferson's vast shipment of books, household goods, furniture, paintings, and papers at long last arrived from Le Havre aboard the *Henrietta* on October 22. His house was not ready to receive his possessions, however, and he had to pay not only a tremendous freight bill but also the storage fee for his belongings. Jefferson paid $544.53 for what he understandably termed "my monstrous bill of freight" for seventy-eight of the eighty-six crates packed by the master packer Grevin on November 30.[18] The remaining eight crates—containing two marbles, the seat and cushion for a carriage, the half-column given to him by Madame de Tessé, two chests of drawers, and other household items—were destined for Monticello. The invoice for Grevin's services totaled sixteen pages of exacting descriptions of Jefferson's possessions, thus revealing what Jefferson brought back to America.[19]

When, at last, work on the Market Street house was sufficiently advanced to receive Jefferson's possessions on December 22 (he noted that two rooms on the third story were ready on the 11th, the stable on the 17th, and the kitchen on the 24th), he paid 12 shillings for carting eight loads of furniture, just the first of twenty-seven wagon loads required to convey the bulky crates from the wharf to his house. The crates from France were not the only boxes to be unpacked; he also had the contents of his New York house, which had arrived in mid-October, a trunk by stagecoach and three boxes containing books and a harpsichord by the ship *Linnet* from Virginia, and another box holding a Wedgwood lamp in the shape of an Etruscan candelabra from John Rutledge, Jr., of Charleston, South Carolina.[20]

For about six weeks in December 1790 and January 1791 Jefferson faced dreadful domestic confusion. Until the bedroom was ready on December 19, he was compelled to lodge again with Mrs. House and take his meals at her popular boardinghouse. On December 23, Jefferson wrote to Martha, "I am still without a house, and consequently without a place to open my furniture."[21] Unpacking the seventy-eight crates of goods packed by Grevin so fastidiously proved an awesome task. Grevin had packed with the utmost precaution, carefully wrapping each item separately and using oilcloth to make the crates weather tight, and he had used a variety of materials and packing techniques: coarse, oil, and strong packing cloths; various kinds of paper; flannel; twine; rope; nearly 400 pounds of shredded paper, 624 bundles of rye straw, and 36 bundles of hay for cushioning; nails; and wood for the crates themselves. Grevin's only failure was that he mixed the contents of the crates; a case containing four silk-covered chairs also held a dozen chafing dishes. Thus, unpacking was inordinately slow.

At long last on January 8, Jefferson wrote in his Memorandum Book, "took possn. drawg. room & parlour. Begin to dine at home." But all was not calm. Jefferson wrote on January 20 that "I am opening my things from Paris as fast as the workmen will make room for me."[22] Miraculously, in the midst of the confusion intensified by the clamorous presence of carpenters and plasterers, Jefferson managed to carry on with affairs of state. He prepared papers on whale and cod fisheries, relations with Great Britain, the French response to the tonnage acts, territorial government, and other matters.

Most remarkably, Jefferson's acquisition of furnishings was not entirely curtailed during the first turbulent months in Philadelphia. He managed to find time to buy a bedstead on January 5—perhaps he had abandoned the hope of locating one among the crates—from the noted cabinetmaker John Aitken, who then had a shop at 50 Chestnut Street, within several blocks of Jefferson's house. Aitken, who had emigrated from Scotland, later provided a tambour secretary and bookcase and two sideboards for President Washington in 1797. Jefferson's other early Philadelphia purchases included a double book press made by cabinetmaker William Long, which Jefferson sold to Judge James Wilson, the next tenant at 274 Market Street, in 1793. The remarkable press, which does not survive, had "not a single nail, screw, nor glue" and could "be taken to pieces and put together again the whole of them in half an hour."[23]

Jefferson also installed the sizable collection of paintings that he had assembled in France; they occupied six separate crates in the shipment of his possessions to America.[24] In the Market Street house, the paintings hung in what Adrien Petit, Jefferson's household manager, called the "Salon," the dining room, in Jefferson's bedroom, and other spaces as well. An amusing anecdote about Alexander Hamilton's response to what Jefferson called his "triumverate of worthies" was recollected by Jefferson years later. Hamilton had paid a call on Jefferson in the Market Street house and saw the portraits of Sir Francis Bacon, Sir Isaac Newton, and John Locke.

[Hamilton] asked him who these men were. They were his "trinity of the three greatest men the world had ever produced," Jefferson said, but they meant little or nothing in Hamilton's philosophy. "The greatest man that ever lived," said the Colonel, "was Julius Caesar."[25]

Home to Monticello

The year 1793 saw complex political events. Louis XVI was guillotined on January 21; news of the execution reached the United States in March. Although Jefferson's opinion of the king's execution later softened, at the time Jefferson wrote that monarchs were "amenable to punishment like other criminals."[26] The relationship between France and the United States occupied much of Jefferson's last year as secretary of state. In spite of Jefferson's French sympathies, he contended that the United States must remain neutral in the war between England and France. He firmly believed that French vessels harbored in American ports should not be armed for war. The scheming minister of the new French republic, Edmund Charles Genêt (Cat. 73), who was later recalled by his government, worked against Washington's administration. The success of Jefferson's neutral position was not recognized, however, until he had left office.

When Jefferson accepted Washington's offer to serve as secretary of state, he advised the president that he could not guarantee the length of his tenure. In January Jefferson thought that he might serve only through the summer. He decided to give up the Market Street residence in the middle of March and move to a country house near Gray's Ferry on the Schuylkill River, just a few miles away from Philadelphia. He wrote Martha, "[I] have sold such of my furniture as would not suit Monticello, and am packing up the rest and storing it ready to be shipped off to Richmond as soon as the season of good sea-weather comes in."[27] As the time for Jefferson's removal to Gray's Ferry approached, he said:

We are packing all our superfluous furniture and shall be sending it by water to Richmond . . . My books too, except a very few, will be packed and go with the other things, so that I shall put it out of my own power to return to the city again to keep house, and it would be impossible to carry on business in the winter at a country residence.[28]

How did Jefferson define the furniture that would not "suit" Monticello? What pieces would he sell and in what categories? He could have decided to sell the most recently purchased American furniture made in New York or Philadelphia, or some of the French furniture, both of which would have fetched high prices. No existing sale records reveal either what was sold or to whom. Surviving furniture, tax lists, and incomplete inventories, however, suggest that Jefferson probably sold relatively little. When he at last departed for the countryside, he wrote Martha that he had loaded his belongings on a boat for Richmond. "I have written to Mr. Brown to hire a Warehouse or rather Ware-room for it, there being 1300 cubic feet of it, which would fill a moderate room."[29]

It seems, however, that Jefferson underestimated the size of the shipment. The actual packing list (prepared mainly in French by Adrien Petit), which, after all, was only a partial shipment of his possessions in Philadelphia, is conspicuously incomplete. Many of the belongings that made their way to Monticello from this period are known yet do not appear on the list. Fifty-one cases, ten of which contained two chairs each, seem unlikely to have filled only a moderate-size room. The boxes contained not only many of the things that Jefferson purchased in France but also the objects that he had acquired in New York and Philadelphia. Six cases contained paintings, which could have been unframed and rolled or wrapped and transported in their frames. A seventh case also contained paintings and had been packed with their glass left intact. The most delicate objects, such as the paintings framed with glass, terra-cotta patinated plaster busts by Houdon, glassware, mirrors, and some marble tops, were singled out for transport by water so as to minimize the bumpy jostling of overland travel.

On July 31, 1793, Jefferson informed Washington that he intended to serve only through the end of September. Nonetheless, he was persuaded to remain until the end of the year. On December 31, Jefferson formally resigned his post, left Philadelphia on January 5, 1794, and arrived at Monticello on January 16.

Without any announced expectation of returning to public service, Jefferson looked forward to a life of domestic tranquillity. He wrote:

I am then to be liberated from the hated occupations of politics, and to remain in the bosom of my family, my farm, and my books. I have my house to build, my fields to farm, and to watch for the happiness of those who labor for mine.[30]

He was happy to be in Albemarle County with his daughter Martha Randolph, her husband, and their two children, Anne Cary and Thomas Jefferson, who shuttled between Monticello and the Randolphs' plantation, Varina, in Henrico County. Although Randolph acquired Edgehill from his father in the spring of 1793, and crops were grown there earlier, the Randolphs did not really dwell there until 1799.

With characteristic seriousness, Jefferson turned his attention to his own plantation. He approached farming with a scientific sensibility. The duc de La Rochefoucauld-Liancourt, who visited in 1796, reported:

Above all, much good may be expected, if a contemplative mind, like that of Mr. Jefferson, which takes the theory for its guide, watches its application with discernment, and rectifies it according to the peculiar circumstances and nature of the country, climate, and soil, and comfortably to the experience which he daily acquires.[31]

Jefferson understood the merits of crop rotation and wanted to abandon the single-crop dependency of the region, both for agricultural and economic reasons. He turned away from tobacco farming at Monticello because it exhausted both the soil and his laborers, but he continued to grow it at Poplar Forest, his plantation in Bedford County. Like many of his neighbors in Virginia, he turned to wheat and other grains because new markets in Europe had been opened through the treaties of commerce that he had helped to negotiate.[32]

Beginning in 1774, Jefferson had kept a Farm Book, in which he recorded all sorts of farm activities—from a census of his slaves to a list of the implements necessary for farming and crops planted, and a conglomeration of notes on goats, sheep, and hogs.[33] Here he listed the names and years of birth of his slaves, and noted where they lived and whether they were laborers on the ground, tithable persons following some other occupation, or discharged from labor on account of age or infirmity.

Jefferson's full-time attention to his farms, though it continued after his return, was not long-lived. Public life again intervened. Although he had little to do with it, he was elected vice president in 1796, and on March 2, 1797, he arrived in Philadelphia.[34] At first, he wanted to take the oath of office at Monticello but then changed his mind; and although he wished his arrival to pass unnoticed, he was instead greeted by a noisy discharge from an artillery company. A flag was hoisted with the words "Jefferson Friend of the People."[35] Wearing a long blue coat and with lightly powdered hair, he took the oath of office on Saturday, March 4. After seeing a Bengal elephant on March 10, Jefferson, who enjoyed curiosities, departed for Monticello on March 13.[36]

Jefferson was an intermittent resident of Philadelphia during his term as vice president. He needed to be there only when Congress was in session in order to preside over the Senate, and over the next four years, he spent about fourteen months there. He lodged in

John Francis's hotel at 12 South Fourth Street rather than procuring more permanent quarters. His presence was so infrequent as to warrant his granting power of attorney to John Barnes, who managed Jefferson's finances, collected his salary of $5,000 per year, and paid his bills.

Most of Jefferson's purchases in this period were personal ones. During his first stay as vice president in early March 1797, he subscribed to Benjamin Franklin Bache's newspaper *Aurora* and bought himself a nautical almanac, a pair of boots from John Bedford, and "a cloth coat and fleecy waistcoat."[37] Later that year, he acquired new gloves, a shaving brush, toothbrush, a facsimile of his name (probably for a calling card), spectacles, an oiled silk coat, and made a tentative agreement to pay for a marble bust of himself by the Italian sculptor Giuseppe Ceracchi, who had made a terra-cotta head sometime in 1791 or 1792 while lodging at Mary House's boardinghouse. The colossal bust was delivered to Monticello in 1795, where it occupied a conspicuous place in the Entrance Hall.

Toward the end of his 1797 stay in Philadelphia (he noted that he left between 8 and 9 A.M. on July 6), Jefferson began to prepare for his journey home. He had some books bound, bought a new trunk and had a lock put on it, collected the oiled silk greatcoats that he had ordered for himself and his son-in-law Thomas Mann Randolph, Jr., settled his account with his washerwoman, and had two packing boxes made. He did not forget to buy toys for his grandchildren.[38]

Among the orders Jefferson gave John Barnes for payments to various shopkeepers and tradesmen was one to Joseph B. Barry, a cabinetmaker who in the first decades of the nineteenth century was known for his elaborate work. He had a shop at 148 South Third Street. Over the course of the next three years, Jefferson patronized Barry heavily, spending a total of $299.25, a sum that would have purchased a sizable amount of furniture. In almost every case, payments were made to Barry just before Jefferson left town, probably indicating that the furniture was to accompany him back to Monticello, since he had no other residence. The orders may have included ten or more side chairs with shield backs (Cat. 134). Some of this furniture might have been destined for his younger daughter Maria, who had married John Wayles Eppes on October 13, 1797, in the Parlor at Monticello.

◆ The Second Monticello ◆

Monticello is a curiosity! Artificial to a high degree; in many respects superb. If it had not been called Monticello, I would call it Olympus, and Jove its occupant.

—Richard Rush
to Charles Jared Ingersoll, October 9, 1816

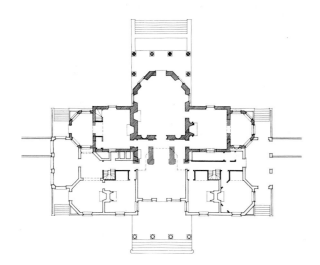

Floor plan of the second Monticello

The shaded portion indicates the outline of the first Monticello.

As early as 1790, Jefferson began to anticipate his permanent return to Monticello by making plans and gathering building materials to enlarge his house. In 1792, he optimistically and unrealistically thought that the cellars would be dug the next year, with brickwork soon to follow; in fact, the brickwork was not begun until 1796, and the house would not be essentially complete until 1809, the year that Jefferson retired from his second term as president. The long building process was far from unpleasant for Jefferson. Once again, he embarked on his favorite pastime of "putting up and pulling down."

By 1794 Jefferson's plans for the enlargement of Monticello were well developed, and he began, in 1796, to knock down parts of the existing, or "first," house. He wrote George Wythe, his Williamsburg mentor, that "we are living in a brick-kiln, for my house, in it's present state, is nothing better."[1] Part of the existing house was to be the core of an expanded, grander dwelling. To make the house larger, he would have to expand in the direction of the East Portico. Jefferson believed that it would be more economical to increase the area of the house by enlarging the plan. A passage would have to be appended between the old rooms and the new ones in order to avoid walking through one room to reach another.

While Jefferson's debt to Andrea Palladio is apparent, his design for Monticello was greatly influenced by contemporary French architecture. Several distinctly French architectural features from the Hôtel de Salm—the impressive town house whose construction Jefferson had so closely scrutinized while he was in Paris—found their way into the new plan. Foremost among these was a dome—the most conspicuous characteristic of the Hôtel de Salm—placed over the existing octagonal bow of the Parlor. Another attribute of the Hôtel de Salm that Jefferson admired was the outward appearance of a single story that cleverly concealed three stories. Jefferson's design for Monticello followed that model. He created a mezzanine level with six bedchambers whose windows were astutely placed immediately above the windows on the chambers below them. Positioned at floor level in the mezzanine chambers, the windows looked like the upper sash of the first-floor windows, thus creating the illusion of one story from the exterior. The third floor contained three additional bedchambers whose only sources of natural light were mullioned, operable skylights.

Nine of Monticello's twelve bedchambers contained bed alcoves, inspired by the rectangular niches that Jefferson had frequently encountered in France, where bedsteads were slipped into alcoves. Jefferson modified the way that the alcoves were used, however, by eliminating the need for a bedstead and replacing it with a built-in support for a mattress. Three U-bolts on each of the facing walls supported three braces; rope was strung across the braces to prop mattresses of feathers, horsehair, or straw.

Jefferson's spatial organization of Monticello placed and linked together all the public rooms on the first floor instead of placing some of them on the second, thus eliminating the need for a grandiose stairway to connect them. To conserve space, Jefferson instead positioned two stairways, like those he had observed in France, in the passages flanking the double-storied Entrance Hall. These narrow, private stairways, measuring only twenty-four inches wide with uncomfortably high risers, were meant to be used only by those who required access to the upper floors—family members, overnight visitors, and house servants. Jefferson thought that great staircases were too expensive and occupied "space that would make a good room in every story."[2]

The best quarters in the house were Jefferson's own. Three rooms, located on the south side of the first floor, were Jefferson's private apartment and became a sanctum sanctorum that only a few designated persons could enter. His bedchamber, which had direct access to the Entrance Hall, contained a privy—another feature copied from modern Parisian dwellings—and a bed alcove. Unlike all the others at Monticello, this bed alcove was open on two sides, with walls only at the head and foot. The sides were situated between the bedroom and the Cabinet, Jefferson's study. The side facing the Cabinet was shielded by a movable screen affixed to a pole. In wintertime, the closed screen helped to contain heat within the bedchamber and alcove.

The Cabinet, where Jefferson spent much of his time writing and reading, had a semioctagonal plan with three windows and a French door. The Cabinet communicated

Monticello

c. 1825
Jefferson Vail (active c. 1825)
watercolor on paper
22.6 × 27.6 (8⅞ × 10⅞ in.)
Musée de Blérancourt

with the Greenhouse, or Conservatory, that contained Jefferson's workbench and flats for sprouting seeds, as well as the fabled Book Room, where much of Jefferson's enormous library was housed. From the Book Room Jefferson could enter a private family sitting room or the South Passage.

The completion of Monticello's ambitious building scheme occupied Jefferson until well after his retirement from the presidency in 1809. Discouraging delays were encountered from the very start of the effort. In 1794, workmen began to demolish some of the existing brick walls. While Jefferson's intention was to salvage 62,000 bricks so that they could be reused, he soon discovered that their strong mortar caused much damage and breakage to the bricks; ultimately, only 29,000 whole bricks were saved. Work crawled to a virtual standstill in 1795 while Jefferson devoted himself to establishing a nail-making operation that employed young male slaves.

By spring of 1796, Jefferson was ready to make the stone foundations for the expanded house. The cellars were excavated and the walls were knocked down. The disarray caused by the construction process seems not to have deterred Jefferson from extending invitations to visitors during the most hazardous and uncomfortable period of construction. The duc de La Rochefoucauld-Liancourt, who visited during June 1796, was unknowingly optimistic when he stated that "the execution . . . will be accomplished before the end of the year."[3] In fact, Anna Thornton, the wife of the architect William Thornton, remarked six years later that

Mr. Jefferson has so frequently changed his plan, and pulled down and rebuilt so often that it has generally made the appearance of a place going to decay . . . A great deal of money must have been expended both above and below the ground but not so as to appear to the best advantage.[4]

Monticello was not Jefferson's only home in Virginia.[5] Eager to experiment with an octagonal design, he designed a second residence at Poplar Forest, his plantation in Bedford County, which he acquired through his wife's dowry from her father, John Wayles. In 1806, Jefferson told his old friend Elizabeth Trist that he was "preparing an occasional retreat in Bedford where I expect to settle some of my grandchildren."[6] Away from the regular influx of visitors, he sought an uninterrupted interval where he could leisurely read, think, and study. He wrote Benjamin Rush that he visited Poplar Forest

three or four times a year. I stay from a fortnight to a month at a time. I have fixed myself comfortably, keep some books here, bring others occasionally, am in the solitude of a hermit, and quite at leisure to attend to my absent friends.[7]

Jefferson's stays at Poplar Forest often coincided with the planting, harvesting, and marketing of the crops grown there, and he usually brought some of his grandchildren with him. The furnishings included a substantial amount of furniture made in Monticello's joinery—four Pembroke tables, for example—as well as bookcases, a dumbwaiter, several of the *fauteuils à la reine* attributed to Georges Jacob (Cat. 162), and two dozen Windsor chairs made in Philadelphia. Poplar Forest was inherited by Jefferson's grandson, Francis Eppes.

◆ The President's House ◆

The United States government moved from Philadelphia to Washington in 1800. The President's House was largely under construction during the four months that it was occupied by John and Abigail Adams. Because the interior of the official residence was for the most part unfinished and incompletely furnished in late March 1801 when Jefferson moved in, the responsibility for completely furnishing it became his. The decorative choices that he made reveal much about his aesthetics and domestic ideas.

Jefferson was elected president by the House of Representatives on February 17, 1801, and had to prepare his inaugural address for March 4. The speech was delivered in the swarming Senate chamber in the Capitol, and not everyone could hear him. Jefferson had made copies of his address available to the *National Intelligencer*, and it was soon widely known; he kept a copy of it at Monticello that was later held by his granddaughter, Ellen Randolph Coolidge. There was no inaugural celebration to speak of in Washington, although festivities were held in Philadelphia and even in Federalist strongholds like Boston. Jefferson was boarding at Conrad & McMunn's, on the south side of Capitol Hill, overlooking Tiber Creek and the Potomac. Years later, he was reported to have taken his usual seat at the boarding table there following the inaugural ceremony. Jefferson stayed at Conrad's for fifteen days, taking his meals in the dining room and conducting business in his chamber, until he could move into the official residence on Pennsylvania Avenue.

Issued almost a year after Jefferson took office, the first medal commemorating the inauguration of a new president (Cat. 109) was struck in February 1802.[1] The artist was John Reich, who may have assisted Robert Scot in the execution of the Indian Peace Medal (1801) with Jefferson's image (Cat. 112). Houdon's bust of Jefferson (1789) (Cat. 101) was the model for both medals, but the likeness was better on the smaller inaugural medal. To honor the President, the goddess Liberty holds the Declaration of Independence in her hand on the medal's reverse.

Architectural Design

Jefferson played a large role in deciding not only how the President's House would be used and improved but also in determining what kinds of furnishings would be purchased. His ideas on the subject also revealed much about his taste. The dwelling into which he moved on March 19 was quite a bit different from the present-day White House. Although the main block of the house remains much the same, the four engaged Ionic columns on the north entry were much more visible (until the distinctive north and south porticoes were appended in the 1820s). The exterior was a soft Virginia stone called Aquia, which had also been used for the north wing of the Capitol; it was painted or whitewashed. Despite its color, it was not called the White House until it was repainted after being burned by the British in 1814, during Madison's tenure.

Jefferson initiated the idea of a competition for the design of the President's House while he was secretary of state. James Hoban, the Irish-born architect, won the contest, which was decided by President Washington and the commissioners of the District of Columbia, apparently without Jefferson's involvement. Before the competition was an-

North Elevation of the
President's House
_____
October 1793
James Hoban (1758?–1831)
ink, wash, and watercolor
on paper, 25.4 × 45.4
(10 × 17⅞ in.)
Maryland Historical Society,
Baltimore

nounced in April 1792, Jefferson made his design preferences for the Capitol and President's House known to Pierre Charles L'Enfant, the engineer and architect who had laid out the plan of the federal city:

Whenever it is proposed to prepare plans for the Capitol, I should prefer the adoption of some one of the models of antiquity which have had the approbation of thousands of years; and for the President's house I should prefer the celebrated fronts of Modern buildings which have already received the approbation of all good judges. Such are the Galerie du Louvre, the Gardes meubles, and two fronts of the Hotel de Salm.[2]

In recommending different stylistic treatments for the seats of the legislative and executive branches, Jefferson drew an interesting distinction. He clearly wanted to establish a symbolic connection between "one of the models of antiquity" and the Capitol, while he wanted the President's House to be a forward-looking "Modern" building equal to the finest buildings of France.

Jefferson's own anonymous submission showed a strong affinity to Palladio, as well as to what he had seen in France. His scheme, with a central dome and four porticoes on each of the façades, prepared less than a year after his letter to L'Enfant, drew heavily on Palladio's Villa Rotonda.[3] The commissioners, however, preferred Hoban's design—also Palladian—with its connection to a plate in James Gibbs's *Book of Architecture*, the work that influenced Jefferson in his design for the first Monticello. Hoban's winning scheme was the sort that would be acceptable to Jefferson.

The First Occupants: John and Abigail Adams

John and Abigail Adams were the first presidential family to occupy the President's House. They moved in on November 1, 1800, and lived there only for four months, spending a decidedly uncomfortable winter without enough wood to keep the fires going. They found only half of the thirty-six rooms plastered and the principal stairs unfinished. Several of the major rooms were wallpapered, including the oval drawing room. Mrs. Adams wrote her daughter that she used "the great unfinished audience-room [East Room] . . . to hang up the clothes in."[4] She thought that the President's House was built "upon a grand and superb scale, requiring about thirty servants to attend and keep the apartments in proper order."[5]

Although bothered by the cold and the lack of a bell system to summon the few servants that they did have, Mrs. Adams recognized that the "house is built for ages to come."[6]

The furniture the Adamses used was acquired by President Washington from cabinetmakers in New York and Philadelphia, where Washington had last served. These pieces, purchased between 1789 and 1797, comprised the shipment transported to Washington from Philadelphia in 1800. Apparently, a good deal of Washington's presidential furniture was sold when he left office, including the entire contents of the Green Drawing Room with its green silk window curtains and matching damask-covered sofa, armchairs, side chairs, and stools.[7] Other suites of seating furniture on Washington's inventory, such as three yellow silk sofas, ten chairs covered with yellow damask, twenty-four mahogany chairs (possibly covered with yellow damask), ten carved chairs, eight plain chairs, and others may have been used by Adams in Philadelphia and later transported to Washington.

Judging from an "Inventory of the Furniture in the President's House, the property of the United States, taken February 26, 1801," few rooms were furnished while the Adamses lived there. On the first floor, only the Dining Room, Levee Room, Breakfast Room, President's Drawing Room, Lodging Room, and Grand Hall were fully functional. The walls of the rooms were unornamented by either paintings or engravings, and only chamber glasses (mirrors) were hung on the walls. The sparingly described furniture suggests that little of it was new or stylish. Seating furniture was adequately supplied in all of the usable rooms where a total of one hundred fifty chairs were used. Some of the seating furniture from Philadelphia was upholstered in crimson. Mrs. Adams wrote her daughter that it had been placed in the handsome upstairs oval Ladies Drawing Room.[8]

Jefferson at the President's House

Although Jefferson was accustomed to the disorder that construction entailed, even he was deterred by the state of the building, which even lacked a "necessary," or privy. Soon after his inauguration, he left for Monticello on April 1 and returned on April 29. While he was gone, James Hoban and a team of workmen, including the fine decorative composition

United States Capitol Under Construction

1800
William Birch (1755–1834)
watercolor on paper
21.8 × 28.7 (8%16 × 11⁵⁄16 in.)
Library of Congress

maker George Andrews—who later made ornament for Monticello—struggled to complete the interior. Their work was not finished for almost a year.

The main entrance was positioned on the north front. Across the hall and opposite the entry was a spacious forty-by-thirty-foot oval room, used by the Adamses as an antechamber and by Jefferson as his main drawing room. Two dining rooms, a large public one at the northwest corner, and a smaller room adjacent to the Oval Drawing Room, were frequently used. Jefferson's own office in the southwest corner looking toward the Potomac, was largely completed. Meriwether Lewis, who was to serve as Jefferson's secretary, lived and worked in the East Room, which was somewhat crudely partitioned, with wood framing and heavy fabric, into an office and bedchamber.

Aided by the new surveyor of public buildings, Benjamin Henry Latrobe, Jefferson made several architectural changes to the President's House. Most significantly, Jefferson and Latrobe collaborated on the addition of the east and west wings, now vastly enlarged. One of the principal problems that they resolved was the placement of discreetly hidden service buildings. As at Monticello, Jefferson thought that one-story wings with terraces atop them would provide an unobtrusive solution. At the President's House, arcaded wings were to contain the dependencies and link the executive residence with the adjacent departments of State and Treasury.

The Jefferson Furnishings

Little is known about the furnishings of the President's House during Jefferson's two terms in office. Regrettably, virtually all of the furnishings that his successors, the Madisons, used—except the silver—perished in the short British invasion during the War of 1812; when on August 24, 1814 they set fire to the President's House, heaping the furnishings in piles and igniting them. Mrs. Madison was able to save only the most important governmental papers and a wagon with the "most valuable portible articles."[9] The scant salvaged property included most of the silver, the red velvet curtains from the Oval Drawing Room, Gilbert Stuart's full-length portrait of Washington that was hastily removed from its frame, and a small clock. Mrs. Madison escaped, sending her pet macaw ahead, to the nearby Octagon, the city home of Colonel and Mrs. John Tayloe III.

Some of the presidential furniture inherited by Jefferson was less than six months old, and the remainder, which had been actively used for ten years, was worn. Although President Adams had expended close to $6,000 for furnishings in August and November 1800, the perception was that the furnishings were tired and outmoded by the early part of Jefferson's first term. Part of the furniture even predated President Washington. One observer wrote that "Amongst the old furniture are articles which were in the use of the Presidents of the old Congress, long before the adoption of the constitution of the United States."[10] President Washington reported that the government's carpets in the Philadelphia house were so worn that they had to be replaced with his own. Margaret Bayard Smith, the observant and articulate wife of Samuel Harrison Smith, the editor of the *National Intelligencer*, reported that Jefferson retained the old furniture out of respect for his predecessor.[11] That supposition may indeed be true, but Jefferson also held on to the presidential furniture because Congress had appropriated $15,000 with which to outfit the entire mansion, the dwelling that Abigail Adams had likened to a "great castle."[12] Just two-thirds of the furnishing funds were left for Jefferson in 1801. By 1805, some of the rooms still had no furniture and others were only partially furnished. Judging by the February 19, 1809 inventory, completed just before he left office, Jefferson did an admirable job of furnishing the residence. He more than doubled the inventory, adding vastly to the collection of objects acquired by his two predecessors.

Through an unusually astute and style-conscious "Agent for furnishing the President's House" named Thomas Claxton, Jefferson acquired furnishings not only for the President's House but for Monticello as well. Claxton, who acted first as Adams's and later as Jefferson's buyer, not only carried out Jefferson's orders but also understood his taste. With his assistance, Jefferson outfitted the President's House and made it a place of great style. When his term was nearly expired, Jefferson commended Claxton on

the satisfactory manner in which you . . . conducted yourself in the purchase of furniture for the house[,] in truth, I say with pleasure that the integrity, diligence and economy with which you have employed the funds destined to that object, have given me perfect satisfaction.[13]

Claxton was also adept at dealing with Congress, and he had in his corner a strong Jefferson ally, Joseph H. Nicholson (1770–1817), the powerful Republican and chairman of the committee for furnishing the President's House. (It was Congressman Nicholson who, ill, was carried into the House to vote for Jefferson in his contest against Aaron Burr in the February 1801 presidential election.) Claxton persuaded Nicholson that the initial appropriation, awarded before the capital had been moved to Washington, was completely inadequate and that a minimum of $14,000 more was needed.[14] The additional funds were appropriated.

Before leaving on a trip to Philadelphia on May 18, 1801, Claxton wrote Jefferson, who had just returned to the President's House from Monticello, about "such articles as appears to me to be necessary for the farther completion of the furnishing of the President's House."[15] At the top of Claxton's list were curtains for windows in the Drawing Room, Meriwether Lewis's lodging and office in the East Room, and the second story of the north front. Claxton also passed on the needs of the steward and cook, who reported that they required five pairs of brass candlesticks, four patent lamps, a large dish kettle of cast iron, three common beds for servants, a Brussels carpet, four girandoles, and three dozen of the cheapest chairs. The kitchen had been well equipped by Washington and Adams; only a kettle was needed. Jefferson gave his approval to buy the fabric for the curtains, Claxton wrote on May 28 that "In consequence of the windows and floors requiring such monstrous large patterns of the same articles, I have been obliged to wait for the unloading of a ship."[16]

On the same trip to Philadelphia Claxton placed an order with the silversmiths Anthony Simmons and Samuel Alexander for one of the most distinctive of Jefferson's possessions, a silver version of a Roman pouring vessel called an "askos" (Cat. 185). Jefferson had seen the original in Nîmes in 1787 and originally intended it as a gift for Charles-Louis Clérisseau. After the first model was lost, Jefferson had his former *valet de place*, Souche, make a second one. Claxton evidently carried it to Philadelphia so that Simmons and Alexander could make a silver version to Jefferson's specifications.

Claxton also found a kind of grass matting in Philadelphia in 1802 that he thought was handsomer and cheaper than common painted floor cloths, but Jefferson rejected it. He preferred painted floor cloths beneath frequently used tables in the President's House. He wanted "to save a very handsome floor from grease and the scouring which that necessitates."[17] While he favored the appearance of straw floor cloths, Jefferson did not think that they were sufficiently durable to withstand repeated rolling and unrolling. Although he later purchased "a canvass floor cloth, painted Green" for the Small Dining Room and covered the whole floor of the Great Entrance Hall with "Canvas painted green," he initially decided against them because of their expense.[18]

Most floors in other rooms were protected by either common or Brussels carpet. At the top of the hierarchy, "elegant" Brussels carpets complemented the Ladies Drawing Room, the large bedroom on the south front, and Jefferson's sitting and drawing rooms.[19] Less-choice Brussels carpets shielded the floors of the large room on the north side, the passage near Jefferson's bedroom, Jefferson's bedroom itself, and on the second floor, the large bedroom on the south front and both bedrooms on the north front. Common carpet, cheaper than Brussels carpet, protected the floors that did not demand constant cleaning in less grand spaces, such as the second-floor passage.

The various kinds of chairs and tables were unmistakably grand. Seating furniture in public rooms was upholstered festively with matching colors for chairs and sofas alike. Jefferson favored crimson, green, or blue. As was the custom, window coverings and upholstery were often made of the same fabric. For example, the five windows of the Ladies Drawing Room featured crimson damask curtains that matched the upholstery of the twenty-two mahogany chairs and two sofas.

Jefferson, who was not bound by tradition, more often chose to mix different kinds of fabrics within one room. In his own Drawing Room in Washington, he combined five "Chints [painted or stained calicoes] window Curtains with cornice" with "4 large Mahogany Sofa's covered with hair cloth" and "24 fashionable Chairs—blue and Gold."[20] Chintz curtains similarly decorated the windows in many rooms.

For bedhangings and curtains Jefferson liked dimity, a stout, undyed cotton fabric woven with raised stripes or small repeating figures. Dimity window curtains hung in the presidential Dressing Room and Bed Room, where it was used with "5 fashionable Chairs—crimson and Gold" and a window stool with a stuffed seat and white dimity cover. Jefferson neither reserved dimity for private use nor restricted its use seasonally. When Claxton prepared the inventory sometime in the early months of 1809, he noted dimity curtains in the Large Dining Room—N.W. Corner, the Large Chamber—South Front, and the Large Bed Room—South Front, as well as on the secretary's bedstead.

Not surprisingly, Jefferson took an interest in the design of the curtains at the President's House, and at least some of the curtains were probably made to his specifications. In a sketch dated January 12, 1803, he diagrammed curtains to be made in dimity and calculated how much yardage would be required for rooms at the President's House in addition to Monticello's Dining Room. Jefferson wrote, "17 yds. of dimity will be requisite for each window at Monticello."[21]

Although cabinetmakers in other cities were equipped to make fashionable furniture,

Claxton probably ordered furnishings for the President's House from Baltimore and Philadelphia. Claxton, who had lived in Philadelphia before coming to Washington, was probably more familiar with Philadelphia makers. Baltimore was far closer, however, and had many talented cabinetmakers.

Not enough is known about the 207 gold-painted chairs placed in various public and private rooms at the President's House. Gilded chairs were exceedingly popular with Jefferson, who was probably still enamored of French furniture, which tended to be either painted or gilded, or both. French furnishings had been popular in Philadelphia during the previous decade, and Jefferson had probably seen the chairs there imported from Versailles by Gouverneur Morris. While Jefferson served in Philadelphia as secretary of state and as vice president, he may also have known that Philadelphia cabinetmakers were making and selling "French chairs."[22] Given Jefferson's experience in France, many of the chairs purchased for the President's House could have been American interpretations of the Louis XVI style.

Whether they were French or English-inspired, the chairs at the President's House were at the cutting edge of fashionable interior decor. The chairs also might have been Federal, a style inspired by a renewed appreciation of ancient Rome and popularized in England by the Scots architects Robert Adam and his brother William. The Neoclassical style, called "Federal" in America, was far more popular than the French Louis XVI style, perhaps because of the greater accessibility of English publications. In any case, American cabinetmakers who wanted to be as smart as London makers had recently discovered delicate chair designs in books such as Thomas Sheraton's *Cabinet-Maker and Upholsterer's Drawing Book* (1791). These designs lent themselves to decorative painting and gilding.

Thirty-six crimson-and-gold, thirty-six green-and-gold, one hundred five black-and-gold, and thirty blue-and-gold chairs were dispersed among seventeen different rooms. The descriptions of the numerous "black and Gold chairs" in the Inventory regrettably does not reveal much information about them. These chairs might have been variously treated. They might have had gilded frames with black upholstery (durable woven horsehair would have been typical) or they could have been "Fancy" chairs with black painted frames embellished with burnished or painted gold.

The standing furniture—dining tables, card tables, side tables, bedsteads, library steps, washstands, dressing tables, wardrobes, commodes, bureaus, sideboards, and even a small child's bedstead—was mahogany without any mention of gilding. Most of the works purchased by Thomas Claxton for Presidents Adams and Jefferson (with the possible exception of the two sideboards), and especially those pieces described as "elegant," were undoubtedly Federal—forms derived from Greek and Roman sources that were sometimes decorated by delicate reeding and varicolored inlays of woods in decorative patterns.

On the other hand, the two sideboards, one each in the Small and Large Dining Rooms, may not have been Federal. One of them was described as "1 elegant side board with pedestals & urns." The prominence of the words pedestal and urn suggest that they figured conspicuously. The sideboards could have been similar to the works of Charles-Honoré Lannuier (1779–1819), a French émigré cabinetmaker who worked in New York and who was known for his bold designs. Similar works were also made in Baltimore.

Dining

At the President's House Jefferson often held small dinner parties and calculated how to use these social occasions to his political advantage. He recognized that his effectiveness as president would be enhanced by frequent informal contact with senators and congressmen. When Congress was in session, Jefferson entertained several times each week, inviting no more than thirteen congressmen and officials to join him and his secretary for dinner. In fact, the Small and Large Dining Rooms each contained only fifteen chairs. With such a small group arranged around an oval table, where all were visible, Jefferson could speak with each person. As host Jefferson made a point of engaging everyone in the conversation.[23] At the President's House, Margaret Bayard Smith reported:

When he had any persons dining with him, with whom he wished to enjoy a free and unrestricted flow of conversation, the number of persons at table never exceed four, and by each individual was placed a dumb-waiter, containing everything necessary for the progress of dinner from beginning to end.[24]

The dinners were renowned for their cuisine as much as for their unconventional approach to traditional social customs. The hierarchy of standard protocol, where dinner guests were seated by rank, was set aside in favor of more democratic behavior; guests sometimes even seated themselves. Offended by what he perceived as an indignity, the new minister from Britain, Anthony Merry, reported that there was "an absolute omission of all distinction" for him and his wife at a dinner.[25] For privacy's sake Jefferson disliked the typical profusion of servants (one for each dinner guest) and did two things to reduce their number. First, a set of revolving circular shelves was set into the wall so that dinner dishes could be removed without opening and shutting doors. Second, parties of four were entertained in the Small Dining Room where self-service was made possible by using four "small Mahogany Dumb Waiters," tiers of shelves on wheels that contained the various dishes of the meal.

The furnishings in the Small Dining Room were chosen with flexibility in mind. The "extra large Mahogany Dining Table in 6 pieces" could be configured to accommodate the exact number of guests. This table, definitely procured during Jefferson's term, replaced either a pine dining table with seven parts or a double breakfast table of the Adams period. The table, with four or six leaves, may have been one of the newly popular ones with four scissor-type legs or the more traditional banquet table with D-shaped ends. The Small Dining Room also contained a large square mahogany table, an oval breakfast table, and two glass cases that held a large number of silver and plated wares. A green-painted canvas cloth protected the floor from spills.

The delicious meals prepared by Jefferson's French chef were exquisitely presented in china or silver serving dishes. The silver included six casseroles, two bread baskets, two punch urns, two coffee urns, a tea urn, two terrines, two pudding dishes, a teapot, and cream and sugar pots. As many as ten branched candlesticks, a candlestick with a double lamp, and two girandoles illuminated the Small Dining Room. Two branched candlesticks were routinely placed atop the sideboard, and two mirrors reflected the sparkling light.

A Federalist reported that he had

sat down to the table at four, rose at six, and walked immediately into another room, and drank coffee. . . . had a very good dinner, with a profusion of fruits and sweetmeats. The wine was the best I ever drank, particularly the champagne, which was indeed delicious. I wish his French politics were as good as his French wines; but to me, at least, they have by no means so exquisite a flavor.[26]

The paucity of dining accoutrements stored there indicates that the Large Dining Room, which could also manage as many as fifteen dinner guests, was used less often. The furnishings were far sparer there than in the Small Dining Room; although a larger room, it contained only two pairs of candlesticks, two girandoles, and three sideboards.

◆ The Public Monticello ◆

Even while president, Jefferson often withdrew to his cherished Monticello, "in order to avoid the bad air of the City of Washington," for two months or so during the heat of summer, when yellow fever and ague were likely to strike.[1] His vision of the home coalesced during his presidency as the building neared completion. Although the overall first impression of Monticello's interior was eclectic, the scheme for it was decidedly purposeful as well as functional. Housed within the structure—Jefferson's reference to the architecture of the Roman republic and what John Dos Passos called "his portico facing the wilderness"—was a disparate collection of the objects associated with the ideas and activities that Jefferson prized. Monticello's interior was a highly idiosyncratic embodiment of the interests that traced his achievements, reflected his immense curiosity, and revealed his view of the world.

Entrance Hall: The Monticello Museum

The Entrance Hall, so often described by visitors as a museum, was planned by Jefferson for precisely that purpose. In 1795, the visitor Isaac Weld commented, before construction of the second Monticello was much under way, that "A large apartment is laid out for a library and museum."[2] In this double-storied room, where the sometimes numerous visitors waited in Windsor armchairs, grew a remarkable collection of paintings, sculpture, bones, minerals, maps, and precious Native American artifacts that had been accumulated by Meriwether Lewis and William Clark on their famous western expedition of 1804–06, which Jefferson had sponsored as president.

◆   ◆   ◆

Several distinctive architectural features heightened the dramatic impression that characterized the Entrance Hall. First, the double-story height lent a sensation of grandeur and expansiveness. The ceiling was decorated by a plaster eagle surrounded by clouds and

eighteen stars, which suggests that it was completed between 1812 and 1816—after Louisiana was admitted as the eighteenth state in 1812 and before Indiana was admitted in 1816. The uppermost section of the wall was decorated with an elaborate entablature with a frieze of urns and marching griffins drawn directly from the "temple d'Antonin et de Faustine," Plate IV, in Antoine Babuty Desgodetz's *Les Edifices Antiques de Rome* (1779). The superbly detailed composition ornament for the frieze was made by George Andrews of Alexandria in 1803. Jefferson knew Andrews's fine craftsmanship from his work at the President's House and might also have seen his composition work at the Tayloes' Octagon house.

Jefferson had determined the color of the Entrance Hall floor while sitting for a portrait by Gilbert Stuart. It was Stuart, Jefferson wrote,

who had first suggested to me the painting a floor green, which he had himself tried with fine effect. He observed that care should be taken to hit the true grass-green, and as he had his pallet and colours in his hand, I asked him to give me a specimen of the colour, which he instantly mixed up to his mind, and I spread it with a knife on the inclosed paper.[3]

On June 8, 1805, Jefferson wrote James Dinsmore, one of his ablest workmen at Monticello, and instructed him that "the floor should be painted the instant you have it ready."[4] Richard Barry, an itinerant painter, was to carry out the work. Nearly two years went by, however, before the green floor was completed. In the interim Barry painted a cloth to protect the floor, and in April 1807 Jefferson wrote Barry and told him to finish the hall floor.

Jefferson's overall guiding principle for the selection and arrangement of objects at Monticello was educational rather than decorative; he believed that the future of the United States absolutely depended upon the informed involvement of each citizen. The only means to assure a population capable of making informed choices was to edify it, and Jefferson seized every opportunity to advance his cause.

The Entrance Hall contained the most dramatic examples of this ambition. Although this public space where visitors were received was crowded with an eclectic mix of objects, Jefferson had organized it with two objectives: first, to trace the history of civilization and human achievement from the earliest moments to the present, and second, to place Monticello within the context of the universe and natural world.

◆ ◆ ◆

Jefferson collected the best and most accurate maps throughout his lifetime, accumulating a collection of more than three hundred fifty different kinds of maps, navigational charts, and city plans. Eight or more large engraved wall maps, varnished and attached to rollers, and two Indian maps on leather dominated the Entrance Hall. Here a visitor could study the geography of the world and then locate Charlottesville on two maps of Virginia (Cat. 239, 240). Jefferson's interest in maps was keen and probably was inherited from his father, the surveyor who had charted the Virginia and North Carolina border. Two maps of Virginia were displayed: the famous Fry–Jefferson map itself, which had become the standard map of Virginia in the later half of the eighteenth century; and Bishop James Madison's map, which was first published in 1807 and featured a vista of Richmond with the prominent State Capitol drawn by the artist Saint-Mémin.

West Front

Margaret Bayard Smith, 1809:

"Monticello is a small mountain, rising six hundred feet above the surrounding country, on the summit of which is a large edifice, built in the modern style . . . a lofty dome of twenty-eight [feet] in diameter rises from the center of the building."

To position Monticello within the larger world, Jefferson displayed his latest and largest acquisitions, including maps of the United States, Europe, Africa, and Asia published between 1796 and 1805 by Aaron Arrowsmith, the celebrated London mapmaker. These were ordered directly from London "varnished and on rollers" so that they could be displayed. At his own expense Jefferson also secured William Faden's map of South America in 1805, nearly twenty years after he had sent Faden his own copy of Cruz Cano's South America to copy for himself and Congress (Cat. 241). The map of the world may have been one of the ancient world by Jean Baptiste Bourguignon d'Anville, mapmaker to Louis XVI, whose specialty was the antique world. Jefferson purchased at least seven maps by d'Anville in 1787, and he may have studied the great collection of ancient maps assembled by d'Anville that Louis XVI acquired in 1782.

◆   ◆   ◆

Steadfastly committed to portraying the natural history of the American continent as well as the history of its human inhabitants, Jefferson collected specimens of many different animals, including examples of extinct species. In late November 1782, as he was about to depart for France, Jefferson was eager to obtain mammoth and other kinds of specimens from George Rogers Clark and told him that "A specimen of each of the several species of bones now to be found is to me the most desireable object in Natural history."[5] He was particularly eager to locate "elkhorns of very extraordinary size, petrifications, or any thing else uncommon."[6] These he wanted not only to satisfy his own curiosity but also to present to scientists in France.

Jefferson urgently wanted the specimens in order to disprove what he thought were the uninformed theories of the comte de Buffon, a prominent naturalist who argued that the species of the New World were literally inferior because the New World itself was intrinsically inferior and thus incapable of producing animal or human populations equal to those of the Old. In an effort to dispute Buffon, Jefferson presented him with a massive skeleton of an American moose or palmated elk, which stood one-third taller than the European elk. In *Notes on the State of Virginia*, Jefferson indicated that he believed that the mammoth, which he calculated was six times the size of an elephant, still existed in the northern parts of America.

Among Jefferson's most prized possessions were the thigh, jawbone, and tusk of the mastodon, then called a "mammoth," which he eventually obtained in 1807 (Cat. 251, 252). His preoccupation with obtaining the bones of a mammoth was not unique. In fact, his curiosity about paleontology may have been piqued by Dr. John Morgan of Philadelphia, who had obtained some fifty bones gathered by his brother George Morgan from Big Bone Lick in 1766, at just about the time that Jefferson met Morgan on his first trip to Philadelphia. The bones drew visitors, including John Adams, who dined with Morgan in 1774, and wrote about them. Although there is no record of it, Jefferson might also have seen Morgan's mastodon bones when he returned to Philadelphia in 1775.[7]

Jefferson's interest in mastodons was shared not only by fellow members of the American Philosophical Society—the eminent Philadelphia learned society of which he served as president from 1797 to 1815—but also by Charles Willson Peale, the painter and

naturalist, who wrote Jefferson a detailed letter about the discovery of a great mastodon near Newburgh, New York. (The mastodon became the subject of one of Peale's greatest works, *The Exhumation of the Mastodon*, 1806–08.)

Jefferson had to wait for twenty-five years to obtain mastodon bones for his own collection. In 1807 George Rogers Clark's younger brother, William, excavated more than three hundred from Big Bone Lick just after he returned from his celebrated trip west with Meriwether Lewis. Most of the bones were collected for the Philosophical Society, but Clark designated some for Jefferson, "particularly the large Tusk and Thy bone, several teeth, and Eliphants tusk and Part of the head."[8] To contrast the animals of the Old and New Worlds, Jefferson placed the upper and lower jawbones and tusks of the mastodon and elephant next to one another.[9] Proud of his quarry, in 1815 Jefferson remarked to George Ticknor, a visitor from Boston, that he had the only *os frontis* that had yet been found.[10]

Without question, the most controversial specimen to be displayed in the Entrance Hall was the fossil remains of the *Megalonyx* (or Great Claw), named by Jefferson, and excavated in Greenbrier County, in what is now West Virginia.[11] Jefferson thought that the three claws, forearm, unbroken radius, and part of the thighbone were from an animal that was to a lion what the mammoth was to an elephant. Just before traveling to Philadelphia in 1797, he prepared a paper that incorporated some tall tales, asserting that the roar of the *Megalonyx* had been heard and seen by hunters. Just before he presented his rather creative findings to the Philosophical Society, Jefferson came upon an account by the young scientist Georges Cuvier that properly classified a similar specimen found in Paraguay, which he called a "megatherium," as a cousin of a sloth. Without abandoning his hypothesis, Jefferson softened the conclusions of his paper and donated the *Megalonyx* fossils to the Philosophical Society. He was not definitively proved wrong for several years.

In addition to the fossils of the *Megalonyx* and mastodon, various other kinds of petrifications were displayed, including "the remains of reptiles and preserved insects."[12] The same visitor reported that the "innumerable relics and curiosities . . . reminded me of the adornments of Romeo's apothecary shop where 'a tortoise hung, an alligator stuffed, and other skins of ill shaped fishes.'"[13]

With considerable effort, more natural-history samples found their way into the Entrance Hall. The Lewis and Clark expedition returned thrilling specimens to President Jefferson and was itself an emblem of Jefferson's own thoughts and interests. His desire to map the American West converged with his curiosity about American natural history and Native American culture. To assure the explorers' familiarity with scientific investigation, Jefferson made sure that Lewis, an unusually intelligent man of twenty-nine, traveled first to Philadelphia to be tutored by the leading members of the Philosophical Society and then to Lancaster to meet Andrew Ellicott, the surveyor and astronomer. Before Lewis visited these experts, Jefferson polled some of his colleagues about the kinds of data that should be gathered.

On their trip Lewis and Clark collected many Native American artifacts; minerals; plants; several live animals, including four magpies and a sharp-tailed grouse; and animal skins, horns, and skeletons. The explorers presented Jefferson with the skins and skeletons of at least three American argali, or bighorn sheep. Jefferson, in turn, sent these to Charles

Willson Peale, who counted taxidermy among his many uncommon skills. Peale mounted one of the bighorn heads for Monticello's Entrance Hall and kept a male and female for his own Peale Museum in Philadelphia.[14]

◆　◆　◆

Keenly interested in Native Americans, Jefferson investigated their burial mounds not far from Monticello along the Rivanna River. He also studied Native American languages, even to the point of collecting vocabularies, which were stolen and mostly destroyed in 1809 en route from Washington to Charlottesville. One of the major achievements of Jefferson's *Notes on the State of Virginia* was his methodical analysis and description of native Virginians and Americans, which he understood was far from complete. He was able to trace the history of the various tribes of Virginia as far back as 1607, when the first English colonists arrived, and to identify some of their lands and languages.

Jefferson explicitly instructed Lewis to learn as much as he could about the diverse peoples he encountered:

make yourself acquainted . . . with the names of the nations and their numbers; the extent of their possessions; their relations with other tribes or nations; their language, traditions, monuments; their ordinary occupations in agriculture, fishing, hunting, war, arts, and the implements for these; their food, clothing and domestic accommodations . . .[15]

Most of the natural-history specimens were shipped back in 1804 and 1805, and the Native American artifacts, distributed between Jefferson and Charles Willson Peale, were sent east in two shipments in 1805 and 1806. In 1805 Jefferson wrote Peale to tell him what he planned for Monticello:

I arrived [in Washington] two days ago, & found the articles which had been forwarded by Capt. Lewis. . . . There are some articles which I shall keep for an Indian Hall I am forming at Monticello, e.g. horns, dressed skins, utensils &c.[16]

His Indian Hall was quickly realized at Monticello. Many of the objects accumulated by Lewis and Clark during the winter of 1804–05 arrived at the President's House in August 1805 and were then shipped to and installed at Monticello. Jefferson instructed Lewis to bring Sheheke, the Mandan chief, to see the "tokens of friendship" that he had assembled there. He also had Native American artifacts in Washington.[17]

Among the three boxes, two cases, and a barrel unwrapped in Washington was the most significant object of the entire expedition, the great painted Mandan buffalo robe portraying a battle between the Mandans, Minitarras, and Ahwahharways against the Sioux and Ricaras (Cat. 259). Jefferson displayed it in the Entrance Hall juxtaposed to an Old Master painting. George Ticknor commented in 1815 that "in odd union with a fine painting of the Repentance of Saint Peter, is an Indian map on leather, of the southern waters of the Missouri, and an Indian representation of a bloody battle."[18] The contrast between the intersecting cultures of Native Americans and Westerners was thus intentionally emphasized.

Jefferson's observations about the specifics of Native American culture and the larger trends among its population were remarkable for their insight. Lamenting the rapid disappearance of many tribes and cultures, Jefferson noted how some tribes were reduced to only ten or twelve people and fifty acres. In *Notes on the State of Virginia*, Jefferson made clear the decline of the Native American population in the state:

What would be the melancholy sequel of their history, may however be augured from the census of 1669; by which we discover that the tribes therein enumerated were, in the space of 62 years, reduced to about one-third of their former numbers.[19]

Although Jefferson respected Native Americans and their distinct cultures, he ultimately looked upon them as savages—albeit noble ones—who would best be served by adopting the agrarian society of the white man if they were to survive in a changed world.

What we now view as his "ethnocentricity" did not lessen Jefferson's historical and scientific interest in Native American culture. Forty artifacts were exhibited in the Entrance Hall, emphasizing Jefferson's crusade to learn about all aspects of the lives and cultures of America's indigenous population. Among the artifacts collected by Lewis and Clark and displayed at Monticello were objects relating to warfare, dress, cooking, and other aspects of domestic life. They consisted of various Mandan specimens, including the buffalo robe, a chief's robe of buffalo hide, a bone whistle, headdress, warrior's dress, six pairs of moccasins, and two pairs of garters. Artifacts from other tribes were a Chippewa knife scabbard; a Winnebago flute; a Crow tobacco pouch; a Sauk/Fox tobacco pouch made from an otter skin (Cat. 254); an Arrickaree necklace; a Sioux dress; three Missouri pipes and stems; and various works of unidentified tribes, including a ladle made from the horn of a mountain sheep, arrows, and a rattle for making music.

Jefferson also displayed a pair of seated figures, which he described as "two busts of Indian figures, male & female by Indians, in hard stone. . . . dug up at a place called Palmyra, on the Tennissee." A report published in 1808 recounted that

the traits are well marked, and characterize those which are peculiar to copper-coloured men; one of them in particular represents an old Savage: the wrinkles in his face and his whole countenance peculiarly expressive.[20]

The more urbane baron de Montlezun, however, found them decidedly crude: "Two stone busts, sculptured by the Indians, one representing a man and the other a woman. The faces are hideous. . . . They were doubtless designated, and have much similarity with those divinities of the Egyptians and orientals . . ."[21]

◆   ◆   ◆

At least four portrait busts and an engraving of John Trumbull's *Declaration of Independence* in the Entrance Hall signaled Jefferson's interest in marking his own intellectual development and political activity. Displayed on brackets affixed to the east wall were terra-cotta patinated plasters by Houdon of Turgot (Cat. 90), the French economist, and Voltaire (Cat. 89), the French philosopher and literary figure. Jefferson brought these back from Paris together with similar plasters by Houdon of himself (Cat. 101), George Washington (Cat. 93), John Paul Jones (Cat. 95), the marquis de Lafayette (Cat. 92), and Benjamin Franklin (Cat. 94). Patriots of the American Revolution were grouped in the Tea Room, and Jefferson placed the two French personalities in the Entrance Hall.

Jefferson evidently saw Turgot and Voltaire as reformers whose views foreshadowed the French Revolution. Turgot was widely known for his recommended revisions of the French system of taxation, which were designed to protect the poor and which Louis XVI rejected. Voltaire, the famed *philosophe* and satirist who was alienated from the French court, came to symbolize the rational spirit of the French Revolution. Voltaire and Turgot symbolically linked the French and American Revolutions.

Jefferson's political struggles were represented by portraits of himself and his political rival, Alexander Hamilton, who "opposed one another in death as in life" on facing sides of the Entrance Hall (Cat. 91). Both were sculpted by Giuseppe Ceracchi. The colossal portrait of Jefferson, draped in Roman costume, towered above the life-size portrait of Hamilton, suggesting that Jefferson's vision of autonomy would overshadow Hamilton's Federalism. Jefferson's portrait was placed atop his gift from Madame de Tessé, a broken column of dark green marble, decorated by the twelve signs of the zodiac and the symbols of the ten lost tribes of Israel.

The collection of sculpture in the Entrance Hall was completed by a reclining portrait of Ariadne (Cat. 107), which was the gift in 1804 of James Bowdoin, then minister to Spain. At first, Jefferson thought that she was Cleopatra and described her as such in his Catalogue of Paintings, but later he corrected his mistake. Whether Ariadne or Cleopatra, she was one of only three references to an ancient civilization in the Entrance Hall. (The other two allusions were a model of the Great Pyramid of Cheops and the frieze derived from the Temple of Antoninus and Faustina.) Except in winter, *Ariadne* was placed directly in front of the fireplace.

◆　　◆　　◆

The acceptance of the Declaration of Independence by the Continental Congress was Jefferson's finest moment and the greatest achievement of the American Revolution. He prominently displayed an engraving of John Trumbull's famous painting of the event in the Entrance Hall (Cat. 31). Jefferson wanted the significance of the Declaration to be recognized, and he urged the young Trumbull to render it and other events of the Revolution accurately. Moreover, he wanted these depictions of American historical milestones to be popularly available. He subscribed to the first engraving of Trumbull's masterpiece, *The Declaration of Independence*, completed by the young Asher B. Durand in 1823, three years after Trumbull finally finished the work that he had begun in Jefferson's house in Paris during the winter of 1787–88.

Eleven paintings—all acquired in France—were hung about the Entrance Hall. The subjects were all biblical. In his Catalogue of Paintings Jefferson even attempted to cite the biblical chapter and verse where the subject appeared. Although the themes of the paintings were predominantly New Testament, two of the most powerful stories of the Old Testament, *David with the Head of Goliath*, copied after Guido Reni, and the *Sacrifice of Isaac* by an unknown artist, were also exhibited. Aside from their biblical significance, both

Pedestal for Ceracchi's bust of Thomas Jefferson

Cornelia J. Randolph
(1799–1871)
ink on paper, 6.7 × 2.9
(2⅝ × 1³⁄₁₆ in.)
Thomas Jefferson Memorial
Foundation Papers (5385-ac),
Special Collections Department,
University of Virginia Library

of these paintings may also have symbolized Jefferson's own political experiences and those of his country. The colonists, like David, rose up to defeat a mightier enemy. Jefferson and his compatriots, like Abraham, were called upon to test their beliefs and principles, and prevailed.

Several of the Christian subjects placed in the Entrance Hall also seem to have been meaningful to Jefferson; their subjects were related to the pursuit of knowledge and truth. For example, Jefferson's selection of *Saint Jerome*, the greatest Christian scholar of his age, known as a writer and a translator of ancient texts, plainly reflected Jefferson's erudite interests (Cat. 16). *Jesus among the Doctors*, in which Jesus at an early age revealed his unusual knowledge to the rabbinic elders of the temple, again drew attention to learning and wisdom. The life of Jesus was further explicated by *Jesus Driving the Money Changers out of the Temple*, copied after Valentin. The temple was polluted by business, and Jesus expelled the offenders—not at all unlike Jefferson's view in his draft of the Declaration of Independence that George III and the British had contaminated the American colonies and therefore must be ousted. *Jesus before Pilate, Jesus in the Praetorium, Ecce Homo* after Guido Reni, and *Saint Peter Weeping* described the flawed judicial process and the suffering that it brought. These pictures, closely related to one another, depict Jesus being judged by Pontius Pilate's court, capped by a crown of thorns after his condemnation, and awaiting execution in the Praetorium, as well as Saint Peter crying at the outcome.

Two additional New Testament paintings—*John the Baptist*, after Leonardo da Vinci, and *Saint Joseph* after an unidentified artist—are less open to political interpretation and probably related more to Jefferson's spiritual beliefs. In his view, Jesus was a great moral teacher. Until Jefferson encountered the work of Joseph Priestley, he thought that he had spurned Christianity; but upon reading Priestley he discovered that "what he had rejected were only its corruptions."[22] While retired at Monticello, Jefferson put together the *Life and Morals of Jesus of Nazareth*, a compilation of the genuine precepts of Jesus in Latin, Greek, French, and English, culled from the New Testament.

◆　　◆　　◆

The Entrance Hall was primarily a reception area for visitors, who waited here to meet Jefferson or members of his family. The large number of chairs confirms that many people journeyed to Monticello, and the Entrance Hall was the only interior space that every visitor was assured of encountering. Twenty-eight Windsor chairs, some of which Jefferson acquired in 1801 from the Philadelphia chairmaker Adam Snyder, probably were those used in the Entrance Hall as they are the ones described in the 1826 inventory made after Jefferson's death. The high price that Jefferson paid Snyder suggests that these fashionable black-painted chairs probably had mahogany arms and were highlighted by gold leaf. Wall space was limited, so presumably the chairs were arranged in rows.

Aside from abundant seating furniture, the Entrance Hall was sparsely furnished. Two marble-top tables with slipper feet (the tops were those brought back from Paris) flanked the double-acting doors leading to the Parlor (Cat. 165). A pair of Argand-type lamps may have been fixed to the wall above the mantel. A lantern hung from the center of the ceiling, but it is not known with certainty if it was the present English four-burner

Argand-type lamp. A marble slab on brackets was positioned on the southeast wall, apparently to hold small objects such as crystals and minerals.

The famous large, double-faced clock with cannonball weights, believed to have been made to Jefferson's design by the Philadelphia clock maker Peter Spruck, an apprentice to Robert Leslie, was completed sometime in late 1793 (Cat. 236). It was installed above the entrance doors and had markers for the days of the week on the southeast wall. The heavy cannonball weights, which still power the clock, descend the wall from Sunday to Thursday and then disappear into the cellar on Friday and Saturday. The second face of the clock, with only an hour hand, was visible on the East Portico. The clock was also connected to a Chinese gong encased in a housing atop the roof. Margaret Bayard Smith reported, "On the top of the house was a *ghan*, instead of a bell—why he preferred this Chinese invention, to our mode of calling people together, I cannot tell, except it is on account of its newness and originality."[23]

Parlor

The elegant Parlor with its high ceiling was one of the principal public spaces of the house, along with the Dining Room, Tea Room, and Entrance Hall. Although the interior was substantially refined after 1796, the Parlor is the only space of the original "first" Monticello to survive largely intact. The marquis de Chastellux described it in 1782 as a "large and lofty *salon*, or drawing room, which is to be decorated entirely in the antique style."[24] The elaborate entablature was based on an illustration of the Temple of Jupiter the Thunderer, published in Roland Fréart de Chambray's *Parallèle de l'architecture antique avec la moderne* (1766) and completed about 1803, when Jefferson paid George Andrews of Alexandria for his composition ornaments. The intricate beech-and-cherry parquet floor, completed in 1806, is an interlocking design of octagons, hexagons, and squares; it was "kept polished as highly as if it were of fine mahogany."[25]

Once the interior features were completed, brilliant crimson draperies were ordered to ornament the tops of four triple-sash windows. Jefferson sent a sketch and precise specifications to the Philadelphia upholsterer John Rea in 1808. He requested "crimson damask silk lined with green and a yellow fringe."[26] Rea was unable to supply damask, so he instead used mantua, an unpatterned fine glazed silk, the same material he used for Jefferson's counterpane, or bedcover.

◆　◆　◆

The Parlor, which contained fifty-seven works of art, offered Jefferson another opportunity to instruct his visitors and family. He said that he wanted to "improve the taste of his countrymen." Although fifteen Old Master paintings and two watercolor drawings of birds were exhibited, the collection in the Parlor predominantly

Sketch of Parlor Window Draperies
March 2, 1808
Thomas Jefferson
ink on paper
Jefferson Papers, Library of Congress

Sketch of Parlor Window Draperies
April 25, 1808
John Rea (active 1799–c. 1829)
ink on paper
Jefferson Papers, Library of Congress

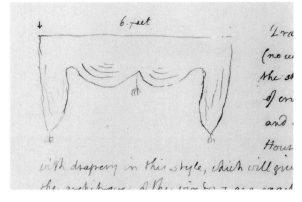

concentrated on historical biography. Here were shown thirty-five portraits of the men (no portraits of women were displayed) who had shaped Jefferson's intellectual development as well as American and world history.

Chief among these portraits, and placed on the uppermost of three tiers on unpainted plaster walls, were the triumverate of Enlightenment thinkers whom Jefferson most admired: John Locke (Cat. 6), Isaac Newton, and Francis Bacon. Of all the works of art in the Parlor, Jefferson named them first in his Catalogue of Paintings and said, "Mr. Trumbul (the painter) procured these copies for Th. J. from originals in England."[27] In his recognition of Locke, Newton, and Bacon, Jefferson acknowledged his enormous intellectual debt to them. From Newton's works Jefferson derived an outlook that was based on science and reason, and Locke influenced him most in shaping his ideas about religious freedom. From Locke, Jefferson learned about "the workings of knowledge, the proper mode of education, and the reasonableness of belief."[28] To Bacon Jefferson was indebted for his systematic classification of knowledge.

Portraits of the explorers Christopher Columbus (Cat. 8), Ferdinand Magellan, Hernando Cortez, and Sir Walter Raleigh (Cat. 11) also hung on the upper tier with a portrait of the person thought to have drawn the first map of America, Amerigo Vespucci (Cat. 9). While Jefferson was serving in France, he had copies of Columbus, Vespucci, Magellan, and Cortez made after portraits in the Uffizi. He said that he "considered it as even of some public concern that our country should not be without the portraits of its first discoverers."[29] The likeness of Sir Walter Raleigh, the English explorer, was copied after a portrait that Jefferson erroneously thought was executed by Holbein, which was secured for him by John Adams's son-in-law, William Stephens Smith in 1787.

Together with the explorers and the triumverate of Jefferson's worthies hung paintings of the eminent heroes of the Revolution George Washington (Cat. 1), John Adams (Cat. 4), James Madison, Benjamin Franklin (Cat. 12), and the marquis de Lafayette (Cat. 10). Jefferson said of Washington:

His mind was great and powerful, without being of the very first order; his penetration strong, though not so acute as that of a Newton, Bacon, or Locke; and as far as he saw, no judgement was ever sounder.[30]

Jefferson commissioned Joseph Wright to paint a large canvas of Washington in 1784 and later acquired at least five other likenesses of him: two busts by Houdon (one plaster and one marble), an engraving by Wright (Cat. 35), an engraving after a drawing by Madame de Bréhan (Cat. 36), and medals made in France (Cat. 113) and England (Cat. 111).

Benjamin Franklin (Cat. 12) hung on the upper tier between *John Locke* and *Herodias Bearing the Head of Saint John*. Jefferson also owned two other images of this respected friend, whom he considered "the greatest man and ornament of the age and country in which he lived."[31] Franklin's appeal to Jefferson stemmed from his intelligence and wit, but especially from his diverse interests that paralleled Jefferson's own.

A large portrait of the marquis de Lafayette was executed by the French painter Joseph Boze for Jefferson in 1790 (Cat. 10). To Jefferson Lafayette exemplified the spirit of friendship and liberty shared by the French and American peoples, and he called

Francis Bacon (1561–1626)
1731 copy after c. 1618 original copy by Johan van der Banck (c. 1694–1739) after unknown artist
oil on canvas
127.6 × 102.6 (50¼ × 40⅜ in.)
National Portrait Gallery, London

Sir Isaac Newton (1642–1727)
1702
Sir Godfrey Kneller (1646–1723)
oil on canvas
75.6 × 62.2 (29¾ × 24½ in.)
National Portrait Gallery, London

Parlor

Jane Blair Smith, 1823–24:

". . . a spacious lofty apartment hung with pictures from floor to ceiling—many fine ones and many inferior—old French mirrors on either side of the door reflected the lawn."

Lafayette "the doyen of our military heroes."[32] As early as 1781 Jefferson recognized Lafayette's dedication to the American cause when he wrote him that "it gives me great Pleasure that we shall be so far indebted for it to a Nobleman who has already so much endeared himself to the Citizens of these States by his past Exertions."[33]

James Madison, Jefferson's friend, political ally, and Presidential successor, was portrayed in a painting in 1790, now lost, by Robert Pine. Jefferson respected him unequivocally, and in his *Autobiography* he wrote:

Of the powers and polish of his pen, and of the wisdom of his administration in the highest office of the nation, I need say nothing. They have spoken, and will forever speak for themselves.[34]

Both Jefferson and John Adams sat in London for Mather Brown, an American student of Benjamin West (Cat. 4, 5). Jefferson obtained a copy of Brown's likeness of Adams, and Adams kept a copy of the portrait of Jefferson (the original is lost). Their interrupted friendship was not without turbulence, but goodwill prevailed at the end of their lives, and Jefferson did not forget their old ties. He wrote, ". . . we were fellow laborers in the same cause, struggling for what is most valuable to man, his right of self-government."[35] They had known one another well as fellow members of the committee to draft the declaration of American independence. By the time they served in Paris together in 1784 Jefferson had a more critical view of Adams. Jefferson found him

vain, irritable and a bad calculator of the force & probably effect of the motives which govern men. This is all the ill which can possibly be said of him . . . he is profound in his views; and accurate in his judgement except where knowledge of the world is necessary to form a judgement.[36]

Subsequently, Adams became a Federalist and, as the departing second president in 1801, made last-minute appointments to federal offices that infuriated Jefferson, who then severed his relationship with him. Their correspondence, on Adams's initiative, was resumed in 1812. Both died in 1826 on the fiftieth anniversary of the acceptance of the Declaration of Independence.

In the middle tier of the Parlor, Jefferson exhibited (among others) two paintings acquired for mysterious reasons; their contentious subjects would seem to have held little interest for him. Nonetheless, portraits were featured of the brilliant naval admiral and unscrupulous leader Andrea Doria (1466–1560) and Castruccio Castracani (1281–1328), the duke of Lucca who defeated the Florentines. The portrait of Castracani was obtained for Jefferson by his friend Philip Mazzei in 1790. Also in the middle tier smaller engraved likenesses were displayed of Lazare Hoche, the young French general; David Rittenhouse, the brilliant scientist from Philadelphia; and Louis XVI, of whom Jefferson said:

The King loves business, oeconomy, order, and justice. He sincerely wishes the good of his people. He is irascible, rude and very limited in his understanding, religious bordering only on bigotry.[37]

The engraving of the king had been a parting diplomatic gift to Jefferson, although he was more inclined to admire General Hoche who had led the Army of the Rhine to the middle Rhine in only four days in 1793, helped defeat the royalists in 1795, and brought peace in 1796 to western France torn by civil war.

David Rittenhouse (Cat. 42), the astronomer, mathematician, and instrument maker, was Jefferson's longtime friend, whom he succeeded as president of the American Philosophical Society in 1797. Jefferson identified Rittenhouse as one of the American geniuses (with Washington and Franklin) in his *Notes on the State of Virginia*; he later told Adams that "Rittenhouse, as an astronomer, would stand on a line with any of his time; and as a mechanician, he certainly has not been equaled."[38]

The lowest of the three tiers on the Parlor walls contained fourteen additional portraits, as well as John Trumbull's depiction of *The Surrender of Lord Cornwallis at Yorktown* (Cat. 7), which signaled the close of the Revolutionary War. This lively sketch in oil on canvas, which Jefferson described as "the premiere ebauche of [Trumbull's] print on that subject," was one of several studies.[39] Trumbull began to sketch his ideas in 1786–87, and it was possible that Jefferson had seen one of the early sketches for the *Surrender* in Paris.

While in Paris, Jefferson had overseen the production of an important series of medals for presentation by Congress to the distinguished officers of the Revolution. Because the cost of gold and silver was so high, Jefferson procured tin proofs of the medals for himself and hung them where they would be visible at eye level on the lowest tier. The ten medals ordered by Congress included likenesses of the officers and a mention of the battle for which they were being honored: General Washington, the Evacuation of Boston, March 17, 1776; Horatio Gates, Saratoga, October 17, 1777; Anthony Wayne, Stony Point, July 15, 1779; John Stewart, Stony Point, July 15, 1779; William Augustine Washington, Cowpens, January 17, 1781; John Eager Howard, Cowpens, January 17, 1781; Nathanael Greene, Eutaw Springs, September 8, 1781; Daniel Morgan, Cowpens, January 17, 1781; John Paul Jones, the engagement of the *Bon Homme Richard* and *Serapis*, September 23, 1779; and François Louis De Fleury, the French soldier who volunteered for the American army and fought at the battles of Fort Mifflin, Brandywine, and Stony Point.

In this tier were portrayed other figures prominent in the American Revolution: Thomas Paine (Cat. 3) and Thaddeus Kosciuszko (Cat. 38), whose likenesses recalled their efforts to achieve American liberty. Paine, the English writer, came to Philadelphia in 1774 at Benjamin Franklin's urging and became the spokesman for the Revolution. His writings popularized the republican cause with the publication of *Common Sense* (1776), and he galvanized the colonists with the words, "These are the times that try men's souls." In 1787, Paine went to Europe to attempt to duplicate his American success. Jefferson acquired the miniature of Paine as a gift from John Trumbull in 1788, who painted it while Paine was in London.

Like Paine, Kosciuszko came to America to assist the Revolution. After military training in his native Poland, he was sent abroad for advanced study and in 1774 returned home. In 1776 he volunteered for the army of the United States. He served with such distinction that General Washington appointed him his adjutant, and he was later granted American citizenship. Jefferson said of Kosciuszko that "he is as pure a son of liberty as I have ever known."[40]

Jefferson's current intellectual activity was represented by a drawing of his friend Constantin François de Chasseboeuf, the comte de Volney, which he purchased in 1801 from the artist, J. J. Barralet. Author of *Voyage en Syrie et en Egypte*, Volney was one of the

Enlightenment *literati* whom Jefferson met at what he called "Notre-Dame d'Auteuil," the salon of Madame Helvetius, the widow of the *philosophe*.[41] Volney visited Monticello in 1796 and presented Jefferson with a model of the pyramid of Cheops, which was later placed in the Entrance Hall. Jefferson later anonymously translated a large portion of Volney's *Les Ruines, ou Méditation sur les Revolutions des Empires* [Paris, 1792] (*The Ruins; or a Survey of the Revolutions of Empires*) for publication in the United States.

Not all of the exhibited portraits were of persons Jefferson admired. Although he later candidly abhorred Napoleon Bonaparte, he nonetheless displayed a bust of him (Cat. 97), which probably was a gift after the purchase of the Louisiana Territory. Jefferson considered Napoleon despicable for his destruction of human life and French liberty. In 1815, after his defeat and imprisonment, Jefferson said that Napoleon

has been the author of more misery and suffering to the world, than any being who ever lived before him. After destroying the liberties of his country, he has exhausted all its resources, physical and moral, to indulge his own maniac ambition.[42]

A plaster bust of Emperor Alexander I (1777–1825) of Russia (Cat. 102) flanked the door to the west front opposite Napoleon; their antithesis was intentional. Jefferson and many others thought that Alexander was an enlightened leader who believed in democracy. To Jefferson, Alexander represented the promise that all the nations of Europe might be governed democratically, but Jefferson apparently knew nothing of the secret internal committee set up to mandate internal reform whose clandestine nature conflicted so greatly with Jefferson's values.

Of the remaining twenty works of art, twelve were biblical subjects, five were classical, two related to natural history, and one was historical. The biblical subjects, placed on all three tiers, were exclusively New Testament. The life of Jesus was portrayed by a copy of *The Baptism of Jesus by John, Christ Bearing His Cross,* a *Crucifixion* by Gerard Seghers, two versions of *The Descent from the Cross* (one after Van Dyke, on canvas and the other, also after Van Dyke, on wood), and a *Transfiguration* after Raphael.

Copies of two important paintings by Coypel were exhibited on the top tier—*Jephtha Leading His Daughter Seila to be Sacrificed* and a very small version, one-eighth the original size, of *Susanna and the Elders.* Two interpretations of *The Return of the Prodigal Son* were also shown: a copy after Benjamin West's painting (*c.* 1771) made by the polyplasiasmos process, which copied the painting in color on canvas; the second *Prodigal Son* was an original painting by an unknown artist, purchased at the sale of the late Dupille de Saint-Séverin's collection in February 1785.

In addition to the *Penitent Magdalen,* which Jefferson thought had been made after José de Ribera's, a copy of *Herodias Bearing the Head of Saint John* by Guido Reni was also purchased at the Saint-Séverin sale (Cat. 19). Jefferson presumed that the artist was Simon Vouet, but recent scholarship has altered the attribution.

One of the classical subjects was *Democritus and Heraclitus,* the laughing and weeping philosophers, which also was among the five paintings acquired from Saint-Séverin's collection. *Cyclops Forging Thunderbolts,* a much smaller painting on wood, had nine eight-inch figures. *Daphne Transformed into a Laurel* depicted a story from Ovid's *Metamorphosis.*

The natural history of Virginia was illustrated by two watercolors of Virginia birds by Alexander Wilson. Wilson, who emigrated from Scotland in 1794, met Jefferson's correspondent William Bartram, the Philadelphia naturalist, in 1802 and began to sketch birds for the publication of *American Ornithology* (1808). Wilson gave Jefferson two drawings that apparently were studies for his eight-volume book: *Two inedited* [unpublished] *birds of Virginia & the Snow sparrow* and *The Singing birds of Virginia, the uppermost inedited.*

◆ ◆ ◆

The light, colorful Parlor with plentiful afternoon sun was furnished for multiple uses, and its furniture typically was arranged to suit the activity and number of persons present. Accumulated over a long period of time, the decorative arts in the Parlor and elsewhere in the house reflected Jefferson's tastes and changing means. The furnishings in the Parlor were not of a single period or style. Instead, they were a pastiche of various styles, including American interpretations of the Rococo or Chippendale style, Louis XVI, Federal, and plantation-made with a strong Jeffersonian influence, crafted in Monticello's own joinery. It was abundantly clear that in his retirement years Jefferson's primary aim was comfort and convenience.

The family gathered here and welcomed visitors to join them to make music, read, play games, or take tea. Virginia Randolph Trist, one of Jefferson's granddaughters recalled:

When it grew too dark to read, in the half hour which passed before candles came in, as we all sat round the fire, he taught us several childish games, and would play them with us. I remember that 'Cross-questions,' and 'I love my Love with an A,' were two I learned from him; and we would teach some of ours to him.[43]

To accommodate Jefferson's large family and visitors, a great number of chairs of different types were placed in the Parlor. In the eighteenth and early nineteenth centuries

Set of Thirty Chessmen

c. 1770–90
Dieppe, France
ivory, H. range: 5.7 to 9.8
(2¼ to 3⅞ in.)
Thomas Jefferson Memorial
Foundation

According to family tradition, this chess set was a gift from the French court to Jefferson, an avid chess player. In later life he taught the game to his granddaughter Ellen, and they played under the trees at Monticello in the summertime.

standing and seating furniture was usually arranged about the walls; chairs typically were moved in from the perimeter as they were needed. In Monticello's Parlor, however, there were so many windows and so many chairs—more than fourteen were identified on the 1826 inventory—that some must have been left standing in the central space of the room or else were arranged in rows. When the Randolph grandchildren assembled in the Parlor to read, the chairs were sometimes arranged in a circle.

The dominant chair design was reflected in a suite of twelve crimson damask uphol-stered mahogany armchairs with sinuous saber legs that Jefferson had acquired in France (Cat. 162). These rather streamlined chairs were probably the work of the noted Parisian *ébéniste* Georges Jacob.

Ten tablet-backed side chairs (Cat. 136, 137) made in the Monticello joinery sometime after 1810 may also have been used in the Parlor. Although no drawing survives for them, the design for the chair was probably Jefferson's and bears a strong resemblance to the *chaise hemicycle* that he had seen in France. Jefferson's chairs, however, have straight rather than saber legs.

In his later years, Jefferson's favorite chair for reclining was a campeachy chair (Cat. 138, 139). Ellen Randolph Coolidge noted:

In the large parlour, with it's parquetted floor, stood the Campeachy chair made of goatskin, sent to him from New Orleans, where, in the shady twilight, I was used to see him resting.[44]

Jefferson had tried to obtain one in 1808, but was initially unsuccessful. After much delay and difficulty, Jefferson finally received one and had it copied by the Monticello slave joiner, John Hemings. Made from a kind of mahogany available in the Campeche province in Mexico, the curule-form chair, with its curved seat made of a single piece of leather, was favored not only by Jefferson but also by James Madison, who had one at Montpelier.

Other seating furniture in the Parlor included a sofa, made in either Paris or Philadel-phia, that was placed on the north side of the double-acting glass doors to the Entrance Hall. Jefferson had six sofas and a *lit de repos* shipped back from France in 1790, and several of these survived until his death. Jefferson also had sofas for sleeping, which could provide both seating and sleeping space. Sofas such as these appeared in inventories of the houses of Virginia gentry during the eighteenth century and typically were placed in passages. Jefferson ordered six sleep sofas in 1801 from an unidentified Philadelphia cabinetmaker. Thomas Claxton asked Jefferson:

please inform me by your answer, whether you wish the cushions to be made for one or two Sophas. If each has a cushion, it will be a handsomer piece of furniture in a room, but when two are placed together for the purpose of sleeping one, one cushion covering, both, would perhaps be more convenient.[45]

A similar sofa, still with its original damask upholstery, has been located at Bremo, the Fluvanna County plantation of John Hartwell Cocke, and may be one of the sofas ordered by Jefferson.

In the Parlor there was minimal standing furniture. Aside from a harpsichord and pianoforte, one of the most consequential pieces of standing furniture was a mahogany

"Universal" table made by Samuel Titt (or Tilt) in London in 1790 (Cat. 126). It is also one of the very few examples of English-made furniture at Monticello. A similar table with sliding leaves was illustrated in Thomas Sheraton's *Cabinet-Maker and Upholsterer's Drawing Book*. The adaptable design was obviously appealing to Jefferson.

A large marble table was catalogued in the Parlor on the 1826 inventory, but its exact placement there is unknown. The largest of the known marble tables, called a *guéridon*, is a round white one with a triangular pedestal base that Jefferson procured in France. Its weight is so great that it must have been stationary. Likely locations for it were the center of the room or in front of one of the windows.

A pair of Federal card tables (Cat. 131) were two of at least thirteen tea and card tables that appeared on the 1815 list of taxable property.[46] This pair, with fine inlaid satinwood, probably made in Philadelphia or Baltimore, may also have been placed in the Parlor where they were most likely to have been used by the family and their guests. When not in use for games or holding lighting devices or small trays, these circular tables were folded into semicircles and placed compactly against the wall.

Incidental tables included at least one of the marble-top tables that Jefferson acquired in France. An almost square marble tilt-top table with a brass band and tripod base was placed against a wall (Cat. 164). Shorter, smaller tables for tea and candlestands were arranged as required for parlor games, reading, or musical ensembles.

Artificial light was used sparingly because of the expense of candles and oil. A lamp was suspended from an ornate bracket on the wall over the double-acting doors. This could have been the alabaster lamp that Jefferson asked his grandson Thomas Jefferson Randolph to purchase in Philadelphia in 1808. A pair of silver-plated branched candlesticks (Cat. 264, 265) were used in the Parlor as one pair was mentioned on the 1826 inventory. Additional lighting was provided by lights affixed to the wall near the mantel, which might have been French sconces (Cat. 269).

Lighting in the Parlor was enhanced by the large reflective surfaces of two rectangular gilded pier mirrors that Jefferson purchased in France (Cat. 169). These mirrors originally hung in one of the salons of the Hôtel de Langeac and were used in Jefferson's Market Street residence in Philadelphia before being transported to Monticello in 1793. They were installed directly on top of two unplastered brick niches for sculpture, apparently never used, that remained from the Parlor of the earlier house.

Dining Room

The Dining Room, with its Doric details, and the adjacent Tea Room were important public rooms where visitors were entertained at breakfast, dinner, and tea. The cubical Dining Room, located on the cold north side of the house, featured two pairs of glazed pocket doors that connected it with the Tea Room. In his scheme to improve Monticello, Jefferson added a double-glazed triple-sash window to conserve heat and a large mullioned skylight. The single window in the Dining Room and those in the Tea Room were likely curtained with dimity made according to his design for curtains at the President's House. He also incorporated a fascinating convenience—two dumbwaiters located on either side of the fireplace to carry bottles of wine from the wine room in the cellar to the Dining Room.

◆   ◆   ◆

Jefferson had more than a passing interest in food and wine. His table was known not only for its conversation but also for its cuisine and style. Daniel Webster noted, "Dinner is served half Virginian, half French style, in good taste and abundance."[47] The French cooking style was the consequence of the training of Jefferson's slave James Hemings, who had accompanied him to Paris in 1784 and studied French cuisine for several years. Hemings was apprenticed first to a caterer named Combeaux and then in 1787 to the prince de Condé's chef, with whom he studied pastry making. When Hemings returned to America with Jefferson in 1789, they brought firsthand knowledge of French cuisine, which was quite different from prevailing English and Virginia traditions. Jefferson even recorded recipes for boiled coffee and *biscuits de Savoye*. Before Hemings was manumitted by Jefferson on February 5, 1796, he trained a new cook to carry on in his place.

The delicate sauces essential to French cuisine were made possible at the Hôtel de Langeac and later at Monticello by Jefferson's acquisition of a complete *batterie de cuisine*. In France, Jefferson purchased a large number of utensils and copper pots and pans that made Monticello's kitchen one of the best equipped in Virginia, equal to that of Governor Botetourt in Williamsburg. Foodstuffs essential to fine cooking, such as "maccaroni, Parmesan cheese, figs of Marseilles, Brugnoles, raisins, almonds, mustard, Vinaigre d'Estragon, and other good vinegar, oil, and anchovies," were exported to Monticello together with Jefferson's belongings in 1790.[48] Once he returned to Monticello, Jefferson ordered special foods from grocers in Richmond and Washington.

The abundant cuisine was in large part the result of the variety of foods produced and preserved at Monticello by slaves. Mutton, pork, beef, and fish were available. In addition to wheat, many kinds of vegetables and fruits were grown for home consumption. These included tomatoes, Jerusalem artichokes, cabbage, lettuce, radishes, carrots, turnips, beets, peas, beans, kale, pears, apples, berries, and peaches. Jefferson tirelessly experimented with varieties of fruits and vegetables to determine the hardiest and tastiest examples.

Only two meals were served each day, breakfast and dinner. The breakfast bell sounded customarily at about eight o'clock. Margaret Bayard Smith, who visited Monticello with her two daughters in August 1809, not long after Jefferson retired, said:

Our breakfast table was as large as our dinner table; instead of a cloth, a folded napkin lay under each plate; we had tea, coffee, excellent muffins, hot wheat and corn bread, cold ham and butter. It was not exactly the Virginian breakfast I expected. Here indeed was the mode of living in general [of] that of a Virginian planter.[49]

Disinclined to waste time, Jefferson read while waiting for his family (it numbered twelve in 1809) to assemble; "on the mantel-piece which was large and of marble were many books of all kinds, Livy, Orosius, Edinburg Review, 1 vol. of Edgeworth's Moral Tales, etc., etc."[50] Jefferson sat on one of a pair of low French armchairs, and between the chairs was a candlestand with candlestick. His great-granddaughter recorded her mother's recollections:

Dining Room

Margaret Bayard Smith, 1809:

"Our breakfast table was as large as our dinner table; instead of a cloth, a folded napkin lay under each plate; we had tea, coffee, excellent muffins, hot wheat and corn bread, cold ham and butter."

The two [armchairs] stood by the fireplace in the dining room with a candle stand between them, and there Mr Jefferson and his daughter used to sit and read, after tea in the cool or winter evenings.[51]

A tripod stand with a tilt top and slipper feet (Cat. 124, 125), probably acquired in New York or Philadelphia, is typical of the kinds of tables that were commonly used as candlestands at Monticello. When not in use, the top tilted to a vertical position for storage against a wall.

At breakfast Mrs. Smith was amazed by the polite behavior of Mrs. Randolph's children who, she said, "eat at the family table, but are in such excellent order, that you would not know, if you did not see them, that a child was present."[52] Daniel Webster reported in 1824 that Jefferson's "breakfast is tea and coffee, bread always fresh from the oven, of which he does not seem afraid, with sometimes a light accompaniment of cold meat."[53]

A large dinner was served in the late afternoon between three-thirty and five o'clock. Jefferson "enjoys his dinner well, taking with his meat a large proportion of vegetables," wrote Webster.[54] Benjamin Henry Latrobe reported that, at the President's House,

Jefferson said little at dinner besides attending to the filling of plates, which he did with great ease and grace for a philosopher, he became very talkative as soon as the cloth was removed.[55]

Beer and cider were served with the meal, but wine was not poured until the cloth was removed from the table. Wines from France, Spain, Portugal, Hungary, Germany, and Italy were served, but the custom of compulsory "healths" or toasts was eliminated because Jefferson believed it caused people to drink more than they desired. Mrs. Smith remarked, "The table was plainly, but genteely and plentifully spread, and his immense and costly variety of French and Italian wines, gave place to Madeira and a sweet ladies' wine."[56] Another visitor, the Bostonian George Ticknor, commented, "The ladies sat until about six, then retired, but returned with the tea-tray a little before seven, and spent the evening with the gentlemen."[57]

The preparation of food at Monticello was not only distinctive, but the way in which dinner was presented was noticeably different from prevailing American social custom. Jefferson disliked the presence of servants at mealtimes and devised a more efficient system that required fewer attendants. He had a serving door with shelves installed in the small passage near the dining room.

Jefferson directed his joiners to make dumbwaiters—sets of shelves on casters—for use at Monticello and at Poplar Forest (Cat. 140, 141) and also brought some from Philadelphia. The dumbwaiters apparently were used for large as well as small dinner parties. George Ticknor said, "The dinner was always choice, and served in the French style," indicating that dinner guests served themselves rather than being served by the host and hostess in the manner of English service.[58]

◆ ◆ ◆

The Dining Room held a group of at least ten prints, eleven oil paintings, one watercolor, three architectural drawings, and a plaster of a small, sleeping Venus. The works were hung in two tiers when Jefferson prepared his Catalogue of Paintings sometime between 1809 and 1815, and more pictures were added later as he acquired additional items. The largest and most commanding works were probably the nine paintings on canvas located on the upper tier. These included two classical and six biblical subjects, and "a Market piece on canvas, to wit, fruit, vegetables, game &c."[59]

Although Jefferson wrote in 1787 that he had little interest in any artist but Jacques-Louis David, the quintessential Neoclassical painter, he acquired paintings in France that revealed a strong captivation with Renaissance, Mannerist, and Baroque art. The upper tier of paintings in the Dining Room held a *Holy Family* after Raphael (Cat. 17), a *Flagellation of Christ* on wood, after de Vos, a *Crucifixion* after Van Dyke, an *Accusation* believed by Jefferson to be a story from ecclesiastical history by an unnamed artist, an *Ascension of Saint Paul into the Third Heaven* after Dominquin (Domenichino), and *The Sacrifice at Lystra* after LeSueur. In his attributions and descriptions of the *Holy Family*, *Ascension of Saint Paul*, *Flagellation of Christ*, and *Diogenes in the Market of Athens*, Jefferson obviously had referred to the first four volumes of the *Manuel du Museum Français* by François Emmanuel Toulongeon, which Jefferson acquired in 1805.

Diogenes, the Cynic philosopher (412–323 B.C.), was portrayed on two canvases, *Diogenes in the Market of Athens*, after the painting by Peter Paul Rubens and *Diogenes Visited by Alexander*, an original work by an unidentified artist. In his description of these paintings in his Catalogue, Jefferson relied on Diogenes Laertius, Diogenes' biographer. Jefferson owned three editions of Laertius' "Lives of the Philosophers," two in Latin and one in French. *Diogenes in the Market of Athens* showed Diogenes holding a lantern and seeking an honest man while *Diogenes Visited by Alexander* showed Diogenes "being desired by Alexander to ask from him whatever he chose, he answered 'stand out of my light.'"[60] Diogenes believed that virtue involved the avoidance of physical pleasure.

The lower tier of works of art, which was closer to the beholder, had an entirely different thematic cast. The eleven smaller works displayed here focused almost exclusively on American subjects. Jefferson particularly wanted to concentrate attention on the spectacular vistas of the American landscape that he had so ardently commended to Maria Cosway. Mrs. Cosway was never persuaded to come to America, and instead Jefferson relied on other artists to render these scenes for him. The American painter William Roberts painted *Natural Bridge* (Cat. 59), which Jefferson called "the most sublime of nature's works" in *Notes on the State of Virginia*, and *The Junction of the Potomac and Shenandoah, Virginia* ("The Passage of the potomak through the Blue Ridge," as Jefferson titled it) (Cat. 60) on canvas. (Both of these paintings are lost.) Next to *Natural Bridge* Jefferson displayed an engraving of the famous Coalbrookdale Bridge (Cat. 54) over the Severn in England, the first cast-iron bridge (1779) and one of the great engineering feats of the age. Two different views of *Niagara Falls* (Cat. 57, 58), from the Indian Ladder and from Table Rock, were engraved after John Vanderlyn's early paintings of what became one of the most popular subjects in the history of American painting.

To document American building, three architectural drawings were mentioned in the Dining Room in the Catalogue, and more were added after the inventory was compiled. As many as three drawings by the young architect Robert Mills (1781–1855) may have been exhibited in the room. On a visit to Monticello and at the President's House Mills made important use of Jefferson's architectural library. He sketched two drawings of Monticello, which he presented to Jefferson (Cat. 24, 25). One hung in the Dining Room, and the second in Jefferson's Book Room. Mills also gave Jefferson ink-and-wash drawings of the principal elevations of St. Paul's Church (Cat. 26) in lower Manhattan (1766 by Thomas McBean) and Benjamin Henry Latrobe's Bank of Pennsylvania (Cat. 27) (1798–1800), a landmark of the emerging Greek Revival style. Jefferson also displayed a watercolor by Nicholas King, the surveyor of the city of Washington, of the President's House (undated and now lost), and a print by William Birch of Mount Vernon (Cat. 53).[61] The growth of American cities was a source of pride for Jefferson, who must have taken considerable pleasure to see a representation of New Orleans (Cat. 56), which symbolized the expansion of the "empire of liberty" made possible by the Louisiana Purchase that was effected during Jefferson's first presidential term.

Interspersed with these mainly American subjects was a print or drawing, now unlocated, that Jefferson described as "the Diocletian Portico." Only Robert Adam's *Ruins of the Palace of the Emperor Diocletian at Spalatro* (1764), a highly influential work, was known in Jefferson's time, and none of the published plates included the portico. Much of the drawing for this study had been accomplished by Clérisseau. The work that Jefferson owned, now lost, may have been an inedited plate or drawing given by Clérisseau to Jefferson or an entirely different work.

Portraits of George Washington and Henri van der Noot completed the Dining Room. Van der Noot, the Belgian-born lawyer and activist, helped to lead the Belgian revolt against the Austrian regime of Joseph II in 1789. His activities concerned Jefferson during his early tenure as secretary of state. The Washington engraving (Cat. 36) was after a drawing by Madame de Bréhan, the French émigré artist whom Jefferson knew.

◆ ◆ ◆

Although Margaret Bayard Smith called "the general mode of living . . . of European elegance," the organizing principle in the Dining Room was overwhelmingly utilitarian. As was typical of the time, furniture was configured to meet the needs of the occasion. Although the general impression leaned toward the Neoclassical, the Dining Room, like the Parlor, was a composite of furnishing styles ranging from Rococo to Federal. Jefferson acquired the accoutrements of dining over a long period of time and from a variety of sources.

The most notable piece of furniture in the Dining Room was a mahogany sideboard (unlocated), with doors and drawers for storing linens and tableware, that stood within the recess in the east wall. The sideboard, which Petit described on his May 12, 1793, packing list of Jefferson's belongings shipped from Philadelphia to Charlottesville as "le Sideboard," is presumed to be of American origin. Lost since its sale to David Lacey at the 1827 Dispersal Sale, the sideboard probably was made in New York City in 1790 or in Philadelphia shortly thereafter. The sideboard could very well have been made by New York cabinetmaker Thomas Burling; Jefferson's expenditures for furniture were greatest in New York where he paid $143 to Burling for unspecified furniture.

Rather than employ a single dining table, Jefferson owned several tables that could be placed together or used independently. When not in use, at least some of the "8 separate parts of dining tables" were positioned against the wall.[62] The earliest one was a two-part Chippendale-style or Rococo dining table (Cat. 120), probably made in England between 1760 and 1770, with eight cabriole legs terminating in ball-and-claw feet.

Other tables used in the Dining Room included a Rococo drop-leaf table (Cat. 115) tentatively attributed to the Williamsburg cabinetmaking shop of Peter Scott.[63] This table with ball-and-claw feet may have been among the three or more that Jefferson purchased from Scott in 1772, or it could have been acquired from the estate of his old friend George Wythe sometime after Wythe's death in 1806. While Jefferson was president, he had its top made smaller either in 1801 by Henry Ingle, first a Philadelphia, then a Washington cabinetmaker and hardware merchant, or later by one of Monticello's slave joiners.

A third highly important table was made in Monticello's joinery and presumably was executed by John Hemings. Made sometime after 1810, this oval drop-leaf table with flylegs (Cat. 147) was crafted of solid mahogany. The design for the movable flylegs was probably derived by Jefferson from the earlier two-part Rococo table.

At mealtimes whatever tables were used were set up atop crumb or floor cloths, which were used universally. These cloths, typically of baize or painted canvas, protected the wood or carpet from spills. After meals, the cloths were swept clean or shaken out of doors. For the President's House Jefferson purchased a crumb cloth to protect the uncarpeted floor from grease "and the scouring which that necessitates"; a carpet was listed in the Dining Room on the 1826 Monticello inventory.[64]

Like the tables in the Dining Room, the side chairs used for dining were comprised of three groups. The oldest among them was a set of at least seven Rococo-style chairs with straight Marlborough legs and scalloped ears at the ends of the crestrail (Cat. 116). On the 1826 Monticello inventory, they were identified as "7 old chairs given by Mr. Wythe." Like the drop-leaf tea table, the chairs are attributed to Williamsburg maker Peter Scott.[65] These chairs may also have been used in the South Square Room, Martha Jefferson Randolph's sitting room.

Two different sets of mahogany shield-back chairs comprised the seating furniture in the Dining Room. At once more modern and classical than the various dining tables, both sets harmonized well with other Neoclassical examples of decorative arts at Monticello. Although their origin is not documented, the carving style of the foliate side chairs (Cat. 134) suggests that they were likely made in New York (or Philadelphia) in the early 1790s.[66] A second set of shield-back chairs (Cat. 133) with reeded stay rails, dating from the 1790s, was more delicately carved. The form was quite popular in New York. A similar chair was owned by George Washington, who was also known to have purchased furniture from Thomas Burling. By 1814 the Dining Room chairs were in considerable disrepair.

On looking around the room in which we sat the first thing that attracted our attention was the state of the chairs. They had leather bottoms stuffed with hair, but the bottoms were completely worn through and the hair sticking out in all directions . . .[67]

Although the accounts of contemporary visitors omit mention of the mantelpiece— aside from the books amassed there—the Dining Room mantelpiece, ornamented by several decorative jasperware plaques set into the front, probably featured a clock and mirror. The mirror may have been the rectangular Neoclassical one with a gilded wood frame and inlaid Greco-Roman–style blue-and-white jasperware plaque showing a sacrifice. During the last quarter of the eighteenth century, plaques bearing antique motifs, such as those made by Josiah Wedgwood, often embellished furniture and architectural elements.

Jefferson was fond of pillar clocks and appreciated them for their low price and Neoclassical design. In 1787, he wrote James Madison:

I have almost been tempted to buy for you one of the little clocks made here mounted on marble columns. They strike, go with a pendulum, a spring instead of a weight, are extremely elegant and can be had for 10. guineas.[68]

Although it is not known how he acquired it, Jefferson owned a similar clock made of alabaster, brass, and ormolu, made by C. N. Vuille and signed 1817. Clocks of this type were made in large numbers for the American market in the early nineteenth century.

◆ ◆ ◆

At dinner, the explicitly cosmopolitan dining table was impressively decorated. The general effect was worldly; references to the antique and reminders of Jefferson's time in Paris abounded. At the center of the table was placed a long oval or rectangular *plateau* (now missing), a mirrored tray with an ormolu or silver-plated gallery designed to reflect light from the candelabra that it held. Jefferson possessed at least two French biscuit (unglazed porcelain) figurines, *Venus with Cupid* (Cat. 105) and *Hope with Cupid* (Cat. 106), which were used as table or mantel ornaments.

The prevailing tableware was either French or Chinese export porcelain. The French porcelain, decorated by sprigs of cornflowers, was derived from the *guirlande de barbeaux–* patterned (cornflower garland) porcelain made at Sèvres for Louis XVI and copied by Paris factories. Jefferson also had at least several fine serving pieces of the authentic *guirlande de barbeaux* pattern made at Sèvres. One of these, a *seau crénelé* (Cat. 191) for rinsing and chilling wine glasses, was signed by the artist who painted it, Madame Geneviève Taillandier.

In addition, Jefferson acquired English creamware and large quantities of Chinese export porcelain. In April 1785 "three cases of China" made its way to Paris. A second large order, presumed to be Chinese export, was requisitioned from William Macarty in June 1787, but it was not received until January 1788. Later, in 1789, Jefferson ordered still more porcelain from a Boston shipmaster, Edward Dowse, who traded in China. In April 1790 Jefferson directed Dowse to send his porcelain order to New York where Jefferson was serving as secretary of state. The shipment was so seriously delayed that it did not reach Jefferson in Philadelphia until 1793, when he refused it.[69] In the interim, Jefferson's possessions had arrived from France, including 120 porcelain plates, 58 cups, 39 saucers, 4 tureens, saltcellars, and various platters. He used these in New York and Philadelphia, and what remained was eventually shipped to Monticello.

Until the more elaborate porcelains arrived at Monticello, Queens ware, a less-expensive earthenware made in England, was one of the kinds used as the household china. Mrs. Randolph wrote her father:

I took an account of the plate china &c. and locked up all that was not in imediate use not recolecting that there was a set of queens ware here I sent to Richmond for some, by which means the china was preserved entire except our beautiful cups which being obliged to leave out are all broke but one.[70]

In 1793 all of Jefferson's tableware was transported to Monticello, and by 1808 the ample supply of china had dwindled. Martha Randolph wrote her father in Washington:

I forgot to mention coffee cups amongst the difficiencies of the house. We have tea cups enough but a dozen coffee cups will be requisite to meet the summer visitations and also 2 or 3 doz shallow plates.[71]

The sophisticated atmosphere for dining was heightened by two silver serving pieces with Neoclassical references. The most exotic of the two was a silver askos (Cat. 184, 185), a modern version of a Roman pouring vessel made in Philadelphia, which the family used for chocolate and nicknamed the "duck." Along with the familiar "Wythe-Jefferson Cups" (silver tumblers, sometimes called "beakers" by Jefferson), it is one of the objects most associated with Jefferson. After his death his grandson-in-law, Joseph Coolidge, Jr., asked if he could purchase the askos at the Dispersal Sale. "Buy for me the *duck*—the silver chocolate-pot—made from the Etruscan Model—and these silver drinking cups which he was wont to use!"[72] After the discovery of Greek and Roman urns and vases in the mid-eighteenth century, urns became popular forms in porcelain and silver. Jefferson purchased two silver, three silver-plated, and at least one copper urn in Paris, but only one is known today (Cat. 182). Its design is closely related to an undated Jefferson drawing.

The best documented of Jefferson's designs for the table were a pair of unadorned Neoclassical silver goblets with gilded interior bowls made to his specifications in May and June 1789 (Cat. 183). Jefferson engaged Jean Baptiste Claude Odiot to make the goblets, but Odiot must have retained Claude-Nicolas Delanoy to produce the goblets as his marks appear on them. Although the drawings made by Jefferson do not precisely match the goblets, they do illustrate his architectonic treatment of the design. He placed an elongated bell-shaped bowl of the goblet on a classical base, perhaps inspired by candlesticks resting on a columnar base.

Years later, in 1810, Jefferson instructed the Richmond silversmith John Letelier to produce eight simple tumblers (Cat. 189) from two silver cups acquired from George Wythe and other sources. This design, made to Jefferson's requirements, was a form popular early in the eighteenth century. The interiors of the treasured silver cups were washed with gold, and the exteriors were engraved either "G.W. to T.J." or "T.J."

Aside from French and English silver flatware, the silver tableware included four French casseroles (Cat. 181), described by Mrs. Randolph as vegetable dishes with tops, four saltcellars, two pudding dishes, two soup ladles, two small ladles, two pairs of sugar tongs, four salt spoons, one sugar dish stand, one lamp for spirits of wine, and one pair of snuffers.[73]

Epergne

c. 1807–1810
cut glass
47.9 × 18.4 (18⅞ × 7¼ in.)
Thomas Jefferson Memorial Foundation

According to family tradition Jefferson gave this epergne, called a "glass tree" by the family, to Martha Burke Jones, second wife of John Wayles Eppes, on the occasion of their marriage.

Tea Room

The polygonal Tea Room located on the north corner was the coldest room in the house. To insulate it and better contain the heat, it was separated from the Dining Room by a double set of glass pocket doors, which was then a novel idea. A "small iron stove which stands in the niche of the tea room," now lost, originally warmed it.[74] When the number of guests at dinner exceeded the capacity of the Dining Room, the pocket doors were slid open to create a single space. The Tea Room also contained an outstanding collection of portraits and a second reading-and-writing arrangement for Jefferson.

◆   ◆   ◆

The works of art in the Tea Room were predominantly portraits of the people who had influenced Jefferson and the American Revolution. Most were visible from the Dining Room. These thirty-four likenesses included four terra-cotta patinated plaster busts by Houdon in Jefferson's "most honourable suite"—John Paul Jones (Cat. 95), Benjamin Franklin (Cat. 94), George Washington (Cat. 93), and the marquis de Lafayette (Cat. 92). These reddish-brown-tinted busts on four elaborate console brackets contrasted with the Tea Room's off-white walls. The sculptures were among the seven portraits by Houdon for which Jefferson paid him 1,000 livres (about $2,000 today).

[Washington] wore a wreath of Immortelles. Some admirer in France sent these to Mr. Jefferson's family, to crown his bust on his birthday. He ordered them, instead, to be placed around the brow of Washington, and there they thenceforth remained until Mr. Jefferson's death.[75]

Washington was portrayed in two additional likenesses in the Tea Room, a tin proof of a medal and an engraved miniature taken from Houdon's bust.

John Paul Jones (Cat. 95), the American naval hero admired for his bravery, sat for Houdon in 1780, and a "buste en platre couleur de terre cuite" was exhibited in the Salon of 1781. Jones gave Jefferson a plaster of himself sometime in 1785 or 1786, and Jefferson transported it to America along with other plasters that Jones wanted to give to American friends.

It seems that Jefferson could not possess enough portraits of the "good old Doctor Franklin, so long the ornament of our country and I may say of the world."[76] Jefferson, who was never more rhapsodic about anyone than he was about Franklin, owned no fewer than four likenesses: the bust by Houdon (Cat. 94), the painting after Duplessis (Cat. 12), a miniature, and a medal in bronze by Augustin Dupré, a designer and engraver of medals and a member of the Académie. Jefferson said of Franklin that

his death was an affliction which was to happen to us at some time or other. We had reason to be thankful he was so long spared: that the most useful life should be the longest also: that it was protracted so far beyond the ordinary span allotted to man, as to avail us of his wisdom in the establishment of our own freedom and to bless him with a view of it's dawn in the east, where they seemed till now to have learned every thing, but how to be free.[77]

Jefferson's old friend the marquis de Lafayette (Cat. 92) also figured heavily in the Tea Room. Lafayette, whose efforts on behalf of American interests in war and peace earned

Tea Room

John Edward Caldwell, 1808:

"In the bow of the dining room are busts of General Washington, Doctor Franklin, Marquis de La Fayette, and [John] Paul Jones, in plaister."

THE WORLDS OF THOMAS JEFFERSON AT MONTICELLO

Jefferson's gratitude, was reunited with him at Monticello in 1824 during his farewell tour of America. Commissioned by the Commonwealth of Virginia, Houdon executed a portrait in marble of Lafayette that was first exhibited in the Salon of 1787. Jefferson subsequently arranged for its transport to Richmond and acquired his own plaster of Lafayette before departing for America.

In February 1820, a fifth portrait bust was added to Jefferson's "most honourable suite," a plaster of General Andrew Jackson (Cat. 98), defender of New Orleans against the British and hero of the War of 1812. William Rush's portrait was the gift of Jefferson's old friend, James Ronaldson, a great admirer of Jackson.

At least three likenesses of Louis XVI were displayed in the four public rooms at Monticello. Two of these were medals placed in the Tea Room: a portrait and *L'Arrivée du roi (Louis XVI) à Paris*.[78] Although grateful to the French government for its support of the American Revolution, Jefferson ultimately had little tolerance for the irascible king, and told John Adams that he was too much governed by his queen and got into the "habit of drowning his cares in wine."[79] He occasionally praised Louis XVI for his honesty and anemic efforts to improve conditions in his country, but the portraits of him at Monticello were more to remind Jefferson of his own part in a critical moment in French history. Jefferson saw Louis XVI re-enter Paris on July 17, 1789 and wrote the Scots philosopher Dugald Stewart, "It is now 35. years since I had the great pleasure of becoming acquainted with you in Paris, and since we saw together Louis XVI. led in triumph by his people thro' the streets of his capital."[80]

A small but potent reminder of Jefferson's presence in France was "the Taking of the Bastile. a medal in bronze."[81] Jefferson was enthralled by the events of July 14, 1789, and three days later he wrote a vivid description of them:

The city committee resolved to embody 48,000 Bourgeois. They asked arms at the [Invalides] and being refused the people forced the place and got here a large supply of arms. They then went to the Bastille and made the same demand. The Governor after hoisting a flag of truce and decoying a hundred or two within the outer drawbridge and fired on them. The people without then forced the place, took and beheaded the Governor and Lt. Governor, and here compleated arming them-selves. . . . The Marquis de la Fayette was made commander in chief of the men raised.[82]

Less than a week later, Jefferson compiled a description for James Madison:

In the rest of Europe nothing remarkable has happened; but in France such events as will be for ever memorable in history. . . . The season is now so advanced towards the Equinox, that if it comes to hand I shall not leave Europe till that be over. Indeed this scene is too interesting to be left at present.[83]

Four cast bronzes, either small freestanding sculptures or bas reliefs, of the Roman emperors Tiberius, Nero, Otho, and Vespasian were exhibited in the Tea Room. The emperors were known to Jefferson through two Roman historians: Tacitus, whose multi-volume works he owned in several editions; and Suetonius.[84] Tiberius Claudius Nero (42 B.C.–A.D. 37), one of two sons of Livia, the powerful wife of the emperor Augustus Caesar, was a legendary soldier.

The diabolical Nero (A.D. 37–68) succeeded Claudius as emperor. Seneca, the historian whose works were in Jefferson's library, was brought back from exile to tutor Nero. He raised money to rebuild Rome by immense taxation of the provinces, which ultimately revolted and caused the Roman Senate to sentence Nero to death. From Tacitus's account of Nero, Jefferson had certainly assimilated the view that unjust provincial taxation was a powerful force for political change.

Vespasian (A.D. 9–79) was a more admirable emperor than Otho (A.D. 32–69). Jefferson's interest in him may have stemmed from his restoration of Rome. Under his leadership the Colosseum and new public baths and forum were begun. Like Jefferson, Vespasian was known to have been precise and regular.

Aside from Thomas Paine, the only English political ally to be displayed (in a wax medallion portrait) was the popular Lord Norborne Berkeley Botetourt (Cat. 108), who briefly served as the colonial governor of Virginia from 1768 until his death two years later. After the Virginia Assembly passed resolutions demanding that Americans determine their own taxation and be tried in American rather than English courts, Lord Botetourt was compelled to dissolve it. He privately approved of the Virginians' resolutions, and corresponded—via an unsealed letter—with the English secretary of state, who promised and failed to obtain repeal of taxes imposed by Parliament. Jefferson, who served in the House of Burgesses from 1769 to 1776, told Daniel Webster that he valued Lord Botetourt for "his great respectability, character for integrity, and his general popularity."[85] Later, he believed that Lord Botetourt's death had hastened the Revolution.

The Tea Room included sixteen engraved miniature portraits: three Revolutionary War heroes, Generals Gates, Dearborn, and Clinton; the patriots and friends Franklin, Gideon Granger, Caesar Rodney, William Burwell, John Wayles Eppes, Meriwether Lewis, Albert Gallatin, Joseph Nicholson, Mahlon Dickerson; and two portraits of Jefferson, one by Saint-Mémin (Cat. 65, 66) and a *verre églomisé* by Amos Doolittle.

Horatio Gates, the Revolutionary War soldier, was represented by two likenesses at Monticello, a tin proof of a medal in the Parlor and a miniature in the Tea Room. Born in England, Gates entered the British army and served under Cornwallis in Nova Scotia and Braddock in Virginia. He took a leave of absence in England in 1765, and in 1772 immigrated to America, where he took up the patriotic cause in 1775. As a friend of Washington, with whom he had earlier served, he was commissioned as a brigadier general. Gates was best known for his victory over Burgoyne at Saratoga in 1777 and his reeling defeat at Camden, South Carolina in 1780. The rout nearly warranted a court inquiry, but Gates was exonerated and again served under Washington's command. During Gates's troubles Jefferson advised him that "the returning justice of your countrymen will remind them of Saratoga, and induce them to recognize your merits."[86]

A miniature portrait of George Clinton, whom Jefferson did not hold in the highest esteem, was also displayed in the Tea Room. He demonstrated little military ability in his defense of the Hudson River, but in 1777 he was made a brigadier general in the Continental Army. Not long after, he was elected to the first of seven terms as governor of New York. When his political base in New York declined, he was elected vice president under Jefferson.

Jefferson admired the ability of Henry Dearborn (Cat. 71). "Should a war come on," Jefferson wrote, "there is no person in the United States to whose management and care I could commit it with equal confidence."[87] Dearborn took part in the battle of Bunker Hill, the assault on Quebec, and served in the army until 1783. As Jefferson's secretary of war for two terms, he assisted in the plan to push Native Americans beyond the Mississippi.

Benjamin Smith Barton (Cat. 70), the naturalist and physician, succeeded Dr. Benjamin Rush as professor of medicine at the University of Pennsylvania. He published the first botanical textbook published in the United States and named the *Jeffersonia diphylla* for him in 1792. Barton shared Jefferson's interest in Native Americans, and Jefferson often turned to him for scientific advice. Jefferson consulted him in preparation for the Lewis and Clark expedition, requesting "a note of those in the lines of botany, zoology or of Indian history; which you think most worthy of enquiry and observation."[88]

Gideon Granger served as postmaster general under Jefferson, an office he held until 1814. He proved to be an able administrator at a time of swift population growth and the expansion of the country as a result of the Louisiana Purchase. A strong Republican, Granger solidly championed Jefferson for the presidency in 1800. Jefferson entrusted him with patronage appointments in his native Connecticut.

Miniature engravings of four of Jefferson's principal congressional supporters reminded him of their loyalty. William Armistead Burwell (Cat. 74), a Virginian, served as Jefferson's trusted private secretary from 1805 to 1807, when he resigned to become a congressman. Together with Jefferson's son-in-law John Wayles Eppes (Cat. 76), Burwell steadily championed Jefferson's policies in Congress. Eppes married Jefferson's daughter Mary (she later was called Maria) in 1797, and later served as congressman and senator from Virginia. Even after his wife's untimely death in 1804, Eppes maintained a close relationship with Jefferson. When Jefferson's finances failed, it was Eppes who offered much-needed financial help.

The third staunch Jefferson supporter was Joseph Nicholson of Maryland. He was elected to Congress in 1799 and served until 1806; he was remarkable for his indefatigable devotion to Jefferson.

Caesar Augustus Rodney (Cat. 72), a Delaware native, ran successfully for Congress in 1802, when he defeated a strong Federalist candidate. He had served only one term when Jefferson selected him as his attorney general, an important position given the prevailing Federalist character of the courts.

Albert Gallatin was appointed secretary of the treasury by Jefferson in 1801 and held that post until 1814. Astute and incisive, no other Republican was his equal in the field of finance. Jefferson said that he was "the ablest man except [Madison] who was ever in the administration."[89]

Jefferson displayed an engraving by Saint-Mémin of Mahlon Dickerson (Cat. 68), whom he appointed commissioner of bankruptcy in 1803. Dickerson dined at the President's House in April 1802 and reported that "he may neglect his person [but] he takes good care of his table."[90]

Meriwether Lewis (Cat. 69) was among Jefferson's dearest associates. Within a week after Jefferson was elected president, he invited Lewis, a fellow native of Albemarle

County, to act as his private secretary. Lewis accepted and moved into the President's House. Before long, Jefferson selected the inquisitive and capable Lewis, who had served in the army on the western frontier, to head the acclaimed expedition to the West. Jefferson said that he was "of courage undaunted, possessing a firmness & perseverance of purpose which nothing but impossibilities could divert from its attention."[91]

◆ ◆ ◆

The Tea Room's most conspicuous feature was a second arrangement for Jefferson's reading and writing. On one side of the Tea Room were placed a revolving Windsor chair (Cat. 127) with an attached writing arm and either a sofa or Windsor couch. Here he could read and write with his legs comfortably outstretched. The comb-back Windsor armchair was made in Philadelphia in 1775 or 1776 and has a celebrated history: Jefferson sat in this chair while he wrote the draft of the Declaration of Independence. A writing arm modified one of the original arms. Sometime later a mechanism with rollers was added so that the chair could swivel, much like the whirligig chair in Jefferson's Cabinet.

The single most important object associated with Jefferson is the small lap desk (Cat. 221), or writing box, upon which he wrote and edited the draft of the Declaration of Independence in 1776. These convenient and portable desks typically consisted of a writing surface and storage space for stationery, writing quills, pens, ink, and sand.[92] Jefferson owned several, but he treasured this one above the others for its "association with the birth of the great Charter of our independence."[93] The desk was made to Jefferson's specifications by Benjamin Randolph.

The reading-and-writing arrangement in the Tea Room was completed by a sofa, possibly an upholstered one (Cat. 130) thought to have been made by Thomas Burling.[94] It was originally a companion to a whirligig chair upholstered in red leather, made in 1790 and also attributed to Burling, that was situated in Jefferson's Cabinet. The Burling sofa had a semicircular end that snugly fit the contour of the round seats of both the Windsor and whirligig chairs.

After Jefferson's death the Tea Room contained a Brescia marble table, a mahogany card table, two sofas, and nine mahogany chairs, most of which were probably placed against the walls.[95] Crafted in France by an unknown maker, the round Brescia marble table (Cat. 167) with a brass gallery was the proper size to hold a coffee urn or tea service. The mahogany card table, either one of two Federal tables (Cat. 131) or one of two later pairs (Cat. 132, 143), would have been pulled away from the wall and its leaf unfolded for the serving of tea. During Jefferson's lifetime, however, the Tea Room may also have held a small dining or tea table for the serving of tea or meals.

The "2 sophas and cushions" mentioned on the 1826 inventory could have originated with any of the three established Jefferson purchases of sofas—the six that Jefferson acquired in France, the one or more that he purchased from Thomas Burling in 1790, and the sleep sofas that he acquired from Philadelphia sources while he was president. At least one of the sofas probably was that made by Burling and used by Jefferson in his reading-and-writing arrangement. Mrs. Randolph's description—"sofas and cushions"—might suggest that the sofas had removable upholstered cushions.

Sitting Room

The public and private uses of Monticello's rooms were exactly circumscribed by Jefferson. To the south, beyond the public Entrance Hall, were a family sitting room and Jefferson's sanctum sanctorum—his Bedroom, Cabinet, Book Room, and the attached Greenhouse. As it was described on the 1826 "Inventory of the furniture in the house at Monticello," the South Square Room was called the "Sitting Room." It then contained "7 old Mahogany chairs given by Mr. Wythe," one old sofa, and a pair of brass andirons.

◆ ◆ ◆

After Jefferson's retirement from the presidency in 1809, the family of his surviving daughter, Martha Jefferson Randolph, joined him at Monticello. The Sitting Room became the Randolphs' principal private space and also functioned as Mrs. Randolph's "office." As the mistress of the sizable Monticello plantation, Mrs. Randolph directed the activities of more than a dozen slaves who were employed as household servants in 1810.[1] "As her daughters grew up, she taught them to be industrious like herself. They used to take turns each day giving out instructions to the servants and superintending the housekeeping."[2] Mrs. Randolph met frequently here with Burwell, the slave butler, to discuss the many activities in which they mutually took part.

One of the domestic occupations that most busied Mrs. Randolph was sewing, which she faithfully taught her own daughters. In an era without sewing machines, this was a necessary occupation for women, but it also provided an opportunity for conversation. Needles, thimbles, and scissors were prized. Needles were safely stored—for those who could afford them—in decorated silver needle cases such as that used by Mrs. Randolph. A sewing table (Cat. 146) with two hinged leaves and drawers for the storage of sewing supplies was made for her in Monticello's joinery after 1809. With its rectangular shape, it closely resembled the joinery-made dumbwaiters in design and construction techniques.

Of the seventy or so adult slaves at Monticello, the Hemings family was the most prominent. Betty Hemings (c. 1735–1807), the matriarch, who had been part of Martha Wayles Jefferson's dowry, was the mother of twelve children, including Nance (1761–1827+), a weaver; Bett (1759–1830+), personal servant to Mrs. Jefferson; Critta (1769–1850), who served in a number of domestic occupations, including nurse to Jefferson's grandson Francis Eppes; Sally (1773–1835), personal servant to Jefferson's daughters and granddaughters; and their brothers Peter (b. 1770), a chef; and John (1775–1830+), a joiner. The relationship of the Hemings and Jefferson families was not only close but also intertwined and complicated. John Wayles, Martha Wayles Jefferson's father, was probably the father of Sally and some of her siblings, which made Martha Wayles Jefferson the half-sister of a number of slaves, but not very much is known about what the Hemings or Jefferson-Randolph families thought about this relationship. Isaac Jefferson, a slave whose recollections were recorded in 1847, said that "Folks said that these Hemingses was old Mr. Wayles's children."[3] In any case, prominent household and artisan positions were occupied by members of the Hemings family.

Needlebook

late 18th c.
ivory, leather, silk, wool twill,
steel, 9.5×6.7×1.3
(3¾×2⅝×½ in.)
Allison C. and B. F. Byrd

Needlecase

c. 1800
Samuel Pemberton
(active 1784–1817)
Birmingham, England
silver, 7.6 (3 in.)
Allison C. and B. F. Byrd

This ivory-covered needlebook and silver needlecase both belonged to Martha Jefferson Randolph.

Undoubtedly, the Jefferson-Randolph family was especially fond of some of the Monticello slaves. Jefferson relayed a message of his young granddaughter Ellen Randolph (1796–1876) to her aunt, Maria Jefferson Eppes: "She always counts you as the object of affection after her mama and unckin [uncle] Juba."[4] Juba, or Jupiter, was Jefferson's personal servant who was with him when his wife died. The family was saddened when he himself died as the result of "a dose from this black doctor who pronounced that it would <u>kill or cure</u>."[5] John Hemings, the gifted joiner and a favorite of the Randolph children, was similarly cherished. He made a wonderful lap desk for Ellen Randolph upon the occasion of her marriage to Joseph Coolidge, Jr., and when it was lost at sea, Jefferson said that "Virgil could not have been more afflicted had his Aeneid fallen a prey to the flames."[6]

Jefferson's views about slavery and slaves were complex and contradictory. Although a slaveholder, he passionately argued for the inalienable rights for all—life, liberty, and the pursuit of happiness. In his draft of the Declaration, he attacked George III for allowing the dreadful institution of slavery to proliferate:

He has waged cruel war against human nature itself, violating it's most sacred rights of life and liberty in the persons of a distant people who never offended him, captivating and carrying them into slavery in another hemisphere, or to incur miserable death in their transportation thither.[7]

But these words were expunged in the final document. Although Jefferson believed that the issue of slavery would inevitably tear apart the country, he also concluded that freed blacks, whom he thought—in the typically paternalistic attitude of the time—were incapable of caring for themselves, would be better off if they were returned to Africa or sent elsewhere. For both financial reasons and what he thought was his moral responsibility to care for the slaves dependent upon him, Jefferson freed only seven slaves, all of whom were male artisans who, Jefferson thought, would be able to succeed independently.

Jefferson strove to improve the standard of living of the slaves at Monticello, and they appear to have lived better there than at many other plantations in Virginia. On the mountaintop they mostly lived in log dwellings with earth floors and wooden chimneys. To store food and special objects, many slaves dug root cellars. Jefferson provided bedding, a few cooking implements, clothing, and a weekly ration of food, which included bacon, dried fish, corn meal, and molasses. In whatever spare time they had, slaves grew vegetables, raised poultry that sometimes was sold to Jefferson, and worked to supplement their rations in whatever ways that they could.

As Isaac Jefferson put it, "Old Master very kind to servants."[8] His daughter Martha spoke compassionately about the plight of slaves but also seemed able to absent herself from her place in the system. As a young girl in Paris, she wrote her father, "I wish with all my soul that the poor negroes were all freed. It grieves my heart when I think that these our fellow creatures should be treated so teribly as they are by many of our country men."[9] Years later, in 1825, her views had not moderated:

The discomfort of slavery I have borne all my life, but it's sorrow in all their bitterness I have never before conceived. . . . the country is overgrown with those trafickers in human blood the negro buyers. . . . nothing can prosper under such a system of injustice.[10]

Only two years later, Mrs. Randolph confronted the unavoidable unpleasantness of her father's financial situation. She, who was so distressed by slavery, was forced to sell Jefferson's slaves to the mainly Virginia buyers who assembled at Monticello in January 1827.

Mrs. Randolph's sympathetic nature won the admiration of everyone who knew her. Monticello's overseer for twenty-six years, Captain Edmund Bacon, wrote:

She had always her father's pleasant smile, and was nearly always humming some tune. I have never seen her at all disturbed by any amount of care and trouble. . . . She was always busy. If she wasn't reading or writing, she was always doing something. She used to sit in Mr. Jefferson's room a great deal, and sew, or read, or talk, as he would be busy about something else.[11]

Mrs. Randolph was admired and revered by her sister, daughters, and sons. Her sister took note of her efficiency:

I found my sister and her children in perfect health; she enjoying the satisfaction arising from the consciousness of fulfilling her duty to the utmost extent. But it is one she has always had. It would please you, I am sure, to see what an economist, what a manager, she has become.[12]

Ellen Randolph Coolidge said that her mother was

Graceful in figure and movement, an accomplished musician, well acquainted with several modern languages, well grounded in all the solid branches of a woman's education, save only the arts of housewifery, to which she afterwards attained with pain and difficulty. . . . Yet she seemed born not only to bless but to shine. She was not only excellent, but captivating to all who came within the sphere of her manifold attractions.[13]

Although her demeanor was serene, Mrs. Randolph's life was far from tranquil. She was deprived of a relationship with her sister, Maria Jefferson Eppes, who had married John Wayles Eppes in 1797 and was dead at twenty-six. While she was blessed with eleven living children (only one died in infancy), her marriage, however promising at its start, was disquieted by her eccentric, troubled spouse, Thomas Mann Randolph, Jr., and the misery brought by the desperately unhappy relationship between her eldest daughter, Anne Cary (1791–1826), and her alcoholic husband, Charles Lewis Bankhead, whom she married in 1808. The sometimes abusive Bankhead was an ungovernable source of distress.

Mrs. Randolph's ten younger children, born between 1792 and 1818 (when she was forty-six), provided more domestic felicity. After Anne Cary and Thomas Jefferson Randolph (1792–1875) came Ellen Wayles (1794–1795)—who died in infancy—Ellen Wayles (1796–1876), Cornelia Jefferson (1799–1871), Virginia Jefferson (1801–1882), Mary Jefferson (1803–1876), James Madison (1806–1834), Benjamin Franklin (1808–1871), Meriwether Lewis (1810–1837), Septimia Anne (1814–1887), and George Wythe (1818–1867).

Educating the children was one of Mrs. Randolph's principal responsibilities, and the Sitting Room was used as a schoolroom. Jefferson said, "My surviving daughter . . . the mother of many daughters as well as sons, has made their education the object of her life."[14] The children had abundant books appropriate for their ages. For example, Mrs. Randolph asked her father to obtain the large-type, four-volume set of Mrs. Barbauld's *Lessons for*

Thomas Jefferson Randolph
(1792–1875)

c. 1808
Charles Willson Peale
(1741–1827)
oil on paper, 68.6 × 58.4
(27 × 23 in.)
Thomas Jefferson Memorial
Foundation

This portrait of Jefferson's eldest grandson, known as "Jeff," was made while he lodged in Philadelphia with Charles Willson Peale.

Sitting Room

Martha Jefferson Randolph schooled her eleven children in this informal family sitting room, located between the Entrance Hall and Book Room.

Children from Four to Five Years Old for Cornelia.[15] As he was involved in educating his own daughters, Jefferson was also concerned—but without being intensely demanding—with the education of his Randolph grandchildren. From Washington he sent Cornelia a primer when she was four. When she was nine, she wrote her "Grandpapa" that she could write (with a goose quill). He replied, revealing his own preferences for the classics and his eagerness for his family to know them:

I congratulate you, my dear Cornelia, on having acquired the valuable art of writing. . . . To this we are indebted for all our reading; because it must be written before we can read it. To this we are indebted for the Iliad, the Aeneid, the Columbiad, Henriad, Dunciad, and now, for the most glorious poem of all, the tarrapiniad [a children's poem], *which I now inclose you.*[16]

Jefferson expected the women of his family to be intellectually informed as well as domestically efficient. What is known about the early education of the female and male Randolph grandchildren suggests that they were similarly schooled in the classics (although not necessarily in Greek and Latin) and modern English and French literature. The list of eighty-three works for female education that Jefferson prepared in 1818 differed little from what he thought necessary for males, except for the omission of technologically oriented works.[17] Jefferson thought that two of his granddaughters were the best pupils. During a visit to Poplar Forest, he said, "Ellen and Cornelia are the severest of the students I have ever met with. They never leave their room but to come to meals."[18] Yet, as was the custom of the time, these talented daughters and their sisters remained at home whereas the sons went off to colleges or universities.

Thomas Jefferson Randolph, called Jefferson, was sent to Philadelphia to study at the University of Pennsylvania for one year in 1808–09. He boarded with Charles Willson Peale, who painted his portrait and sent it as a gift to the president in February 1809. Instead of returning to Philadelphia, Jefferson Randolph completed his studies in Richmond at the school of Louis H. Girardin, who later used Jefferson's library to write the fourth volume of the history of Virginia series begun by John Daly Burk.[19] Two Randolph brothers, James Madison and Benjamin Franklin, eventually attended the new University of Virginia. Their cousin Francis Eppes (1801–1881), Maria's only living child, studied at South Carolina College until his father was no longer able to finance his studies.

Book Room

A comfortable apartment consisting of four connected spaces comprised Jefferson's private suite of rooms, a sanctum sanctorum at the south end of the house. Jefferson's territory was rarely entered except by Mrs. Randolph, who was often seen there talking to her father as she sewed, and by occasional invited scholars. Mrs. Anna Thornton, who visited in 1802, noted, "The president's bedchamber is only separated from the Library by an arch, he keeps it constantly locked, and I have been disappointed much by not being able to get in to day."[20] Mrs. Thornton was not the sole aggrieved guest. Sir Augustus John Foster remarked:

If the Library had been thrown open to his Guests, the President's Country House would have been as agreeable a Place to stay at as any I know, but it was here he sat and wrote and he did not like of

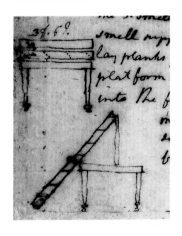

Drawing of folding stairs

1784–1789
Thomas Jefferson
ink on paper
Massachusetts Historical Society

Jefferson sketched these library steps, which fold to form a table, next to a drawing showing the arrangement of bookcases in the library of the first Monticello.

course to be disturbed by Visitors who in this Part of the world are rather disposed to be indiscreet.[21]

The Book Room, linked to the Sitting Room by a door, was adjacent to Jefferson's Cabinet (or study) and Bedroom. The unheated, mostly glazed Greenhouse where Jefferson sprouted seedlings and sat at a workbench was located outside the Book Room and Bedroom.

◆　◆　◆

In 1815 Jefferson's extensive library was among the largest in the nation.[22] Much of Jefferson's life and a high percentage of his financial resources were spent acquiring books. At fourteen he had inherited forty or so from his father, and they became the nucleus of his first library. He added to it considerably while a student at the College of William and Mary between 1760 and 1762, and later while studying law under George Wythe. He bought many titles, including *Bacon's Philosophy*, from the Virginia Gazette, the best bookstore in Williamsburg. He secured still more books from abroad. His Literary Commonplace Book, in which he recorded favorite passages, shows that he was then reading eighteenth-century poets in addition to Lord Bolingbroke's *Philosophical Works*. During this early period he also studied Lord Kames's *Principles of Equity*, as well as John Locke, Montesquieu, and Burlamaqui. A fire at Shadwell in 1770 destroyed the house and virtually every book in it. "I was unlucky enough to lose the house in which we lived, and in which all it's contents were consumed. A very few books, two or three beds &c. were with difficulty saved from the flames."[23]

Jefferson began to replace the lost library with extraordinary rapidity. By August 1773 he noted in a Memorandum Book entry that he had accumulated 1,256 volumes at Monticello, not including his music or his other books in Williamsburg. Among other noted Virginia libraries, Jefferson was able to buy opportunely all the collections of the intellectual Richard Bland and the celebrated Peyton Randolph, which were among the best. The books that he purchased from Randolph even came in their bookcases "as they stood."

One of the things that attracted Jefferson to Philadelphia and Paris was, undoubtedly, the access that he would have to more cosmopolitan bookstores.

While residing in Paris, I devoted every afternoon I was disengaged, for a summer or two, in examining all the principal bookstores, turning over every book with my own hand, and putting by everything which related to America, and indeed whatever was rare and valuable in every science. Besides this, I had standing orders during the whole time I was in Europe, on it's principal book-marts, particularly Amsterdam, Frankfort, Madrid and London, for such works relating to America as could not be found in Paris.[24]

While in Paris, he added approximately two thousand volumes, so that when he returned to America he owned about five thousand titles.[25]

After the British burned part of the Capitol in 1814, destroying its book collection, Jefferson immediately offered to sell his library to Congress for whatever price it was willing to pay. He then supposed that he owned between nine and ten thousand volumes, but the actual number was closer to seven. Francis Calley Gray, a Harvard graduate, said that "the history of North and South America is the most perfectly displayed in this library. The collection on this subject is without a question the most valuable in the world."[26] After some partisan wrangling, the purchase was approved at a cost of $23,950, in spite of the Federalist Cyrus King's comments that "Jefferson's books would help disseminate his 'infidel philosophy' and were 'good, bad, and indifferent, old, new, and worthless, in languages which many can not read, and most ought not."[27] This collection forms the nucleus of the present Library of Congress.

After the departure of his prized library, Jefferson assembled a third library of favorites—poetry, politics, philosophy, Christianity—to occupy him in his retirement. He told John Adams, "I cannot live without books; but fewer will suffice where amusement, and not use, is the only future object."[28] The collection for "amusement" numbered more than one thousand titles. Ellen Randolph Coolidge reported that Jefferson's reading in his later years was largely devoted to the classics.

Books were at all times his chosen companions. . . . he derived more pleasure from his acquaintance with Greek and Latin than from any other resource of literature. . . . I saw him more frequently with a volume of the classics in his hand than with any other book.[29]

◆   ◆   ◆

The books sold to Congress, packed as they had been shelved in book boxes at Monticello, traveled in ten wagons. Most had been shelved in five different sizes of open wooden boxes with a shelf in the middle. These book boxes were so much tailored to Jefferson's use that it seems likely that they were made in Monticello's joinery. Books were placed on the bottom of the box and on the shelf, and then were stacked by size. Folios were on the bottom, followed by quartos, octavos, duodecimos, and petit-format books at the top. To move them, the boxes were taken down from their stacks, boards were nailed across the front of the boxes, and then the boxes were wrapped in oilcloth.

The Book Room literally spilled over with books. Since it was not mentioned on the 1826 inventory, comparatively little is known about the other contents of this room, which was only seldom visited and described by others. Other than the book boxes and the one or more presses acquired with Peyton Randolph's library, the Book Room also probably contained a tall reading desk, an octagonal filing table, and two or more chairs. The reading desk (Cat. 119), which could have been used as a table for drawing or writing, was one of several purchases from Virginia cabinetmakers dating from the late 1760s and early 1770s. Capable of supporting a book as large as a folio, this table with Chinese fretwork details matches the description of a desk "to have [Chinese?] railing at the back and ends of top" that was purchased in 1767 from George Donald of Williamsburg and Richmond.[30]

An octagonal filing table (Cat. 118) dating from the last decade of the eighteenth century was acquired in Philadelphia or New York. The letters of the alphabet in groups of three were inlaid in light wood on eight drawers, which could be locked by rotating a ring under the top. The table was highly prized by the family; both Ellen Coolidge and Thomas Jefferson Randolph wanted it after their grandfather's death. Virginia Trist said that Randolph "set his heart on having it, and he said it was the only thing in the house he would bid against Joseph [Coolidge] for."[31]

Greenhouse

Jefferson to William Hamilton, March 1, 1808:

"My green house is only a piazza adjoining my study, because I mean it for nothing more than some oranges, Mimosa Farnesiana and a very few things of that kind." The Greenhouse also contained Jefferson's workbench and tools.

Side Chair

Monticello joinery
mahogany
91.4 × 50.4 × 42.9
(36 × 19⅞ × 16½ in.)
Thomas Jefferson Memorial
Foundation

The Book Room may also have contained a small walnut desk (Cat. 149) made in the Monticello joinery. Simple in style, the desk has straight, tapering legs with casters that are emblematic of Monticello-made works. The top was hinged to reveal a green baize-covered writing surface and storage compartment.

Little is known about the seating furniture in the Book Room. Presumably, there were at least several side chairs that could have been from any one of several sets. A mahogany joinery-made example with straight legs and vase-shaped splat, typical of provincial Virginia makers, is one possibility.

In the Book Room annex, nearly opposite the door to the Greenhouse, a walnut cupboard or press with double doors and mahogany shelves held many of his precious seeds. During her 1802 visit Margaret Bayard Smith said:

He opened a little closet which contains all his garden seeds. They are all in little phials, labeled and hung on little hooks. Seeds such as peas, beans, etc. were in tin cannisters, but everything labeled and in the neatest order.[32]

The closet, or seed press, put together with the readily available nails from Monticello's own nailery, contains a row of holes for hooks.

Greenhouse

A passionate gardener, Jefferson encouraged his daughters and grandchildren to share his enthusiasm. After his retirement he described himself to Charles Willson Peale as "an old man but a young gardener" and told him that "no occupation is so delightful to me as the culture of the earth, and no culture comparable to that of the garden."[33] He exchanged seeds with scientists and farmers from around the world and thought nothing as important to a country as the cultivation of useful plants.

Jefferson variously called the Greenhouse the "South Piazza," and "S. E. Piazza." Here he kept flowers, plants, and flats for sprouting seeds. It was "divided from the other by glass compartments and doors; so that the view of the plants it contains, is unobstructed."[34] The room was not yet completed in January 1808 and was only just finished when Margaret Bayard Smith visited in 1809. "The arched piazza beyond, was ultimately sashed with glass, and converted into a flower conservatory, so that the windows and glass doors of the library opened upon both its beauty and its fragrance."[35] In 1796, Isaac Weld, Jr., noted that Jefferson planned to create an aviary, but no evidence of it has been found.

Before Monticello was expanded and the Greenhouse was built, Jefferson kept a large rectangular workbench in the middle of a room adjacent to his upstairs library. He had a chest of tools that had been acquired in London.[36] The caliber of his workmanship was evident to visitors. George Tucker, one of Jefferson's earliest biographers, recorded his impressions of a visit in 1824:

Mr. Jefferson was fond of exercising himself in mechanical employments. He had a small room adjoining his bed room, in which was a complete assortment of tools, in the use of which he had acquired much practical skill, to find an agreeable relaxation for his mind, to repair any of his various instruments in physical science, and to execute any little scheme of the moment in the way of furniture or experiment.[37]

The slave Isaac Jefferson said:

My Old Master was neat a hand as ever you see to make keys and locks and small chains, iron and brass. He kept all kind of blacksmith and carpenter tools in a great case with shelves to it in his library, an upstairs room [in the 1782 house].[38]

Only one example of Jefferson's workmanship is thought to have survived; family tradition has it that Jefferson made the small press and bookcase (Cat. 150) in his Bedroom.

The windows in the Greenhouse were shielded by special venetian blinds that Jefferson designed. He made several drawings for them in 1804, but the blinds are not extant. Also no longer extant is a jalousie that stretched from the east wall of the Greenhouse along the south wall of the Book Room.

Cabinet

The most private part of Jefferson's sanctum sanctorum was the Cabinet, or study, where he spent much of the morning and late afternoon reading and answering correspondence. Immediately adjacent to the open alcove of his bed, the room was illuminated by three windows and a French door. It was ringed by presses squeezed full with papers and letters. At the center of the room was an entirely idiosyncratic reading-and-writing arrangement that included a whirligig chair, a Windsor couch, a writing table with a rotating top, and a revolving bookstand that could hold five volumes simultaneously. Atop the writing table was a copying press to duplicate Jefferson's letters. Everything was organized for efficiency.

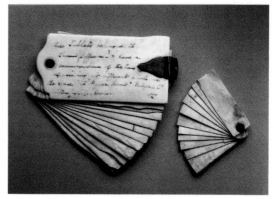

Ivory Notebooks

Philadelphia
10.2 × 5.2 (4 × 2 1/16 in.)

France
5.1 × 1.7 (2 × 11/16 in.)
Thomas Jefferson Memorial Foundation

Jefferson carried pocket notebooks made of leaves of ivory; penciled notes could be erased after they were transferred to paper.

Correspondence was one of Jefferson's principal activities; during his lifetime he wrote approximately twenty thousand letters. In retirement the burden of responding to all the letters he received—the number of which he sometimes exaggerated—inundated him. To John Adams he confessed in 1817:

From sun-rise to one or two o'clock, and often from dinner to dark, I am drudging at the writing table. And all this to answer letters into which neither interest nor inclination on my part enters; and often from persons whose names I have never before heard. Yet, writing civilly, it is hard to refuse them civil answers. This is the burthen of my life, a very grievous one indeed, and one which I must get rid of.[39]

Five years later, he reiterated his unchanged distress to Adams, "At best it is the life of a mill-horse, who sees no end to his circle but in death. To such a life that of a cabbage is paradise."[40]

◆ ◆ ◆

Jefferson's novel reading-and-writing arrangement was set up to make him both productive and comfortable. Troubled by an aching wrist, Jefferson liked to place as little stress as possible on it while writing. The whirligig chair (Cat. 129) and a Windsor couch (Cat. 128) were used to make him more comfortable while he wrote.[41] Jefferson purchased

the whirligig, or swivel, chair together with an upholstered sofa (Cat. 130), attributed to Thomas Burling, in New York in 1790. A concave piece of the sofa's end was cut out so that the two could fit together, creating a two-piece chaise longue. If Jefferson wanted to sit upright, he could do so simply by pushing the sofa away. Although they worked in tandem, the chair and sofa could not have been used together at Monticello for writing because the sofa, with its back, could not be straddled by a table.

To create a workable arrangement, Jefferson matched the whirligig chair with a Windsor couch (Cat. 128) without arms or back that could slide perfectly under his writing table. The couch, which he described as "a stick sopha and mattras," had a tufted cushion and bamboo legs.[42] It was made in Philadelphia in 1798 by Lawrence Allwine, a chair maker and manufacturer of paints. In the Tea Room Jefferson created a second arrangement by adding a writing arm to the revolving Windsor and using it with the Burling sofa.

The Cabinet, which was not finished and used by Jefferson until 1801, was largely furnished with utilitarian pieces made at Monticello. The other parts of the reading-and-writing arrangement—a writing table and a revolving bookstand—were obviously made or altered to Jefferson's specifications in the Monticello joinery. For example, the unusual mahogany writing table (Cat. 144) was made there. The design features two tops held together by an iron bolt and nut. The original skirt was cut away and stretchers and rollers were added to help the top pivot.

Jefferson also may have designed a compact revolving bookstand (Cat. 148), which also appears to be the product of the Monticello joinery. The bookstand smartly folds into a cube when the rests are closed. Five books, no larger than octavos, can be supported on four rests on each upright side and one on the top of the cube. The precedent for this ingenious design is not known, nor does a drawing for it survive.

A joinery-made table (Cat. 142), possibly used to support the bookstand, echoed the decorative treatment of a French architect's table that also may have been used in the Cabinet or Book Room. The carving on the legs of the Monticello-made table copied the carved panels of the legs on the considerably more delicate table by Denis-Louis Ancellet. The architect's table (Cat. 166) has an adjustable top; extra notches were cut into the supports to raise the height for Jefferson, who was six feet two and one half inches tall.

Filing presses (Cat. 152, 153) are still other examples of joinery-made furniture used in the Cabinet. The five filing presses were packed with letters, receipts, invoices, and other papers. Several of these presses, with a door covering movable shelves and a drawer at the bottom, were produced in the joinery. The letters inside them apparently were kept folded, tied together in small bundles, and then were filed chronologically and alphabetically. One of the presses, for example, was marked "Paris." From Poplar Forest Jefferson wrote his daughter at Monticello:

In my Cabinet, and in my window on the right of my writing table you will see 4. or 5. cartoons of papers, and in the 2nd where the alphabet begins you will find Cathalan's papers in one or more bundles.[43]

Even five presses could not hold Jefferson's voluminous correspondence, which spilled over the room in boxes.

Cabinet

Margaret Bayard Smith, 1809:

"[Jefferson] asked us into what I had called his *sanctum sanctorum*, into which it is very seldom any one is admitted. This suit of apartments open from the hall, and occupy the *south wing*—it consists of three rooms, formerly filled by his valuable and extensive library . . . another opening from these for his cabinet, which is furnished with every convenience for a man of letters—communicating with his chamber in which he sleeps."

The works of art displayed in the Cabinet are unmentioned in the Catalogue of Paintings, and so only a little is known about them. Apparently a "gallery of presidents" was set up here after 1820. In a letter to John Adams, who presented him with a plaster copy (now lost) of his portrait (Cat. 100) by the French sculptor J. B. Binon (1818), Jefferson said that he would place it in his cabinet between his predecessors and successors. Because Jefferson owned two Houdon busts of Washington, as well as busts of James Madison (Cat. 96) and James Monroe by Peter Cardelli, and busts of himself by Houdon and William John Coffee (as well as the one by Ceracchi in the Entrance Hall), he very easily could have placed the busts on the tops of the five presses in the Cabinet.

◆ ◆ ◆

Jefferson was part of a community of "practical philosophers," or scientists, who tried to learn as much as they could about the natural world and scientific phenomena. From his Cabinet he corresponded with the leading scientists and inventors of his age: Baron Friedrich Heinrich Alexander von Humboldt, the Prussian geographer; the Abbé José Correia da Serra, the Portuguese botanist; Dr. Benjamin Rush, the eminent Philadelphia professor of medicine; Charles Willson Peale, the artist and naturalist; David Rittenhouse, the astronomer and mathematician; and the Abbé Alexis Marie de Rochon, the physician and astronomer. In a lifelong effort to establish a statistical base of information about the weather, he systematically recorded temperature and weather conditions twice each day. He studied climatology, astronomy, and he applied scientific methods to farming and gardening—in short, he did everything in his power to improve the lives of his countrymen through the practical application of science.

One of the devices that was most useful to him was a polygraph (Cat. 223), a kind of copying machine, patented by Charles Willson Peale and John Isaac Hawkins, an inventor. Jefferson, who kept a copy of virtually every letter that he wrote from 1785 and on, said that it was "the finest invention of the present age," and he used one at the President's House and a second at Monticello.[44] This copying machine replaced one by James Watt that Jefferson had acquired in 1785. The Watt machine (Cat. 222) used a special ink that reproduced the writing by running the original letter and a piece of dampened tissue through a press. The polygraph was far easier to use; it created a duplicate, as Jefferson described it, by "copying with one pen while you write with the other."[45] Jefferson carried out a lengthy correspondence with Peale to help him modify some early defects in the polygraph's design. He liked it so much that he ordered them as gifts for the comte de Volney, Edward Preble, and James Bowdoin.

At his disposal in the Cabinet were the tools necessary for surveying: a theodolite (Cat. 214) for measuring horizontal and vertical angles, chains, a micrometer (Cat. 211) for computing short distances, and a circumferentor (Cat. 217), a surveyor's compass that had projecting arms with a vertical slit sight. With them he calculated distances and boundaries of various parts of the Monticello plantation.

Jefferson was interested in astronomy and said that "No inquisitive mind will be content to be ignorant" of the sciences of astronomy, natural philosophy, natural history, chemistry, and anatomy.[46] His large holdings on astronomy ranged from a French edition of the stars according to Ptolemy to the latest scientific studies. Although Jefferson sent his observations of the solar eclipse to Nathaniel Bowditch, the astronomer and navigator, he mainly watched solar and lunar eclipses for enjoyment.[47]

But aftr 40. years of abstraction from it, and my mathematical acquirements coated over with rust, I find myself equal only to such simple operations & practices in it as serve to amuse me. But they give me great amusement, and the more as I have some excellent instruments. My telescope however is not equal to the observation of the eclipses of Jupiter's satellites, nor my best time piece sufficiently to be depended on.[48]

Jefferson kept several telescopes (Cat. 212, 213), an astronomical clock (Cat. 238), a celestial globe, and an orrery (Cat. 210), a kind of miniature three-dimensional planetarium, in his Cabinet. The largest telescope, an achromatic refracting type made by Dollond of London, was used for stargazing. With a handheld "spyglass," he is reported to have tracked the construction of the University of Virginia from Monticello.

The University of Virginia, which Jefferson founded, was chartered in 1819. In his "last act of usefulness,"[49] he dedicated the remaining years of his life to "this institution of my native state, the hobby of my old age, . . . based on the illimitable freedom of the human mind to explore and to expose every subject susceptible of its contemplation."[50] As the university's first rector, Jefferson not only helped to select an internationally distinguished faculty and to recommend books for the library but he also both conceived the idea of the model campus and designed it. Seated at his architect's desk with his drafting instruments before him, on coordinate paper Jefferson devised an ideal "academical village" with ten pavilions—"models of taste and good architecture, and of a variety of appearance, no two alike, so as to serve as specimens for the architectural lectures"—connected by dormitories for the students—"giving to each a room."[51] The centerpiece of the university was the Rotunda, the library, modeled after the Pantheon.

Jefferson's Bedroom

The Bedroom was lighted by a triple-sash window on the west and a large skylight that could be opened. The intricate frieze motifs with putti, bucrania, and urns and swags ornamented by ribbons were inspired by the Ionic order of the Temple of Fortuna Virilis in Rome, which Jefferson had seen illustrated in Plate IV of Desgodetz's *Les Edifices Antiques de Rome*. The double-height Bedroom was separated from the Cabinet by a door and an unusual bed alcove that was open on two sides, thus perforating the barrier between the two adjacent rooms. The alcove on the Cabinet side, however, was apparently closed off, particularly in winter, by a glazed mahogany sash until it was replaced in 1809 by a lightweight folding screen of wood and wallpaper, supported by a pole affixed to the ceiling and floor.

Jefferson's out-of-season clothing as well as extra bedcovers were stored in a closet on top of the bed alcove that was reached by a ladder. From Poplar Forest, he wrote his daughter on one occasion that he was troubled by the cold: "In the closet over my bed you will find a bag tied up, and labelled 'Wolf-skin pelisse,' and another labelled 'fur-boots,'

Counterpane

1809
John Rea (active 1799–c. 1829)
silk, silk fringe, wool batting,
linen and cotton backing,
215 cm square (84½ in. square)
excluding fringe
Thomas Jefferson Memorial
Foundation

wherein those articles will be found."[52] Garments for everyday wear were hung on a "turning machine, upon wh. He hung his clothes—his coats and waistcoats &c—which stands between the library and the bed-chamber."[53] Augustus John Foster reported:

In a recess at the foot of the bed was a horse with forty-eight projecting hands on which hung his coats and waistcoats and which he could turn round with a long stick; a Knick-knack that Jefferson was fond of showing with many other little mechanical Inventions.[54]

◆ ◆ ◆

At the foot of Jefferson's bed and presumably inside the alcove was a superb clock (Cat. 235) supported by two black marble obelisks that was probably placed on a bracket made in the Monticello joinery. Jefferson's own design was carried out by the expert Paris clock maker Chantrot in 1790. The clock was closely associated with Jefferson not only because he designed it but also because his regimen depended upon it: "Mr. Jefferson rises in the morning as soon as he can see the hands of his clock, which is directly opposite his bed," Daniel Webster wrote in 1824.[55] Mrs. Randolph, who retained her father's bedroom furniture, said of the clock, after her daughter and son-in-law acquired it:

The marble clock I should have prized beyond anything on earth, and if, in our circumstances, I had felt justifiable in retaining a luxury of that value, that clock, in preference to everything else but the immediate furniture of his bedroom, I should have retained.[56]

Happily, the Trists purchased the clock at the Dispersal Sale and gave it to Mrs. Randolph, who later bequeathed it to Nicholas Trist.

The bed itself was covered with a brilliant crimson silk mantua counterpane, made to Jefferson's exact specifications in 1808 by the Philadelphia upholsterer John Rea, who had recently provided the Latrobe-designed draperies for the House of Representatives chamber at the Capitol. Jefferson requested "a counterpane of such crimson Mantua silk such as the draperies which Mr. Rea formerly furnished to Th: Jefferson."[57] Rea edged the counterpane with a handknotted fringe of gold and crimson silk rather than the plain gold that he supplied for the Parlor curtains. The bed hangings of an unidentified fabric did not match the counterpane; Jefferson "remarked that the curtains of his bed had been purchased from the first cargo that arrived [presumably from England] after the peace of 1782."[58]

One of the Bedroom's most distinctive features was the gilt-and-gesso-on-wood mirror with a round arched top (Cat. 170) that hung opposite the triple-sash window. The mirror, which reflected the abundant afternoon light, was one of seven mirrors that Jefferson brought back with him from Paris. Commanding mirrors such as this one were made in pairs, and its separated mate may have been suspended above the sideboard in the Dining Room where a hook has been found. A semicircular girandole mirror (Cat. 168) with two brass candle sconces, also of French origin, hung above the mantel.

Cornelia Jefferson Randolph's drawing of Monticello's first floor indicates that Jefferson kept a dressing table opposite the window and "a chair, with a small bookcase near it" next to the fireplace.[59] The character of his lost dressing table is unknown; it could have

Jefferson's Bedroom

Sir Augustus John Foster,
1804–5:

"The President had his Bed placed in a Door way: and in a Recess at the foot of the Bed was a Horse with forty Eight projecting Hands on which hung his Coats and Waistcoats and which he could turn round with a long Stick."

Bedroom Frieze

Jefferson based the
ornamental frieze in his
bedroom on a design from the
temple of Fortuna Virilis,
taken from Claude-Antoine
Jombert's edition of Antoine
Desgodetz's *Les Edifices
Antiques de Rome* (Paris, 1779).

been acquired in France or may have been made in America. While in Philadelphia he
used one with a broken marble top, but he may not have bothered to bring it back to
Monticello. Jefferson's granddaughter Cornelia also placed "Mrs. Jefferson's dressing
table" (Cat. 123) in the Bedroom. No purchases of dressing tables were recorded in
Jefferson's Memorandum Books while his wife was alive, and thus it is assumed that she
already owned one at the time of her marriage in 1772. Although no documentation is
known, the fashionable Rococo-style block-front kneehole bureau table with a Massachusetts origin could have been Mrs. Jefferson's. Case pieces by New England cabinetmakers
were known to have been sold in Virginia.

A small joinery-made mahogany press surmounted by an unmatched tall narrow
bookcase (Cat. 150) is reputedly the one that Jefferson used in his Bedroom. The dark
finish, possibly original, corresponds to the finish on other joinery-made works; the brass
handles are identical to those on one of the Dining Room dumbwaiters. At least one chair
was used here. A likely candidate, other than a campeachy, is the low cherry armchair (Cat.
117) in the Rococo style made in Virginia in the 1770s. The chair's straight legs were
shortened to accommodate a set of casters, now missing.

◆　◆　◆

Less is known about the works of art and artifacts displayed in Monticello's private
rooms than those in the four public rooms, which were described in Jefferson's Catalogue of
Paintings. A visitor in 1807 described an important Native American artifact in the Book
Room:

*a picture representing a battle, painted by one of the Big-bellied tribe of Indians, who live upon the
Missouri, on a buffalo hide, very grotesque, as may be supposed, but extremely interesting. It
represents several Indians in single combat, with tomahawks or spears and shields, fighting on
horseback. Where a white man was intended to be represented he is painted with the accompani-
ments of a gun and cocked hat. The whole is rudely sketched, and the men seem sliding off instead
of sitting on their horses.*[60]

The robe could have been fastened to the wall or draped over a chair or table, as the tiered book boxes probably occupied most of the available wall space.

Judging from Jefferson's "Memorandum of Taxable Property" of March 1815, substantially more framed works of art were exhibited than were listed in the undated Catalogue. The 1815 inventory listed a total of 183 works, "144 pictures, prints, engravings with frames, more than 12 i[nches]" and "39 do. under 12 i. with gilt frames," compared to approximately 102 paintings and prints (but not sculpture and medals) identified in the Catalogue. Among the few firmly documented works was an elevation of the west front of Monticello (Cat. 24), one of two drawn by Robert Mills. Joseph Coolidge wanted it after Jefferson's death and said of it, "I remember, dear N. [Nicholas Trist], nothing more of the furniture of these rooms (the chamber and library,) but the simple drawing—a front view, I think of Monticello itself."[61]

Jefferson obtained engravings of John Trumbull's principal historical works, and these could have been displayed in any of Monticello's private rooms, particularly the rooms occupied by Jefferson. In addition to Asher B. Durand's engraving of *The Declaration of Independence, July 4th, 1776* (1823) (Cat. 31), Jefferson owned *The Battle at Bunker's Hill Near Boston* (1798) (Cat. 33), engraved by Johann Gotthard Muller and published in London, and *The Death of General Montgomery in the Attack of Quebec, December 1775* (1798) (Cat. 34), engraved by Johann Frederick Clemens and also published in London.

The only British subject among the Trumbull works owned by Jefferson celebrated the outstanding valor of a defeated Spanish officer. Trumbull completed *The Sortie Made by the Garrison of Gibraltar in the Morning of 27 November 1781* (Cat. 32) while he studied under Benjamin West in London in 1787. The subject was the victorious British assault of Spanish troops, and the dying Spanish officer who charged the British alone after being abandoned by his own company.

◆　◆　◆

The Jefferson-Randolph-Eppes family owned many portraits of its members. Unmentioned on Jefferson's Catalogue of Paintings of Monticello's four public rooms, numerous family portraits were unquestionably displayed throughout the many other private rooms, presumably including Jefferson's sanctum sanctorum. One of the most significant of these likenesses was James Westhall Ford's *Martha Jefferson Randolph* (Cat. 15). In 1823, Jefferson commissioned "the attendance of Mr. Ford at Monticello to take the portrait of Mrs. Randolph when it shall suit his convenience."[62] He was pleased with Ford's result and wrote that "His good execution, and the reasonableness of his terms render him worthy of encouragement and patronage."[63]

Jefferson thought highly of sculpture and made arrangements in 1819 for a particularly talented itinerant sculptor, William John Coffee, to make not only his terra-cotta bust (now lost) but also to depict his granddaughters Anne Cary Randolph Bankhead (Cat. 104), Ellen Randolph, and Cornelia Jefferson Randolph (Cat. 103), and Mrs. Wilson Cary Nicholas, his grandson, Jefferson Randolph's, mother-in-law.

Jefferson sat for many more portraits than were displayed at Monticello.[64] Among the likenesses exhibited throughout the house were four busts: Giuseppe Ceracchi's colossal marble (1791) in the Entrance Hall, and three lost works, a life-size terra-cotta patinated plaster by Houdon that may have been one of the presidential group in the Cabinet; a half-life-size terra-cotta by Coffee (1818), and a plaster by Peter Cardelli (1819) for whom Jefferson sat at the urging of John Adams. Painted likenesses included two works by Gilbert Stuart, the classicized Medallion profile (1805) (Cat. 14) and the Edgehill (1805) (Cat. 13), so called for its later association with the Randolph family home in Albemarle County; a miniature by John Trumbull (1787); and possibly two other lost portraits, one by William Joseph Williams (1792) and the second by Mather Brown (1786). An unusual *verre églomisé* portrait by A. B. Doolittle (1803) hung in the Tea Room. Jefferson also paid for a drawing by Saint-Mémin in 1804 (Cat. 65) that also may have been at Monticello.

Madison's and the Abbé Correia da Serra's Rooms

Monticello was visited by Jefferson's family and friends for long periods of time during his retirement. For example, the Carys of Carybrook made frequent long stays as did Aunt Hackley. Jefferson's sister, Anna, or "Aunt Marks," moved into Monticello after the death of her husband. Unannounced callers often appeared, and Mrs. Randolph once had to contend with as many as fifty guests at one time. A family member reported:

We had persons from abroad, from all the States of the Union, from every part of the State, men, women, and children. In short, almost every day for at least eight months of the year, brought its contingent of guests. People of wealth, fashion, men in office, professional men military and civil, lawyers, doctors, Protestant clergymen, Catholic priests, members of Congress, foreign ministers, missionaries, Indian agents, tourists, travellers, artists, strangers, friends.[65]

Not all of the visitors were polite. People sometimes lined the passage waiting to catch a glimpse of Jefferson, and "a female once punched through a window-pane of the house, with her parasol, to get a better view of him."[66]

Among the family's favorite visitors was the Abbé José Correia da Serra, the Portuguese botanist and diplomat whom Jefferson said was "one of the most learned men of the age."[67] He visited seven times between 1813 and 1820—often enough for the North Square Room on the first floor to be named for him. Introduced to Jefferson by the marquis de Lafayette, baron von Humboldt (Cat. 81), and Pierre Samuel Dupont de Nemours, the Abbé had helped to found the Academy of Science in Lisbon. Jefferson quickly developed considerable affection for this "modest, good-humored, familiar, plain as a country farmer" man of science, and entreated him to remain at Monticello.[68] He extended "a comfortable room . . . for retirement when you choose it, and a sociable family, full of affection and respect for you, when tired of being alone."[69] While at Monticello, Correia da Serra read and "passed his time in the fields and woods."[70] The Abbé was designated Portugal's minister plenipotentiary to the United States in 1816 and left the country in 1820.

James Madison and his wife Dolley Payne Todd Madison were particular friends of Jefferson and his family, and they frequently visited Monticello. The family named the North Octagonal Room at the end of the north passage for them. Madison was Jefferson's

James Madison (1751–1836)
1804
Gilbert Stuart (1755–1828)
oil on canvas, 73.7 × 70
(29 × 24 in.)
Colonial Williamsburg
Foundation

North Octagonal Room
Ellen Randolph Coolidge, 1856:

Monticello was overrun by throngs of visitors, mostly uninvited, that descended upon Jefferson after his retirement from the presidency. His granddaughter recalled that "they came of all nations, at all times, and paid longer or shorter visits . . . In short, almost every day, for at least eight months of the year, brought its contingent of guests."

Abbé José Correia da Serra
(1750–1823)

1881
Designed by Jùlio Costa
engraving
Fundaçào Luso-Americana,
Lisbon

Dome Room

Margaret Bayard Smith, 1809:

"[Jefferson] afterwards took us
to the drawing room, 26 or 7
feet diameter, in the dome. It
is a noble and beautiful
apartment, with eight circular
windows and a sky-light. It
was not furnished and being in
the attic story is not used,
which I thought a great pity as
it might be made the most
beautiful room in the house."

hand-picked successor to the presidency, and he said of him that "There is no sounder judgment than his."[71] No one shared Jefferson's values and commitment to his country as closely as did Madison. As a token of "the cordial and affectionate friendship, which . . . has united us in the same principles and pursuits of what we have deemed for the greatest good of our country," Jefferson bequeathed Madison a gold-topped walking stick (Cat. 275).[72] Near the end of his life he also asked Madison to take over as rector of the University of Virginia "to leave that institution under your care, and an assurance that it will not be wanting."[73]

Madison served as secretary of state under Jefferson. In Washington the old ties of friendship were strengthened by proximity. Before Mrs. Madison had set up her own house in 1801, she stayed at the President's House, acting as hostess so that Jefferson could "begin an acquaintance with the ladies of the place."[74] The first child to be born in the President's House, the Randolphs' second son, was named James Madison. Mrs. Madison and Mrs. Randolph and her daughters were especially close. Mrs. Randolph asked her father to ask Mrs. Madison to select "a fashionable wig of the colour of the hair inclosed, a set of combs for dressing the hair, a bonnet shawl and white lace veil for making morning visits."[75]

◆   ◆   ◆

The Madison Room was decorated with a colorful trellis wallpaper that William Short purchased for Jefferson in Paris in 1790. Jefferson had specified, "22. rouleaux of lattice or treillage do. [wallpaper] (This is in imitation of a treillage, with vines &c. on it.)" from "Arthur's, on the Boulevards."[76] Although other rooms at Monticello were wallpapered with some of the plain sky-blue, plain pea-green, plain crimson, or brick-patterned papers from the same order, the Madison room is the only room with a well-documented pattern.[77]

The rooms of both the Abbé and Madison contained bed alcoves. The furnishings on the 1826 inventory revealed essential rather than deluxe appointments in these rooms. Each contained brass andirons; mirrors; and a Pembroke table, a compact design with two hinged leaves that could be used for writing, reading, or to hold a tray. Correia da Serra's room contained "2 old Mahogany chairs" and a black walnut stand, possibly a washstand or candlestand. Madison's room may also have been used as a sitting room, since it contained "8 rush bottomed chairs." The furnishings included a painted toilet table for holding, among other things, combs, toothbrushes, and hairbrushes.

Upper Floors

The second and third floors, reached by identical narrow stairways in the north and south passages, were mainly reserved for bedrooms, which were occupied by the Randolph children, visiting family members, and other houseguests. The second floor has six rooms. Four bedrooms on this floor echo the plan of the rooms below (two square rooms and two rooms with semioctagonal ends). Anna Thornton, the wife of William Thornton, said:

When we went to bed we had to mount a little ladder of a staircase about 2 feet wide and very steep, into rooms with the beds fixed up in recesses in the walls—the windows square and small turning in pivots. Every thing has a whimsical and droll appearance.[78]

A rectangular fifth room, above the South Piazza, was used for storage, extra sleeping space, and a nursery. Little is known about the function of the sixth room, sometimes called the "appendix" by family members, but presumably it was also a bedroom. Four of the bedrooms, heated by cast-iron stoves, had bed alcoves. The 1826 inventory indicates that the bedrooms were modestly outfitted, probably with chintz, calico, checked blue-and-white, white knotted, or white homespun counterpanes.[79] The octagonal room on the south side contained a table, a chest of drawers, two black walnut stands, and a pair of iron andirons.

The third floor contains three bedrooms illuminated by skylights and what Jefferson called the "Dome room." Margaret Bayard Smith reported that "it was designed for a lady's drawing-room when built, but [it was] soon found, on account of its situation in the dome, to be too inconvenient for that use, and was abandoned to miscellaneous purposes."[80] Thomas Jefferson Randolph and his new bride, Jane Hollins Nicholas, lived there briefly after their marriage in 1815 until they moved to Tufton, one of Jefferson's nearby farms, in 1817.[81] Virginia and Cornelia Randolph made a little hideaway in the space above the portico in 1823. Virginia told her future husband, Nicholas Trist:

Since the columns to the portico have been completed, Grand-Papa has had the great work bench removed from it, and a floor layed. Cornelia's ingenuity in conjunction with mine formed steps from the dome into this little closet with a pile of boxes, and [we have] furnished this apartment with a sopha to lounge upon, though alas! without cushions, a high and low chair and two small tables . . .[82]

After Jefferson's death and possibly earlier, the Dome Room was used for storage. The 1826 inventory mentions that it then contained a truckle bed (perhaps for a slave), three painted toilet tables, a dumbwaiter, a couch and cushion, mahogany chair, three stools, a carding machine, three old screens, and old maps and buffalo robes (Appendix V).

The unheated three bedrooms on the third floor include a rectangular bedroom on the north side with two bed alcoves and two skylights. Each of the other two bedrooms has a skylight, but no bed alcove.

◆ Monticello Dispersed ◆

The last great enterprise of Jefferson's life was the founding of the University of Virginia, as he said, "the hobby of my old age"; it occupied him during the last decade of his life. Ever determined to assure the spread of information freely among men so as to create a natural aristocracy based on virtue and talent, Jefferson founded an institution "based on the illimitable freedom of the human mind to explore and to expose every subject suscepti-ble of its contemplation" and devoted his energy to realizing this last goal.[1]

After realizing his great achievement, Jefferson died in his bed in 1826 on the fiftieth anniversary of the acceptance of the Declaration of Independence. He had been acutely ill for at least ten days. His personal physician, Dr. Robley Dunglison, was summoned on June 24 and spent the last week attending him. Mrs. Randolph spent her days with her father, while his grandson Jefferson and grandson-in-law Nicholas Trist stayed with him at night. He remained lucid until the evening of July 2, when he slipped into unconsciousness, periodically awakening and inquiring if it were the Fourth. With his daughter Martha, his slave Burwell, Trist, and grandson Jefferson nearby, he died at 12:50, at about the same time fifty years earlier that the Continental Congress had received the Declaration of Independence from Adams, Livingston, Sherman, Franklin, and Jefferson. In an extraor-dinary coincidence, his old friend John Adams died later that day, believing Jefferson was still alive. His last words were "Jefferson still survives."

Although sometimes burdened by the chore of oppressive correspondence, Jefferson relished the last years of his life "in the bosom of my family," surrounded by his daughter, sister, grandchildren, nieces, and nephews. He had the satisfaction of watching the numerous Randolph children mature. One of his grand-daughters recollected:

My grandfather's manners to us, his grandchildren, were delightful. . . . He talked with us freely, affectionately, never lost an opportunity of giving a pleasure or a good lesson. He reproved without wounding us, and commended without making us vain. He took pains to correct our errors and false ideas, checked the bold, encouraged the timid, and tried to teach us to reason soundly and feel rightly. . . . My Bible came from him, my Shakespeare, my first writing-table, my first handsome writing-desk, my first Leghorn hat, my first silk dress. What, in short of all my small treasures did not come from him? Our grandfather seemed to read our hearts, to see our invisible wishes, to be our good genius, to wave the fairy wand, to brighten our young lives by his goodness and his gifts.[2]

Jefferson also derived great pleasure from gardening, reading, and corresponding with John Adams. Reconciled in 1812 after an eleven-year rift, they conducted a stimulating exchange, the subjects of which ranged from religion, philosophy, politics, and history to family matters.

Obelisk for the Grave of
Jefferson with His Epitaph

Thomas Jefferson
ink on paper, 12.4 × 19.5
(4⅞ × 7¹¹/₁₆ in.)
Library of Congress

After Jefferson's death a family member found this sketch specifying the design and inscription of his tombstone among his papers.

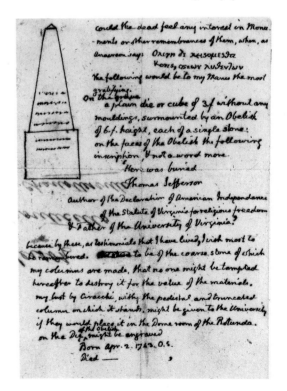

Jefferson had peacefully contemplated his death for a long time. In 1816, he wrote Adams, "I enjoy good health; I am happy in what is around me. Yet I assure you I am ripe for leaving all, this year, this day, this hour."[3] Jefferson later designed his tombstone, an obelisk of plain stone, for placement in the Monticello graveyard next to his wife. He prepared his own simple epitaph, wishing to be remembered for what he had given his country: "Here was buried Thomas Jefferson, Author of the Declaration of American Independence, of the Statute of Virginia for religious freedom, and Father of the University of Virginia."

Jefferson's serenity was sadly disturbed during the last five years of his life by increasing anxiety over his desperately bad financial situation; he owed debts that he could not pay. He wrote Jefferson Randolph in 1816:

You kindly encourage me to keep up my spirits but oppressed with disease, debility, age and embarrassed affairs, this is difficult. For myself, I should not regard a prostration of fortune. But I am overwhelmed at the prospect of the situation in which I may leave my family. My dear and beloved daughter, the cherished companion of my early life, and nurse of my age, and her children, rendered as dear to me as if my own, from having lived with me from their cradle, left in a comfortless situation, hold up to me nothing but future gloom.[4]

Cornelia wrote her sister Ellen in 1825, describing the miserable financial circumstances:

I know I wish I could do something to support myself instead of this unprofitable drudgery of keeping house here, but I suppose not until we sink entirely will it do for the graddaughters of Thomas Jefferson to take in work or keep a school, and we shall hold out for some time yet; ours is not a galloping consumption but one of those lingering diseases which drags on for years and years . . .[5]

At the time of his death, Jefferson owed more than $107,000 to creditors. The largest portion, about $60,000, was owed to Jefferson Randolph, who had acted as manager of Jefferson's affairs. Other creditors included James Leitch, a Charlottesville merchant; Andrea Pini, the daughter of Philip Mazzei, for a personal loan; and various banks for debts predating the Revolution that involved both Jefferson's portion of the Wayles inheritance from his wife and loans incurred after the Revolution. The pressure on Jefferson was so severe that his family and friends pressed the Commonwealth of Virginia to conduct a lottery to benefit him. Although it never came to pass, at the time of his death Jefferson believed that the lottery would save his heirs from financial ruin.

Martha Jefferson Randolph, heir to Monticello, was compelled to sell the entire plantation and its contents. Her son Thomas Jefferson Randolph continued to manage the financial affairs. After advertising in newspapers, a great sale of the furnishings was begun on January 15, 1827. The financial demands dictated that nearly everything—all of the slaves but five, all household furnishings, farm animals, memorabilia, some engravings, grain, and farm equipment—except Jefferson's personal effects, would be sold. Even family members were forced to buy most of what they wished to retain. The only records of the sale are family letters describing their own acquisitions and some odd receipts for money owed Mrs. Randolph for various purchases.

The Randolph family undoubtedly engaged in some spirited haggling over the pieces that they wanted. Ellen and Joseph Coolidge had the means to purchase more than the other siblings. Second to the Coolidges were Virginia and Nicholas Trist, who acquired a number of important objects, including the obelisk clock designed by Jefferson, a sofa, and the last chair that Jefferson sat in before his death. Francis Eppes, now living at Poplar Forest, which he had inherited, also purchased a few items. By 1830 some resentment flared up between Jefferson Randolph and his unmarried sisters. Mrs. Randolph tried to soothe her son when she wrote him from Washington in 1830:

With regard to the Monticello furniture you seem to be under a strange misapprehension when you say 'the girls took everything worthy of retention' of your grandfather's. They have nothing my dear Jefferson but a light table which raising and lowering, was convenient to draw at and which I gave Cornelia. The others have not a solitary article of furniture that ever belonged to him.[6]

After the sale was over, the family believed that their neighbors had been generous to them, giving good prices for their valuables. *The Niles' Weekly Register* reported that the executors raised $12,840 to pay the interest on the debt and $35,000 of the principal.[7] Even this was not sufficient for the family to hold on to Monticello, and in 1828 Mrs. Randolph resolved that it must be sold. Until August 1829 Monticello was occupied by Nicholas and Virginia Trist and intermittantly visited "in this bare castle of ours" by other members of the family.[8] Visitors continued to flock to Monticello. Seeking mementos, they grabbed everything that they could, digging up plants and nicking chips of stone from Jefferson's tomb.

In 1831 a buyer was finally located. James Turner Barclay, who then ran an apothecary shop in Charlottesville, purchased Monticello and 552 acres for $4,500, less the value of his own house. Monticello still contained the great clock in the Entrance Hall, a folding ladder, a lamp, a few books, and the enormous pier mirrors in the Parlor. Barclay's aim was to develop the grounds to raise silkworms. Although he and his wife took fine care of the house, he reportedly destroyed many of Jefferson's rare specimens to plant mulberry trees.

The works of art and books were sold separately in Boston and Washington. The family agreed that the paintings would be more likely to fetch higher prices in a city. Accordingly, Ellen Coolidge and her husband, Joseph, made the arrangements for an exhibition and sale of paintings at the Boston Athenaeum. The works of art were shipped to Boston, but not all of the paintings were in good enough condition to be put up for sale. Ellen Coolidge wrote to her mother:

It made my heart swell to see so many of my old friends the paintings from Monticello. They had been new varnished and Jones has done his best to set them off, but they are evidently in a state of

Lottery ticket

April 1826
6.7 × 14.6 (2⅝ × 5¾ in.)
Thomas Jefferson Memorial Foundation

Executor's Sale Advertisement

January 6, 1827
Richmond Enquirer
Virginia State Library and Archives

Martha Jefferson wrote of the Dispersal Sale: "I know it is necessary; I do not repine; but I cannot but remember that such things were and are most dear to me." She purchased most of the furniture of her father's bedroom and some objects that belonged to her children.

Sale of Monticello

in Atkinson's Saturday
Evening Post, *Philadelphia*
October 19, 1833

Uriah Phillips Levy (detail)
(1792–1862)

c. 1815
oil on canvas, 82.6 × 68.6
(32½ × 27 in.)
American Jewish Historical
Society, Waltham, Mass.

decay and ruin, which must prevent their bringing anything like what was expected. . . . Time,
and damp, and dust, and flies, and Mr. Coffee [the sculptor who restored the paintings] have done
their work too effectually.[9]

Only one painting—the portrait of Benjamin Franklin—was sold at the May 1828 sale at the
Athenaeum. A second effort was made five years later when "The Collection of the late
President Jefferson" was auctioned at Mr. Chester Harding's Gallery on School Street on
July 19, 1833. The books were sold by a Washington bookseller, Nathaniel P. Poor, in 1829.

After nearly two years of ownership, the Barclays decided to put Monticello up for
sale.[10] The next buyer was Uriah Philips Levy, an impassioned admirer of Jefferson. Levy,
a Jew and an officer in the United States navy, cherished Jefferson's memory and was
determined to honor it. In 1832, before Monticello was again up for sale, he had commissioned the prominent sculptor Pierre Jean David (known as David d'Angers) to sculpt a
full-length portrait of Jefferson for the United States Capitol. Levy said:

I consider Thomas Jefferson to be one of the greatest men in history—author of the Declaration
and an absolute democrat. He serves as an inspiration to millions of Americans. He did much to
mould our Republic in a form in which a man's <u>religion</u> does not make him ineligible for political
or governmental life.[11]

Levy acquired Monticello in May 1834 and owned it until his death in 1862. He bequeathed
it to the United States government so that it could be used as a training school for children of
deceased warrant officers of the navy. During the Civil War Monticello was seized by the
Confederate government, which, in turn, sold it.

At the war's end the United States government rejected Levy's bequest, and Monticello's ownership was contested by Levy's numerous heirs. In 1878, Jefferson Monroe
Levy, Uriah's nephew, finally gained control and clear title in 1879. Levy found the house
and grounds in wretched disrepair and devoted his life to their restoration, including the
acquisition of original Jefferson furnishings for the house. He owned Monticello until 1923,
when the Thomas Jefferson Memorial Foundation was formed to acquire it and commemorate Jefferson's legacy. Since 1834 (with a notable break between 1862 and 1878), Jefferson's
Monticello has been protected, studied, and preserved for future generations in an effort to
recognize "one of the most notable champions of freedom and enlightenment in recorded
history."[12]

◆ Catalogue ◆

PAINTINGS

1

**GEORGE
WASHINGTON
(1732–1799)**

1784; 1786

*Joseph Wright (1756–1793);
completed by John Trumbull
(1756–1843)
oil on canvas
94.5 × 77.5 (37³/₁₆ × 30½ in.)
Massachusetts Historical Society*

PROVENANCE:
Thomas Jefferson; by purchase to
Israel Thorndike at the Harding
Gallery sale in 1833; by gift to the
Massachusetts Historical Society in
1835.

In Paris Jefferson had two portraits of George Washington, a full-length by Charles Willson Peale and a half-length portrait by Joseph Wright that he had commissioned while he was briefly in Philadelphia on his way to sail from Boston for France between May 14 and 28, 1784. The Peale portrait was sent to Jefferson in Paris in 1785 by Virginia Governor Benjamin Harrison for Jean-Antoine Houdon to use as a model for his sculpture for the Virginia legislature in 1784.[1] Jefferson thought that the Peale was more painterly—"better coloured, more softly painted, more flattering, but less like."[2] Before leaving Paris, Jefferson apparently presented the Peale to Madame de Tessé.[3] Wright's portrait of Washington became part of the collection at Monticello. Jefferson considered it

dryer, however, but more like. The painter has seised the gravest lineaments of the General's face, so that tho' it is a faithful likeness at certain times, it is an unfavourable one. It shews him as he was in the moments of his gravest difficulties.[4]

Although Jefferson thought that he was purchasing an original portrait, the likeness that he received was probably derived from Wright's first life study of General Washington, for which he sat in October 1783.[5] Jefferson apparently saw this portrait in Philadelphia in the possession of a fellow signer of the Declaration of Independence, Francis Hopkinson. On May 28, 1784, the day that Jefferson departed Philadelphia, he noted, "left with F. Hopkinson for Wright for drawg Go. Washington £17.10."[6]

Wright immediately began to work on the painting so that Hopkinson could ship it to Jefferson in Boston. Two days after Jefferson had left Philadelphia, Hopkinson reported:

Mr. Wright has made a most excellent Copy of the Generals Head; he is much pleased with it himself, and I think it rather more like than the Original. In Order to admit of it's being pack'd up at all he has been oblig'd to expose it all this Day in the Sun. The Consequence is that the Coulours will sink in, as the Painters call it, that is, it will look dead and without Brilliancy or Gloss. This is the Case with all Pictures. All the Colours are brought out again by a Varnish. This Operation must be performed in France, as it can not be done till the Picture is thoroughly dry, for which you know there was not Time in the present Case.[7]

Many months later the picture was still unfinished. On July 6, 1785, Jefferson asked Hopkinson, "I also petitioned you to know whether I am yet at liberty to permit a copy to be taken of Genl. Washington's picture. Because till I am I cannot trust it in the hands of a painter to be finished."[8] In 1786, the portrait was finally finished by John Trumbull, who rendered the uniform in the correct colors but mistakenly used a European epaulet that was not worn in the United States.[9]

At Monticello, Washington's portrait by Wright hung in the upper tier in the Parlor. In a c. 1789 list of his paintings Jefferson wrote:

A Washington half length of full size or larger, an original taken by Wright (son of Mrs. Wright, famous for her works in wax), when Genl. Washington attended the meeting of the Cincinnati in Philadelphia May 1784. Passing then through that city on my way from Annapolis to Boston to embark for Europe I could only allow Wright time to finish the head and face and sketch the outlines of the body. These and the drapery were afterwards finished in Paris by Trumbull.[10]

Joseph Wright, who was born in Bordentown, New Jersey, was the son of Patience Wright, the prominent sculptor and secret American agent in Europe during the Revolution. After the death of her husband she settled in London in 1772 with her children, thus enabling Joseph to enroll at the Royal Academy in 1775 to study painting. Wright returned to America in 1782, where he launched a brief but successful career as a portrait painter, sculptor, and die-sinker. He died during the yellow fever epidemic in Philadelphia in 1793.

S.R.S.

John Trumbull began to work on his masterpiece, *The Declaration of Independence, July 4, 1776*, while he stayed with Jefferson at the Hôtel de Langeac in Paris between December 1787 and February 1788, when he returned to London.[11] Jefferson described the scene in the Assembly Room at Independence Hall in great detail—including the exact placement of the representatives to the Continental Congress—and sketched the room for Trumbull. Trumbull planned to obtain life portraits of all the living representatives, and he made Jefferson his first subject.

On December 19, 1788, Trumbull presented Jefferson with "a little case with two pictures, one of which I hope you will do me the honor to accept, and the other I beg you to be so good as offer to Miss Jefferson."[12] The gift for Jefferson was a miniature of Thomas Paine and the second was a miniature of Jefferson for his daughter Martha. Trumbull made three different miniatures of Jefferson derived from the life portrait in the *Declaration of Independence*. In the *Declaration* Jefferson is seen as he would have looked in 1776 with unpowdered reddish hair and wearing clothes then fashionable. On the other hand, in the three miniatures, each distinct from the other, Jefferson is depicted more formally with rolled and powdered hair, waistcoat, and jabot.

William Short, Jefferson's secretary, knew that Trumbull had painted miniatures for Jefferson's friends Maria Cosway and Angelica Schuyler Church, and he encouraged him to paint a third. He asked Trumbull:

Shall I put you in a way to do a very clever gallant thing? You have not time to think of people so far off and therefore you will excuse my giving you the hint—make what you please of it. Send a copy of the same to Miss Jefferson. Dont say that the hint came from me or from any body.[13]

Jefferson reported that Martha was delighted to have the portrait of her father:

I am to thank you a thousand times for the portrait of Mr. Paine, which is a perfect likeness, and to deliver you, for the other, on the part of my daughter, as many more as the sensations of the young are more lively than of the old.[14]

[1958-38]   S.R.S.

A miniature of Thomas Paine was a present for Jefferson from John Trumbull who painted it in 1788 while Paine and Trumbull were both in London. Trumbull knew that Jefferson wanted a portrait of "the first public advocate of the American Revolution" for he had asked Trumbull the previous year if he could get Mather Brown, the American painter then in London for whom Jefferson and Adams sat in 1786, to draw his picture.[15] When Jefferson received the miniature, he wrote Trumbull, "I am to thank you a thousand times for the portrait of Mr. Paine, which is a perfect likeness . . ."[16]

Paine, who was born in England, came to America in 1774 with a letter of introduction from Benjamin Franklin. He edited the *Pennsylvania Magazine* and wrote *Common Sense*, the famous political pamphlet that galvanized support for America's separation from England. Paine's popular work, written for all to understand, paved the way for the writing of the Declaration.

[1957-28]   S.R.S.

4

JOHN ADAMS
(1735–1826)

1788

Mather Brown (1761–1831)
oil on canvas
90.2 × 71.3 (35½ × 28¹⁄₁₆ in.)
The Boston Athenaeum

PROVENANCE:
Thomas Jefferson; by sale
to an unidentified buyer at the
Harding Gallery sale in 1833; by
descent to George Francis
Parkman; by bequest to the Boston
Athenaeum in 1908.

5

THOMAS
JEFFERSON
(1743–1826)

1788

Mather Brown (1761–1831)
oil on canvas
91.4 × 71.1 (36 × 28 in.)
Charles F. Adams

PROVENANCE:
John and Abigail Adams; by
descent to Charles F. Adams.

One of the more promising students of Benjamin West in London was Mather Brown, a young American who was active in London for a period of time after 1781. Born in Massachusetts, he was an early pupil of Gilbert Stuart. By 1785 Brown's popularity in London was such that he attracted the patronage of John and Abigail Adams.[17] Their daughter, Abigail, wrote her brother:

A rage for Painting has taken Possession of the Whole family, one of our rooms has been occupied by a Gentleman of this profession, for nearly a fortnight, and we have the extreme felicity of looking at ourselves upon Canvass.[18]

Jefferson visited England in the spring of 1786. He not only sat for Brown for a portrait for John and Abigail Adams but also must have seen Brown's likeness of Adams (1785). Once Jefferson had returned to Paris, he asked William Stephens Smith, Adams's son-in-law, to obtain a portrait of Adams.

Will you undertake to prevail on Mr. Adams to set for his picture and on Mr. Brown to draw it for me? I wish to add it to those of other principal American characters which I have or shall have: and I had rather it should be original than a copy.[19]

More than a year later, Jefferson still had no picture. Mrs. Adams told him: "Mr. Adams will write you. He has not a portrait that he likes to send you. Mr. Trumble talks of taking one. If he succeeds better than his Brethren, Mr. Adams will ask your acceptance of it.[20]

Although Jefferson later was enthusiastic about John Trumbull's abilities as a painter, he thought that he was not equal to the task of taking Adams's portrait. Jefferson informed Smith:

With Mr. Adams's picture, I must again press it to be done by Brown, because Trumbul does not paint of the size of life, and could not be asked to hazard himself on it. I have sent to Florence for those of Columbus (if it exists) of Americus Vesputius, Magellan &c. and I must not be disappointed of Mr. Adams's.[21]

Realizing that Adams would soon return to America, Jefferson pressed hard to secure Adams's portrait before his departure. In March 1788, Smith at last reported that the portrait was under way: "Brown is busy about the pictures. Mr. Adams's is like. Yours I do not think so well of."[22]

Jefferson finally received both portraits, together with a "polyplasiasmos" and a picture of George Washington for the marquis de Lafayette, in late August or early September of 1788.[23] In Brown's portrait of Adams, probably at Adams's suggestion, the artist showed Jefferson's *Notes on the State of Virginia*, which Jefferson had sent to his friend in 1785. Adams told him that the book "is our Meditation all the Day long . . . I think that it will do its Author and his country great Honour."[24]

S.R.S.

Jefferson called Bacon, Newton, and Locke, who had so indelibly shaped his ideas, "my trinity of the three greatest men the world had ever produced."[25] While in Paris in January 1789, Jefferson launched an effort to obtain portraits of his "trinity" as well as of Algernon Sidney (1622–1683), British author and politician; John Hampden (1594–1643), British statesman; and Shakespeare. Jefferson wrote John Trumbull in London:

What would it cost to have them copied by some good young hand, who will do them well and is not of such established reputation as to be dear? Those of Columbus, Vespucius, Cortez, and Magellan are well done and cost a guinea and a half each. I do not expect as cheap work in England, tho' I do not expect better. Do the busts of the same persons, Newton, Locke &c. exist, and what would they cost in plaister?[26]

In February 1789 Trumbull replied:

I have made enquiry about the pictures for which you enquire. Several of them exist, and are to be got at:—and a young man whom I know and who will do these Copies as well as most copiers: undertakes to do them for three Guineas each. . . .—I do not think tolerable copies can be procur'd for less.—The Busts in Plaister of Newton, Locke, Bacon, and Shakespeare may be had from 25/ to 30/ each, the size of life.[27]

Anticipating that he would soon be in America for several months, Jefferson responded with his approval to proceed with the portraits of his "trinity" and a sketch.

I will put off till my return from America all of them except Bacon, Locke, and Newton, whose pictures I will trouble you to have copied for me: and as I consider them as the three greatest men that have ever lived, without any exception, and as having laid the foundation of those superstructures which have been raised in the Physical and Moral sciences, I would wish to form them into a knot on the same canvas, that they may not be confounded at all with the herd of other great men. To do this I suppose we need only desire the copyist to draw the three busts in three ovals all contained in a larger oval in some such forms as this each bust to be the size of the life. The large oval would I suppose be about between four and five feet. Perhaps you can suggest a better way.[28]

In fact, Trumbull disliked Jefferson's idea. He told him:

I have given your Commission for the three pictures:—but I cannot say I think you will like the arrangement you propose when you see it executed:—The blank spaces between the three ovals will have a very awkward look. Besides that the whole be unweildy either to transport or to hang:—I should certainly have them seperate and of the common size and distinguish the three by the manner of hanging them.—I have order'd the copyist to go on with only one of the heads untill I have your answer.[29]

Jefferson concurred with Trumbull's suggestion, saying, "I submit the plan of the pictures implicitly to your opinion and therefore adopt your advice to have them separate. In this case they had better not be oval."[30]

On April 12, 1789 Trumbull made arrangements with the naturalist Joseph Banks, president of the Royal Society, for Stewart, who was presumably the copyist, to make copies of portraits of Newton, Bacon, and Locke in the Society's apartments.[31] By May 26 the paintings were completed, and Trumbull reported that

the Pictures are less good than I wish, but the fault is more in the originals than in the copyist.—
Originality is indeed all their merit—to this I believe they have the best claim. They hang in the
Apartments of the Royal Society and I am assured by Sr. J: Banks that they are genuine.[32]

The three portraits left England on the *Diligence* on May 30, 1789.[33]

It is not known if Jefferson ever hung the three portraits at the Hôtel de Langeac. They were exhibited together at his house in Philadelphia and later at Monticello where they hung in the upper tier in the Parlor. *John Locke* was sold at the Harding Gallery sale in Boston in 1833 for thirty-five dollars.[34] The paintings of Newton and Bacon are unlocated.

[1960-13]   S.R.S.

7

**STUDY FOR THE
SURRENDER OF
LORD CORNWALLIS
AT YORKTOWN**

1787; 1791

John Trumbull (1756–1843)
oil on canvas
37.5×55.9 (14¾×22 in.)
Private collection

PROVENANCE:
Thomas Jefferson; by purchase to
Nathan Appleton at the Harding
Gallery sale in 1833; by purchase
or gift to Jessee Appleton; by
descent to David Aiken, Timothy
Aiken, and Penelope Aiken
Emory; by purchase to an
unidentified buyer in 1986.

John Trumbull began *The Surrender of Lord Cornwallis at Yorktown* in 1786 and later gave Jefferson a "première ébauche" or first sketch because many of the portraits of French officers for the *Surrender* were taken in Jefferson's house in Paris. From London in August 1787 Trumbull wrote to Jefferson:

Will you do me the favor to inform me at what season I shall most probably meet the principal Officers who serv'd in America, at Paris. I shall soon be ready to paint my picture of the surrender of York Town, and must then come to paris. . . . I shall wish to see the Marquis L Fayette, Count Rochambeau, Chatellux, the two Viomenils, De Grass and D Bar[ras].[35]

A month later Trumbull reported that he was busy with a new work, *The Sortie Made by the Garrison at Gibraltar,* as well as the composition of the *Surrender:* "I wish to have decided exactly in my own Mind and even in a sketch, the composition for the Surrender at York; that I may have no embarrassment and lose no time when I come to you."[36]

Trumbull came to Paris in December 1787, bringing with him the canvases for *The Declaration of Independence* and *The Surrender of Lord Cornwallis at Yorktown.* He also probably brought along at least some of the preliminary drawings and one or more of the three known oil sketches that he completed. While staying at Jefferson's house, Trumbull painted Jefferson's life portrait in the *Declaration* and the portraits of the French officers who had served at Yorktown. By February 1788 Trumbull informed his brother Jonathan:

I have been in this capital of dissipation and nonsense near six weeks for the purpose of getting the portraits of the French Officers who were at York Town, and have happily been successful as to find all whom I wished in town. I have almost finished them . . .[37]

Before Trumbull went back to America to finish the picture, he wrote Jefferson from London:

When I was with you last, you remember I promis'd to send you the little sketch of Yorktown which I had with me:—tho' I have not fulfilld this promise, I have not forgotten it; the truth is, I have not touch'd the larger picture from that day: I hope soon to proceed with it on the other side of the Atlantic. The sketch will then find its destination.[38]

Two years later Trumbull honored his pledge and sent Jefferson the sketch.

I had not forgotten my promise, tho' it was made so long since. The first days of liesure which I enjoyed among friends in Connecticut, were devoted to render this little picture more worthy of your acceptance that it was when you saw it.[39]

Trumbull is known to have completed three or more sketches in oil. In his *Autobiography* he noted:

I also made various studies for the Surrender of Cornwallis, and in this found great difficulty; the scene was altogether one of utter formality—the ground was level—military etiquette was to be scrupulously observed, and yet the portraits of the principal officers of three proud nations must be preserved . . . I drew it over and over again, and at last, having resolved upon the present arrangement, I prepared the small picture to receive the portraits.[40]

Three of the oil sketches are known today. Two of them, now in the Detroit Institute of Arts, are too preliminary to have been the one given to Jefferson. The third (in a private collection), which more closely approximates the final painting, was probably the presentation sketch.[41]

In his Catalogue of Paintings, Jefferson described the sketch, located on the lower tier in the Parlor, as "The surrender of York by Trumbull. It was the premiere ebauche of his print on that subject. On canvas." The picture was included but not sold in the exhibition and sale at the Boston Athenaeum in 1828, and later, presumably, it was sold at Harding's Gallery in Boston in 1833 to Nathan Appleton. Jefferson also owned an engraving of the same subject.

S . R . S .

8

**CHRISTOPHER
COLUMBUS
(1451–1506)**

1788

*copy by Giuseppe Calendi (active
c. 1800) after an anonymous
portrait in the Gioviana
Collection of the Gallery of the
Uffizi, Florence
oil on canvas
61.2 × 47.2 (24⅛ × 18⁹⁄₁₆ in.)
Massachusetts Historical Society*

PROVENANCE:
Thomas Jefferson; by purchase to
Israel Thorndike at the Harding
Gallery sale in 1833; by gift with
Jefferson's portrait of Washington
to the Massachusetts Historical
Society in 1835.

9

**AMERICUS
VESPUCIUS
(1454–1512)**

1788

*copy after an anonymous
portrait in the Gioviana
Collection of the Gallery of the
Uffizi, Florence
oil on canvas
60.5 × 48.1 (23⅞ × 18¹⁵⁄₁₆ in.)
Massachusetts Historical Society*

PROVENANCE:
Thomas Jefferson; by purchase to
unidentified buyer at the Harding
Gallery sale in 1833; in the collec-
tion of Massachusetts Historical
Society by 1838.

$\mathbf{W}$hile in Paris, Jefferson wrote his friend Philip Mazzei in 1787 to obtain portraits of "Americus Vespucius, of Columbus, of Magellan and Cortez." He told Mazzei:

I should wish extremely to obtain copies of the two first, and even of the two last also, if not too expensive. Painters of high reputation are either above copying, or ask extravagant prices. But there are always men of good talents, who being kept in obscurity by untoward circumstances, work cheap, and work well.[42]

Mazzei was successful, for on January 12, 1789, Jefferson advised John Trumbull that the pictures had arrived in Paris.

I was much gratified to receive yesterday from Italy the portraits of Columbus, Americus Vespuciu[s], Cortez, and Magellan. Observing by the list of the pictures in the gallery of the Grand duke at Florence that these were there, I sent to have them copied.[43]

Jefferson valued these works very highly. In 1814, Joseph Delaplaine, who was preparing *Delaplaine's Repository of the Lives and Portraits of Distinguished American Characters* (1815–16), asked Jefferson if he might borrow the portraits of Columbus and Vespucius. Jefferson told him:

While I resided at Paris, knowing that these portraits and those of some other of the early American worthies were in the gallery of Medicis at Florence, I took measures for engaging a good artist to take and send me copies of them. I considered it as even of some public concern that our country should not be without the portraits of its first discoverers. These copies have already run the risks of transportations from Florence to Paris, to Philadelphia, to Washington, and lastly to this place, where they are at length safely deposited. . . . I think that these portraits ought not to be hazarded from their present deposit.[44]

Jefferson offered, however, to make the paintings available for copying, if Delaplaine were to send an artist to Monticello. Jefferson eventually loaned Delaplaine an engraving of Vespucius from one of his books. In 1816, Delaplaine commissioned Bass Otis to paint Jefferson for inclusion in his *Repository*.

S . R . S .

MARQUIS DE LAFAYETTE
(1757–1834)

1790

Joseph Boze (1745–1826)
oil on canvas
92.1 × 72.4 (36¼ × 28½ in.)
Massachusetts Historical Society

PROVENANCE:
Thomas Jefferson; by purchase to Mrs. John W. Davis at the Harding Gallery sale in 1833; by gift to the Massachusetts Historical Society in 1835.

As Jefferson was getting settled in New York as secretary of state in 1790, he wrote William Short, his secretary in Paris:

My pictures of American worthies will be absolutely incomplete till I get the M. de la fayette's. Tell him this, and that he must permit you to have it drawn for me. I do not like Madme. Le Brun's fan colouring, and of all possible occasions it would be worst applied to a hero. This therefore is an additional reason to that of her extravagant price. I must leave it to you to find a good clear hand of both objections. It should be the size of Genl. Washington's half length picture in the Dining room.[45]

Joseph Boze began work on the portrait by November 7. Short reported to Jefferson: "I have advice that also the Mis. de la fayette's picture is finished and I have directed it to be sent also to Havre."[46] The cost was "16. guineas for the painting, 3½ for the gilt frame."[47]

Short informed Jefferson that he had selected Joseph Boze, "who I think has taken by far the best likenesses of the Marquis."[48] Boze had completed an oval miniature of Martha Jefferson before her return to America in 1789. Having been a portrait painter at the court of Louis XVI, he was imprisoned during the Revolution and later released.

Correspondence between Short and Jefferson suggests that the portrait of Lafayette may not have been painted from life. Short wrote Jefferson:

It has been impossible as yet to get the Marquis de la fayette to set for his picture. He always says he will do it, but never keeps his word and indeed he has not time—not even one moment to spare. Still if it is possible it shall be done.[49]

Boze depicted Lafayette in the military uniform of the Parisian National Guard wearing the medals of the Society of the Cincinnati, the Vainqueurs de la Bastille, and the Cross of Saint Louis.

At Monticello Jefferson placed this portrait of his dear friend in the top tier of the Parlor between Sir Walter Raleigh and James Madison. Lafayette undoubtedly saw it there in 1824 when he was reunited with Jefferson during his triumphant farewell tour of the United States. At a speech at a dinner honoring Lafayette in Charlottesville, Jefferson said:

His deeds in the War of Independence you have heard and read. . . . When I was stationed in his country, for the purpose of cementing friendship with ours and advancing our mutual interests, this friend of both was my most powerful auxiliary and advocate. . . . Honor him, then, as your benefactor in peace as well as in war.[50]

S.R.S.

11

SIR WALTER RALEIGH
(1552?–1618)

1787

possibly Edward Alcock
(active 1757–1778)
oil on canvas
64.8 × 50.2 (25½ × 19¾ in.)

PROVENANCE:
Thomas Jefferson; by purchase at
the Harding Gallery sale in 1833 to
Colonel James W. Sever; by gift to
the Pilgrim Society in Plymouth,
Massachusetts in 1868; by
purchase to TJMF in 1965.

Although Sir Walter Raleigh was a historian and poet, Jefferson's interest in him stemmed from his early exploration of the North Carolina coast in 1584 and his premature attempt to colonize America. Jefferson owned *Sir Walter Raleigh's Essays* (1650) and Raleigh's *History of the World* (1736). To explain government in Virginia, Jefferson used Queen Elizabeth's agreement with Raleigh in *Notes on the State of Virginia*, which was published in English at about the same time that Jefferson acquired the portrait of Raleigh.

In 1786 Jefferson toured English country estates and gardens with John Adams, who was then serving as the American minister to Great Britain. Together they saw a picture of Sir Walter Raleigh at Birmingham. Jefferson then asked either Adams or Colonel Smith to obtain a likeness of Raleigh for him. He wanted "to add it to those of other principal American characters which I have or shall have."[51] In October and December of the same year, Jefferson renewed his request to Smith for both "Mr. Adams's [by Mather Brown] and Sir. Walter Raleigh's pictures."[52] When neither painting had appeared by February 19, Jefferson wrote a third reminder, "—Remember Mr. Adams's picture, I pray you; and Sir Walter Raleigh's too."[53] On May 19 Smith notified Jefferson that the portrait was on its way; "Sir Walter Raleigh I immagine will be at your House to receive you."[54] Apparently Smith located a copy of a different portrait of Raleigh, probably from a London collection, rather than the one Jefferson had seen at Birmingham. Nearly a year after the painting was shipped to Jefferson in Paris, Smith wrote, "You have never informed me whether the picture I send [sent] you was the one you saw at Bermingham or Brumigum, and whether the price I gave, was anything near what you could have obtained for it, previous to its visit to the Capital."[55]

The portrait of Raleigh was exhibited on the top tier of the Parlor next to Cortez and adjacent to other early explorers of America—Columbus, Vespucci, and Magellan. In his Catalogue of Paintings Jefferson mistakenly wrote "copy from an Original of Holben," but Hans Holbein predeceased Raleigh by nearly ten years.

The copyist may be Edward Alcock, who was active in Bath in 1757 and living in Birmingham in 1759–60, after an unidentified artist.[56]

[1965-14]   S.R.S.

12

BENJAMIN FRANKLIN
(1706–1790)

c. 1786

copy attributed to Jean Valade
(1709–1787) after 1778 original
by Joseph-Silfrede Duplessis
(1725–1802)
oil on canvas
73 × 58.9 (28¾ × 23³⁄₁₆ in.)

PROVENANCE:
Thomas Jefferson; by purchase to
the Boston Athenaeum at the sale
of Jefferson's art collection at the
Athenaeum in 1828; by loan to the
Museum of Fine Arts, Boston, in
1876; by purchase to TJMF in 1977.

Although Jefferson identified this painting as "Doctr. Franklin. an original drawn for the Abbe Very by Greusz," it is a copy of Duplessis' famous fur-collar portrait, now in the Metropolitan Museum of Art. Duplessis, a respected portrait painter, exhibited it in the Salon of 1779, and numerous copies of it were made by Duplessis as well as other artists.

Jefferson purchased "a picture 96 f." from Jean Valade, a painter, member of the Académie Royale, and sometime dealer, on September 10, 1786. Nearly a year later Jefferson received a note from Valade who then offered him a portrait of Louis XVI "bien proportionné pour le Cabinet" and reminded Jefferson that he had secured the portrait of Franklin for him.[57] The September 1786 payment was probably for that picture.

Jefferson's attribution of the portrait to Greuze is curious because his Franklin more closely resembles Duplessis' likeness (1778) than Greuze's (1779). Charles Coleman Sellers suggested that Valade used the better-recognized names of Greuze and the Abbé de Veri to help make the sale.[58] Jefferson, however, could have seen Greuze's *Franklin* (1777) in the Abbé de Veri's collection (he was then living in Paris) and recognized the difference between the Duplessis and Greuze portraits.

At Monticello *Franklin* hung in the upper tier in the Parlor. After Jefferson's death it was shipped to the Boston Athenaeum in 1828 where it was the only painting sold. The Athenaeum paid $200 for it to Joseph Coolidge, Jr., Jefferson's grandson-in-law. He reported to Mrs. Randolph, "the exhibition has closed, and only one has as yet been sold, the Franklin to the Athenaeum."[59]

[1977-80]   S.R.S.

138

Before his first portrait, taken in Philadelphia in May 1800 by Gilbert Stuart, had been delivered, Jefferson sat again for the noted portraitist in his Washington studio shortly before June 7, 1805. Jefferson wrote that he sat for the second likeness upon Stuart's insistence.

With respect to Mr. Stuart, it was in May, 1800, I got him to draw my picture and immediately paid him his price, one hundred dollars. He was yet to put the last hand on it, so it was left with him. When he came to Washington in 1805 he told me he was not satisfied with it, and therefore begged me to sit again, and he drew another which he was to deliver me instead of the first, but begged permission to keep it until he could get an engraving from it.[60]

From the beginning Jefferson knew that it would be difficult to wrest a finished portrait from Stuart's studio. Of the three portraits, only the Medallion would be placed expeditiously in the sitter's hands. Ultimately, it was to take Jefferson sixteen years and considerable effort to obtain the second, or Edgehill, portrait.[61]

In October 1818, more than thirteen years after the second portrait was made, Jefferson called on his old friend Henry Dearborn, the former secretary of war, to obtain the portrait from Stuart. Dearborn informed Jefferson:

An interview took place and after many trifling excuses for the long detention of the portrait and its unfinished situation, he said that he could not finish it, in cold weather but would certainly complete it in the Spring.[62]

The portrait was still undelivered in January 1820. Dearborn again pressed Stuart, who now, remarkably, said that "he painted this for himself. That he had no commission from any one to paint it."[63] Jefferson sent Stuart a letter that refreshed his memory of the situation, and Stuart agreed to provide either a common portrait or a half-length. Jefferson told Dearborn:

I shall be perfectly content to receive the original he drew in Philadelphia in 1800, which was of the common size (that the painters call I believe a bust). It will suit me better in the line of my other portraits not one of which is half-length. I have no doubt that Mr. Stuart's justice will think me entitled to the original and not merely a copy. There was something pleasanter in the aspect of that portrait which I liked better than the second drawn at Washington.[64]

On August 17, 1821, Jefferson finally reported, "The portrait by Stuart was received in due time and good order and claims, for this difficult acquisition, the thanks of the family."[65] Although he did not specify which portrait he received from Stuart, he was clearly pleased with the result. Whether or not it was the original 1800 life portrait, which Jefferson favored, or the 1805 portrait, or a work of 1821, is a matter of debate.

In any case what came to be known as the "Edgehill" portrait for its long association with the Jefferson Randolphs and their home, Edgehill, this portrait is one of Gilbert Stuart's best works and one of the most compelling portraits of Thomas Jefferson.

[1982-53]   S.R.S.

13
THOMAS JEFFERSON (1743–1826)

1805

Gilbert Stuart (1755–1828) oil on wood 66.7 × 55.2 (26¼ × 21¾ in.) National Portrait Gallery, Smithsonian Institution, and Thomas Jefferson Memorial Foundation; gift of the Regents of the Smithsonian Institution, The Thomas Jefferson Memorial Foundation, and the Enid and Crosby Kemper Foundation

PROVENANCE:
Thomas Jefferson; by descent to Thomas Jefferson Randolph; by purchase to Burton Harrison; by purchase to the Babcock Galleries and John B. Winant; by purchase to Percy S. Straus; by descent to Donald B. Straus; by purchase to the National Portrait Gallery and TJMF in 1983.

Jefferson kept two portraits of himself by the celebrated American portrait painter Gilbert Stuart at Monticello, this one, which is called the "Medallion," and the "Edgehill" portrait, named for its later place in the home of the Jefferson Randolphs. Both were family favorites. Ellen Coolidge remarked to her sister Virginia Trist that the Medallion "is an incomparable portrait, and the only likeness of him I think that gives a good idea of the original."[66]

Jefferson sat for Stuart twice, and from these sittings the artist produced three important life portraits. In 1813 Jefferson told Joseph Delaplaine, who was then preparing publication of Delaplaine's *Repository of the Lives and Portraits of Distinguished American Characters* (1815–16):

Mr. Stuart has drawn two portraits of me, at different sittings. Of which he prefers the last. Both are in his possession. He also drew a third in watercolours a profile in the medallion stile, which is in my possession. Mr. Rembrandt Peale also drew a portrait in oil colours on canvas while I lived in Washington. Of the merit of these I am not a judge. There being nothing to which a man is so incompetent as to judge of his likeness. He can see himself only by reflection, and that of necessity, full-faced or nearly so.[67]

Jefferson called on Stuart in his studio in Washington on June 7, 1805, for he noted in his Memorandum Book that he then paid Stuart one hundred dollars for his portrait. After he sat for the second, or Edgehill, portrait, Jefferson persuaded Stuart to sketch him in the medallion form,

which he did on paper with crayons. Although a slight thing I gave him another 100 dollars, probably the treble of what he would have asked. This I have; it is a very fine thing, though very perishable.[68]

On June 18 he thanked Stuart for "taking the head a la antique."[69] In 1815 Jefferson loaned the painting to William Thornton who first copied it in "Swiss crayons" for the Library of Congress and later made three painted versions.[70]

S.R.S.

14 (left)

THOMAS JEFFERSON (1743–1826)

1805

Gilbert Stuart (1755–1828) grisaille of aqueous medium on blue laid paper on canvas 46 × 46.7 (18.1 × 18.4 in.) The Fogg Art Museum, Harvard University, Cambridge, Massachusetts (not exhibited)

PROVENANCE:
Thomas Jefferson; by descent to Martha Jefferson Randolph; by gift to Nicholas P. Trist; by loan and later gift to Ellen and Joseph Coolidge; by descent to T. Jefferson Newbold; by gift to the Fogg Art Museum in 1960 by Mrs. T. Jefferson Newbold and family in memory of Thomas Jefferson Newbold, class of 1910.

c. 1815

copy by William Thornton (1759–1828) after 1805 original by Gilbert Stuart (1755–1828) oil on panel 61 × 47.6 (24 × 18¾ in.) Diplomatic Reception Rooms, United States Department of State

PROVENANCE:
Meriwether Lewis Randolph (Jefferson's grandson); by descent to Alexander Donelson; by bequest to Buffy Hooper Donelson Mizelle; by sale to Graham Gallery, New York; by sale to State Department.

15

**MARTHA
JEFFERSON
RANDOLPH
(1772–1836)**

1823

*James Westhall Ford
(1806–1866)
oil on canvas
48.3 × 38.7 (19 × 15¼ in.)*

PROVENANCE:
Martha Jefferson Randolph; by
descent to Septimia Randolph
Meikleham; by descent to Mrs.
Henry P. Meikleham; by gift to
TJMF in 1957.

Jefferson wrote James Westhall Ford on September 1, 1823 that he requested "the attendance of Mr. Ford at Monticello to take the portrait of Mrs. Randolph when it shall suit his convenience."[71] Mrs. Randolph, then the mother of eleven children, was fifty-one years old. Ford must have come to Monticello almost immediately, for he painted not one but two portraits—Mrs. Randolph and her eldest daughter Anne Cary Randolph Bankhead—by the end of the month. Jefferson paid "Ford for 50 D. for 2 portraits" on September 29, 1823.[72]

Jefferson evidently was pleased with young Ford's work (he was only seventeen) and recommended him to others as soon as he had finished the portraits at Monticello.

with general approbation he has drawn two portraits for me, both esteemed . . . His good execution, and the reasonableness of his terms render him worthy of encouragement and patronage.[73]

Ford's career, much of it spent as an itinerant portrait painter in Virginia, was advanced by Jefferson's endorsement. The artist later wrote that he "promised Mr. Jefferson to paint the faculty of the University of Virginia—which has been done some years past."[74]

[1936-2]   S.R.S.

Saint Jerome was the best known Christian scholar of the fourth century. He translated the Bible into Latin, then the lingua franca of the literate. At Monticello Jefferson placed *Saint Jerome in Meditation* in the Entrance Hall. In his Catalogue of Paintings, he described it as "A bust of St. Jerom in meditation, his head reclined on his right hand, and a book in his left. of full size, on Canvas. Copied from Goltzius."[75]

Goltzius, a Dutch artist of German ancestry, is chiefly known as an outstanding engraver, who, in addition to his own work, successfully imitated the styles of Dürer and Lucas van Leyden and other Old Masters. He traveled to Rome in 1590, thus coming into contact with the work of Michelangelo and Raphael. In Haarlem Goltzius turned to painting after his return from Rome. Although some of his work was in Parisian collections in the late eighteenth century, it is not known with certainty if Jefferson's painting was copied from a painting or an engraving. The painting bears some resemblance to an engraving of St. Jerome (1596) by Goltzius based on a drawing by Jacopo Palma il Giovane.[76]

[1952-61]   S.R.S.

16

SAINT JEROME IN MEDITATION

*copy after Hendrick Goltzius
(1558–1617)
oil on canvas
62.2 × 49.5 (24½ × 19½ in.)*

PROVENANCE:
Thomas Jefferson; by purchase
to an unidentified buyer at the
Harding Gallery sale in 1833;
by gift or purchase to Eleanor
Melville Metcalf; by gift to TJMF
in 1952.

17

HOLY FAMILY
(*also called*
**MADONNA OF
FRANCIS I**)

c. 1785

*copy after 1518 original by
Raphael (1483–1520)
oil on canvas
97.8 × 67.3 (38½ × 26½ in.)*

PROVENANCE:
Thomas Jefferson; by descent to
Ellen and Joseph Coolidge; by
descent to Ellen Dwight; by gift
to Frances M. Burke; by gift or
purchase to the Washington
Committee; by gift to TJMF.

Jefferson obtained two copies of paintings after Raphael while he was in France, a *Transfiguration* (now lost) and the *Holy Family*. The *Holy Family*, which was commissioned by Lorenzo de'Medici for Francis I, was one of the jewels of the royal collection at the Louvre.[77]

At Monticello the *Holy Family*, roughly half the size of Raphael's original, hung in the Dining Room on the upper tier. A descendant reported that "the painting of 'Holy Family' from 'Raphael' which Mr. Jefferson had copied in the 'Louvre' and which Ellen Dwight left to me, hung on the *left* of the arch in the dining room at 'Monticello' . . ."[78] After Jefferson's death the painting was one of the works of art held back from sale by Ellen Randolph Coolidge "because I thought it a pity to sacrifice them as the others were sacrificed."[79]

[1955-45]   S.R.S.

On of only three examples of northern Renaissance painting in Jefferson's collection was a *Descent from the Cross* by Frans Floris that Jefferson purchased before 1789. It is not known where Jefferson purchased the *Descent*. He could have acquired it in the Netherlands in the early spring of 1788 when he visited Rotterdam, The Hague, and Amsterdam—or elsewhere.

Frans Floris, who was active in Antwerp, visited Rome where he studied the works of Michelangelo and Tintoretto. Once Floris returned to Antwerp, he became known for transplanting Italian Mannerism to the north. One of his followers was Martin de Vos whom Jefferson also admired for he owned a copy of de Vos's *Flagellation of Christ* (unlocated).

Jefferson described the painting in his Catalogue as:

a Descent from the cross on wood. A groupe of 5. figures. The body of Jesus is reclined on the ground, the head and shoulders supported in the lap of his mother, who with four others, women from Galilee, are weeping over him. The figures are whole lengths; the principal one 13.I. It is an original by Francis Floris.[80]

Undoubtedly because of its small size, the *Descent from the Cross* hung where it would be most visible on the lowest of three tiers in the Parlor at Monticello.

[1974-43]   S.R.S.

18

DESCENT FROM THE CROSS

Frans Floris (1516–1570)
oil on wood
44.1 × 34.9 (17⅜ × 13¾ in.)

PROVENANCE:
Thomas Jefferson; by purchase to an unidentified buyer at the Harding Gallery sale in 1833; by gift or purchase to Sarah S. Schellens; by gift to TJMF in 1974, still bearing its label from the Harding sale on its back.

HERODIAS
BEARING THE
HEAD OF SAINT
JOHN

copy after c. 1631 original by
Guido Reni (1575–1642)
oil on canvas
143.5 × 102.9 (56½ × 40½ in.)

PROVENANCE:
Thomas Jefferson; by descent to
Ellen and Joseph Coolidge; by
descent to Harold Jefferson
Coolidge; by gift to TJMF in
1939.[85]

Jefferson acquired this painting with four others at a sale of works of art belonging to the late Dupille de Saint-Séverin at his residence in the Marais between February 2 and 26, 1785.[81] Saint-Séverin's collection, which was expanded throughout the eighteenth century, included works by Guercino, Luca Giordano, and José de Ribera.

Described as "l'un des plus beaux de ce maitre," *Herodias Bearing the Head of Saint John* was billed as an original work by Simon Vouet (1590–1649).[82] Jefferson thought otherwise. When he prepared his Catalogue of Paintings, he wrote, "Herodiade bearing the head of St. John in a platter, a ¾ length of full size on canvas, copied from Simon Vouett. Purchased from St. Severin's collection. Catal. No. 248."[83] *Herodias* depicts the biblical account of Salome presenting the head of John the Baptist to her mother, Herodias; Jefferson wrote that the subject was Matthew 14:11 and Mark 6: 2–8.

The painting that Jefferson purchased, however, was neither Simon Vouet's *Herodias* nor a copy of it. Jefferson's *Herodias* is instead a copy of Guido Reni's version of the same subject, much known and admired during the eighteenth century, that hung in the Corsini Gallery in Rome. For example, Benjamin West painted a copy of it in 1763, which he described as "a copy of Guido's finest, Herodias in Cardinal Corsini's Palace."[84]
[1939-5]
S.R.S.

JESUS IN THE
PRAETORIUM

copy after 1527 original by Jan
Gossaert ["Malbodius"]
(1478–1533/6)
oil on wood
95.3 × 71.1 (37½ × 28 in.)
New-York Historical Society

PROVENANCE:
Thomas Jefferson; by purchase to
an unidentified buyer at the
Harding Gallery sale in 1833; by
gift from Louis Durr to the New-
York Historical Society in 1882; by
loan to TJMF since 1949.

Jefferson acquired this copy while he was in France, as it appeared on a brief list of his collection that he prepared in 1789. At that time he identified it as an "Original Malbodius." It hung in the Entrance Hall. In his later Catalogue of Paintings Jefferson described it as

Jesus in the Praetorium, stripped of the purple, as yet naked, and with the crown of thorns on his head. He is sitting. A whole length figure of about 4. feet. The persons present seem to be one of his revilers, one of his followers, and the superintendant of the execution. The subject from Mark 15. 16.-20. an original on wood, by M[albo]dius.[86]
[1947-5]
S.R.S.

21

VIEW OF THE WEST FRONT OF MONTICELLO AND GARDEN

22

VIEW FROM MONTICELLO LOOKING TOWARD CHARLOTTESVILLE

1825

Jane Braddick Peticolas
(1791–1852)
watercolor on paper
(West Front view)
34.6 × 46 (13⅝ × 18⅛ in.)
(view toward Charlottesville)
31.8 × 52.1 (12½ × 20½ in.)
Inscription: Verso of View of the West Front of Monticello: *"To Mrs. Ellen Coolidge, from a friend, Washington—1827"*

PROVENANCE:
Ellen Wayles Randolph Coolidge; by descent to Catherine Coolidge Lastavica; by gift to TJMF in 1986.

Monticello was only rarely depicted in Jefferson's lifetime. Consequently, these watercolors have become important documents recording the appearance of Monticello and its surrounding landscape. According to Ellen Randolph Coolidge's grandson, these watercolors of Monticello were painted for Mrs. Coolidge by her friend, the Richmond artist Jane Braddick Peticolas.

The *View of the West Front of Monticello* shows Monticello with three of the Randolph children. George Wythe, the youngest boy, rolls a hoop, and two of his sisters, Mary and Cornelia, stand in the middle ground. An unidentified young man sits at the left sketching the scene. The *View from Monticello Looking Toward Charlottesville* looks toward the small town of Charlottesville and a clearing through which is seen the construction of the University of Virginia.

The artist, Jane Pitford Braddick, probably of Scots descent, married Edward F. Peticolas, a painter and the second son of the established Richmond artist Philippe Abraham Peticolas on October 17, 1822.[87]

The Randolph daughters, who frequently visited cousins in Richmond, knew Jane Braddick when she ran a school in Richmond before her marriage to Peticolas. Virginia Randolph wrote:

I heard with great surprise that Miss Braddick intended to break up her school and marry Mr. Petticola—hitherto I have believed her too ambitious if not too prudent to make this match, but sister Ellen who knew her better expected it to take place. I feel interested in her fate, which will not at least be as forlorn as it has been and I hope she may be happy.[88]

Although very little of her work is known today, Mrs. Peticolas was chiefly recognized as a copyist of portraits. Her best-known work is a copy of Cephas Thompson's portrait of *John Marshall*.

[1986-13-30 and 29] S.R.S.

DRAWINGS

23

**THE FRIGHT OF
ASTYANAX**
(*also called*
**HECTOR TAKING
LEAVE OF
ANDROMACHE**)

1797

*Benjamin West (1738–1820)
pen and brown ink, brown
wash, and blue and white
gouache on brown prepared
paper
31.8 × 46 (12½ × 18⅛ in.)
J. Paul Getty Museum, Malibu,
California*

PROVENANCE:
Benjamin West to General
Thaddeus Kosciuszko, June 1797;
General Kosciuszko to Thomas
Jefferson until 1826; by descent to
Ellen and Joseph Coolidge; to a
private collection; by sale at
Christie's, New York, January 7,
1981 to Paul Magriel; by sale to
Hirschl & Adler Galleries; to the
J. Paul Getty Museum in 1984.

Benjamin West, the American-born painter who forged a brilliant career in London, was represented by two works in Jefferson's collection, *The Prodigal Son* (unlocated) done in the polyplasiasmos manner and what Jefferson referred to as "Hector and Andromache." The subject is based on the sixth book of Homer's *Iliad* and shows Hector bidding good-bye to his wife, Andromache, and young child, Astyanax, who is frightened by his father's helmet.[1] West painted two paintings, both lost, of this subject. In his Catalogue of Paintings Jefferson described it as "Hector and Andromache, in water colours, an original by West. The scene is their meeting in Homer 6.494.&c. Given by West to Genl. Kosciuzko, and by him to Th.J." West signed the watercolor at the top left, "From Benj.n West esq/ to Genl Kosciusko/London June 10th./1797."

The accomplished *Fright of Astyanax* was a gift on June 10, 1797 from the artist to General Kosciuszko, the Polish nobleman who volunteered for service and became one of Washington's best officers. Trained in military studies in Poland and France, Kosciuszko strengthened the immature Revolutionary army. He was on his way to America when he met West in London. In Philadelphia during the winter of 1798, he met Jefferson, who was then vice president. Kosciuszko presented him with West's watercolor drawing before he returned to Europe in May 1798.[2]

Jefferson noted in his Catalogue of Paintings that the watercolor was exhibited on the lowest tier in the Parlor, although a descendant reported that it was hung in the Dining Room on the right side of the arch to the Tea Room. After Jefferson's death the drawing was held back from sale at the Harding Gallery in 1833 by Ellen Coolidge, who wrote her mother, "I kept back the Ariadne . . . Hector and Andromache and the soap-stone Indian, because I thought it a pity to sacrifice them as the others were sacrificed."[3]

S.R.S.

24

WEST FRONT OF MONTICELLO

1803?

Robert Mills (1781–1855)
ink and wash on paper
20.9 × 36.8 (8¼ × 14½ in.)
Massachusetts Historical Society

PROVENANCE:
Thomas Jefferson; by descent to
Ellen and Joseph Coolidge; by
descent to Thomas Jefferson
Coolidge, Jr.; by gift to the
Massachusetts Historical Society.

Robert Mills left Charleston, South Carolina, for Washington in 1800 at age nineteen and entered the architectural office of James Hoban, who was then supervising the construction of the President's House and the Capitol.[4] Years later Mills recalled in an essay on his architectural career that "fortunately for the author, Mr. Jefferson, then President of the United States (befriended him), to whose library he had the honor of having access."[5] Mills probably consulted the books at Washington for, very likely, Jefferson kept on hand those needed to produce detailed drawings for his workmen at Monticello. Jefferson had completed, with the construction of the dome in 1800, the framing and closing-in of the building and was now engaged in the long process of finishing the joinery work. Mills noted that "the details were all drawn and proportioned by Mr. Jefferson and with an accuracy which astonished the workmen engaged in carrying them into execution."[6]

Although this drawing of the west elevation of Monticello is without signature or date, it is likely the one that hung in the lower tier in the Dining Room and was identified by Jefferson in his Catalogue of Paintings as "an elevation of the house at Monticello by Mills."[7] The provenance was written on the back of the drawing in 1911:

Received from my father. My father received it from his mother. His mother received it from Mr. Jefferson, her grandfather. T. Jefferson Coolidge, Jr. Unframed by me, March, 1911, to put with portfolio of Jefferson architectural drawings, letters, etc. recently purchased by me from the Randolph family. T.J.C.Jr.

Further attribution to Mills is based on other drawings in Jefferson's possession exhibiting similar technique. One drawing for a house based on the Villa Rotonda bears Mills's inscription "T. Jefferson, Archt. R. Mills, Delt. 1803."[8] Mills stated that "previous to entering Mr. Latrobe's office at Washington [1803] the author made the drawings of the general plan and elevations of Monticello."[9] It is not unreasonable to conclude that this drawing dates from that time, but what is not clear is whether Mills made the drawing after visiting Monticello. In fact, it is uncertain when he was there and for how long. His notes, entitled "Description of Monticello House," mention the incomplete northwest range of dependencies and some particulars of landscape design, suggesting firsthand observation.[10] He also noted that Jefferson had ordered a single sheet of glass to cover the dome oculus. Jefferson placed the order in June 1804.[11]

Regardless of whether the drawing is based on observation, if it dates from 1803, or even 1804, then it shows features that were not yet constructed. These include the balustrade, which was not built until 1807–08, and the West Portico columns, which were not up by 1807 when a visitor remarked that the "pediment had in the meanwhile to be supported on the stems of four tulip trees, which are really, when well grown, as beautiful as the fluted shafts of Corinthian pillars."[12]

The drawing is not without inaccuracies, such as the number of steps; the size of the cellar, dome, and pediment windows; the height of the main roof (shown here too low); the diminished height of the dome and proportion of the dome plinths. Mills also failed to show Jefferson's famous triple-sash windows, although that may be because he drew the double-sash windows too low and the basement too high.[13]

Perhaps of greater significance are the omissions, for if Mills produced this rendering from only what notes, drawings, or instruction Jefferson provided, then it could be a fairly accurate record of what Jefferson envisioned at that time. It is known that Jefferson's first reference to wanting sash for the arched openings of the South Piazza was in the fall of 1804, after which came the idea of louvered enclosures for the landings to the east and west of the piazza.[14] However, omitting the parapet that continued the line of the balustrade onto the pedimented portico and omitting the pediment over the portico doorway may very well mean that they had not yet been incorporated in Jefferson's design.

According to Mills, it was with Jefferson's advice and recommendation that in 1803 he entered the office of Benjamin Latrobe, who had just been appointed by the president to the office of surveyor of public buildings.[15] Mills remained with Latrobe until 1808 and then moved to Philadelphia. During his career, he designed churches, courthouses, jails, and hospitals, and he worked on engineering projects. He is known for his design of the Washington monuments at Baltimore (1814) and at Washington (1836), and for his design of the Treasury Building at Washington, also from 1836. Mills claimed to be the "first native American who directed his studies to architecture as a profession"—a training guided in its early stage, in part, by Jefferson.[16]

W.L.B.

This study for a version of Monticello very different from the one built is attributed to Robert Mills. Fiske Kimball, who first published the drawing in 1916, considered it "probably little more than a practice exercise" by the young architect.[17] He noted that it "showed little regard for expense or practical consideration," and that some of the details were "inconsonant with Jefferson's academic and classical ideals."[18]

Mills drew a house equal in length to Monticello but taller by about six feet to the top of the balustrade. The drum of the dome is also higher and Mills's dome begins where the dome, as constructed, is capped by the oculus. A second story (mezzanine) is indicated above all the west front rooms, and the north and south piazzas rise only to the height of one story. The handling of the architectural order, the dome, and the window and door enframements are among the stylistic differences.

In plan the differences that are readily noticeable from the house as built are the porticoes; the octagonal parlor ("saloon-room"); the elliptical piazzas; the alignment of the passages that connect the dependencies to the house; the series of rooms with fireplaces in the northwest dependencies; and the arcades indicated along the face of the dependencies. There are many other intriguing differences, such as the configuration of the interior stairs; the location of interior doorways; and the number and location of windows.

The labeling is also of interest. The square room south of the Entrance Hall is labeled part of the Library rather than bedroom or sitting room. "Greenhouse" is written faintly in pencil for the South Piazza and "bedroom" penciled under "Tea-room" and "Parlour." Jefferson's writing appears in the identification of the three indoor privies. The perplexing notations for the rooms in the northwest dependencies have not been deciphered.

The drawing may very well be an "exercise" by Mills, but the coincidence, in plan and elevation, of several key features once considered by Jefferson but abandoned by 1796, raises the possibility that Mills was working from sources provided by Jefferson. Mills shows an octagonal parlor as did Jefferson in a preliminary study drawing before construction of the new walls in 1796.[19] The choice of distinctive fenestration for the upper stories is a striking coincidence. In 1792 Jefferson attempted to order ten circular window sashes from England, hoping to have them made by the same man who produced the double-sash windows for the first house.[20] Mills also shows square sashes in the drum of the dome and a circular sash centered over the pediment, which is exactly what Jefferson first planned but later changed.[21]

The extent to which Mills drew on sources from Jefferson is not known, but nowhere are there drawings and notes by Jefferson that suggest the complete plan and elevation rendered by Mills.[22]

W.L.B.

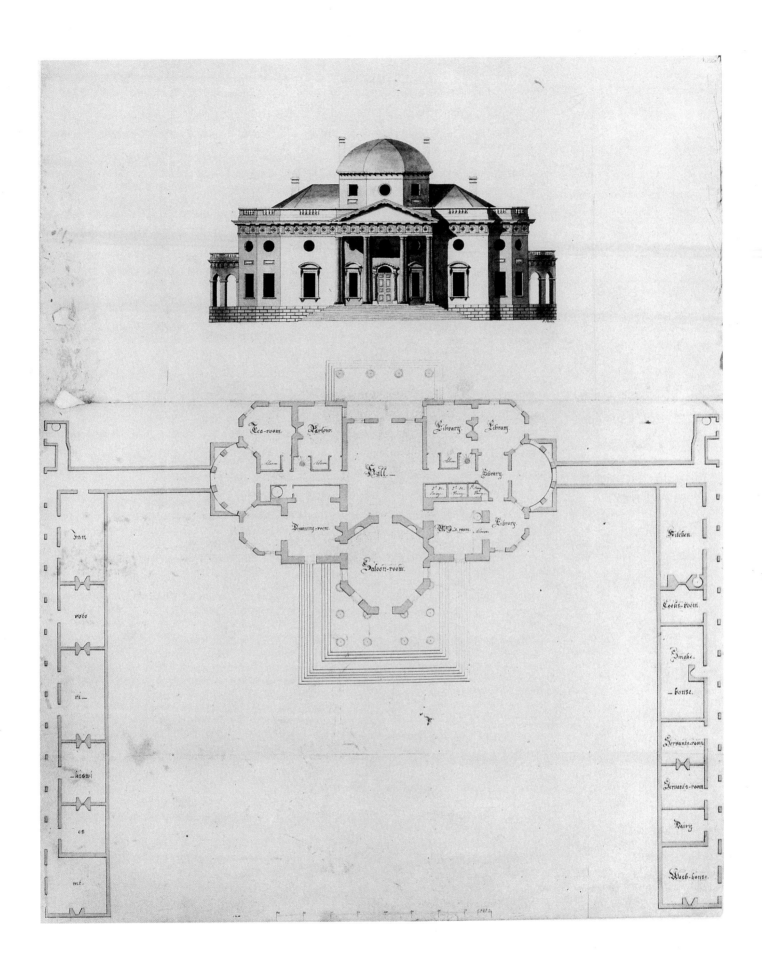

26

ST. PAUL'S CHURCH

c.1802

Robert Mills (1781–1855)
ink and wash on paper
23.2 × 18.9 (9⅛ × 7⁷⁄₁₆ in.)

27

BANK OF
PENNSYLVANIA

c.1807–08

Robert Mills (1781–1855)
after Benjamin Henry Latrobe
(1764–1820)
ink and wash on paper
21.1 × 21.1 (8⁵⁄₁₆ × 8⁵⁄₁₆ in.)

PROVENANCE:
Thomas Jefferson; by descent to
Virginia and Nicholas Trist; by
descent to a private collection; by
gift to TJMF in 1956.

These drawings of two consequential American buildings were gifts to Jefferson from Robert Mills. Mills probably made his drawing of Thomas McBean's St. Paul's Church (1764–66) in lower Manhattan on his 1802–03 trip through the northern states to study architecture. The design was much influenced by the London church St. Martin-in-the-Fields (1722–26), designed by McBean's teacher James Gibbs.[23] Mills probably gave the drawing to Jefferson when he returned to Washington in 1803.[24]

The most important advancement of Mills's career came in 1803, when Jefferson introduced him to the British émigré architect Benjamin Henry Latrobe—whom he had just appointed surveyor of public buildings in Washington. Mills later told Jefferson that when he began working with Latrobe, "I began first to imbibe the true and correct principles of Architecture."[25]

My present ideas of the nobel art and science, which are dramatically opposite to those I enter'd Mr. L[atrobe]'s office with, I trust are founded on the dictates of Reason and nature, because these are the only true foundations of correct taste and real beauty.[26]

Mills worked under Latrobe for five years as a draftsman and clerk. When Mills entered his office, Latrobe's Bank of Pennsylvania, completed about two years earlier (1801), was commanding enormous attention. Latrobe's goal for the building had been "to produce a pure specimen of Grecian simplicity in design, and Grecian permanence in execution."[27] It quickly became a landmark in American architecture and furthered the Greek Revival.[28]

Mills's drawing of the Bank of Pennsylvania was sent to Jefferson at Monticello in October 1808.[29] Jefferson also owned an engraved perspective of the bank that was part of William Birch's *The City of Philadelphia* (Cat. 55).

When Mills decided to leave Latrobe's office in 1808 to establish a practice in Philadelphia, he wrote a characteristically complimentary letter to Jefferson. In seeking his help, Mills appealed to the president's well-known belief in the ability of the citizens of his country:

My wish is to endeavor to shew to the European who visits us from the metropolis of his country that the American talent for architecture is not a whit inferior to the Europeans, under the same advantages.[30]

He also reminded Jefferson of his own "anticipations" on the future of American architecture as described in *Notes on the State of Virginia:*

perhaps a spark may fall on some young subjects of natural taste, kindle up their genius, and produce a reformation in this elegant and useful art.[31]

Mills believed himself to be one of the "young subjects" of which Jefferson spoke. His architecture helped set in motion the Greek Revival that Jefferson and Latrobe so vigorously championed.[32]

[1956-29; 1956-28]   A.M.L.

St. Paul's Church N. Y.

Bank of Pennsylvania

157

28

**UNITED STATES
CAPITOL**

1806

*Benjamin Henry Latrobe
(1764–1820)
pencil, pen and ink, and
watercolor on paper
49.5 × 68.9 (19½ × 27⅛ in.)
Inscription: "To Thomas
Jefferson Pres U.S./B.H. Latrobe.
1806."
Library of Congress*

PROVENANCE:
Benjamin Henry Latrobe; by gift
to Thomas Jefferson; by purchase
or gift to John Neilson; to an
unidentified person; by purchase
to Nicholas Latrobe Roosevelt;
by descent to William Morrow
Roosevelt; by gift to the Library
of Congress.

When Jefferson appointed the English-born architect Benjamin Henry Latrobe to the difficult position of surveyor of public buildings in the new city of Washington in 1803, his most pressing project was the completion of the United States Capitol, which was not yet one-third finished. He found that the Capitol project lacked a cohesive design and direction. There were no definitive drawings for the building, only early plans by William Thornton that had been heavily modified by Thornton himself, Jefferson, Etienne Sulpice Hallet, and others.[33]

Jefferson played an important role in the design and construction of the Capitol. He mediated between Latrobe's proposed changes and Thornton's original plan, which had received the approval of George Washington a decade earlier. This delicate situation was further complicated by Jefferson's extensive knowledge of architecture; Latrobe respected, but did not always agree with Jefferson's opinions.

Latrobe's presentation of this drawing to Jefferson is indicative of their working relationship.[34] This perspective demonstrated that Latrobe had followed Jefferson's suggestion to incorporate elements from one of his favorite ancient buildings, Diocletian's Portico, into the design of the east front of the Capitol. The drawing was also meant to convince the president of the practicality of using cupolas (termed "lanterns" by Latrobe), to which Jefferson replied:

You know my reverence for the Graecian and Roman styles of architecture. I do not recollect ever to have seen in their buildings a single instance of a lanthern, Cupola, or belfry. I have ever supposed the Cupola an Italian invention . . . and one of the degeneracies of modern architecture.[35]

Jefferson displayed this drawing in the President's House, with two others, the "Portico of Diocletian," and an unidentified plan of the Capitol.[36] He left all three drawings in Washington after his departure from the presidency in 1809, so that Latrobe could refer to them. As late as 1811, he requested that they be returned to him at Monticello. Apparently, the works arrived by 1815, when Jefferson listed "Diocletian's Portico" in his Catalogue as being in the Dining Room next to Robert Mills's elevation of Monticello (Cat. 24). The Capitol drawings were more likely kept in Jefferson's private suite of rooms.

Despite his differences with Latrobe, Jefferson paid a high compliment to him for his work on the Capitol:

I believe that the work when finished will be a durable and honorable monument of our infant republic, and will bear favorable comparison with the remains of the same kind of the antient republics of Greece and Rome.[37]

Jefferson's involvement with Latrobe did not end when he left Washington. Shortly after Jefferson returned to Monticello, Latrobe sent him a model of the capital from an architectural order that he had created especially for the interior of the Capitol. It was composed of ears of corn, in tribute to the indigenous American plant. Jefferson praised Latrobe's "handsome and peculiarly American capital," and made a sundial to sit on top of it.[38] Although Latrobe's son saw the corn capital on a visit to Monticello in 1832, neither it nor the sundial are extant.[39]

A second capital designed by Latrobe and sent to Monticello, based on the foliage and flowers of the tobacco plant, does survive. Latrobe created the tobacco-leaf order during

29

TOBACCO LEAF CAPITAL

1816

Designed by Benjamin Henry Latrobe, executed by Francisco Iardella (1793–1831)
sandstone
45.7 × 53.3 × 53.3
(18 × 21 × 21 in.)

PROVENANCE:
Benjamin Henry Latrobe; by gift to Thomas Jefferson; by purchase to James T. Barclay; by purchase to Uriah P. Levy; by descent to Jefferson M. Levy; by purchase to TJMF in 1923.

the Capitol's second building campaign, after its destruction by the British in 1814. In an 1816 letter to Jefferson, he sketched and described his creation:

I have therefore composed a capital of leaves and flowers of the tobacco plant which has an intermediate effect of approaching a Corinthian order and retaining the simplicity of the Clepsydra or Temple of the Winds. [Francisco] Iardella a sculptor who has just arrived, has made an admirable model for execution in which he has well preserved the botanical character of the plant, although it has been necessary to enlarge the proportion of the flowers to the leaves, and to arrange them in clusters of three.[40]

In 1817 he sent this capital to Jefferson and recommended that it be painted like those in the Capitol, "the leaves of the upper tier, be colored in the lower part a faint brown (umber) . . ."[41] The capital is among the few original objects from Monticello that have remained with the property through its history.

[1923-4]   A . M . L .

30
SELF-ACTING BELIER HYDRAULIC

1810

Robert Fulton (1765–1815)
ink and wash on paper
36 × 35.2
(14³/₁₆ × 13⁷/₈ in.) by sight
Mrs. Joseph C. Cornwall

PROVENANCE:
Thomas Jefferson; by descent to Virginia and Nicholas Trist; by descent to Charles B. Eddy Jr.; by bequest to Mrs. Charles B. Eddy, Jr. (now Mrs. Joseph C. Cornwall).

In Jefferson, Robert Fulton (Cat. 41) found an enthusiastic supporter of innovation, and one eager to share all sorts of knowledge. Their correspondence covered topics ranging from Fulton's torpedo designs to Jefferson's work on the mouldboard plow of least resistance. Fulton sent a drawing of a "self acting Bélier Hydraulic" (or hydraulic ram) to Jefferson in March 1810.[42] He wrote Jefferson:

I have long since made the drawing for your Bélier hydraulic but I wished to do more than make a drawing, I wished to send you a working model but together with procrastinating workmen and my own moving from place to place I have not yet been able to accomplish it. If your men can work from the drawing I will forward it from New York.[43]

Jefferson found the design "simple and ingenious," and assured Fulton that a model was unnecessary because his workmen could "execute from the drawing."[44]

As early as 1805, Jefferson owned a hydraulic ram made after the design of its French inventor, Joseph de Montgolfier. He planned to use this pump "for watering hill sides from the streams at the foot," but there is no indication that he carried out this idea.[45] Fulton's design differed from Montgolfier's in that it pumped water from a cistern instead of a running stream.[46] At the time that Jefferson and Fulton were corresponding about the pump, four cisterns were under construction at Monticello. Jefferson designed them to contain rainwater gathered in the accordion-pleated "rooflets" of the terraces that covered the all-weather passageway and dependencies. Although the cisterns were completed by the end of 1810, Jefferson was still struggling to make them waterproof as late as 1822, and it seems doubtful that they ever held water consistently.[47] We do not know if Jefferson employed Fulton's design for the "Bélier Hydraulic" at Monticello. After Jefferson's death, his grandson-in-law and secretary Nicholas P. Trist found Fulton's drawing among his papers.

A . M . L .

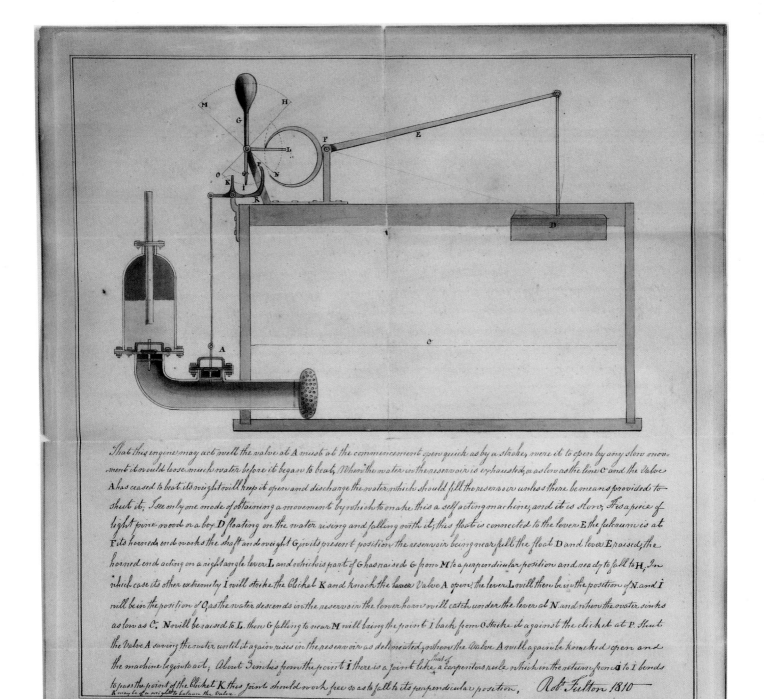

That this engine may act well the valve at A must at the commencement open quick as by a stroke, were it to open by any slow movement it would loose much water before it began to beat, When the water in the reservoir is exhausted, or as low as the line c and the Valve A has ceased to beat its weight will keep it open and discharge the water which should fill the reservoir unless there be means provided to shut it; I see only one mode of obtaining a movement by which to make this a self acting machine, and it is slow; F is a piece of light pine wood or a box D floating on the water rising and falling with it; this float is connected to the lever E the fulcrum is at F its horned end works the shaft and weight G, in its present position the reservoir being near full the float D and lever E raised, the horned end acting on a right angle lever L and which is part of G has raised G from M to a perpendicular position and ready to fall to H, In which case its other extremity I will strike the Clicket K and knock the lever Valve A open, the lever L will then be in the position of N and I will be in the position of O, as the water descends in the reservoir the lower horn will catch under the lever at N and when the water sinks as low as C, N will be raised to L then G falling to near M will bring the point I back from O strike it against the clicket at P, shut the Valve A saving the water until it again rises in the reservoir as delineated, when the Valve A will again be knocked open and the machine begins to act; About 3 inches from the point I there is a joint like that of a carpenters rule which in the return from i to I bends to pass the point of the clicket K this joint should work free so as to fall to its perpendicular position. Rob Fulton 1810

K may be of a weight to balance the Valve.

Scale one inch to a foot but may be varied at pleasure.

31

**THE DECLARATION
OF INDEPENDENCE
OF THE UNITED
STATES OF AMERICA,
JULY 4TH, 1776**

1823

*Asher B. Durand (1796–1886),
engraver, after John Trumbull
(1756–1843)
engraving
image: 55.6 × 77.2
(21⅞ × 30⅜ in.)*

Iohn Trumbull's masterpiece, *The Declaration of Independence of the United States of America, July 4th, 1776*, was begun at Jefferson's residence in Paris.[1] Trumbull later reported, "I began the composition of the Declaration of Independence, with the assistance of his [Jefferson's] information and advice."[2] Jefferson contributed a firsthand description of the Assembly Room and made a rough sketch of it. Later, Trumbull painted Jefferson from life for the *Declaration*, and made three miniatures of the likeness (Cat. 2). The committee responsible for the draft—John Adams, Roger Sherman, Robert R. Livingston, Jefferson, and Benjamin Franklin—was depicted to the right of center.

Trumbull dedicated himself to portraying from life as many of the forty-eight signers as he could. Consequently, the original painting, located in the Yale University Art Gallery, was not completed until 1820. The young artist Asher B. Durand was selected to make the engraving, which was published in 1823. The small number of subscribers greatly disappointed Trumbull, who had worked for more than thirty-three years on it.

Jefferson's engraving of *The Declaration of Independence* was exhibited in the Entrance Hall at Monticello. Reverend Henry Thweatt, a visitor, wrote that Jefferson was happy to explain the scene.

In a free and somewhat playful manner I said—"and how Mr. Jefferson—did you feel amid—all being as you were—the author of the instrument—being thus signed by all"—why—my son—(he very pleasantly replied with an arch look)—"pretty much as you may imagine with a halter around his neck to be hung—for such—doubtless would have been my fate—and that too of all who signed this instrument—had we been taken by the British."[3]

[1923-8]   S . R . S .

32

**THE SORTIE MADE BY
THE GARRISON OF
GIBRALTAR IN THE
MORNING OF
27 NOVEMBER 1781**

1799

*William Sharp (1746–1824),
engraver, after John Trumbull
(1756–1843)
engraving with gouache
65.7 × 86.7 (25⅞ × 34⅛ in.)*

In the hope that he could generate interest in his work in England, John Trumbull depicted the recent victory of the British over the Spanish at Gibraltar. Benjamin West, Trumbull's mentor, recommended the subject to him, perhaps to rival John Singleton Copley's huge *Siege of Gibraltar*.[4] The *Sortie* portrays the death of a valiant Spanish officer, Don José de Barboza, who alone rushed British troops after he was abandoned by his own men. He refused aid offered by the British, preferring to die on the battlefield. Trumbull made three versions of this painting, but none achieved the unequivocal acclaim in London that Trumbull desired. In May 1789 Trumbull reported to Jefferson,

With your books I took the liberty to enclose three or four descriptions of my picture of Gibraltar. There are People here foolish enough to be half affronted that I have paid so much compliment to the Spanish Officer.[5]

Although Jefferson sent Trumbull a subscription for "a copy of your print of Gibraltar" on June 21, 1789, the engraving was not published until 1799.[6] Jefferson's engraving is unlocated.

[1967-161]   S . R . S .

The DECLARATION of INDEPENDENCE of the UNITED STATES of AMERICA.
July 4th 1776.

The Sortie made by the Garrison of Gibraltar in the Morning of the 27 of November 1781.

The Battle at Bunkers Hill, near Boston
June 7 1775

The Death of General Montgomery
In the Attack of Quebec 2 Dec 1775

In late 1785 John Trumbull resolved to devote himself to the depiction of Revolutionary War scenes "which have since been the great objects of my professional life."[7] Benjamin West encouraged Trumbull's objectives, as did Jefferson. From the outset Trumbull intended to paint the pictures so that they could be engraved for sale. Through Benjamin West, Trumbull made the acquaintance of "an Italian artist, by the name of Antonio di Poggi, of very superior talents as a draughtsman, and who had recently commenced the business of publishing."[8]

The first two works that Trumbull completed of the series of eight were *The Battle at Bunker's Hill* and *The Death of General Montgomery in the Attack of Quebec*, which were much influenced not only by West, but also by the dramatic action of John Singleton Copley's *Death of Chatham* (1781) and *Death of Major Pierson* (1782–84). *Bunker's Hill* was begun in 1785 and completed in March 1786; *Quebec* was begun in February 1785 and finished before Trumbull brought it to Paris in 1786.

As soon as *Bunker's Hill* and *Quebec* were completed, Trumbull tried to find a suitable engraver in London. He was unsuccessful and instead decided to look for an engraver in Paris, where Jefferson had invited him to stay with him at the Hôtel de Langeac. Finding acceptable engravers for the series proved to be a difficult task. In 1786 Trumbull journeyed through Germany and the Low Countries to look for an engraver. He then returned to London to work on the *Declaration of Independence* and to begin a new work, *The Sortie Made by the Garrison of Gibraltar*. After meeting little success, he went back to the United States in November 1789, traveling everywhere to compile portraits for the historical series. Discouraged, he temporarily abandoned the project in 1793, saying that "my great enterprise was blighted."[9] Trumbull accepted a post with John Jay on the diplomatic mission to Great Britain, and returned to London. While there, *Bunker's Hill* and *Quebec* were finally published in 1798. Jefferson's worn copies are in Monticello's collection; the ones exhibited and pictured are duplicates.

[1941-3 and 1941-10 (originals); 1970-65-2 and 1970-65-1 (pictured)]   S.R.S.

33

THE BATTLE AT BUNKER'S HILL NEAR BOSTON, JUNE 7TH, 1775

1798

Johann Gotthard Muller (1747–1830), engraver, after John Trumbull (1756–1843) engraving
62.2 × 84.5 (24½ × 33¼ in.)

34

THE DEATH OF GENERAL MONTGOMERY IN THE ATTACK OF QUEBEC, DECEMBER 1775

1798

Johann Frederick Clemens (1749–1831), engraver, after John Trumbull (1756–1843) engraving
62.2 × 84.5 (24½ × 33¼ in.)

PROVENANCE (originals): Thomas Jefferson; by descent to Virginia and Nicholas Trist; by descent to an anonymous donor; by gift to TJMF in 1941.

35

**GEORGE
WASHINGTON
(1732–1799)**

1790

*Joseph Wright (1756–1793)
drypoint etching
image: 7×5.1 (2¾×2 in.)
McAlpin Collection, The
Miriam and Ira D. Wallach
Division of Art, Prints and
Photographs, The New York
Public Library, Astor, Lenox
and Tilden Foundations.*

Jefferson judged Joseph Wright's portrait of George Washington very highly. "I have no hesitation in pronouncing Wright's drawing to be a better likeness of the General than Peale's," he wrote in 1785.[10] Wright painted a portrait of Washington for Jefferson in 1784 and planned to have a drawing, which was made at the same time, engraved in London by Patience Wright, his mother and a prominent sculptor.

In January 1786, the engraving still had not been made. Jefferson wrote:

before the painter would agree to draw it for me, he made me promise not to permit any copy of it to be taken till his mother in London should have time to have an engraving from one which he drew at the same time, and also to dispose of the engravings. Twenty months have now elapsed, and I can neither learn that they have made any engraving from the picture, nor get an answer from the painter.[11]

The engraving apparently was never made.

Wright, however, did make a small drypoint etching in New York in 1790, and Jefferson acquired two of them. He purchased the first on June 10, noting in his Memorandum Book, "pd for print of the President by Wright 8/." and the second on June 23, "pd. for another engraving of General Washington by Wright 8/." On June 27, he sent one to his daughter Martha: "I now inclose you an engraving of the President done by Wright who drew the picture of him which I have at Paris."[12] Jefferson displayed his in the Tea Room at Monticello.

This image, showing Washington in profile, "was widely copied in prints, medallions, relief cuts, and medals both here and abroad."[13] Jefferson's engravings are unlocated.

S.R.S.

The French minister to the United States, the comte de Moustier, arrived in New York in 1787 with his sister-in-law, Madame de Bréhan. Jefferson, then in Paris, knew both Moustier and de Bréhan.[14] He sent glowing letters of introduction for them to John Jay and James Madison. "I think it impossible," Jefferson wrote to Jay, "to find a better woman, more amiable, more modest, more simple in her manners, dress, and way of thinking."[15]

Jefferson described de Bréhan to Madison as "goodness itself. . . . The way to please her is to receive her as an acquaintance of a thousand years standing."[16]

George Washington received Moustier and de Bréhan at Mount Vernon in November 1788.[17] After their meeting, de Bréhan began drawing a profile of Washington, which she finished on October 3, 1789, when she and Moustier visited the newly elected President Washington in New York. Washington recorded in his diary that he "sat about two Oclock for Madam de Bréhan to complete a miniature profile of me which she had begun from Memory and which she had made exceedingly like the Original."[18]

Madame de Bréhan brought with her to Paris the original profile of Washington, done in watercolor on ivory, and there Moustier had it engraved. He sent proofs of the prints to Washington in May 1790, and promised that de Bréhan would send the original as a gift to Martha Washington once it returned from the engraver. The Washingtons were apparently enamored with the prints and presented several to their friends and associates.[19] Jefferson may have been among the recipients. He displayed Washington's profile by de Bréhan in the Dining Room at Monticello; his copy is unlocated.[20]

[M-40]   A.M.L.

36
GEORGE WASHINGTON (1732–1799)

———

1801

Barthelemy Joseph Fulevan Roger (1767–1841), engraver, after P. F. Tardieu (1711–1771), from a drawing by Madame de Bréhan (active in U.S. 1788–89) stipple engraving image: 15.1 × 10.2 (5¹⁵⁄₁₆ × 4 in.)

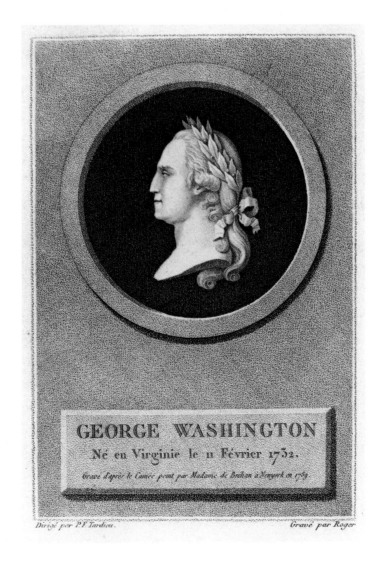

LOUIS XVI

1790

Charles-Clément Bervic (1756–1822), engraver, after Antoine-François Callet (1741–1823)
engraving
70.5 × 52.7 (27¾ × 20¾ in.)

PROVENANCE:
Unknown prior to purchase by Mr. and Mrs. Fillmore Norfleet; by gift to TJMF in 1980.

On the occasion of Jefferson's departure from France in 1789, Louis XVI gave him a "miniature picture of the king set in brilliants."[21] Though diplomatic gifts were routine in European courts, the lavish present with diamonds caused Jefferson considerable anguish. He was acutely aware of the United States policy that forbid the acceptance of gifts from foreign monarchs without the consent of Congress. Yet for reasons of protocol, Jefferson was reluctant to have the matter publicly debated.[22]

The problem was further complicated because Jefferson had already returned to the United States when the gift arrived at his Paris home. He was therefore forced to rely upon his capable secretary, William Short, to handle the matter. Under Short's supervision, the diamonds were removed from the case and sold. The proceeds went to offset Jefferson's moving expenses, and his diplomatic gifts to members of the court.[23] Short sent the print and its stripped frame to the United States in 1791 with the remainder of Jefferson's furniture. "I send you by Petit [Adrien Petit, Jefferson's maitre d'hotel] the remains of what I received for you, agreeably to your desire. The secrecy you requested is fully observed."[24]

The miniature print arrived in Philadelphia on July 19, 1791.[25] That same summer the new French minister, Jean Baptiste Ternant, brought with him to Philadelphia twenty engravings of Louis XVI by Charles-Clément Bervic, after the portrait by Antoine-François Callet. Ternant presented these to members of the United States government, including President Washington, whose copy in its original frame is still extant.[26] Presumably Jefferson, then secretary of state, would also have received a print from Ternant. Jefferson displayed one image of Louis XVI in the Parlor at Monticello, next to an engraving of Napoleon, and listed it in his Catalogue of Paintings as "a present from the King to Th.J."[27] Whether this was the miniature print sent from Paris or Ternant's gift is undetermined; unfortunately, neither of Jefferson's engravings of the king has been located.
[1980-58]   A.M.L.

LOUIS SEIZE
ROI DES FRANÇAIS, RESTAURATEUR DE LA LIBERTÉ.
PRÉSENTÉ AU ROI et à L'ASSEMBLÉE NATIONALE. Par l'Auteur

38

**THADDEUS
KOSCIUSZKO
(1746–1817)**

c. 1796

*Christian Josi (d. 1828),
engraver, after Joseph Grassi
(1756–1838)
stipple engraving
paper: 37.1 × 26
(14⅝ × 10¼ in.)
Library of Congress*

39

**THOMAS
JEFFERSON
(1743–1826)**

1798–99

*Michel Sokolnicki (1760–1816),
engraver, after Thaddeus
Kosciuszko (1746–1817)
colored aquatint
36 × 25.4 (14³⁄₁₆ × 10 in.)
University of Virginia School of
Architecture*

Jefferson found the Polish revolutionary Thaddeus Kosciuszko to be "as pure a son of liberty as I have ever known and of that liberty which is to go to all and not to the few or to the rich alone."[28] A print of Kosciuszko, probably taken after his portrait by Christian Josi, hung in the Parlor at Monticello as evidence of their friendship. This portrait celebrates Kosciuszko's leadership of the Polish Revolution and shows him in his uniform of the hat and coat of the peasants he led.[29]

Jefferson's portrait by Kosciuszko, engraved by Michel Sokolnicki, occupied a much less public position at Monticello, according to Jefferson's grandson Thomas Jefferson Randolph:

The portrait of Jefferson by Kosciusko hung in a room occupied at Monticello by my mother when I was a small boy. . . . I thought it a good likeness; my mother did not. It had under it a philosopher, a patriot, and a friend printed conspicuously. This subscription I presume kept it out of the public rooms.[30]

Likewise, a second copy of the print was kept at the President's House in Jefferson's private cabinet.[31] His daughter Martha was not alone in her dislike of this image of Jefferson. William Thornton complained that it was an "injustice," and wrote:

when I saw it, I did not wonder that he lost Poland—not that it is necessary a Genl. should be a Painter, but he should be a man of such Sense to discover that he is not a Painter.[32]

Jefferson did not meet Kosciuszko, one of the heroes of the American Revolution, until 1797, when he returned to the United States after being imprisoned by the Russians, who had crushed the Polish Revolution that he led.[33] Jefferson, who was then serving as vice president, was living in Philadelphia when Kosciuszko arrived there, and the two men immediately became friends. They saw one another almost daily, and it was during this time that Kosciuszko made his portrait of Jefferson (now lost) from which Michel Sokolnicki made this aquatint.[34] Jefferson helped Kosciuszko claim payment from the United States government for his services in the Revolution, a sum that totaled more than $20,000. He also aided Kosciuszko in obtaining a passport under another name, so that he could secretly leave the country for France in the spring of 1798. Kosciuszko wanted to return to Europe to help organize Polish émigrés to fight for a reunited Polish state.[35]

Kosciuszko left his financial matters in Jefferson's hands. In a remarkable will, in which he named his new friend executor, Kosciuszko provided for the purchase and emancipation of American slaves:

I, Thaddeus Kosciuszko, being just in my departure from America, do hereby declare and direct that. . . . I hereby authorise my friend Thomas Jefferson to employ the whole thereof in purchasing Negroes from among his own or any others and giving them liberty in my name, in giving them an education in trades or otherwise and in having them instructed for their new condition in the duties of morality which may make them good neighbours good fathers or moders, husbands, or vives and in their duties as citisens teeching them to be defenders of their Liberty and Country and of the good order of Society and in whatever may make them happy and useful, and I make the said Thomas Jefferson my executor of this.[36]

Until his death in 1817, Kosciuszko maintained a friendly correspondence with Jefferson. Although twenty years earlier Jefferson had agreed to serve as his friend's executor, he asked to be released from the responsibility because of his age (he was then seventy-four) and the probability of prolonged litigation.[37] He best described his affection for Kosciuszko in a letter responding to the news of his death:

To no country could that event be more afflicting nor to any individual more than myself. I had enjoyed his intimate friendship and confidence for the last 20 years, and during the portion of that time which he spent in this country, I had daily opportunities of observing personally the purity of his virtue, the benevolence of his heart, and his sincere devotion to the cause of liberty.[38]

A . M . L .

JAMES MONROE
President of the United States.

ROBERT FULTON ESQ.ᴿ

40

JAMES MONROE
(1758–1831)

_____

1817

Thomas Gimbrede (1781–1832),
engraver, after John Vanderlyn
(1775–1852)
engraving
image: 30.2 × 19.4
(11⅞ × 7⅝ in.)
James Monroe Museum and
Memorial Library

In 1822 Jefferson instructed his granddaughter Ellen Randolph, who was then in Washington, to purchase an engraving of President James Monroe based on the portrait by John Vanderlyn, and busts of Monroe and James Madison by the Italian émigré sculptor Pietro (Peter) Cardelli (Cat. 96). Although Ellen acquired all three works of art, none survives.[39]

Jefferson had a profound influence on Monroe's political career. They first met in Williamsburg, in about 1779, while Jefferson served as governor. He encouraged Monroe, fifteen years his junior, to further his political career by studying law.

Both were elected to Congress in 1783. Before Jefferson left for France in 1784 he introduced Monroe to James Madison. Jefferson encouraged both to move near Monticello, in Albemarle County, so that they could create there "a society to our tastes."[40] Although Madison never accepted Jefferson's offer, Monroe twice owned homes in Albemarle, one of which, Highland, is located only two and one-half miles from Monticello.[41]

A.M.L.

The publisher Joseph Delaplaine sent Jefferson this engraving of Robert Fulton, along with engravings of Dr. Benjamin Rush, James Madison, Columbus, and the frontispiece of *Delaplaine's Repository* (1815–16), to thank him for his assistance in its preparation.[42] Delaplaine turned to Jefferson for portraits of himself, Columbus, and Amerigo Vespucci for the biographical series. Jefferson declined to send his paintings to Philadelphia, but he did forward Delaplaine an engraving of Vespucci along with suggestions of appropriate images of Columbus that were readily available. Jefferson refused Delaplaine's request to choose his favorite portrait of himself, insisting that there is "nothing to which a man is so incompetent as to judge of his likeness."[43] After several failed attempts to secure permission to reproduce either of Gilbert Stuart's portraits of Jefferson, Delaplaine accompanied the artist Bass Otis to Monticello to take Jefferson's portrait for the *Repository*.[44]

Robert Fulton's portrait by his mentor Benjamin West was particularly appropriate because it suggests Fulton's dual careers as an artist and a scientific inventor, and was in Jefferson's opinion, "a good likeness and elegantly executed."[45] Fulton began studying painting under West in London in 1786 at the age of twenty-one and sought to support himself by painting portraits until about 1794, when he abandoned art for scientific pursuits in Paris.[46] Fulton's experiments there with torpedoes and submarine navigation drew the attention of the American Joel Barlow, who alerted President Jefferson to Fulton's efforts "to demonstrate the practicability of destroying military navies altogether."[47]

Through the window of this portrait West depicts Fulton's successful 1805 London demonstration of a torpedo destroying a ship. The next year Fulton returned to the United States. In 1807 he demonstrated his torpedo in New York Harbor to Jefferson's secretary of war, Henry Dearborn.[48] Jefferson responded favorably to Fulton's experiment, writing, "I consider your Torpedoes as very valuable means of the defence of harbours, and have no doubt that we should adopt them to a considerable degree."[49] In addition to his work with defense, Fulton pioneered steamboat navigation. Several years after the *Clermont*'s successful voyage up the Hudson, Jefferson wrote to Fulton:

I rejoice at your success in your steamboats and have no doubt they will be the source of great wealth to yourself and permanent blessing to your country. I hope your torpedoes will equally triumph over doubting friends and presumptuous enemies.[50]

A.M.L.

41

ROBERT FULTON
(1765–1815)

1815

W. S. Leney (1769–1831), engraver, after Benjamin West (1738–1820), published in Joseph Delaplaine's Delaplaine's Repository of the Lives and Portraits of Distinguished Americans, *vol. 1, Philadelphia, 1815.*
stipple engraving
12.9 × 10.3 (5 1/16 × 4 1/16 in.)
Mrs. Joseph C. Cornwall

PROVENANCE:
Thomas Jefferson; by descent to Virginia and Nicholas Trist; by descent to Charles B. Eddy, Jr.; by bequest to Mrs. Charles B. Eddy, Jr. (now Mrs. Joseph C. Cornwall).

DAVID RITTENHOUSE, L. L. D. F. R. S.

President of the American Philosophical Society.

LIBERTY.

In the form of the Goddess of Youth; giving Support to the Bald Eagle.

42

**DAVID
RITTENHOUSE
(1732–1796)**

1796

*Edward Savage (1761–1817),
engraver, after Charles Willson
Peale (1741–1827)
mezzotint
paper: 54.8 × 39.4
(21⁹⁄₁₆ × 15½ in.)
Philadelphia Museum of Art,
lent by Mr. Robert Maskell
Patterson*

On the occasion of Jefferson's departure from Philadelphia in 1793, David Rittenhouse wrote:

I shall ever remember with pleasure, whilst memory continue to perform its office, that I have counted the name of Mr. Jefferson in the very short list of my friends.[51]

More than fifteen years earlier, Jefferson met the American-born inventor and astronomer in Philadelphia, where both were attending the Continental Congress.[52] Rittenhouse was a member of the Pennsylvania Assembly and President of the American Philosophical Society. Both Jefferson and Rittenhouse were devoted to science. Jefferson displayed a print of Rittenhouse in Monticello's Parlor with his collection of American worthies.[53]

Rittenhouse's reputation as a scientist was principally linked to his clockwork-driven orrery, a model that showed the solar system. In *Notes on the State of Virginia,* Jefferson used

Rittenhouse's achievements to counter the Abbé Raynal's contention that America "has not yet produced . . . one able mathematician, one man of genius in a single art or a single science."[54]

We have supposed Mr. Rittenhouse second to no astronomer living: that in genius he must be the first, because he is self-taught. As an artist he has exhibited as great a proof of mechanical genius as the world has ever produced. He has not indeed made a world; but he has by imitation approached nearer its Maker than any man who has lived from the creation to this day.[55]

Rittenhouse and Jefferson's correspondence centered on scientific pursuits and the instruments necessary for them. Jefferson sent Rittenhouse his report on the 1778 eclipse and requested an astronomical clock for future observations.[56] Among the instruments that Jefferson bought from Rittenhouse were a universal equatorial, made by the Englishman Jesse Ramsden, an odometer (Cat. 219), and a camera obscura (Cat. 274).[57]

After Rittenhouse's death in 1796, Jefferson was elected to succeed him as president of the American Philosophical Society. In his letter of acceptance to the Society, he praised the former president: "Genius, Science, modesty, purity of morals, simplicity of manners, marked him one of Nature's best samples of the Perfection she can cover under the human form."[58]

A.M.L.

Edward Savage's *Liberty,* a potent symbol of the triumph of the United States over tyranny, hung in the Parlor at Monticello among Jefferson's collection of historical, religious, and allegorical art.[59] Jefferson counted the preservation of liberty among those "sacred and undeniable rights" belonging to all men, and considered liberty to be above politics.[60] "Our attachment to no nation on earth should supplant our attachment to liberty," Jefferson wrote in the 1775 "Declaration of the Causes and Necessity for Taking Up Arms."[61] He believed that the role of the United States was to promote liberty throughout the world.

Jefferson left no record of how he obtained this print, but it was probably available at Savage's Columbian Gallery on Chestnut Street in Philadelphia when Jefferson returned to that city in March 1797.[62] As early as 1760 the Goddess of Liberty became associated with the American cause and was often depicted with figures representing the American continent, such as the Indian Princess. Gradually Liberty herself came to symbolize the young United States and she was often shown as she is in Savage's print, surrounded with icons such as the bald eagle, the American flag, the liberty pole, and the liberty cap, while trampling the symbols of monarchy.[63]

Edward Savage was an American-born artist who worked in Philadelphia, New York, and Boston, and traveled to England to study engraving. He is best known for his portraits of the Washington family.[64] Jefferson's copy of *Liberty* is unlocated.

A.M.L.

43

LIBERTY IN THE FORM OF THE GODDESS OF YOUTH GIVING SUPPORT TO THE BALD EAGLE

1796

Edward Savage (1761–1817)
stipple engraving
62.7 × 38.1 (24¾ × 15 in.)
Library of Congress

MARIA COSWAY

as the Act directs my Jan.l 1785 by G.Bartolozzi & Co his how. at M. Torres Hay Market 23

44

**MARIA COSWAY
(1759–1853)**

1785

*Francesco Bartolozzi
(1725–1815), engraver, after
Richard Cosway (1742–1821)
stipple engraving
image: 21.3 × 13.8
(8³⁄₈ × 5⁷⁄₁₆ in.)*

PROVENANCE:
Thomas Jefferson; by descent to
Virginia and Nicholas Trist; by
descent to Gordon T. Burke; by
gift to TJMF in 1961.

Maria Hadfield Cosway, an artist and musician, was part of Jefferson's intimate circle of friends during his time in France. Jefferson described her as having "qualities and accomplishments, belonging to her sex, which might form a chapter apart for her: such as music, modesty, beauty, and that softness of disposition which is the ornament of her sex and charm of ours."[65] Her knowledge of art and immense popularity in Paris and London no doubt contributed to Jefferson's fondness for Mrs. Cosway's companionship.

Mrs. Cosway and her husband, Richard, the celebrated English miniaturist, were introduced to Jefferson in Paris in the fall of 1786 by the American artist John Trumbull. According to Trumbull, the entourage "was occupied with the same industry in examining and reviewing whatever related to the arts . . . Mr. Jefferson joined our party almost daily."[66] Their excursions included sites such as the Halle aux Bleds, Versailles, the Louvre, Louis XIV's retreat Marly, the Palais Royal, St. Germain, and the Column at the Désert de Retz. Jefferson was enchanted by Maria, and her departure from Paris in October 1786 compelled him to write the only existing love letter in the vast collection of his correspondence, "The dialogue between my Head and my Heart."[67]

Maria Hadfield was born of English parents in Italy, where she spent her youth and was schooled in drawing, music, and languages. She furthered her study of drawing in Florence and Rome, and was elected to the Academy of Fine Arts in Florence at nineteen.

Maria met her mentor Angelica Kauffmann when she returned to England after her father's death, and her circle of English friends included Francesco Bartolozzi, the engraver of this portrait.

Kauffmann introduced Maria to her future husband Richard Cosway, a member of the Royal Academy who was famous for his portrait miniatures of London's aristocracy, including the royal family. Cosway was also a collector and connoisseur of Old Master paintings and drawings, prints, sculpture, and decorative art, and his duties as principal painter to the Prince of Wales included overseeing the royal collection. The Cosways frequently hosted members of London's literary and artistic circles at fashionable salons, or musical evenings, at Schomberg House in Pall Mall, which was filled with their eclectic collection.[68]

Mrs. Cosway exhibited forty-two works at the Royal Academy between 1781 and 1801 but complained that, because her husband would not permit her to rank professionally, she lost the drawing skills from her early Italian training.[69] Mrs. Cosway and Jefferson corresponded intermittently following their time in Paris until a year before Jefferson's death. Her letters told of the birth and short life of her only child, Angelica, and her founding of a girl's convent school in Lodi, Italy, where she died in 1838.

[1961-37-35]   A.M.L.

LE DÉJEUNÉ DE FERNEY.

De N.on d'après Nature à Ferney le 4 Juillet 1775.   Gravé par Née et Masquelier même Année.

According to family tradition, Jefferson presented this engraving to his grandson-in-law Joseph Coolidge on the occasion of his marriage to Ellen Randolph in 1825. The image shows Voltaire having lunch at his summer home in Ferney, France. Jefferson, a great admirer of Voltaire's writing, returned from France with this print and Jean-Antoine Houdon's bust of the writer (Cat. 89). The frame for this work has traditionally been attributed to the Monticello slave cabinetmaker John Hemings.[70]

[1963-19-2]   A.M.L.

45

LE DEJEUNE DE FERNEY

1775

Denis Née (c. 1732–1818) and Louis Masquelier (1741–1811), engravers, after Baron Dominique Vivant Denon (1747–1825)
engraving
14.3 × 18.1 (5⅝ × 7⅛ in.)

PROVENANCE:
Thomas Jefferson; by gift to Joseph Coolidge; by descent to Ellen Coolidge Dwight; by gift to Martha Jefferson Trist Burke; by descent to Ellen Coolidge Burke Eddy; by descent to James Eddy; by purchase to TJMF in 1963.

L' Ara Canga male. Pl. 2. (bis).

46

L'ARA CANGA MALE

1801

"Langlois," engraver, (possibly Jacques-Louis Langlois), from François Levaillant, Histoire Naturelle des Perroquets, *vol. 1, Paris, 1801, pl. 2.*
hand-colored engraving
32.4 × 24.8 (12¾ × 9¾ in.)
by sight
Mrs. Joseph C. Cornwall

PROVENANCE:
Thomas Jefferson; by descent to Virginia Randolph and Nicholas Philip Trist; by descent to Charles B. Eddy Jr.; by bequest to Mrs. Charles B. Eddy, Jr. (now Mrs. Joseph C. Cornwall)

This print of a scarlet (or red) macaw is from François Levaillant's *Histoire Naturelle des Perroquets*, published in Paris in 1801.[71] Jefferson apparently purchased this work before November 1804, when John Quincy Adams saw it at the President's House. Adams recorded in his diary that "[Jefferson] showed us, among other things, a Natural History of Parrots, in French, with colored plates very beautifully executed."[72] Jefferson may have only purchased the first part of Levaillant's work, and he apparently never bound the prints with the text. Twelve "prints of parrots" were included on a packing list of items sent from the President's House to Monticello in 1807.[73] *L'Ara Canga Male* is the only one known to have survived.

A.M.L.

Count Dugnani, the papal nuncio in Paris during Jefferson's time there, sent this engraving and one of Francisco de Moncada to Jefferson at Monticello by way of two American students whom he met in Rome.[74] Jefferson hung the prints in the Tea Room and, in writing the count, called them "chef d'oeuvres of that art, which, placed among the ornaments of my house, renew to me daily the memory of your friendship."[75]

As early as 1782, before his journey to Europe, Jefferson wanted a copy of Salvator Rosa's painting *Belisarius Demanding Alms* to include in his Monticello gallery.[76] The story of the Roman general Belisarius was popularized by the French writer Marmontel, and Jefferson owned a 1768 London edition of his novel, *Belisarius*.[77] After a successful military career under Emperor Justinian I, Belisarius fell out of favor, and according to tradition, his eyes were put out, reducing him to a life of begging. This engraving after Rehberg's painting shows the moment when Belisarius is recognized by a soldier who once served under him.

[1958-20]   A . M . L .

47

DATE OBOLUM BELISARIO

1790

Pietro Bettilinie (1763–1828), engraver, after Frederic Rehberg (1758–1835)
engraving
image: 43.5 × 34
(17⅛ × 13⅜ in.)

PROVENANCE:
Count Dugnani, by gift to Thomas Jefferson; by descent to Ellen and Joseph Coolidge; by descent to T. Jefferson Coolidge III; by gift to TJMF in 1958.

48

FAÇADE DU PALAIS DES TUILLERIES DU COTE DU JARDIN

18th c.

published by F. Chereau
engraving
25 × 86.4 (9¹³/₁₆ × 34 in.)
Inscription on verso:
"H R Burke Jefferson Library"

PROVENANCE:
Thomas Jefferson; by descent to
Virginia and Nicholas Trist; by
descent to Harry Randolph Burke;
by gift or purchase to TJMF.

49

FAÇADE DE LA GALLERIE DU LOUVRE DU COSTE DE LA RIVIERE

18th c.

published by F. Chereau
engraving
24.8 × 130.8 (9¾ × 51½ in.)

PROVENANCE:
Thomas Jefferson; by descent to
Thomas Jefferson Randolph; by
descent to Olivia Taylor; by gift
and bequest to TJMF.

50

VUE GEOMETRALE DU PORTAIL DE LA NOUVELLE EGLISE DE STE. GENEVIEVE PATRON DE PARIS

1757

Francois-Philippe Charpentier
(1734–1817), engraver, after
Jacques-Germain Soufflot
(1713–1780)
engraving
40 × 48.9 (15¾ × 19¼ in.)
Mrs. James C. Moyer

PROVENANCE:
Thomas Jefferson; by descent to
Thomas Jefferson Randolph; by
descent to Mrs. James C. Moyer;
by loan to TJMF since 1972.

The Louvre and the Château des Tuilleries were at the center of many of Jefferson's social activities in Paris. On September 19, 1784, shortly after his arrival in the city, he witnessed from the Tuilleries gardens a manned hot-air balloon ascension.[78] The gardens came to be a favorite spot for Jefferson, where he could sit on the parapet overlooking the Seine and admire his favorite building, the Hôtel de Salm.[79] He attended more than twelve "concerts spirituels" held in the Tuilleries' "Salle de Machines." Here the Paris symphony presented works by French and Italian composers, performed by some of the most famous musicians of the day.[80]

No longer a royal residence, the Louvre served multiple purposes during Jefferson's time in France. There he visited the studios of the artist Jacques-Louis David and the architect Clérisseau, met with members of various royal academies, and attended the Salon of 1787. The "new" east façade of the Louvre (designed by the architects Louis Le Vau, Charles Le Brun, and Claude Perrault from 1667 to 1670) impressed Jefferson as one of the "celebrated fronts of modern buildings, which have already received the approbation of all good judges."[81] He recommended it many years later as a model for buildings in the United States capitol.[82]

[1970-93; 1969-8]   A . M . L .

During Jefferson's stay in Paris, the skyline was dominated by the scaffolding surrounding the nearly completed dome of Soufflot's Ste. Geneviève, which was secularized after the Revolution. Arguably the most important Neoclassical building erected in France during the last half of the eighteenth century, the building is now known as the Panthéon.[83] In 1744 Louis XV initiated the construction of a church dedicated to the patron saint of Paris whose prayers once saved the city from Attila the Hun. Soufflot began working on the project in 1755. This engraving by Charpentier was after one of the drawings in a set presented to the king for his approval. As it was built, the project varied from the preliminary design especially in the dome.[84] Jefferson owned at least two engravings of the church, and these were framed and glazed for display at Monticello.[85]

[1972-74]   A . M . L .

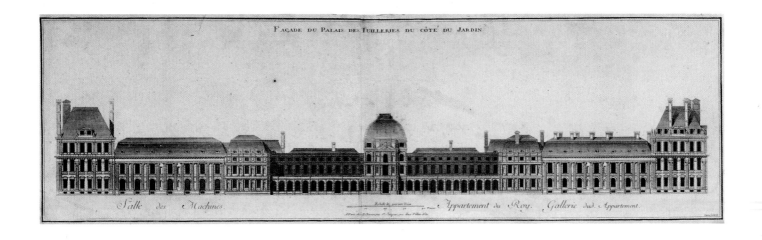

FAÇADE DU PALAIS DES TUILLERIES DU CÔTÉ DU JARDIN

Salle des Machines. Appartement du Roy. Gallerie dud. Appartement.

FAÇADE DE LA GALLERIE DU LOUVRE DU COSTE DE LA RIVIERE.

VUE GEOMETRALE DU PORTAIL DE LA NOUVELLE EGLISE DE S.te GENEVIEVE PATRONE DE PARIS.

These two prints of scenes from William Shakespeare's *A Midsummer Night's Dream* and *The Taming of the Shrew* are among the rare survivors from Jefferson's print collection, the only ones that have been located from the 1827 Dispersal Sale of his belongings. Jefferson was well acquainted with Shakespeare's works; he recommended them to his friends and gave them to his grandchildren.[86] "Read the best of the poets . . . ," he advised a young friend, "But among these Shakespeare must be singled out by one who wishes to learn the full powers of the English language."[87] Jefferson owned anthologies of Shakespeare's plays, as well as a concordance and books of criticism. Though Jefferson asked John Trumbull to obtain a copy of Shakespeare's portrait for his collection, it seems that these prints were the only representation of the writer at Monticello.[88]

The engraving from *A Midsummer Night's Dream* depicts Act IV, Scene I where Titania, Queen of the Fairies—who is enamored of Bottom because of the love potion she has taken—waits upon the donkey-headed man with her attendants. The scene shown from *The Taming of the Shrew* is the induction, Scene II, in which the tinker, Christopher Sly, is fooled into thinking he is a wealthy lord who has been asleep for many years. The attendants pose as courtiers and the page as his worried wife.

These two works were among 100 prints that were published by John and Josiah Boydell as part of their monumental Shakespeare Gallery project. Financed completely by the Boydells, the gallery operated from 1789 until 1803 and exhibited as many as 170 specially commissioned paintings of scenes from Shakespeare's plays, from which engravings were made. John Boydell attracted England's finest painters and engravers to his project, and the paintings by Robert Smirke and Henry Fuseli are considered to be masterpieces of their kind.[89]

[1965-47-1; 1965-47-2]   A . M . L .

51

**A MIDSUMMER-
NIGHT'S DREAM**

1796

*J. Peter Simon (active late 18th–
early 19th c.), engraver, after
Henry Fuseli (1742–1825)
stipple engraving
image: 43.8 × 59.7
(17¼ × 23½ in.)
Private collection*

52

**THE TAMING OF
THE SHREW**

1791

*Robert Thew (1758–1802),
engraver, after Robert Smirke
(1752–1845)
stipple engraving
image: 43.8 × 59.7
(17¼ × 23½ in.)
Private collection*

PROVENANCE:
Thomas Jefferson; by purchase at
the Dispersal Sale in 1827 to
Colonel Alexander R. Holladay; by
descent to a private collection; by
loan to TJMF since 1965.

MOUNT VERNON, *the Seat of the late* GEN.ʳ G.WASHINGTON.

**MOUNT VERNON, THE
SEAT OF THE LATE
GENL. G.
WASHINGTON**

original c. 1801–03;
engraved 1804

*Samuel Seymour (active 1796–
1823), engraver, after William
Birch (1755–1834)
stipple and line engraving,
colored
image: 32.2 × 40.6
(12¹¹⁄₁₆ × 16 in.)
Mount Vernon Ladies' Association*

In October 1790, while serving as George Washington's secretary of state, Jefferson made his first of at least six visits to Mount Vernon, Washington's plantation home on the Potomac River.[90] On one occasion Jefferson, his daughter Maria, and James Madison stopped by on their return to Philadelphia, and Maria completed the trip with Martha Washington.[91] Jefferson visited Mount Vernon for the last time in 1801, two years after Washington's death.[92]

Washington first acquired land at Mount Vernon in 1754. Over the course of thirty years he transformed a one-and-a-half-story farmhouse into the mansion shown in Birch's view. His estate grew to more than eight thousand acres, which were divided into five farms. Washington was keenly interested in agricultural experiments such as crop rotation, which he discussed with Jefferson at Mount Vernon in 1792.[93]

William Birch was an English-born painter who came to America in 1794. He is best known for *The City of Philadelphia*, a series of engravings published in 1800, to which Jefferson subscribed (Cat. 55). Jefferson displayed Birch's view of Mount Vernon in the Dining Room at Monticello; his copy is unlocated.[94]

A . M . L .

This View of the CAST-IRON-BRIDGE, near COALBROOK-DALE

The first iron bridge in the world was constructed between 1777 and 1781 over the Severn River gorge at Coalbrookdale, a center of the iron industry in England. Even while under construction, the bridge became a symbol of the relationship between man and nature in the Industrial Revolution. The bridge's design was the collaborative effort of the Shrewsbury architect Thomas Pritchard and Abraham Darby III, owner of the Darby Ironworks where the bridge was cast. Its single span covered over 100 feet, a distance unimaginable in wood or stone, and allowed for uninhibited barge traffic on the river below.[95]

While living in Paris, Jefferson purchased prints of the iron bridge through a friend in London. He later exhibited one in the Dining Room at Monticello next to a painting of Virginia's Natural Bridge.[96] The most popular print in Jefferson's time, and likely the one he exhibited, was engraved by William Ellis after a watercolor drawing by Michael Angelo Rooker. Darby commissioned Rooker to draw the bridge just after its opening in January 1781. Although better known as a painter, Rooker was skilled in engraving. He exhibited at the Society of Artists and served as scene painter for the Haymarket Theater.[97]

Jefferson discussed iron-bridge construction with Thomas Paine. While living in Philadelphia in 1783, Paine had designed an iron bridge. He visited Jefferson in Paris in 1787 on his way to England, and showed him a model of his iron bridge, which he believed could span 400 feet in a single arch—four times that of the Coalbrookdale Bridge.[98]

[1985-4-1]   A . M . L .

54

**COALBROOKDALE
BRIDGE**

1782

*William Ellis (1747–1810),
engraver, after Michael Angelo
Rooker (1746–1801)
etching
57.8 × 78.1 (22¾ × 30¾ in.)*

BACK OF THE STATE HOUSE, PHILADELPHIA

1799

From The City of Philadelphia, in the State of Pennsylvania, North America; as It Appeared in the Year 1800
Engravings executed 1798–1800
published December 31, 1800
William Birch (1755–1834) and Thomas Birch, artists and engravers, with Samuel Seymour (active 1796–1823), engraver, and William Barker (active 1795–1803), engraver
folio containing engraved map of the city of Philadelphia; hand-colored line-engraved frontispiece and 28 plates
27.9 × 33 (11 × 13 in.)

PROVENANCE:
Dr. Milton A. and Joan P. Wohl; by gift to TJMF in 1992.

William Birch's monumental publication *The City of Philadelphia* captured the vibrant capital as Jefferson knew it during his vice presidency (1797–1801). Birch and his son Thomas immigrated to Philadelphia from England in 1794, and in 1798 they produced their first engravings for the series. Birch's twenty-nine scenes of the city were innovative in their high level of detail, which conveyed a cross-section of city life. New vantage points for familiar sites, evident in the three plates of the Statehouse, set Birch's work apart.[99]

The collection was published on the last day of 1800 and celebrated Philadelphia's progress over the preceding century. In his introduction, Birch wrote of the city:

The ground on which it stands, was, less than a century ago, in a state of wild nature, covered with wood, and inhabited by Indians. It has, in this short time, been raised, as it were, by magic power to the eminence of an opulent city, famous for its trade and commerce, crouded in its port, with vessels of its own producing, and visited by others from all parts of the world . . . This Work will stand as a memorial of its progress for the first century; the buildings, of any consequence, are generally included, and the street scenes all accurate as they now stand; the choice of subjects are those that give the most general idea of the town . . .[100]

Jefferson was among 156 original subscribers to the work, which ranged in price from $28 for an uncolored, unbound copy to $44.50 for a colored, bound copy.[101] Other subscribers included Gilbert Stuart and the architect Latrobe, whose Philadelphia Waterworks and Bank of Pennsylvania were represented. According to Birch, Jefferson prominently displayed his bound copy of *The City of Philadelphia* in the President's House:

During the whole of [Jefferson's] presidency it layed on the sophia in his visiting Room at Washington till it became ragged and dirty, but was not suffered to be taken away.[102]

Once he returned to Monticello, Jefferson kept the folio outside of his library.[103] In 1815 he sold Birch's *City of Philadelphia*, along with most of his library, to help form the Library of Congress. It was likely destroyed in the 1851 fire that devastated the Library.[104]
[1991-29]   A . M . L .

56

A VIEW OF NEW ORLEANS TAKEN FROM THE PLANTATION OF MARIGNY

1804

John L. Boqueta de Woiseri (active in America 1797–1815)
colored aquatint
image: 29.5 × 54.5
(11⅝ × 21⁷⁄₁₆ in.)
The Historic New Orleans Collection, Museum/Research Center, Acc. No. 1958.42

A View of New Orleans and its companion plan celebrated the acquisition of New Orleans by the United States. The print was dedicated to Jefferson, the engineer of the 1803 Louisiana Purchase that more than doubled the size of the United States and also prevented a potential war with France over port rights at the mouth of the Mississippi River.[105]

While negotiations were still under way, Jefferson sent out queries about the Louisiana Territory to government officials in the area requesting maps and graphic representations of the region. The lack of available images may have encouraged Boqueta de Woiseri to undertake his painting of the view from Marigny's estate and its companion piece, a plan of the city. Both were advertised by de Woiseri in the February 21, 1804 *General Advertiser*.[106] These engravings (now missing), the only ones available, were probably those listed by Jefferson in his Catalogue of Paintings. They hung on the lower tier in the Dining Room.[107] The view exhibited is from The Mariners' Museum.

A . M . L .

Drawn Engraved & Published by W. Birch & Son   Sold by R. Campbell & C°. N°. 30 Chesnut Street Philad°. 1799.

BACK *of the* STATE HOUSE, PHILADELPHIA.

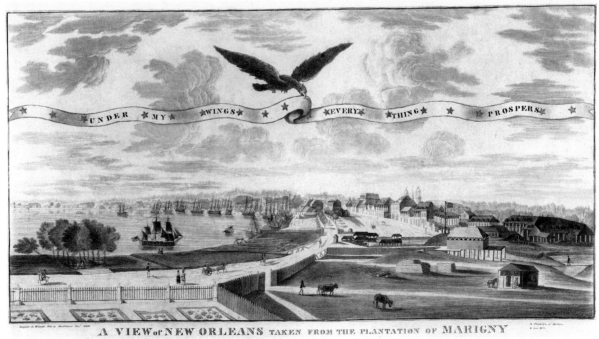

UNDER MY WINGS EVERY THING PROSPERS

A VIEW of NEW ORLEANS TAKEN FROM THE PLANTATION OF MARIGNY

**A VIEW OF THE
WESTERN BRANCH
OF THE FALLS OF
NIAGARA, TAKEN
FROM THE TABLE
ROCK, LOOKING UP
THE RIVER, OVER
THE RAPIDS**

1804

*Frederick Christian Lewis
(1779–1856), engraver, after
John Vanderlyn (1775–1852)
engraving
57.8 × 77.5 (22¾ × 30½ in.)
The Octagon Museum, The
American Architectural
Foundation*

58

**A DISTANT VIEW OF
NIAGARA,
INCLUDING BOTH
BRANCHES WITH THE
ISLAND AND
ADJACENT SHORES,
TAKEN FROM THE
VICINITY OF INDIAN
LADDER**

1804

*J. Merigot (late 18th–early
19th c.), engraver, after John
Vanderlyn (1775–1852)
engraving
57.8 × 77.5 (22¾ × 30½ in.)
The Octagon Museum,
The American Architectural
Foundation*

Jefferson included the "Cascade of Niagara" among America's natural wonders "worth a voiage across the Atlantic," and he displayed these two engravings in the Dining Room at Monticello alongside images of the Natural Bridge and Harpers Ferry.[108] Jefferson's knowledge of Niagara was only through written descriptions and early engravings. He owned what is thought to be the first engraved image of the falls, which was contained in the missionary-explorer Louis Hennepin's *Nouvelle Découverte d'un très grand Pays situé dans l'Amerique,* published in 1697.[109]

John Vanderlyn was an American-born artist who with the help of his patron Aaron Burr (who later was Jefferson's vice president) studied painting with Gilbert Stuart and then traveled to Paris to study art. After his return to America in 1801 Vanderlyn planned to support himself by selling views of Niagara Falls. He made a series of sketches at the falls in late 1801 and completed the first painting, *A Distant View of the Falls of Niagara,* in 1802. He finished the second work, *A View of the Western Branch of the Falls of Niagara* while on a second trip to Paris.[110] There he met James Monroe (Cat. 40) and the two traveled together to London, where Vanderlyn engaged the engravers Frederick Lewis and J. Merigot.[111]

Vanderlyn began collecting subscriptions for the engravings in 1803; Jefferson paid $20 for both prints on March 2.[112] The engravings were completed in London in 1804, and Vanderlyn wisely decided against dedicating the prints to Burr, who conspired against Jefferson and was replaced as vice president that same year by George Clinton.[113] The venture proved on the whole to be unprofitable largely due to mismanagement. Though the subscription list was lost, Jefferson received his two prints, framed and glazed, in December 1805.[114] Their whereabouts today are unknown.

A.M.L.

A VIEW of the WESTERN BRANCH of the FALLS of NIAGARA, taken from the TABLE ROCK, looking up the RIVER, over the RAPIDS.
To the Society of Fine Arts of New York, this Print is respectfully Inscribed by their most obedient humble Servant

A DISTANT VIEW of the FALLS of NIAGARA, including BOTH BRANCHES with the ISLAND, and ADJACENT SHORES, taken from the VICINITY of the INDIAN LADDER.
To the Society of Fine Arts of New York, this Print is respectfully Inscribed by their most obedient humble Servant

59 (opposite)

NATURAL BRIDGE

1808

J. C. Stadler (active early 19th c.), engraver, after William Roberts (active early 19th c.) colored aquatint 69.2 × 52.1 (27¼ × 20½ in.)

60 (overleaf)

THE JUNCTION OF THE POTOMAC AND SHENANDOAH, VIRGINIA *(also called* HARPERS FERRY)

c. 1810

Joseph Jeakes (active early 19th c.), engraver, after William Roberts (active early 19th c.) aquatint 28.6 × 35.6 (11¼ × 14 in.) Museum of Early Southern Decorative Arts; Douglas Battery Purchase Fund and G. Wilson Douglas Purchase Fund

Jefferson considered the Natural Bridge and the passage of the Potomac River through the Blue Ridge Mountains at Harpers Ferry to be two of the most incredible natural sites in America and described them as "monuments of a war between rivers and mountains, which must have shaken the earth to its center."[115] While president, Jefferson received oil paintings of the two wonders as a gift from the artist William Roberts, who also sent two copies of his engraving of the Natural Bridge. The two paintings hung in Monticello's Dining Room alongside the Coalbrookdale Bridge, England's feat of engineering, and Niagara Falls, another of America's natural wonders. Neither the oil paintings nor Jefferson's copies of the engravings are located.[116]

Little is known of Roberts's life and work, but he referred to himself as a Virginian and met Jefferson at least twice. The two were first introduced in Europe in 1786 by the naturalist Michel Guillaume Jean de Crèvecoeur, and it seems likely that Jefferson suggested Harpers Ferry and the Natural Bridge as subjects for Roberts's work.[117] Jefferson described both places in *Notes on the State of Virginia*, and he encouraged artists such as John Trumbull and Maria Cosway to paint them.

In *Notes on the State of Virginia* Jefferson praised the Natural Bridge as "the most sublime of Nature's works."[118] It was a site well known to him: he purchased it and the surrounding 157-acre tract in 1774 and owned it until his death. He visited the Natural Bridge at least four times.[119] On his first visit in 1767, he sketched the bridge and recorded its dimensions and setting on the inside back cover of his Memorandum Book.[120] These notes were the basis for his famous description in *Notes* of the bridge's sublime qualities:

It is impossible for the emotions, arising from the sublime, to be felt beyond what they are here: so beautiful an arch, so elevated, so light, and springing, as it were, up to heaven, the rapture of the Spectator is really indiscribable![121]

Jefferson shared his admiration for the bridge with his grandchildren, two of whom he took to see it on an adventurous journey in 1817. He often considered building a "little hermitage" there.[122] Although he attempted to sell the bridge during a financially difficult year, he later decided never to part with the property. "I view it," he wrote, "in some degree as a public trust, and would on no consideration permit the bridge to be injured, defaced or masked from public view."[123]

Jefferson visited Harpers Ferry in October 1783 and climbed a hill behind a tavern there to get the vantage point that inspired his powerful description in *Notes on the State of Virginia* of "one of the most stupendous scenes in nature."[124]

You stand on a very high point of land. On your right comes up the Shenandoah, having ranged along the foot of the mountain an hundred miles to seek a vent. On your left approaches the Patowmac, in quest of a passage also. In the moment of their junction they rush together against the mountain, rend it asunder, and pass off to the sea.[125]

In Jefferson's time Harpers Ferry was the home of the United States arsenal. The town was later famous as the site of John Brown's 1859 rebellion.

[M-69]   A.M.L.

THE NATURAL BRIDGE.

191

Drawn by Wm Roberts Esqr.

Engraved by J. Jeakes

JUNCTION OF THE POTOMAC AND SHENANDOAH, VIRGINIA.

Jefferson kept the rough draft of the Declaration of Independence, "scored and scratched like a schoolboy's exercise," at Monticello all his life.[126] He counted his authorship of what he called "an expression of the American mind" first among the achievements for which he wished to be remembered.[127] An engraving of John Trumbull's *Declaration of Independence* hung in Monticello's Entrance Hall (Cat. 31). One visitor reported that Jefferson used the print to illustrate a discussion of the historic event.[128] He also owned at least three different prints of the document itself. All three were published more than forty years after the original, during a time of fierce nationalism following the War of 1812.[129]

Although the first published copy of the Declaration was made on the evening of July 4, 1776, by the Philadelphian John Dunlap, it was not until 1818 that Americans could see the text in engraved writing as opposed to print. A virtual war ensued between rival printers John Binns and Benjamin Owen Tyler to be the first to publish and garner Jefferson's endorsement.[130] Binns was the publisher of the Republican Philadelphia newspaper *The Democratic Press*. In June 1816, he began taking subscriptions for his print of the Declaration, which was to be surrounded by portraits of John Hancock, George Washington, and Jefferson, and the seals of all thirteen states, but he failed to produce the work until 1819.

In the meantime Tyler took advantage of Binns's publicity and produced a less expensive and unornamented print in April 1818, complete with facsimile signatures and a dedication to Jefferson. Tyler was a self-taught calligrapher and penmanship instructor.[131] When he asked Jefferson for permission to dedicate the engraving to him, Jefferson consented but reminded Tyler that he was "but a fellow laborer" with the other signers:

For the few of us remaining can vouch, I am sure, on behalf of those who have gone before us, that notwithstanding the lowering aspect of the day, no hand trembled on affixing its signature to that paper.[132]

Tyler sent Jefferson a copy of his work on parchment, and sometime after May 1818, paid a visit to Monticello, where he spent the day teaching penmanship to Jefferson's family.[133]

Binns's response to Tyler's success was to dedicate his work to the people of the United States. He sent a proof of the print to Jefferson in 1819 soliciting comments. "The dedication to the people is peculiarly appropriate," Jefferson wrote, "for it is their work, and particularly entitled to my approbation with whom it has ever been a principle to consider individuals as nothing in the scale of the nation."[134] Jefferson added that the print's "great value will be in it's exactness as a fac-simile to the original paper," a comment that foreshadowed Binns's next struggle.[135]

Binns had hoped to sell 200 copies of his print to the government but was disappointed in 1820 by then secretary of state John Quincy Adams's commission of an exact facsimile of the original by William J. Stone. When completed in 1823 Stone's print was considered the "official" copy for government use; two copies were sent to each of the three remaining signers, Jefferson, John Adams, and Charles Carroll, as well as to the marquis de Lafayette. Other copies were distributed to governors and presidents of colleges and universities.[136]

Jefferson's prints of the Declaration were dispersed among his family following his death in 1826, and none are known to survive today.

[1992-11]   A.M.L.

61–63 (overleaf)

DECLARATION OF INDEPENDENCE

1819

John Binns (1772–1860), publisher; James Barton Longacre (1794–1869) engraver of portraits engravings
plate: 89.7 × 61 (35⁵⁄₁₆ × 24 in.)

1818

Benjamin Owen Tyler (b. 1789) engraving
78.7 × 68.6 (31 × 27 in.)
Massachusetts Historical Society

1823

William J. Stone (1798–1865) engraving
overall 85.7 × 69.2 (33¾ × 27¼ in.)
Dr. William R. Coleman

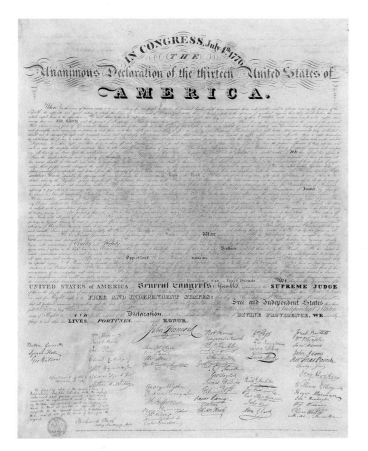

64

**THE UNIVERSITY
OF VIRGINIA**

1825 (second edition)

*Peter Maverick (1780–1831),
engraver, after a drawing by
John Neilson (d. 1827)
line engraving
46.4 × 51.8 (18¼ × 20⅜ in.)
Manuscripts Division, Special
Collections Department,
University of Virginia Library*

Jefferson's plan for the buildings and grounds at the University of Virginia, published first in 1822 and again in 1825, reveals his innovative design for an "academical village." With the assistance of the architects Benjamin Henry Latrobe and William Thornton, Jefferson designed a complex of buildings for functional and didactic purposes. He disliked the large institutional buildings of other American universities, such as his alma mater, the College of William and Mary:

Large houses are always ugly, inconvenient, exposed to the accident of fire, and bad in case of infection. A plain small house for the school and lodging of each professor is best . . . in fact an University should not be an house but a village.[137]

At the center of Jefferson's plan of the university is the Rotunda, modeled after the Roman Pantheon and intended by Jefferson to be used as a library. Flanking it are two parallel rows of five pavilions, each with school rooms on the lower floors and housing for the professor and his family above. All ten pavilions have a different classical façade, "so as to serve as specimins for the Architectural lectures."[138] Connecting the pavilions are single-celled dormitory rooms fronted by a colonnade, so that the students can be protected from the weather as they walk between classes. The pavilions and dormitories open onto a shared "lawn" and behind the pavilions are private yards and gardens enclosed by serpentine walls. The two outer "ranges" consist of six "hotels," or dining halls also connected by dormitories.

Construction at the university was ongoing in 1821 when the Board of Visitors of the university ordered the engraving of a plan for sale to the public; only six of the ten pavilions were complete, and the Rotunda had yet to be begun.[139] The sculptor William Coffee, who was working at Monticello at the time, recommended to Jefferson the New York engraver Peter Maverick, and he acted as intermediary between them. In the summer of 1821 Coffee carried to Maverick a plan of the university that was probably drawn by John Neilson, a skilled house joiner who worked for Jefferson at Monticello, Poplar Forest, and the university.[140]

Jefferson received the first printing of 250 plans from Maverick on December 7, 1822, along with his bill totaling $150 for engraving, printing, paper, and shipping.[141] Maverick retained the copperplate, at Jefferson's instruction, for future impressions. In the fall of 1824, when the university's opening was imminent and construction was nearing an end, the engraved plans were again in demand. Jefferson wrote to Maverick requesting a second set of 200 engravings with a few alterations to the original design. He asked that the pavilions and dormitories be numbered, that an additional room be added to the end of the West Range (room no. 55), and that the Rotunda portico be connected to the upper level of the lawn terraces. Maverick executed these changes and sent 250 engravings (50 more than requested) to Virginia. Jefferson recorded paying for one of the revised plans on March 29, 1825.[142] Its whereabouts today are unknown.

A . M . L .

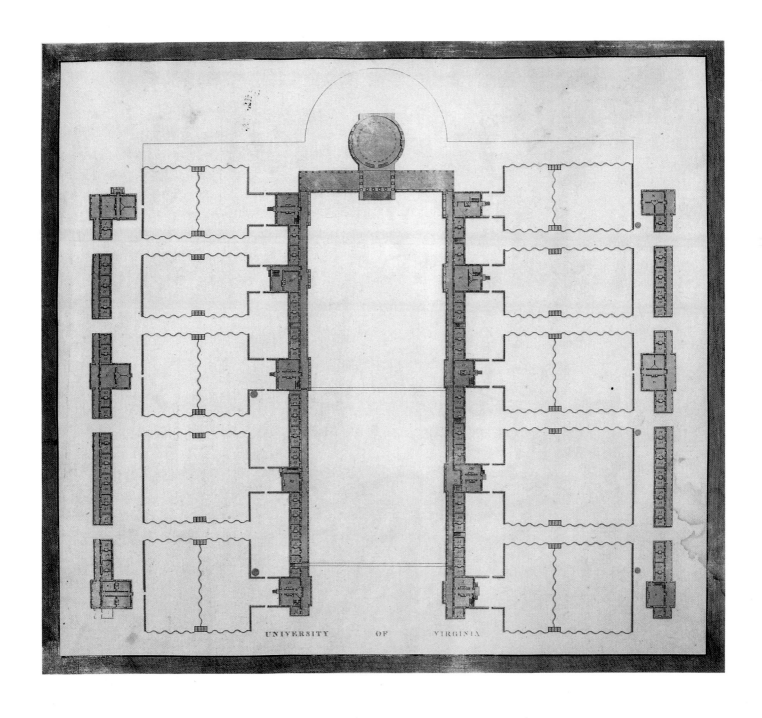

UNIVERSITY OF VIRGINIA

When the French émigré Charles Fevret de Saint-Mémin introduced physiognotrace portraits to the United States in 1797 Jefferson was already acquainted with the use of a mechanical device to trace a sitter's profile. Eight years earlier in Paris, Jefferson sat for a life-size crayon physiognotrace portrait by the machine's inventor, Gilles-Louis Chrétien. Using a pantograph, Chrétien then reduced the original profile to a miniature copperplate from which multiple engravings could be printed.

Jefferson was probably the first American to have his profile taken by the physiognotrace. He and Gouverneur Morris (Cat. 67) went together to the Palais Royal on April 22, 1789 to purchase tickets for sittings. The next day Jefferson sat for Chrétien and his partner Edmé Quenedey (1756–1830) at their studio. Six days later Jefferson picked up the copperplate of his portrait and twelve prints taken from it. Curiously, Jefferson made no further reference to these prints, and none are known to survive within his family.[1]

On the other hand, the portrait of Jefferson done by Saint-Mémin in 1804 was widely distributed both by the artist and Jefferson, and it became one of the best-known likenesses of Jefferson in his day.[2] Saint-Mémin came to the United States from Dijon, France in 1793.

The cost and size of Saint-Mémin's engravings made them immensely popular gifts among friends, relatives, and colleagues. Jefferson's print collection included at least a dozen of the artist's miniatures, many of which were exhibited in the Tea Room. For twenty-five dollars ($250 today) a gentleman could purchase his original crayon drawing, the engraved copperplate, and twelve engravings. The cost for ladies was ten dollars more, and an additional twelve prints cost only one dollar and fifty cents.[3]

Jefferson's children entreated their father to have his portrait taken by the Frenchman. In February 1804, Maria Jefferson Eppes, the younger of Jefferson's two daughters, wrote to her father in Washington from her sickbed:

We had both thought you had promised us your picture if ever St. Mimin went to Washington. If you did but know what a source of pleasure it would be to us while so much separated from you to have so excellent a likeness of you you would not I think refuse us. It is what we have allways most wanted all our lives and the certainty with which he takes his likenesses makes this one request I think not unreasonable.[4]

Maria did not live long enough to see her father's portrait, but her sister Martha was very fond of the likeness. Both she and her eldest daughter, Anne Cary Bankhead, requested additional prints for friends and associates near Monticello.[5] Jefferson purchased a total of forty-eight prints from Saint-Mémin after his November sitting, which he gave to his family, members of his Cabinet, and friends, including the comte de Volney and the marquis de Lafayette.[6] Saint-Mémin produced additional prints in an oval frame on the eve of Jefferson's second inauguration for sale to the public.[7]

[1962-1-38]   A . M . L .

67

GOUVERNEUR
MORRIS
(1752–1816)

1789

*Gilles-Louis Chrétien (1754–
1811), engraver, after Edmé
Quenedey (1756–1830)
engraving
D: 5.1 (2 in.)
Print Collection, The Miriam
and Ira D. Wallach Division of
Art, Prints and Photographs,
The New York Public Library,
Astor, Lenox and Tilden
Foundations.*

The amiable New York lawyer Gouverneur Morris was active in American politics beginning with the Revolution. He was a staunch supporter of Washington and a member of numerous Continental Congresses, where he helped frame the Constitution. Private business matters brought Morris to Paris in 1789, just before Jefferson returned to the United States.[8] Although the two had political differences, Jefferson and Morris were frequent companions and went together to have their portraits taken by Chrétien and Quenedey.[9] Later that year Jefferson included Morris among the guests at his farewell dinner, which was attended by distinguished Frenchmen, such as the marquis de Lafayette, and several Americans. "Mr. Jefferson lives well," Morris wrote in his diary, "keeps a good table and excellent wines which he distributes freely and by his hospitality to his countrymen here possesses very much their good will."[10]

Following Jefferson's departure from Paris, Morris was the most influential American in that city. Despite opposition to Morris from Jefferson and many senators, President Washington appointed him minister to France in 1792. The opposition to Morris's nomination centered on three issues, according to Jefferson:

1. His general character, being such that we would not confide in it. 2. His known attachment to monarchy and contempt of republican government and 3d his present employment abroad being a news vender of back lands and certificates.[11]

Morris's term as minister during the height of the French Revolution was brief but turbulent. After returning to the United States, he served a short term in the Senate before retiring in 1803 to his home in Morrisania, New York. Through his 1809 marriage to Anne Cary Randolph, Thomas Mann Randolph's sister, Morris became part of the extended Jefferson family.[12] Jefferson displayed Morris's miniature in the Tea Room at Monticello; it is unlocated today.

A.M.L.

Mahlon Dickerson recorded in his diary that he sat for this portrait in Philadelphia on a cloudy and rainy May 18, 1802. He may have been accompanied by Meriwether Lewis (Cat. 69), whom he had met the month before at a dinner hosted by Jefferson at the President's House. Dickerson, a New Jersey native, had just graduated from the College of New Jersey law school and was practicing in Philadelphia when he made his visit to Washington. He and Jefferson discussed Pennsylvania and New Jersey politics at dinner, and their meeting led to Dickerson's appointment as commissioner of bankruptcy in Philadelphia.

Of his visit with Jefferson, Dickerson wrote: "He is accused as being very slovenly in his dress, and to be sure he is not very particular in that respect, but however he may neglect his person he takes good care of his table. No man in America keeps a better."[13] Dickerson had an active political career as New Jersey's governor, United States senator for sixteen years, and secretary of the navy under Martin Van Buren.[14]

[1962-1-44]   A.M.L.

68
MAHLON DICKERSON (1770–1853)

1802

Charles Fevret de Saint-Mémin (1770–1852)
engraving
D: 8.6 (3⅜ in.)

PROVENANCE:
Thomas Jefferson; by descent to Virginia and Nicholas Trist; by descent to Charles, James, and John Eddy; by gift to TJMF in 1962.

Jefferson described the leader of the Lewis and Clark expedition as having undaunted courage and "possessing a firmness and perseverance of purpose which nothing but impossibilities could divert from it's direction . . ."[15] Jefferson knew Lewis and his family from his native Albemarle County, Virginia. As early as 1792 Lewis expressed his desire to lead a western expedition. He was serving as Jefferson's presidential secretary when Congress approved the 1803 expedition to explore the northwest, and Jefferson did not hesitate to name Lewis leader of the exploring party.

Under Jefferson's direction Lewis studied with leading scientists in preparation for the expedition. Lewis recruited his fellow Albemarle County native William Clark to accompany him. From 1803 to 1806 these two men led the expedition to the Pacific Ocean and back, all the while making meticulous notes on their activities. Lewis and Clark's journals

69
MERIWETHER LEWIS (1774–1809)

1802

Charles Fevret de Saint-Mémin (1770–1852)
engraving
D: 5.6 (2³⁄₁₆ in.)
Library of Congress

contain descriptions and drawings of virtually everything they encountered: plants, animals, minerals, weather activity, landscapes, and Indians. Jefferson was the recipient of three shipments of artifacts from the expedition, which he distributed to the Peale Museum and the American Philosophical Society. Select specimens, many specifically procured by the explorers for the president, were displayed at the President's House and remained in Jefferson's collection at Monticello (Cat. 253–259).[16]

Jefferson appointed Lewis governor of Louisiana after his return in 1806. Lewis held that position until his mysterious death in 1809, the cause of which remains undetermined. Although many believed that Lewis was murdered, Jefferson concluded that he died by his own hand:

About 3. oclock in the night he did the deed which plunged his friends into affliction and deprived his country of one of her most valued citizens . . .[17]

Lewis sat for Saint-Mémin twice, before and after the expedition, and Jefferson may have owned both images.

A . M . L .

70

BENJAMIN SMITH BARTON (1766–1815)

1820

Christian Gobrecht (1785–1844), after Charles Fevret de Saint-Mémin (1770–1852)
stipple engraving
D: 5.7 (2¼ in.)
The Library Company of Philadelphia

Jefferson and Benjamin Smith Barton, the physician and botanist, shared an interest in many aspects of natural history and Native American languages. Together with Barton's brother William and his uncle, David Rittenhouse (Cat. 42), both were members of the American Philosophical Society. Barton was born in Lancaster, Pennsylvania, and studied medicine in Edinburgh and London, where he became a member of the Royal Medical Society. Upon his return to America, Barton taught natural history and botany at the College of Philadelphia, and later succeeded Benjamin Rush in the chair of medicine at the University of Pennsylvania.[18]

In his 1792 paper to the American Philosophical Society, Barton praised Jefferson's contribution to the study of natural history and renamed *Podophyllum diphyllum*, a wildflower of eastern North America, *Jeffersonia binata* in his honor.

In imposing upon this genus the name of Mr. Jefferson, I have had no reference to his political character, or to his reputation for general science, and for literature. My business was with his knowledge of natural history. In the various departments of this science, but especially in botany and zoology, the information of this gentleman is equalled by that of few persons in the United-States.[19]

Jefferson had keen respect for Barton and sent Meriwether Lewis (Cat. 69) to consult with him about botany, natural history, and Native Americans, to prepare for the northwest expedition. He wrote Barton, "I know that the same wish to promote science which has induced me to bring forward this proposition, will induce you to aid in promoting it."[20] After Lewis and Clark's return in 1806, Barton was engaged to compile a scientific report for publication from their journals, but died before completing the work.

Barton and Jefferson believed that the key to discovering the origin of Native Americans was a comparative study of their languages with those of Europe and Asia. They actively sought examples of Native American vocabularies. Barton published his findings in 1797 in a work dedicated to Jefferson, *New Views of the Origin of the Tribes and Nations of America.*[21] Jefferson planned to publish his comparative vocabularies in 1800, but presidential demands caused him to delay his work on the subject until his retirement. Tragically, most of the fifty vocabularies he had collected over thirty years were destroyed en route from the President's House to Monticello in 1809.[22] Barton had asked Jefferson to send him samples of the vocabularies collected by Lewis and Clark, but these, too, were mostly destroyed. Jefferson shared with his friend Barton "the only morsel of an original vocabulary" that survived: Lewis's record of the Pani language.[23]

A . M . L .

As Jefferson's secretary of war, Henry Dearborn helped form policy on Native Americans, the goal of which was to establish a strong western boundary by procuring lands along the Mississippi and its tributaries. "The Indians," Jefferson wrote to Dearborn in 1803,

being once closed in between strong settled countries on the Mississippi and Atlantic, will, for want of game, be forced to agriculture, will find that small portions of land well improved, will be worth more to them than extensive forests unemployed, and will be continually parting with portions of them, for money to buy stock, utensils and necessities for their farms and families.[24]

71

HENRY DEARBORN
(1751–1829)

c. 1805

Charles Fevret de Saint-Mémin (1770–1852)
engraving
D: 5.6 (2 3/16 in.)

PROVENANCE:
Thomas Jefferson; by descent to Virginia and Nicholas Trist; by descent to an anonymous donor; by gift to TJMF in 1956.

Dearborn assisted in planning the Lewis and Clark expedition and was also in charge of frontier trading posts, or "factories," which reinforced the government's presence on these boundaries.

Jefferson praised Dearborn for the "integrity, attention, skill, and economy with which you have conducted your department," adding, "should a war come on, there is no person in the United States to whose management and care I could commit it with equal confidence."[25] Although Dearborn had enjoyed a celebrated military career prior to joining Jefferson's cabinet, his poor performance in the War of 1812 as a major-general led to his removal from command and honorable discharge from the army. Madison tried unsuccessfully to return Dearborn to the post of secretary of war. In 1822 Monroe appointed Dearborn as minister to Portugal, a post he held for two years before retiring from public service.[26]

[1956-38]

A.M.L.

72

CAESAR RODNEY
(1772–1824)

1800

Charles Fevret de Saint-Mémin
(1770–1852)
engraving
D: 5.6 (2³⁄₁₆ in.)
Library of Congress

Jefferson appointed Delaware Congressman Caesar Rodney as United States attorney general in January 1807. Almost immediately Rodney was given the task of organizing the government's case in the impending treason trial of Aaron Burr.[27] He secured William Wirt and Alexander McRae to represent the United States, directed the summoning of witnesses, and gathered depositions.[28] Jefferson also charged Rodney with leading the investigation into Burr's activities.[29]

A warm letter from Rodney, enquiring after Jefferson's health during his retirement, prompted Jefferson to recall

the sociability, the friendship, and the harmony of action which united personal happiness with public duties, during the portion of our lives in which we acted together. Indeed, the affectionate harmony of our Cabinet is among the sweetest of my recollections.[30]

Rodney's career after Jefferson left office was an active one. He served as attorney general during Madison's administration, fought in the War of 1812, and was appointed minister to Argentina by Monroe.[31]

A.M.L.

PHYSIOGNOTRACE PORTRAITS

Genêt came to the United States in 1793 as French envoy during Jefferson's term as secretary of state. He probably presented this miniature to Jefferson as a routine diplomatic gift—possibly the only routine act of his short, controversial career. Genêt attempted to draw the United States into aggressions on land and sea, against Spain and England. His disregard for the authority of the United States government, particularly Washington's power as president, led Jefferson to complain to James Madison:

Never in my opinion was so calamitous an appointment made, as that of the present Minister of France here. Hot headed, all imagination, no judgement, passionate, disrespectful and even indecent toward the P[resident] in his written as well as verbal communications. . . . He renders my position immensely difficult.[32]

After suffering through Genêt's many diplomatic and political indiscretions, Jefferson, Washington, Alexander Hamilton, and Henry Knox (Washington's secretary of war) agreed that to maintain peace between the United States and France, Genêt's appointment must be recalled. Jefferson particularly feared that Genêt's threatened appeals to the people of the United States would "enlarge the circle of those disaffected to his country."[33]

Jefferson summarized the minister's actions in his report to the French government:

When the government forbids their citizens to arm and engage in the war, he undertakes to arm and engage them. When they forbid vessels to be fitted in their ports for cruising on nations with whom they are at peace, he commissions them to fit and cruise. When they forbid an unceded jurisdiction to be exercised within their territory by foreign agents, he undertakes to uphold that exercise, and to avow it openly.[34]

Genêt was removed from his post in the same year in which he began.[35] He remained in the United States and became an American citizen.

[1968-58-1]   A.M.L.

73
EDMOND CHARLES EDOUARD GENET (1763–1834)

1793

Gilles-Louis Chrétien (1754–1811) engraving D: 5.1 (2 in.) Private collection

PROVENANCE:
Thomas Jefferson; by descent to Virginia and Nicholas Trist; by descent to a private collection; by loan to TJMF since 1968.

74

WILLIAM BURWELL
(1752–1821)

1806

Charles Fevret de Saint-Mémin
(1770–1852)
engraving
D: 5.7 (2¼ in.)
Library of Congress

Jefferson's secretary William Burwell, a Virginia native, was part of the Presidential "family" from 1804 until 1806. Jefferson described the position as "more in the nature of an Aid de camp, than a mere Secretary."[36] Burwell needed to do very little writing since Jefferson wrote his own letters and copied them by aid of a polygraph. The secretary assisted Jefferson with the care of his company, the execution of commissions in Washington, messages to Congress, and meetings with particular members of Congress. Burwell was promised a salary of $600 a year, a servant to answer to his needs, and a horse for his use kept in the stables at the President's House.[37]

Burwell left Jefferson's employ because of his poor health and commitments as a member of Virginia's General Assembly.[38] In 1806 he won a seat in Congress, where he served until his death in 1821. Burwell's support for Jefferson was steadfast, and he led Jefferson's defense in 1805 against the accusations of the journalist James Callender.[39] Jefferson and Burwell maintained a warm personal and political correspondence for years after Jefferson's departure from the President's House.

A . M . L .

75

MARY RANDOLPH
(1762–1828)

1807

Charles Fevret de Saint-Mémin
(1770–1852)
engraving
D: 5.6 (2³⁄₁₆ in.)

PROVENANCE:
Possibly a gift from Mary
Randolph to Martha Jefferson
Randolph; by descent to Charles,
James, and John Eddy; by gift to
TJMF in 1962.

Although members of Jefferson's extended family, Mary Randolph and her husband, David Meade Randolph, were among his most bitter political critics. Jefferson recommended David for the post of United States marshal for Virginia during Washington's presidency, but his suspicion that Randolph packed a jury with Federalists led Jefferson to dismiss him in 1801. The couple remained in close contact with Jefferson's family because Mary Randolph was Thomas Mann Randolph's sister (the husband of Jefferson's daughter Martha). Following his dismissal from office, the Randolphs opened a boardinghouse in Richmond, and there Mrs. Randolph gained a reputation for her culinary skills.[40] Both Randolphs continued to be outspoken critics of Jefferson.

In 1825, Mrs. Randolph capitalized on her skills and published one of the best-known cookbooks of the nineteenth century, *The Virginia House-wife*. She sent a copy to Jefferson who thanked her for the book, writing that it was "one of those which contribute most to the innocent enjoyments of mankind . . . a greater degree of merit few classes of books can claim."[41] Manuscript cookbooks kept by Jefferson's granddaughters reveal that Mrs. Randolph was the source of over forty dishes that were served at Monticello, including catfish soup and floating island.[42]

[1962-1-39]   A . M . L .

Jefferson was delighted when John Wayles Eppes proposed marriage to his daughter Maria, and he wrote glowingly of his future son-in-law: "A long acquaintance with him has made his virtues familiar to me and convinced me that he possesses every quality necessary to make you happy and to make us all happy."[43] John and Maria were married at Monticello in October 1797, after a lifelong courtship. When her mother died, the four-year-old Mary Jefferson (later called Maria) went to live with her aunt, Elizabeth Wayles Eppes, at Eppington in Chesterfield County, Virginia. There she met her cousin John, five years her elder. The two renewed their friendship after Maria's return from France, and both lived with Jefferson in Philadelphia when he was secretary of state.

Jefferson greatly influenced John's education by recommending that he attend his alma mater, the College of William and Mary, and later directed his study of law in Philadelphia. Eppes was admitted to the Virginia bar in 1794 and began his political career in 1800, when he was elected to the Virginia House of Delegates. He served his first term in Congress in the fall of 1803 with his brother-in-law Thomas Mann Randolph, and returned to Monticello the next spring, just before his wife died at the age of twenty-five after the birth of their third child. Only one of their children, Francis, lived to adulthood. Jefferson remained close to his grandson and son-in-law.[44]

A . M . L .

76

**JOHN WAYLES
EPPES
(1 7 7 3 – 1 8 2 3)**

1805

*Charles Fevret de Saint-Mémin
(1770–1852)
engraving
D: 5.7 (2¼ in.)
Library of Congress*

SILHOUETTES

Two types of silhouettes from Monticello survive today: those that were cut by anonymous hands, some possibly taken at Monticello using the camera obscura (Cat. 274), and those that were the product of Charles Willson Peale or his children. Silhouettes provided striking likenesses and were easily transmitted through the mail, making them popular remembrances exchanged between family members and close friends. Jefferson's granddaughter Ellen Coolidge, living in Boston and separated from her Virginia relatives, asked her sister to send her silhouettes: "I wish if any opportunity occurs you would have them cut. I like to have such things to remind me in after years what my friends have been."[1] The Monticello silhouette collection is appropriately dominated by profiles of Jefferson's family, and contains only a few neighbors, friends, and associates.

Surviving silhouettes include several of Jefferson, his eldest daughter Martha Randolph at several ages, her husband Thomas Mann Randolph, their children Anne Cary Bankhead, Thomas Jefferson Randolph, Ellen Randolph Coolidge, Cornelia Jefferson Randolph, Virginia Jefferson Randolph Trist, and an unidentified profile labeled "Miss Randolph." Though Jefferson's younger daughter Maria's silhouette is unlocated, those of her husband John Wayles Eppes, mother-in-law Elizabeth, and son Francis all survive. Jefferson's sister Martha Carr (Cat. 78) and her son Peter are also represented in the collection, as are silhouettes of Jefferson's Albemarle County neighbors Col. and Mrs. Ruben Lindsay. Lafayette also left a silhouette with Jefferson on his last visit to Monticello in 1824.[2]

Subjects among the Peale silhouettes are Mrs. Nicholas Waters (neé Esther Ritten-house), a Philadelphia friend of Martha Randolph; Thomas Jefferson Randolph, Jeffer-son's grandson who lived with Charles Willson Peale for over a year while studying in Philadelphia; Nicholas Trist (Cat. 80), the husband of Jefferson's granddaughter Virginia Randolph; and his brother Hore Browse Trist (Cat. 79). The silhouettes of Baron von Humboldt, Aimé Jacques Alexandre Bonpland, Dr. Nicholas Collin, and Dr. Anthony Fothergill were given to Jefferson by Charles Willson Peale on the occasion of their visit to the President's House in 1804 (Cat. 81–84).

Though little is known about silhouette cutting at Monticello, Charles Willson Peale's success with the silhouette is well documented. With the help of the English inventor Isaac Hawkins, Peale created a rage in America for silhouettes cut with the aid of the physiog-notrace, or "Facieatrace," a device based on the principle of Chrétien's machine that allowed a sitter to trace the outline of his own face. This outline was reduced by a pantograph to miniature size and impressed on twice-folded banknote paper, from which four identical silhouettes were cut. Peale installed the machine in the long gallery of his Philadelphia museum, and though it was designed to be self-operating, most sitters pre-ferred to have some assistance; Peale's servant Moses Williams, a former slave, cut over 8,500 silhouettes in the first year.[3]

Peale's advertisement for Hawkins's machine intrigued Jefferson, who was in the process of helping Hawkins and Peale perfect another innovation, the polygraph (Cat. 223). Peale sent Jefferson a drawing and an explanation by Hawkins of the physiognotrace, and dispatched his son Raphaelle to the President's House in 1804 to cut Jefferson's profile using a portable machine. Peale had already been distributing a silhouette of the President taken from the profile of his bust by Jean-Antoine Houdon (Cat. 101) but preferred this image from life. He made thousands of copies to give to visitors to his Philadelphia museum.[4] Raphaelle Peale also toured the south with his portable machine, taking silhouettes in Virginia, South Carolina, and Georgia. When the novelty began to fade, Raphaelle and others offered profiles of Washington, Adams, or Jefferson as enticements to silhouette customers.[5]

[1962-1-26]   A . M . L .

78

**MARTHA
JEFFERSON CARR
(1746–1811)**

after 1782

paper
7 × 3.8 (2¾ × 1½ in.)

PROVENANCE:
Thomas Jefferson; by descent to
Virginia and Nicholas Trist; by
descent to Charles, James, and
John Eddy; by gift to TJMF in
1962.

In 1765 Jefferson's older sister Martha married his closest childhood friend, Dabney Carr. After Carr's premature death in 1773, Jefferson acted as a father to his six children and directed the education of Peter, the eldest. "Aunt Carr" was an important presence following the death of Jefferson's wife in 1782, and she helped take care of Monticello while her brother served in France between 1784 and 1789.[6] She was described as "a gifted woman, and every way worthy of her husband; and their married life was one of peculiar felicity."[7]

[1962-1-35]   A . M . L .

The Trist brothers were born in Charlottesville but moved to New Orleans in 1803 to join their father, whom Jefferson had appointed port collector for the lower Mississippi River. The boys remained close to their grandmother in Charlottesville, Eliza House Trist, a close friend of Jefferson's. At his invitation Nicholas and "Browse" returned to Charlottesville in December 1817, and spent nearly a year at Monticello where Nicholas began his six-year courtship of Jefferson's granddaughter Virginia Randolph. After Nicholas had attended West Point, and studied law in Louisiana, the pair were married at Monticello in 1824. They lived in the North Pavilion at Monticello, and Nicholas became Jefferson's personal secretary, companion, and ultimately one of the executors of his estate.[8]

These silhouettes were probably cut at Peale's Philadelphia Museum around 1820, when Hore Browse sent two of his profiles to his grandmother Eliza Trist, who wrote to Nicholas of the resemblance between the brothers:

Browse enclosed me two of his Profiles one for Mrs. Randolph [Martha Jefferson Randolph], she says that it is so excellent a likeness of you that they can scarsely discover a trace of him self and but for Peals Museum which is stamp'd on the paper they wou'd have thought it intended for you.[9]

Nicholas may have brought his silhouette with him to Monticello on his return there from West Point in 1821.

[1962-1-8; 1962-1-30]   A.M.L.

Inspired by the Prussian explorer Alexander von Humboldt's desire to meet Jefferson, Charles Willson Peale led a delegation composed of Humboldt and his partner, Alexandre Bonpland, and two physicians, Nicholas Collin and Anthony Fothergill, from Philadelphia to the President's House, arriving on June 1, 1804. Peale recorded every detail of his trip in his diary, including their several visits with Jefferson. Peale presented Jefferson with this group of silhouettes during one of their visits:

I had brought with me sundry Profiles of the Baron and of Doctr Fothergill and myself—Doctr Collin, these I distributed to such Persons as I thought they would be most acceptable.[10]

Although Peale's diary entry mentions a silhouette of himself, none from Jefferson's collection is known to survive.[11]

Humboldt had just completed his famous explorations in South and Central America, accompanied through South America by the botanist Bonpland who had collected plant specimens. When he arrived in the United States, Humboldt requested a meeting with

Jefferson, and wrote praising "your writings, your actions, and the liberalism of your ideas, which have inspired me from my earliest youth."[12] Jefferson was more than happy to oblige, congratulating Humboldt on the success of his travels and writing:

The countries you have visited are those least known, and most interesting, and a lively desire will be felt generally to receive the information you will be able to give. No one will feel it more strongly than myself, because no one person views this new world with more partial hopes of it's exhibiting an ameliorated state of the human condition.[13]

The boundaries with Spanish possessions were of immediate importance to Jefferson following the Louisiana Purchase, and Humboldt's providential visit supplied him with the data he needed to compose his fall congressional message on negotiations with Spain over Louisiana, Mobile, and the Mexican border.[14] Humboldt and Jefferson intermittently corresponded on scientific and political subjects for the remainder of Jefferson's life.

[1962-1-5; 1962-1-7; 1962-1-20; 1962-1-18]   A.M.L.

85–88

CHIEFS FROM THE MISSOURI AND MISSISSIPPI

1806

cut by either Charles Willson Peale (1741–1827) or Moses Williams (active 1813–1820), employing the physiognotrace at the Peale Museum, Philadelphia.
paper embossed "Museum"
average 7.6 × 3.8 (3 × 1½ in.)
National Anthropological Archives, Smithsonian Institution

(upper left)
Wasconsca, Counsel of Nations

(upper right)
Sagessaga, Great Chief of the Osages

(lower left)
Possibly Mechenecka of the Sack Nation. (This chief's identity is in question because Peale mistakenly labeled two silhouettes with the same number.)

(lower right)
Tahawarra, Nation Sourie

The 1803–06 Lewis and Clark expedition was not only a journey of discovery but also a diplomatic mission from the United States government to the Native Americans who inhabited the newly acquired Louisiana Territory. Jefferson instructed Lewis and Clark to treat the Native Americans "in the most friendly and conciliatory manner."[15]

If a few of their influential chiefs, within a practicable distance, wish to visit us, arrange such a visit with them, and furnish them with authority to call on our officers, on their entering the U.S. to have them conveyed to this place [Washington] at the public expence.[16]

The first delegation of Native Americans came from the Osage nation, and arrived in Washington in the summer of 1804.[17] The following fall, a second delegation of about twenty-seven "Chiefs from the Missouri and Mississippi"[18] departed from St. Louis for the capital. They arrived there two months later, on December 22, 1805.[19]

Sir Augustus John Foster, Secretary of the British legation, witnessed their entry into the city:

They all rode on miserable little horses with saddles and bridles like our own. The interpreters and Americans who came with them went first, and the Orator went before the rest: he was in a great coat but his left eye was surrounded by a circle of green and white paint and the rest of his face was red. . . . Next followed two, naked to the waist and painted reddish yellow, their hair shaved as far as the crown where it was ornamented with feathers and formed into a tail behind inclosed in silver; they wore blankets about their middles and Mocassins and Pantaloons of Deer's skin. They carried instruments in their hands made of hollow gourds with something to rattle in them, singing or rather bawling all the while as loud as they could. . . . Others of the savages wore quantities of feathers hanging from their hair behind and the rattles of the rattle-snake at the end of some of them. There was one very handsome young man with black hair and on his forehead was a broad streak of light green paint, highly rouged cheeks and green ears. He could not be more than 16 or 17 years old and wore a crest of red feathers on his head.[20]

Jefferson received this delegation at the President's House on New Year's Day, 1806 at the annual open house. Also present were Jefferson's daughter and grandchildren, and the full diplomatic corps, including Foster and the British Minister Anthony Merry. Foster described Jefferson as

much attached to [the Native Americans] from Philanthropy and because they were Savages as if they were his own children, while he paid them infinitely more attention than he ever vouchsafed to shew a foreign Minister, a circumstance which annoyed not a little Mr. Merry.[21]

Merry and Foster left the reception after staying only five minutes because Jefferson "appeared wholly taken up with his natives."[22] Margaret Bayard Smith, a prominent member of the Washington social scene and wife of the founder of the *National Intelligencer*, Samuel Harrison Smith, responded to Foster's account.

On one occasion described by Sir A. Foster in his "Notices of the U.S." he seems to think the President failed in paying due respect to the gentlemen of the diplomatic corps. . . . It really may have been so, and not only the President but the whole assembled company may have participated in this neglect, so lively was the interest and the curiosity excited by the appearance of the Osage-Chiefs and their attendant squaws.[23]

Jefferson officially addressed the delegation on January 4, as "My friends and children, Chiefs of the Osages, Missouris, Kanzas, Ottos, Panis, Ayowas, and Sioux. I take you by the hand of friendship and give you a hearty welcome to the seat of the govmt. of the U.S."[24] In his speech, Jefferson also invited the Native Americans to visit other cities, such as Baltimore, Philadelphia, and New York, and offered to provide carriages for their journey.[25] Late in January, about a dozen Native Americans traveled to Philadelphia. There they visited Charles Willson Peale's Museum, and sometime before February 8, eleven had their silhouettes taken by Peale's physiognotrace.[26]

These silhouettes, which show the Native Americans in European dress, are among the earliest-known representations of many tribes west of the Mississippi. Peale sent his friend Jefferson a set of the silhouettes that included the two interpreters who accompanied the Native Americans.

Even as Peale sent the silhouettes to Jefferson, there was some doubt as to the identity of number ten, as Peale found that he had labeled two profiles with that number.[27] Identifying the subjects today is infinitely more difficult. Many Native Americans had more than one name, and there was no standard orthography for recording Native American words.[28] Although Jefferson's set of silhouettes is not located, eight of the original eleven profiles of the chiefs, and the profiles of the two interpreters, survive in a duplicate set at the Smithsonian Institution.[29]

A . M . L .

SCULPTURE

Jean-Antoine Houdon (1741–1828)

Jefferson identified ten sculptures in his Catalogue of Paintings &c. at Monticello. Seven were terra-cotta patinated busts by the eminent French sculptor Jean-Antoine Houdon; four of these busts were displayed on brackets in the Tea Room.

Houdon, one of the greatest eighteenth-century sculptors, was much admired by Jefferson, who in 1785 urged the Virginia legislature to engage Houdon to portray George Washington. From Paris, Jefferson wrote to the Virginia Delegates that Houdon "is without rivalship the first statuary of this age; as a proof of which he receives orders from every other country for things intended to be capital."[1]

Houdon was born in Versailles in 1741 and is reported to have had an early interest in sculpture. Of his earliest surviving works, a bust of Denis Diderot exhibited in the Salon of 1771 is the best known. By the age of thirty-two, Houdon's ability was sufficiently established for him to sculpt *Catherine the Great* (1773). The number of his commissions rapidly increased in the later part of the decade with works such as *Turgot* (1775), *Molière* (1779), *Voltaire* (1778), *Franklin* (1778), and *Jean-Jacques Rousseau* (1778). Houdon, like Jefferson, was at the peak of his powers in the 1780s as he completed portraits of *John Paul Jones* (1781), *George Washington* (1785), and the *Marquis de Lafayette* (1787), as well as *Thomas Jefferson* (1789).

Houdon's sitters were selected carefully, and he seemed to choose those who would be popular with the public. Boilly's painting *Houdon in His Studio, Working on the Portrait Bust of Laplace* (1803) illustrates the availability of Houdon's work. Once a model was completed, Houdon copied it in plaster, marble, or bronze as clients and their means demanded. When Jefferson returned from France, he brought back plasters of Houdon's portraits of Benjamin Franklin, John Paul Jones, the marquis de Lafayette, George Washington, Turgot, Voltaire, and several of himself. The busts were definitely terra-cotta patinated. "One vial of paint for the busts" was shipped back to the United States with Jefferson's belongings. Later, when he returned to Virginia in 1793, he wrote, "4. bustes de terre cuite, & 3. pieds pour les bustes."[2]

Voltaire, the great French philosopher and writer, died six years before Jefferson arrived in Paris. Jefferson admired his works and included them among a list of books of ancient and modern history, mathematics, astronomy, and religion recommended for the education of his nephew, Peter Carr, in 1787.[3] Jefferson's library included Voltaire's works published by Beaumarchais at Kehl, which he visited. A little more than a year after Jefferson arrived in Paris, he wrote, "I find the general fate of humanity here most deplorable. The truth of Voltaire's observation offers itself perpetually, that every man here must be either the hammer or the anvil."[4]

The last twenty years of Voltaire's life were spent in partial exile at his estate at Ferney, near the Swiss border. In February 1778 he came back to Paris where he sat for Houdon, who took a life mask. Houdon made an array of variations, which were immediately popular, including a seated version and a bust. H. H. Arnason called the bust "one of the most famous if not the most famous portrait sculpture in history."[5] While in Paris, Jefferson saw it in the lobby of the Théâtre Français, now the Odéon.[6]

It is not known which of the known five versions of the bust was acquired by Jefferson; the bust now in Monticello's collection is a modern plaster. No record of the original can be found after Cornelia Randolph's drawing of the plan of Monticello's first floor, made after Jefferson's death, which records its location in the Entrance Hall.

[1945-17]   S.R.S.

89

**VOLTAIRE
(FRANÇOIS MARIE
AROUET DE
VOLTAIRE)
(1694–1778)**

copy after 1778 original

*copy after Jean-Antoine Houdon
(1741–1828)*
plaster
*68.6 × 45.7 × 29.2
(27 × 18 × 11½ in.)*

PROVENANCE:
Although no mention of it is made in either the Boston Athenaeum or Harding Gallery sales, it is presumed that the Voltaire was among the paintings and sculpture sent to the Coolidge family for sale in Boston after Jefferson's death.

A terra-cotta patinated plaster bust of Turgot—economist, intellect, and political figure—was among the portraits by Houdon acquired by Jefferson upon his departure from France. It was displayed in the Entrance Hall. Turgot was a physiocrat, one of a school of political economists who believed that "society should be governed according to an inherent natural order, that the soil is the sole source of wealth and the only proper object of taxation, . . ."[7] Turgot's discharge as controller-general of finances in 1776 by Louis XVI presaged bankruptcy in France.

In a letter to James Madison, Jefferson described Turgot as the head of ". . . the sect called the oeconomists . . ."[8] When Jefferson learned that his son-in-law, Thomas Mann Randolph, Jr., planned to study law, he advised, "There are some excellent books of Theory written by Turgot and the economists of France."[9]

[1945-5]   S.R.S.

90

**TURGOT (ANNE-
ROBERT-JACQUES
TURGOT)
(1727–1781)**

copy after 1775 original

*copy after Jean-Antoine Houdon
(1741–1828)*
plaster
*78.7 × 59.7 × 34.3
(31 × 23½ × 13½ in.)*

PROVENANCE:
The original plaster is unlocated. Presumably it was shipped to Boston for sale with other works of art at the Boston Athenaeum or Harding Gallery sales. The copy in Monticello's collection is modern.

Jefferson placed two busts, a likeness of himself and his political opponent Alexander Hamilton, opposite one another in the Entrance Hall. Both were modeled by the Italian sculptor Giuseppe Ceracchi in Philadelphia in 1793 and 1794. One of Jefferson's grandchildren said:

the eye settled with a deeper interest on busts of Jefferson and Hamilton, by Ceracchi, placed on massive pedestals on each side of the main entrance—"opposed in death as in life," as the surviving original sometimes remarked, with a pensive smile, as he observed the notice they attracted.[10]

Visitors to Monticello found the juxtaposition particularly amusing because the colossal-size Jefferson bust on its green marble pedestal decorated with the signs of the zodiac and the twelve tribes of Israel was larger than the life-size Hamilton. Although both works were identified by Cornelia Jefferson Randolph on her undated plan of the first floor, neither was mentioned by Jefferson in his Catalogue of Paintings.

Jefferson first came into contact with Ceracchi during his visit to the United States in 1791–92. Ceracchi proposed a monument to the American Revolution and appealed to Congress to finance the project. Jefferson favored the idea and tried to advance the project with the Federal District Commissioners, but it was turned down in Congress on May 7, 1792. When Ceracchi attempted to raise private funds for the memorial, Jefferson endorsed him to Robert Livingston, calling him "a very celebrated sculptor of Rome."[11]
[1923-12]   S.R.S.

On July 3, 1789, just before the storming of the Bastille and two months before he returned to America, Jefferson purchased a number of busts from Houdon. Among these was a terra-cotta patinated plaster of Jefferson's trusted friend, the marquis de Lafayette.

Lafayette sat for Houdon in 1786, who had been commissioned by the State of Virginia to make two marble busts of one of the noblest heroes of the American Revolution. One of the busts was to be placed in the Virginia State Capitol, near Houdon's full-length portrait of Washington, and the second was installed at the Hôtel de Ville in Paris on September 18, 1786. Although the marble bust of Lafayette remains in the Virginia State Capitol, the bust at the Hôtel de Ville was destroyed in 1792 along with three other portraits by Houdon.[12] Jefferson's plaster shows Lafayette in uniform, while the Richmond marble has a drapery on top of a uniform.

At Monticello, Jefferson owned at least three portraits of Lafayette—the half-length portrait by Joseph Boze (1790), a full-length engraving, and the bust by Houdon, which was installed in the Tea Room in Jefferson's "gallery of worthies." After Jefferson's death, the bust was transported to Boston where it was sold to the Boston Athenaeum for $100 in 1828. In 1830, Joseph Coolidge reported to his brother-in-law, Thomas Jefferson Randolph, "Franklin's portrait, you knew, was sold; and the bust of Lafayette also, and the money appropriated to Mother a year or two since."[13]

                                                                S.R.S.

91

ALEXANDER HAMILTON (1757–1804)

1794

after Giuseppe Ceracchi (1741–1801)
marble
61×33×24.1 (24×13×9½ in.)

PROVENANCE:
Thomas Jefferson; by purchase to James Barclay; by purchase to Uriah P. Levy; by descent to Jefferson Monroe Levy; by purchase to TJMF in 1923.

92

MARQUIS DE LAFAYETTE (1757–1834)

1789

Jean-Antoine Houdon (1741–1828)
plaster
74.7×51×50.2
(29⅜×20 1/16×19¾ in.)
The Boston Athenaeum

PROVENANCE:
Thomas Jefferson; by purchase to the Boston Athenaeum in 1828.

Jefferson exhibited not one, but two portrait busts of George Washington at Monticello, a terra-cotta patinated plaster that he obtained in 1789 and a marble copy that was a later gift. In a letter to the sculptor Pietro Cardelli, he said that the plasters "are of a brick dust color."[14] The plaster version was displayed in Jefferson's "most honourable suite" in the Tea Room at Monticello. A family member said:

Washington's (by Houdon) wore a wreath of Immortelles [dried flowers]. Some admirer in France sent these to Mr. Jefferson's family, to crown his bust on his birthday. He ordered them, instead, to be wreathed around the brow of Washington.[15]

Jefferson was responsible for persuading the Virginia Assembly to commission Houdon to portray General Washington, a native Virginian. Jefferson told Governor Benjamin Harrison that "There could be no question raised as to the sculptor who should be employed, the reputation of Mons. Houdon, of this city, being unrivaled in Europe."[16] The initial plan, devised in Virginia, called for Houdon to model the likeness after a full-length portrait by Charles Willson Peale that was shipped to Jefferson. Recognizing how much better a life portrait would be, Jefferson prevailed upon the Virginians to finance Houdon's trip to America. Houdon arrived at Mount Vernon on October 2, 1785 and stayed until October 19, returning to France on December 25, 1785.[17] The bust was shipped separately and arrived in Paris in May 1786.

Houdon made many versions of Washington's bust in marble and plaster. Jefferson's plaster, acquired in 1789, was undraped, *à l'antique*.

S.R.S.

Jefferson served with Franklin, the senior statesman of the Continental Congress, in Philadelphia in 1775, calling him "the greatest man and ornament of the age and country in which he lived."[18] He was a printer, author, inventor, statesman, scientist, and diplomat, and these accomplishments could not have failed to impress Jefferson.

Franklin's popularity in France increased French support for American independence. His image was well known and appeared in engravings and even in jewelry. Later, when Jefferson succeeded Franklin as minister to France in 1784, he said:

The succession to Doctor Franklin, at the court of France, was an excellent school of humility. On being presented to any one as the minister of America, the commonplace question used in such cases was "c'est vous, Monsieur, que remplace le Docteur Franklin"? "It is you, sir, who replace Doctor Franklin"? I generally answered, "no one can replace him, sir; I am only his successor."[19]

This portrait of Franklin is one of two completed by Houdon. Franklin first sat for Houdon in 1778 and again in 1782, or later.[20] In the earlier portrait Franklin is clothed in simple Quaker dress; in the later work Franklin is classically draped. The earlier bust, whose size and treatment matches the other Houdon busts acquired by Jefferson, is probably the one that Jefferson selected for Monticello.

S.R.S.

John Paul Jones, the naval commander of the Revolutionary War, was born John Paul in Scotland.[21] He began a naval career at twelve; "Jones" was appended to John Paul sometime later.

At the beginning of the Revolution, Jones was jobless, but he received a commission in December 1775. After considerable success Jones was given command of a French ship, which he renamed the *Bonhomme Richard* (Poor Richard) to honor Franklin, who was then America's minister to France. Sailing under American colors, Jones went to sea in August 1779 with a small squadron. The *Bonhomme Richard* took on the much larger British vessel *Serapis* in a bitter sea fight. Jones's ship was sunk, but only after the *Serapis* was surrendered. The battle made Jones a naval hero.

The Freemason Lodge of the Nine Sisters commissioned Houdon to complete Jones's portrait upon his triumphant return to Paris in 1779. A terra-cotta patinated plaster was not shown until the Salon of 1781; the date of the sitting is not known.[22] Jones presented Jefferson with a plaster in February 1786 and wrote to thank him for his letter (unlocated):

I have received the kind Note you wrote me this morning, on the occasion of receiving my Bust. I offered it to you as a mark of my esteem and respect, for your virtues and talents. It has been marked by professed judges, that it does no discredit to the talents of Mr. Houdon; but it receives its value from your acceptance of it.[23]

In 1788, Jones ordered at least eight plasters from Houdon to present to American friends. He wrote Jefferson:

Some of my Friends in America did me the honor to ask for my Bust. I inclose the Names of eight Gentlemen, to each of whom I promis'd to send one. You will oblige me much, by desiring Mr. Houdon to have them prepared and pack'd up two and two . . .[24]

William Short was instructed by Jefferson to send busts to General St. Clair and Mr. Ross of Philadelphia; John Jay, General Irvine, Secretary Charles Thomson, and Colonel Wadsworth of New York; and James Madison and Colonel Carrington of Virginia.[25] Of these eight busts, only two can now be located—Jefferson's and General Irvine's, now in the collection of the Pennsylvania Academy of Fine Arts in Philadelphia.

Jefferson placed Jones's bust in the Tea Room, and later recommended it to John Sherburne as the basis for an engraving. Jefferson disliked the Jones engraving that Sherburne had sent him in 1825 and wrote that "it does not recall one single feature of his face to my perfect recollection of him. Houdon's bust of him is . . . an excellent likeness."[26]

After Jefferson's death the Jones bust was shipped to Boston. It was accepted as a deposit at the Boston Athenaeum from Joseph Coolidge, Jr. on March 11, 1828, together with Jefferson's busts of Franklin and Washington. Coolidge said that he would "be very glad to add to the valuable collections of busts [at] the Boston Athenaeum."[27] No record of it appears on the Athenaeum records after 1867, and it is thought to be the plaster in the Museum of Fine Arts, Boston, which was the gift of Charles H. Taylor in 1931. The bust was once among the effects of Moses Kimball, proprietor of the Boston Museum theater that often borrowed sculpture in the 1860s and 1870s for stage sets.[28]

S.R.S

96

JAMES MADISON
(1751–1836)

1819

Pietro Cardelli (d. 1822)
plaster
48.9 × 25.4 × 24.1
(19¼ × 10 × 9½ in.)
Virginia Historical Society

PROVENANCE:
A bust of Madison, now unlocated, was purchased by Edward Coles, an Albemarle County neighbor, for $10 at the Dispersal Sale in 1827. It may have been either the Cardelli bust or the smaller-than-life-size bust by William Coffee, which Jefferson also owned.

In October 1820 Jefferson wrote the sculptor Pietro Cardelli to tell him that he wanted to purchase two portraits. Although he already owned Robert Edge Pine's portrait of his respected ally James Madison, whom he said had at his command "the rich resources of his luminous and discriminating mind, & of his extensive information," he wanted a second likeness.[29]

I understand you have taken the busts in plaister of the President of the US. and of Mr. Madison of the size of the life and have to request the favor of you to send me a copy of each. As they are to stand en suite of those of Genl. Washington and Dr. Franklin which perhaps you may have noted in our tea-room and these are of a brick dust color, I should be glad that those you send me should be of the same color.[30]

More than a year passed and Jefferson was still without the busts of Madison and Monroe. Cardelli, who had worked as a sculptor on the United States Capitol, had since departed for New Orleans. Jefferson turned to his granddaughter Ellen Randolph to help him locate the busts while she visited Washington. In December 1821 she wrote:

After a great many inquiries I have at length discovered two copies of Cardelli's busts of Mr. Madison and Mr. Monroe which I think I shall be able to obtain for you; as the lady in whose possession they are, seems not averse to the idea of parting with them. Upon a second examination I am by no means so well pleased with these busts, as when I saw them at Montpellier; I think now that they are both caricature likenesses, but if you wish it I can obtain them for you, I believe for ten dollars each.[31]

In January Jefferson told his granddaughter that he would be happy to have them.[32] About one month later he sent fifty dollars to her "to pay for the busts of Misters Madison and Monroe, and for their package, the balance for yourself for your commission on the transaction."[33]

When at last Ellen Randolph sent the busts to her grandfather, she also sent along an engraving of Monroe copied after John Vanderlyn's portrait (Cat. 40), and reported:

The busts are second hand, and one of them somewhat soiled, but none others could be had. . . . These copies have become very scarce, and are to be found only in private families, and Cardelli himself is believed to have left the country.[34]

Once they arrived, Jefferson may have put them in his Cabinet for he later told John Adams that he intended to display his bust there together with his predecessors and successors. Jefferson did not find Cardelli's likenesses meritorious. He wrote, "The only merit of Cardelli's busts of Madison and Monroe is a strikingly faithful resemblance. The [drawing] of the busts is against all rules of nature and art . . ."[35]

S.R.S.

It is not known how or when Jefferson acquired this portrait of Napoleon, although he must have owned it before 1815 when he identified it as "65. Bonaparte a bust in Marble" in his undated Catalogue of Paintings, which was completed between 1809 and 1815. The bust of Napoleon probably came into his possession late in his presidency to commemorate the Louisiana Purchase.

Although Jefferson later considered Bonaparte "a cold-blooded, calculating, unprincipled usurper, without a virtue,"[36] he told Lafayette in 1807, "Your emperor has done more splendid things, but he has never done one which will give happiness to so great a number of human beings as the ceding of Louisiana to the United States."[37]

No matter what Jefferson may have thought of Bonaparte, his family prized the marble bust. It was sent to Boston for sale with other works of art, but "Ellen aware that they would be sacrificed kept back the . . . Bonaparte."[38] It appears to be a copy after Chaudet's portrait, which was widely copied by various artists in Carrara marble. The identity of the copyist is unknown.

[1953-5]

S.R.S.

97

**NAPOLEON
BONAPARTE
(1769–1821)**

after 1807

*copy after Antoine-Denis
Chaudet (1763–1810)
marble*
*62.2 × 33 × 25.4
(24½ × 13 × 10 in.)*

PROVENANCE:
Thomas Jefferson; by descent to
Ellen and Joseph Coolidge; by
descent to Robert, Lawrence, and
Nathaniel Coolidge; by gift to
TJMF in 1953 in memory of their
father Lawrence Coolidge.

James Ronaldson, an old friend of Jefferson's who visited Monticello in the 1790s, was a Philadelphian and admirer of General Jackson. Ronaldson presented a plaster cast of Jackson's portrait by the Philadelphia sculptor William Rush to Jefferson in 1820.[39] Ronaldson wrote Jefferson:

With sentiments of respect & esteem, I beg you to accept a bust of Genl. Andrew Jackson, the hero of New Orleans, a citizen whose devotion to his country has proved worthy of her highest confidence. It is the chef d'Oeuvre of Rush, and an evidence of this nation being destined to not less celebrity in arts than in arms . . .[40]

Jefferson shared Ronaldson's admiration for General Jackson. He responded:

I thank you, dear Sir, for the present of the bust of Genl. Jackson. He holds a high place in my esteem, as an undeviating patriot and a military character who has deserved well of his country. I shall give his bust a place in my most honourable suite, with those of Washington, Franklin, Fayette &c. Its' value is moreover heightened as from the hand of an artist of whom our country has a high and just admiration.[41]

Little is known about which—if any—of William Rush's works were known to Jefferson, or how Jefferson knew of his work. A bust of George Washington by Rush in the collection of the Art Museum at Princeton University has a history of belonging to Jefferson's collection. Although Rush's earliest portrait bust (of Franklin) is dated 1787, Rush's portraits of sitters such as Samuel Morris (1812), and Benjamin Rush (1812), and Caspar Wistar (1812–13) were not made until after Jefferson retired from the presidency. At Monticello, Jefferson had no access to new works of art.

Jackson apparently sat for Rush during a four-day visit to Philadelphia in February 1819.[42] Jackson, a major hero of the War of 1812, defended New Orleans against the British in 1815 and had captured two Spanish forts in Florida. At the time that Rush portrayed Jackson, he was a popular champion with obvious political potential. To capture the interest in Jackson, Rush's portrait of him was advertised in places as distant as Charles Town, West Virginia.

It is the intention of Mr. Rush, if the public patronage should be adequate, to furnish any number of casts, at a reasonable price; and we cannot but hope, that patriotism and a love of the arts combined, will insure him success in the undertaking.[43]

Other plasters, all now unlocated, were in the collections of the Boston Athenaeum, the State Library of South Carolina, Peale's Museum, and the American Academy of Fine Arts. Only two plasters are known today, the illustrated example in the Art Institute of Chicago and the one in the exhibition owned by Historic Hudson Valley from the collection of Montgomery Place.

S.R.S

227

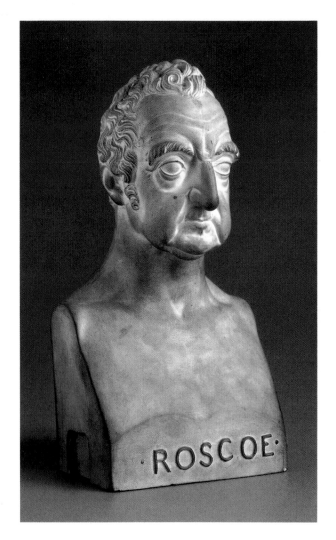

99

WILLIAM ROSCOE
(1753–1831)

c. 1820

copy after William Spence
(1793–1849)
porcelain
26.7 × 14 × 8.9
(10½ × 5½ × 3½ in.)

PROVENANCE:
James Maury; by gift to Thomas
Jefferson; by purchase at the
Dispersal Sale in 1827 to Dr.
Charles Austin; by descent to Mrs.
Douglas Harnish; by purchase to
TJMF in 1963.

The small porcelain bust of the historian and Liverpool resident William Roscoe was given to Jefferson in 1820 by his old friend and classmate James Maury, who was serving his country in Liverpool. He recalled that years before Jefferson had written Roscoe under Maury's care as United States consul.

In passing a Porcelain Warehouse the other day, I was so struck with a correct likeness of Wm. Roscoe in a small Bust that I thought it would be pleasing to you to have the opportunity of giving it a place in your collection at Monticello . . .[44]

The bust that Maury sent was produced by the Liverpool firm of Franceys. In 1813 the young William Spence exhibited a bust of Roscoe at the Liverpool Academy that won him wide recognition and evidently served as the model for the version produced for commercial sale by Franceys.[45]

Once Jefferson learned that Maury planned to send the bust, he wrote Roscoe that he would receive it "with great pleasure and thankfulness, and shall arrange it in honorable file with those of some cherished characters."[46]

Roscoe and Jefferson exchanged several letters between 1805 and 1820. Roscoe first contacted Jefferson in 1805 when he sent him a copy of *The Life and Pontificate of Leo X* (1805), which Jefferson said would "stand worthily on the shelf with the Life of Lorenzo de Medici [by Roscoe] and both will contribute to mark honorably the age we live in."[47] Roscoe was not only a historian but also a banker and botanist who wrote *A Catalogue of Plants in the Botanic Garden, at Liverpool* (1808), which he also sent to Jefferson.

[1963-17]   S.R.S.

100

**JOHN ADAMS
(1735–1826)**

---

copy after 1818 original

*copy after J. B. Binon
(1775–1875?)
plaster
63.5×50.8×35.6
(25×20×14 in.)*

Adams's portrait for Faneuil Hall in Boston was financed by 215 public subscribers, each of whom contributed two dollars so as to transmit "to our Children the Features of the Man, whose patriotic energies were so strenuously exerted for the Independence of our common Country."[48] Adams described Binon as

a French artist from Lyons who has studied Eight Years in Italy has lately taken my Bust. He appears to be an Artist and a Man of Letters. I let them do what they please with my old head.[49]

Binon studied with the sculptor Joseph Chinard (1756–1813) in France and was the American sculptor Horatio Greenough's first teacher. Binon sculpted a marble bust for Faneuil Hall and hoped to sell plaster versions for profit, although Adams thought it "so hopeless a speculation."[50] Binon made at least six plasters, including those given to Adams, his son John Quincy Adams, the Boston Athenaeum, and Jefferson.

Jefferson was presented with a plaster as a gift from Benjamin Gould, who wrote him:

I have sent by the schooner Virginia, Capt. Otis, a Box containing a plaister Bust of Mr. Adams, which I beg you will do me the honor to accept. It is taken from the marble bust of Binon . . . The likeness is considered most striking. No one can hesitate an instant in recognizing it, who has seen the original within ten years.[51]

The bust (now unlocated) was received at Monticello in August 1825. Jefferson thanked Gould and reported:

Without knowing exactly the precise period at which it was taken I think it a good likeness of what he was a little after he had passed the middle age of life. It received a little injury by fracture but the parts are preserved, and being behind can be repaired without disfiguring it. I place it with pleasure in the line in my cabinet of his predecessor and successors . . .[52]

[1959-64]   S.R.S.

101

**THOMAS
JEFFERSON
(1743–1826)**

1789

*Jean-Antoine Houdon
(1741–1828)
terra-cotta patinated plaster
H: 73 (including white marble
socle) (28¾ in.)
Mr. and Mrs. E. G. Nicholson*

PROVENANCE:
Jean-Antoine Houdon; by purchase
by Comte Peres at the auction of
Houdon's studio on December 15–
17, 1828; by descent to Comte
Franceschini d'Accianelli; by
purchase to J.L. Souffrice, Paris
art dealer, to Roy Chalk in 1962;
by purchase at Christie's to Mr.
and Mrs. E.G. Nicholson in 1987.

Houdon's portrait of Jefferson is one of the best known and admired of all of the likenesses of Thomas Jefferson. It served as the model for John Reich's Indian Peace Medal (1801) and the nickel (1943). It is a superb likeness—sensitive, intellectual, aristocratic, and idealistic. Jefferson apparently thought well of it because he acquired at least one for himself. He apparently took it with him when he returned to America.

Several months before he departed from Paris in 1789, Jefferson sat for a portrait by Jean-Antoine Houdon, whom he thought to be the finest sculptor of the age. He had known Houdon for four years since he had personally made the arrangements with Houdon for his trip to America to portray George Washington (1785). The precise date of Jefferson's sitting is not documented, but it definitely occurred before the end of August as the bust was exhibited in the Salon of 1789. It was identified in the *Livret* of the Salon as "No. 241. buste platre of M. Sefferson [sic], Envoye des Etats de Virginie."[53]

To create a "gallery of worthies" at Monticello, Jefferson acquired ten or twelve terra-cotta patinated plasters by Houdon before he left Paris: the marquis de Lafayette, John Paul Jones, Benjamin Franklin, George Washington, Turgot, Voltaire, and several of himself. On July 3, 1789, he "Gave Houdon order on Mr. Grand for 1000 livres for busts made for me."[54] Jefferson may have presented several likenesses to friends before leaving France.

Houdon always worked from life. He first modeled his sitter in terra-cotta, a soft, unfired clay.[55] A more durable plaster cast was made from this terra-cotta model; Houdon could then create a marble or more plasters. High-quality atelier or studio plasters were usually made after the marble was completed. These were made on demand with varying degrees of finishing by hand. A painting of Houdon's studio by Louis-Léopold Boilly (1761–1845) illustrates that many different works were available for sale, including busts of Franklin and Jefferson.[56]

Houdon's portrait of Jefferson in marble is now in the Museum of Fine Arts, Boston. Five early plasters, of three different dates, survive. The earliest and finest—now belonging to Mr. and Mrs. E. G. Nicholson—bears its original terra-cotta patination as well as the official red-wax seal of the Académie Royale de Peinture et Sculpture. Examples in the collections of the American Philosophical Society (acquired in 1811) and the New-York Historical Society apparently were made next. Although lacking the clarity of the plaster exhibited at the Salon of 1789, they more closely resemble it than the marble, which was made next. Plasters attributed to Houdon in a private collection and at the University of Virginia seem to have been made after the marble, which they more closely resemble. A sixth plaster is in the Musée de Blérancourt, but it has not been examined for dating.

Jefferson's portrait by Houdon probably was placed in his Cabinet in his gallery of presidents. It is unlocated.

S.R.S.

102

ALEXANDER I
(1777–1825)

copy 1955; original c. 1803

*Fedot Shubin (1740–1805), copy
by Alexander T. Savinsky*
plaster
83.8 × 48.3 × 31.8
(33 × 19 × 12½ in.)

Jefferson received a plaster copy of a bust of Tsar Alexander I as a gift from the American consul general at St. Petersburg, Levett Harris, in 1804. Harris, like Jefferson, held a high opinion of the monarch, whose "greatness and goodness which he so remarkably unites."[57] The bust was transported from Washington to Monticello in March 1806. Jefferson wrote Harris to thank him in April.

It will constitute one of the most valued ornaments of the retreat I am preparing for myself at my native home. I had laid it down as a law for my conduct while in office, and hitherto scrupulously observed, to accept of no present beyond a book, a pamphlet, or other curiosity of minor value; as well as to award imputation on my motives of action, as to shut out a practice susceptible of such abuse. But my particular esteem for the character of the Emperor, places his image in my mind above the scope of the law. I receive it, therefore, and shall cherish it with affection. It nourishes the contemplation of all the good placed in his power, and his disposition to do it.[58]

Jefferson's instructions in 1806 were to place the bust of Alexander in the then-unfinished Cabinet. Later, to dramatize the contrast between evil and virtue, the bust of Alexander was installed opposite Napoleon's likeness, flanking the Parlor doors to the West Portico. Jefferson identified it in his Catalogue of Paintings as "Alexander of Russia. A bust in plaister."

Jefferson began to correspond with Alexander I in 1804, three years after his accession to the throne. He believed that Alexander was a person of noble character with Enlightenment values, and wrote laudatory comments about him to many people, including Joseph Priestley.

The apparation of such a man on a throne is one of the phaenomena which will distinguish the present epoch so remarkable in the history of man. But he will have a herculean task to devise and establish the means of securing freedom and happiness to those who are not capable of taking care of themselves. Some preparation seems necessary to qualify the body of a nation for self government. . . . Alexander will doubtless begin at the right end, by taking means for diffusing instruction and a sense of their natural rights through the mass of his people, and for relieving them in the meantime from actual oppression.[59]

Although Jefferson was full of optimism for what Alexander might accomplish, his reign was far from the success that Jefferson envisioned.

The original portrait by Shubin is in the collection of the Voronezh Museum of Plastic Arts in Voronezh, Russia. Jefferson's plaster is unlocated; the present copy was made in 1955 by Alexander Terentevich Savinsky.

[1955-18]   S.R.S.

William John Coffee (c. 1774–c. 1846)

Jefferson described William Coffee as "an English gentleman of eminence in the arts of sculpture and painting."[60]

He has been for sometime an intimate with us at Monticello, having been engaged in making the busts in plaister of myself and all the grown members of our family. He has done the same at Mr. Madison's and some other families of our neighborhood and much in Richmond.[61]

Coffee sculpted the busts of Jefferson and his family between 1818 and 1820, and was intermittently hired for various tasks until Jefferson's death in 1826.

Coffee first arrived in the United States about 1817 from his native England. There he had worked in several porcelain factories, and eventually owned his own company, where he produced china, terra-cotta ornaments, and figurines. He was also a painter, and exhibited at the Royal Academy of Arts in London in 1808, 1811, and 1816.[62]

He must have made contact with Jefferson shortly after his arrival in the United States. His first visit to Monticello took place before March 4, 1818, when he wrote Jefferson thanking him for his hospitality. Coffee added that he would again be visiting Jefferson for two or three days.[63] He arrived at Monticello on April 5, 1818, and within the course of a week he completed busts of Jefferson, his daughter Martha, and granddaughter Ellen, for which Jefferson paid him $105.[64] At the same time, Jefferson ordered a copy of James Madison's bust, which Coffee had yet to sculpt, and twelve copies of his daughter's bust, apparently one for himself and each of her eleven children.[65]

Possibly at this same time, or on a later visit, Coffee executed busts of "Mr. Randolph,"[66] and Jefferson's granddaughters Cornelia Randolph, and Anne Cary Randolph Bankhead.[67] Coffee also branched out to other area families, such as the Coleses of Enniscorthy.[68] Jefferson wrote a letter of introduction for Coffee to Madison:

Mr. Coffee . . . is a Sculptor lately from England, and really able in his art. He makes busts in plaister or terra cotta he came from Richmond to take you[r] bust and mine and gives less trouble than any artist painter or sculptor I have ever submitted myself to . . .[69]

By July 1818, Coffee had sculpted busts of Madison, his wife Dolley, and her son John Payne Todd.[70]

Jefferson employed Coffee to provide classical architectural frieze ornaments in lead and composition for the University of Virginia and his Bedford County retreat, Poplar Forest.[71] Coffee was also engaged to "repair" Jefferson's painting collection at Monticello.[72] In the opinion of Jefferson's granddaughter Ellen Randolph Coolidge, Coffee's work was "ruthless," and one of several reasons why Jefferson's paintings were in such poor condition at the time of his death. "[Coffee's] brush has been traced on several of them where after scratching off the old paint he has daubed on new."[73] Coffee, who resided in New York, also assisted Jefferson with commissions in that state, such as procuring Roman cement for the cisterns at Monticello, and engaging the New York engraver Peter Maverick to execute plans of the University of Virginia (Cat. 64).[74]

A.M.L.

Cornelia Jefferson Randolph was the fifth child of Martha Jefferson Randolph and Thomas Mann Randolph. Jefferson wrote to Cornelia before she could even pen a reply and sent her poems for her scrapbook, such as the "Grasshopper's Ball," that he cut from newspapers and magazines.[75] She accompanied her grandfather on his trips to Poplar Forest. In 1817 Jefferson wrote to Martha from his retreat and described Cornelia and her sister Ellen as "the severest students I have ever met with. They never leave their room but to come out to meals. About twilight of the evening, we sally out with the owls and bats, and take our evening exercise on the terras."[76]

During their stay at Poplar Forest Jefferson took Ellen and Cornelia to visit nearby Natural Bridge (Cat. 59). In two letters to her sister Virginia, Cornelia vividly described their eventful trip. She shared her grandfather's affection for the bridge, writing that "the scene was beyond anything you can imagine possibly."[77]

Cornelia, who never married, was an amateur artist. She operated a ladies school at Edgehill with her sister Mary in the 1830s and 40s, where she taught drawing, painting, and sculpture.[78]

[1985-28]   A.M.L.

103

CORNELIA JEFFERSON RANDOLPH (1799–1871)

c. 1819

William Coffee (c. 1774–c. 1846)
terra-cotta
34 × 20.5 × 9
(13½ × 8¼ × 3½ in.)
Mrs. James C. Moyer and a
private collection, in memory of
Margaret Randolph Taylor and
Olivia Alexander Taylor

PROVENANCE:
Thomas Jefferson; by descent to Thomas Jefferson Randolph; by descent to a private collection and Mrs. James C. Moyer; by loan to TJMF since 1985.

Anne Cary Randolph, daughter of Martha and Thomas Mann Randolph, was Jefferson's first grandchild and chief gardening correspondent when he was absent from Monticello. "How stands the fruit with you in the neighborhood and at Monticello," Jefferson wrote twelve-year-old Anne from Washington,

and particularly the peas, as they are what will be in season when I come home. The figs also, have they been hurt? You must mount Midas and ride over to Monticello to inform yourself or collect the information from good authority and let me have it by next post.[79]

Anne tended Monticello's flower garden as well, and Jefferson sent one of two extant drawings of the flower beds there to his granddaughter, on the back of a letter describing his plans.[80]

From yourself I may soon expect a report of your first visit to Monticello, and the state of our joint concerns there. I find that the limited number of our flower beds will too much restrain the variety of flowers in which we might wish to indulge, and therefore I have resumed an idea . . . of a winding walk surrounding the lawn before the house, with a narrow border of flowers on each side.[81]

During the winter of 1805–06, when Anne was fifteen, she lived in the President's House with her grandfather, along with her mother and five brothers and sisters. Just a year before Jefferson's retirement from the presidency, Anne married Charles Lewis Bankhead, a twenty-year-old law student. Their first home was at Carlton, on the western slope of Monticello.[82] Anne and Charles's marriage was a troubled one, marred by his alcoholism

104

ANNE CARY RANDOLPH BANKHEAD (1791–1826)

c. 1818–20

William Coffee (c. 1774–c. 1846)
terra-cotta
31.75 × 20.32 × 10.16
(12½ × 8 × 4 in.)

PROVENANCE:
Thomas Jefferson; by descent to Thomas Jefferson Randolph; by descent to Mrs. Pattie Cary Kean Morris; by gift to TJMF in 1927.

and violence. After one particularly serious episode at Monticello, Jefferson wrote to Bankhead's father hoping to convince him that his son's recovery could only be effected by his moving home, where his sobriety could be constantly enforced.[83]

Unfortunately, Charles's behavior toward Anne and their children continued to distress the family greatly.[84] Following a bloody street fight between Bankhead and his brother-in-law Thomas Jefferson Randolph in 1819, Jefferson wrote that Bankhead deserved to be in a penitentiary. Anne was so attached to her husband that she could not be persuaded to leave him to live at Monticello.[85] She died in February 1826, at the age of thirty-five, two weeks after the birth of her fourth child. Jefferson, who was present at Anne's death, "abandoned himself to every evidence of intense grief."[83]

[1927-1]   A.M.L.

Statuettes made of biscuit for the decoration of tables were much favored in the eighteenth century. The milky surface of unglazed soft paste porcelain lent itself well to fine modeling. The figures, which were mass produced in molds, ranged from mythological subjects—the most popular—to the seasons, portraits, playful children's games, and contemporary events. The renowned Sèvres porcelain factory, the Manufacture Royale de Porcelaine de France, made some of the best examples.

Jefferson acquired at least ten biscuit statuettes. Four—Minerva, Diana, Apollo, and Mars—were purchased for Abigail Adams from Bazin, a Paris merchant who sold tablewares, in late September 1785. Jefferson purchased more than six for himself, including a Hercules purchased from Bazin in 1784, which might have been the Farnese Hercules produced at Sèvres.[87] Only *Venus with Cupid* and *Hope with Cupid* are known today.[88] *Hope with Cupid* was signed by Jossé-François-Joseph Le Riche, who had been one of two principal assistants to the director Etienne-Maurice Falconet at Sèvres and later became *chef de sculpteurs* there. After Falconet left Sèvres in 1766, his assistants, including Le Riche, carried on similar work, but in a more stylized manner.

At Monticello, the figures may have been used in the Parlor or in the Dining Room as table decorations.

[1938-13-2; 1938-13-1]   S.R.S.

105

VENUS WITH CUPID

c. 1785

biscuit
30.5 × 19.7 × 13.3
(12 × 7¾ × 5¼ in.)

106

HOPE WITH CUPID

c. 1785

Jossé-François-Joseph Le Riche
(1741–1812)
biscuit
31.8 × 19.1 × 14
(12½ × 7½ × 5½ in.)

PROVENANCE:
Thomas Jefferson; by gift to Martha Jefferson Carr; by descent to Hetty Cary Harrison; by gift to TJMF in 1938.

ARIADNE

*unknown copyist after an
ancient work*
marble
*68.5 × 95.3 × 34.3
(27 × 37½ × 13½ in.)*
T. Jefferson Coolidge, Jr.

PROVENANCE:
Thomas Jefferson; by descent to
Ellen and Joseph Coolidge; by
descent to T. Jefferson Coolidge,
Jr.; by loan to TJMF since 1928.

James Bowdoin III of Maine was appointed American minister to Spain by President Jefferson in 1804. An admirer of Jefferson, Bowdoin had secured the services of Gilbert Stuart to paint a portrait of Jefferson for him in March 1805. Bowdoin visited Paris where he saw an ancient sculpture of *Ariadne*, one of many Italian works of art confiscated by Napoleon that were exhibited at the Louvre. He wrote Jefferson:

Accident having thrown in my way a handsome piece of modern Sculpture, a Cleopatra copied and reduced from the ancient one now at Paris, which for many years lay at the Palace of Belvidere at Rome, as I think it for the fineness of its marble and the neatness of its workmanship and finishing, among the best of the modern pieces of Sculpture. . . . I was told it was purchased of a french commissary in Italy, who wanted money, and that it had been taken from the apartments in the vatican.[89]

Jefferson replied, "It shall be deposited [at Monticello] with the memorials of those worthies whose remembrance I feel a pride and comfort in consecrating there."[90] *Ariadne* arrived at Monticello in 1805, but for ten years or so Jefferson thought, as Bowdoin did, that she was Cleopatra. Jefferson initially described the reclining sculpture as "A Cleopatra in marble" in the Catalogue of Paintings. It wasn't until he turned to the appropriate page and illustration in his own copy of Augustine Legrand's *Galeries des Antiques* (1803), which he acquired in December 1804, that he changed his mind and revised his description in the Catalogue, translating Legrand's comments into English. Jefferson also noted that the sculpture was placed in the Belvedere Gallery at the Vatican by Julius II, where it remained for three centuries.

After Jefferson's death *Ariadne* was shipped to Boston for sale there, but Ellen Coolidge decided to hold on to it. She wrote her mother, "I kept back the Ariadne, Bonaparte . . . because I thought it a pity to sacrifice them as the others were sacrificed."[91]

[1928-4]   S.R.S.

108

**NORBORNE
BERKELEY, BARON
DE BOTETOURT
(c. 1718–1770)**

c. 1770–73

Isaac Gossett (1713–1799)
wax
Field: 11.4 × 8.6 (4½ × 3⅜ in.)
Image: 7.6 × 3.8 (3 × 1½ in.)
Carter Family, Shirley
Plantation

Jefferson was a twenty-five-year-old lawyer living in Williamsburg when the royal governor Botetourt arrived in that city in October 1768. During Botetourt's short but popular tenure, Jefferson was first elected to the Virginia House of Burgesses, and commissioned as a Lieutenant of the Albemarle County militia. Years later, Jefferson recalled to Daniel Webster that Botetourt was "an honourable man" of great respectability and integrity.[1] Jefferson was attending the general court in Williamsburg when Botetourt died on October 15, 1770, and likely attended the funeral services in Bruton Parish Church and at the chapel of the College of William and Mary, where the Governor was interred.[2]

Shortly after Botetourt's death the Virginia General Assembly voted to erect a statue of him in Williamsburg. Botetourt's nephew in England lent the statue's sculptor a small wax profile of his uncle by the English artist Isaac Gossett to use as a model. The profile caught the eye of a merchant involved with the statue commission, and he sent four copies of the memento to his customers in Virginia. Soon the medallions were in high demand, and Jefferson no doubt purchased his in Williamsburg about 1773. Jefferson displayed Lord Botetourt's "medallion in wax" in the Tea Room at Monticello; its location today is unknown.[3]

A.M.L.

109

**THOMAS
JEFFERSON
COMMEMORATIVE
MEDAL**

1802

John Reich (1768–1833)
solid silver
D: 4.5 (1¾ in.)
American Numismatic Society

Jefferson's presidential medal was among the first commemorative works to be struck at the United States mint and probably the first medal executed here by the recent German émigré engraver John Reich.[4] The medal's obverse is based on Jean-Antoine Houdon's 1789 bust of Jefferson (Cat. 101), and the reverse celebrates twenty-five years of American independence and the documents that secured it, the Declaration of Independence and the Constitution.

The medals were available to the public in February 1802, and Jefferson sent one each to his daughters Maria and Martha, and his sister-in-law Elizabeth Eppes. His letter to Martha best describes his opinion of Reich's work: "I inclose you a medal executed by an artist lately from Europe and who appears to be equal to any in the world."[5] Martha thought the medal was a good likeness, but "as I found fault with Houdon for making you too old I shall have the same quarrel with the medal also. You have many years to live before the likeness can be a perfect one."[6] Maria's letter of thanks to her father reveals the medal's importance to the family from which Jefferson was often absent: "I received your last with the medals which I think very much like you. Mine will be very precious to me dear Papa during the long separations from you to which I am doomed . . ."[7] None of the medals owned by Jefferson's family are known to survive.

A.M.L.

110

EDWARD PREBLE
(1761–1807)

1806

John Reich (1768–1833)
copper-bronzed medal
D: 6.4 (2½ in.)

PROVENANCE:
Thomas Jefferson; by purchase to
John Hartwell Cocke at the
Dispersal Sale in 1827; by descent
to Mrs. Mazyck Wilson Shields; by
bequest to TJMF in 1943.

In tribute to his successful attack on the city of Tripoli during the fall of 1804, Congress commissioned this medal honoring navy commodore Edward Preble.[8] President Jefferson may have received this medal as a gift from the United States mint, where John Reich designed the dies from which two hundred copper medals and one gold one were struck. After Preble's return to the United States in 1805, Jefferson praised his actions to Congress:

The energy and judgment displayed by this excellent officer, through the whole course of the service lately confided to him, and the zeal and bravery of his officers and men . . . cannot fail to give high satisfaction to Congress and their country, of whom they have deserved well.[9]

Preble began his career with the navy as a midshipman and lieutenant in the Revolutionary War and rose to the rank of captain in 1799. He joined the forces fighting the Barbary pirates in Tripoli in 1803 and commanded the third squadron to be sent to the Mediterranean. His actions at Tripoli laid the groundwork for the 1805 peace treaty.[10] Jefferson undoubtedly remembered Preble fondly not only for his military success but also for his gift of a hogshead of Marsala wine from Madrid. Jefferson reciprocated by sending Preble a polygraph, a letter-copying machine that he purchased from Charles Willson Peale in Philadelphia.[11]

[1943-2]   A.M.L.

111

GEORGE
WASHINGTON
(1732–1799)

1805

David Eccleston
gold-plated bronze
D: 7.62 (3 in.)

PROVENANCE:
David Eccleston; by gift to
Thomas Jefferson; by purchase to
John Hartwell Cocke at the
Dispersal Sale in 1827; by descent
to Mrs. Mazyck Wilson Shields; by
bequest to TJMF in 1943.

David Eccleston sent Jefferson this medal honoring Washington in 1807, along with two others that he wished forwarded to Bushrod Washington, George Washington's nephew, and the chief justice of the Supreme Court, John Marshall.[12] Eccleston believed the medal to be the largest and in the highest relief that had been struck in England "for some time."[13] Jefferson was all the more pleased with Eccleston's work because the artist was British:

That our own nation should entertain sentiments of gratitude and reverence for the great character who is the subject of your medallion, is a matter of duty. His disinterested and valuable services to them have rendered it so; but such a monument to his memory by the member of another community, proves a zeal for virtue in the abstract, honorable to him who inscribes it, as to him whom it commemorates.[14]

This medal was one of at least six images of Washington at Monticello; its location in the house in Jefferson's time is unknown.[15]

[1943-7]   A.M.L.

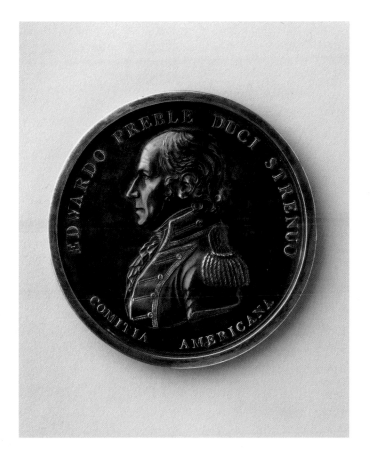

112

**INDIAN PEACE
MEDAL**

1801

*Robert Scot (d. 1823) possibly
with assistance from John Reich
(1768–1833)[16]
silver (hollow)
D: 10 (3¹⁵⁄₁₆ in.)
American Numismatic Society*

Indian peace medals were part of what Jefferson called "an ancient custom from time immemorial" of giving "marks of friendship" to influential members of Native American nations.[17] Native Americans had been wearing medals showing their allegiance to England, France, or Spain for decades before the United States began making these medals in 1789.[18] Jefferson's Indian Peace Medal, which served as a model for medals throughout the nineteenth century, had an enormous distribution because of the Lewis and Clark expedition and the many Native American delegations that visited the President's House.

The medal's obverse shows the profile of Jefferson taken from his bust by the French sculptor Houdon (Cat. 101). William Thornton wrote, "The Figure of Mr. Jefferson on the medal is like nothing human or divine."[19] The clasped hands on the medal's reverse symbolize "Peace and Friendship" between the Native Americans and the United States.

Lewis and Clark took three sizes of the medal with them on their expedition and presented them to chiefs and warriors according to their importance.[20] The first presentation of medals to the Oto and Missouri tribes on August 2, 1804, was also the first meeting between Plains Indians and representatives of the United States government. Lewis and Clark first spoke to the Native Americans and then gave seven medals to their chiefs as presents from "the great Chief of the Seventeen great nations of America":

He has sent by us, one of his flags, a medal and some cloathes . . . which he directed should be given to the great chief of the Ottoe nation, to be kept by him, as a pledge of the sincerity with which he now offers you the hand of friendship.[21]

Lewis and Clark also instructed the Native Americans to visit Jefferson in Washington and surrender to him any flags and medals "received from your old fathers the French and Spaniards, or from any other nation whatever . . ."[22] Several delegations of Native Americans visited Jefferson at the President's House, wearing their medals. Between 1804 and 1807 the French émigré artist Saint-Mémin painted members of these delegations, and his portraits of the Chief of the Great Osages and the Chief of the Little Osages show both wearing their peace medals.[23] An 1804 newspaper account of the delegation described the

Native Americans as having "the likeness of Jefferson, engraved in silver, I believe, hanging at their breasts . . ."[24] The medals were generally prized among the Native Americans (though there is at least one account of a medal being discarded in a time of conflict) and were passed down through families or buried with their owner.[25]

A . M . L .

Set of Seven Medals Presented to *Jefferson by George Erving*

George Erving sent this set of seven medals, which arrived at Monticello in early April 1823, to Jefferson through James Madison.[26] While President, Jefferson appointed Erving chargé d'affaires in Spain. Erving and Jefferson corresponded regularly after Jefferson left the President's House, and their letters covered topics ranging from politics to Merino sheep.[27]

Four medals in the set were restrikes of works Jefferson saw executed in Paris: John Paul Jones, William Augustine Washington, George Washington, and John Eager Howard. Jefferson also knew the medal of Benjamin Franklin, as it was included in the sets of silver and gold medals that he presented to George Washington in 1790.[28] Erving likely included Christopher Columbus and Thaddeus Kosciuszko in the set because of their importance to the history of America. He may have remembered from his visit to Monticello that Jefferson displayed a portrait of Columbus and a print of Kosciuszko in the Parlor.[29]

Erving apologized to Jefferson for the small size of the set and expressed his frustration at the lack of medals of Americans available in Europe:

But a narrow compartment in the temple of fame is allotted to this hemisphere, by the envy and jealousy of Europe. . . . Perhaps when our mint shall be brought to perfection, we shall do that justice to ourselves, which is denied to us by the old world:—but tho' the effigies of our sages and heros may never be stamped on bronze, the records of their labors cannot be effaced from history, nor can they fade or be superseded . . . they must on the contrary acquire fresh lustre as the principles which have been firmly secured here, shall extend their influence over yet enslaved and bigotted nations of the European continent.[30]

A . M . L .

113
(center)

GEORGE WASHINGTON
(1732–1799)

1790

Pierre Simon Benjamin DuVivier (1731–1819) copper-bronzed medal D: 7 (2 ¾ in.)

(upper right)

BENJAMIN FRANKLIN
(1706–1790)

1786

Augustin Dupré (1748–1833) copper-bronzed medal D: 4.7 (1⅞ in.)

(center right)

WILLIAM AUGUSTINE WASHINGTON
(1752–1810)

1789

Pierre Simon Benjamin DuVivier (1731–1819) copper-bronzed medal D: 4.7 (1⅞ in.)

(lower right)

JOHN EAGER HOWARD
(1752–1827)

1789

Pierre Simon Benjamin DuVivier (1731–1819) copper-bronzed medal D: 4.7 (1⅞ in.)

English and American Furniture

FURNITURE

114

CARD TABLE

1730–60

England
mahogany; oak and beech
71.8 × 82.5 × 39
(28¼ × 32½ × 15⅜ in.)
The Maryland Historical
Society, Baltimore

PROVENANCE:
Thomas Jefferson; by purchase to
an unknown buyer; by purchase to
Joshua Cohen; by gift to Bertha
Cohen; by gift to the Maryland
Historical Society from Bertha
Cohen, Mrs. Harriet Cohen Coale,
Mrs. Arnold Burges Johnson, and
Mrs. Grisby Long in 1920.

115

TABLE

c. 1770

Williamsburg
mahogany; yellow pine
71.1 × 83.8 × 45.7
(28 × 33 × 18 in.) closed

PROVENANCE:
Thomas Jefferson; by gift to Peter
Carr; by descent to Mrs. Jacqueline
A. Caskie; by purchase to Mrs.
Hollins N. Randolph; by purchase
to TJMF in 1938.

This card table, if its provenance is true, is the oldest surviving work from Monticello and one of only three pieces of furniture with Queen Anne features. The table has cabriole legs terminating in pad feet, and a fly leg to support the opened top. Made in England, the table may have been owned by Martha Wayles Skelton Jefferson, whose father, John Wayles (1715–1773) had access to English furniture through Virginia merchants. Mrs. Jefferson may have brought this card table with her to Monticello after her marriage to Jefferson in 1772. Because so few of Jefferson's belongings survived the 1770 fire at Shadwell, this table is more likely to have belonged to Mrs. Jefferson than to her husband.

The table was purchased in 1836 in Charlottesville by Dr. Joshua Cohen (1801–1870).[1] If the table was still at Monticello, he may have bought it from James Barclay or Commodore Uriah P. Levy, who took title from Barclay in 1836, or from any of the many local residents who purchased Jefferson's possessions at the Dispersal Sale in 1827. Cohen and his brother were later named executors of Levy's will (1862).

S.R.S.

This drop-leaf table might be one that Jefferson ordered from the Williamsburg cabinetmaker Peter Scott in 1772.[2] He contracted with Scott "to make table 4. f. 1.I. sq. & 2 f. 4.I. high" and "tea tables . . . 3 f. by 2.f. & 2.f. 3.2I. high."[3] The table has claw-and-ball feet, rather straight cabriole legs, and thick ankles.

Once a much larger table, it was made smaller by cutting down the top on all four sides. The modifications may have been performed by joiners at Monticello or by Henry Ingle in Washington, who altered several tables in 1801. Ingle told Jefferson, "The table to be altered appears very good and as the alteration will exceed my expectation as to cost, I shall forbear cutting it untill I hear further from you."[4]

Henry and Joseph Ingle, whom Jefferson first employed to do cabinetwork in Philadelphia in January 1791, were joiners and cabinetmakers. Later Henry was a hardware merchant in Washington, D.C. Without specifying what was accomplished, Jefferson made payments for work done in Philadelphia to both, or one or the other, of the Ingles each year from 1791 through 1794. Jefferson modified the rented house that he occupied on High Street in Philadelphia. The disbursements in 1791 might have covered interior cabinetwork for these changes, but little is known about the work conducted between 1792 and 1794; Jefferson only indicated "cabinetwork" in his Memorandum Book. Ingle, who made furniture for President Washington in Philadelphia in 1794, may have made several dumbwaiters for Jefferson.[5]

While Jefferson was President, he paid Ingle for cabinetwork, including the making of a writing box in 1802, the alteration of several tables, and for unidentified cabinetwork in 1809, which might have been a pair of D-shaped card tables (Cat. 132). He also bought tools, cupboard locks, tacks, sandpaper, and picture rings from Henry.[6]

[1938-23]

S.R.S.

c. 1770

*attributed to Peter Scott
(1694–1775), Williamsburg
cherry; oak slip seat
99.1 × 43.2 × 50.8
(39 × 17 × 20 in.)
Mrs. Lucy Buck LeGrand and
Thomas Jefferson Memorial
Foundation*

PROVENANCE:
Thomas Jefferson; [1965.22] by
purchase to an unidentified buyer
at the Dispersal Sale in 1827; by
gift or purchase to Dr. William
Cox; by gift to Mrs. E. H.
McPherson and Mrs. Annie Leroy
Cox Dennis; by descent to Albert
P. Dennis, Jr.; by gift to TJMF in
1965. [1935-3-1 through 4] by gift
or purchase to an unidentified
owner by purchase to Mrs. Martha
Farish; by bequest to TJMF in
1935. The sixth chair: by gift or
purchase to a Mr. Farish of
Albemarle County; by gift to
Samuel Henry Buck; by descent to
Mrs. Lucy Buck LeGrand.

117

ARMCHAIR

1770–80

*Virginia
cherry; southern pine
96.5 × 58.4 × 49.2
(38 × 23 × 19⅜ in.)
Missouri Historical Society,
St. Louis*

PROVENANCE:
Thomas Jefferson; by descent to
an unnamed descendant of Charles
Lewis Bankhead; by gift to Colonel
James C. Broadhead; by descent
to Mrs. Edwin M. Harford; by gift
to the Missouri Historical Society;
by loan to TJMF in 1982.

Martha Jefferson Randolph mentioned "7 old Mahogany chairs given by Mr. Wythe" in the Sitting Room in her 1826 inventory of the contents of Monticello. Six of what are believed to be these chairs are known today and are attributed to the Williamsburg cabinetmaker Peter Scott. The chairs, numbered on the inside of the rear seat rail as high as XX, may have been part of a larger set, but none of Jefferson's sets of chairs contained as many as that.

Jefferson's long friendship with George Wythe began in 1768 when Jefferson enrolled in the College of William and Mary and studied law with him. Upon Wythe's death, Jefferson was bequeathed his "books and small philosophical apparatus" as well as his "silver cups and gold headed cane." The large silver cups were melted down to make what are now called the "Wythe-Jefferson cups" (Cat. 189), and the books were sold to Congress in 1815 together with Jefferson's library. The whereabouts of the scientific instruments, or what they were, is not known. Just how Jefferson acquired the chairs is not established, and no mention of Wythe furniture was made in any correspondence. Family tradition indicates that the chairs may have been a wedding gift.

Jefferson patronized five Williamsburg cabinetmakers between 1768 and 1773 but seems to have had more pieces made by Peter Scott than by his peers Benjamin Bucktrout, Edmund Dickinson, George Donald, and Anthony Hay. In November 1772, ten months after his marriage to Martha Wayles Skelton, he purchased several tables from Scott.[7] The chairs may have been a gift from Wythe at this time.

In spite of the fact that Peter Scott's prosperous career spanned five decades, no documented works have been located.[8] Wallace Gusler, however, has attributed a number of works to him, and these range from elaborately to more modestly carved chairs.

The Rococo chairs owned by Jefferson evidently began as a more ambitious design. The pierced splat is relatively elaborate, but the serpentine crest rail with scallop-cut ears is simpler than it might have been had the entire decorative scheme been executed. An extra thickness of wood was cut to allow shells to be carved at the ears, but this was never carried out. To disguise the thickness, Scott or his assistant cut a curve to hide the difference. The straight Marlborough legs have a box stretcher. The seat rails have a thumbnail molding.
[1935-3-1/4; 1965–22]   S.R.S.

This simple Rococo armchair with a subtle serpentine crest rail and a vertically pierced splat is typical of many chairs made in Virginia's piedmont. Before Jefferson traveled to Europe in 1784, most of his furniture was supplied by Virginia cabinetmakers, principally in Williamsburg. The chair might have been made for him there—or in the piedmont region. If the chair was made in Williamsburg, two possibilities are likely: first, that the chair came from the workshop of the celebrated Williamsburg cabinetmaker Anthony Hay (d. 1770), from whom Jefferson may have purchased some furniture as early as 1768, or Hay's successors, Benjamin Bucktrout (d. 1813) and Edmund Dickinson.[9] Bucktrout took over Hay's shop in 1767 and Dickinson succeeded him in 1771. Jefferson made several purchases from Bucktrout between 1768 and 1773, and later from Dickinson.[10] An attribution to Hay and Bucktrout based on documentary evidence can only be tentative because Hay was also the proprietor of the Raleigh Tavern, patronized by Jefferson, and Bucktrout also was a merchant.[11] The references in Jefferson's Memorandum Book might refer to payments for things other than furniture.

Dickinson or his assistants might also have executed Jefferson's chair. Dickinson apparently made a very similar armchair now in the Fredericksburg Masonic Lodge in around 1775.[12] Jefferson's chair, however, is more restrained and linear than the Masonic Lodge example. It has box stretchers and Marlborough legs, which have been shortened to accommodate casters, now missing. The chair was improperly upholstered over the rail, but a slip seat has been restored.

[1982-28]   S.R.S.

118

FILING TABLE

1790–1800

Mid-Atlantic
mahogany; poplar
H: 71.1 D of top: 78.7
(28 × 31 in.)
Massachusetts Historical Society

PROVENANCE:
Thomas Jefferson; by descent to
Ellen and Joseph Coolidge; by
descent to Thomas Jefferson
Coolidge; by gift to the
Massachusetts Historical Society in
1912; by loan to TJMF since 1929.

This octagonal filing table, with eight drawers marked with the letters of the alphabet, stood in the Book Room at Monticello and was highly prized by the family. After Jefferson's death both Thomas Jefferson Randolph and Ellen Randolph Coolidge vied for it. From Boston, Joseph Coolidge wrote Randolph, who was administering the sale, that he would pay as a stranger for "the octagon table with drawers for Ellen which stands in his library."[13] Concerned that he would not be able to obtain it, Coolidge restated his case to Nicholas Trist, who would be present at the sale on January 15, 1827:

I want you to understand that Ellen is very anxious to have, for <u>her own use</u>, something wh. he habitually used in his chamber; and I can recollect nothing which will answer so well as the <u>octagon</u> table upon which <u>I</u> used to read, and where his papers were kept . . .[14]

Yet Jefferson Randolph wanted it, too. Virginia Trist told her sister Ellen that her brother "has long set his heart on having it, and he said it was the only thing in the house he would bid against Joseph for . . . his intention was . . . to give it to Mama to keep during her life time . . ."[15] The conflict was decided by Martha Randolph, who decided to give the table to Ellen Coolidge.

The table, with four square and four triangular drawers, is supported by a tripod base with snake feet. The form of the table is modeled after the English rent table.
[1936-3]   S.R.S.

119

DESK

1770–85

Virginia
mahogany; yellow pine
116.5 × 91.4 × 58.4
(45⅞ × 36 × 23 in.)

PROVENANCE:
Thomas Jefferson; by descent to
Thomas Jefferson Randolph; by
descent to Hollins N. Randolph;
by bequest to Mrs. Hollins N.
Randolph; by purchase to TJMF
in 1938.

One of the more interesting pieces of furniture owned by Jefferson is this tall, adaptable desk for reading or drawing. The angle of the top, hinged at the front, can be adjusted with a ratchet stand. A bail handle pulls forward the front of the desk to reveal a flat, lined writing surface. Supported by six legs, the desk has mostly replacement Chinese fretwork brackets beneath the skirt. The original—presumably brass—list to prevent books, papers, or writing implements from slipping is missing. The straight legs sit on casters.

The desk, whose angled top is large enough to accommodate a folio, is similar to a partially illegible description of one that Jefferson ordered from the Williamsburg cabinetmaker George Donald.[16] The dimensions specified by Jefferson, however, do not exactly match the existing desk.
[1938-22]   S.R.S.

120

DINING TABLE
ONE OF TWO

1760–70

England
mahogany; pine and poplar
69.9 × 147.3 (extended) × 119.4
(27½ × 58 × 47 in.)

PROVENANCE:
Thomas Jefferson; by descent to
Thomas Jefferson Randolph; by
descent to Alex B. and Burton H.
Randall; by gift to TJMF in 1927
in memory of Jane Harrison
Randolph Randall.

This Rococo dining table consists of two freestanding rectangular drop-leaf tables that were intended to be put together to form a larger table. When fully extended, the table could seat twelve. In an eighteenth-century house a table such as this was typically placed against the wall when not in use. At Monticello this dining table and others were adaptably arranged to suit the number of diners. The number of dining tables suggests that at least some of them would have been placed against the wall when not in use.

The table might have come to Jefferson from George Wythe. An account of a descendant indicates that Jane Nicholas Randolph Harrison (1862–1926), the sixth child of Thomas Jefferson Randolph, said that it was referred to as the "Wythe table," but no documentation is known to confirm the story.[17] It might have been given to Jefferson as a wedding gift, or he may have purchased it after Wythe's death. In 1806 Jefferson corresponded with William DuVal, the executor of Wythe's estate, and expressed an interest in acquiring some of Wythe's belongings. Other than the objects that Jefferson received by bequest (chairs [Cat. 116], two large silver cups, a cane, books, a celestial globe, and scientific apparatus), he received a profile portrait of Wythe made with a physiognotrace (unlocated) in 1804. A table was not mentioned.

Each part of the table has a fixed central board with two broad hinged drop leaves, four cabriole legs with plain knees, and claw-and-ball feet. Two of the legs are stationary, and the other two, called "fly legs," are movable in order to support the leaves.

[1927-59-1 and 2]   S.R.S.

121

SLAB TABLE

1760–70

England
mahogany
76.2 × 96.5 × 50.8
(30 × 38 × 20 in.)

PROVENANCE:
[Thomas Jefferson]; by purchase
to Jefferson Monroe Levy; by
purchase to TJMF in 1923.

Slab tables, known variously in eighteenth-century America as marble tables, marble sideboards, and sideboard tables, were commonly placed against a wall in dining rooms or parlors for serving food and drink. Marble, although not impervious to stains, was a far more durable surface than wood. In the Hôtel de Langeac Jefferson attached a marble slab for serving directly to the wall of the dining room.

This table was at Monticello when the house was acquired from Jefferson Monroe Levy in 1923. Little is known about its history, except that Levy attempted to acquire original Jefferson furnishings. If the table was Jefferson's, it is one of the earliest surviving pieces of furniture. It may have been one of the rare items to endure the fire at Shadwell in 1770.

The table has a straight skirt and rather straight cabriole legs terminating in claw-and-ball feet. The knees of the front legs are carved with acanthus leaves. The marble is a later replacement.

[1923-20]   S.R.S.

HIGH CHEST OF
DRAWERS

1750–60

Philadelphia
mahogany; yellow pine
194.3 × 112.3 × 61
(76½ × 44¼ × 24 in.)

PROVENANCE:
Elizabeth House Trist; by purchase
or gift to Martha Jefferson Randolph;
by descent to Frances Maury
Burke; by purchase of the
Washington Committee; by gift to
TJMF in 1926.

Tʜɪs simple high chest of drawers was made in Philadelphia for a member of the House family, the keepers of the boardinghouse in Philadelphia where Jefferson sometimes lodged. The chest became the property of Eliza House, a friend of Jefferson's, and was later nicknamed "Grandmama Trist" by her family. Miss House married Nicholas Trist, who with his brother, Hore Browse Trist, was a leader of the Royal Irish Regiment at the battle of Bunker's Hill. Mrs. Trist's grandson Nicholas Philip Trist (Cat. 80) married Jefferson's granddaughter Virginia. Jefferson had persuaded Trist's parents, Mary Brown and Hore Browse Trist, to settle in Albemarle County, where they lived at Birdwood, until Jefferson appointed Hore Browse Trist collector of the port of New Orleans.

The chest is in two parts. The upper case, with a flat top, has a molded cornice with chamfered corners and stop-fluted pilasters along the chamfered front corners of the chest. There are eight graduated drawers. The lower case has five drawers and fluted pilasters on the chamfered front corners. A carved shell embellishes the knees of the cabriole legs terminating in trifid feet.
[1926-3]   S.R.S.

123
BUREAU TABLE

1750–70

Massachusetts
walnut; white pine
74.3 × 83.5 × 52.1
(29¼ × 32⅞ × 20½ in.)
Miss Sara Lois Jordan

PROVENANCE:
Martha Wayles Skelton Jefferson;
to Thomas Jefferson; by descent to
Septimia Meikleham; by descent to
Julia Graves Cantrell; by bequest
to Emma Kane Jordan; by gift to
Sara Lois Jordan; by loan to TJMF
since 1977.

Tʜɪs block-front bureau table is believed to have belonged to Jefferson's wife, Martha. After her marriage to Jefferson in January 1772, she undoubtedly would have brought it with her to Monticello, where it would have been used to store valuable clothing and toilet articles in the bedroom. After her death the table was kept in Jefferson's bedroom for the duration of his life. In 1830, Martha Jefferson Randolph reported, "The younger girls use my mother's dressing table . . ."[18] It was inherited by Septimia Anne Randolph Meikleham, the seventh and youngest daughter.

Block-front kneehole tables with six legs were extremely fashionable in Massachusetts and elsewhere in America during the third quarter of the eighteenth century.[19] The form consists of one shallow wide top drawer, a "kneehole" or central opening with a cupboard at the back, and two tiers of narrow lower drawers on either side of the kneehole. The drawers typically each had locks to protect expensive textiles and toiletries. The cupboard is tall enough to accommodate a wig and wigstand.
[1977-56]   S.R.S.

TRIPOD TABLE

New York or Philadelphia
walnut
H: 78.1 D of top: 59.7
(30¾ × 23½ in.)

PROVENANCE:
Thomas Jefferson; by descent to
Benjamin Franklin Randolph; by
purchase to Jefferson Randolph
Anderson in 1896; by descent to
Mrs. Henry Norris Platt; by
purchase to TJMF in 1971.

TRIPOD TABLE

New York or Philadelphia
mahogany
H: 73.7 × D of top: 44.5
(29 × 17½ in.)

PROVENANCE:
Thomas Jefferson; by descent to
Virginia and Nicholas Trist; by
descent to Martha Jefferson Trist
Burke; by gift to Fanny E. Cole in
1882; by descent to Mrs. M. T.
Barrier; by purchase to TJMF in
1938.

Tables or stands such as these were typically used to hold candlesticks. Jefferson may have bought three or more such tables with "bird-cage" turning mechanisms in New York or Philadelphia. They might have been altered later by Monticello's joiners.

The table pictured at left, which is very similar to two others that belonged to Jefferson, may have been used as a writing surface, as it contains a small pivoting drawer partitioned to hold writing implements. The Rococo vase-shaped base terminates in ribbed snake feet on casters. The birdcage revolving mechanism is engaged by pulling a peg to allow the table top to revolve on the turned pedestal.
[1971-71-2]

The table at right is one of several tilt-top tables with a family history connecting it with the Monticello joinery. Although its construction suggests that it was made in New York or Philadelphia, a descendant wrote:

This little Mahogany Table was made at Monticello—by Thomas Jefferson's cabinetmaker— "Daddy" Hemmings a slave of T. Jefferson who had his capable servants taught—so that if they ever were forced by circumstances to leave the family—to be able to support themselves—. . . . The Table a Candle-Stand and so arranged as to be either a light source or fire screen . . .[20]

[1938-25]   S.R.S.

126

UNIVERSAL TABLE

1790

Samuel Titt [or Tilt], London
mahogany; oak
68.6 × 91.4 × 75
(27 × 36 × 29½ in.)

PROVENANCE:
Thomas Jefferson; by descent to
Thomas Jefferson Randolph; by
gift from a descendant of Thomas
Jefferson Randolph to Mrs. Barton
Hall; by descent to Charlotte
Noland; by gift to TJMF in 1961.

On his way home from France in November 1789, for what he thought was a brief visit, Jefferson's interest was piqued by a novel, multipurpose table that he saw aboard the ship *Clermont.* The table had two sliding leaves that when opened, doubled the area of the top. With the understanding that the finished tables would be shipped to him in Paris, Jefferson asked the ship's captain, Nathaniel Colley, to obtain two such tables for him in London.[21]

When Captain Colley learned that Jefferson had been appointed secretary of state by President Washington, he delayed placing an order for the tables, not knowing where they should be shipped or if Jefferson would still want them. When Jefferson had not heard from Colley for nine months, he renewed his request for the tables.

From Norfolk in September 1790, Captain Colley informed Jefferson that he had received his memorandum and would proceed at once.

I Did not Get the Tables made when in London last As Mr. Cutting informed me you did not Return to France again and I thought they might attend with trouble transporting them there and back. . . . But you may Depend on my Bringing them when I return and will Send them to Philadelphia Imeadatly.[22]

In January 1791, Captain Colley reported that the tables had been shipped. They arrived in Norfolk on Captain Anderson's ship *Isabella* on January 21, 1791.[23]

Your Tables which I had made in London for you Which I hope will meet your Approbation, as I made it a point to find out the Mr. Titt you Recommended me to, he has Remov'd from Cheapside to Hatten Garden. I think that they are well made but he has charged too high a price for them.[24]

Colley enclosed an invoice from Titt, London, dated November 25, 1790, for £6 6s. for "a fine Solid Mahogony Secret flap Table Taper feet fluted and Therm'd" and £3 18s. for the smaller one.[25]

The idea of a "Secret Flap Table" achieved some popularity among London cabinet-makers. A similar design, called a "Universal Table," was illustrated and described in Thomas Sheraton's *The Cabinet-Maker and Upholsterer's Drawing Book,* published in November 1791. Sheraton wrote that the table could serve both as a breakfast and dining table. Jefferson may have used his tables for dining, writing, or drawing; only the larger of the two tables has been located. It has a front drawer with a felt-lined slider and various sized compartments, and fluted and tapered legs, terminating in spade feet.

[1961-23]   S.R.S.

Windsor Furniture

When an inventory of Monticello was taken after Jefferson's death, the Entrance Hall contained "28 black painted chairs."[26] Although none of the chairs survive, the black Windsors were an important feature of the room. They also represent a fraction of the many Windsor chairs that Jefferson acquired during his lifetime. Sets of painted Windsors, widely popular in America in the eighteenth and early nineteenth centuries, were practical and affordable; they were a common choice of seating furniture for entrance halls or other rooms of the house. They were also used outside as garden furniture.

Between 1790 and 1809 Jefferson recorded purchases of at least 132 Windsor chairs in his Memorandum Book. These chairs were acquired in five different sets, the first of which came from New York in 1790.[27] Shortly after buying these thirty green-painted Windsors, Jefferson had them shipped to Monticello.[28] The following year he shipped eighteen more chairs from Philadelphia, America's largest center of Windsor-chair production.[29] In 1793, 1800, and 1801, three additional sets of Philadelphia-made Windsors were purchased.[30]

Green was the standard color for Windsor chairs in the mid to late eighteenth century. The New York Windsors were green, yet after 1800 Jefferson clearly preferred black-painted Windsors with bamboo turnings such as the three dozen bow-back Windsors "painted black with yellow rings" that he ordered for Poplar Forest in 1809 (below).[31]

The twenty-eight black chairs for Monticello's Entrance Hall came from the sets of Windsors purchased in 1800 and 1801. On May 10, 1800, Jefferson recorded a payment for six "stick chairs" at a cost of two dollars and sixty cents each. The chairs were made by John Letchworth, one of Philadelphia's leading makers of Windsor furniture between 1785 and 1824.[32] By June 24, 1800 Jefferson had returned to Monticello and he wrote to his Philadelphia agent, "All the articles forwarded by you have come to hand except the half dozen square railed Windsor chairs bought in 4th. street."[33] In July Jefferson still had not received his chairs, and he sent a letter to George Jefferson, his agent in Richmond.

Drawing of a table and bow-back Windsor Chair

c. 1817
Cornelia Jefferson Randolph
Poplar Forest, Bedford County,
Virginia
ink and wash on paper
20.3 × 21.6 (8 × 8½ in.)

This chair is believed to be one of the Windsors that Jefferson purchased for Poplar Forest in 1809.

Jefferson asked if he had seen the chairs, which were "painted of a very dark colour, and were in this style." He sketched a rod-back Windsor side chair with double crest rails in the center of his letter (right).[34] The rod-back Windsor chair with bamboo turnings, first introduced about 1799, was very popular throughout the first decade of the nineteenth century. Although Jefferson's somewhat crude sketch shows nothing in the space between the two crest rails, this type of Windsor chair back was usually strengthened with a central medallion or alternating spindles that projected through the secondary crest rail in what is now called the "bird-cage" design.[35] At least one other bird-cage Windsor side chair bearing both Letchworth's brand and a strong resemblance to Jefferson's sketch is known.[36]

A year after buying the six side chairs, Jefferson ordered a much larger set of forty-eight Windsor armchairs. An invoice dated July 31, 1801, (below) arrived from Adam Snyder, another Philadelphia maker of both Windsor and fancy chairs, active from about 1798 to 1820: "To 4 Dozen of Armd Chairs Blak & Gould for the President of the United States—$192."[37] Thomas Claxton shipped the chairs to Jefferson at Monticello, and although there is no further description of their form, they were almost certainly of the popular rod-back type and similar to the Letchworth chairs. Snyder is known to have made rod-back chairs with an octagonal medallion centered between the double crest rails. Gold leaf was probably used to mark the bamboo rings. In 1815, Virginia law required that every chair "ornamented with gold or silver leaf" be included on personal property taxes; forty-four chairs with gold leaf appeared on Jefferson's list of taxable property.[38] Jefferson also paid four dollars per armchair; in 1801, that substantial amount for a Windsor chair probably meant that they had more costly scrolled mahogany arms in addition to their gilt decoration.

Many of Jefferson's Windsor chairs were apparently sold at the Dispersal Sale in 1827. Although few receipts from the sale survive, one mentions "6. Windsor chairs @ 1.95" sold to Lilbourn Railey.[39]

S.M.O.

Sketch of a rod-back Windsor side chair made by John Letchworth of Philadelphia

Thomas Jefferson to George Jefferson
19 July 1800
Massachusetts Historical Society

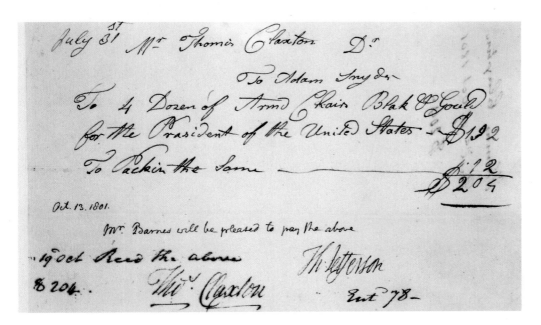

Invoice from Adam Snyder of Philadelphia for forty-eight Windsor armchairs

31 July 1801
Massachusetts Historical Society

127

WINDSOR ARMCHAIR

c. 1775

Philadelphia
poplar, mahogany, maple, oak,
and hickory
H before restoration 101.6; H of
seat 36.8; D of seat: 58.4
(40 × 14½ × 23 in.)
The American Philosophical
Society

PROVENANCE:
Thomas Jefferson; by descent to
Martha Jefferson Randolph; by gift
to J. R. Kane; by gift to the
American Philosophical Society in
1838.

When Jefferson returned to Monticello in 1776, he brought with him an uncommon revolving Windsor chair which he used "at Philadelphia while preparing the Declaration of Independence."[40] At Monticello this consequential chair was used to form one of two reading-and-writing arrangements. The chair was apparently first used with a Windsor bench (Cat. 128), and later with a sofa believed to have been made by Thomas Burling (Cat. 130).

This comb-back chair, so called for the resemblance of the crest rail to a hair comb, is rare for its highly remarkable revolving mechanism, which probably was specified to the (unidentified) maker by Jefferson. The chair has two seats and "rotates on a central iron spindle and on rollers made of window sash pulleys set in a groove between the two seats."[41] The chair has volute-carved ears at the ends of the crest rail and knuckle handholds on the arms. Unlike most comb-back Philadelphia Windsors, Jefferson's chair has eleven spindles rather than the usual nine forming its back. The seat is round—rather than the customary D-shape with a pommel and "dished out" seat.

Later the chair was vastly altered in Monticello's joinery. A new base with bamboo-turned legs, made either in the joinery or taken from another chair, replaced the original baluster-turned legs. The writing paddle was probably added when Jefferson switched the Windsor couch for the sofa (Cat. 130).

S.R.S.

128

WINDSOR BENCH

1798

Lawrence Allwine
black paint on unidentified wood
36.5 × 135.9 × 58.4
(14⅜ × 53½ × 23 in.)

PROVENANCE:
Thomas Jefferson; by descent to
Thomas Jefferson Randolph; by
descent to Carolina Ramsay
Randolph; by bequest to R.T.W.
Duke; by descent to Helen and
Mary Duke; by purchase to TJMF
in 1951.

On April 2, 1798, Jefferson purchased a Windsor bench from a Philadelphia maker of Windsor furniture, Lawrence Allwine. He noted in his Memorandum Book, "gave Lawrence Allwine ord. on Barnes for 26 D. for a stick sopha and mattras." The bench with turned stretchers and six bamboo legs (later shortened) with casters, was eventually placed near his chair to support his legs while he read or wrote in the Cabinet at Monticello. Both ends were cut out to allow the round bottom of the chair to fit against the couch.

Initially, Jefferson may have used the Windsor bench with a comb-back Windsor chair with a writing arm, but later he used the bench with a revolving, or whirligig, chair that was made by Thomas Burling (Cat. 129).[42]

Once some shipping difficulties were resolved, the bench presumably arrived at Monticello later in 1798.[43] In 1800, Jefferson wrote his son-in-law, Thomas Mann Randolph, to find a book catalogue, and said that it might be found "under the window by the red couch in the cabinet."[44]

Allwine, who also made his own patented paint, produced Windsor chairs in Philadelphia between 1786 and 1800. In the *Aurora*, May 3, 1800, Allwine advertised that he made paints for ships, buildings, and furniture superior for its brilliance and durability. The "stick sopha" was Jefferson's only known purchase from him.

[1951-1]

S.R.S.

While serving as secretary of state in New York in 1790, Jefferson purchased a good deal of furniture from local cabinetmakers, particularly Thomas Burling, who had a shop on Beekman Street. In his Memorandum Book, Jefferson carefully recorded two payments totalling £143 to Burling in July and August 1790 but did not identify his purchases. Among other articles, Jefferson evidently acquired a sofa and a revolving chair. The attribution of both sofa and chair to Burling is based upon a very similar chair, now at Mount Vernon, that Burling made for President Washington.[45] He called it an "Uncomn Chr" and paid £7 for it in 1790.[46]

Although Washington eluded the enmity of the Federalist critic William Loughton Smith, Jefferson did not escape ridicule for his politics and his chair. Smith wrote, "Who has not heard from the Secretary of the praises of his wonderful Whirligig Chair, which had the miraculous quality of allowing the person seated in it to turn his head without moving his tail?"[47]

The source for the design appears to be French. Jefferson certainly was familiar with the concave *fauteuil de bureau*, the prevailing form for desk chairs during the Louis XVI period, typically upholstered in leather.[48] The comte de Moustier, who sold many of his furnishings to Washington, may have owned such a chair. The general contour also foreshadows the concave easy chairs later made fashionable in America by French-influenced Thomas Sheraton and his *Cabinet-Maker and Upholsterer's Drawing Book*, but the origin of the design is more likely to have been French than English.

The idea to combine a revolving chair with a *fauteuil de bureau* might have been hatched by Jefferson, whose penchant for mechanical apparatuses is well known, but no documentation exists to prove his authorship of the Burling-made chairs. He already owned a revolving Windsor (Cat. 127), then at Monticello, that he purchased in Philadelphia during the 1770s. The turning mechanism on this chair is similar to the others, which might suggest Jefferson's involvement with the later design.

The revolving chairs enjoyed by Washington and Jefferson are much alike, except that Jefferson's is more than a foot taller. The back on Jefferson's is higher, and the legs on Washington's have been shortened. The chairs have the same kind of turning mechanisms. The upper part of the seat pivots on a spindle supported by four rollers on each of the tops of the legs. The heavy legs on Jefferson's chair terminate in applied spade feet.

At the same time that Jefferson purchased his "uncommon" chair from Burling, it is believed that he also acquired a unique sofa. Made with movable arms and concave ends, the sofa neatly fit the round bottom of the chair. If Jefferson wanted to put his legs up while reading or writing on his lap with a portable writing box, he could push the sofa and chair together to create a rather awkward version of a *duchesse, brisée en deux*.[49]

The sofa and revolving chair were apparently used together as a pair until Jefferson decided that he wanted to rest his legs while reading or writing at a table. He then purchased a Windsor couch, which he switched with the Burling sofa, thus creating two distinct reading-and-writing arrangements—the revolving Burling chair, revolving Monticello-made table, and Windsor couch in the Cabinet, and the revolving Windsor and Burling sofa in the Tea Room.

[1951-2] S.R.S.

129
CHAIR

1790

New York
attributed to Thomas Burling
(active 1787–1800)
mahogany, mahogany veneer;
white oak
123.2 × 64.1 × 61
(48½ × 25¼ × 24 in.)

PROVENANCE:
Thomas Jefferson; by descent to Thomas Jefferson Randolph; by descent to Carolina Ramsay Randolph; by bequest to R.T.W. Duke; by descent to Mary and Helen Duke; by purchase to TJMF in 1951.

130
SOFA

1790

New York
attributed to Thomas Burling
mahogany, mahogany veneer
95.3 × 142.9 × 61
(37½ × 56¼ × 24 in.)
Private collection

PROVENANCE:
Thomas Jefferson; by descent to Virginia and Nicholas Trist; by descent to a private collection.

131
CIRCULAR CARD TABLE
ONE OF A PAIR

1800

Baltimore or Philadelphia
mahogany, mahogany veneer,
satinwood; beech and poplar
75.6 × 95.3 × 31.8
(29¾ × 37½ × 12½ in.)

PROVENANCE:
Thomas Jefferson; by purchase to
Dr. Addison Dold of Augusta
County at the Dispersal Sale in
1827; (table 60-59) by descent to
Charles J. Connolly; by bequest to
Ruth G. Connolly; by gift to
TJMF in 1976; (table 82-34) by
descent to G. Woodbridge
Williams; by purchase to TJMF
in 1982.

These matching Federal card tables were two of thirteen tea and card tables identified on Jefferson's 1815 Memorandum of Taxable Property. They appear stylistically compatible with similar tables made in Baltimore, but the maker and place of origin are unknown.[50] Although no specific mention of them is known, they might have been secured for Jefferson while he was president by his purchasing agent, Thomas Claxton.

The tables have four square, tapering legs. The right rear one is a flyleg, which swings to support the top when the table is opened. The circular playing surface is covered with green baize. The inlaid ornamentation includes satinwood oval panels (characteristic of Baltimore) above the legs, bell-flowers on each leg, a fan on the closed top, and satinwood stringing encircling the top and skirt panels.

[1960-59; 1982-34]   S . R . S .

132
CARD TABLE
ONE OF A PAIR

---

c. 1810

Mid-Atlantic
mahogany, mahogany and
rosewood veneers
75 × 94 × 45.7
(29½ × 37 × 18 in.)

PROVENANCE:
[Thomas Jefferson]; by purchase to
Jefferson Monroe Levy; by
purchase to TJMF in 1923.

If the provenance of this pair of Sheraton-style card tables is accurate, they are the latest works made by an urban cabinetmaker to be acquired by Jefferson, as most of his furniture made after 1810 was produced in the Monticello joinery. The tables were acquired from Jefferson Monroe Levy, the last private owner of Monticello, who attempted to furnish Jefferson's house with authentic works.

The tables may have been purchased for Jefferson while he was president by Claxton. They might have come from Philadelphia, where Claxton was known to have acquired furnishings for the President's House, or possibly from the shop of Henry Ingle, a Philadelphia cabinetmaker who had moved to Washington. Jefferson had employed Ingle in the early 1790s in Philadelphia and later while he was president, but not enough is known about the work that he completed. In 1809, about the time that these tables were made, Jefferson paid Ingle for "cabinet work 16.11."[51]

Each of the D-shaped tables has four turned and reeded legs terminating in bulbous feet. The top is hinged at the back, and when extended, is supported by one of the rear legs, which pivots 90°.

[1923-21-1/2]   S . R . S .

While living in New York, Jefferson purchased a set of shield-back chairs with fine carved ornament on the ribs. The design of this chair was especially popular in New York.[52] One similar pair may have been purchased from Thomas Burling by George Washington, who paid just over £47 for unnamed furniture from Burling in June 1790.[53] Although the chairs may be the product of another cabinetmaker, Jefferson's chairs very well could have been made by Burling, from whom Jefferson made two sizable purchases in 1790. He paid Burling £100 on July 17, and £43 on August 30, 1790, which would have provided a substantial amount of furniture. A similar pair of armchairs made by Robert Carter, another New York cabinetmaker, cost £8 4s, and a set of ten side chairs cost £33.[54] Thus, Washington and Jefferson made payments to Burling of approximately £47 and £43—the approximate cost of ten side chairs and two armchairs.

From Jefferson's set, two armchairs are known. Much influenced by Plate 2 of George Hepplewhite's *The Cabinet-Maker and Upholsterer's Guide*, these chairs have delicate bead and petal-carved ribs, reeded legs terminating in spade feet, and a rounded bottom on the shield back. The four ribs radiate from a foliate-carved lunette. The surviving chairs show that the chairs were upholstered over the rail in two tacking patterns, one straight across and the second with a swag configuration; it is not known which was done first.
[1949-4] S.R.S.

Ten side chairs, possibly of a set of twelve, were used in the Dining Room at Monticello. Jefferson probably acquired them in New York during the spring of 1790 for his house on Maiden Lane. His household goods from Paris had not yet arrived, and he needed to furnish his residence. Jefferson made purchases from both New York and Philadelphia merchants while as secretary of state he resided in these temporary United States capitals between 1790 and 1793, but his expenditures in New York outnumbered those in Philadelphia. In Philadelphia, he anticipated the forthcoming arrival of his vast household inventory and thus would not have wished to duplicate what he already owned.

Jefferson purchased two sets of shield-back chairs from two different unidentified makers. The designs for these chairs were influenced by Plate 5 of George Hepplewhite's *The Cabinet-Maker and Upholsterer's Guide*. The interpretation of this design varied.[55] Jefferson's set had pointed shield bottoms and square, tapered legs supported by stretchers. The seats were originally upholstered over the rail and tacked in a swag pattern.

Placed in the Dining Room at Monticello, the chairs were terribly worn by 1814.

On looking around the room in which we sat the first thing that attracted our attention was the state of the chairs. They had leather bottoms stuffed with hair, but the bottoms were completely worn through and the hair sticking out in all directions.[56]

The poor condition of most of the chairs prevented their inclusion in the Dispersal Sale in 1827. The chairs were retained by the family; nine of the ten known chairs descended in the family of Thomas Jefferson Randolph. The tenth descended through Benjamin Franklin Randolph to the Carter family of Redlands in Albemarle County.
[1955-30-1/8; 1958-16; 1987-26] S.R.S.

133

**ARMCHAIR
ONE OF TWO**

1790–1800

*New York, possibly Thomas Burling
mahogany; ash
95.9 × 55.2 × 46.3
(37¾ × 21¾ × 18¼ in.)*

PROVENANCE:
Thomas Jefferson; by purchase to John Cochran at the Dispersal Sale in 1827; by descent to Nelly Cummings Preston; by purchase to TJMF in 1956.

134

**SIDE CHAIR
ONE OF TEN**

1790–1800

*Mid-Atlantic
mahogany; oak
91.4 × 52.1 × 41.9
(36 × 20½ × 16½ in.)
Mr. and Mrs. Robert Carter and Thomas Jefferson Memorial Foundation*

PROVENANCE:
Thomas Jefferson; by descent to Thomas Jefferson Randolph; [1955-30-1/3] by gift of Alex B. Randall and Burton H. R. Randall in 1927; [1955-30-4] by gift of Sarah Randolph Anderson in 1928; [1955-30-5 and 6] by purchase from Mrs. Hollins N. Randolph in 1938; [1955-30-7] by gift of Mrs. M. Ritchie Harrison Cocke and Burton H. R. Randall in memory of Eleanor Wayles Randolph Harrison in 1941; [1955-30-8] by purchase from Burton H. R. Randall in 1951; [1958-16] by bequest of Ethel Patterson Randolph in 1958; [1987-26] by loan of Mr. and Mrs. Robert Carter in 1987.

EASY CHAIR

1800–10

Mid-Atlantic
mahogany; maple and poplar
147.3 × 73 × 59.7
(58 × 28¾ × 23½ in.)
University of Virginia

PROVENANCE:
Thomas Jefferson; by descent to
Thomas Jefferson Randolph; by
gift to the University of Virginia;
by loan to TJMF since 1926.

This exceptionally tall easy chair has a high, curved barrel back, no wings, and reeding on the turned arms and front legs. The rear, slightly curving saber legs are uncarved. The red leather upholstery is a replacement of the original. The unusual height of the back may indicate that the chair had a ceremonial purpose. Tradition says that it was used by Jefferson while he served as vice president, although no documentation is known to support this claim.

The form of the chair was influenced by Thomas Sheraton, whose publication *The Cabinet-Maker and Upholsterer's Drawing Book* popularized the use of carved reeding on the arms and legs of furniture. By 1810 the motif, which had its origins in ancient Rome, was popular in America.[57] This chair may have been derived from Sheraton's Plate 8, "Various easy Chairs with their sizes in Inches."[58]

[1926-1]   S.R.S.

The Joinery at Monticello

Although trade with merchants was imperative to obtain various kinds of materials, foodstuffs, and manufactured products, Monticello was intended to be a self-sufficient enterprise. The plantation community, chiefly comprised of slaves, included not only field workers, but also skilled blacksmiths, nail makers, sawyers, weavers, spinners, cobblers, as well as many others with accomplished skills in cooking, dairymaking, butchering, preserving food, sewing, laundering, and other essential vocations. Among these talented artisans were many highly competent joiners, workers "in wood who do lighter and more ornamental work than that of carpenters, as the construction of furniture and the fittings of a house."[1] Workers with such skills were indispensable in the construction of Monticello between 1770 and 1810. After the house was completed, the joiners more often turned their considerable proficiency with wood to the production of furniture for Jefferson and some of his neighbors.[2]

Joinery

An enclosed workshop for woodworking would have been necessary for the construction of the first Monticello, but the site of it is not known. By 1796 a "joiner's shop, 57. feet by 18. feet, the underpinning and chimney of stone, the walls and roof of wood," was located at the west end of the principal plantation "street," Mulberry Row; only the ruins of the joinery— a chimney and partial stone foundations—survive today.[3] Located nearby were a nail factory, saw pit, timber yard, dairy, blacksmith's shop, washhouse, and dwellings for both slaves and free white workmen.

The joiner's shop was furnished with the tools required for basic carpentry as well as fine furniture. It was surprisingly well equipped, an indication of the sophisticated skills that Jefferson's workmen possessed. One of the earliest documented devices (1775) was a turning wheel or lathe, the only piece of large equipment in the shop, which was used to make balusters for the roof and staircases. The range of hand tools is impressive and rivals the equipment used in the shops of Williamsburg cabinetmakers. James Dinsmore, one of the men hired as a house joiner at Monticello, prepared an inventory in 1809 that mentioned many different kinds of planes—including fifteen pairs of "hollows and rounds," "rabbitt," astragal, bead, raising, and eleven kinds of cornice planes; straight and circular smoothing planes; two plow planes and bits; a bench vise; six augers; three hand saws; pocket chisels; and more.[4] In addition, the hired joiners had their own specialized equipment, which must have added considerably to the sizes and kinds of tools that were available. The variety of implements demonstrates that the Monticello joinery had the mechanical capability to turn out detailed furniture designs.

Hired Joiners

With its intricate entablatures (which varied from room to room), differing ceiling heights, complex roof, and ornamental scheme, Monticello's ambitious architecture demanded skilled artisans. Jefferson imported several highly trained craftsmen to carry out the most complicated aspects of construction as well as to teach Monticello slaves the joinery craft. At

Monticello, a team of unusually able joiners—both slave and free—was assembled to realize Jefferson's vision.

Among the first hired joiners was Thomas Walker, who was employed for only a year. In 1773, Walker presumably worked on the construction of the house and also made two spinning wheels, "a pine press for papers 6. f. by 4. f," and "1 large safe 5 f. square."[5] In 1778, Jefferson remarked, "I retain for instance among my domestic servants a gardener (Ortolano), weaver (Tessitore di lino e lan[o]), a cabinet maker (Stipettaio) and a stonecutter."[6]

Jefferson hired a skilled workman named David Watson, "a British deserter, house joiner by trade."[7] Jefferson found him in Richmond in April 1781. He worked at Monticello until at least the middle of 1784, came back briefly for several weeks in 1792, and was again employed from October 1793 until December 1797. Watson was also a skilled wheelwright and fashioned wheels for a mule cart, two ox carts, wheelbarrow, wagons, and Jefferson's phaeton. It was Watson who gave John Hemings, Jefferson's slave, his first instruction. In 1793, Jefferson noted, "Johnny is to work with him for the purpose of learning to make wheels and all sorts of work."[8] Watson was capable of supervising Monticello's carpenters, who were "to be employed in splitting, planing, jointing and rounding shingles, which may be under the eye of Watson."[9] He must also have been known to Jefferson as a talented cabinetmaker because Jefferson authorized him to make a writing desk for his daughter Maria.[10] After leaving Jefferson's employ in 1797, Watson worked for Thomas Mann Randolph.

The second of the important joiners at Monticello was James Dinsmore (c. 1771–1830), whom Jefferson hired in Philadelphia shortly after he became a naturalized citizen in June 1798. Jefferson purchased tools for him in June of that year and paid the cost of his journey to Charlottesville in October.[11] He worked at Monticello until 1809, and later at Montpelier and the University of Virginia, where he was chief master carpenter for many structures. In recommending Dinsmore to Benjamin Henry Latrobe for work on the Capitol, Jefferson remarked that he had never known "a more faithful, sober, honest and respectable man."[12] Jefferson said that he and his fellow craftsman, John Neilson, were "house joiners of the very first order both in their knolege [sic] in architecture, and their practical abilities."[13] Little detailed comment is recorded, however, about Dinsmore's particular involvement with the making of furniture, except for a reference to his obtaining mahogany in 1807 from James Oldham, a former Monticello joiner, for some tables to be made at Monticello.

Another experienced joiner, James Oldham, was engaged to complete Jefferson's challenging scheme to enlarge Monticello. Oldham was hired in 1801 to replace the only fatality of Monticello's construction, John Holmes, who fell from a scaffold in 1801. Daniel Trump, a Philadelphia window sash maker, recommended James Oldham, who "Studied Architecture under Me and made Great Progress for the time he was with me . . . he is a Genteel well behaved young man and I have not a Doubt but he will answer you very well."[14] Not only did Oldham put up the cornice around the South Piazza as he did in January 1802 but he also had ample skills to make window sashes. As it turned out, Oldham served Jefferson well until 1804, when he left to establish a business of his own in Richmond. Almost immediately, Jefferson placed an order for "a pair of folding doors, mahogany, for partition between the Hall & Parlour," and a great deal of sash, which indicates that Oldham had exceptionally fine skills as a joiner and was capable of making furniture.[15] Jefferson endorsed him to a Richmond friend, Colonel John Harvie: "James Oldham has lived with me several years, is an able workman in housejoinery, skilled in the orders of architecture, honest, sober and industrious."[16] He was also ambitious and asked Jefferson to help him procure a copy of Palladio's *Four Books of Architecture*, which he no doubt knew from Jefferson's library. Jefferson told him:

The chance of getting one in America is slender. In the meantime, as you may be distressed for present use, I send you my portable edition, . . . It contains only the 1st book on the orders, which is the essential part.[17]

In October 1807, Jefferson wrote to Oldham in Richmond to instruct him to buy enough mahogany to make four Pembroke tables, again suggesting that Oldham had particular knowledge of the requirements of the manufacture of furniture. Jefferson very carefully described exactly what would be required.

I have a job of 4. Pembroke tables on hand at Monticello, but we have the Mahogany for the tops; they are to be 2f. 3I. square in the bed, and the leaves half the [width] of the beds, so as to be 4f by 2f 3 when the leaves are up. 2 planks of Mahogany 10 f. by 2f4I each would make the tops of the 4 tables. will you be so good as to chuse and procure for me the 2. planks.[18]

Two months later Oldham informed Jefferson that he had not been able to find sufficient "San demingo," a high quality mahogany from Santo Domingo, that Oldham reported was little used in Richmond.[19] To complete Jefferson's order, he also sent some bay wood plank, which he thought would suit the production of furniture at Monticello.

Not enough is known about John Neilson (d. 1827), a talented housejoiner who labored on the last phase of Monticello's enlargement. Neilson became a naturalized citizen in Philadelphia on September 28, 1804.[20] In his Memorandum Book, Jefferson noted on May 11, 1806, "Agreed that John Neilson's wages shall be 270D. from the commencement of the 2d. Year." Neilson worked at Monticello through 1808, when he went to work at Montpelier, James Madison's house in Orange County. He later worked for John Hartwell Cocke on the construction of Bremo in Fluvanna County. Neilson was evidently a learned individual. He possessed a substantial library of 248 titles, including several carpenter's guides and works on ancient and modern history, and had a large collection of prints and drawings.[21] From Jefferson, either before or after his death, he acquired Diocletian's Portico (unlocated). He made the drawing of the University of Virginia that was engraved by Peter Maverick in 1822 (Cat. 64).

African-American Joiners

All three of the hired white joiners—Dinsmore, Oldham, and Neilson—worked hand-in-hand with slaves. Thomas Mann Randolph, Jefferson's son-in-law, observed, "I think it would be better to employ some industrious white person to labor with them [slave out-carpenters who felled trees and built farm buildings] and lay off their work for them."[22] Jefferson described a little of how hired joiners and slaves worked together when he sought a replacement for John Holmes after his fatal accident. He wrote, "He will have a black man under him to rough out his work."[23] Jefferson's statement indicates that slaves were sufficiently well trained to carry out many carpentry functions.

Jefferson also clearly expected that the hired joiners would train Monticello slaves in the joinery trade. Proficient joiners required many years of instruction. For example, aspiring white joiners were apprenticed under a master joiner and his journeyman helpers for at least seven years. Although without a fixed period of study, the training of slave carpenters and joiners at Monticello was apparently rigorous.

The eighteen-year-old John Hemings (1775–1830 +) was first instructed in carpentry work under Watson in 1793. He later worked with Dinsmore and become a remarkably capable joiner and cabinetmaker in his own right, recognized by family members and plantation workers for his skill. One of Monticello's overseers, Edmund Bacon, said:

John Hemings was a carpenter. He was a first-rate workman—a very extra workman. He could make anything that was wanted in woodwork. He learned his trade of Dinsmore. He made most of the woodwork of Mr. Jefferson's fine carriage.[24]

The son of Betty Hemings, the matriarch of the slave Hemings family, Hemings labored on many aspects of Monticello's construction, often working side by side with Dinsmore. In September and October 1799, "Dinsmore and Johnny prepared and put up the oval arch" in the Cabinet in twelve days.[25] Among other accomplishments he worked on the Chinese railing, venetian blinds, cellar sashes, bedchamber closet, and window shutters; recovered Monticello's roof in the 1820s; and made repairs to Poplar Forest after it was damaged by fire in 1825. Jefferson wrote his grandson Francis Eppes, "I will spare J. Hem. to you and his two aids and he can repair every thing of wood as well or perhaps better than any body there."[26]

Hemings probably made a substantial amount of the furniture crafted in the Monticello joinery after 1809, although only eight works are positively attributed to him—a campeachy chair (Cat. 139), the boxes for the books sold to the United States Congress (destroyed), a traveling desk for Ellen Randolph Coolidge (destroyed), a bedstead (unlocated), a table for playing chess (unlocated), Pembroke tables for Poplar Forest, a hanging cabinet (Cat. 154), and a dressing table (unlocated). When the superb writing desk that Hemings had made for Ellen Randolph Coolidge was lost at sea, Jefferson wrote his granddaughter:

John Hemmings was the first who brought me the news. He was au desespoir! That beautiful writing desk he had taken so much pains to make for you! Everything else seemed as nothing in his eye, and that loss was everything. Virgil could not have been more afflicted had his Aenid fallen a prey to the flames. I asked him if he could not replace it by making another? No. His eyesight had failed him too much, and his recollection of it was too imperfect.[27]

Hemings was manumitted in a codicil to Jefferson's will:

I give also to my good servants John Hemings and Joe Fosset their freedom at the end of one year after my death and to each of them respectively all the tools of their respective shops.[28]

A lesser known slave joiner was Lewis (1758/60–1822), who came to Jefferson as part of the Wayles estate. In 1799, he dressed and laid the plank for the floor in the upper southwest bow. Like John Hemings, he worked with Dinsmore.[29] After the house was largely completed, he helped John Hemings make furniture. In 1818, Jefferson noted:

Johnny Hem. and Lewis began a dressing table and finished it in exactly 6. weeks, of which 4. weeks was such dreadful weather that even within doors, nothing like full work could be done.[30]

Furniture Made at Monticello

When Jefferson stepped down from the presidency in 1809, Monticello's interior was not entirely finished, but the complex expansion had been accomplished. Dinsmore and Neilson were gone, and the joinery was left in the capable hands of John Hemings, who by then had sixteen years of experience.

Jefferson found himself in an unusual predicament. He had a "new" and larger Monticello that realized his Neoclassical vision, but he also had tired furniture and not enough of it. Most of his furniture had been purchased while he was in France between 1784 and 1789, and in New York and Philadelphia, between 1790 and 1793. In 1809, many of the furnishings were twenty-five to thirty years old and had survived storage or use in a house that was under construction for more than fifteen years.

With his financial resources substantially diminished and without easy access to urban furniture-making centers, Jefferson turned to adept slave craftsmen at Monticello's own joinery to make furniture both for Monticello and Poplar Forest. John Hemings, Lewis, and their assistants fabricated tables, dressing tables, dumbwaiters for serving food, several kinds of chairs, candlestands, a bedstead, boxes for storing and transporting books, a small cupboard, presses for storing papers, a seed press, and other works.

The designs for the furniture made in the joinery were probably Jefferson's, but only a few drawings by him survive to substantiate his involvement. Although the actual piece of furniture is not known, a drawing for a work table proves Jefferson's direction of the design of the Monticello-made furniture. His drawing, showing the characteristic straight, slightly tapering legs, bears remarkable similarity to the Monticello-made work table (Cat. 146) and dumbwaiters (Cat. 140, 141). The work produced in the joinery characteristically was spare and utilitarian in its approach—distinctly unlike the fashionable inlaid furniture then being produced in urban centers such as Philadelphia, New York, and Charleston. John Hemings and Lewis, after all, had been trained by house joiners, not cabinetmakers; their work could not be expected to demonstrate technical virtuosity or a familiarity with the stylish designs of the published cabinetmakers such as Hepplewhite, Sheraton, or Hope.

The remarkable achievement of the Monticello slave joiners was not only their craftsmanship but also their ability to realize Jefferson's ideas. The few surviving drawings suggest that Jefferson probably handed them a small, casual sketch, made known the finished size, and left the production to them. The result was a piece of furniture that expressed the skill of its maker and the straightforward, functional values of its designer, Thomas Jefferson.

S . R . S .

Marble Top Table

c. 1784–89
Thomas Jefferson
(1743–1826)
ink on paper
Massachusetts Historical Society

Monticello joinery
walnut
87.6 × 48.3 × 39.4
(34 ½ × 19 × 15 ½ in.)

PROVENANCE:
Thomas Jefferson; by purchase
to John Hartwell Cocke at the
Dispersal Sale in 1827; by descent
to Mrs. Mazyck Wilson Shields; by
bequest to TJMF in 1945.

Monticello joinery
cherry
88.9 × 47.6 × 39.4
(35 × 18¾ × 15 ½ in.)
Private collection

PROVENANCE:
Thomas Jefferson; by gift to
Joseph C. Cabell; by descent
to private collection; by loan
to TJMF since 1929.

Tradition in the family of Joseph C. Cabell, a longtime friend of Jefferson's who helped him establish the University of Virginia, states that the cherry chairs were given to Cabell by Jefferson. Jefferson called Cabell "the main pillar" of support for the university. It appears that the chairs were part of a larger set that may have included ten or more chairs.[31]

Two almost identical chairs, made of walnut, are also known and may have comprised a second tablet-backed set. The cherry chairs, however, have ovolo molded seat rails. The walnut pair was purchased at the Dispersal Sale in 1827 by John Hartwell Cocke of Bremo in Fluvanna County; ten additional chairs from this set are in a private collection.

According to family tradition, the walnut chairs with leather seats were made at Monticello from a drawing [Jefferson] made from chairs excavated at Pompeii. Although the general idea of the chairs seems to have been influenced by a "Klismos" type, it is very likely that Jefferson had seen—or owned—Georges Jacob's *siège hemicycle*, the first models of which Jacob made for Montholon in 1786.[32] This type of chair, with a concave back, similar to a Klismos chair, was very popular in the first quarter of the nineteenth century but was also known earlier. Jefferson might also have seen Klismos chairs in Washington, or drawings of them such as Benjamin Henry Latrobe's sketches for furniture in the Greek style made for the Madison Dining Room at the President's House.

The chairs executed by Monticello's joiners conform to the French *chaise hemicycle*. While many of the French examples have saber legs, the Monticello-made examples have straight, slightly tapering legs, characteristic of Jefferson's furniture designs.
[1945-1-1/2; 1929-1-1/2]

S.R.S.

CAMPEACHY CHAIRS

---

after 1809

New Orleans or possibly
Monticello joinery
unidentified wood
114.3 × 71.1 × 81.3
(45 × 28 × 32 in.)
Private collection

PROVENANCE:
Thomas Jefferson; by purchase
to John Hartwell Cocke at the
Dispersal Sale in 1827; by descent
to a private collection.

before August 1819

John Hemings
mahogany
100.1 × 61 × 83.8
(39⁷/₁₆ × 24 × 33 in.)

PROVENANCE:
Thomas Jefferson; by descent to
John H. Burke; by bequest to the
Pennsylvania School for the Deaf;
by purchase to TJMF in 1970.

In his later years Jefferson was most comfortable in a campeachy chair. When suffering from a serious attack of rheumatism at Poplar Forest, Jefferson specifically requested a siesta, or campeachy, chair:

While too weak to sit up the whole day, and afraid to increase the weakness by lying down, I long for a Siesta chair which would have admitted the medium position. I must therefore pray you to send by Henry the one made by Johnny Hemmings. . . . John or Wormly should wrap it well. . .[33]

Ellen Randolph Coolidge, a granddaughter, recollected that she often saw him reclining in one at Monticello:

In the large parlour, with it's parquetted floor, stood the Campeachy chair made of goatskin, sent to him from New Orleans, where, in the shady twilight, I was used to see him resting.[34]

The unusual form of this chair, variously called a "lolling chair," "siesta chair," "sling-seat armchair," "hammock chair," "Spanish chair," or "campeachy," had its origins in ancient Egypt. Versions of the design with its characteristic X-shaped stretchers were known in ancient Greece and Rome and were fashionable in France and Spain during the seventeenth century. The campeachy form that was popular in New Orleans was apparently derived from Spanish sources. The name "campeachy" is an anglicized spelling of Campeche, a Mexican state, where a kind of mahogany called "bloodwood" or "logwood" was grown that was often used to make the chair.

Although it is not known how or where Jefferson first saw a campeachy, he tried to obtain several in 1808. He wrote to William Brown, "the Campeachy hammock, as made of some vegetable substance netted, is commonly to be had in New Orleans. . . . I take the liberty of asking you to procure me a couple of them."[35] Brown shipped three chairs, but they were lost at sea. The chairs were intended for Jefferson, Thomas Mann Randolph, and Eliza House Trist. "The hammocks from Campeachy were sent on in the month of October so William Brown wrote to Mrs. Trist, directed to you, but she has never heard of their arrival."[36] Ten days later Jefferson reported that "the Schooner Sampson, Capt. Smith, with the Campeachy hammocks etc. . . . has never been heard of since."[37]

Ten years later, Jefferson finally obtained his long-awaited New Orleans campeachy chair. Thomas Bolling Robertson, a native Virginian who was then a representative to Congress from Louisiana, told his father in June 1819, "I have sent by the North Star . . . for Richmond a Campeachy chair. I have sent one also to Mr. Jefferson; he asked me many years ago to procure him one."[38] The chair was shipped in August.[39] Once it arrived, Jefferson thanked Robertson for his effort, "Age, its infirmities & frequent illnesses have rendered indulgence in that easy kind of chair truly acceptable."[40]

Although John Hemings probably copied the New Orleans chair later, he also probably made two campeachy chairs for Jefferson before the New Orleans example arrived. The origin of the prototype—or drawing—that Hemings used is not known. Seven campeachy chairs with a Monticello association are mentioned in various documents; two chairs descended in the family, four were sold at the 1827 Dispersal Sale, and a seventh was given to Peachy Gilmer in 1821. Of these, five are known today.

[1970-91]   S.R.S.

DUMBWAITERS

Monticello joinery
walnut; pine
88.9 × 47 × 46.7
(35 × 18½ × 18⅜ in.)

PROVENANCE:
Thomas Jefferson; by descent to
Francis Eppes; by purchase to
William Cobbs; by descent to Mr.
and Mrs. Charles S. Adams; by
gift to TJMF in 1975.

Monticello joinery or Henry and
Joseph Ingle
mahogany with King of Prussia
marble
88.9 × 47 × × 47
(35 × 18½ × 18½ in.)

PROVENANCE:
Thomas Jefferson; by descent to
Robert M. Graham; by gift to
TJMF in 1983.

In Paris, Jefferson became accustomed to the French practice of using "dumbwaiters," small tiers of shelves on casters, for small dinner parties. These étagères were also known in England throughout the eighteenth century. Later, as president, Jefferson continued to employ dumbwaiters when he received dinner guests at the President's House. Margaret Bayard Smith remarked:

When he had any persons dining with him, with whom he wished to enjoy a free and unrestricted flow of conversation, the number of persons at the table never exceeded four, and by each individual was placed a dumbwaiter, containing everything necessary for the progress of the dinner from beginning to end, so as to make the attendance of servants entirely unnecessary, believing as he did, that much of the domestic and even public discord was produced by the mutilated and misconstructed repetition of free conversation at dinner tables, by these mute but not inattentive listeners.[41]

In Paris, where Jefferson could entertain as many as twenty guests at dinner, he owned five dumbwaiters, but these were sold because they "were of the more common kind."[42] To replace them, he purchased four or more in Philadelphia as they were among his furnishings at his house at Gray's Ferry.[43]

Two of the five extant dumbwaiters have features that suggest that they are the products of the Monticello joinery; straight, slightly tapering legs; astragal molding on the top rails; ovolo molding on the side rails; and a double-scratch bead on the open end of the shelf. The other two dumbwaiters differ slightly. They have King of Prussia marble tops, brass bail handles on two sides, and legs that terminate in applied spade feet resting on casters. Only one of the mahogany dumbwaiters has its original spade feet; the others are later replacements. The fifth dumbwaiter has a wood and marble top but no spade feet. The comparatively unrefined workmanship suggests that they were made either in Monticello's joinery or possibly by two Philadelphia joiners named Joseph and Henry Ingle who performed cabinetwork for Jefferson in the early 1790s.

The dumbwaiter pictured at left was made in the Monticello joinery for Jefferson's use at Poplar Forest, his farm and retreat in Bedford County. The dumbwaiter descended in the family of William Cobbs, who acquired Poplar Forest together with some of Jefferson's furnishings in 1828.

[1975-45; 1976-129]   S.R.S.

142

SIDE TABLE

---

after 1793

Monticello joinery
mahogany; oak
71.1 × 71.1 × 52.1
(28 × 28 × 20½ in.)

PROVENANCE:
Thomas Jefferson; by descent to
Septimia Meikleham; by descent to
William A. Meikleham; by gift to
TJMF in 1938.

This occasional table was made in the Monticello joinery sometime after 1793. The uncommon ovolo-headed raised ornament on the legs imitates the decorative details on a Paris-made architect's table (Cat. 166), which was brought to Monticello in 1793. The table, with an unusually thick top and rather heavy legs, has a drawer with brass bail handle. The legs originally had casters (now missing).

[1938-24]   S . R . S .

This plain card table in the Federal style was one of thirteen tea and card tables mentioned by Jefferson on his 1815 Memorandum of Taxable Property. The simplicity of the unornamented design suggests that it might have been made in the Monticello joinery, possibly modeled after more elaborate card tables acquired in Philadelphia or Baltimore (Cat. 131). The table has four straight, slightly tapering legs. The right rear leg is a fly leg and supports the hinged, unlined top when it is opened.

S.R.S.

143

CIRCULAR CARD TABLE

after 1790

mahogany and mahogany veneer
73.7 × 91.4 × 45.1
(29 × 36 × 17¾ in.)
Miss Mary Frances Petty

PROVENANCE:
Thomas Jefferson; by purchase to Alexander Pollock at the Dispersal Sale in 1827; by descent to Miss Mary Frances Petty.

Together with a revolving chair and a Windsor bench, this table was one of three essential components that comprised the novel reading-and-writing arrangement in Jefferson's Cabinet. The table was substantially altered in the Monticello joinery and probably was made there as well.

The initial table top was rectangular. A round revolving top was later attached with a bolt in the center. The table's apron was cut away on two sides so that Jefferson could sit comfortably, and two stretchers were appended to stabilize the legs. To allow the table to be easily moved, small wheels were affixed to the slightly tapering legs.

[1951-3]   S . R . S .

Jefferson, who cherished efficiency and mechanical innovation, apparently was fascinated by revolving furniture. He owned not only two revolving tables but also two revolving chairs. Both revolving tables and chairs were unusual in the late eighteenth and early nineteenth centuries.

This table was made in the Monticello joinery for Jefferson's use at Poplar Forest. It may be the very table that Jefferson referred to in a letter to his Monticello overseer, Edmund Bacon, in 1811: "Tell Johnny Hemmings to finish off immediately the frame for the round table for this place that it may come by the waggon."[44] Cornelia Randolph, Jefferson's artistically inclined granddaughter, sketched the table and a Windsor chair at Poplar Forest (see p. 262).

Fabricated entirely of native woods, the table has a segmented decorative top. A cove mold beneath the outer edge of the lower top effectively minimizes the height of the two tops. The straight legs, which taper to the bottom, are characteristic of Monticello joinery-made furniture.

[1976-34]   S . R . S .

Monticello joinery
mahogany
73.7 × 94 × 75.2
(29 × 37 × 29⅝ in.)

PROVENANCE:
Thomas Jefferson; by descent to Thomas Jefferson Randolph; by descent to Carolina Ramsay Randolph; by bequest to R.T.W. Duke; by descent to Helen Duke; by purchase to TJMF in 1951.

145

TABLE WITH REVOLVING TOP

Monticello joinery
cherry; walnut and southern pine
H: 71.1 D: 91.4 (28 × 36 in.)

PROVENANCE:
Thomas Jefferson; by descent to Francis Eppes; by purchase to William Cobbs; by sale to Fred Harris in 1877; by trade to Christian S. Hutter in 1891; by purchase to James Owen Watts, Jr. in 1946; by purchase to Claudine Hutter in 1946; by purchase to the Buckley-Lunati Galleries, Atlanta, Georgia; by purchase to TJMF in 1976.

146

WORK TABLE

c. 1800

*Monticello joinery
mahogany; yellow pine and
tulip poplar
69.9 × 39.7 closed (77.5
extended) × 45.4 (27¼ × 15⅝
closed [30½ extended] × 17⅞
in.)*

PROVENANCE:
Martha Jefferson Randolph; by
descent to Virginia and Nicholas
Trist; by descent to Frances Maury
Burke; by gift to TJMF in 1929.

This small drop-leaf work table was used by Martha Jefferson Randolph for sewing. The faces of the drawers have a scratch bead, and the base is surrounded by a large astragal molding; both features are typical of Monticello joinery craftsmanship. Among Monticello-made furniture, the reeding on the front is unique. The dust board is attached in exactly the same manner as the shelves on the joinery-made dumbwaiters.

[1929-2]

S . R . S .

147

TABLE

c. 1810

*Monticello joinery
mahogany; cyprus and oak
71.8 × 207 × 138.4
(28¼ × 81½ × 54 in.)
Private collection*

PROVENANCE:
Thomas Jefferson; by descent to
Martha Jefferson Randolph; by
descent to a private collection.

One of the more ambitious products of Monticello's joinery is this oval mahogany table with ten legs, which was said to have been placed in the Tea Room. The design is likely Jefferson's. He is known to have favored ovals, as he selected one to outline the dinner invitation card that he used while president and also chose to have his initials "Th:J" engraved on an oval brass plaque that was affixed to one of his writing boxes.

The table has square, tapering legs, an attribute characteristic of Monticello joinery workmanship and Jefferson's designs. The rounded ends of the table are each supported by two fly legs.

S . R . S .

This revolving bookstand, once thought to be a music stand, was probably made to Jefferson's design and specifications in the joinery. As many as five books could be placed on it at a time. Jefferson may have conveniently placed it next to his chair in his reading-and-writing arrangement in the Cabinet. It is one of three known "revolving" works made in the joinery; the other two are tables.

Constructed of solid walnut, the cube-shaped stand has five adjustable rests for holding books; it has one book rest on the top and one on each of the four sides. The rests can be folded down to form a cube. A central pole enables the bookstand to rotate at the bottom. A hole in the bottom suggests the possibility that the bookstand originally was supported by a tripod base.[45]

[1938-20]   S.R.S.

This very modest and unadorned desk is said to have been a gift for William A. Burwell (Cat. 74), the young man who served as Jefferson's secretary for the later part of his first term as president. The desk, attributed to the Monticello joinery, has straight, tapering legs, and two hinged surfaces. The first hinged surface exposes a writing surface with a scratch-beaded edge, and the second reveals an area for storage.

[1947-4]   S.R.S.

149

DESK
_____

c. 1810

Monticello joinery
mahogany and pine
77.5 × 92.7 × 50.8
(30½ × 36½ × 20 in.)

PROVENANCE:
Thomas Jefferson; by gift to William A. Burwell; by descent to Frances Steptoe Todd; by purchase to TJMF in 1947.

292

This unusual piece has two distinct parts that have been paired together: a tall, narrow bookcase with five shelves set atop a press. The bookcase has a strong family tradition that states that it was actually made by Jefferson, "he having made the upper part of the Bookcase with his own hands and having kept it in his bedroom with a reading chair standing by, keeping in this Bookcase such books as he was currently reading."[46] According to family tradition, the press with four interior shelves was used by Jefferson to store memoranda concerning the farm and observations on the weather.

The bookcase and press are identified on Cornelia Randolph's drawing of Monticello's floor plan, which reveals a small bookcase next to the mantelpiece in Jefferson's bedroom.

The top of the press features an astragal molding typical of Monticello-made furniture. One of the two unmatched bail handles on the sides of the press exactly matches a dumbwaiter. The interior of the door has an inscription in Jefferson's handwriting, beginning with the words "Dead Papers" (the rest is illegible).

[1988-1]   S.R.S.

150

**BOOKCASE
AND PRESS**

c. 1810

Monticello joinery
Bookcase: mahogany
Press: mahogany, mahogany
veneer over pine on door, walnut
breadboard ends, and tulip
poplar
Bookcase: 125.1 × 36.8 × 16.8
(49¼ × 14½ × 6⅝ in.)
Press: 81.3 × 41.3 × 34.9
(32 × 16¼ × 13¾ in.)

PROVENANCE:
Thomas Jefferson; by descent
to Thomas Jefferson Randolph;
by descent to Lyne Moncure
Shackelford; by purchase to
TJMF in 1987.

Jefferson used this press, which he kept in his Cabinet, to hold garden seeds in packets and vials. He may have first installed the press and seeds in May 1809, for he asked Thomas Jefferson Randolph, his grandson who was then studying in Philadelphia, to obtain "a gross of vial-corks of different sizes, and 4. dozen phials of 1.2.3. and 4. ounces, one dozen of each size. The largest mouth would be the best as they are for holding garden seeds."[47] On a visit to Monticello in August 1809, Margaret Bayard Smith noted:

He opened a little closet which contains all his garden seeds. They are all in little phials, labled and hung on little hooks. Seeds such as peas, beans, etc. were in tin cannisters, but everything labeled and in the neatest order.[48]

The back of the seed press shows the holes made by the hooks on which the phials hung.

The press was crafted in the Monticello joinery, and the nails were made in Monticello's own nailery. The press has two paneled doors, each with two recessed panels. The moldings on the right-hand door (the left is a replacement) and the double-scratch beading on the mahogany shelves precisely duplicate those on Septimia Randolph's small cabinet.

[1942-9]   S.R.S.

151

SEED PRESS

c. 1809

Monticello joinery
walnut and mahogany; yellow
pine
168 × 100.6 × 35.4
(66⅛ × 39⅝ × 13¹⁵/₁₆)

PROVENANCE:
Thomas Jefferson; by descent to
Septimia Meikleham; by descent to
Mrs. H. P. Meikleham; by bequest
to TJMF in 1957.

152 and 153

FILING PRESSES

1800–20

Monticello joinery
cherry and walnut
88.1 × 48.3 × 32.4
(34¹¹⁄₁₆ × 19 × 12¾ in.)

1800–20

Monticello joinery
mahogany
88.3 × 52.1 × 35.9
(34¾ × 20½ × 14⅛)

Mrs. Cynthia K. Barlowe

PROVENANCE:
Thomas Jefferson; by descent to
Thomas Jefferson Randolph; by
loan to George Tucker; by descent
to Dr. Janet Kimbrough; [1] by gift
to TJMF in 1970; [2] by descent to
Mrs. Cynthia K. Barlowe.

Jefferson was not only a prolific correspondent, but also was an exemplary recordkeeper. With the help of various copying presses, he was able to produce copies of his own letters. These copies were kept in more than six presses, made by the Monticello joinery especially for filing. In addition to the letters that he wrote and received, Jefferson also kept law cases, papers of the old Congress, state papers, household accounts, plantation papers, pocket memorandum books, bank accounts, diplomas, and documents that he used in preparing *Notes on the State of Virginia.*

Five of the original presses are known today. Each consists of a rectangular cabinet with fixed shelves resting on a wide plinth containing a drawer. Without feet, the base sits directly on the floor. The presses feature construction details characteristic of the Monticello joinery. For example, just as on the work table (Cat. 146), one of the presses has a drawer with a scratch bead at the top and bottom, but not on the sides. The shelves are notched to fit into the sides of the cabinet.

These presses and another, which contained Jefferson's correspondence, were loaned to George Tucker by Thomas Jefferson Randolph. The correspondence was returned, but Tucker kept the filing presses, which have descended in his family.

[1970-85]   S.R.S.

154

CABINET

Monticello joinery
walnut and poplar
57.1 × 57.8 × 20.3
(22½ × 22¾ × 8)

PROVENANCE:
Septimia Randolph (later
Meikleham); by descent to Mrs.
H. P. Meikleham; by bequest to
TJMF in 1957.

A descendant reported that this small cabinet was made in the Monticello joinery to hold dolls' clothes for Septimia Anne Randolph, one of Jefferson's granddaughters. The interior contains two shelves with edges ornamented by a scratch-molded double bead. The glazed door, with four panes, has sash molding that is similar to the treatment on the petit-format bookcase in the collection of the Winterthur Museum. A concealed hole for a staple reveals that the cabinet was intended to be wall mounted.

[1938-3]   S.R.S.

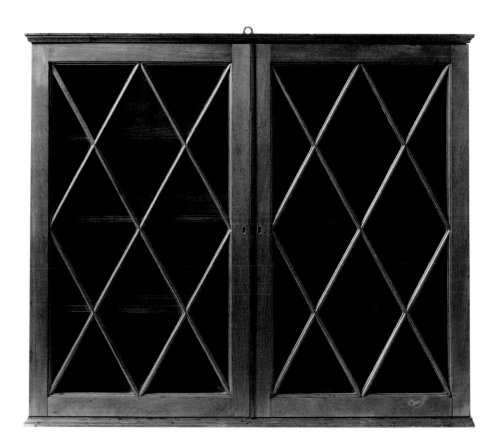

This wall-mounted bookcase with four shelves for petit-format books may have been one of several bookcases made at the Monticello joinery for Poplar Forest.

In the drawing-room there was what Mr. Jefferson called his petit-format library, contained in four cases, each of which was perhaps between three and four feet in width and height. The books, to economize space, were generally of the smallest sized editions published. It contained upwards of one hundred volumes of British, a considerable collection of Italian and French, and a few favorite Greek and Latin poets, and a larger number of prose writers of the same languages—all, it is unnecessary to say, in the original.[49]

Three of the four bookcases were put up for sale with the books from the Poplar Forest library in 1873. Included were ninety-eight petit-format books with the description "Principally from the press of Wetstein, Elzavir, and Jansonii."[50] The bookcase in the collection of the Winterthur Museum has a tradition of Jefferson ownership, "to hold his choice little collection of Elzevirs and Aldines (small pocket-sized books)."[51]

The attribution to the Monticello joinery is based upon the detailed molding on the three bookshelves, which is identical to the seed press (Cat. 151), another joinery-made piece, and the mullions, which are similar to Septimia Randolph's cabinet (Cat. 154).

S . R . S .

155

BOOKCASE

c. 1810

*Monticello joinery
mahogany; southern pine
64.3 × 76.5 × 13.3
(25⁵⁄₁₆ × 30⅛ × 5¼ in.)
Winterthur Museum*

PROVENANCE:
Thomas Jefferson; by descent to Francis Eppes (?); by purchase to David Francis in 1827; by descent to D. G. Francis; by purchase to Barclay Dunham; by purchase to Mrs. W. H. Burr; by purchase to Mrs. Glen Wright; by purchase to Mr. and Mrs. Archibald Millikan; by purchase to Mr. and Mrs. O. Hakola; by purchase to Winterthur Museum in 1967.

WALL BRACKET

c. 1810

Monticello joinery
mahogany
58.4 × 41 × 22.5
(23 × 16⅛ × 8⅞ in.)

PROVENANCE:
Thomas Jefferson; by descent to
Francis Eppes; by purchase to
William Cobbs; by descent to Mr.
and Mrs. Charles S. Adams; by
gift to TJMF in 1977.

This hanging shelf with decorative pierced and scrolled fretwork is attributed to the
Monticello joinery and was made for Poplar Forest. The large astragal molding is characteristic of Monticello-made works. In the eighteenth century decorative shelves such as this
one were often used to hold busts or clocks.

[1977-55]   S . R . S .

This compact folding ladder, attributed to the Monticello joinery, closes into an unobtrusive pole. This type of ladder was frequently used in libraries in the late eighteenth century.[52] When closed, the two uprights of the ladder fit together, forming a single shaft of wood. According to tradition, the ladder was used to reach the great clock in the Entrance Hall for its weekly winding. Although the source for the design is not known, Jefferson noted seeing "a folding ladder" in Bergen, Germany during a trip there in 1788.

Efficient and portable ladders such as these were also helpful outside. In *Rural Affairs* (1877), J. J. Thomas recommended a similar design for pruning trees.

[1923-15]   S.R.S.

157
LADDER

after 1790

Monticello joinery
oak
424.2 × 33 open; 8.9 closed
(167 × 13 open; 3½ in. closed)

PROVENANCE:
Thomas Jefferson; [by purchase to Uriah P. Levy]; by descent to Jefferson Monroe Levy; by purchase to TJMF in 1923.

French Furniture

**FAUTEUILS
A LA REINE**

Paris
beech, leather or silk upholstery
87.3 × 58.4 × 55.9
(34⅜ × 23 × 22 in.);
87.6 × 57.2 × 50.8 cm
(34½ × 22½ × 20 in.)
Mrs. John C. Parker and
Thomas Jefferson Memorial
Foundation

PROVENANCE:
Thomas Jefferson; by purchase to
John A. G. Davis at the Dispersal
Sale in 1827; two chairs by descent
to Mrs. Richard H. Dabney; by
descent to Mrs. John C. Parker.

Thomas Jefferson; by purchase to
an unidentified member of the
Randolph family at the Dispersal
Sale; by descent to Mrs. Nannie
Shackelford Block; by gift to
TJMF in 1940.

The traditions of two families indicate that these Louis XVI armchairs by an un-known maker were purchased in Paris between 1794 and 1796 by James Monroe, who acquired much French furniture at auction while he served as minister to France. Although the chairs differ in the shape of their seats, they are part of the same suite. The chairs supposedly were later sold to Jefferson, but no documentation has been located to confirm this account. They might have been among the forty-eight chairs that Jefferson transported from Paris to Philadelphia in 1790.

[1940-6]   S.R.S.

FAUTEUILS EN CABRIOLET

c. 1785

Paris
painted beech
83.9 × 56.5 × 47
(33 × 22¼ × 18½ in.)

PROVENANCE:
Thomas Jefferson; by descent to
Virginia and Nicholas Trist; by
descent to Charles B. Eddy, Jr.; by
bequest to Mrs. Charles B. Eddy,
Jr. (now Mrs. Joseph C. Cornwall);
by gift to TJMF in 1988.

c. 1785

Paris
painted beech
86.4 × 57.1 × 50.8
(34 × 22½ × 20 in.)

PROVENANCE:
Thomas Jefferson; by purchase to
John A. G. Davis at the Dispersal
Sale in 1827; by gift to Martha
Jefferson Minor; by descent to
Mrs. Jacqueline A. Caskie; by sale
to [1946-3-2] William MacCorkle
and [1946-3-1] Mrs. Hollins N.
Randolph; by purchase to TJMF.

Jefferson's grandson-in-law
carved the initials "TJ" in the
arm of the last chair in which
Jefferson sat.

Two pairs of related unstamped and unattributed *fauteuils* are known from a suite of eighteen chairs that Jefferson probably used in the dining room and adjacent petit salon in the Hôtel de Langeac.[1] These chairs, typical of the Louis XVI period, may have been made by Jacques Upton, who made a great deal of furniture for Jefferson. Upton, a *menuisier*, was made a master in 1782 and had a shop on the rue de Chaillot not far from the Hôtel de Langeac.[2]

Jefferson's original set was comprised of ten *chaises*, six large *fauteuils*, and two *bergères*, all upholstered in blue silk, presumably damask. These two pairs of armchairs feature trapezoidal and oval backs and deeply fluted legs, arms, and crest rail. At Monticello they may have been used in the Parlor or family sitting room.

One of these chairs, with a slightly curving oval back, was the last chair in which Jefferson sat before he died. Immediately after his death on July 4, 1826, his grandson-in-law, Nicholas P. Trist, carved Jefferson's initials in the inside of the chair's left arm. Another chair like it is in Monticello's collection.

[1964-36-1; 1988-2; 1946-3-1 and 2]   S.R.S.

162

**FAUTEUIL
A LA REINE
ONE OF SEVEN**

c. 1785

*attributed to Georges Jacob
(1739–1814)
mahogany
95.3 × 61.6 × 61
(37½ × 24¼ × 24 in.)*

PROVENANCE:
Thomas Jefferson; by descent to
Septimia Meikleham; by descent to
William A. Meikleham; by gift to
TJMF in 1940.

Among the four suites of seating furniture that Jefferson acquired in France was one by the celebrated cabinetmaker Georges Jacob, one of the finest *menuisiers* of the last quarter of the eighteenth century. Jacob, whose business was carried on by his sons, was renowned for the versatility of his designs. He was capable not only of creating highly ornamented, gilded furniture for Marie Antoinette, as he did for her at Versailles, but he could also fabricate much simpler and less pretentious designs.[3] The *fauteuils*, or armchairs, made in his shop that Jefferson acquired are so streamlined that they have been confused with later Directoire works.

Jacob is better known for his painted and gilded furniture, but he was also one of the first French cabinetmakers to use mahogany. As an American, Jefferson was more accustomed to unpainted furniture of woods such as mahogany, walnut, and cherry, and it was mahogany that he selected for a suite of twelve chairs made by Jacob. The suite, upholstered in crimson damask, included two *bergères* (upholstered easy chairs) and ten *fauteuils*. Of the ten *fauteuils*, seven are extant, but no *bergères* from this suite are known.

The form of the chair, with its elegant saber legs, is reminiscent of classical design, and that was probably the basis of the appeal of this design for Jefferson. The unusually sinuous effect is heightened by the flatness of the chair's members. Only a double bead surrounds the seatback. Although there is little carved ornamentation, the supports for the arms have a characteristically Jacob feature of incised colonettes. The chair is also decorated with two bronze leaves at the junction of the arms and back, and two bronze buttons at the top end of the arms.

Monticello's collection includes seven of the original ten *fauteuils;* all descended in Jefferson's family.

[1940-5-1/2; 1957-24; 1957-26; 1971-71-3; 1981-48; 1981-49]   S.R.S.

Jefferson owned a number of marble tables, and this one, supported by a marble pedestal, is the largest of those that survive. It may have been the one that Jefferson purchased on July 29, 1789, not long before he left France to return to America. He noted in his Memorandum Book, "pd for marble table 54 f."[4]

This table, called a *guéridon,* was so heavy that it was disassembled before it was shipped to rejoin Jefferson in Philadelphia in 1790. The base was packed in crate number twenty-three and the top in crate number sixty-three. "One large marble table" was located in the Drawing Room on Martha Jefferson's inventory taken after Jefferson's death.

At the Dispersal Sale on January 15, 1827, the table was purchased by George Blaetterman, professor of modern languages at the University of Virginia, who also acquired four bronze busts of the Roman emperors Otho, Vespasian, Nero, and Tiberius, a campeachy chair, and two dumbwaiters, together with "1 large Marble Table."[5]

[1967-118]   S.R.S.

163
PEDESTAL TABLE

1789

Paris
marble
77.5 × 105.4 (30½ × 41½ in.)

PROVENANCE:
Thomas Jefferson; by purchase to George Blaetterman at the Dispersal Sale in 1827; by descent to Mrs. A. F. McKnight; by gift to TJMF in 1967.

164

MARBLE TOP
TRIPOD TABLE

1785–90

top, Paris; base, Philadelphia [?]
marble, brass, mahogany
75.6 × 71.1 × 53.3
(29¾ × 28 × 21 in.)
Yale University Art Gallery, gift
of De Lancey Kountz, B.A.
1899

PROVENANCE:
Thomas Jefferson; by descent to
Thomas Jefferson Randolph; by
descent to [Carolina Ramsay
Randolph]; by purchase to De
Lancey Kountz; by gift to the Yale
University Art Gallery; by loan to
TJMF since 1945.

165

MARBLE TRESTLE
TABLE
ONE OF A PAIR

---

c. 1785

tops, Paris; bases, Philadelphia
and Monticello joinery
mahogany; oak; marble
75 × 77.2 × 73.7
(29½ × 30⅜ × 29 in.)
Mr. and Mrs. Robert Carter and
Thomas Jefferson Memorial
Foundation

PROVENANCE:
Thomas Jefferson; by descent to
Thomas Jefferson Randolph; by
descent to Wilson Randolph
Porterfield; by bequest to Mrs.
Wilson Randolph Porterfield; by
purchase to TJMF in 1978.

Thomas Jefferson; by descent to
Benjamin Franklin Randolph; by
gift or bequest to Sarah Champe
Carter Randolph; by gift or
bequest to Robert Carter family;
by descent to Mr. and Mrs. Robert
Carter.

This table top was one of four marble table tops with a brass border that Jefferson brought back to America from France. It is not known if the tops were accompanied by bases. The tilt-top base may have been joined to the top after Jefferson's return in 1790, possibly in Philadelphia. The pillar and slipper feet bear a striking similarity to a Pennsylvania-made stand in the collection of the Metropolitan Museum of Art said to have been designed by Benjamin Franklin.[6]

[1945-16]   S.R.S.

Jefferson acquired eight marble-topped tables while he was in France. Four were marble table tops with gilt borders, which returned to America in crate number forty-seven, identified as "quatre dessu de marbre de table avec bordure dores."[7] Grevin, the fastidious master *emballeur* who packed Jefferson's belongings, made no mention of the bases for the four tables on his list. A reference to bases does appear, however, on the list of goods to be shipped from Philadelphia to Monticello in 1793, "plusiers pieds de table" (several table bases). Nonetheless, the origin of the bases is unknown; they may have been made in France or America.

Only three of the original four table tops are known today, two rectangular and one nearly square (Cat. 164). The rectangular pair with trestle bases and snake feet stood in the Entrance Hall flanking the double-acting doors leading to the Parlor. (A fourth marble top table [Cat. 167] was returned to America with its base intact.) One of the tilt-top trestle tables, now in a private collection, survives in its nearly original state—with the brass band intact, but without a gilded perforated gallery. The trestle on this table, like the tripod base on the squarer marble tilt-top table (Cat. 164) appears to have been made by an urban cabinetmaker, possibly in Philadelphia. Without specifying the nature of the work, payments were recorded in Jefferson's Memorandum Books to several Philadelphia cabinetmakers including Henry and Joseph Ingle, Joseph Barry, and John Aitken.

The second table, in Monticello's collection, lacks its original border and gallery, and has a top that has been entirely reworked. The border was replaced by a Monticello joinery-made band of wood with mitered corners. The trestle and slipper feet appear to have been copied after the other table. The trestle has a distinctive astragal molding.

[1978-49]   S.R.S.

166

DESK WITH ADJUSTABLE TOP

c. 1785

Denis Louis Ancellet
mahogany; oak
70.5 × 86.4 × 58.4
(27¾ × 34 × 23 in.)

PROVENANCE:
Thomas Jefferson; by descent to
Thomas Jefferson Randolph; by
descent to Alex B. Randall and
Burton R. H. Randall; by gift to
TJMF in 1927.

This unusual mahogany table was specifically conceived for drawing. The adjustable top lifts up, and can be tilted to the angle desired by the user. The sliding supports for the top, encased in the front legs when closed, have had extra notches cut into them to allow the top to be raised higher for Jefferson, who was six feet two and a half inches tall. The square, very slightly tapering legs have a carved panel topped by a semicircle; it was this ornamental motif that was copied on a Monticello-made side table by John Hemings and his helpers in the joinery (Cat. 142). The legs terminate in brass cup casters. The brass bail pull on the single drawer is a replacement.

The desk's maker was Denis Louis Ancellet, whose stamp is impressed on the bottom of the left side rail. Ancellet was an *ébéniste*, who was made a master in 1766. While Jefferson lived in Paris, his establishment was located on the rue Saint-Nicolas. Ancellet was successful, and his works were popular with furniture merchants.[8] Jefferson's Memorandum Book does not mention Ancellet by name. It is presumed that he purchased this desk, properly called a *table à la tronchin* as he did most of his furniture, through a merchant. It may have been the *table en pupitre* for which he paid 36 livres on July 24, 1789 and transported to America in case thirty-nine.[9] The desk was shipped to Monticello in 1793; it might have been one of "deux tables de la bibliotheque" that were packed in the first crate among Jefferson's belongings shipped to Richmond for Monticello.[10]
[1927-61]   S.R.S.

167

BRESCIA MARBLE TABLE

Paris
marble, brass, and cherry
71.3 × 65.1 (28¹/₁₆ × 25⅝ in.)
Private collection

PROVENANCE:
Thomas Jefferson; by descent to
Robert Mann Randolph; by
purchase to Jefferson Randolph
Anderson; by descent to a private
collection.

This marble table top was one of four that returned to America with Jefferson's household furnishings in 1790.[11] It is the only one made of Brescia marble and also the sole top to survive with its perforated gallery intact. The skirt, a simple drum, is supported by square, slightly tapering legs terminating in wooden rollers affixed to the legs with metal collars. The table has no carved ornamentation of any kind.

S.R.S.

168

MIRROR

c. 1785

Paris
gilt, gesso, wood, mirrored glass,
brass
61 × 111.8 (24 × 44 in.)

PROVENANCE:
Thomas Jefferson; by descent to
Thomas Jefferson Randolph; by
descent to Carolina Ramsay
Randolph Joslin; by gift to TJMF
in 1950.

Designed to be placed over a mantelpiece, this semicircular mirror also functions as a girandole, as it features two brass candleholders on either side. The amount of light was doubled by placing candles next to a reflective surface. This mirror, with its plain gilded border, may have been the one identified as "une glace à demi-ovale" on the list of Jefferson's goods to be transported to Richmond and eventually to Monticello in 1793.[12] It was among nine mirrors taxed in 1815.[13]

[1950-1]   S.R.S.

Four mirrors, believed to be two different pairs, were shipped from France in 1790 in case number forty-eight, described as "quatre glaces avec parquet et bordure dure."[14] The smaller, round-headed pair was separated at Monticello. One mirror was hung opposite the window in Jefferson's Bedroom (this mirror is now owned by Mr. and Mrs. Robert Carter) and the second in the Dining Room above a sideboard (both mirror and sideboard are unlocated).

The larger rectangular pair was installed in the Parlor, flanking the double-acting doors to the Entrance Hall, sometime before 1809. Jefferson noted that he had two mirrors greater than five feet high on his 1815 list of taxable property.[15] The design of the mirrors consists of a central glass, made of two plates, surrounded by a border of smaller rectangular mirrors. The joints are concealed by molding. A visitor reported that she saw them in 1830 after the family had departed:

There was no furniture in the room, with the exception of two massy pier glasses attached to the partition one on each side of the opening into the round parlor. They were covered with gauze and nearly the size of those in the east room, but much better stuff—they go with the free hold.[16]

Since their installation, the mirrors have been taken down only once, exposing two brick niches remaining from the first Monticello.

The French were capable of producing large sheets of glass by the middle of the eighteenth century, and they were the first to enhance interiors with large mirrors to reflect daylight and candlelight. Jefferson admired what he had seen in France and incorporated more and larger windows in his scheme for the revised Monticello. Adding pier mirrors to create a lighter interior was an important part of his plan.

[1923-18-1/2]   S.R.S.

169 (overleaf, left)

**PIER MIRROR
ONE OF A PAIR**

c. 1785

*France
gilt, gesso, wood with mirrored glass
284.5 × 121.9 (112 × 48 in.)*

PROVENANCE:
Thomas Jefferson; by purchase to James Barclay; by purchase to Uriah P. Levy; by descent to Jefferson Monroe Levy; by purchase to TJMF in 1923.

170 (overleaf, right)

PIER MIRROR

c. 1785

*France
gilt, gesso, wood, with mirrored glass
176.8 × 110.5
(69⅝ × 43½ in.)
Mr. and Mrs. Robert Carter*

PROVENANCE:
Thomas Jefferson; by descent to Benjamin Franklin Randolph; by gift or bequest to Sarah Champe Carter Randolph; by gift or bequest to Robert Carter family; by descent to Mr. and Mrs. Robert Carter.

171

PAIR OF SALTS

1768/69

Elizabeth Muns (active c. 1768)
London
H: 3.3 (1⁵⁄₁₆ in.);
D (rim): 6 (2⅜ in.)
Total wt: 83 g (2 oz. 13 dwt.
10 gr.)

When Thomas Jefferson married the young widow Martha Wayles Skelton in January 1772, she brought to their household a number of items acquired during her first marriage to Bathurst Skelton, 1766–68. On January 18, 1772, Jefferson made a list in his Fee Book, "By sundry European goods on hand at the death of B. Skelton & taken by me." The list mentions many household items, including one silver ladle, one dozen tablespoons, one dozen teaspoons, two pairs "gaderoon salts" with four glass liners and four "salt shovels."[1]

The surviving silver from the Skelton estate is the work of at least three London silversmiths. The pair of circular tripod salts (below) with gadrooned and scalloped rims was made in 1768/69 by Elizabeth Muns, a smallworker whose only mark was entered in the London registry that same year.[2] Though unmarked, the two salt spoons (near right) were probably purchased at the same time and are believed to be part of the same set; the unusual handles might be shaped in the form of an S for Skelton. Silversmith James Tookey made the Onslow pattern soup ladle (p. 316) in 1764/65. The set of teaspoons (far right) with spiral gadrooned handles also bear his mark, but with no date letter or other hallmarks. They were probably made about 1768 when his wife, Elizabeth Tookey, made the similar set of tablespoons with downturned handles (middle right). The silver must have arrived in Virginia shortly before or just after Bathurst Skelton's death in October 1768. With the exception of the salt spoons, all of the objects are engraved with the block letters $_B{}^S{}_M$ for Bathurst and Martha Skelton.

**PAIR OF SALT
SPOONS**

c. 1768

probably London
L: 8.4 (3⁵⁄₁₆ in.)
Total wt: 12.9 g (8 dwt. 7 gr.)

**TABLESPOON
ONE OF TWO**

1768/69

Elizabeth Tookey
(active c. 1767–1774), London
L: 21.6 (8½ in.)
Total wt: 109.9 g (3 oz. 10 dwt.
16 gr.)
Yale University Art Gallery, Gift
of De Lancey Kountze, B.A.
1899, and Thomas Jefferson
Memorial Foundation

**TEASPOON
ONE OF FIVE**

c. 1768

James Tookey, London
L: 11.4 to 12.4
(4½ to 4⅞ in.)
Total wt: 68.9 g (2 oz.
4 dwt. 7 gr.)
Mrs. Joseph C. Cornwall and
Thomas Jefferson Memorial
Foundation

LADLE

1764/65

James Tookey
(active 1750–c. 1772), London
L: 34.3 (13½ in.)
Wt: 183.3 g (5 oz. 17 dwt. 21 gr.)

PROVENANCE:
Thomas Jefferson; all pieces by
descent to Martha Jefferson
Randolph. SALTS, SALT SPOONS,
AND LADLE: by descent to Thomas
Jefferson Randolph; by descent to
Francis Meriwether Randolph; by
purchase to General Meredith
Read in 1884; by descent (?) to
Mrs. John Bergan; by purchase in
1978 to TJMF. TABLESPOONS: by
descent to Thomas Jefferson
Randolph; one spoon by descent to
Carolina Ramsay Randolph; by
purchase to De Lancey Kountze;
by gift to Yale University Art
Gallery; by loan to TJMF since
1945; second spoon by descent to
Francis Meriwether Randolph; by
descent to Carolina Ramsay
Randolph Joslin; by purchase to
TJMF in 1958. TEASPOONS: one
teaspoon by descent to Septimia
Randolph Meikleham; by descent
to Frances Louise Meikleham; by
purchase to TJMF in 1954; four
teaspoons by descent to Ellen
Randolph Coolidge Dwight; by gift
to Martha Jefferson Trist Burke;
one spoon by descent to Frances
Maury Burke and three spoons by
descent to Ellen Coolidge Burke
Eddy; two of the three spoons by
descent to James Henry Eddy; by
purchase to TJMF in 1963; the
third of the three spoons by
descent to John Burke Eddy; by
purchase to TJMF in 1965; a
fourth spoon by descent to Charles
B. Eddy; by bequest to Mrs.
Charles B. Eddy, Jr. (now Mrs.
Joseph C. Cornwall); one of the
four preceding spoons is probably
the teaspoon once owned by Fanny
Maury Burke.

With such ornamental features as shells, gadrooning, and cabriole legs, the Skelton silver is typical of the Rococo style that was popular in America in the third quarter of the eighteenth century. These are some of the few items in the Rococo taste that Jefferson kept at Monticello throughout his lifetime. While he had other pieces of old silver melted down and formed into Neoclassical objects more to his liking, the Skelton items were saved, perhaps for sentimental reasons. In the safekeeping of Martha Jefferson Randolph, they appeared in part on two lists she made of Monticello silver. On her "housewife list," c. 1823, are "9 twist handle tea spoons."[3] About 1833 she made another inventory of silver packed in a pine chest. This sheet was pasted to the inside of the chest's lid, and among the 135 pieces included were "4 salt cellars" and "4 salt spoons, 1 broken," plus two ladles, thirteen English tablespoons, and a number of teaspoons.[4]

[1978-32-1/2; 1978-33-1/2; 1945-15; 1958-6; 1954-11; 1963-19-1a/b; 1965-6-1; 1978-31]   S.M.O.

Decanter and bottle stands, or "bottle sliders" as they were often called, were essential to the well-appointed dinner table of the late eighteenth or early nineteenth century. In 1815 a visitor to Monticello wrote, "The dinner was always choice, and served in the French style; but no wine was set on the table till the cloth was removed."[5] With the custom of removing the tablecloth before the dessert of fruit, nuts, and wine, decanter and bottle stands with wooden bases and baize-covered bottoms protected the table surface and no doubt made it easier to slide a bottle from one gentleman to the next.

Decanter stands are usually of greater diameter than bottle stands; great quantities of both were produced in fused silverplate, particularly by Sheffield manufactories. Jefferson included "4. bottle sliders" on his dinner canteen list of about 1789, but he did not record the purchase of any while in Paris.[6] Jefferson's acquisition of this later decanter stand is also unrecorded, but it was probably included in one of his many purchases of "plated wares." "4 plaited sliders with mahogany bottoms" appear on the inventory of Monticello made after Jefferson's death.[7] The arched silver plaque set into the wood base and inscribed "Th Jefferson" in a facsimile signature is believed to be a later addition.

[1985-6]   S.M.O.

176

DECANTER STAND

c. 1815

England, probably Sheffield
fused silverplate with mahogany
base
H: 5.1 (2 in.); D: 15.9 (6¼ in.)

PROVENANCE:
Thomas Jefferson; by descent to
Thomas Jefferson Randolph; by
descent to Jefferson Randolph
Kean II; by gift to TJMF.

FORK
ONE OF TWELVE

1784

Louis-Julien Anthiaume
(active 1779–1806), Paris
L: 19.4 (7⅝ in.)
Total wt: 1093 g (35 oz. 2 dwt.
19 gr.)

178 (center)

TABLESPOON
ONE OF FOUR

1784

Louis-Julien Anthiaume, Paris
L: 20.3 (8 in.)
Total wt: 327 g (10 oz. 10 dwt.
6 gr.)

179 (right)

FORK

1784

Pierre-Nicolas Sommé
(active 1760–1806), Paris
L: 20 (7⅞ in.)
Wt: 87.5 g (2 oz. 16 dwt. 6 gr.)
Yale University Art Gallery, Gift
of De Lancey Kountze, B.A. 1899

PROVENANCE:
Thomas Jefferson. FORKS BY
ANTHIAUME: by descent to George
Wythe Randolph; by bequest to
Sarah N. Randolph; by gift to
Jefferson Randolph Anderson; by
descent to Mrs. Henry N. Platt,
Henry N. Platt, Jr., Page Platt
Allen and Jefferson R. Platt; by
purchase to TJMF in 1972.
SPOONS BY ANTHIAUME: by
descent to Mary Hubard Mathewes
and Izaetta Hubard Ambler; three
spoons by descent to Thomas
Waring and Mary Beretta; by gift
to TJMF in 1983; one spoon by
descent to Izaetta Slaughter
Mundy; by purchase to TJMF in
1958. FORK BY SOMMÉ: by descent
to Carolina Ramsay Randolph; by
purchase to De Lancey Kountze;
by gift to the Yale University Art
Gallery; by loan to TJMF since 1945.

When Jefferson arrived in Paris in early August 1784, he quickly set about acquiring necessary household items. Among his first purchases were two groups of "table furniture." On August 21 he recorded in his Memorandum Book, "Pd. [for] 1 doz. spoons and 12 silver forks 600f." Two days later he expanded the service, buying an additional "1 doz. silver forks" and "1 doz. tablespoons" at the same price.[8] Although different silversmiths may each have supplied Jefferson with a dozen forks and spoons, the heavy tablespoons and four-tined table forks have matching handles in the common fiddle and thread pattern. Most of the extant pieces bear the mark of Parisian silversmith Louis-Julien Anthiaume, who specialized in making spoons and forks and whose mark was first cited in the Paris registry in 1779.[9] The forks made by Anthiaume are slightly longer than the single fork by Pierre-Nicolas Sommé.

According to a list written in 1788 or 1789, Jefferson included some of this flatware in his dinner canteen, the traveling box or boxes outfitted with all the accoutrements required for dining en route. The forks and spoons came to America with Jefferson's many belongings and were in use at Monticello for the remainder of his life. Twenty-four silver forks and twenty French tablespoons appeared on Martha Jefferson Randolph's housewife list written about 1823; on her silver inventory of about 1833 she listed "24 forks" and "16 table spoons (french)."[10]

The flatware, along with most of the family silver, was distributed among the four Randolph brothers in 1837. The monograms engraved on the handles of the forks were added sometime later. George Wythe Randolph wrote to his niece in 1855 about what he had done to the twelve forks by Anthiaume in his possession:

I have never ceased to regret that my name was put upon the forks and shall take your father's [Thomas Jefferson Randolph's] advice and have it scratched out provided it can be done without injury. The thing was done without reflection. . . . If the name can be taken off I shall have T.J. cast in its place.[11]

[1971-71-1a/l; 1981-20-4a/c; 1958-3; 1945-8]   S.M.O.

On January 8, 1787, Jefferson wrote to Matthew Boulton, the best-known manufacturer of silverplated wares in England. He requested estimates on plated soup tureens as well as "10 dishes, round, of 10½ Inches diameter" and six oval platters.[12] He never purchased these items, but his letter attests to a need for serving pieces in silver or silverplate.

These four silver plates were acquired in Paris a short time later, probably in February 1787 when Jefferson paid a merchant named Cellier 657 livres for a quantity of silver.[13] The plates are a little more than ten inches in diameter, slightly larger than typical dinner plates yet similar to the ten round dishes mentioned in the inquiry to Boulton. Their style suggests a much earlier date than that indicated by their 1786–87 Paris guild marks. Plates and platters with a shaped and reeded edge first appeared in France in the 1730s and remained popular for the rest of the century.

Serving dishes were commonly placed on a table in symmetrically arranged pairs, so they were usually purchased in pairs or even-numbered sets. Round dishes were particularly suitable for serving second-course fare such as cakes, pies, and puddings, but meat dishes and first-course entrées called for larger oval or oblong platters.[14] The packing list of Jefferson's goods shipped to America in 1790 mentioned the four silver platters ("quatre plats d'argents").[15] The silver plates were used at Monticello for many years. Martha Jefferson Randolph included "4 flat ditto [dishes]" on a list of family silver made about 1823. The "4 round dishes" were still in her possession in the 1830s, according to another silver inventory.[16] For Jefferson's family, the plates had a very strong personal association, and together with four silver vegetable dishes (Cat. 181) were considered among the most precious objects passed down in the Randolph family.

[1958-11-3/4; 1957-32; 1957-33]   S.M.O.

While in London in 1786 Jefferson looked for silver vegetable dishes. He noted a price on the back of an engraved trade card from the silversmith Thomas Whipham, "Silver dishes for vegetables &c about 16£ each including the cover which may serve occasionally for another dish."[17] Some serving dishes of the period do have lids that could be inverted for use as an extra shallow serving dish, but Jefferson made no such purchases in England. He waited until his return to Paris, and in early 1787, midway through his five-year stay, he paid over 1300 livres in two installments for "4. Casserolles."[18] This acquisition was his largest single purchase of French silver.

The round, flat-bottomed vegetable dishes each have two handles and a domed lid with reeded rim and central handle. In contrast to much French silver of the Louis XVI period, they are almost devoid of ornamentation. The handles, in the form of a bead supported by two husks rising from rosette junctures, are their only truly decorative feature. The clean, simple lines and understated ornamentation of these dishes exemplify Jefferson's Neoclassical taste. He would repeatedly express these preferences in future purchases of silver in France and America.

The silver vegetable dishes came to America in 1790 with the rest of Jefferson's household items. Used first at Jefferson's Philadelphia residence, they came to Monticello in 1793 where they continued in service for many years.[19] They appear as "4 vegetable dishes with cov[ers]" on Martha Jefferson Randolph's list of silver, circa 1823, and again as "4 vegetable dishes [and] 4 tops. 1 handle & a half lost," on her silver inventory made about 1833.[20] The fact that the vegetable dishes are one of only two specific bequests of silver made in Martha Randolph's will attests to the strength of their association with Jefferson. They passed to Mrs. Randolph's eldest son, Thomas Jefferson Randolph, who in turn passed them to his youngest daughter, Sarah Nicholas Randolph, who wrote *The Domestic Life of Thomas Jefferson* in 1871. He wrote in his will, "To my daughter Sarah I give the four silver vegetable dishes with their plates and covers bequeathed me by my mother, as a reward for her successful vindication of the Character of my Grandfather in her Domestic life of him."[21]

In addition to the dishes' substantial size and value, the special regard for the silver vegetable dishes may be in part due to Jefferson's fondness for vegetables. He himself wrote in 1819, "I have lived temperately, eating little animal food, & that, not as an aliment so much as a condiment for the vegetables, which constitute my principal diet."[22]

[1958-11-1/2; 1957-30; 1957-31]   S.M.O.

VEGETABLE DISHES TWO OF FOUR

1786–87

Antoine Boullier (active 1775 to post-1806), Paris
H: 13.3 (5¼ in.);
D: 20 (8 in.)
Total wt: 4346 g (139 oz. 14 dwt. 12 gr.)
Mrs. Richard R. Mullings and Lawrence R. Greenough, and Thomas Jefferson Memorial Foundation

PROVENANCE:
Thomas Jefferson; by descent to Thomas Jefferson Randolph; by descent to Sarah Nicholas Randolph; by bequest to Carolina Ramsay Randolph; by gift or bequest to Margaret Randolph Anderson Rotch; by descent, TWO VEGETABLE DISHES each to Margaret Randolph Rotch Storrow and Katherine Lawrence Rotch Greenough. TWO DISHES by descent to James Jackson Storrow; by gift to TJMF in 1958. ONE DISH by descent to Malcolm Whelen Greenough, Jr.; by purchase to TJMF in 1979. ONE DISH by descent to Lawrence Rotch Greenough; by descent to Mrs. Richard R. Mullings and Lawrence R. Greenough; by loan to TJMF since 1957.

Design for an Urn

*c. 1789
Thomas Jefferson (1743–1826)
ink on paper
Massachusetts Historical Society*

This coffee urn is the only surviving example of several tea and coffee urns that Jefferson owned. Marked by the silversmith Jacques-Louis Auguste Leguay, it bears the Paris guild mark of issue between July 1787 and November 12, 1788.²³ It is believed to be the "silver coffee pot" that Jefferson purchased in February 1789. He recorded a payment of 309 livres in his Memorandum Book on February 6 but later crossed out the line that stated it was a "present for Clerissault [*sic*] for his trouble about the draughts & model of Capitol & prison . . . to be chargd. to Virginia."²⁴ Jefferson first intended to thank the architect Charles-Louis Clérisseau for his assistance with the Virginia State Capitol by giving him a silver copy of a Roman askos, but the model for it never reached him (Cat. 184). He bought this coffee urn as a substitute but apparently decided to keep it for himself when he learned that he might be able to have the askos for Clérisseau after all. By May, with the askos still not in his hands and in the midst of preparations to return to America, Jefferson commissioned another silver coffee urn, again intended for Clérisseau.²⁵ On June 7, 1789, Jefferson wrote to Clérisseau, explained about the trouble with the askos, and begged him to accept the substitution of a "Fontaine à caffé" which he described as a vase "moins singulier, mais antique et beau."²⁶

The urn given to Clérisseau is unlocated, but it was purchased at the shop of Jean-Baptiste-Claude Odiot (1763–1850) with Jefferson's two silver goblets (Cat. 183). Odiot, one of a prominent family of Parisian silversmiths, was just beginning a long, highly successful career as a goldsmith and merchant of fine gold and silver work.²⁷ According to the invoice Jefferson received from him on June 3, 1789, the urn was made "like the drawing," weighed just over four marcs seven ounces (about 1200 grams), and cost 423 livres.²⁸ The undated Jefferson drawing of an urn (left) is believed to be the one mentioned in the invoice.²⁹ It is strikingly similar to the Leguay urn, differing only in the shape of its lid and the fullness of its body. Jefferson probably based his drawing on the Leguay urn already in his possession.

On June 3 Jefferson's Memorandum Book entry recorded his payment to Odiot for "a coffee pot as a present to Clérissault" plus an extra one hundred livres "to correct error of addn. in my acct. Feb. 6." Evidently the silver urn bought in February also came from Odiot's shop.³⁰

Jefferson's coffee urn, "une fontaine d'argent," came to America with Jefferson's household goods in 1790.³¹ It is one of the two silver coffee pots included on Jefferson's 1815 list of taxable property, as well as being the "1 coffee urn" and "1 urn" Martha Jefferson Randolph mentioned in her silver inventories of about 1823 and 1833 respectively.³² The urn remained in the Randolph family until the late nineteenth century when Jefferson M. Levy, then owner of Monticello, acquired it. The coat-of-arms was probably added around this time.

Of Jefferson's other coffee and tea urns, most were silverplated and likely came from Sheffield, England. Jefferson mentioned a plated tea urn on his summary of French purchases, 1788–1789.³³ In 1815, "2 Plated Urns, & 1 Plated Coffee Pot" appeared on the inventory of taxable property.³⁴ One plated tea urn was sold at the 1827 Monticello dispersal sale to George W. Spotswood for $4.25.³⁵

[1940-10]   S.M.O.

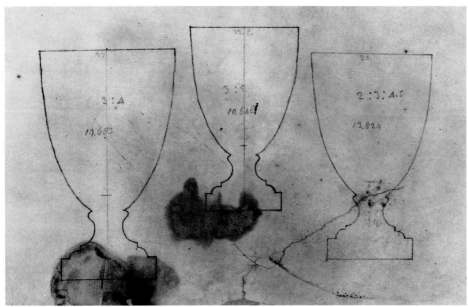

Profiles for Goblets

c. 1789
Thomas Jefferson (1743–1826)
pencil on paper
Massachusetts Historical Society

On June 3, 1789, Jefferson recorded in his Memorandum Book the sum of 229 livres paid for a "pr. goblets &c."[36] Jefferson made his purchase at the shop of Odiot on the rue St. Honoré in Paris. On an invoice from Odiot dated that same day, Jefferson bought a silver coffee urn, a present for the architect Clérisseau (Cat. 182), and "Deux Goblet, Pareille au Model." The silver for the two goblets cost 109 livres. Sixty livres was charged for labor, plus some other small amounts, including 36 livres for gilding the interior of the bowls. The goblets made "like the model" are based on a Jefferson drawing that shows three goblets of varying proportions (lower left).[37] The silver goblets differ slightly from Jefferson's drawing in the shape of their bowls; they differ from each other in size and particularly in stem shape. They are distinctive for their unembellished surfaces and architectural form, quite unlike other contemporary examples of French silver cups. *Timbales*, or beakers with no stem, typically had much gadrooning and other decoration.

Both goblets bear the Paris guild mark used from November 1788 to September 1789, charge and discharge marks, and the mark of their maker, Claude-Nicolas Delanoy. Delanoy, born about 1735, became a master silversmith in 1766 and was listed at six different addresses between 1783 and 1793, including the rue Neuve St. Méderic where he was working in 1789.[38] Nothing is known about his relationship with Odiot, but it seems likely that Odiot assigned Jefferson's commission, a relatively small job, to the capable but lesser-known master.

In September 1789 Jefferson returned to the United States; the two "silver and vermeil goblets" were shipped with his other belongings the following year.[39] At Monticello, during the years of Jefferson's retirement, they were used at table with the set of eight silver tumblers made by John Letelier in 1810 (Cat. 189). Jefferson included "10 Silver Cups" on his 1815 list of taxable property.[40] These were undoubtedly the "8 becars, 2 goblets" specified on Martha Jefferson Randolph's silver inventory of about 1823.[41]

After Jefferson's death the family silver was taken to the Randolph home, Edgehill. In 1837, the year after Martha Jefferson Randolph's death, her eldest son received news of his brother Meriwether Lewis Randolph's death. He wrote to the widowed Mrs. Randolph:

The morning of the day on which we received the afflicting intelligence we had divided the family plate between my brothers. Of itself not of much value to him, it would have been valuable from association. You will direct what shall be done with his share."[42]

The pair of silver goblets were among the items sent to Elizabeth Martin Randolph in Tennessee.

[1982-33]   S.M.O.

183
GOBLETS

1789

Claude-Nicolas Delanoy (active 1766–c. 1793), Paris designed by Thomas Jefferson silver with gilt interior H: 11.7 (4⅝ in.); D (rim): 7.5 (2¹⁵⁄₁₆ in.); Base: 5.1 (2 in.) square Wt: 227.5 g (7 oz. 6 dwt. 7 gr.) Dr. and Mrs. Benjamin H. Caldwell, Jr.

1789

Claude-Nicolas Delanoy, Paris; designed by Thomas Jefferson silver with gilt interior H: 12.4 (4⅞ in.); D (rim): 7.6 (3 in.); Base: 5.1 (2 in.) square Wt: 218.6 g (7 oz. 13 gr.)

PROVENANCE:
Thomas Jefferson; by descent to Elizabeth Martin Randolph, widow of Meriwether Lewis Randolph; by gift to Bettie M. Donelson; by purchase to Mr. and Mrs. Stanley Horn; by descent to Stanley F. Horn, Jr. and Ruth Crownover; FIRST GOBLET by purchase to Dr. and Mrs. Benjamin H. Caldwell, Jr.; SECOND GOBLET by purchase to TJMF in 1982.

Jefferson's search for an appropriate gift for the architect Charles-Louis Clérisseau began in Nîmes, where he had helped Jefferson with the preparation of drawings and a model of the Maison Carrée for his design of the Virginia State Capitol. Jefferson found a fitting present in the form of a Roman askos, a bronze pouring vessel that had been excavated at the ruins in Nîmes. He commissioned a local craftsman named Souche and paid him 18 livres to make a model of the askos in the collection of Jean François Seguier (1703–1784), the scholar and antiquarian who had excavated the Maison Carrée.[43]

Souche's model never reached Jefferson in Paris, and he was compelled to select another gift for Clérisseau, a coffee urn made according to his own design (Cat. 182). Yet it was the "vase antique" that he preferred for "sa singularité et sa beauté,"[44] and engaged Souche to make a second model, which arrived in Paris on May 18, 1789.[45] This was crated among the vast shipment of wines, books, and furnishings shipped to rejoin Jefferson in Philadelphia in 1790.

More than ten years later, just after he became president in 1801, Jefferson directed his purchasing agent, Thomas Claxton, to have a silver copy made after Souche's wooden model. Claxton engaged the Philadelphia silversmiths Anthony Simmons and Samuel Alexander and instructed them to engrave an inscription on the lid: "Copied from a model / taken in 1787 by / Th. Jefferson / from a Roman Ewer in the / Cabinet of Antiquities at / Nismes."

The model and the silver copy were at Monticello after Jefferson's retirement. They differ in that the silver askos has a lid, a simplified handle, and a floret or rosette instead of a mask at the base of the handle. At Monticello the family called the askos "the silver duck" and used it as a chocolate pot.[46] The wooden model was given to the painter Thomas Sully in 1821 when he journeyed to Monticello to take Jefferson's portrait for the United States Military Academy. Sully had it inscribed, "Presented/by Ex-Pres. Thos./Jefferson to Thos./Sully." The model was lost until it mysteriously appeared at an auction in Bucks County, Pennsylvania in 1972. The silver askos was inherited by Martha Jefferson Randolph who bequeathed it to Joseph Coolidge.

[1974-20; 1957-29]   S.R.S.

On July 11, 1805, Martha Jefferson Randolph wrote to her father, "I must beg your pardon for having omitted till this moment to inform you of the dismantled state of our tea equipage . . . the plated ones [cream pots] being so much worn as to shew the copper."[47] The plated cream pots Martha mentions were probably the two that Jefferson had bought in Paris eighteen years earlier, and perhaps the letter prompted Jefferson to purchase a solid-silver cream pot as a replacement.[48] Although unrecorded in Jefferson's Memorandum Books, two silver cream pots made by the successful Richmond partnership of Reuben Johnson (1782–1820) and James Reat (1782–1815) descended in Jefferson's family with a history of his ownership.[49]

The first cream pot is helmet-shaped with a flared spout and strap handle resting on a round trumpet-shaped foot and square plinth. The second cream pot has an oval, boat-shaped body with concave shoulder, flared spout, reeded rim and strap handle on a rectangular footed base. The monogram "TJ" on the side is probably a later addition, as the same style monogram also appears on a single French fork that descended in the same line. The "1 cream dit. [pot]" and "1 cream ewer" mentioned in Martha Jefferson Randolph's silver inventories, c. 1823 and 1833 respectively, might refer to either of these pieces.[50] The 1826 inventory of Monticello furnishings included "2 plated cream pots" among numerous items of silverplate, most of which appear to have been sold at the 1827 Dispersal Sale.[51]

[1981-20-2; 1945-3]   S.M.O.

186
CREAM POT

c. 1805

Johnson and Reat (partnership c. 1805–15), Richmond, Virginia
H: 16.2 (6⅜ in.);
W: 14.1 (5⁹⁄₁₆ in.)
Base: 6.4 (2½ in.) square
Wt: 173 g (5 oz. 11 dwt. 6 gr.)

187
CREAM POT

c. 1810

Johnson and Reat (partnership c. 1805–15), Richmond, Virginia
H: 15.2 (6 in.); W: 14 (5½ in.)
Base: 6.4 (2½ in.);
Wt: 172.3 g (5 oz. 10 dwt. 19 gr.)
Yale University Art Gallery, Gift of De Lancey Kountze, B.A. 1899

PROVENANCE:
FIRST CREAM POT: Thomas Jefferson; by descent to Benjamin Franklin Randolph; by descent to Thomas Waring and Mary Randolph Waring Beretta; by gift to TJMF in 1983. SECOND CREAM POT: Thomas Jefferson; by descent to Thomas Jefferson Randolph; by descent to Carolina Ramsay Randolph; by sale to De Lancey Kountze; by gift to Yale University Art Gallery; by loan to TJMF since 1945.

**DESSERT SPOON
ONE OF FOURTEEN**

1808–09

*Charles A. Burnett (active c.
1793–1849), Georgetown
L: 19.1 (7½ in.)
Total wt: 516.6 g (16 oz. 12
dwt. 4 gr.)
Mrs. James Hubard Mathewes
and Thomas Jefferson Memorial
Foundation*

PROVENANCE:
Thomas Jefferson; by descent to
Benjamin Franklin Randolph; SIX
SPOONS by descent to James
Hubard Mathewes; by loan to
TJMF since 1961; EIGHT SPOONS
by descent to Thomas Waring and
Mary Randolph Waring Beretta;
by gift to TJMF in 1983.

Charles A. Burnett was a prominent silversmith in Alexandria, Virginia, and then in Georgetown, District of Columbia, from 1800 to about 1849. He did considerable business with the government, manufacturing large quantities of Indian ornaments for frontier trading stations in the 1820s and 30s.[52] His first dealings with Jefferson probably occurred when he was commissioned to craft a two-handled urn-shaped sugar bowl inscribed, "Presented to Camilla Franzoni by Thomas Jefferson, 1808." Camilla Franzoni was the wife of Italian sculptor Giuseppe Franzoni who had been commissioned to work on the United States Capitol.[53] The occasion for presenting such a gift and the extent to which Jefferson was involved in procuring it is not known. There is no doubt, however, that Jefferson went directly to Burnett the following year to acquire a set of dessert spoons for his own use.

Jefferson wrote from Washington to Martha Jefferson Randolph at Monticello in September 1808, "I forgot to bring with me the gravy spoons to be converted into dessert spoons. I must therefore pray you to send them to me. I think you mentioned a spare ladle."[54] Martha replied, "I have sent the 4 spoons and a large french ladle, there being 2 others left, one french and one english belonging to the BSM spoons (Cat. 173)."[55] Sometime after receiving the old silver, Jefferson noted Burnett's prices for making a pudding dish and eighteen dessert spoons on an undated slip of paper. He also calculated the cost of both items, using their estimated weight and the price of silver, minus the value of the objects to be melted down. "He [Burnett] sais [*sic*]," wrote Jefferson, "they charge 10½D. the doz. for making Dessert spoons, plain, but double that if with beaded edges." Jefferson chose the plainer, less expensive option as his calculations and the finished spoons prove.[56]

The dessert spoons with pointed oval bowls and downturned spatulate ends inscribed with a cipher J were paid for in February 1809. Jefferson recorded in his Memorandum Book, "Drew orders on the bank U.S. . . . in favr . . . Charles A. Burnet. plate 39.615."[57] After Jefferson's presidency, the dessert spoons and the pudding dish went to Monticello. Both items appeared on Mrs. Randolph's housewife list (c. 1823) and her silver chest inventory (c. 1833).[58] Although most of the dessert spoons survive, the pudding dish is unlocated.

[1961-36-1/6; 1981-20-3a/h]   S . M . O .

In 1806 Jefferson's friend and teacher, George Wythe, died, leaving him a bequest that included his "silver cups." Correspondence between the executor of Wythe's estate and President Jefferson reveals that there were two cups but provides no further description.[59] They might have had outmoded Rococo decoration. For that or another reason, Jefferson decided to have them melted down. The Wythe cups and two of Jefferson's own canns (round-bellied mugs) were converted into a new set of eight tumblers in 1810.[60]

Tumblers, a popular form of silver cup from the seventeenth through the eighteenth century, were a type of low round-bottomed cup hammered from a disk of silver with a base proportionately thicker than the sides. The heavier bottom to the cup provided stability and helped prevent spilling. Tumblers were often used in traveling sets, or canteens.[61]

Jefferson contacted a silversmith named John Letelier in 1810 to reshape his cups. The son of a Philadelphia silversmith of the same name, John Letelier began working with his father in that city in the 1790s. Father and son often used the same marks, making the younger Letelier's work and history difficult to distinguish from the elder's. Both Leteliers moved to Wilmington, Delaware, then to Chester County, Pennsylvania, and back to Wilmington around 1799 where John Letelier, Jr. began to practice dentistry in addition to silversmithing.[62]

Jefferson's first known contact with John Letelier came in 1806 when he purchased an etui for himself (Cat. 225) and a silver cann to give to Rev. Charles Clay, an Albemarle County minister who had presided over family funerals at Monticello and who now lived near Jefferson's Poplar Forest in Bedford County.[63] Letelier appears to have been working in Richmond at that time but probably moved to Washington or Alexandria, and Jefferson again sought him out when he wrote to his Richmond agent, George Jefferson, in 1808:

Mr. Letelier, a goldsmith, who lived a considerable time in Washington and did a good deal of work for the President's house and to great satisfaction is said to have removed to Richmond. Is he there and in a situation to execute a considerable job say two silver tureens and some other things.[64]

Letelier, who was again in Richmond, agreed to do the work for Jefferson. When confirming the order, Jefferson sent Letelier two designs for tureens, "the upper being that preferred," but neither the drawings nor the tureens survive, apparently destroyed when the President's House was burned in 1814.[65]

Pleased with Letelier's work, on March 27, 1810, Jefferson, who was now retired to Monticello, wrote to him again:

Being just setting out on a journey, I have directed . . . a pair of Cans and a pair of Beakers to be sent to you to be melted and put into the form of a plated cup, which will be sent with them as a model. The Cans and beakers weigh a little over 40. oz. avoirdupoise, the model a little over two ounces and a half. But it is too thin and weak for common use. I think those to be made should be of 5. oz. avoirdupoise weight nearly. They must also be about half an inch higher, in order to hold a little more than the model does. In every other respect I would wish the model to be exactly imitated. I suppose the metal of the Cans and beakers will make about 8. cups such as desired. That number however I would wish to receive even if additional metal should be necessary. Mark 4. of them if you please G.W. to T.J. and the others simply T.J. all in the cypher stile. If you can gild the inside

1810

John Letelier (also Letellier, Le Tellier), (active c. 1790–1810), Richmond, Virginia
silver with gilt interior
H: 6.7 (2⅝ in.);
D (rim): 8.1 (3³⁄₁₆ in.)
Total wt: 759.5 g (24 oz. 8 dwt. 9 gr.)

PROVENANCE:
Now known as the Wythe-Jefferson cups, the set of tumblers descended from Thomas Jefferson to Martha Jefferson Randolph. FIRST CUP: by gift to Virginia Jefferson Randolph (inscribed V.J.T.); by gift to Esther Alice Meikleham; by gift or bequest to William A. Meikleham; by gift to TJMF in 1938. SECOND CUP: by gift to Thomas Jefferson Trist; by bequest to John P. Walker; by bequest to Anna A. Walker; by purchase to Grace Thompson; by purchase to TJMF in 1953. THIRD CUP: by gift to Ellen Coolidge, by descent to Thomas Jefferson Coolidge, Jr.; by loan to TJMF since 1986. FOURTH CUP: by gift to George Wythe Randolph; by bequest to George Randolph Kean who died at age three; by descent from his parents to Robert H. Kean; by bequest to Mrs. Robert H. Kean; by loan to TJMF since 1988. FIFTH CUP: by gift to Cornelia Jefferson Randolph (inscribed C.J.R. on bottom); by gift or bequest to Hore Browse Trist; by descent to Mary Helen Trist; by gift to Henry Randolph Burke; by descent to Rosella Trist Graham Schendel.

as the model is it would be desirable. . . . I am too well acquainted with the stile of your execution to suppose it necessary to add any recommendations on that subject. Accept the assurances of my esteem.[66]

The model to which Jefferson refers is almost certainly the unornamented two-inch-high tumbler of fused silverplate with gilt interior that descended in the Randolph family. As he described, its sides are very thin, and it weighs about 2.2 ounces avoirdupois. Jefferson probably acquired this cup in Paris; in 1787 he recorded thirty livres paid for "a silver cup for me."[67]

Each of Letelier's tumblers is 2⅝ inches high and weighs about 4.8 ounces avoirdupois, corresponding quite closely to Jefferson's instructions. With five of the eight original tumblers exhibited, three are marked "G.W. to T.J." and two simply "T.J."; all of them are inscribed on the bottom: "J. L.'T. Maker."

The silver tumblers remained at Monticello for the rest of Jefferson's life. They were apparently part of his regular dining table equipage, for a visitor to Monticello in 1815 wrote, "The drinking cups were of silver marked G.W. to T.J., the table liquors were beer and cider and after dinner wine."[68] In the 1830s Martha Jefferson Randolph apparently distributed the cups among her family, giving one cup each to six of her children and one to a grandson. Six of these cups survive. The seventh cup is unlocated and the descent of the eighth cup is unknown.

Jefferson is not known to have made any further purchases from Letelier, but he did write to him once more in 1817: "I live about three miles from a pleasant & respectable village called Charlottesville. . . . We want a good silversmith in the town & such an one would find more work than he could do, and ready money always."[69] Letelier, however, politely declined Jefferson's offer, explaining that he was prevented from doing so because of the positions he held as Keeper of the Poorhouse and Keeper of the City Magazine in Richmond.[70]

[1938-10; 1953-2; 1986-13-2; 1988-3; 1962-1-55]   S.M.O.

190 (bottom opposite)

TUMBLER

c. 1787

probably Paris
fused silverplate with gilt interior
H: 4.8 (1⅞ in.);
D (rim): 6.7 (2⅝ in.)

PROVENANCE:
Thomas Jefferson; by descent to
James, Charles, and John Eddy;
by purchase to TJMF in 1962.

191
SEAU CRENELE

1787

Geneviève Taillandier,
(active 1774–1798),
Sèvres
hard-paste porcelain
14.6 × 31.8 × 20.6
(5¾ × 12½ × 8⅛ in.)

PROVENANCE:
Thomas Jefferson; by descent to
Septimia Meikleham; by descent to
Henry P. Meikleham; by bequest
to TJMF in 1957.

While he served in Paris, Jefferson acquired at least two pieces from a dessert service—a *seau crénelé* and a *sucrier* (sugar bowl)—in the *guirlande de barbeaux* (cornflower garland) pattern made at the royal porcelain factory at Sèvres. This pattern, introduced in 1783 and replenished until the early 1790s, was almost exclusively used for tableware for Louis XVI, who used it to equip one of the dining rooms at Versailles.[1] How Jefferson came to acquire parts of this royal service is not precisely documented; he might have purchased slightly damaged pieces from a merchant in Paris or was given or found them at Versailles.

Jefferson's purchases of porcelain tableware in France were numerous, but little is known about the design or manufacture of the lost and presumably destroyed works. Among the many crates of goods ferried back to America were ten dozen porcelain plates, two *soupières* (soup tureens), five large porcelain platters, forty-two cups and thirty-nine saucers, and other pieces not enumerated on the packing list of 1790, such as the *seau crénelé* and sugar bowl. Jefferson's chinaware might have consisted of additional pieces of the *guirlande de barbeaux* of the Sèvres service for Louis XVI, other Sèvres designs, or entirely different designs made by other factories. Jefferson's largest single acquisition of "6½ doz. china plates, a sallad dish & 3 doz. caraffes 166f18."[2] could very well have been Sèvres porcelain, purchased from Dominique Daguerre (d. 1796), a merchant prominent for his sale of Sèvres porcelain in his shop on the rue St.-Honoré.[3]

The *seau crénelé*, a crenelated bucket used for cooling wine glasses, typically was part of a dessert service that might include several dozen plates, twelve to sixteen *compotiers*, two sugar bowls, twelve to fourteen *tasses à glace* (ice cream dishes) and two trays to hold them, two *seaux à glace* (serving containers for ice cream), and two *seaux crénelés*.[4] Jefferson's surviving *seau* was decorated by Geneviève Le Roy Taillandier, the wife of Vincent Taillandier (1736–1790), a Sèvres painter, gilder, and burnisher. Until her marriage, she was a painter in the factory. Later, Mme. Taillandier was paid *à la pièce* for work that she did at home, chiefly painting garlands, flower sprays, and bouquets on tea and service wares and plaques.[5] The *seau* bears the mark of her husband, a fleur-de-lis.[6] Although it is not known when Jefferson's *seau* was painted, Mme. Taillandier was paid for painting *guirlandes de barbeaux* on twenty-two *seaux à verres* on December 14, 1782 and four *seaux* on April 9, 1788.[7]

A similarly decorated elaborate sugar bowl, which also belonged to Jefferson, is marked with the symbol of the Sèvres factory, two interlaced Ls, "jj" signifying the year 1786, and the mark of the painter, "Y."[8] The painter was probably Geneviève-Louise Bouilliat, the wife of Edmé-François Bouilliat (1739/40–1810). Bouilliat was a well-known painter of ceramics who did quite elaborate work in the 1780s such as allegories, landscapes, flying birds, as well as floral decorations. His wife, who began her career in 1777, is more likely to have painted the *sucrier*. She was paid for applying *guirlandes de barbeaux* to three *sucriers de table* on January 15, 1786, which were fired on February 5, 1786.[9]

[1942-8]   S.R.S.

Paris Porcelain Decorated with
Cornflower Sprigs

early 19th c.
Possibly made by André et Cie,
Foëscy
Clockwise from left: sauce
tureen, tureen, serving dish,
covered sauce boat, custard cups.

At the end of his stay in France, Jefferson copied several of his favorite recipes. One of them explained how to make "Wine jellies." Boiled calves-feet or isinglass was combined with egg whites and a pint of madeira. The mixture was sweetened and flavored with lemon, cloves, and nutmeg. "Strain it 2 or 3 times thro' a flannel till clear," wrote Jefferson; then, "Put it in glasses or moulds."[10]

In the eighteenth and early nineteenth century, the second course of dinner typically featured a number of sweet dishes such as cakes, custards, creams, and jellies. Although sometimes made in large, elaborate molds, jellies served in individual glasses were equally popular. Round, trumpet-shaped, and footed jelly glasses corresponded to other fashionable glassware in shape and decoration.[11]

Three different styles of Monticello jelly glasses are known. Two are plain free-blown glasses, one with a knopped stem. A third type of free-blown jelly glass has cut decoration on the rim and bowl.

On August 18, 1791, in New York, Jefferson wrote in his Memorandum Book, "Pd. for jelly glasses 3. doz. 3 D[ollars]."[12] Among the items inventoried at Monticello after his death were "21 cut & 3 plain jelly glasses."[13]

[1986-31-10; 1986-31-9; 1986-31-11 and 12]   S.M.O.

192 (left)

JELLY GLASS

late 18th c.

England
glass
H: 10 (3¹⁵⁄₁₆ in.)
D (rim): 6.5 (2⁹⁄₁₆ in.)

193 (center)

JELLY GLASS

late 18th c.

England
glass
H: 10.8 (4¼ in.)
D (rim): 6.4 (2½ in.)

194 (right)

JELLY GLASS
ONE OF TWO

late 18th c.

England
lead glass
H: 10.8 (4¼ in.);
D (rim): 6.7 (2⅝ in.)

PROVENANCE:
Thomas Jefferson; by descent to Margaret Randolph Taylor and Olivia Alexander Taylor; by bequest to TJMF in 1985.

DECANTER

1760–70

England
glass
H: 24.8 (9¾ in);
D (base): 8.9 (3½ in.)
Provenience: Dry Well

This labeled Madeira decanter was excavated from the dry well site of the Monticello kitchen yard in 1981. The dry well, intended to be a cool, dry storage place, was dug in 1770 to a depth of almost nineteen feet. Jefferson's plans for the dependency structures soon changed, however, and the large hole was refilled over the next two years. A number of discarded domestic artifacts dating from the earliest years of Jefferson's habitation on the mountain top were found in the backfill during archaeological excavation.[14] One of the finest objects unearthed was an English decanter with wheel-engraved cartouche and grapevine motifs dating from the 1760s. Decanters of this type were made with various labels for all types of alcoholic beverages.[15]

Although Jefferson's purchase of this early decanter is unrecorded, he acquired many others in later years. Eight crystal decanters were among the household goods shipped from France in 1790. In 1815 Jefferson listed "4 cut glass decanters" in his list of taxable property.[16] The inventory of Monticello made after his death included "12 decanters 6 of them a little broken."[17]

Jefferson once noted how many glasses of Madeira a cask would yield and which type was the most economical to drink. In 1775 he wrote in his Memorandum Book:

If a pipe of Madeira yeilds 30 doz. bottles, we drink it at 7. years old for 3/ a bottle, which includes the 7. years interest. Such a bottle holds 15 common wine glasses. . . . A pipe of new Madeira will yeild 40. doz, which brings the price (there being no interest) to 20/ a doz. or 20d the bottle when drank new.[18]

[1981–92]   S.M.O.

TWO WINE GLASSES

1790–1810

England
lead glass
H: 15.6 (6⅛ in.); 14.6 (5¾ in.)

PROVENANCE:
Thomas Jefferson; by descent to
Frances Maury Burke; by gift or
purchase to Rose Gouverneur
Hoes; by descent to Laurence G.
Hoes; by bequest to Camilla Hoes
Pope; by purchase to TJMF in
1984.

197

TUMBLER

1770–1810

England or America
glass
H: 8.9 (3½ in.);
D (rim): 7.6 (3 in.)

198

TUMBLER

1810–25

America, possibly Pittsburgh
lead glass
H: 7.3 (2⅞ in.);
D (rim): 7 (2¾ in.)

PROVENANCE:
Thomas Jefferson; by descent to
Virginia and Nicholas Trist; by
descent to Frances Maury Burke;
by gift or purchase to Rose
Gouverneur Hoes; by descent to
Laurence G. Hoes; by bequest to
Camilla Hoes Pope; by purchase to
TJMF in 1984.

In a letter to M. de Neuville in 1818, Jefferson commented:

I rejoice, as a moralist, at the prospect of a reduction of the duties on wine, by our national legislature. . . . No nation is drunken where wine is cheap; and none sober, where the dearness of wine substitutes ardent spirits as the common beverage. . . . Fix but the duty at the rate of other merchandise, and we can drink wine here as cheap as we do grog, and who will not prefer it? It's extended use will carry health and comfort to a much enlarged circle.[19]

Jefferson, a connoisseur of wines and patron of viticulture in America, acquired a well-developed palate during his years abroad. The well-stocked cellar at Monticello was supplied with wines from France, Portugal, Spain, Hungary, Germany, and Italy.[20] "He has a strong preference for the wines of the continent, of which he has many sorts of excellent quality, having been more than commonly successful in his mode of importing and preserving," noted Daniel Webster in 1824.[21]

At the Monticello dinner table, wine was not served until "after the cloth was removed," with the dessert of fruit, nuts, and sweetmeats served on the bare tabletop. These two lead-glass vessels, each with a band of wheel-cut sprig and oval engraving, illustrate just one of the many styles of stemware that Jefferson owned, some of which still survive. The packing list of Jefferson's goods shipped from France in 1790 included twelve crystal goblets and "39 footed glasses."[22] Purchases of glassware were recorded in Jefferson's Memorandum Books between 1767 and 1821. From Monticello Martha Jefferson Randolph reminded her father in Washington in 1803, "When you send the groceries on will you remember glasses, tumblers and wine glasses both are much wan[ting here]."[23] By 1826, when a household inventory was made following Jefferson's death, only seventeen wine glasses remained among the household goods.[24]
[1984-44-3a/b]   S.M.O.

"Malt liquors and cyder are my table drinks," wrote Jefferson to a friend in 1819.[25] During his lifetime, tumblers were a common drinking vessel for beer and cider. The low, usually cylindrical and slightly tapering glasses were adapted from rounded silver cups of the same name as early as the seventeenth century.[26]

Tumblers were made and decorated in many styles. The first example (near right) was mold-blown with vertical fluting extending more than half way up its sides. The second tumbler (far right) has fourteen cut panels around its base surmounted by a band of vertical wheel-cut engraving. Numerous fragments of other kinds of tumblers have been recovered in archaeological excavations at Monticello.

Jefferson first recorded buying tumblers in 1767 when he ordered three dozen of them in the half-pint size.[27] In an 1801 letter to his agent in Philadelphia, Jefferson wrote from Monticello, "if you could procure and send at the same time a couple of dozen of [barrel?] glass tumblers (I mean of this shape [a rough outline of a barrel-shaped tumbler]) they would be acceptable as none of any kind are to be had here."[28] According to the inventory of Monticello made in 1826, "13 tumblers" remained in the house after Jefferson's death.[29]
[1984-44-1; 1958-32-1]   S.M.O.

This portable chest with iron lock, bail handles, and fittings, is divided into ten compartments for holding eight large and two small square case bottles. Eight original mold-blown bottles with spherical stoppers and gilded grapevine decoration on the shoulders remain with the case; one bottle is a replacement. In October 1772 Jefferson recorded, "Pd. Mr. Jones for case of bottles and glass cylinders bot. by Ogilvie £10-11-3."[30] These items were probably bought by Jefferson's friend, James Ogilvie, in England. This is his only recorded acquisition of case bottles, but he likely bought others.

Case bottles were frequently used as shipping and storage containers, although decorated bottles such as these were usually intended for domestic use. Jefferson said he did not use "ardent spirits in any form," so these bottles probably did not hold gin and rum as was common. Case bottles were, however, equally useful for storing and transporting non-alcoholic beverages, as well as other liquids and oils. They remained popular throughout the eighteenth and early nineteenth century.[31]

During his retirement Jefferson traveled to Poplar Forest three times a year, a three-day journey of ninety-three miles. A case of bottles might have traveled with him. One of his granddaughters described their picnics en route:

Our cold dinner was always put up by his own hands; a pleasant spot by the road-side chosen to eat it, and he was the carver and helped us to our cold fowl and ham, and mixed the wine and water to drink with it.[32]

[1961-41]   S.M.O.

SPIRIT CHEST

1770–1800

England or America
oak with iron fittings; glass
26.4 × 40 × 27.3
(10⅜ × 15¾ × 10¾ in.)

Provenance:
Thomas Jefferson; by descent to Susan Ware Eppes and Alice Bradford Eppes; by purchase to TJMF in 1961.

WHITE SALTGLAZE STONEWARE TANKARD

1740–80[33]

reconstruction[34]
England
H: 12.1 (4¾ in.)
Provenience[35]: *Dry Well*[36]
[ER 354AC, 354AD, 357AD (SC503)]

---

201 (center)

CHINESE EXPORT PORCELAIN PATTY PAN

18th c.

reconstruction
Chinese export
H: 4 (1½ in.) D: 10.8 (4½ in.)
Provenience: Garden Wall[42]
[ER 294C (SC 550)]

---

202 (middle left)

CREAMWARE BASKET

after 1760

reconstruction
England
H: 6.8 (2⅝ in.) D: 12.6 (7 in.)
Provenience: Dry Well
[ER 352L, 354F, 354M, 356E, 357G (SC 266)]

This form is a common drinking pint tankard, found in private homes and taverns alike.[37] White saltglaze stoneware became the most popular American tableware in the period 1740–1770.[38] Unlike its earthenware contemporary, delft, white saltglaze did not have the problem of easily losing its glaze, nor was it unduly fragile. White saltglaze was extremely well suited for the molding of elaborate shapes. This characteristic allowed it to be sold in an impressive variety of forms and made possible a much wider range of impressed and sprigged decoration than could ever have been achieved on tin-glazed earthenware. As early as 1710, Staffordshire potters were producing slip-cast and thrown wares for both the domestic and foreign markets.[39] These vessels are rarely marked.

M.D.P.

This Chinese export porcelain patty pan is an example of a vessel form made solely in response to the needs of the Western market. "Pastry dishes" were ordered from China as early as 1620, and in 1797 a Rhode Island merchant imported Chinese porcelain "Patty pans" in sets of three.[40] These small round pans were used for the baking of small tarts and pies. Since they were transported from oven to table, they were often made out of those ceramics that were also used for tableware. Jefferson recorded a purchase of patty pans in 1812 while at Poplar Forest.[41]

M.D.P.

Creamware was often referred to as "cream colored ware" or "queensware" by eighteenth-century English potters.[43] By the 1760s creamware, decorated and undecorated, was the dominant English ceramic on the market, both at home and in America. Like saltglaze, it was produced in a wide variety of forms, and was often sold in large sets. Although Chinese porcelain held the market in teaware; creamware cups and saucers were also available, and very popular. Although Jefferson himself makes no reference to creamware, a 1791 letter from his daughter, Martha Randolph, mentions her inadvertent purchase of a second set of "queensware."[44] This double purchase may account for the two separate rim patterns, feather and royal (Cat. 203, 205) recovered at Monticello. By the time Mrs. Randolph sent to Richmond for creamware, pearlware was already popular,[45] and by her own admission the purchase was made in order to protect the "china" (most likely Chinese export porcelain) from harm. This is evidence of the changing role of creamware, whose aesthetic and qualitative value was waning. In the nineteenth century, creamware was not only much cheaper than other wares on the market, but its suppliers now relied on selling the most basic of tableware forms and toiletry items, especially chamberpots, ewers, and basins.[46]

M.D.P.

203 (front left)	204 (lower right)	205 (middle right)

CREAMWARE PLATE, FEATHER EDGE RIM

CREAMWARE CUP AND SAUCER

CREAMWARE PLATE, ROYAL RIM

1760–80

after 1760

1760–1800

reconstruction
England
D: 24.8 (9¾ in.)
Provenience: Dry Well
[ER 354 AD, 356AD (SC 193)]

reconstruction
England
cup: D: 8.9 (3½ in.);
saucer: D: 13.2 (5¼ in.)
(cup) Provenience: Building "O"
[ER 831E2, 831E1, 831E3, 831K1,
831K3, 962D1, 987C1.]
(saucer) Provenience: Building "S"
[ER 831E1, 831E2]

reconstruction
England, marked: impressed "M"[47]
D: 24.8 (9¾ in.)
Provenience: Building "M"
(Smokehouse/Dairy)
[ER 345D (SC 190)]

206 (rear right)

CHINESE PORCELAIN SLOP BOWL

mid-18th c.

reconstruction
Chinese "Imari";[48] *underglaze*
blue with overglaze enamel in
red and gold; pagoda, bridge
and dock
H: 8.2 (3¼ in.)
D: 16.5 (6½ in.)
Provenience: Dry Well
[ER 352L, 354M, 357G]

207 (front left and front center)

CHINESE EXPORT PORCELAIN CUP AND SAUCER

18th c.

reconstruction
underglaze blue with overglaze
enamel in red and gold
cup: D: 8.9 (3½ in.)
saucer: D: 13.9 (5½ in.)
Provenience: Garden Wall
[ER 294C (SC 550)]

208 (rear left)

CHINESE EXPORT PLATE

after 1750

reconstruction
underglaze blue,[49] *"peony"*
pattern[50]
D: 23.9 (9⅜ in.)
Provenience: Building "O"
[ER 1), 2), 3) 407AA, 410AA 4)
407AA 5) 400AA, 401AA, 407AA,
410AA, 540AA, 548AA, 548AA (SC
508 +)]

Although it was the Portuguese who fostered the opening of lucrative trade relations with the Far East in the sixteenth century, it was not long before the importation of Chinese porcelain became a productive business for other European nations as well.[51] Porcelain's hard, translucent body was a mystery that English potters tried unsuccessfully to solve for many years. A number of interesting and innovative ware types were attempted, although until the nineteenth century none approached the look of Chinese export.

The variety of porcelain available to the Western market was tremendous, as was the volume. Much of what reached America, first through Europe, and after 1784, directly from Canton, was not the best of what was available in China. By the eighteenth century this was especially true, when Chinese export such as the "peony" pattern found at Monticello was typical of imports to America. Lavish, but rarer, examples of Chinese porcelain, with overglaze enamel painting added to blue underglaze patterns, were also imported at higher prices. Much of the decoration on early Chinese porcelain was based on traditional Chinese motifs, but the exposure to Western ceramic forms and decoration created new vessel types and often merged Chinese and Western decoration in new and different ways.

Jefferson did not habitually make much detailed comment on his ceramic purchases for his various households. One exception to this surrounds his acquisition of Chinese porcelain. While in Paris, Jefferson made a number of references to "East India" porcelain. These include correspondence that seeks to match existing porcelain "as nearly like the pattern as they can be found."[52]

It would appear that Jefferson, like most who ordered stock Chinese porcelain in the eighteenth century, relied on the tenacity of the middleman, and the nature of the current inventory in China.

M.D.P.

This overglaze pattern is also occasionally referred to as the "Valentine" pattern. Although a number of variations are recorded, most include flaming hearts on an altar, two love birds, and a quiver of cupid's arrows and his bow. This pattern is believed to have been taken from a 1743 drawing by Piercy Brett, an artist who traveled in China with Admiral Lord Anson.[53]

M.D.P.

209 (front right)

CHINESE EXPORT PORCELAIN SAUCER

after 1743

reconstruction
overglaze enamel in red, black
and gold; "Altar of Love" pattern
D: 11.4 (4½ in.)
Provenience: Garden Wall
[ER 294C (SC 550)]

SCIENTIFIC INSTRUMENTS

Jefferson's "Mathematical Apparatus"

At the age of fourteen, Thomas Jefferson inherited from his father a collection of "mathematical Instruments" valued at £6, as well as about twenty books, including a work on astronomy.[1] Peter Jefferson undoubtedly passed on to his son some of his knowledge of surveying and mathematics before his early death. It was another man, however, who gave Jefferson his "first views of the expansion of science and of the system of things in which we are placed." The Scotsman William Small, professor of natural philosophy at the College of William and Mary, "fixed the destinies of my life."[2] Small, who transmitted the Enlightenment principles that underlay all of Jefferson's future actions, inspired him with a lifelong passion for mathematics and astronomy. Jefferson believed in science as an instrument for improving the condition of mankind and observed with delight the universal laws of nature demonstrated by Sir Isaac Newton, one of his trinity of the "greatest men that ever lived."[3]

In astronomy, Jefferson did not review the heavens in the manner of Halley and Herschel. He, like many of his American contemporaries, used the celestial bodies to learn about the earth. As he wrote in 1816, "we cannot know the relative position of two places on the earth, but by interrogating the sun, moon, and stars."[4] To fix his own position in the universe and to contribute to an understanding of the geography of his country, Jefferson repeated his heavenly interrogations over the course of a long life.

He began at Monticello, by fixing its meridian, calculating its elevation and latitude, and trying to find its longitude. He then extended these operations to other Virginia sites as part of his larger purpose of contributing to precise geographical information about America. Instruments of the finest workmanship were essential for these purposes.

Little is known of Jefferson's instrument collection before his European residence. The small stock inherited from his father may have been destroyed in the Shadwell fire of 1770. By the time of his departure for France in 1784, he had at least a spyglass, a microscope, and a fine Ramsden theodolite. His journey in the spring of 1786 to London, where the mechanical arts were "carried to a wonderful perfection," inspired him to draw up a list of his "Mathematical Apparatus."[5] He visited the shops of the most famous opticians and instrument makers—Jesse Ramsden, Peter and John Dollond, John Jones, Edward Troughton, Henry Shuttleworth, and William Cary—and carried back to France an assortment of instruments worth £56, including his first achromatic telescope, an air pump, and compound and solar microscopes. He later added to his collection an equatorial telescope and reflecting circle, also of English workmanship.

Throughout his years of public service, Jefferson yearned to pursue the scientific studies for which he had no time. As he wrote Dr. Caspar Wistar in 1817, "I have been drawn by the history of the times from physical and mathematical sciences, which were my passion, to those of politics and government towards which I had naturally no inclination."[6] On his retirement in 1809, he was able to return to the "tranquil pursuits of science," primarily astronomy.[7] In 1812 he wrote that he had been "for some time rubbing up my Mathematics from the rust contracted by 50. years pursuits of a different kind, and thanks to the good foundation laid at College by my old master and friend Small, I am doing it with a delight and success beyond my expectation."[8]

Jefferson passed his surveying skills and knowledge of astronomy on to younger friends and relations and shared his findings and some of his best instruments with mapmakers. At the end of his life he intended to give to the University of Virginia part of his collection—instruments both technically advanced and of the highest quality workmanship.[9] Four of the finest survive—his Ramsden theodolite (Cat. 214), two Dollond telescopes (Cat. 213), and an astronomical clock (Cat. 238). Two of the most valuable—an equatorial telescope and a reflecting circle—are now unlocated.

L.C.S.

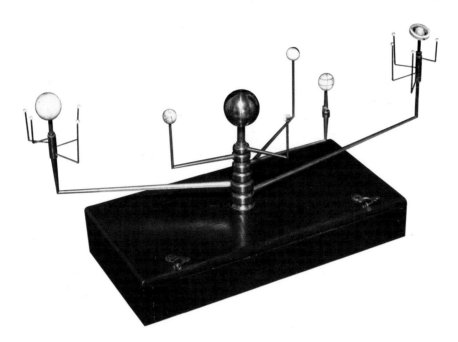

210
PORTABLE ORRERY
---
c. 1792

*William Jones (1763–1831);
Samuel Jones
undetermined materials
dimensions not known
unlocated*

PROVENANCE:
Thomas Jefferson; by unknown route to Charles Sinkler; by gift to the Franklin Institute in 1938; stolen in 1961 and still unlocated.

This portable orrery was ordered by Jefferson in 1792 from a prominent London firm of mathematical instrument makers. These operating models of the solar system demonstrated the diurnal and annual motion of the planets and their satellites and were dramatic visual expressions of the rational order of nature's laws in a Newtonian universe.

Like most of his countrymen, Jefferson marveled at the "amazing mechanical representation of the solar system" he encountered at the College of Philadelphia in 1775.[10] The orrery recently made by David Rittenhouse performed with unparalleled precision and complexity. Wishing to send proof of American genius to the rest of the world, Jefferson proposed that the American Philosophical Society commission one of Rittenhouse's orreries for presentation to the king of France.[11]

Jefferson may have had an orrery representing just the earth and the moon by 1793, when a packing list prepared by his French butler included "une machine qui est la boule du monde."[12] By the end of that year he received from William Jones a "New Manual orrery and Planetarium," costing three guineas.[13] A later reference suggests that Jefferson may have had it in his cabinet at the President's House.[14]

L.C.S.

211

MICROMETER WITH CASE AND COVER

c. 1780

Alexis Marie Rochon
(1741–1817)
brass, glass; case: pressed board,
paper; cover: textile, leather
L: 35.6 (14 in.) closed;
48.3 (19 in.) extended;
case: L: 35.6 (14 in.)
D: 5.2 (2¹/₁₆ in.) cover:
36.8 × 41.9 (14½ × 16½ in.)

PROVENANCE:
John Hartwell Cocke; by descent
to John Page Elliott; by gift and
purchase to TJMF in 1992.

Jefferson's list of "Mathematical Apparatus" includes "a telescope of Iceland chrystal by the abbé Rochon & Herbage."[15] This "lunette," as he sometimes called it, combined an achromatic telescope with a prismatic micrometer, based on the use of double-refracting rock crystal.

Jefferson was in Paris while the Abbé Rochon was making his important new discoveries in optics at La Muette, the royal Cabinet de Physique in Passy. At Benjamin Franklin's house nearby, he had seen Rochon demonstrate his micrometer and had learned its principles from the inventor himself. "I was intimate with him in France," Jefferson wrote in 1812, adding that he possessed "one of his lunettes, which he had given to Doctor Franklin and which came to me thro' Mr. [Francis] Hopkinson."[16] Later he lamented that Rochon's micrometer had not been widely adopted in navigation and land armaments, commenting that "it is one of the remarkable proofs of the slowth with which improvements in the arts and sciences advance."[17]

John Hartwell Cocke's known interest in Jefferson's scientific instruments suggests the possibility that Cocke acquired this micrometer from Jefferson's estate after his death.
[1992-4-2]   L.C.S.

212

HAND TELESCOPE

c. 1768–1800

Jesse Ramsden (1735–1800)
mahogany, silver plate
L: 19.1 (7½ in.); 52.1
(20½ in.) extended

PROVENANCE:
Thomas Jefferson; by descent to
Thomas Jefferson Randolph; by
descent to Jefferson Randolph
Kean II; by gift to TJMF in 1986.

Although "perspective" glasses and "pocket telescopes" make scattered appearances in Jefferson's records, no certain reference to this fine portable instrument can be found. The upper silver band bears the inscription "Thomas Jefferson."

Several family stories describe Jefferson with spyglass in hand; the one accompanying this telescope relates that Jefferson used it to see British soldiers swarming in the streets of Charlottesville in 1781, when he barely escaped capture by Tarleton's dragoons. It would also be a likely instrument for his walks on the North Terrace of Monticello to view the progress of the building of the University of Virginia.[18]
[1955-72]   L.C.S.

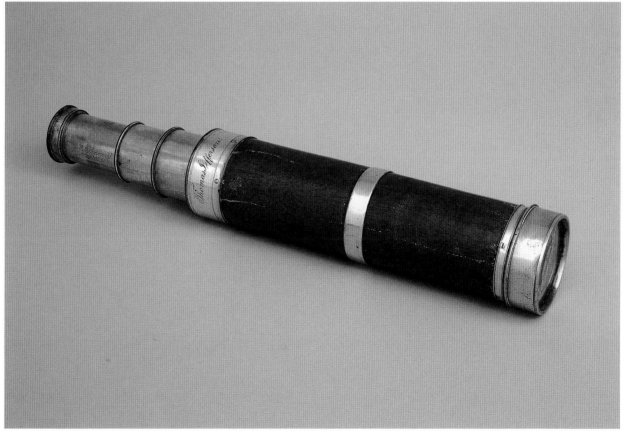

213

PEDESTAL ACHROMATIC TELESCOPE

1786–93

Peter Dollond (1730–1820)
and John Dollond (d. 1804)
mahogany, brass
L: 74.9 (29½ in.)

PROVENANCE:
Thomas Jefferson; by descent to Thomas Jefferson Randolph; by descent to Arthur Rotch; by gift to TJMF, in memory of Margaret Randolph Rotch, in 1943.

While in London in 1786, Jefferson purchased his first achromatic telescope from Peter and John Dollond, who continued to make the instrument perfected by their father, John Dollond (1706–1761). This refracting telescope, with "three object glasses," cost £10-10.[19] Jefferson acquired a second Dollond telescope for an unknown price in 1793.[20] Both instruments survive, although it has not been determined which was purchased first.

In 1793 Jefferson acquired the most valuable instrument in his collection, an equatorial telescope by Jesse Ramsden (1735–1800), whom he considered preeminent among makers. With "this noble instrument," as he called it, he fixed the meridian at Monticello and viewed the solar eclipse of 1811.[21] Judged by one scholar to be "unquestionably the most sophisticated astronomical instrument in the United States" at the time, Jefferson's equatorial was the foundation of his favorite theory of a method for determining longitude by lunar distances without a timepiece.[22]

Although he often expressed a desire for a more powerful telescope, Jefferson apparently never acquired one capable of viewing the eclipses of Jupiter's satellites, a requisite for the other common method of determining longitude.

In the 1820s Jefferson lent his "best" telescope to Hermann Böÿe, then engaged in mapping Virginia. When attempting to recover it, he wrote that he intended to give it to the University of Virginia.[23] The telescope illustrated here descended through the family of Thomas Jefferson Randolph and bears the inscription "Thomas Jefferson Monticello" on the band near the eyepiece.

[1943-4]. L.C.S.

Peter Jefferson, active for many years as a county surveyor, almost certainly gave his older son some instruction in surveying. For a few months Thomas Jefferson filled the position of Albemarle County surveyor once occupied by his father, apparently carrying out his duties entirely through deputies. When he resigned in 1774, he did not let his surveying skills decay. He used them for the rest of his life to map his lands and measure his landscape.

Dozens of Jefferson's plats survive of his lands in both Albemarle and Bedford counties. In 1793, with theodolite and Gunter's chain, he revised the boundaries of his fields at Monticello to fit his crop-rotation schemes. In 1806 he surveyed a new entrance road from the Rivanna River to the house. He also enjoyed passing on the secrets of surveying to apt young men; at age sixty-six he was running lines on the rugged slopes of Monticello, while instructing a grandson.

In 1778 Jefferson purchased from mathematician Robert Andrews perhaps the most sophisticated surveying instrument then available, a telescopic theodolite made by Jesse Ramsden.[24] In one of several tributes to this celebrated instrument maker, Jefferson wrote that "the measure of angles, by the wonderful perfection to which the graduation of instruments has been brought by a Bird, a Ramsden, a Troughton removes nearly all distrust from that operation."[25]

Since this "most excellent" instrument could be used for measuring both horizontal and vertical angles and was equipped with telescopes, Jefferson employed his theodolite for far more than land surveying.[26] In the months after he bought it, he made observations on the variation of the needle, fixed the true meridian of Monticello, calculated the position of features of the Monticello landscape and surrounding mountains, and may have used it in his observation of the solar eclipse in June 1778. In 1815, in one of his most elaborate trigonometric exercises, he used the theodolite to determine the elevation of the Peaks of Otter in the Blue Ridge Mountains.

[1952-67]   L.C.S.

214

THEODOLITE WITH CASE AND TRIPOD

1770s

*Jesse Ramsden (1735–1800)
brass, copper; case: mahogany
theodolite: 35.6 × 19.7 × 17.1
(14 × 7¾ × 6¾ in.); case:
30.5 × 19.7 × 19.7
(12 × 7¾ × 7¾ in.); tripod:
115.6 (45½ in.)*

PROVENANCE:
Thomas Jefferson; by purchase to John Hartwell Cocke at the Dispersal Sale in 1827; by descent to Mrs. Lucy Cocke Elliott; by gift to TJMF in 1952.

HAND MAGNIFIER

1780s

William Jones? (1763–1831)
brass, glass
H: 4.4 (1¾ in.) D: 3.8 (1½ in.)

This small instrument, with a vertically adjustable double-convex lens, may be the "botanical microscope" Jefferson purchased from William Jones in London in April 1786 for ten shillings.[27] On the same visit he bought a Dollond solar microscope and a Jones compound microscope, as well as some devices for concentrating light for microscope use.

This small magnifier was probably always at hand for close observation of objects of natural history. An undated list of the contents of a small traveling box, in which Jefferson planned to pack everything from razors and a toothbrush to a corkscrew and a platting scale, includes a "microscope," very possibly this one.[28]

"I view no science with more partiality than natural history," Jefferson wrote in 1807.[29] He was described at this time by a friend as "passionately fond" of botany, riding out of Washington in search of interesting plants.[30] He could use his little lens to place botanical specimens in the order of the Linnaean classification system or to examine "in all their minutest particles" the "perfectly organised" structures of insects and other small creatures.[31]

[1955-50]   L.C.S.

In 1806 Jefferson ordered from the London firm W. & S. Jones "a 12. Inch concave glass mirror in a plain black frame" costing £2-5.[32] He had acquired a larger concave mirror in a more elaborate frame while living in France in the 1780s, for which this was probably a replacement.[33]

Jefferson intended using his concave mirrors, as well as the condensing lenses and scioptric ball he bought in London in 1786, with his microscopes. As he wrote in 1822, "in microscopic observations, the enlargement of the angle of vision may be indulged, because auxiliary light may be concentrated on the object by concave mirrors."[34] The reflecting mirror of a compound microscope would be placed at the focal point of the mirrors.

When a viewer stands outside the focal point of a concave mirror, his image is reflected upside down. This optical phenomenon may account for the mirror's location in the Entrance Hall in an inventory prepared shortly after Jefferson's death.[35] It might have become a source of family entertainment in Jefferson's last years, when he had abandoned more complex scientific experiments.

[1961-15]   L . C . S .

216

CONCAVE MIRROR

c. 1807

*William Jones (1763–1831);
Samuel Jones
glass, with walnut frame
D: 30.5 (12 in.); 33.7 (13¼ in.) with frame*

PROVENANCE:
Thomas Jefferson; by purchase to George Toole at the Dispersal Sale in 1827; by descent to Mrs. John Toole; by purchase to Henry Polkinhorn; by gift to William Wilson Corcoran; by purchase to an unidentified Washington dealer; by purchase to Mr. and Mrs. Parry Borgstrom; by gift of Ruth D. Borgstrom to TJMF in 1961.

PLAIN SURVEYING COMPASS IN CASE

1791–1829

John Bleuler (1757–1829)
brass, steel, glass; case: wood
(probably pine), paper
L: 39.4 (15½ in.); H: 5.1 (2
in.); 17.8 (7 in.) with sights;
dial: D: 15.2 (6 in.); Depth: 2
(¾ in.); case: 29.4 × 17.1 × 6.7
(15½ × 6¾ × 2⅝ in.)

PROVENANCE:
John Hartwell Cocke; by descent
to John Page Elliott; by gift and
purchase to TJMF in 1992.

Although no references to the English maker John Bleuler appear in Jefferson's records, this instrument may have been his, as John Hartwell Cocke purchased other surveying equipment from Jefferson's estate in 1827.[36]

Jefferson almost certainly owned and used a plain surveyor's compass—in England it was known as a circumferentor. It would have been his major surveying tool before he acquired his Ramsden theodolite in 1778. He later expanded his surveying equipment by purchasing more portable circumferentors—called graphometers in England. While in London in 1786 he bought "a pocket graphometer by Cole," and in 1805 he asked Thomas Freeman, leader of the Red River exploring expedition, to buy him "an accurate compass for surveying, with two pair of sights moving concentrically, an outer graduated circle with a Nonius to take angles accurately without regard to the needle, with its ball and socket and staff." He reflected the still-present confusion in terminology when he added that he believed "they are called Circumferentors, but is not certain." He added it to his instrument list as "a common Theodolite or Graphometer," eight inches in diameter and costing $54.[37]

[1992-4-3]   L . C . S .

PORTABLE SCALES

c. 1790

Young & Son, London
brass, with wooden case
case: 17.6 × 8.7 × 3.2
(6¹⁵⁄₁₆ × 3⁷⁄₁₆ × 1¼ in.);
pans: D: 5.1 (2 in.);
balance: L: 12.4 (4⅞ in.)

PROVENANCE:
Thomas Jefferson; by descent to
Elizabeth Martin Randolph, widow
of Meriwether Lewis Randolph; by
gift to Bettie M. Donelson; by
purchase to Mr. and Mrs. Stanley
Horn; by bequest to Ruth Horn
Crownover; by purchase to TJMF
in 1992.

The place and date of Jefferson's purchase of these portable scales cannot be determined. A practically identical set, without case, also survives, as does a folding pocket money scale.

Jefferson's Memorandum Books contain surprisingly few references to the purchase of scales or steelyards. They and other records are full, however, of signs of the daily use of weighing devices. On the plantation there was constant weighing of wheat and cornmeal, hogs and beef, or nails made in the nailery. Jefferson himself used smaller scales to weigh a silver coffee pot used in payment, his newborn daughter Lucy, a new pair of silk stockings, and the amount of sugar he added to his coffee.[38] Coins had to be frequently weighed to test their value, and Jefferson's specifications for a traveling box include "money scales" and "money steelyards" among the contents.[39]

[1992-9-1]   L . C . S .

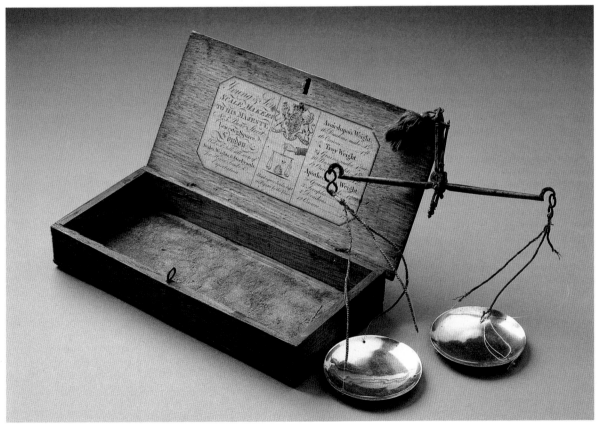

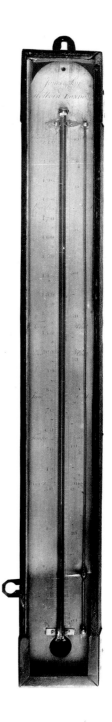

219

ODOMETER

n.d.

Nairne & Blunt, London
mahogany, metal
27.9 × 23.2 × 8.1
(11 × 9⅛ × 3³⁄₁₆ in.)
University of Virginia
School of Medicine

PROVENANCE:
Thomas Jefferson; University of
Virginia; by loan to TJMF since
1949.

Jefferson often wrote of his great experience in traveling. Long hours on the road in his legal and public careers made him eager to find the shortest routes to his common destinations. This, and an innate passion for measurement, prompted his desire for a means of knowing the distances he traveled.

During his longest journey, a three-month tour through France and Italy in 1787, he heard of "a pendulum Odometer for the wheel of a carriage."[40] The next year he inquired about English odometers, but found them—at seven to ten guineas—too expensive.[41]

After another long journey to New York and New England in 1791 he purchased his first odometer, for ten dollars, from the Scottish clockmaker Robert Leslie, "the most ingenious workman in America." He attached it immediately to his phaeton and recorded the mileages of his route from Philadelphia to Monticello. This odometer merely counted the revolutions of the wheel.[42]

The odometer pictured here, made by London instrument makers Nairne & Blunt, may be the one he purchased from David Rittenhouse in 1794.[43] This very sophisticated instrument measured the distance in chains, links, and poles as well as miles, so it could be mounted on either a hand-propelled waywiser or a carriage.[44]

Jefferson, having failed in his own efforts to develop the ideal odometer, received one in 1807 from its inventor, James Clarke of Powhatan County, Virginia. Clarke's odometer had two features that were particularly pleasing to Jefferson. It chimed after every ten miles, and it subdivided the miles decimally, into dimes and cents. Jefferson found "great satisfaction in having miles announced by the bell as by milestones on the road," and as one of the fathers of the American decimal system, he liked being able to use the decimal point in making his itineraries.[45] His Clarke odometer also proved the efficacy of the decimal system for measures other than money. "The people on the road," he wrote, "inquire with curiosity what exact distance I have found from such a place to such a place; I answer, so many miles, so many cents. I find they universally and at once form a perfect idea of the relation of the cent to the miles as a unit."[46]

[1949-9]   L . C . S .

In his Memorandum Books Jefferson recorded the purchase of almost twenty thermometers. On July 4, 1776, he bought one from Philadelphia merchant John Sparhawk for £3-15. Three days earlier he had begun his first surviving "meteorological diary."[47] For the rest of his life his daily routine included a thermometer check at dawn and in late afternoon—in his opinion, the coldest and warmest times of day. His temperature record was sometimes supplemented with barometer and hygrometer readings, as well as notes on what he called "indexes of climate," like the blooming of plants and migrations of animals.

As one of the first systematic observers of the American climate, Jefferson tried to enlist others in his activities and even envisioned a national network of weather watchers. He realized that, for the formation of a reliable theory of climate, many others would have to provide what he had: years of "steady attention to the thermometer, to the plants growing there, the times of their leafing and flowering, its animal inhabitants, beast, birds, reptiles and insects; its prevalent winds, quantities of rain and snow, temperature of mountains, and other indexes of climate."[48]

Marked "Jones & Son/Holborn London," this thermometer is probably the one received from William Jones early in 1789. Jefferson had asked for a thermometer "not less than 18. inches long" for mounting outside a window, with Fahrenheit and Reaumur scales and graduations precise enough for occasional "nice" experiments.[49]

L . C . S .

220

THERMOMETER

1788

John Jones (active late 18th c. to early 19th c.); William Jones (1763–1831)
brass, glass, mercury, wood
48.3 × 5.7 (19 × 2¼ in.)
The Historical Society of Pennsylvania

PROVENANCE:
Thomas Jefferson; by gift to Dr. Robley Dunglison; by descent to John Alden Tifft; by gift to The Historical Society of Pennsylvania in 1945.

WRITING AND DRAWING INSTRUMENTS

One of the most precious historical relics of the United States is the lap desk or writing box upon which Jefferson wrote his draft of the Declaration of Independence in 1776.[1] He presented the desk to his grandson-in-law Joseph Coolidge, Jr., of Boston, who had married Ellen Wayles Randolph, one of his favorite granddaughters. He attached an affidavit to the desk:

Th. Jefferson gives this Writing desk to Joseph Coolidge, Jr. as a memorial of affection. It was made from a drawing of his own, by Ben. Randall, cabinet maker of Philadelphia with whom he first lodged on his arrival in that city in May 1776 and is the identical one on which he wrote the Declaration of Independence. Politics as well as Religion has its superstitions. These, gaining strength with time, may, one day, give imaginary value to this relic, for its association with the birth of the Great Charter of our Independence.

Monticello, Nov. 18, 1825.[2]

Although the affidavit was addressed to Joseph Coolidge, the writing box was intended for both Ellen and Joseph, at least in part to console her for the loss in a shipwreck of her belongings en route from Virginia to Boston—among those irretrievable items was a lap desk made especially for her by John Hemings, Monticello's proficient slave joiner. Commiserating with his granddaughter, Jefferson tendered her a priceless replacement.

It has occurred to me however, that I can replace it, not indeed, to you, but to Mr. Coolidge, by a substitute, not claiming the same value from it's decorations, but from the part it has borne in our history and the events with which it has been associated. . . . If then things acquire a superstitious value because of their connection with particular persons, surely a connection with the great Charter of our Independence may give a value to what has been associated with that; and such was the idea of the enquirers after the room in which it was written. It was made from a drawing of my own, by Ben. Randall, a cabinet maker in whose house I took my first lodgings on my arrival in Philadelphia in May 1776. And I have used it ever since. It claims no merit of particular beauty. It is plain, neat, convenient, and taking no more room on the writing table than a moderate 4to. volume, it yet displays it self sufficiently for any writing. Mr. Coolidge must do me the favor of accepting this. Its imaginary value will increase with the years, and if he lives to my age, or another half century, he may see it carried in the procession of our nation's birthday, as the relics of the saints are in those of the church.[3]

Once Coolidge had received the desk, he expressed his gratitude to Jefferson.

When I think of this desk, 'in connection with the great charter of our independence,' I feel a sentiment almost of awe, and approach it with respect; but when I remember that it has served you fifty years, been the faithful depository of your cherished thoughts; that upon it have been written your letters to illustrious and excellent men, your plans for the advancement of civil and religious liberty, and of Art and Science; that it has, in fact, been the companion, of your studies, and instrument of diffusing their results; that it has been the witness of a philosophy which calumny could not subdue, and an enthusiasm which eighty winters have not chilled, I would fain consider it as no longer inanimate, and mute, but as something to be interrogated, and caressed.[4]

This uncommon desk, made entirely of mahogany, was made to Jefferson's specifications by the prominent Philadelphia cabinetmaker, Benjamin Randolph, with whom Jefferson lodged when he first came to Philadelphia in July 1775 and when he returned in May 1776.[5] Although a payment was recorded for Randolph's workmen for three boxes in September, the purchase of a writing box or lap desk was not noted in Jefferson's Memorandum Books. Jefferson's drawings for the desk do not survive. The desk consists of a rectangular box with a drawer containing compartments for storing writing implements and paper. A hinged writing board is attached to the upper surface of the box.

S.R.S.

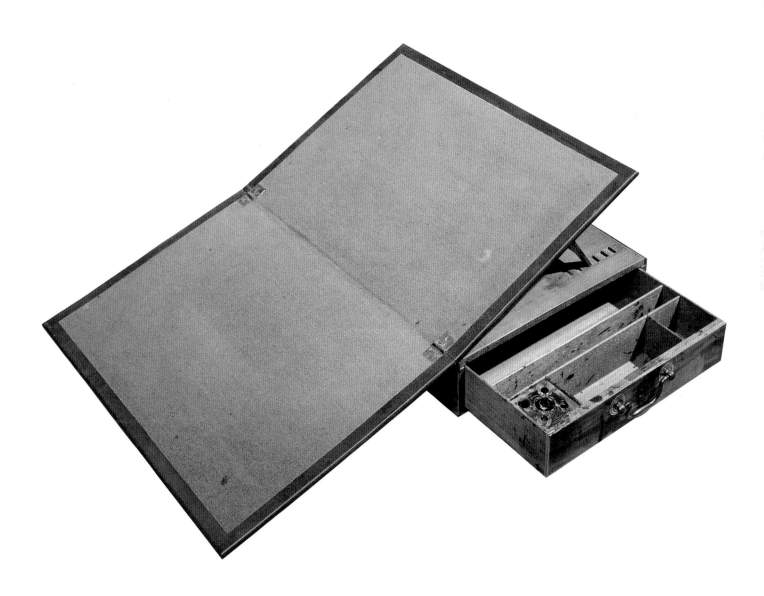

Duplicating Devices

Jefferson was one of the few active advocates of the preservation of written records in his day. He championed efforts to publish public records and collected and copied those of his own state. "The lost cannot be recovered," he wrote in 1791, "but let us save what remains . . . by such a multiplication of copies, as shall place them beyond the reach of accident."[6]

Correspondence, too, was important to preserve as a part of the historical record. "The letters of a person," wrote Jefferson in 1823, "form the only full and genuine journal of his life."[7] As soon as word reached America from Benjamin Franklin in Europe of a new mechanical method of duplication, Jefferson took steps to acquire it. In 1783 he ordered a copying press patented in 1780 by James Watt (1736–1819).[8]

Because he left for France before it arrived, Jefferson did not receive a press for another two years—his first letter copy dates from June 3, 1785. He could now abandon his custom of summarizing each letter in a record book and, instead, take a copy from each letter "at a single stroke."[9] Watt's patent machine consisted of a pair of iron rollers operated by a crank and required the use of a special water-soluble ink. When the original letter and a dampened sheet of paper were passed between the rollers, the writing was transferred—reversed—to the copying paper, which was thin enough for the letter to be read through the back.

This large office model, which cost about fourteen guineas, did not suffice for a man who wrote daily. While in London in 1786, Jefferson "formed a portable copying press on [the] principles of the large one. . . . I had a model made there and it has answered perfectly."[10] Made in the form of a traveling lap desk, the portable press pleased Jefferson so much that he had many made for friends. He carried his own on his journeys through southern France and Germany and was thus able to continue keeping file copies of all his letters.

Jefferson used his portable copying press for almost twenty years, evidently refining the design so that, within the compass of a small box, he could store not only the complete apparatus for copying but also all his traveling needs, from razors and nightcap to tape measure, thermometer, and money scales.[11]

In 1804, Jefferson welcomed the invention of the polygraph, which dispensed with the need for any operation beyond the writing of the letter. He abandoned his copying press and was only momentarily enticed by the precursor of carbon paper, Ralph Wedgwood's patented "Stylographic Manifold Writer." The most portable of available duplication methods, it was rejected because of the "fetid" smell of the "carbonated paper."[12]

Jefferson rarely made use of an amanuensis. As president he told a prospective secretary that "the writing is not considerable, because I write my own letters and copy them in a press."[13] Even late in life, when writing was painful because of wrist injuries, he penned most of his own correspondence. Because of his forty-year use of letter-copying machines, thousands of his letters are now part of an archive called by one biographer "the richest treasure house of historical information ever left by a single man."[14]

L.C.S.

Jefferson's design for a portable copying press was first executed by a London workman, for £5-10, in 1786. When it arrived in Paris, Jefferson immediately set about having it duplicated for his friends by François Philippe Charpentier, a *mécanicien* working in the Louvre.[15] Jefferson was not the first to make the copying press portable, but he had apparently not seen the portable presses being made by a London cabinetmaker when he conceived his own design.[16]

Neither the English press nor any of Charpentier's presses are known to survive, but several of Jefferson's designs and specifications for portable presses have been preserved in his papers. This machine, similar to the one Jefferson designed, was made by James Watt & Company. James Watt, Jr., developed the portable version of the large table model in 1794 and Watt portable presses were sold for many years.

L.C.S.

222

COPYING PRESS

---

early 19th c.

James Watt & Company
mahogany, brass
12.7 × 35 × 29.2
(5 × 13¾ × 11½ in.)
Mary S. Allen

Marked "Hawkins & Peale's Patent Polygraph No. 57," this machine was used by Jefferson from 1806 until his death. Jefferson first acquired the letter-copying device he called "the finest invention of the present age" in March of 1804.[17] Invented and named by Englishman John Isaac Hawkins, the polygraph used the principles of the pantograph (Cat. 224), a draftsman's tool for reducing or enlarging drawings. The writer's hand moves one pen, whose action is duplicated by the second one, producing a copy strikingly like the original.

Before he returned to England in 1803, Hawkins assigned his American patent rights to Charles Willson Peale, who developed and marketed the invention. Jefferson was one of his most eager clients, purchasing one for the President's House and one for Monticello. He soon exchanged these machines for new ones, as Peale continued to perfect the design—often according to Jefferson's suggestions. By 1809 Jefferson wrote that "the use of the polygraph has spoiled me for the old copying press the copies of which are hardly ever legible. . . . I could not, now therefore, live without the Polygraph."[18]

A second Jefferson polygraph, made in England for Hawkins, survives at the American Philosophical Society. It was given by Jefferson's grandson-in-law and last secretary, Nicholas P. Trist.

[1949-10]   L.C.S.

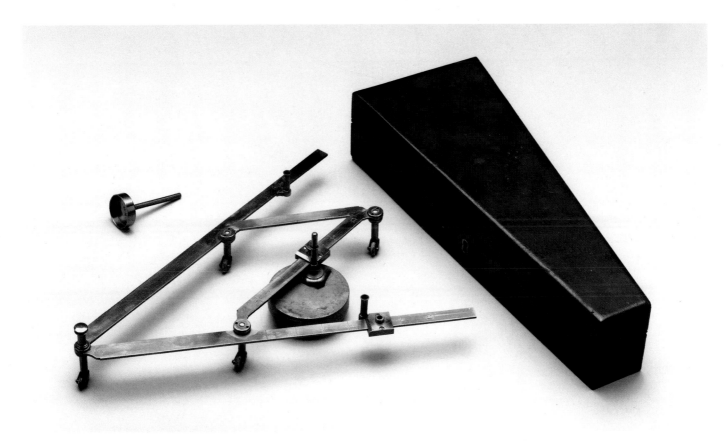

This device for reducing and enlarging drawings is probably the same pantograph that Jefferson purchased from the London mathematical instrument maker Henry Shuttleworth in 1786.[19] It consists of four flat brass bars made movable by four ivory wheels and hinged in the form of a flexible parallelogram, to which pens or styluses can be attached. The bars work in tandem as the user traces a drawing with a stylus, to produce a second drawing at a reduced or enlarged scale. Jefferson may have used this instrument to make copies of drawings and maps. The polygraphs made by Peale and Hawkins that Jefferson used to copy his correspondence employed a type of pantograph in their operation, though in that application the pantograph copied writing at the same size, instead of altering it (Cat. 223). Jefferson was also familiar with the pantograph's popular use to reduce profile drawings to miniature scale for engravings and silhouettes. Between 1789 and 1804, he sat for three artists who incorporated it in their techniques: Gilles-Louis Chrétien, Charles Fevret de Saint-Mémin, and Charles Willson Peale (see Physiognotrace Portraits).

[1985-30]   A.M.L.

224

PANTOGRAPH

1786?

maker unknown; possibly Henry Shuttleworth, London
brass, wood, ivory, lead
4.5 × 24.2 (1¾ × 9½ in.)
Private collection, in memory of Margaret Randolph Taylor and Olivia Alexander Taylor.

PROVENANCE:
Thomas Jefferson; by descent to Thomas Jefferson Randolph; by descent to a private collection.

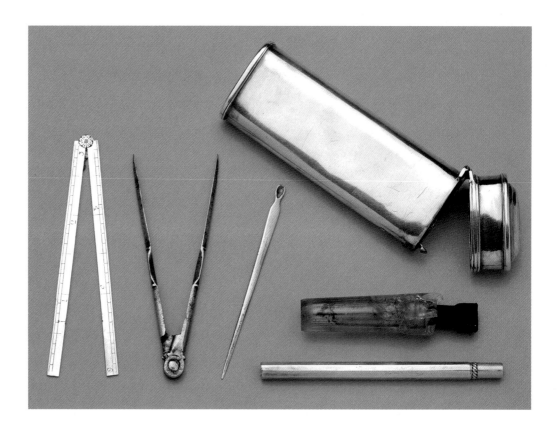

225

**DRAWING
INSTRUMENTS AND
SILVER POCKET
CASE**

---

case: c. 1806
John Letelier (c. 1790–1810),
Philadelphia
silver
8.9 × 3 × 1.6
(3½ × 1³⁄₁₆ × ⅝ in.)
instruments: possibly 1786
maker unknown, possibly Peter
(1730–1820) and John Dollond
(d. 1804)
silver dividers, penholder, tracer,
and rule; brass nib; glass bottle.
dividers: L: 7.6 (3 in.)
penholder including tip: L: 7.5
(2¹⁵⁄₁₆ in.)
rule: L open: 15.2 (6 in.); L
closed: 7.9 (3⅛ in.)
bottle: L: 5.6 (2¼ in.); D (at
base): 1.0 (⅜ in.)

PROVENANCE:
Thomas Jefferson; by descent to
Virginia and Nicholas Trist; by
descent to Edmund Jefferson
Burke; by gift to Charles M.
Storey; by gift to TJMF in 1958.

Jefferson purchased the etui for these pocket-size drawing instruments in 1806 from the Philadelphia silversmith John Letelier.[20] Pocket cases, also known as gentlemen's traveling cases or "etuis," were common in Jefferson's time. The contents of holders varied according to an individual's needs, and it was not uncommon to purchase the contents and case separately.[21] Jefferson probably ordered the case to accommodate instruments that he had purchased two decades earlier from the mathematical instrument maker Peter Dollond in London. On March 29, 1786, Jefferson noted that he paid Dollond for a silver "drawpen, pocket divider, etc."[22] He may have added the silver rule to the case in 1808, when he recorded purchasing one for seventy-five cents.[23]

Jefferson's set enabled him to make measured or free-hand drawings while he traveled, possibly using a portable drawing board.[24] Descriptive sketches often accompanied Jefferson's explanations of mechanical devices, but he also drew objects and sites that simply caught his attention. For example, hasty sketches of buildings, furniture, stoves, wheelbarrows, castle ruins, and maps punctuated Jefferson's diary of his travels in the Netherlands and Rhine Valley.[25]

While only pen, ink, and paper are necessary for sketching, measured drawings require more particular tools, such as a rule, tracer, and dividers. Jefferson used a tracer, a blunt tapered instrument, to create score marks on paper that could be filled in later with ink or graphite.[26] Dividers were used for marking off distances, taking measurements off scale rules, or transferring dimensions from one drawing to another.[27]

[1958-44-4]   A . M . L .

Jefferson preferred to buy drawing instruments from the best English makers. In 1786, while living in Paris, he ordered four instruments from England. His list included:

A pair of brass dividers, 6. Inches long, with a leg to slide out.
A draw pen, and pencil leg, both made to slide into the leg of the dividers occasionally . . . they have these in the mathematical shops in London.
A pair of brass dividers with a moveable center, for reducing draughts . . . I think they have been not long invented, and are under a patent.[28]

The large dividers, ruling-pen tip, lead-holder tip, and proportional dividers that are in this set are probably the ones sent to Jefferson from London.

After he left Europe, Jefferson continued to patronize English mathematical shops, in particular William & Samuel Jones. From that firm Jefferson purchased George Adams the Younger's *Geometrical and Graphical Essays* (1803), which contained a catalogue of instruments and their prices.[29] In an 1806 letter to William and Samuel Jones, Jefferson placed an order for two compasses, and referenced the catalogue's illustrations: "2 pair of hair compasses, one larger one small. [Adams' geom. & graph. essays.] Pl. 1. fig. L & H."[30] The compasses were sent to Jefferson in October 1807 and are likely the two in this set.
[1992-9-2]   A.M.L.

226

CASE WITH DRAWING INSTRUMENTS

c. 1786–1806

English
brass and steel; mahogany
veneer case with brass hinges,
lock, and inlay
bow compass: 6.8 (2¹¹⁄₁₆ in.)
divider: 9.4 (3¹¹⁄₁₆ in.)
Dr. and Mrs. Benjamin H.
Caldwell, Jr.
case: 21 × 12.7 × 3.3
(8¼ × 5 × 1¹⁵⁄₁₆ in.)
ruling-pen tip (pen insert): 5.9
(2⁵⁄₁₆ in.)
lead-holder tip (pencil insert):
4.9 (1¹⁵⁄₁₆ in.)
ruling pen: 10 (3¹⁵⁄₁₆ in.)
divider: 16 (6⁵⁄₁₆ in.)
ruling-pen tip (pen insert): 10
(3¹⁵⁄₁₆ in.)
lead-holder tip (pencil insert):
7.6 (3 in.)
extension arm: 10.2 (4 in.)
proportional divider: 17.5
(6⅞ in.)
Thomas Jefferson Memorial
Foundation

PROVENANCE:
LARGE COMPASS AND SMALL
DIVIDER: Thomas Jefferson; by
descent to Elizabeth Martin
Randolph, widow of Meriwether
Lewis Randolph; by gift to Bettie
M. Donelson; by purchase to Mr.
and Mrs. Stanley Horn; by
purchase to Dr. and Mrs.
Benjamin H. Caldwell, Jr.;
CASE AND REMAINDER OF
INSTRUMENTS: Thomas Jefferson;
by descent to Elizabeth Martin
Randolph, widow of Meriwether
Lewis Randolph; by gift to Bettie
M. Donelson; by purchase to Mr.
and Mrs. Stanley Horn; by bequest
to Ruth Horn Crownover; by
purchase to TJMF in 1992.

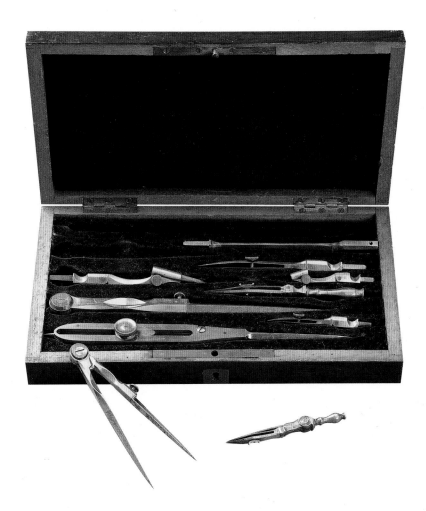

Over the course of his life, Jefferson made hundreds of drawings, ranging from rather wobbly freehand sketches to measured drawings on coordinate paper. He drew plats, maps, city plans, garden designs, and furniture, as well as sections, elevations, and floor plans for numerous buildings.[31] He may have learned the rudiments of drafting from his father, the surveyor and mapmaker Peter Jefferson. Upon his father's death Jefferson inherited his mathematical instruments, which certainly included the tools for drawing maps and plats.[32]

As with scientific instruments, Jefferson preferred English-made drawing instruments. His first recorded purchases are from London firms in 1786.[33] As late as 1806, Jefferson purchased drawing instruments from the same merchants with whom he first became acquainted in 1786, William and Samuel Jones.[34]

Jefferson likely used the instruments illustrated here to make measured drawings, which were usually architectural. Recent studies of Jefferson's drawings reveal two techniques that he employed: pricking and scoring. Using a "pricker," a sharp pinlike object, Jefferson punctured sets of points in his drawings. These may have been used to lay out a new drawing or copy an existing one. Scoring employed a small, blunt tool called a scorer or tracer, to make indentations in paper that could later be filled in with ink or graphite.[35]

Prior to 1784, when Jefferson arrived in France, most if not all of his drawings were

made in ink. In Paris, Jefferson began to use pencil for drawing, and adopted the use of coordinate, or graph, paper. He treasured the coordinate paper that he brought back to the United States with him and used it sparingly over the course of many years. He gave a few sheets to his good friend David Rittenhouse, the astronomer and inventor:

I send for your acceptance some sheets of drawing-paper, which being laid off in squares representing feet or what you please, saves the necessity of using the rule and dividers in all rectangular draughts and those whose angles have their sines and cosines in the proportion of any integral numbers. Using a black lead pencil the lines are very visible, and easily effaced with Indian rubber to be used for any other draught.[36]

A few precious sheets of this paper survive today.

In addition to designing and improving his own houses, Jefferson was a willing contributor to public buildings, such as the Virginia State Capitol. He was involved in the planning of the city of Washington, D.C. and contributed an anonymous design in the competition for the President's House. His architectural knowledge was well known, and friends such as James Monroe solicited his help in designing their houses.[37]
[1962-1-53; 1961-37-7; 1961-37-6; 1927-34-4; 1974-34-29; 1927-34-5; 1927-46; 1984-44-5]

A.M.L.

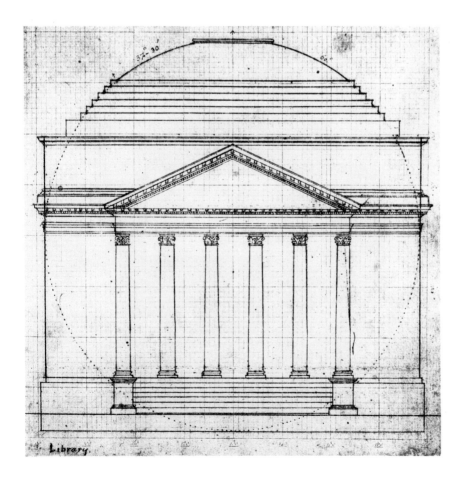

232 (top)

ARCHITECT'S SCALE

early 19th c.

possibly English
ivory
L: 34.6 (13⅝ in.); W: 4 (1⁹⁄₁₆ in.)

233 (top left)

SINGLE-HANDED DIVIDER

early 18th c.

iron, brass
L: 15.2 (6 in.); W: 3.8 (1½ in.)

234 (center)

PROTRACTOR

late 18th or early 19th c.

brass
L: 4.8 (1⅞ in.) W: 9.5 (3¾ in.)

PROVENANCE:
RULED PAPER: Thomas Jefferson; by descent to Charles, James, and John Eddy; by purchase to TJMF in 1962. PARALLEL RULE AND DIVIDER: by descent to Gordon T. Burke; by purchase to TJMF in 1968. SINGLE-HANDED DIVIDER AND SCRAPER: by descent to Frances Maury Burke; by gift to TJMF in 1927; ARCHITECT'S SCALE: by descent to Mrs. Robert W. Graves; by bequest to TJMF in 1975; PROTRACTOR: by descent to Frances Maury Burke; by descent to Burton H. R. Randall; by purchase to TJMF in 1970; FOLDING RULE: by descent to Frances Maury Burke; by purchase or gift to Laurence G. Hoes; by purchase to TJMF in 1984.

Ink drawing by Jefferson of the "Library" (Rotunda) of the University of Virginia, c. 1821.

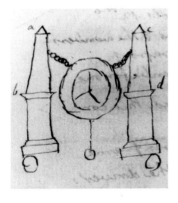

Jefferson's sketch of his design
for an obelisk clock in his
April 6, 1790 letter to William
Short.
College of William and Mary

The obelisk clock was constructed to Jefferson's design after his return to the United States to replace a similar mantel clock that had been stolen from his Paris home. Before his trip to Paris, Jefferson knew of obelisks from architectural treatises and even considered incorporating them into the design of Monticello.[1] While in Europe he commented on obelisks he saw in the gardens at Lord Burlington's Chiswick House and at Alexander Pope's garden at Twickenham.[2] His preoccupation with this ancient Egyptian form never flagged, and in his later years he chose an obelisk as the marker for his grave.

Jefferson instructed William Short, his secretary in Paris, to have the clock made there:

This, Mr. Short may recollect, was the form of the little clock which was stolen from the chimney of my study. The parts a.b.c.d. were parts of a cone, being round and tapering to the top, where a gilt head was put on. I would wish one to be made like that, as to the pedestal part, but with obelisks as is represented here a.b.c.d. instead of conical columns as the former had. No gilt head to be on the obelisk, but to be in plain marble, cut off obliquely as is always done in the obelisk.[3]

He went on to prescribe the works:

The clock to have a pendulum vibrating half seconds exactly. To have a second hand, but none for the days of the week, month or moon. To strike the hours and half hours. The dial plate to be open work, or as the French workmen say, le cadran à jour, of black marble. The superintendant of the Salle des ventes (where I bought mine) undertook to have a clock on the above plan made for me, for either 12. or 15. guineas, I forget which.[4]

Short engaged the eminent Parisian clockmaker Louis Chantrot (or Chantereau) to make the timepiece. Chantrot completed the clock in the early fall of 1791, and Jefferson received it on October 22, while living in Philadelphia.[5]

The clock returned to Monticello with Jefferson in 1794. According to accounts by family members and a visitor, Daniel Webster, it was mounted on a bracket opposite the head of Jefferson's bed, presumably inside the alcove.[6] "Mr. J. rises in the morning," Webster wrote, "as soon as he can see the hands of his clock (which is directly opposite his bed) . . ."[7] Because of its close association with her father, Martha Randolph desired the obelisk clock "beyond anything on earth"[8] and was initially disappointed when Nicholas Trist, her son-in-law, bought it at the Dispersal Sale of Jefferson's estate.

If, in our circumstances, I had felt myself justifiable in retaining a luxury of that value, that clock, in preference to everything else but the immediate furniture of his bedroom, I should have retained. However, in addition to the loss of the clock, which I regret the more bitterly since I know how near we were getting it, let us not alienate so near a relation and friend . . .[9]

After learning of his mother-in-law's keen desire to own the clock, Trist presented it to her. She bequeathed it to him.[10]

[1985-43]   A . M . L .

1792–93, installed at
Monticello in 1804–05

designed by Thomas Jefferson;
executed by Peter Spruck (also
spelled Spurck, Spurch, Sprunk,
active 1794–1806), apprentice to
Robert Leslie (active 1789–1803),
Philadelphia
wood, wrought iron, cast iron,
brass
115.3 × 74.9 × 41.3
(45⅜ × 29½ × 16¼ in.)

PROVENANCE:
Thomas Jefferson; by purchase to
James Barclay; by purchase to
Uriah P. Levy; by descent to
Jefferson Monroe Levy; by
purchase to TJMF in 1923.

With its dual faces and hour-striking gong, the Great Clock at Monticello served the residents of the house as well as the workers in the field. Its design evinces Jefferson's desire for order, which he exerted in equal but different ways over his family and his slaves. It also reveals his love of innovation and his ability to modify the traditional to suit his needs. It was as much a topic of conversation in Jefferson's time as it remains today.

The seven-day clock is mounted in the Entrance Hall and has a second face on the east front of the house. Jefferson's instructions for the clock's construction explain his intent for the exterior face, which has only an hour hand:

a toothed wheel of 2.I. [inches] on the back end of the axis of the hour hand . . . may turn an hour hand on the reverse face of the wall on a wooden hour plate of 12 I. radius. There need be no minute hand, as the hour figures will be 6.I. apart. But the interspace should be divided into [qu]arters and 5. minute marks.[11]

The Entrance Hall face indicates the hours and minutes on a larger dial, and the seconds on a smaller one. The clock is powered by two sets of cannon-ball–like weights (eighteen pounds each), which drive its ticking and the striking of a gong on the roof. The weights are strung on ropes and descend in the corners of the room on either side of the clock, through holes in the floor to the cellar below. Jefferson placed labels next to the path of the ticking (or running) weights to indicate the days of the week, which he also did on the inside case of his astronomical clock (Cat. 238). The clock was wound every Sunday with a cranklike key, and a folding ladder was made in the Monticello joinery for that task (Cat. 157).

Jefferson began planning the Great Clock in 1792, while in Philadelphia. He wrote to Henry Remsen, chief clerk of the foreign desk of the department of state, to inquire about Chinese gongs for the clock:

The chinese have a thing made of a kind of bell metal, which they call a Gong, and is used as a bell at the gates of large houses etc. . . . I wish for one to serve as the bell to a clock, which might be heard all over my farm.[12]

Benjamin Franklin's use of a gong in place of a bell, may have inspired Jefferson.[13]

By the beginning of 1793, the clock had been completed to Jefferson's specifications in Philadelphia by Peter Spruck, an apprentice to Robert Leslie, whose workmanship was less than satisfactory. Jefferson wrote to Leslie in December 1793:

My great clock could not be made to go by Spruck. I ascribe it to the bungling manner in which he had made it. I was obliged to let him make the striking movement anew on the common plan, after which it went pretty well . . .[14]

The clock was probably installed in Jefferson's Philadelphia house at Gray's Ferry before it was transported to Virginia.[15] It was brought to Monticello when Jefferson returned there in 1794, and he soon solicited clockworkers to undertake its repair.[16] At this same time he finally procured a gong for use with the clock.[17]

It was not until 1804, while president, that Jefferson ordered the weights for the clock from the Foxall Foundry in Washington, D.C.[18] In January of that year, Jefferson was first

confronted with the fact that the length of the descent of the clock weights, which he planned to have enclosed in a box, was greater than the height of the Entrance Hall. In a letter to James Dinsmore Jefferson arrived at the notable solution:

I do not approve of cutting the wall, not even the cellar wall to make a space for the descent of the clock weights, but would have them advanced into the room so as to descend clear even of the cellar wall. Should the box in this case encroach too much on the window we may avoid the eye sore by leaving them unboxed, to descend naked till they get to the floor where they may enter a square hole and go [on?] to the cellar floor . . .[19]

The Great Clock has never been removed from Monticello since its installation in 1804–5.

[1923-6]   A.M.L.

Jefferson purchased this plain, eight-day case clock in 1803, and it was probably used in the Monticello kitchen. Isaac Briggs, a surveyor then residing in Philadelphia, arranged for the purchase from the prominent clockmaker Benjamin Ferris. The clock case has little ornamentation other than the freestanding columns supporting its flat-topped hood. Curiously, the dial bears the name of Thomas Dring, a little-known West Chester, Pennsylvania clockmaker who returned to his native England just before 1800.[20]

Whether Dring or Ferris made the clock works is unclear. Although Dring's signature is on the clock dial, Ferris clearly completed the clock in 1803 to Jefferson's order:

Pursuant to the directions of Isaac Briggs I have completed a Clock for thee. He informed me that it was not in any degree for ornamental purposes, and particularly requested that it might be made plain; the workmanship is good, and the regulation nearly perfected. I had the rod of the pendulum made of well seasoned wood, it being less affected by the changes of the weather than either Brass or Steel.[21]

Jefferson paid Ferris seventy dollars for the clock, its case, and shipping costs.[22] It was certainly intended for use in a room outside of the main house at Monticello, as Jefferson thought that the Great Clock in the Entrance Hall "renders all chamber clocks unnecessary."[23] The fact that the clock suffered considerable smoke damage in Jefferson's time suggests the kitchen as a likely site for its placement. Isaac, one of the Monticello slaves, recalled that the only time Jefferson went into the kitchen was to wind the clock.[24] A kitchen clock is also listed in Jefferson's Memorandum Book as one of four clocks repaired in 1817.[25]

John Hartwell Cocke, a friend of Jefferson's who was instrumental in founding the University of Virginia, purchased the clock at the Dispersal Sale in 1827 for fifty-five dollars.[26] His construction superintendent, Robert Jones, picked it up from Monticello, and wrote to Cocke of its poor condition:

I have gotten the clock from Monticello; and indeed it was the most smoke dried thing of the kind I ever saw. Ned gave the case a rubbing over with hot water and soap which helped it but a little—I find the cap of the case to be mahogany the other parts walnut. . . . The face and inside works of the clock were almost as badly smoked as the case and it is a task to get them in order, I have however gotten Cullen at work on the clock who says it is a most excellent piece of work and that there is no doubt of its being a regular good time piece when put in good order.[27]

A.M.L.

Jefferson wanted an accurate clock for use in making astronomical observations from the time he had observed an eclipse of the moon in 1778. He then ordered a clock from the scientist and inventor David Rittenhouse. The Revolutionary War left Rittenhouse little time to work on Jefferson's clock, and the project was forgotten. Jefferson's desire for an astronomical clock was renewed more than thirty years later, when he expressed his regret at not having an accurate timepiece to use during the annular eclipse in 1811.[28] In

237 (left)

TALL CASE CLOCK

c. 1803

*Thomas Dring
(active 1786–1799), West Chester, Pennsylvania
Benjamin C. Ferris
(1780–1867), Philadelphia
black walnut case; brass dial
229.9 × 53.3 × 26.7
(90½ × 21 × 10½ in.)
Private collection*

PROVENANCE:
Thomas Jefferson; by purchase to John Hartwell Cocke at the Dispersal Sale in 1827; by descent to a private collection.

238 (right)

ASTRONOMICAL CASE CLOCK

1812

*works by Thomas Voight (active 1811–1836), Philadelphia
mahogany veneer, walnut
238.8 × 45.7 × 27.9
(94 × 18 × 11 in.)
The Historical Society of Pennsylvania*

PROVENANCE:
Thomas Jefferson; by purchase to Martha Jefferson Randolph; by gift to Robley Dunglison; by descent to William Ladam Dunglison; by gift to The Historical Society of Pennsylvania in 1894.

Jefferson marked the weight path inside the case of his astronomical clock with the days of the week.

September of that year, Jefferson asked his friend Robert Patterson, a Philadelphia mathematician and director of the United States Mint, for his recommendations on clocks available in that city:

I extremely regret the not being provided with a time-piece equal to the observations of the approaching eclipse of the sun. Can you tell me what would be the cost in Philadelphia of a clock, the time-keeping part of which should be perfect? And what the difference of cost between a wooden and gridiron pendulum? To be of course without a striking apparatus, as it would be wanted for astronomical purposes only.[29]

Patterson recommended the Philadelphian Thomas Voight (also spelled "Voigt"), a young "ingenious artist" who would make a clock for sixty-five dollars.[30] Jefferson knew and patronized Voight's father Henry, a clock and watchmaker who was also the chief coiner at the United States Mint.

With Patterson's recommendation and firsthand knowledge of the capability of Voight's father, Jefferson gave Thomas Voight the commission. He specified that the clock should be "as good as hands can make it, in everything useful, but no unnecessary labor to be spent on mere ornament. A plain but neat mahogany case will be preferred."[31] Voight completed the timepiece by the end of 1812, but shipping complications caused by the War of 1812 delayed the clock's arrival at Monticello until December 1815.[32]

The final cost for the clock was $115.50—almost double Voight's estimate. The clock is a masterpiece, although more ornamented than Jefferson had requested. Its dial, decorated with gilt and black lunettes, is surmounted by a festooned medallion. The clock's hood is supported by freestanding reeded columns and topped by a scrolled, broken pediment. Reeded pilasters flank oval veneer reserves on the clock's trunk and base. This veneering added to the cost of the clock, as it required repair even before the clock was shipped to Jefferson.[33]

Jefferson placed the eight-day clock in his private suite of rooms, probably in his Bedroom. It has no striking mechanism and operates with a single weight. Jefferson marked the inside of the clock's case with the days of the week, so that as the weight dropped it would indicate the passing of the days, just as the wall in the Entrance Hall is marked with the days for the weights of the Great Clock (Cat. 236).

After Jefferson's death, his granddaughter Ellen Coolidge wanted to purchase the clock because it was one of the objects that Jefferson "habitually used in his chamber."[34] Jefferson's daughter Martha, however, had already decided that she wanted to present the clock to the physician Robley Dunglison, who had faithfully attended Jefferson during his final illness.[35] Jefferson had recruited Dunglison, who was born and educated in England, to be professor of medicine at the University of Virginia.

Three persons bid on the clock at the sale of Jefferson's estate in 1827: Jefferson's grandson-in-law Nicholas Trist, John Hartwell Cocke (who purchased another clock, Cat. 237), and Robley Dunglison. Trist, who was bidding on Martha's behalf, prevailed against Dunglison's unwitting bids. Dunglison recalled the event in his diary:

I had no knowledge of the intention of Mrs. Randolph to bestow this clock on me; but had determined to possess it, if it went at a reasonable rate, at the sale. General Cock, of Fluvanna, bade, I think, 145 dollars. I bade 150; and it was knocked down to Mr. Trist for one hundred and fifty-five dollars. I immediately went up to Mr. Trist, apologizing for having opposed unwittingly the desire of the family to possess the clock, when he told me I might make my mind easy, as he had been commissioned by them to buy it, in order that they might present it to me.[36]

Dunglison left his post at the university in 1833 and began teaching at Jefferson Medical College in Philadelphia in 1835. His son presented the clock to The Historical Society of Pennsylvania in 1894.

A.M.L.

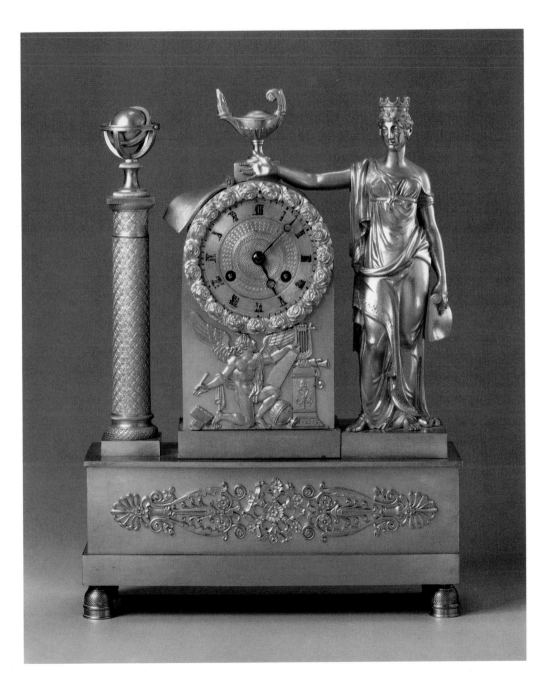

Gilt Brass Mantle Clock

late 18th–early 19th c.
Louis Moinet (1758–1853),
Paris
gilt brass, ormolu
35.6 × 26 × 9.2
(14 × 10¼ × 3⅝ in.)

MAPS

In a quest to fix his position in the larger world, Jefferson compiled a collection of more than 350 maps, atlases, and writings on the geography of near and distant lands. Jefferson credited his father, the surveyor Peter Jefferson, and Joshua Fry with producing the "1st map of Virginia ever made, that of Capt. Smith being merely a conjectural sketch."[1] Jefferson knew how to survey, a skill that he used throughout his life in matters both practical and amusing, such as determining the boundaries of his farms and calculating the altitude of neighboring mountains.[2] Through his travels, reading, and surveying, he also developed considerable knowledge of the emerging science of geography. He strove to disseminate precise geographical knowledge by his authorship of *Notes on the State of Virginia*, encouragement of American mapmakers, and direction of the Lewis and Clark expedition to the American northwest.

Jefferson's map collection ranged from road maps and city plans to navigational charts and wall maps. His account books reveal that he collected maps as he traveled through Europe, integrating them with his notes in his travel log. Jefferson advised Americans traveling in Europe to "buy beforehand the map of the country you are going into. On arriving at a town, the first thing is to buy the plan of the town, and the book noting it's curiosities."[3] In April 1791, Jefferson lent his collection of city plans to Pierre Charles L'Enfant to aid in his planning of the federal city of Washington, D.C.

In compliance with your request I have examined my papers and found the plans of Frankfort on the Mayne, Carlsruhe, Amsterdam, Strasburg, Paris, Orleans, Bordeaux, Lyons, Montpelier, Marseilles, Turin and Milan, which I send in a roll by this post.[4]

Plans from this same collection were probably among those bound into an atlas in 1805 by a Georgetown bookbinder. John March charged Jefferson $10.00—more than the price of a four-sheet map—for the "difficult" binding of "towns" into a 16 × 22-inch atlas.[5]

At the President's House, Jefferson displayed "maps, globes and charts around the walls" of his Cabinet.[6] He traveled very rarely during his two terms as president, and his map collecting shifted from city plans and road maps, to wall maps. From 1802 to 1805 he purchased at least six large-scale wall maps, including two of the United States, the boundaries of which changed dramatically with the Louisiana Purchase. Lewis and Clark's careful mapping of the northwest territory provided the first accurate picture of the topography of that portion of the American continent, including the disappointing reality that a northwest passage to India was impossible.[7]

Lewis and Clark's findings whetted Jefferson's appetite for geographical knowledge. "A great deal is yet wanting to ascertain the true geography of our country," he wrote in 1812. "Towards this we have done too little for our selves and depended too long on the ancient and inaccurate observations of other nations."[8] American mapmakers such as John Melish often consulted Jefferson on the accuracy of their work. Melish sent Jefferson a copy of his 1816 *Geographical Description of the United States* with its map of the United States and contiguous countries. In his acknowledgment of Melish's gift, Jefferson prefaced his page-long list of corrections by complimenting Melish's work:

[The map] is handsomely executed and on a well chosen scale; giving a luminous view of the comparative possessions of different powers in our America. It is on account of the value I set on it that I will make some suggestions . . .[9]

At least eight engraved wall maps and two Indian maps on leather hung in the Entrance Hall at Monticello, serving as illustrations of the origin of objects composing Jefferson's eclectic "cabinet of curiosities." According to an inventory made by Jefferson's daughter Martha Randolph following his death, the engraved maps were those of "Europe, Asia, Africa, South America, Map of the World, United States, 2 of Virginia."[10]

A.M.L.

Survey Showing Monticello
Mountaintop within the
Fourth Roundabout

1809
Thomas Jefferson (1743–1826)
ink on paper
25.4 × 41.3 (10 × 16¼ in.)
Massachusetts Historical Society

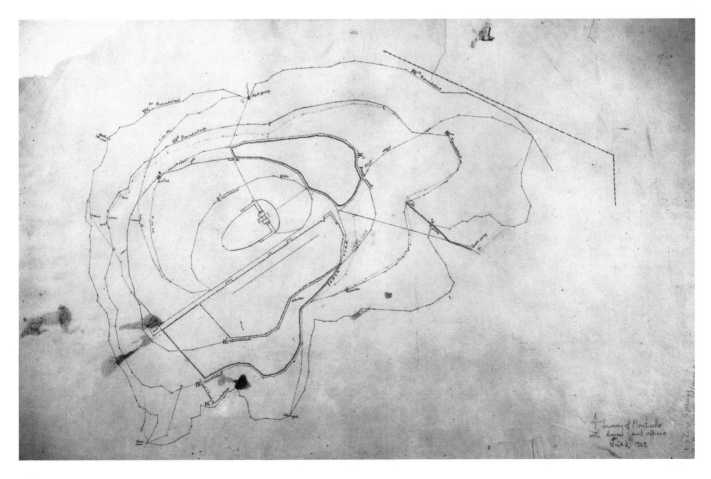

The best description of Peter Jefferson's role in the creation of the Map of Virginia came from his son:

My father's education had been quite neglected; but being of a strong mind, sound judgment and eager after information, he read much and improved himself insomuch that he was chosen with Joshua Fry professor of Mathem. In W.[William] and M.[Mary] college to continue the boundary line between Virginia and N. Caroline . . . and was afterwards employed with the same Mr. Fry to make the 1st accurate map of Virginia which had ever been made, that of Capt. Smith being merely a conjectural sketch. They possessed excellent materials for so much of the country as is below the Blue Ridge, little being known beyond that ridge.[11]

Jefferson was eight years old when his father finished his work on this map, and its importance seems to have been indelibly marked in his mind. Regardless of filial pride, the Fry-Jefferson map was the most accurate record of Virginia in the eighteenth century, and Jefferson used it as the basis for the map he compiled for *Notes on the State of Virginia.*[12]

Joshua Fry and Peter Jefferson were commissioned to draw a map of Virginia by the acting Virginia governor, Lewis Burwell, in 1750. The two men were obvious candidates for the job. Both were proven surveyors and established landholders in Albemarle County. They formed a kind of partnership, with the more prominent Fry attracting commissions, and the capable Jefferson carrying out much of the work.[13]

They first began working together in 1746, when in his post as commissioner of the Crown, Fry caused Jefferson to be chosen as one of four surveyors to map the boundaries of Virginia's Northern Neck. Although Jefferson already had considerable surveying experience, working with Fry probably contributed to his knowledge of mathematics. Their next project, in 1749, was a survey to extend the dividing line between North Carolina and Virginia. The men met with great hardships as they crossed mountains and rivers, and tales of their journey were passed down to Thomas Jefferson's great-grandchildren:

Colonel Jefferson and his companions had often to defend themselves against the attacks of wild beasts during the day, and at night found but a broken rest, sleeping—as they were obliged to do for safety—in trees. . . . Jefferson's courage did not once flag, but living upon raw flesh, or whatever could be found to sustain life, he pressed on and persevered until his task was accomplished.[14]

These two projects laid the groundwork for their map of Virginia, published first in England in 1752.[15] It was to be their last collaboration.

The two men went separate ways after the map's publication. Jefferson returned to his Shadwell farm, and Fry was appointed commander-in-chief of the Virginia Forces. Jefferson became an Albemarle County magistrate, and after Fry's death in 1754 assumed his offices as county surveyor and member of the House of Burgesses. Fry bequeathed his surveying tools to Peter Jefferson, and some of these tools were undoubtedly among the mathematical instruments that Thomas Jefferson inherited from his father, along with a map of the state of Virginia.[16] This map was probably lost in the fire at Jefferson's birthplace, Shadwell, in 1770. Jefferson likely owned several copies of his father's map, and this later 1775 edition may have been the one that hung in the Entrance Hall at Monticello.

[1975-7-2]   A.M.L.

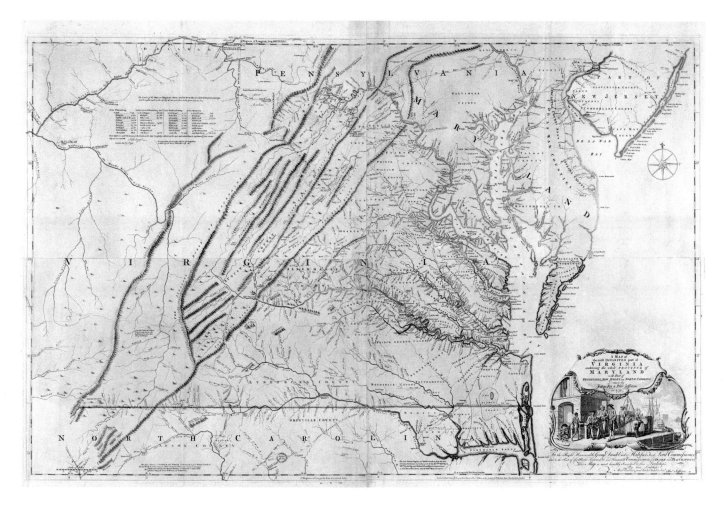

**A MAP OF VIRGINIA
FORMED FROM
ACTUAL SURVEYS,
AND THE LATEST AS
WELL AS MOST
ACCURATE
DESCRIPTIONS**

1807

*Bishop James Madison
(1749–1812)
engraved on 4 sheets
114.6 × 173.8 (45⅛ × 68⁷⁄₁₆ in.)
Library of Congress*

*(opposite below: View of
Richmond, Virginia, c. 1805,
Charles Fevret de Saint-Mémin
[1770–1852], detail from
Bishop Madison's Map of
Virginia.)*

While serving as president of the College of William and Mary, Bishop James Madison, first cousin of President James Madison, determined the need for an updated map of Virginia. Familiar with the local surveyors that the college licensed and examined, Madison sponsored the work, although he himself had no training as a draftsman or surveyor. Under the supervision of William Prentis, William Davis began drafting the map in 1803. Two years later Madison began collecting subscriptions for the work.[17]

Madison advertised the map in the April 15, 1805 *Richmond Enquirer:* "The price to subscribers will be eight dollars, neatly mounted, colored and glazed. One dollar, (to lighten the great expense of publication) to be paid on subscribing."[18] Jefferson subscribed in June 1805, for two copies, and paid for them in full in 1807, when the map was published.[19] He supported Madison's efforts to produce an accurate map of the state, and offered his assistance with a second edition:

Do you think of ever giving us a second edition of your map? If you do, I may be able to furnish you with some latitudes. I have a pocket sextant of miraculous accuracy, considering its microscopic graduation . . .[20]

In 1818, after Madison's death, Davis redrafted a second edition of the map, which remained the authoritative work on Virginia until about 1827.[21]

A.M.L.

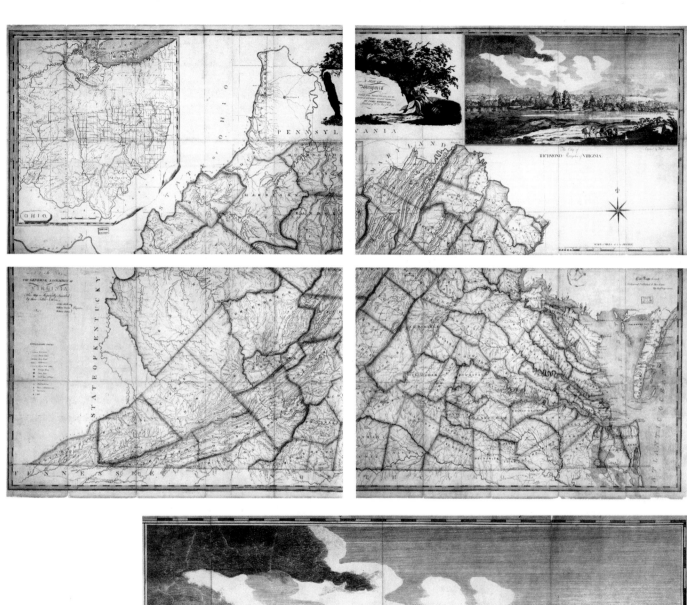

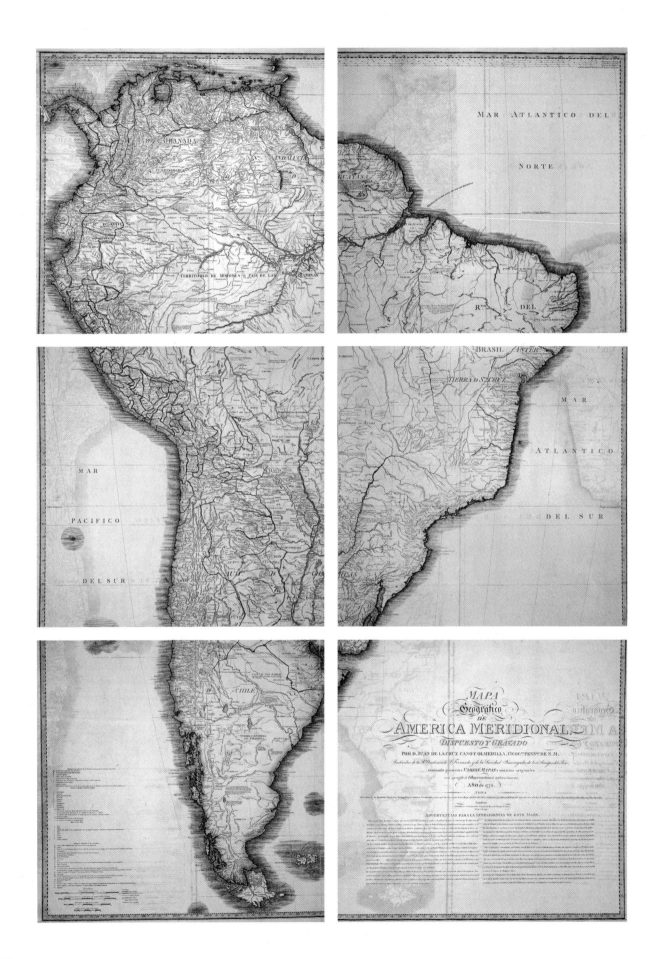

In 1786, while serving as minister to France, Jefferson received Cruz Cano's map of South America from William Carmichael and sought to have copies made for himself and Congress.[22] Jefferson enlisted William Stephens Smith, John Adams's son-in-law who was then living in London, to help him commission the London mapmaker William Faden to make these copies. In a letter to Smith, Jefferson described the map and its importance:

The government of Spain at first permitted the map, but the moment they saw one of them come out, they destroyed the plates, seized all of the few copies which had got out and on which they could lay their hands, and issued the severest injunctions to call in the rest and to prevent their going abroad. Some few copies escaped their search. A friend has by good management procured me one, and it is arrived safe through all the searches that travellers are submitted to.[23]

Sight unseen, Faden agreed to reproduce all twelve sheets of the map.[24] In December 1786, Jefferson sent the map to Faden in care of Smith, and drew up a set of suggestions for republishing the map, including three sketches of the proposed layout of the sheets.

Thirteen years later, in 1799, Faden published his copy of Cruz Cano's work, but he neither sent Jefferson the copies he requested nor returned the original. Jefferson, who had enlisted friends such as James Madison[25] to inquire as to Faden's progress, resorted to buying a copy from a London map dealer in 1805—nineteen years after sending the original to Faden.[26] Publication of the controversial map may have been delayed because of Faden's position as geographer to the King.[27]   A . M . L .

Jefferson's Entrance Hall map collection was dominated by the wall maps of the London mapmaker Aaron Arrowsmith. In Jefferson's day, Arrowsmith's maps were renowned for their clarity and large scale. He was particularly skilled in producing maps from a wide variety of source material, ranging from visitor's accounts of terrain, to sketch maps and triangulations.[28] His map of the United States was compiled largely from Native American maps and information supplied by the Hudson Bay Company.[29] Arrowsmith began his career as a surveyor, and worked with the prominent map and globe maker John Cary. His success led to an appointment as hydrographer to King George IV.[30]

Jefferson made all of his purchases of Arrowsmith maps while serving as president. The first, in 1803, was "A Map of the United States of North America," published in London in 1802. Apparently satisfied with Arrowsmith's work, in 1805 Jefferson ordered maps of Europe, Asia and Africa "on linen, with rollers and varnished," from a London agent, William Tunnicliff.[31] These three, along with the map of the United States, were probably among the maps that hung in Jefferson's Cabinet at the President's House.[32]

Jefferson's copies of Arrowsmith's maps remain unlocated, with the possible exception of his maps of Asia and the United States. These two maps, varnished and on rollers as Jefferson specified, descended through the Cabell family of Nelson County, and may have been purchased by Joseph Cabell at the Dispersal Sale in 1827.[33] Much of the Monticello map collection may have been used after Jefferson's death at the Edgehill School, which was operated from 1829 until around 1900 by his granddaughters at a nearby farm.[34]

A . M . L .

241

MAPA GEOGRAFICO DE AMERICA MERIDIONAL (SOUTH AMERICA)

1779

William Faden (1750–1836)
after Don Juan de la Cruz Cano
y Olmedilla (1731–1802)
engraved on 6 sheets
184.8 × 130.8 (72¾ × 51½ in.)
Library of Congress

242 (overleaf)

ASIA

1801

Aaron Arrowsmith (1750–1833)
engraved on 4 sheets
121.9 × 143.8 (48 × 56⅝ in.)
Library of Congress

243 (overleaf)

AFRICA

1802

Aaron Arrowsmith (1750–1833)
engraved on 20 sheets
125.9 × 145.4 (49⁹⁄₁₆ × 57¼ in.)
Library of Congress

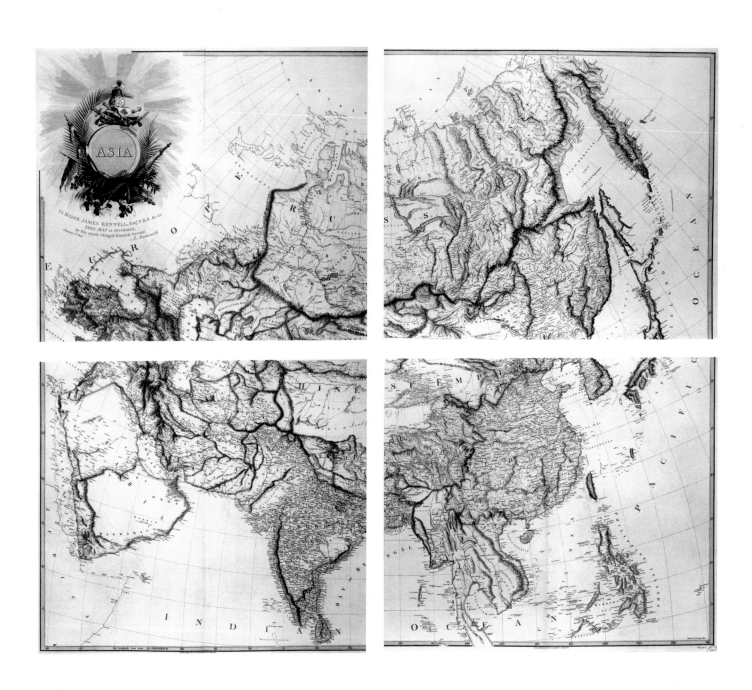

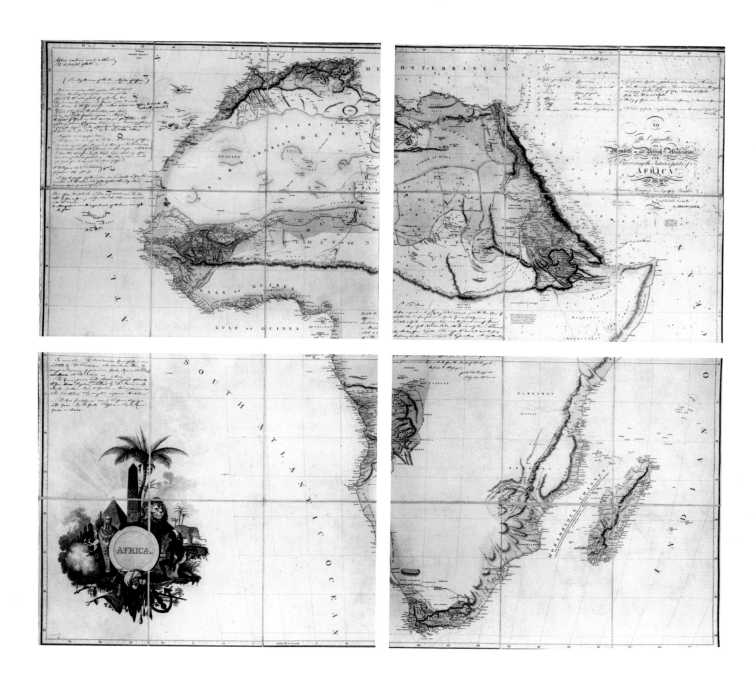

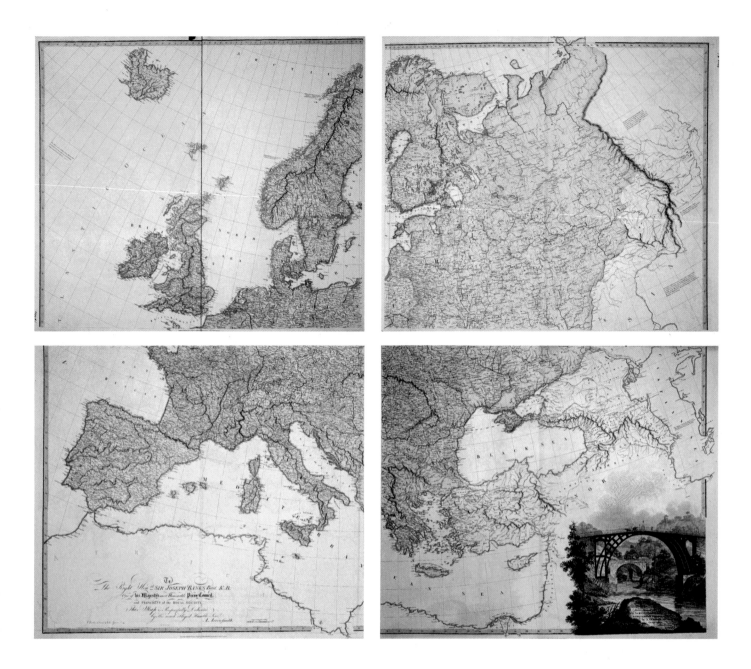

244

**MAP OF EUROPE,
DRAWN FROM ALL
THE BEST SURVEYS
AND RECTIFIED BY
ASTRONOMICAL
OBSERVATION**

1798

*Aaron Arrowsmith (1750–1833)
engraved on 4 sheets
123.7 × 144 (48¹¹⁄₁₆ × 56¹¹⁄₁₆ in.)
Library of Congress*

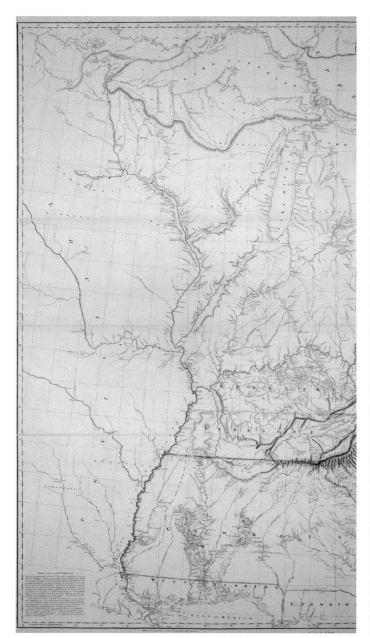

245

**A MAP OF THE
UNITED STATES OF
NORTH AMERICA
DRAWN FROM A
NUMBER OF
CRITICAL
RESEARCHES**

1802

*Aaron Arrowsmith
engraved on 4 sheets
129.5 × 143.5 (51 × 56½ in.)
Library of Congress*

Jefferson purchased this map in 1803 for use in planning the Lewis and Clark expedition. Considered the most accurate representation to date of the land west of the Mississippi, the map shows the United States, parts of Canada, and the Louisiana Territory.[35] In his order for the map, Jefferson wrote that he would prefer the English edition, "because I know the engraving is superiorly well done."[36]

A.M.L.

NATURAL HISTORY SPECIMENS

The most likely source for the moose antlers now at Monticello is either William Whipple or John Sullivan, both residents of New England from whom Jefferson requested moose antlers, bones, and skins. Jefferson became interested in the possibility that the American moose might be a species distinct from the European moose while he was writing *Notes on the State of Virginia*.

In the winter of 1783–84, when Jefferson was revising *Notes*, he sent queries about the moose to Sullivan and Whipple. Eager to refute the comte de Buffon's assertions about the inferiority of American species, Jefferson wanted the answers to such questions as

Is not the Caribou and the Black Moose one and the same Animal? Has it a Sollid or Cloven Hoof? Do their feet make a loud ratling as they run? Do they sweat when run hard or only drip at the tongue?[1]

Whipple passed the survey on to three men better acquainted with the moose, and Jefferson received four replies.[2]

At the same time that Jefferson sent the survey, he apparently requested a specimen of the moose. Sullivan wrote to him in June 1784:

I have procured from the head of the province of Main a Large pair of Mooses horns and a pr. of the [caribou], together with a pair of the Largest Deer horns . . . This will Demonstrate the great difference between these Animals.[3]

No record survives indicating whether Jefferson received the horns.

In 1786, Jefferson met Buffon in Paris and, among other topics, they discussed the American moose. Jefferson renewed his request for the "skin, the skeleton, and the horns of the Moose, the Caribou, and the Orignal or Elk" to both Sullivan and Whipple, adding that they would be "an acquisition here, more precious than you can imagine."[4] Sullivan succeeded in procuring a moose from Vermont, dressing it to Jefferson's specifications and, with great difficulty, shipped the moose—skeleton and all—to France.[5]

The moose, along with horns from the caribou, elk, deer, spiked horned buck, and roebuck, arrived in late September 1787. Jefferson presented them to Buffon on October 1, with a copy of *Notes* and a letter describing the species. "I really suspect," Jefferson wrote,

that you will find the Moose, the Round horned elk, and the American deer are species not existing in Europe. The Moose is perhaps of a new class. I wish these spoils, Sir, may have the merit of adding any thing new to the treasures of nature . . .[6]

Jefferson hoped that Buffon would mount the moose and place it on display in the King's Cabinet, but it is not known if it was exhibited there.[7] Although Jefferson's efforts helped to disprove Buffon's theory of the degeneracy of animals in America and dismiss the notion that the moose was the same as a Lapland deer, Buffon did not live to correct his errors.[8] As Jefferson related to Daniel Webster many years later, Buffon "promised in his next volume, to set these things right also: but he died directly afterwards."[9]

[1949-1]   A.M.L.

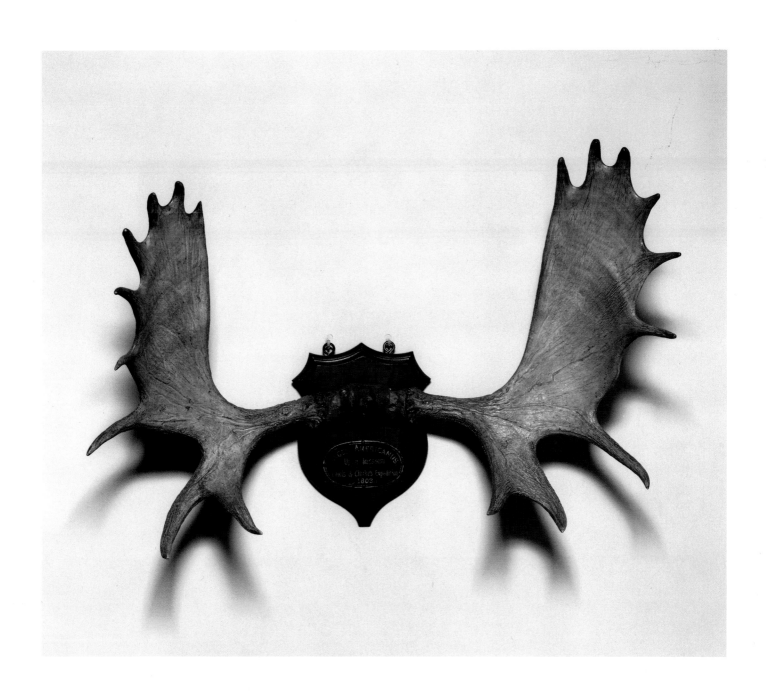

CERVUS CANADENS
Upper
Lewis & Clark
1805.

Of the many natural history specimens sent to Jefferson by Lewis and Clark, only one is extant: the elk antlers now in the Entrance Hall at Monticello, listed on Lewis's invoice as "1 large par [*sic*] of Elk's horns connected by the frontal bone."[10] These antlers probably came from one of the fifty elk the expedition members killed over the winter of 1804–5 in the Fort Mandan area.[11] After display at the President's House over the winter, the antlers came to Monticello in March 1806, with various other items from Lewis and Clark's 1805 shipment.[12] Descriptions left by visitors in Jefferson's lifetime place the antlers on the walls of the Entrance Hall beside those of the moose and deer.

Through careful study of Lewis and Clark's notes and drawings, modern scholars have credited the explorers with the discovery of at least twenty-five species of mammals.[13] In his parting instructions to Lewis, Jefferson wrote that "the animals of the country generally, & especially those not known in the U.S." were worthy of notice.[14] Lewis and Clark explicitly followed Jefferson's instructions. Along with recording in detail their sightings of all types of animals, the exploration party collected skins, horns, entire skeletons, and even live specimens to send back to Jefferson in Washington.

It seems likely that Lewis obtained some instruction from Charles Willson Peale prior to the expedition on the preservation of animal skins, bones, and skeletons, but Lewis's attempt to send back six live animals (four magpies, a "burrowing squirel of the praries," and a "hen of the prarie") was an exceptionally bold idea.[15] The animals were part of a shipment sent by Lewis and Clark from Fort Mandan in April 1805. After traveling to St. Louis, New Orleans, and Baltimore, only one magpie and the "burrowing squirel" survived. The animals arrived in Washington in August, while Jefferson was at Monticello.[16]

Etienne Lemaire, Jefferson's maître d'hôtel at the President's House, alerted Jefferson of the arrival of Lewis and Clark's shipment in August 1805, writing that he had just received a barrel, four boxes and a kind of cage "in which there is a little animal very much resembling the squirrel, and in the other a bird resembling the magpie of Europe."[17] Lewis included an invoice with the shipment. Upon his return Jefferson used it to verify the contents of the shipment and designate which items should go to the American Philosophical Society and which to Charles Willson Peale. Those objects that were simply marked as "came," such as these elk antlers, thirteen red fox skins, and the horns and ears of the black tail deer, were most likely kept by Jefferson for exhibition in the President's House and later Monticello.[18]

[1949-2]   A . M . L .

247

ELK ANTLERS (CERVUS ELAPHUS CANADENSIS)

c. 1804–05

acquired by Meriwether Lewis (1774–1809) and William Clark (1770–1838)
tip to tip: 75.2 (29⅝ in.)
University of Virginia Department of Biology

Provenance:
Lewis and Clark; by gift to Thomas Jefferson; by gift to the University of Virginia; by loan to TJMF since 1949.

Big Horn Sheep (Ovis Canadensis)

1830–33
engraving
Thomas Doughty (1793–1856)
The Cabinet of Natural History and American Rural Sports
The American Philosophical Society

Charles Willson Peale preserved the head and horns of a big horn sheep brought back by Lewis and Clark for the Entrance Hall at Monticello. This early example of taxidermy remained at Monticello until after Jefferson's death, when it was transferred to the collection of the University of Virginia. It is now unlocated.

248

**MEGALONYX
JEFFERSONII
(JEFFERSON'S
GROUND SLOTH)**

Bones of Hand
excavated c. 1796

*Cromer Cave, Greenbrier
County, West Virginia
8.9 to 30.5 (3½ to 12 in.)
The Academy of Natural
Sciences, 12507*

PROVENANCE:
Col. John Stuart; by gift to
Thomas Jefferson in 1796; by gift
to the American Philosophical
Society in 1797; by transfer to The
Academy of Natural Sciences in
1849.

249

**BISON ANTIQUUS
(AMERICAN BISON
OR BUFFALO)**

Partial Skull with Horn Core
excavated 1807

*Big Bone Lick, Kentucky
12.7×40.6×17.8
(5×16×7 in.)
The Academy of Natural
Sciences, 12990*

PROVENANCE:
William Clark; to Thomas
Jefferson in 1807; by gift to the
American Philosophical Society
c. 1808; by transfer to The
Academy of Natural Sciences in
1849.

Jefferson's collection of fossils in the Entrance Hall at Monticello demonstrated his patronage of the study of American vertebrate paleontology, which grew out of his desire to learn more about the animals of the American continent. As president of the United States and of the American Philosophical Society, Jefferson encouraged the study of fossils with his commission of a dig at Big Bone Lick, Kentucky, his analytical writings submitted to the American Philosophical Society, and his distribution of fossils to major American and French repositories. By bringing together the materials necessary for its advancement, Jefferson furthered the developing science of paleontology.[19]

He first seriously considered fossils while researching the animals of America in 1781 for *Notes on the State of Virginia*, when he asked his friend and fellow Albemarle County native George Rogers Clark for teeth and other bones of the "great animal" found on the Ohio River. He called them "the most desireable object in Natural history."[20] Jefferson actively sought fossilized bones to further his understanding of particular animals, especially the *Mammut americanum* (mastodon), then known commonly as the "mammoth."[21]

In *Notes on the State of Virginia* Jefferson included the mammoth in a description of animals native to America, correctly identifying it as a relative of the elephant that had adapted to a colder climate. "It may be asked," Jefferson wrote,

why I insert the Mammoth as if it still existed? I ask in return, why I should omit it, as if it did not exist? Such is the oeconomy of nature, that no instance can be produced of her having permitted any one race of her animals to become extinct; of her having formed any link in her great work so weak as to be broken.[22]

Jefferson concluded that until the West had been explored there was no reason to assume that the mammoth did not still exist; his Enlightenment belief in the "chain of being" precluded the idea that an animal could become extinct.[23]

Megalonyx jeffersonii

Once *Notes on the State of Virginia* was available in the United States in 1787, Jefferson's interest in fossils became widely known. For more than two decades Jefferson received fossils from friends and acquaintances who knew of his curiosity. An odd gift came from Col. John Stuart of Greenbrier County, Virginia (now West Virginia):

Being informed you have retired from Public Business and returned to your former residence in Albemarle, and observing by your Notes your very curious desire for Examining into the antiquity of our Country, I thought the Bones of a Tremendious Animal of the Clawed kind lately found . . . might afford you some amusement.[24]

Stuart added that he thought the animal was "of the Lion kind."[25] Jefferson began preparing a paper on the bones for submission to the American Philosophical Society based on Stuart's hypothesis.

While waiting in vain for Stuart to send a thigh bone of the animal that could indicate its full size, Jefferson was elected to two important offices: vice president of the United States

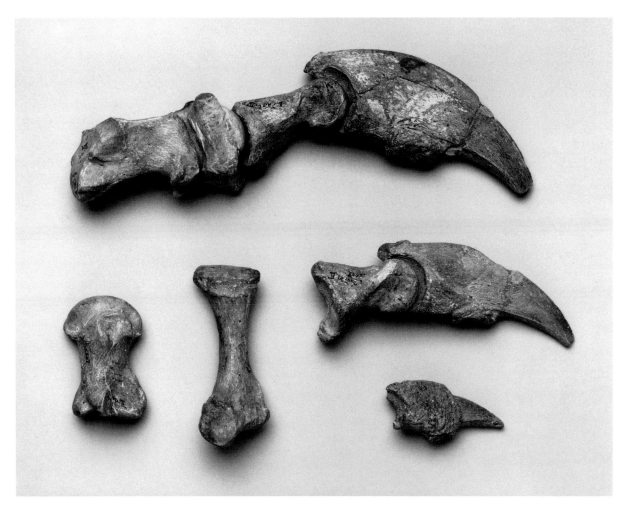

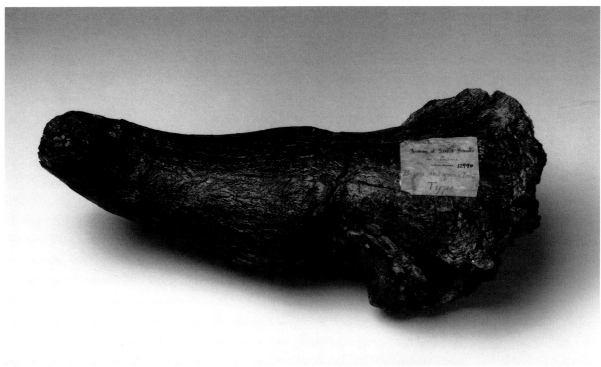

under John Adams and president of the American Philosophical Society. With his induction as Society president pending, Jefferson completed his paper on the bones with the information at hand and carried the fossils with him on the journey to Philadelphia. He had reached the conclusion that the bones were from an animal "of the lion kind, but of most exaggerated size." Because of the animal's bulk—three times that of a lion—Jefferson called it "the Great-claw, or Megalonyx."[26]

Sometime after his arrival in Philadelphia in March 1797, Jefferson went to a bookstore where he happened to peruse the September 1796 issue of London's *Monthly Magazine*. By incredible coincidence the issue contained an engraving of a fossilized skeleton that was strikingly similar to Jefferson's "Megalonyx," but it was identified as a relative of the sloth. The fossils from Paraguay illustrated in the *Magazine* had been mounted in the Royal Cabinet of Natural History in Madrid. Realizing that his classification of the fossils as part of the cat family was probably wrong, Jefferson quickly revised his paper on the day of his presentation. He deleted all references to "Megalonyx" and substituted instead the more general term, an animal "of the clawed kind."[27]

The bones were deposited into the Society's collection. The renowned Dr. Caspar Wistar noted both similarities and differences between the bones at hand, those of a sloth, and those illustrated in the *Monthly Magazine*, leaving the identification of the specimen unanswered.[28] In 1804 Jefferson was credited as the discoverer of the *Megalonyx*, an animal that is indeed related to the sloth family, and in 1822 the French naturalist Anselme Desmarest gave the extinct animal its formal name: *Megalonyx jeffersonii*.[29]

Big Bone Lick, Kentucky

Inspired by Jefferson's presentation of the *Megalonyx* bones, the American Philosophical Society formed a committee, headed by Jefferson with Charles Willson Peale and Dr. Wistar as members, whose mission was "to collect information respecting the past and present state of this country." In a circular letter sent out by the committee in 1798 to "lovers of science," the first item on a list of priorities was "to procure one or more entire skeletons of the Mammoth, so called, and of such other unknown animals as either have been, or hereafter may be discovered in America." The Great Salt Lick on the Ohio, known as Big Bone Lick, was a rich site for fossil finds. Jefferson probably knew Big Bone Lick as early as 1766 when he met Dr. John Morgan in Philadelphia who had collected "mammoth" (now known as mastodon) specimens from it. He also described the ancient salt lick, now in Kentucky but originally part of Virginia, in *Notes on the State of Virginia*.[30]

As president of the United States, Jefferson established the same objective for the explorers Meriwether Lewis and William Clark's expedition to the Northwest as that held by the American Philosophical Society: Learn more about all aspects of America. One of Meriwether Lewis's stops on the westward journey was at Cincinnati, Ohio, where he sent a group of Big Bone Lick fossils to Jefferson (which were lost in transit) and wrote a detailed report of Dr. William Goforth's excavation of the Lick.[31] The return of the explorers in 1806 provided another opportunity for gathering fossils for the Society. Jefferson financed William Clark's return to Big Bone Lick in 1807 to collect mostly head

and foot bones missing from the Society's "mammoth" skeleton that Charles Willson Peale was assembling.[32]

Clark's dig was an immense success. It netted over 300 bones of various species, including the coveted "mammoth" cranium. The bones were sent to Jefferson at the President's House. The sheer volume of the collection gave Jefferson the idea to send duplicate specimens to the National Institute of France.[33] He enlisted his old friend Dr. Wistar to come from Philadelphia to assist in the selection process.[34] With bones spread out in the rooms of the President's House, Wistar spent the early part of July 1807 writing a report on the collection and selecting the contents of three boxes to be sent to France. There the fossils became part of the Museum of Natural History, where they became critically important to the study of paleontology in France.[35]

The remainder of Jefferson's collection was divided between the Society and Monticello, where the fossils were displayed in the Entrance Hall. "There is a tusk and a femur which Genl. Clarke procured particularly at my request for a special kind of Cabinet I have at Monticello," Jefferson wrote to Wistar.[36] Visitors to Monticello recorded seeing upper and lower jawbones, tusks, thigh bones, a head, and teeth of the "mammoth" in particular, as well as bones from other animals as well as petrifications.[37]

After Jefferson's death the Monticello collection was transferred to the University of Virginia, where it was first exhibited in the Rotunda. The American naturalist Richard Harlan recorded seeing the collection in 1831, and that same year one fossil from the university was lent to the American Philosophical Society for study there.[38] No record of the fossil collection at the university exists after 1848 and many surviving specimens today remain unidentified.[39]

The specimens given to the American Philosophical Society were transferred to the Academy of Natural Sciences in Philadelphia in 1849, where over fifty bones from Jefferson's collection remain today.[40]

A . M . L .

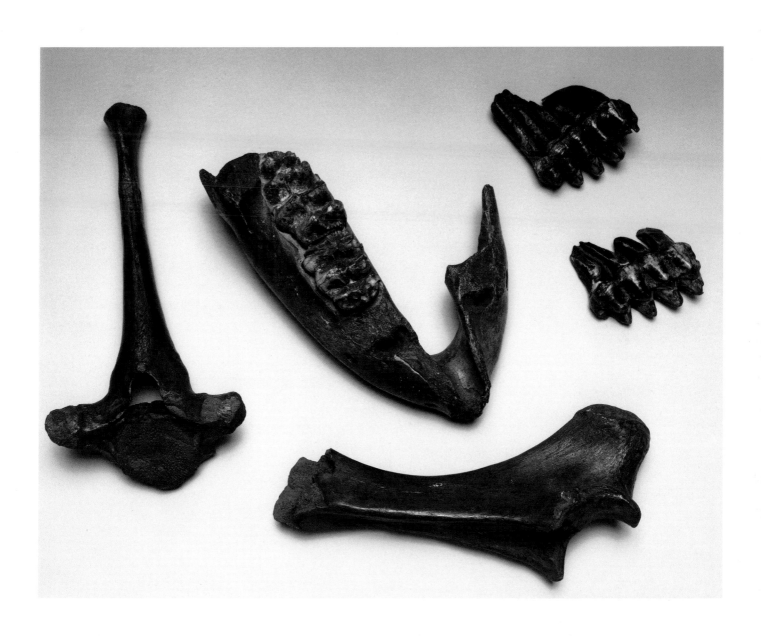

253

EAGLE BONE
WHISTLE

---

c. 1803–05

Attributed to Mandan
eagle bone, hide, hematite,
quill, resin, sinew, glass beads
20.3 × 1.7 (8 × ¹¹/₁₆ in.) Strap L:
approx. 20.3 (8 in.)
Peabody Museum of Archeology
and Ethnology, Harvard
University

254

TOBACCO POUCH

---

c. 1803–05

Attributed to Sauk/Fox
otter skin, deer skin, quill,
sinew, tin-plated sheet iron
tinklers, fiber, glass beads
110 × 23.5 (43⁵/₁₆ × 9¹/₄ in.)
Peabody Museum of Archaeology
and Ethnology, Harvard
University

NATIVE AMERICAN ARTIFACTS

In 1805 Jefferson began to create what he called an "Indian hall" at Monticello, using Native American artifacts sent to him by the explorers Lewis and Clark.[1] At the conclusion of the Lewis and Clark expedition in 1806, Jefferson invited Lewis and the Mandan chief Sheheke to view his collection:

Tell my friend of the Mandane also that I have already opened my arms to recieve him. Perhaps while in our neighborhood, it may be gratifying to him, and not otherwise to yourself to take a ride to Monticello and see in what manner I have arranged the tokens of friendship I have recieved from his country particularly as well as from other Indian friends: that I am in fact preparing a kind of Indian hall.[2]

Jefferson's collection, which he maintained for more than twenty years, was the culmination of his lifelong fascination with Native Americans and symbolized the new age of western expansion made possible by the Louisiana Purchase.[3] Visitors to Monticello marveled at the display of Native American painting, sculpture, clothing, weapons, and domestic utensils, which were interspersed with natural history specimens, scientific curiosities, and European art. "That which excites the curiosity of visiters," an 1824 visitor wrote of Monticello, "is the rich museum, which is placed at the entrance of the house."[4]

It contains offensive and defensive arms, clothes, ornaments, and utensils of the different savage tribes of North America; the most varied and complete collection that has ever been made.[5]

"In the very early part of my life," Jefferson wrote in 1812 to John Adams, "I was very familiar, and acquired impressions of attachment and commiseration for [the Indians] which have never been obliterated."

Before the revolution they were in the habit of coming often, and in great numbers to the seat of our government, where I was very much with them. I knew much the great Outassete, the warrior and orator of the Cherokees. He was always the guest of my father, on his journeys to and from Williamsburg.[6]

In *Notes on the State of Virginia*, Jefferson defended the Native American from the French naturalist Comte Georges-Louis de Buffon's assertions that the "savage of the new world" was "feeble," lazy, having no ardor and "no vivacity, no activity of mind."[7] Jefferson viewed Buffon's attack on Native Americans as an attack on the viability of the American continent.[8] In his refutation of Buffon's theories, Jefferson argued that the eloquence of Native American oratory and their art and domestic artifacts were evidence of their potential.

The Indians will often carve figures on their pipes not destitute of design and merit. They will crayon out an animal, a plant, or a country, so as to prove the existence of a germ in their minds which only wants cultivation. They astonish you with strokes of the most sublime oratory; such as prove their reason and sentiment strong, their imagination glowing and elevated.[9]

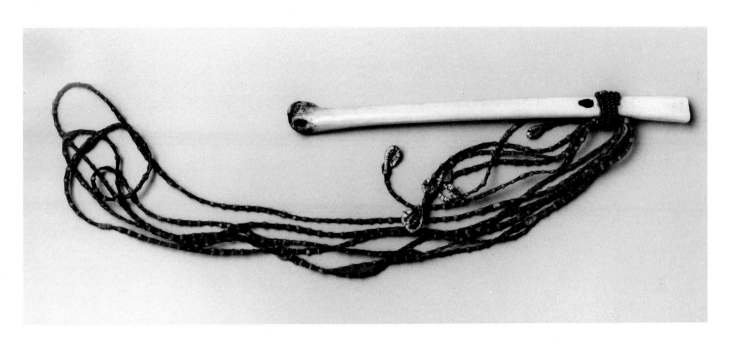

Jefferson believed that when more facts were gathered about Native Americans "we shall probably find that they are formed in mind as well as body, on the same module with the 'Homo sapiens Europaeus.'"[10] His curiosity about the function and composition of Indian burial mounds led him to make an archaeological investigation of a mound on the Rivanna River in Virginia, and he sought to discover the origin of Native Americans by studying their languages.[11]

The Lewis and Clark expedition, proposed by Jefferson and authorized by Congress in 1803, just prior to the purchase of the Louisiana Territory, best combined Jefferson's political and scientific interests. Jefferson explicitly instructed the explorers that "The object of your mission is single, the direct water communication from sea to sea formed by the bed of the Missouri and perhaps the Oregon,"[12] but he also recognized the expedition as an opportunity to gather knowledge of all kinds, including facts about Native Americans.

Jefferson consulted leading scientists and members of the government to compose a list of instructions for the explorers.[13] They were to record such details as the names and numbers of the Indian nations, their physical characteristics, diseases, and the boundaries of their lands. In addition, Jefferson directed the explorers to record their

language, traditions, monuments; their ordinary occupations in agriculture, fishing, hunting, war, arts, and the implements for these; their food, clothing and domestic accomodations; and articles of commerce they may need or furnish, and to what extent.[14]

Jefferson cautioned Lewis and Clark to "treat [the Indians] in the most friendly and conciliatory manner which their own conduct will admit," and he urged the explorers to extend an open invitation to all Indian chiefs to visit him in Washington.[15] The first of three delegations of Native Americans to visit Jefferson arrived in Washington in July 1804. A St. Louis fur trader, Pierre Chouteau, accompanied fourteen members of the Osage nation, and brought with him the first of many artifacts from the explorers.

During their expedition, Lewis and Clark sent three large shipments of artifacts to Jefferson in Washington. The largest and best-documented group left Fort Mandan in April 1805 and reached the President's House in August, while Jefferson was at Monticello.[16] According to Lewis's instructions, Jefferson divided the Native American artifacts between himself and Charles Willson Peale's Philadelphia Museum.[17] Jefferson retained a Mandan bow with a quiver of arrows, four buffalo robes, one pot "such as the Mandans manufacture and use for culinary purposes," various articles of "Indian dress," and "1 Buffalow robe painted by a Mandan man representing a battle which was faught 8 years since, by the Sioux & Ricaras, against the Mandans, Minitarras & Ahwahharways."[18]

After the expedition had safely concluded at St. Louis in the fall of 1806, Lewis and Clark sent Jefferson a third shipment containing artifacts gathered from the West Coast as well as the Midwest: hats made by the Clatsop Indians, baskets, Mandan robes, a sheepskin blanket, several boxes of miscellaneous articles, and nine additional Indian vocabularies. The last installation of artifacts came from Jefferson's privately funded dig at Big Bone Lick, Kentucky, supervised by Clark in 1807. Although Lewis primarily sent fossils and natural-history specimens to Jefferson, he also sent a small number of Sioux artifacts, most likely left over from the expedition.

As late as 1825 Jefferson contacted William Clark in an effort to augment his collection before giving it to the University of Virginia.[19] Whether Jefferson ever gave the artifacts to the university is undetermined, and their history after his death is unclear. In June 1828 Colonel C. J. Hutter donated a group of artifacts to the Peale Museum in Philadelphia, including the painted Mandan buffalo robe (Cat. 259) believed to have been displayed at Monticello.[20] How Hutter obtained the artifacts is unknown.[21] Moses Kimball purchased Peale's collection in 1847, and it was exhibited in the Boston Museum until 1889 when it was acquired by the Peabody Museum of Archaeology and Ethnography at Harvard University.

A . M . L .

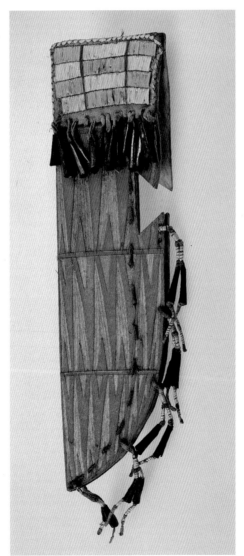

257

CRADLE

c. 1803–05

Attributed to Crow
wood, semi-tanned hide, hide,
glass beads, wool trade cloth,
sinew
13 × 66 × 25
(5⅛ × 26 × 9¹³/₁₆ in.)
Peabody Museum of Archaeology
and Ethnology, Harvard
University

258

KNIFE SHEATH

c. 1803–05

Attributed to Chippewa/Ojibwa
hide, bird quill, tin tinkler,
sinew
31.4 × 9.5 × 1.5
(12⅜ × 3¾ × ⅝ in.)
Peabody Museum of Archaeology
and Ethnology, Harvard
University

259

MANDAN BUFFALO ROBE

c. 1798

Mandan
semi-tanned buffalo hide,
porcupine quill work, pigments
259.1×238.8×2.5
(102×94×1 in.)
Peabody Museum of Archaeology
and Ethnology, Harvard
University

Meriwether Lewis sent this robe to Jefferson in April 1805 from Fort Mandan, in what is now North Dakota, where the expedition had spent the previous winter. He described it as "1 Buffalow robe painted by a Mandan man representing a battle which was faught 8 years since, by the Sioux and Ricaras, against the Mandans, Minitarras, and Ahwahharways."[22] The robe became part of Jefferson's extensive collection of Native American artifacts and attracted the attention of many visitors to his "Indian hall."[23] George Ticknor, who visited Jefferson in 1815, noted that in the Entrance Hall, "in odd union with a fine painting of the Repentance of Saint Peter . . . [is] an Indian representation of a bloody battle, handed down in their traditions."[24]

A.M.L.

260 and 261

CARVED STONE
HEADS

n.d.

Anglo or African-American
probably sandstone
17.8 × 16.5 × 16.5
(7 × 6½ × 6½ in.)
Valentine Museum

PROVENANCE:
Thomas Jefferson; by purchase to
Captain Stockton; acquired by Col.
Wertenbaker of Charlottesville; by
gift to the Valentine Museum prior
to 1892.

n.d.

Anglo or African-American
probably sandstone
18.4 × 15.2 (7¼ × 6 in.)
National Museum of Natural
History, Smithsonian Institution

PROVENANCE:
Thomas Jefferson; by purchase to
Captain Stockton; by descent to
John N. C. Stockton; "picked up"
by Dr. William C. Dabney; by gift
to the Smithsonian Institution in
1875.

These two stone heads, which Jefferson believed were made by Native Americans, were part of his eclectic collection of art and artifacts in the Entrance Hall. When a visitor to Monticello wrote to Jefferson in 1820 asking the origin of "some curious, I believe *hindoo* figures in your collection of natural and artificial curiosities," Jefferson replied that the figures could not be "Hindoo," but "must be Indian of our own continent as I possess no others."[25]

Jefferson's grandson, Thomas Jefferson Randolph, remembered that one of these heads (now in the collection of the Smithsonian) sat on a stand in the Entrance Hall, and that it had been sent to his grandfather from "the West."[26] According to tradition, both heads were sold at the Dispersal Sale in 1827 to Captain Stockton of Albemarle County.

Jefferson displayed at least four "Indian" sculptures in the Entrance Hall. The most remarkable were a pair of bust-length statues of a man and woman, carved in hard stone (now unlocated). Morgan Brown, a lieutenant during the Revolutionary War, sent the statues to Jefferson from Palmyra, Tennessee in 1799.

They were found on a high bluff on the north side of Cumberland river standing side by side facing to the East, the tops of their heads about six inches under the surface of the earth; there were two large mounds a little to the West of them and a quantity of human bones under and near them.[27]

Jefferson displayed the statues on brackets in the Entrance Hall on either side of the busts of Voltaire (Cat. 89) and Turgot (Cat. 90).[28] The busts may have remained at Monticello and been sold with the house to James Barclay in 1831.[29]

A.M.L.

411

STONE STATUE OF A KNEELING WOMAN

Late Mississippian (c. 1400)

Cumberland River Valley;
Middle Cumberland Culture
unidentified stone
24.1 × 10.8 × 14
(9½ × 4¼ × 5½ in.)
National Museum of the
American Indian, Smithsonian
Institution

PROVENANCE:
Harry Innes; by gift to Thomas
Jefferson in 1790; by gift to the
American Philosophical Society in
1791; by transfer to the National
Museum of the American Indian.

In 1790 Harry Innes renewed his "slight acquaintance" with Jefferson by sending him this statue. He wrote that it had been found five or six inches below the surface of the ground by a farmer plowing near the Cumberland River:

It is the Image carved of Stone of a naked Woman kneeling; it is roughly executed, but from the coarseness of the Stone the instruments which it was probably carved and its antiquity I think shews the maker to have had some talent in that way, the design being good.[30]

Innes hoped to search the site where the statue was found for evidence of habitation to help determine its age.

Jefferson was very pleased with Innes's gift:

It is certainly the best piece of workmanship I ever saw from their [Indian] hands. If the artist did not intend it, he has very happily hit on the representation of a woman in the first moments of parturition.[31]

Jefferson presented the statue to the American Philosophical Society in 1791, and it was recorded in their proceedings as "a curious piece of Indian sculpture representing an Indian woman in labor, found near Cumberland, Va."[32] Although Jefferson believed the statue depicted a woman in labor, the kneeling position was a typical ceremonial posture for both females and males of high status during the Mississippian period.[33]

A . M . L .

According to family tradition, this "Portrait of a young chief of the Sack nation of Indians" was part of Jefferson's collection at Monticello. It was most likely given to him by a member of the delegation of Native Americans from the "Missouri and Mississippi," which arrived in Washington late in 1805 (Cat. 85–88).

The portrait may depict Wa Pawni Ha, a seventeen-year-old Sack chief who was befriended in Washington by Sir Augustus John Foster, secretary to the British minister there. Foster described Wa Pawni Ha as having "dark hazel eyes, short blunt teeth, the upperlip a little pressed upwards, straight nose and very fat cheeks . . . the young Sac chief wore his hair down on the forehead which indicates the age of youth . . ."[34] At Foster's request the Swiss miniaturist David Boudon (also Bourdon, active in the United States 1797–1816) took Wa Pawni Ha's portrait in late December.[35] Wa Pawni Ha may have presented the image to Jefferson when the delegation visited the President's House on January 4, 1806.[36]

[1927–82]   A.M.L.

263

**YOUNG CHIEF OF
THE SACK NATION**

c. 1805

watercolor on paper
D: 7.1 (2¹³⁄₁₆ in.)

PROVENANCE:
Thomas Jefferson; by descent to Virginia and Nicholas Trist; by descent to Frances Maury Burke; by descent to Virginia Randolph Burke and Ellen Burke Eddy; by loan and then gift to TJMF in 1941.

LIGHTING

CANDELABRUM ONE OF A PAIR

c. 1770 and 1789

John Hoyland and Company (active 1764–1779), Sheffield fused silverplate
H: 35.6 (14 in.); W: 46.7 (18⅜ in.); Base: 12.1 (4¾ in.) square
Private collection

PROVENANCE:
Thomas Jefferson; by descent to Thomas Jefferson Randolph; by descent to a private collection.

Jefferson's sketch in the margin of his letter to John Trumbull, August 5, 1789.
Library of Congress

On August 4, 1789, just a few weeks after the storming of the Bastille, Jefferson wrote from Paris to John Trumbull in London:

About a week before those tumults began, I suffered by common robbers, who broke open my house and rifled two apartments. One article they took obliges me to trouble you. This was my candlesticks, all of which I lost. I have searched every shop in Paris and cannot find a tolerable pattern: therefore I will beg the favor of you to send me 4. pair plated from London. Mine were plated and came from there, and I am sure the pattern is common there. It was a fluted Corinthian column, with the capital of it's order, and the bottom of the form in the margin. I recollect to have once seen the undermost form, which I thought very handsome. Mine were about 12 Inches high. I must trouble you therefore to find one of these patterns for me, and indeed I think you will find them in any great shop of plated ware. I think no form so handsome as that of the column.[1]

Trumbull responded to Jefferson on September 18, and his letter contained an itemized list of his purchases and planned purchases for Jefferson. He had obtained one pair of Corinthian column and pedestal candlesticks, fifteen inches high, and two similar pairs of twelve-inch candlesticks. A fourth pair of candlesticks he had yet to buy. The candlesticks were bought second-hand for about thirteen pounds. He explained to Jefferson:

To have had them all of one pattern and new, I must have waited to have them done at Sheffield, which is an uncertain time and they would have cost . . . £18. 8. 0. . . . I hope you will think I have done rightly to sacrifice something to this difference of price, if the want of entire uniformity be any sacrifice. These will be sent early next week.[2]

Trumbull also bought Jefferson "2 Branches for 3 lights new." The term "branch" describes the upper section of a candelabrum with a candle cup in the center and two arms, each supporting an additional socket. The branch fits into the candle cup of a regular candlestick, converting it to a three-light candelabrum, or "girandole."[3] The Corinthian column candlestick on a stepped pedestal base illustrated here is almost certainly one of the four twelve-inch candlesticks, paired with a new "branch for three lights," bought by Trumbull.

The branches, though unmarked, stylistically date from the late 1780s or 1790s. The Corinthian column candlesticks with stepped bases, most popular in the 1760s, bear the marks of John Hoyland and Company. They were made before 1773, as marks on plated wares were prohibited between 1773 and 1784 and the formation of Younge, Greaves and Hoyland in 1779 superceded the earlier manufactory.[4]

The final bill for the candlesticks, dated October 10, 1789, indicates that Trumbull acquired the four pairs from four different merchants.[5] By the time they arrived in Paris, Jefferson had already sailed for America. Four silver-plated candlesticks and two girandoles, carefully packed in one of the many crates of household items, made the same trans-Atlantic journey the following year.[6] Used first in Jefferson's Philadelphia house, they were shipped to Monticello in 1793 in a case containing ten candlesticks and two girandoles.[7]

S.M.O.

CANDELABRUM
ONE OF A PAIR

c. 1818

England, probably Sheffield
fused silver plate
H: 30.5 (12 in.);
D (base): 14.3 (5⅝ in.)
The Maury Family

PROVENANCE:
Thomas Jefferson; according to
family tradition, by purchase to
Jesse Maury at the Dispersal Sale
in 1827; by descent to the Maury
family.

In addition to the four pairs of silver-plated candlesticks that Jefferson obtained through John Trumbull in London in 1789, other plated candlesticks such as this pair were acquired for use at Monticello. Jefferson bought a pair of plated candlesticks in New York in May 1790, and in 1801 some candlesticks were included in his $273 purchase of "silver and plated ware bot for me in Phila[delphia]."[8] Although no candlestick purchases after 1801 are mentioned in Jefferson's Memorandum Books, the style of this pair of candelabra suggests that they must have come to Monticello after his retirement from the presidency.

Thirteen silver-plated candlesticks were listed on Jefferson's 1815 list of taxable property.[9] An inventory taken shortly after his death included two plated candelabra and two plated candlesticks in the Parlor, four plated candlesticks in the Dining Room, and ten plated candlesticks as well as six brass and two japanned candlesticks elsewhere in the house.[10] At least some of these candlesticks were sold at the Dispersal Sale in 1827. Receipts survive for two pairs of plated candlesticks bought by John Gorman and George W. Spotswood, but no receipts exist for the people who paid cash for their purchases.[11]

These plated candelabra in the late Federal style with bands of floral and foliate decoration on the bobeches, knops, and bases present an obvious contrast to the columnar candlesticks that Jefferson favored in the 1780s. As Sheffield wares were one of the first products of the Industrial Revolution made for a mass market, Jefferson's acquisitions of silver plate reflect popular stylistic trends more so than objects in solid silver, which he was often able to design and have made according to his own taste.

For versatility, each of these candelabra could be used as a single candlestick by removing the branches from the socket just below their juncture. Until 1791 Jefferson apparently used tallow and spermaceti candles exclusively for illuminating Monticello. After 1791 he began to order myrtle wax, or bayberry, candles and stated with at least one order of molded candles, "myrtle wax would be greatly prefered, but if not to be had, good tallow would be next desired . . ."[12]

S . M . O .

HANGING BRASS
ARGAND LAMP

c. 1805

probably English
brass
H (overall): 104.1 (41 in.);
main housing: 44.5 × 59.7
(17½ × 23½ in.);
chimneys H: 19.1 (7½ in.); D:
5.1 (2 in.); upper canopy H:
19.1 (7½ in.); D: 24.8 (9¾ in.)

PROVENANCE:
Thomas Jefferson; by purchase to
James Barclay; by purchase to
Uriah P. Levy; by descent to
Jefferson Monroe Levy; by
purchase to TJMF in 1923.

This four-branch brass hanging Argand lamp, with a central oil reservoir, and acanthus-leaf ornaments, was probably made in England.[13] It may be the "passage lanthern" that Jefferson purchased for Monticello in 1805 from the Philadelphia stationers Caldcleugh and Thomas.[14] "Lanthern" then referred to lamps of this type, as well as hanging lamps for candles consisting of glass panes in a metal frame. Two years later, Jefferson bought "lanthern ornaments" from the same firm, including a balance shell, brass chain and double pullies, suggesting that at this time the Entrance Hall ceiling was prepared for hanging the lamp.[15]

The inventory taken after Jefferson's death fails to mention this hanging lamp in the Entrance Hall, but it does include some wall-mounted lamps that were probably also Argand types. Jefferson sent some of the first Argand lamps from England to the United States in 1786 (Cat. 268).

[1923-16]   A . M . L .

This unusual form of lighting device, sometimes called a "reading lamp," reflected candlelight downward for ease of reading or writing. Jefferson, who said of his daily routine that "from candle light to early bed-time, I read," would no doubt have found such a light useful. The completely adjustable candelabrum has two pivoting brass candle cups. The arms are attached to a piece with fixtures for holding candle snuffers and extinguisher; this piece can be raised or lowered on the central steel shaft. The height and angle of the rectangular reflector, attached to the shaft above the candle branches, are also adjustable. The turned brass base is lead weighted for stability, and at the top of the shaft is a brass handle for carrying.

When and where Jefferson purchased this item has not been established. George Washington owned a similar device, and both might have been obtained in New York or Philadelphia. The inscription, "Thomas Jefferson, Monticello," is a later addition. [1978-79-2]   S.M.O.

During his tenure in France Jefferson constantly observed and made note of all kinds of innovations, which he eagerly shared with his correspondents in the United States. His interest in promoting the "new" and "innovative" led him in several instances to become a supplier of goods not yet available in the United States. Jefferson wrote to James Madison and Charles Thomson (secretary of the Continental Congress) in 1784 about the Swiss scientist Ami Argand's invention of a bright-burning lamp with a hollow wick, describing it as giving "a light equal as is thought to that of six or eight candles."[17]

Jefferson was particularly intrigued by Argand's idea because he had accomplished an advance that Benjamin Franklin had only attempted. Jefferson wrote to Thomson:

The improvement is produced by forming the wick into a hollow cylinder so that there is a passage for the air through the hollow. The idea had occurred to Dr. Franklin a year or two before: but he tried his experiment with a rush, which not succeeding he did not prosecute it.[18]

Both Madison and Thomson, as well as Richard Henry Lee, requested that Jefferson procure Argand lamps for them. Jefferson found during a visit to John Adams in London that the lamps there were superior to the Parisian examples.[19] While Argand was working in London with Matthew Boulton and James Watt to perfect the manufacture of his lamp, numerous Parisian lampmakers were producing lesser-quality versions.[20]

In March and April 1786, while in London, Jefferson purchased a total of three "plated reading lamps," possibly from Matthew Boulton, and "blue lamp chimneys."[21] He sent one lamp to Charles Thomson, another to Richard Henry Lee, and presumably kept the third for himself.[22] Of the three, only Thomson's lamp is known to survive. After receiving the lamp in July 1786, Thomson acknowledged Jefferson's gift:

The [lamp] you have now sent is an elegant piece of furniture, if it were not otherwise valuable on account of its usefulness. I am informed this kind of lamp is coming into use in Philadelphia and made there.[23]

A.M.L.

267
**CANDELABRUM
WITH REFLECTOR**

1770–1800

*England
brass, steel
H: 50.2 (19¾ in.);
W: 33 (13 in.)
D (base): 15.2 (6 in.)*

PROVENANCE:
Thomas Jefferson; by descent to
Edward Cabot Rotch, Abbott
Lawrence Rotch and Ann R.
Magendantz; by gift and purchase
to TJMF in 1985.

268
ARGAND LAMP

1786

*English, possibly Matthew
Boulton (1728–1809)
Sheffield plate
17.8 × 9.5 (7 × 3¾ in.)
Winterthur Museum*

PROVENANCE:
Thomas Jefferson; by gift to
Charles Thomson; by descent to an
unidentified Thomson descendant;
by purchase to Harrold E. Gillingham;
by purchase to Henry Francis du
Pont.[16]

269

PAIR OF LOUIS XV BRAS DE CHEMINEE (CHIMNEY SCONCES)

mid to late 18th c.

French
gilt-bronze
47 × 27.9 × 27.9
(18½ × 11 × 11 in.)
Mr. and Mrs. Robert Carter

PROVENANCE:
Thomas Jefferson; by descent to Benjamin Franklin Randolph; by gift or bequest to Sarah Champe Carter Randolph; by gift or bequest to Robert Carter family; by descent to Mr. and Mrs. Robert Carter.

270

ALABASTER HANGING LAMP

c. 1808

purchased in Philadelphia
alabaster, brass
H: 15.2 (6 in.)
D: 33 (13 in.)

PROVENANCE:
Thomas Jefferson; by descent to Thomas Jefferson Randolph; by descent to Mrs. Page Kirk; by gift to TJMF in 1954.

Jefferson purchased the gilt-bronze sconces illustrated on page 313 while living in Paris, sometime between 1784 and 1789. Their naturalistic "rocaille" style dates to the earlier Louis XV period, but this form of lighting was so popular that it was produced well into the nineteenth century.[24] It is difficult to determine whether the sconces that Jefferson purchased were of the Louis XV period or a contemporary imitation.

Pairs of sconces typically were placed on either side of a mirror to increase their luminescence. The account of the *emballeur* who packed Jefferson's Paris household recorded these sconces as "deux bras de Cheminée," identifying their placement over a fireplace.[25] The sconces were also included on Petit's 1793 packing list of Jefferson's furniture shipped from Philadelphia to Monticello, where they were likely used in the Parlor.[26]

A.M.L.

Thomas Jefferson Randolph, the eldest son of Martha Jefferson Randolph, purchased this alabaster lamp in Philadelphia in the fall of 1808. Randolph was then beginning a nearly year-long stay with Jefferson's good friend Charles Willson Peale. In his parting instructions to his sixteen-year-old grandson, Jefferson wrote, "Should you be able at any time to find in the shops of Philadelphia a handsome Alabaster lamp, inform me of it, and it's price, and describe it's form, that I may judge whether to buy it or not."[27]

Randolph fulfilled that commission quickly, sending Jefferson "designs" of two lamps from which to choose. Jefferson responded on October 28, 1808, specified a thirteen-inch bowl lamp, and enclosed a ten-dollar bill for payment.[28] The lamp was still in transit in January of the next year, but apparently made it to Monticello before May 6, 1809, when Jefferson asked Randolph to send him "9 feet of brass chain to hang the alabaster lamp you got for me . . ."[29]

The shape of the lamp, Jefferson's reference to it as a "vase" lamp, and the current lack of provision for a flame all suggest that the alabaster lamp employed a floating wick, which was floated on the surface of the oil by some buoyant device or supported there by wires. Benjamin Franklin described the wick for a float lamp he made as being held by a "little wire hoop . . . furnished with corks to float it on the oil."[30]

This alabaster lamp was a replacement for an earlier one, as Jefferson wrote to Randolph, "I shall not need chains or bands, having them on the lanthern which this will replace."[31] An account by Sir Augustus John Foster (then secretary to the British minister) of his visit to Monticello in 1807 suggests that tending the first alabaster lamp was a way for the women of the house to gain popularity with Jefferson. In his "Notes on the United States," Foster wrote:

After breakfast Mrs. Randolph and her amiable daughters as well as the other female relations of the house set about cleaning the tea things and washing the alabaster lamp, which I took to be designed as a catch for popularity: after this operation the President retired to his books . . .[32]

[1954-8]

A.M.L.

MUSICAL INSTRUMENTS AND AMUSEMENTS

271
CITTERN

1760–80

English
maple, pine and other woods,
gilded metal rose
L: 77.5 (30½ in.)

PROVENANCE:
Thomas Jefferson; by gift to
Virginia Jefferson Randolph in
1816; by descent to Ellen Coolidge
Burke; by gift to TJMF in 1946.

The cittern, or English guitar, was a popular drawing-room instrument in the second half of the eighteenth century. Although it has straight sides and a generally flat back like instruments in the guitar family, it is more closely related to the lute. Its metal strings are plucked with the fingertips in the same manner.[1] Until about 1825 the term "guitar" referred almost exclusively to the English guitar, while the Spanish guitar was normally identified as "Spanish." The English guitar was not, however, a specifically English product. They were also made in other countries and were especially popular in France as well as in Virginia.[2]

As early as 1776, Jefferson recorded the purchase of guitar strings in Philadelphia, suggesting perhaps that his wife played the instrument.[3] When his younger daughter Maria joined him in Paris in 1787, he paid eighty-four livres for a guitar and regularly recorded payments to the "Guitar master for Polly."[4] Maria Jefferson's guitar came to America with the rest of the family's baggage, but this cittern appears to have been purchased by Jefferson in Virginia in 1816.[5] His granddaughter, Virginia Randolph Trist, recalled in 1839:

I had for a long time a great desire to have a guitar. A lady of our neighborhood was going to the West, and wished to part with her guitar, but she asked so high a price that I never in my dreams aspired to its possession. One morning, on going down to breakfast, I saw the guitar. It had been sent up by Mrs.— for us to look at, and grandpapa told me that if I would promise to learn to play on it I should have it. I never shall forget my ecstacies. I was but fourteen years old, and the first wish of my heart was unexpectedly gratified.[6]

In 1824 Virginia Randolph received another guitar, possibly the guitar from Paris that Jefferson had given to his daughter Maria. In a letter to Nicholas Trist, her future husband, Virginia wrote that her father had come from Richmond and brought "a spanish Guitar," a gift from a cousin named Wayles Baker. She explained:

It belonged formerly to Aunt Maria Eppes, and she gave it to Mrs. Baker. It appears to be a very sweet toned instrument, and looks all spanish. I have practised but little on it as yet, because I have not much time for music this month. Did you ever hear a Spanish Guitar, and do you think it agreable? Perhaps it will support my voice, which is, you know, very weak, and somewhat cracked.[7]

The Spanish guitar is unlocated, but the cittern descended in the family of Virginia Trist. The maple and pine instrument with wood inlay has watch-key tuning invented in the 1760s by John N. Preston of London.[8]

[1946-6]   S.M.O.

In 1786, Jefferson advised John Paradise, an old friend from Williamsburg then in London, "to get Kirckman to make for me one of his best harpsichords with a double set of keys, and the machine on top resembling a Venetian blind for giving a swell."[9] This superb harpsichord, made by the celebrated London maker Jacob Kirckman (also spelled Kirkman or Kirckmann), was one of the finest harpsichords available at the time. It was acquired for his older daughter, Martha, while she was a student at the Abbaye de Panthemont. Evidently pleased with the first harpsichord, a second one, made by Joseph Kirckman, successor to Jacob and Abraham, was ordered for Maria in 1798.

Although the pianoforte was solidly gaining acceptance, Jefferson remained steadfastly loyal to the harpsichord during its declining popularity. He wanted, however, to improve upon the plucked sound of the harpsichord. He specified that Martha's harpsichord was to have a patented "Celestina stop" by Adam Walker, a mechanism of revolving silk bands that added a bowed-string sound, as well as a Venetian swell for crescendos.[10] Dr. Charles Burney, the famous organist and musical historian whom Jefferson had briefly met earlier that spring, acted as his intermediary with Jacob Kirckman. Burney reported that Kirckman had no objection to the Venetian swell but was "a great enemy" to the Celestina, believing that

the Resin, used on the silk thread that produces the tone, not only clogs the wheels and occasions it to be frequently out of order, but in a short time, adheres so much to the strings as to destroy the tune of the instrument.[11]

Against Kirckman's wishes, the Celestina stop was installed.

Jefferson also wanted an exceptionally durable harpsichord that was easy to tune and maintain. Burney wrote Jefferson that Kirckman reported that "he has sent Harpsichords to every part of the Globe where the English have any commerce, and never has heard of the wood-work giving way."[12]

After the family returned to Monticello, Martha's instrument was placed in the Parlor beneath the pier mirror on the southeast wall. Jefferson, advocating three hours per day of practice, was a great stimulus to his daughters and granddaughters. In 1790, he reminded Martha, "Do not neglect your music. It will be a companion which will sweeten many hours of life to you."[13] By 1825 the once-prized harpsichord was in terrible condition, and one granddaughter stated that it was "an old instrument too far gone even to learn on."[14] Martha's harpsichord was left at Monticello after Jefferson's death, and reportedly was made into furniture. John Wayles Eppes, Maria's widower, returned her harpsichord (unlocated) to Poplar Forest in 1820 for Martha and her daughters to enjoy there.

Jacob Kirckman, the maker of the first instrument, worked for Hermann Tabel, a Flemish harpsichord maker in London. After Tabel's death, Kirckman married his widow and took over his business.[15] In 1772 Jacob entered into a partnership with his nephew, Abraham. They were succeeded by Joseph Kirckman after 1790. Although thousands of Kirckman harpsichords were made, only about 110 are known today. The harpsichord exhibited at Monticello, inscribed "Jacobus Kirckman Londini Fecit 1762," is a single manual instrument.

[1990-13]   S.R.S.

1762

Jacob Kirckman (1710–1792),
London
mahogany, mahogany veneer
89.8 × 92.7 × 218.4
(35⅜ × 36½ × 86 in.)

PROVENANCE:
Pelham Galleries; by purchase to Patricia M. Kluge; by gift to TJMF in 1990.

Another instrument for observation, in this case of engraved prints or maps rather than the landscape, was the perspective glass, or *vue d'optique*. The combination of magnifying lens and angled mirror provided enlarged views of heightened perspective of prints placed on a table below. Because the mirror reversed the image, engravers of the period produced prints in reverse particularly destined for use with perspective glasses or their public form, traveling peep shows.

No certain documentary reference to a *vue d'optique*, also known as a "zograscope" or an "optical diagonal machine," has been found in Jefferson's records, nor have any reversed-image prints survived among the collections of his descendants. His Memorandum Book does note a 1769 payment to James Craig in Williamsburg for the repair of a "perspect. glass."[16] This could represent a *vue d'optique*, but might also be a simple spyglass.

[1942-16]   L.C.S.

The camera obscura, the device that led to the invention of photography, served many purposes in the eighteenth century—from the scientific uses of viewing sunspots or demonstrating the nature of vision, to serving the needs of engravers or traveling landscape artists. It could also be enjoyed for the heightened effect of the scene in miniature that appeared on the viewing glass—a "picture drawn by nature's hand," as Benjamin Martin described it in 1740.[17]

Jefferson's instrument is a reflex camera obscura. The movable lens projects an inverted image onto an interior mirror, which reflects an upright, but reversed, image onto the glass viewing plate. It may be the instrument he bought in 1794 from David Rittenhouse, after borrowing it a few months earlier so that his daughter Maria could "take a few lessons in drawing from nature."[18]

For Jefferson, drawing was an important part of female education, "an innocent and engaging amusement, often useful, and a qualification not to be neglected in one who is to become a mother and an instructor."[19] His own drawing activities, beyond his notable architectural draftsmanship, are less clear. The only nonarchitectural drawings that survive are simple sketches of furniture or farm equipment, meant solely as aids to craftsmen or his own memory. He did, however, have an active interest in devices that assisted in drawing directly from life. While in Europe, he purchased a "perspective machine" to aid in drawing objects and landscapes.[20]

In London in 1786 Jefferson bought a scioptric ball, which could be fitted to a window shutter to turn a darkened room into a camera obscura. The previous day he had visited Alexander Pope's grotto at Twickenham and must have recalled Pope's famous description of it in 1725, when it could be turned into a camera obscura providing a "moving Picture" of traffic on the Thames. Jefferson may also have seen the room camera obscura at the Greenwich Observatory when he stopped there three weeks later on his way back to France.[21]

It is not known just why Jefferson commissioned the purchase of a second instrument in 1805. Geographer William Tatham (1752–1819) procured for him in London "A Camera

Obscura, with Extra Glasses constructed in the best manner by Adams" and costing £10-10. It arrived at the President's House just in time for the visit of Jefferson's daughter Martha and her children, and it may have been purchased to provide amusement for this extended winter visit.[22]

Three years later, after "revising" his collection of scientific instruments, Jefferson gave one of his camera obscuras to his son-in-law John Wayles Eppes for the future use of his grandson Francis, then aged eight.[23] Although there are no references to the camera obscura's use in making silhouettes, the survival of a large number of unsigned silhouettes suggests the possibility that some were made with the assistance of this instrument.

[1938-4]   L . C . S .

PERSONAL OBJECTS

**BONE WALKING
STICK**

c. 1806

unidentified bone, gold
108 (42½ in.)
T. Jefferson Coolidge, Jr.

PROVENANCE:
Thomas Jefferson; by bequest to
James Madison; by bequest to
Thomas Jefferson Randolph; by
gift or purchase to an unidentified
member of the Coolidge family; by
descent to T. Jefferson Coolidge,
Jr.; by loan to TJMF since 1986.

In the summer of 1805, while Jefferson was in residence at the President's House, this "elegant walking staff" arrived for him at Monticello with no hint of the name of the benefactor.[1] On a visit to Monticello that summer, Jefferson's fourteen-year-old granddaughter, Anne Cary Randolph, was shown the walking stick by some workmen there, who told her that it was a gift from Napoleon. She dutifully passed this "fact" on to her grandfather:

They showed me a cane which they said Buonaparte sent you. It is a very handsome one but I hope you never will have ocassion for it. It is made of fish bone I believe as it is too long to have been the horn of any animal, although it has that appearance. It is capped and pointed with gold very handsomely embost.[2]

It was not until February the following year that Jefferson learned that the walking stick had been the gift of John F. Oliveira Fernandes, a Norfolk physician and wine merchant from whom Jefferson purchased wine for Monticello. Jefferson considered it

the most elegant thing of the kind I have ever seen; and worthy of place, as a curiosity, in any Cabinet whatever. I perceive that it is of the horn of some animal, but cannot conjecture of what.[3]

Fernandes told Jefferson that the cane was in thanks for his "bounty and generosity":[4]

It was my hope that your Love of Natural Philosophy would render so rare a production of the Animal Kingdom acceptable to you, While it might be an usefull companion in your retired and rural excursions at Monticello.[5]

Jefferson bequeathed this walking stick to his friend James Madison, who expressed his appreciation for the gift in a letter to Jefferson's grandson Thomas Jefferson Randolph:

The article bequeathed to me by your grandfather . . . [I] received with all the feelings due to such a token of the place I held in the friendship of one, whom I so much revered and loved when living and whose memory can never cease to be dear to me.[6]

Madison, in turn, bequeathed the stick to Thomas Jefferson Randolph.[7]

[1986-13-3]   A . M . L .

In 1809, the young Virginia congressman Joseph Cabell presented this walking stick (engraved "TJ," "Joseph C. Cabell to his friend Christmas 1809") to Jefferson, who had just recently retired from the presidency. Jefferson was first introduced to this fellow Virginian by the Philadelphia physician and botanist Benjamin Smith Barton (Cat. 70). Barton sent Cabell to meet Jefferson at the President's House in June 1806, bearing a generous letter of introduction, in which he called him "a young Virginian of uncommon merit."[8] Like Jefferson, Cabell graduated from the College of William and Mary and then studied law. He spent over three years in Europe, where he met many of Jefferson's friends, including Thaddeus Kosciuszko (Cat. 38), Robert Fulton (Cat. 41), and the comte de Volney.[9]

Cabell entered the Virginia Senate in 1810. Within a few years he became the "main

276

WHALEBONE AND IVORY WALKING STICK

c. 1809

whalebone, ivory, gold
92.7 (36½ in.)

PROVENANCE:
Thomas Jefferson; by gift or purchase to an unidentified person; by gift or purchase to The Hon. Breckenridge Long; by gift to TJMF in 1955.

pillar of support" for Jefferson's plan for a state system of elementary, intermediate, and higher education.[10] Jefferson described his plan to Cabell as

culling from every condition of our people the natural aristocracy of talents and virtue, and of preparing it by education, at the public expense, for the care of the public concerns.[11]

Most importantly, Jefferson relied on Cabell to generate support in the Virginia legislature for funding a school that he hoped to begin in Albemarle County. First named the Albemarle Academy, then Central College, this school became the University of Virginia after years of negotiations led by Cabell and Jefferson.

In his last letter to Cabell, in April 1826, Jefferson wrote:

We have now 166 students; and, on the opening of the law school, we expect to have all our dormitories filled. Order and industry nearly complete, and sensibly improving every day.[12]

Cabell continued to shape the young university after Jefferson's death. He was a member of the Board of Visitors from its inception in 1816 until 1856, and also held the position of rector from 1834 to 1836, and again in 1845 until his death in 1856.[13]

[1955-74]   A . M . L .

(clockwise from upper left): silver spectacle case, c. 1798; tinted spectacles, 1790–1820; sets of spectacle lenses in paper wrappers, 1806 and 1808; spectacles, 1806, designed by Thomas Jefferson and made by John McAllister, Sr. in Philadelphia.

In 1819, Jefferson remarked in a letter that "a stiff wrist, the consequence of an earlier dislocation, makes writing both slow and painful."[14] In Paris in 1786, he had fallen and dislocated his right wrist.[15] The injury took many months to heal, and in later years, pain and stiffness in the joint returned to trouble him. A fall from the steps to one of Monticello's terraces in 1822 resulted in a broken bone or dislocation in his other wrist, which further disabled him.[16] He wrote to Robert Mills in March 1826:

My own health is quite broken down. For the last 10 mo. I have been mostly confined to the house. . . . The dislo[catio]n of both my wrists has so far injured the use of my hands that I can write but slowly & laboriously.[17]

Feeling obligated to carry on much correspondence, Jefferson sought devices to ease his pain and make the many hours spent at his writing table more comfortable. About ten years before the injury to his left arm occurred, he apparently acquired two small lead dumbbells and used them to strengthen and exercise his right wrist. The crude lead forms were probably made at Monticello. Both are marked in block letters, "THOMAS JEFFER-SON" on the end. One also has "DUMBELL" around the edge, and "1812 MONTICELLO VA." on the opposite end.

Accompanying the dumbbell is a one-inch-wide leather strap fastened with a large brass button. Its presumed purpose was to give extra support to Jefferson's wrist. The red woolen and linen cushion has three pairs of loops on the bottom by which it could be securely tied to the arm of a chair. Perhaps fastened to the writing arm of the revolving Windsor chair (Cat. 127) where he often worked, it provided a comfortable rest for his arm. [1961-37-22; 1927-57; 1983-14-34]
S.M.O.

277
DUMBBELL ONE OF A PAIR

1812

America, probably Monticello
lead
L: 8.9 (3½ in.); D: 6.7 (2⅝
in.); Wt: 4 lb. 5 oz.
Mrs. Martina Graham Creger
and Thomas Jefferson Memorial
Foundation

278
WRIST STRAP

c. 1812

America, probably Monticello
leather, brass
L: 19.1 (7½ in.); W: 2.5 (1 in.)

279
WRIST CUSHION

c. 1812

America, probably Monticello
wool, linen
3.8 × 24.1 × 12.1
(1½ × 9½ × 4¾ in.)

PROVENANCE:
DUMBBELLS: Thomas Jefferson; by descent to Virginia and Nicholas Trist; by descent to Harry Randolph Burke; ONE DUMBBELL (illustrated) by descent to Gordon Trist Burke; by purchase to TJMF in 1968; SECOND DUMBBELL by descent to Mrs. Martina Graham Creger. STRAP: Thomas Jefferson; by descent to Thomas Jefferson Randolph; by descent to Agnes Dillon Randolph; by gift to TJMF in 1927. CUSHION: Thomas Jefferson; by descent to Thomas Jefferson Randolph; by descent to Margaret Randolph Taylor and Olivia Alexander Taylor; by purchase to TJMF in 1983.

POCKETKNIFE

1800–25

England, probably Sheffield
steel, wood
8.9 × 1.9 (3½ × ¾ in.)
National Museum of American
History, Smithsonian Institution

PROVENANCE:
Thomas Jefferson; by descent to
Ellen and Joseph Coolidge; by
descent to Harold Jefferson
Coolidge; by acquisition to the
National Museum of American
History, Smithsonian Institution;
by loan to TJMF since 1986.

(opposite) Inside Jefferson's
pockets (clockwise from upper
right): key ring and trunk key,
gold toothpick, goose quill
toothpick, pocket knife, ivory
rule, watch fob, steel pocket
scissors, and red-leather
pocketbook.

Jefferson recorded purchases of several knives in his Memorandum Books between 1767 and 1819, but it is not clear when this particular pocketknife with wooden sides and multiple blades was acquired. The handy device has twelve tools, including saw, file, drill, corkscrew, and knife blades. It is very similar to pocketknives illustrated in a patternbook of the predominant Sheffield cutlery manufacturers issued in 1816.[18]

This pocketknife and the others that Jefferson owned were no doubt often carried in his coat pocket. He recorded in his Memorandum Book in 1810, "Pd. Clasby [for] finding knife 1. [dollar]."[19]

[1986-15]   S.M.O.

APPENDICES

APPENDIX I

Memdm. of Carpenters tools belonging to Mr. Jefferson
James Dinsmore
April 15, 1809
Massachusetts Historical Society

15 pair hollows and rounds, and 1 plane for making spouts
1 pair <hollow & r> quarter rounds, 1 Do. [ditto] Snipe Bills
1 Do. side rabbitt planes—4 rabbitt planes & astragal
3 philasters. & one Spring plane—
4 pair Groveing [Grooving] planes & 1 Cut & thrust—
2 Plow planes & 9 plow bits
5 bead planes 9, ogees & 2 quarter rounds—
2 Sash ovolas [ovolos], 2 astragal Do.—
1 scotia & ovola & 1 ogee & ovola
1 raising plane. 2 pair Base and surbase planes—
1 architrave Do.—11 Cornice planes of different kinds
3 Straight & 3 Circular Smoothing planes—1 toothing do.
4 Sets of Bench planes—3 in each set & 1 double Iron jointer
3 try planes for Circular work, 3 steel blade squares—
1 bench vice 2 plated gages & 1 mortise do. 1 brace & 15 bits
2. pair pincers & 1 pair cutting plyers [pliers]—
2 Drawing knives 2 pair Compasses
4 Sockett chishels 4 mortise Do. & 13 firmer Do.
19 gouges, 2 rasps 4 files, 15 gimblets
3 pair hand screws, 3 iron screws for joining up work
6 augres: 3 hand saws 1 pannel do 1 table Do 1 tenor Do—
1 Sash Do. 1 dove tail Do 1 frame Do & 2 lock saws. 9 new plane irons
3 saw files 1 axe 1 adz 1 bevel 1 miter [illeg.] 1 turkey [s]et stone &c.

April 15th 1809   Jas. Dinsmore

planes borrowed by Jas. Dinsmore.
1 Tuscan Cornice plane
1 Sash astragal
1 ogee & quarter round
    Bot [bought]
1. Screw. worth 9/. by J Dinsmore £ 0.9
2 flooring Do. worth 4/[6 each?] by J Nelson [Neilson]
                Memdm. of Carpenters
                tools

APPENDIX II

Catalogue of Paintings &c. at Monticello
Thomas Jefferson
c. 1809–15
Thomas Jefferson Papers (#2958-b), Special Collections Department,
University of Virginia Library

Hall.

1. An Ecce homo. A bust of Jesus of about ⅔ the natural s[cale] on canvas. He is clothed with a robe of purple, and a crown of thor[ns] on his head. Copied from Guido.
2. A bust of St. Jerom [sic] in meditation, his head reclined on his right hand, and a book in his left. Of full size on Canvas. Copied from Goltzius.
3. Jesus driving the money changers out of the temple. 7. [fi]gures of full length, and about half the natural module. The su[b]ject Matthew 21.12. On Canvas. Copied from Valentin.

4. St. Peter weeping. His hands are pressed together, and nea[r] him the cock shews it was in the moment of Matthew 26.75 'and Peter remembered the words of Jesus, which said unto h[im] before the cock crow thou shalt deny me thrice. And he wen[t] out and wept bitterly.' A half-length figure of full size, on Canvas, copied from Carlo Lotti. Purchased from St. Severin collection. Catalogue No. 36.
5. John Baptist, a bust of the natural size. The right han[d] pointing to heaven, the left, deeply shaded, is scarcely s[een] pressing his breast, which is covered by his hair flowin[g] thickly over it. It is seen almost in full face, on canv[as] copied from Leonardo da Vinci.
6. Jesus among the Doctors and disputing with them. The subject Luk[e] 3.46. His right hand pointing to heaven, the left pressing his breas[t] the drapery blue and purple, the hair flowing loose. A half length figure of full size, seen in profile, on Canvas.
7. St. Joseph the husband of Mary, the mother of Je[su]s, a ¾ len[gth] of full size on Canvas. A book is laying open before him. [His] hands interlocked with energy, his head and eyes turned up to heaven, and his mouth open, as in the act of fervent prayer.
8. Jesus in the Praetorium, stripped of the purple, as yet naked, and with the crown of thorns on his head. He is sitting. A whole length figure of about 4. feet. The persons present seem to be one of his revilers, one of his followers, and the superintendant of the execution. The subject from Mark 15.16.-20. An original on wood, by M[albo]dius.
9. David with the head of Goliah, copied on canvas from Guido, who has given his own picture in the person of David. A whole length of 2.f.6.I.
10. The sacrifice of Isaac. He is placed on the pile, on his knees, his wrists bound, Abraham with his left hand grasping the back of his neck, a naked sworn [sword] in his right, uplifted and ready to strike the fatal stroke. In that instant an Angel hovering above him, stays his hand, and Abraham looks up with distraction to see by what power his his [sic] hand is witheld. In a bush on the right hand is seen the ram. The figures are whole length. That of Abraham on a scale of not quite half the natural size. On canvas, an original. The subject Gen. 22.
11. Jesus before Pilate. The subject Mark 27.27.28. On canvas, copied from Pordononi.
12. & 15. Two busts of Indian figures male and female by Indians in hard stone. 18 I. high. They were dug up at a place called Palmyra, on the Tennessee.
13. A bust of Turgot in plaister, by Houdon.
14. A bust of Voltaire in plaister, by Houdon.
16. A fac simile of the largest of the Pyramids of Egypt, called Cheops.
17. A Cleopatra in marble. see this corrected pa. 11. [p. 238 in this volume]
An Indian painting of a battle between the Panis and Osages, on a buffalo pelt.
An Indian map of the Southern waters of the Missouri, by a Ricara chief on a buffalo pelt.

Parlour. upper tier

18. Lord Bacon.   } Mr. Trumbul (the painter) procured these copies for
19. Sr. Isaac Newton   } Th.J. from originals in England.
20. John Locke   }
21. Doctr. Franklin. An original drawn for the Abbe Very by Greusz.
22. Herodiade bearing the head of St. John in a platter. A ¾ length of full size on canvas, copied from Simon Vouett, purchased from St. Severin's collection, Catal. No. 248. The subject Matt. 14.11. Mark 6.28.
23. Democritus and Heraclitus, or the laughing and weeping philosophers, the former smiling, the latter railing at the follies of mankind. The figures are ¾ lengths, larger than life, on canvas. An Original purchased from the collection of St. Severin. Catal. No. 215.
24. Christopher Columbus.   }
25. Americus Vesputius.   } Copied from Originals in the gallery of Medicis, for
26. Ferdinand Magellan   } Th.J.
27. Fernando Cortez.   }
28. Sr. Walter Raleigh. Copy from an Original of Holben.
29. La Fayette. Original done in 1789 for Th.J.
30. James Madison. An original by Pine. Taken in 1790.
[Number 31 is erased.]
32. John Adams. An original by Brown. Taken in London in 1785.
33. George Washington. An original by Wright. Taken in Philadā in 1784.
34. The Prodigal son. He is in rags, kneeling at the feet of his father, who extends his hands

to raise him. The mother and sister appear shocked at his condition, but the elder son views him with indignation. The figures of full size on Canvas. Purchased from St. Severin's collection. Catal. 306. An Original.

35. A Magdalen penitent, sitting, her hair dishevelled, her eyes looking up to heaven, a book in her right hand, and the left resting on a skull. A ¾ length of full size on Canvas, copied from Joseph de Ribera, called Espagnolet, purchased from St. Severin's collection. Catal. No. 59.

Middle tier.

36. A Transfiguration. Copied from Raphael. Whole length figures of 6.I. on Canvas. The subject Matt. 17.1-8. See 4. Manuel du Museum. Pl. 1.
37. The Baptism of Jesus by John. Figures whole length of 10. I. on wood, from Devoes. The subject Luke 3.21.22.
38. A Crucifixion. Whole length figure on wood. An original by Gerard Seggers. The moment is that of Luke 23.44.45.
39. Liberty. A print. Designed and engraved by Savage.
40. Daphne transformed into a laurel. Apollo is siesing her round the waist to bear her off; but her father, the river-god Peneus, who is present, transforms her, in that instant, into a laurel, the branches of which are seen shooting from her fingers. On the left are two female figures, struck with dismay; and above a Cupid flying off in consternation. The figures are whole length. That of Daphne of 12.I. on canvas. An Original. The subject is from Ovid's Metamorphosis L.1—tergoque fugaci Imminet: et crinem sparsum cervicibus afflat. Viribus assumptis expalluit illa: citaeque Victa labore fugae, spectans Peneïdas undas. Fer, pater, inquit, opem; si flumina numen habetis. Vix prece finitâ torpor gravis alligat artus: Mollia cinquntur tenui praecordia libro. In frondem crines, in ramos brachia crescunt.
41. Susanna and the elders. Three figures of about an eighth of the natural module. On Canvas, copied from Coypel.
42. Louis XVI. A print. A present from the king to Th.J.
43. Bonaparte. A print.
44. Castruccio Castracani. } copied from the originals in the gallery of Medicis, for Th.J.
45. Andrea Doria }
46. Hoche. A print.
47. David Rittenhouse. A print.
48. Jesus bearing his cross. A half length on wood. Scale about ⅖ of the life. Subject John 19.17.
49. Jephtha leading his daughter Seïla to be sacrificed. On one side is the altar and the high priest with the implements of sacrifice: on the other the mother, sisters, and by-standers weeping and holding the victim by the one hand, while Jephtha pulls her towards the altar by the other. There are 17. figures the principal of which is 16½ I. On Canvas. Copied from Coypel. The subject from Judges.11.

Lower tier.

50. The Prodigal son from West. Done on canva[s] in the manner called Polyplasiasmos, or the Polygraphic art.
51. A Descent on Copper. The Christ is of about 10.I. Behind him is the virgin weeping. On each side angels. It is copied from Vandyke by Diepenbec. See Rubens' management of the same subject 3. Manuel du Museum. 483.
52. A Descent from the cross on wood. A groupe of 5. figures. The body of Jesus is reclined on the ground, the head and shoulders supported in the lap of his mother, who with four others, women from Galilee, are weeping over him. The figures are whole lengths; the principal one 13.I. It is an original by Francis Floris.
53. The Cyclops forging thunderbolts. A groupe of 9 figures of about 8.I. on wood.
54. The surrender of York by Trumbul. It was the premiere ebauche of his print on that subject. On canvas.
55. The Medals given by the revolutionary Congress to the officers who distinguished themselves on particular occasions. To wit Genl. Washington, Gates, Stewart, Wayne, De Fleury, Paul Jones, Colo. Washington, Morgan, Howard, Greene & [space] tin proofs.
56. Zenobia. A print.
57. Hector and Andromache, in water colours. An original by West. The scene is their meeting in Homer 6.494. &c. given by West to Genl. Kosciuzko [*sic*], and by him to Th.J.
58. Kosciuzko. A print.
59. Thomas Paine. An original on wood by Trumbul.
60. Count Rumford. A print.
61. Two inedited birds of Virginia and the Snow sparrow. } watercolors by Wilson
62. The Singing birds of Virginia, the uppermost inedited. }
63. Volney. In pencil.
64. A Cutting in paper.
65. Bonaparte a bust in Marble.
66. Alexander of Russia. A bust in Plaister.

No. 17. corrected. Ariadne reclined on the ro[ck]s of Naxos, where Theseus had just abandoned her. She is represented asleep, as in the moment when Bacchus discovers and becomes enamoured of her. Her tunic is half loosed, her veil negligently thrown over her head. The disorder of the drapery in which she is wrapped manifests the anguish which had preceded this moment of calm. On the upper part of her left arm is a bracelet in the form of the small serpent called Ophis: this bracelet, taken for an asp, long occasioned the belief that this figure represented Cleopatra procuring death by the bite of this reptile.

This statue was placed by Julius II. in the Belvedere of the Vatican, of which it was, for three centuries, the principal ornament. See Notice de la Galerie des Antiques du Musée Napoleon. No. 60.

Dining room. upper tier.

67. A sleeping Venus in plaister. small.
68. Diogenes in the market of Athens. Laertius in the life of this philosopher tells us that appearing in a public place in mid-day with a lanthern in his hand he was asked by the crowd what he was doing? He answered that he was seeking if he could find a man. This anecdote is the subject of this piece. It is a groupe of 6. figures, half lengths, of full size on canvas. Copied from Rubens. See 3. Manuel du Museum. 495.
69. The Sacrifice at Lystra, by the Priest of Jupiter to Paul and Barnabas, on canvas, copied from Le Sueur. See Acts of the Apostles. 14.8.-13.
70. An Accusation, a groupe of 9. figures of about ⅓ the natural height. It is an original on canvas, known to be by Solimeni, but the subject not certainly known. It is believed however to be taken from Ecclesiastical history, and to be the story of a young woman accusing a young man of violence committed on her, before a bishop, who is sitting in judgment on him and raises a person from the dead to be a witness.
71. Diogenes, visited by Alexander. An Original on canvas. Being desired by Alexander to ask from him whatever he chose he answered 'stand out of my light.' Laertius VI.38.
72. An Ascension of St. Paul into the third heaven. From Dominiquin. On canvas. The original is in the collection of the king of France. The principal figure is 22.I. The head is inspired. The Saint sees the heavens open, and expands his arms towards the glorious light he sees. He is supported by angels. The groupe is no longer ascending, but in a state of rest to give him time to contemplate the scene. see 2. Manuel. 778.
73. The holy family copied from Raphael on canvas. The figures are whole lengths, the Virgin and infant Jesus, Joseph, Elizabeth and the infant John and 2. angels. See the 4. Manuel du Museum. Pl.3.
74. A crucifixion. The instant siesed is that of the expiration, when the sun is darkened, the temple rent, the atmosphere kindled with lightning, the tombs open and yield their dead. On one side is the Centurion, struck with awe, and seeming to say 'verily, this was a righteous man.' On the other the two Marys, one of them her hair bristled with fear, the other in adoration. The subject is taken from Matt.27.51.52 and Luke 23.45. The figures are whole lengths, the largest of 16.I. copied on canvas from Vandyke. <see>
75. A Flagellation of Christ, a groupe of 10. figures, the principal of which is 21. I. He is bound to a post, two souldiers whipping him with bundles of rods, and a third binding up another bundle. On the right are the Superintendants and Spectators. The subject. Matt. 27.26. It is copied on wood from Devoes. See the same subject treated very similarly by Rubens. 3. Manuel du Musee. 501.
76. A Marketpiece on canvas, to wit, fruit, vegetables, game &c.

Lower tier

77. Vandernoot. A print.
78. Washington. A print from a drawing by Made de Brehan.
79. New Orleans a print.
80. Colebrook-dale bridge. A print.
81. The Natural bridge of Virginia on Canvas by Mr. Roberts.
82. The passage of the Patomak through the Blue ridge. do.
83. A distant view of the falls of Niagara from the Indian ladder.

84. A view of the falls of Niagara from the table rock. Both of these are prints from designs of Vanderlin.
85. The President's house at Washington, in water colours by King.
86. Mount Vernon. A print from a design of Birch.
87. An elevation of the house at Monticello. By Mills.
88. The Diocletian Portico, a print [vice the Environs of N. Orleans].

The Tea-room.

Paul Jones.
Franklin.   } Busts in plaister by Houdon
Washington.   } size of the life.
Fayette.

Moncada. A print remarkeable for it's execution.
Le bon Odeur
Le bon Gout   } Models of fine execution with the pen.
Date obolum Belisario. A print from Rheberg at Rome.
Morgan's and Colo. Washington's medals. Tin proofs.
Infant America protected by Minerva from the lion. A medal designed by Dr. Franklin.
    Ld. Botetourt. A medallion in wax.
Franklin. A medal of bronze by Dupré.
Louis XVI. A medal. Tin-proof.
Genl. Gates. A miniature print.
The Entry of the King (Louis XVI.) into Paris. A medal bronz[e]
The Taking of the Bastile. A medal in bronze.
Dr. Barton. Franklin. Granger.
Rodney. Burwell. Gallatin.   } Miniatures.
Tiberius. A cast bronzed.
Capt. Lewis. Th.J. a print. Th.J. by Doolittle. Miniatures.
Nero. A cast bronzed.
Genl. Clinton. Nicholson. Madison. Miniatures.
Otho. A cast bronzed.
J.W. Eppes. Dickerson. Dearborne. Miniatures.
Vespatian. A cast bronzed.
Pius VII. Gouvr. Morris. Washington by [blank space] at Paris,
                                            from Houdon's bust.

APPENDIX III

A list of the taxable property of the subscriber
in Albemarle Mar. 1815 [rates deleted]
Thomas Jefferson
Massachusetts Historical Society

5640. acres of land (including 400. a. on Hardware held jointly with Hudson and others).
  90. slaves of or above the age of 12 years
  12. do. [ditto] of 9. and under 12. years of age
  73. head of cattle
  27. horses, mares, mules and colts
   1 Ice house
   1. gigg and harness
   1. 4-wheeled carriage (Landau) House
   4 clocks
   1. Bureau or Secretary. mahogany
   2. book cases   do.
   4. chests of drawers   do.
   1. Side board with doors & drawers. mahogany
   8. separate parts of Dining table   do.
  13. tea and card tables   do.
   6. Sophas with gold leaf
  36. Chairs. mahogany
  44. do. gold leaf
  11. pr. window curtains. foreign.
  16. portraits in oil.
   1. do. Crayon.

64. picture, prints and engravings with frames more than 12.I.
39. do. under 12. I. with gilt frames
 3. looking glasses 5.f. long.
 3. do. 4.f. and not 5.f.
 1. do. 3.f. and not 4f.
 2. do 2f. and not 3.f.
 1. harpsichord
 2. silver watches
 2. silver coffee pots
 3. plated urns and coffee pots
13. plated candlesticks
 4. cut glass decanters
10. silver cups
 1. manufacturing mill renting at 1280.D. @ 2¾ p.c.
 1. toll grist mill
 1. saw-mill

APPENDIX IV

Untitled list of silverware from Martha Jefferson Randolph's
"Housewife," or pocket notebook
c. 1823
Thomas Jefferson Memorial Foundation

20 french spoon   } table
12 english   } table
18 dessert spoons
 2 soup Ladles
 2 small dit [ditto]
24 silver forks
 2 twisted handle teaspoons
10 french
 6 plain dit
 4 vegetable dishes with cov.
 4 flat dit
 1 pudding dish
 1 chocolate pot
 1 cream dit
 1 coffee urn
 1 waiter
 8 becars
 2 goblets

APPENDIX V

Inventory of the furniture in the house at Monticello
[Martha Jefferson Randolph?]
c. 1826
Massachusetts Historical Society

Hall

2 small marble tables
1 mahogany dit. [ditto]
28 black painted chairs
1 concave mirror
1 old broken globe
8 maps. (1) Europe, (2) Asia, (3) Africa, (4) South America, (5) Map of the world, (6.)
    United States, (7. & 8.) 2 of Virginia. these maps we should like to have for the school,
    and particularly the map of South America. lamps and marble bracket fixed to the
    wall.

Drawing room

1 large marble table
1 sofa and cushion

14 Mahogany chairs
2 Campeachy ditto
2 plated branch candlesticks
2 dit not branched.
The Mirrors and lamps are fixed to the wall.

Dining room

Mahogany sideboard
1 round marble table
1 oblong marble table
Mahogany Dining tables in 7 pieces.
1 very small round mahogany table
1 dumb waiter
12 leather bottomed chairs
1 small arm chair.
carpet.
1 pr brass andirons
clock
2 green painted lamps
4 plated candlesticks

Tea Room

Brescia table
Mahogany card table
2 sofas and cushions
9 Mahogany chairs

Octagon room Downstairs

1 Pembroke table
1 painted toilet table
8 rush bottomed chairs
1 pr brass andirons   Mirrors fixed to the wall.

Square room downstairs

1 Pembroke table
1 black walnut stand
2 old Mahogany chairs
2 black framed mirrors.
1 pair brass andirons.

Passage

1 painted table

Sitting room

7 old Mahogany chairs given by Mr. Wythe.
1 old sofa
1 pr brass andirons

Storeroom
Kitchen Furniture

3 iron pots*	1 bread toaster
2 pr pothooks	4 bread moulds
1 iron ladle	1 coffee mill
1 skimmer	1 coffee toaster
1 spit & spit rack	1 pr kitchen andirons
1 cleaver	1 pr tongs
1 knife	1 shovel
1 flesh fork	6 copper saucepans
1 tin roaster (for meat)	2 fish kettles
1 frying pan.	1 pestle & mortar
3 dutch ovens	1 ice cream freezer
2 skillets	1 ice cream ladle
2 hoes	1 tin coffee pott
1 grid iron	3 pewter dishes
2 waffle irons	37 patty pans
*Edy has one of these	& some old worn out copper moulds

Dairy Utensils

7 tin pans	2 wooden spoons	1 stone churn
3 butter prints	1 wooden churn	1 broken set of candle moulds

---

10 plated candlesticks	2 old plated salt cellars
6 brass do. [ditto]	1 old plate urn
2 japan do.	1 Japan do.
2 pr. snuffers	1 wedgewood teapot
4 plated coolers	1 wedgewood sugar dish
1 leaden fountain basin	9 pink & white coffee cups
one part of this fountain	8 saucers belonging to them
is in the cellar	7 french china coffee cups
9 water plates	6 saucers belonging to them
10 dishes for holding hot sand	12 china teacups
2 old waters	13 saucers belonging to them
2 old knife boxes	13 tumblers
4 plaited sliders with	17 wine glasses
mahogany bottoms	12 decanters 6 of them
2 coasters 1 mahogany, 1 japan	a little broken
1 plated bread basket	21 cut & 3 plain jelly
2 sets of casters with cruets	glasses
1 plated fish knife	1 glass finger bowl
2 plated cream pots	3 glass shades for candles
8 old plaited beakers	2 glass lanterns
	1 large square case bottle
1 demijohn	3 liverpool dishes smaller
1 refrigerator	8 middle sized dishes
12 stone pots	6 do different from all the
	others
1 funnel	5 small dishes
1 qt measure	1 liverpool dish smallest size
1 gill measure	26 dishes in all
1 patent balance & weights	1 salad bowl
1 pr scales & weights	1 sauce boat & ladle
1 small tin bucket	2 sauce boat dishes
1 bread rasp	3 pickle dishes
1 hammer	2 fish dishes
2 sleighs	12 custard cups
1 sizing brush	3 doz & 1 dinner plates
3 boxes of glass	22 breakfast plates
1 box of tin	30 deep plates
1 broken Mahogany table	7 butter plates
1 painted wood do.	5 vegetable dish tops
1 wooden do. not painted	2 brown & white pitchers
6 bottles of anchovies	
tin canisters	

blue liverpool

3 tureens & 1 tureen dish
1 very large dish
1 do smaller
1 large China dish

Passage

1 painted toilet table.   1 small Mahog. reading stand

Square room up stairs on the south side of the house.
11 feather beds
10 matrasses   several of the beds are on the alcove.
7 straw bed covers several of them filled
1 small child's matras

1 small childs bolster, hair

12 bolsters

14 pillows

16 woolen blankets on the alcove

4 cotton do. 3 on the alcove 1 on the floor under the beds.

10 chintz and calico counterpanes.

7 checked blue and white counterpanes ⎫
4 white knotted cotton do. ⎪
2 white homespun do. ⎬ In the alcove
2 dimity do. ⎪
     25 in all ⎭

18 pillow cases. folded up and lying on the pillows

8 pr and 1 cotton sheets ⎫
6 pr linen dit. old and new. ⎬ on the couch
1 pr old osnaburgs sheets. ⎭

6 sets of curtains and the draperies to 2 windows. ⎫
   3 curtains for the lower parts of the windows ⎬ on the couch

5 table cloths. linen and cotton. on the table.

8 toilet covers of one shape ⎫
6 dit. of another shape ⎬ on the table

12 damask napkins   on the table

12 basins

9 ewers

4 looking glasses

3 shovels

8 pr tongs

1 couch and cushion

1 Pembroke table.

Octagon room up stairs on the south side.

1 chest of drawers

1 Pembroke table

2 black walnut stands

1 pr iron andirons

Double room

1 painted toilet table.   4 Mahogany chairs

Long passage
Mat of the Dining room floor

Dome

Truckle bedstead	1 Mahogany chair
3 painted toilet tables	3 stools
1 dumb waiter	Carding machine
1 couch and cushion	3 old screems [*sic*]

old maps and buffalo robes.

APPENDIX VI

Untitled inventory of silver written on a piece of paper pasted to the inside of the lid of a pine chest
in which the silver was stored
Martha Jefferson Randolph
c. 1833
Thomas Jefferson Memorial Foundation

Plate	Plated Ware.
4. round dishes	1 sugar dish stand.
4 vegetable dishes	1 lamp for spirits of wine
4 tops. 1 handle & a half lost.	1 pr snuffers
1 urn	
1 Ewer.	
1 waiter	
8 beakers	
4 salt cellars	
2 pudding dishes	
1 cream ewer	
2 soup ladles. 2 small ladles.	
16 tablespoons (french) (George has one)	
13 dit [ditto] English.	
24 forks (George has one)	
18 desert spoons	
11 teaspoons (several others broken)	
8 dit very thin. 2 pr. sugar tongs	
4 dit. dit [ditto] smallissimo.	
4 salt spoons, 1 broken.	

BIBLIOGRAPHY

Short List of Abbreviations

Published Sources

Antiques	*The Magazine Antiques*, New York
Bear	Bear, James A., ed. *Jefferson at Monticello*, containing "Memoirs of a Monticello Slave," as dictated to Charles Campbell by Isaac, and "Jefferson at Monticello: The Private Life of Thomas Jefferson," Rev. Hamilton Wilcox Pierson. Charlottesville: University Press of Virginia, 1967.
Bedini	Bedini, Silvio A. *Thomas Jefferson, Statesman of Science*. New York: Macmillan Publishing Co., 1990.
Bush	Bush, Alfred L. *The Life Portraits of Thomas Jefferson*. Charlottesville: University Press of Virginia, 1987.
Cappon	Cappon, Lester J., ed. *The Adams-Jefferson Letters*. 2 vols. Chapel Hill: University of North Carolina Press, 1959.
Cunningham	Cunningham, Noble E., Jr. *The Image of Thomas Jefferson in the Public Eye: Portraits for the People 1800–1809*. Charlottesville: University Press of Virginia, 1981.
DAB	Johnson, Allen, ed. *Dictionary of American Biography*. New York: Charles Scribner's Sons, 1964.
Domestic Life	Randolph, Sarah N. *The Domestic Life of Thomas Jefferson, Compiled from Family Letters and Reminiscences by His Great-Granddaughter*. 1871. Reprint. Charlottesville: University Press of Virginia, 1985.
Family Letters	Betts, Edwin M., and James A. Bear, Jr., eds. *The Family Letters of Thomas Jefferson*. Charlottesville: University Press of Virginia, 1966.
Ford	Ford, Paul Leicester, ed. *The Writings of Thomas Jefferson*. 12 vols. New York: G. P. Putnam's Sons, 1904–1905.
Greene	Greene, John C. *American Science in the Age of Jefferson*. Ames: Iowa State University Press, 1984.
Jackson	Jackson, Donald, ed. *Letters of the Lewis and Clark Expedition*. 2nd ed. 2 vols. Chicago: University of Illinois Press, 1978.
L and B	Bergh, Albert Ellery, ed. *The Writings of Thomas Jefferson*. 20 vols. Washington, D.C.: Thomas Jefferson Memorial Association, 1907. Andrew A. Lipscomb was co-editor of the first edition, 1903–1904.
Malone	Malone, Dumas. *Jefferson and His Time*. 6 vols. Boston: Little, Brown and Co., 1948–1981.
	1. *Jefferson the Virginian*
	2. *Jefferson and the Rights of Man*
	3. *Jefferson and the Ordeal of Liberty*
	4. *Jefferson the President: First Term, 1801–1805*
	5. *Jefferson the President: Second Term, 1805–1809*
	6. *The Sage of Monticello*
MB	Bear, James A., Jr., and Lucia C. Stanton, eds. *Jefferson's Memorandum Books: Accounts, with Legal Records and Miscellany, 1767–1826*. Princeton, NJ: Princeton University Press, forthcoming.
Notes	Jefferson, Thomas. *Notes on the State of Virginia*. London, 1787. Reprint with notes edited by William Peden. Chapel Hill: University of North Carolina Press, 1955.
Papers	Boyd, Julian, et al., eds. *The Papers of Thomas Jefferson*. 23 vols. in 1992. Princeton, NJ: Princeton University Press, 1950–.
Paris	Rice, Howard C., Jr. *Thomas Jefferson's Paris*. Princeton, NJ: Princeton University Press, 1976.
Randall	Randall, Henry S. *The Life of Thomas Jefferson*. 3 vols. New York: Derby and Jackson, 1858.
Smith	Smith, Margaret Bayard. *The First Forty Years of Washington Society*. Edited by Gaillard Hunt. 1906. Reprint. New York: Frederick Ungar Publishing Co., 1965.
Sowerby	Sowerby, E. Millicent, comp. *Catalogue of the Library of Thomas Jefferson*. 5 vols. Charlottesville: University Press of Virginia, 1983.
Visitors	Peterson, Merrill D., ed., *Visitors to Monticello*. Charlottesville: University Press of Virginia, 1989.

Manuscript Sources

Catalogue	Thomas Jefferson, "Catalogue of Paintings &c. at Monticello," [c. 1809–1815]. Private collection.
1815 Tax List	Thomas Jefferson, "A list of the taxable property of the subscriber in Albemarle Mar. 1815." MHi.
1826 Inventory	[Martha Jefferson Randolph?], "Inventory of the furniture in the house at Monticello." MHi.
1790 Packing	Grevin packing list, 17 July 1790. Short Papers, DLC.

Manuscript Collections

Unless otherwise noted, all citations refer to the Jefferson Papers in each repository.

CSmH	Henry E. Huntington Library, San Marino, CA
CtY	Yale University Library, New Haven, CT
DLC	Library of Congress, Washington, D.C.
MHi	Massachusetts Historical Society, Boston
MoSHi	Missouri State Historical Society, St. Louis
NcU	University of North Carolina, Chapel Hill
NHi	New-York Historical Society, New York
NjHi	New Jersey Historical Society, Newark
NNP	The Pierpont Morgan Library, New York
PHi	Historical Society of Pennsylvania, Philadelphia
PPAP	American Philosophical Society, Philadelphia, PA
ScHi	South Carolina Historical Society, Charleston
Vi	Virginia State Library, Richmond
ViMo	Thomas Jefferson Memorial Foundation (Monticello), Charlottesville
ViU	Alderman Library, University of Virginia, Charlottesville. See Douglas W. Tanner, ed. *Guide to the Microfilm Edition of the Jefferson Papers of the University of Virginia 1732–1828*. Charlottesville: University of Virginia Library, 1977.
ViWC	Colonial Williamsburg, VA

Published Works

Ackerman, James S. *The Villa: Form and Ideology of Country Houses*. Princeton, NJ: Princeton University Press, 1990.

Adams, Abigail. *Letters of Mrs. Adams, the Wife of John Adams*. 2d. ed. 2 vols. Boston: C. C. Little and J. Brown, 1840.

Adams, William Howard. *Jefferson's Monticello*. NY: Abbeville Press, 1983.

Adams, William Howard, ed. *The Eye of Thomas Jefferson*. Charlottesville: University Press of Virginia, 1976.

———. *Jefferson and the Arts: An Extended View*. Washington, D.C.: National Gallery of Art, 1976.

Arnason, H. H. *The Sculptures of Houdon*. NY: Oxford University Press, 1975.

Bedini, Silvio A. *Declaration of Independence Desk: Relic of Revolution*. Washington, D.C.: Smithsonian Institution Press, 1981.

———. *Thomas Jefferson and American Vertebrate Paleontology*. Virginia Division of Mineral Resources, Publication 61. Charlottesville, Department of Mines, Minerals and Energy, 1985.

———. *Thomas Jefferson and His Copying Machines*. Charlottesville: University Press of Virginia, 1984.

Belden, Louise Conway. *The Festive Tradition: Table Decoration and Desserts in America, 1650–1900*. NY: W. W. Norton & Company, 1983.

Betts, Edwin M., and Hazlehurst Perkins. *Thomas Jefferson's Flower Garden at Monticello*. 3rd ed. Rev. and enl. by Peter J. Hatch. Charlottesville: University Press of Virginia, 1986.

Betts, Edwin M., ed. *Thomas Jefferson's Garden Book*. Philadelphia: The American Philosophical Society, 1944.

———. *Thomas Jefferson's Farm Book*. Princeton, NJ: Princeton University Press, 1953.

Bradbury, Frederick. *History of Old Sheffield Plate*. London: Macmillan and Co., Ltd., 1912.

Brownell, Charles, and Jeffrey A. Cohen. *The Architectural Drawings of Benjamin Henry Latrobe*. The Papers of Benjamin Henry Latrobe, Series 2. New Haven, CT: Yale University Press, forthcoming.

Brownell, Charles, et al. *The Making of Virginia Architecture*. Richmond: Virginia Museum of Fine Arts, 1992.

Bryan, John M., ed. *Robert Mills, Architect*. Washington, D.C.: American Institute of Architects Press, 1989.

Bullock, Helen Duprey. *My Head and My Heart: A Little History of Thomas Jefferson and Maria Cosway*. NY: G. P. Putnam's Sons, 1945.

Burroughs, Raymond D. *The Natural History of the Lewis and Clark Expedition*. East Lansing: Michigan State University Press, 1961.

Chastellux, Marquis de. *Travels in North America in the Years 1780, 1781, and 1782*. Translated and edited by Howard C. Rice, Jr. 2 vols. Chapel Hill: University of North Carolina Press, 1963.

Chinard, Gilbert. *Thomas Jefferson: The Apostle of Americanism*. Boston: Little, Brown and Company, 1929.

Chinard, Gilbert, ed. *The Letters of Lafayette and Jefferson*. Baltimore: The Johns Hopkins Press, 1929.

Comstock, Helen. *American Furniture*. Exton, PA: Schiffer Publishing Ltd., 1962.

Cooper, Helen A. *John Trumbull: The Hand and Spirit of a Painter*. New Haven, CT: Yale University Press, 1982.

Cripe, Helen. *Thomas Jefferson and Music*. Charlottesville: University Press of Virginia, 1974.

Crone, G. R. *Maps and Their Makers: An Introduction to the History of Cartography*. London: Hutchinson, 1986.

Cunningham, Nobel E., Jr. *In Pursuit of Reason: The Life of Thomas Jefferson*. Baton Rouge: Louisiana State University Press, 1987.

————. *Popular Images of the Presidency from Washington to Lincoln*. Columbia, MO: University of Missouri Press, 1991.

Cutright, Paul Russell. *Lewis and Clark: Pioneering Naturalists*. Urbana: University of Illinois Press, 1969.

Cutten, George Barton. *The Silversmiths of Virginia*. Richmond, VA: Dietze Press, Inc., 1952.

de Guillebon, Plinval. *Porcelain of Paris 1770–1850*. Translated by Robin R. Charleston. NY: Walker and Company, 1972.

de Longpré, Hayot. "Catalogue d'une belle Collection de tableaux . . . du Cabinet du Sieur Dupille de Saint-Severin." Paris: Imprimerie de Clousier, 1785.

de Reyniès, Nicole. *Le mobilier domestique: vocabulaire typologique*. 2 vols. Paris: Imprimerie Nationale, 1987.

de Salverte, Comte François. *Les ébénistes du XVIII siècle: leurs oeuvres et leurs marques*. Paris: F. De Nobele, 1985.

de Treville, Lawrence R., Sr., ed. *Jefferson and Wine*. The Plains, VA: Vinifera Wine Growers Association, 1976.

Dumbauld, Edward. *Thomas Jefferson, American Tourist*. Norman: University of Oklahoma Press, 1946.

Dumonthier, Ernest. *Les Sièges de Georges Jacob*. Paris: Éditions Albert Morancé, 1922.

Fede, Helen Maggs. *Washington Furniture at Mount Vernon*. Mount Vernon, VA: The Mount Vernon Ladies Association, 1966.

Flanigan, J. Michael. *American Furniture from the Kaufman Collection*. Washington, D.C.: National Gallery of Art, 1986.

Foley, John P., ed. *The Jefferson Cyclopedia*. NY: Funk & Wagnalls Company, 1900.

Foster, Sir Augustus John. *Jeffersonian America: Notes on the United States of America Collected in the Years 1805–6–7 and 11–12*. Edited by Richard Beale Davis. San Marino, CA: Huntington Library, 1954.

Fowble, E. McSherry. *Two Centuries of Prints in America, 1680–1880: A Selective Catalogue of the Winterthur Museum Collection*. Charlottesville: University Press of Virginia, 1987.

Frégnac, Charles, ed. *Les Grands orfèvres de Louis XIII à Charles X*. Paris: Hachette, 1965.

Fried, Michael. *Absorption and Theatricality: Painting and Beholder in the Age of Diderot*. Berkeley and Los Angeles: University of California Press, 1980.

Gallagher, H. M. Pierce. *Robert Mills, Architect of the Washington Monument*. NY: Columbia University Press, 1935.

Garrett, Elisabeth D. *At Home: The American Family, 1750–1870*. NY: Harry N. Abrams, 1990.

Garrett, Wendell D. *Jefferson Redivivius*. Barre, MA: Barre Publishers, 1971.

Garvan, Beatrice B. *Federal Philadelphia 1785–1825*. Philadelphia: Philadelphia Museum of Art, 1987.

Gentle, Rupert, and Rachael Feild. *English Domestic Brass, 1680–1810, and the History of Its Origins*. NY: E. P. Dutton & Co., Inc., 1975.

Gilreath, James, and Douglas L. Wilson. *Thomas Jefferson's Library*. Washington, D.C.: Library of Congress, 1989.

Greene, John C. *American Science in the Age of Jefferson*. Ames: Iowa State University, 1984.

Gusler, Wallace B. *Furniture of Williamsburg and Eastern Virginia 1710–1790*. Richmond: Virginia Museum of Fine Arts, 1979.

Hambly, Maya. *Drawing Instruments 1580–1980*. London: Sotheby's Publications, 1988.

Harding, Jonathan P. *The Boston Athenaeum Collection: Pre–Twentieth Century American and European Painting and Sculpture*. Boston: The Boston Athenaeum, 1984.

Harris, Eileen. *British Architectural Books and Writers 1556–1785*. NY: Cambridge University Press, 1990.

Heckscher, Morrison H. *American Furniture in the Metropolitan Museum of Art*. Vol. 2, *Late Colonial Period: The Queen Anne and Chippendale Styles*. NY: Metropolitan Museum of Art and Random House, 1985.

Hepplewhite, George. *The Cabinet-Maker and Upholsterer's Guide*. 1794. Reprint. NY: Dover Publications, Inc., 1969.

Hodgson, Adam. *Letters from North America, Written during a Tour in the United States and Canada*. 2 vols. London: Hurst, Robinson & Co., 1824.

Hornor, William MacPherson, Jr. *Bluebook of Philadelphia Furniture*. Alexandria, VA: Highland House Publishers, 1935.

Hunt-Jones, Conover. *Dolley and the "great little Madison"*. Washington, D.C.: American Institute of Architects Foundation, 1977.

Jackson, Donald. *A Year at Monticello, 1795*. Golden, CO: Fulcrum, Inc., 1989.

Jaffe, Irma B. *John Trumbull: Patriot-Artist of the American Revolution*. Boston: New York Graphic Society, 1975.

————. *Trumbull: The Declaration of Independence*. NY: Viking Press, 1976.

Jefferson, Thomas. *The Jefferson Bible: the Life and Morals of Jesus of Nazareth*. Boston: Beacon Press, 1989.

Julian, R. W. *Medals of the United States Mint: The First Century, 1792–1892*. Edited by N. Neil Harris. El Cajon, CA: The Token and Medal Society, Inc., 1977.

Kane, Patricia E. *Three Hundred Years of American Seating Furniture: Chairs and Beds from the Mabel Brady Garvan and Other Collections at Yale University*. Boston: New York Graphic Society, 1976.

Kimball, Fiske. *The Capitol of Virginia: A Landmark of American Architecture*. Edited by Jon Kukla. Richmond: Virginia State Library and Archives, 1989.

————. *Thomas Jefferson, Architect*. New York: Da Capo Press, 1968.

Kimball, Marie. *Jefferson: The Road to Glory: 1743–1776*. New York: Coward-McCann, Inc. 1943.

————. *Jefferson: War and Peace: 1776–1784*. New York: Coward-McCann, Inc., 1947.

————. *Jefferson: The Scene of Europe: 1784–1789*. New York: Coward-McCann, Inc. 1950.

Latrobe, Benjamin H. *The Papers of Benjamin Henry Latrobe: Correspondence and Miscellaneous Papers*. Edited by John C. Van Horne and Lee W. Formwalt. 3 vols. New Haven, CT: Yale University Press, 1984–1988.

Latrobe, John H. B. *The Capitol and Washington at the Beginning of the Present Century*. 1881. Reprint. Woodbridge, CT: Research Publications, 1973. Microfilm.

Lehmann, Karl. *Thomas Jefferson, American Humanist*. NY: The Macmillan Company, 1947.

Lewis, Jan. *The Pursuit of Happiness: Family and Values in Jefferson's Virginia*. NY: Cambridge University Press, 1983.

Loubat, J. F. *The Medallic History of the United States of America: 1776–1876*. 1878. Reprint. New Milford, CT: N. Flayderman & Co., Inc., 1967.

Maddex, Diane, ed. *Master Builders: A Guide to Famous American Architects*. Washington, D.C.: Preservation Press, 1985.

Malone, Dumas. Introduction to *The Fry & Jefferson Map of Virginia and Maryland: Facsimiles of the 1754 and 1794 Printings*. Charlottesville: University Press of Virginia, 1966.

————. *The Story of the Declaration of Independence*. Bicentennial edition. NY: Oxford University Press, 1975.

Mayo, Bernard, ed. *Jefferson Himself*. NY: Houghton Mifflin Company, 1942; Charlottesville: University Press of Virginia, 1970.

McCormick, Thomas J. *Charles-Louis Clérisseau and the Genesis of Neo-Classicism*. NY: The Architectural History Foundation; Cambridge, MA: MIT Press, 1990.

McLaughlin, Jack. *Jefferson and Monticello: The Biography of a Builder*. NY: Henry Holt and Company, 1988.

Meuvret, Jean, and Claude Frégnac. *Les Ébénistes du XVIII siècle français*. Paris: Hachette, 1963.

Miller, Charles A. *Jefferson and Nature: An Interpretation*. Baltimore, MD: The Johns Hopkins University Press, 1988.

Miller, John Chester. *The Wolf by the Ears: Thomas Jefferson and Slavery*. 1977. Reprint. Charlottesville: The University Press of Virginia, 1991.

Mills, Robert. *Guide to the Capitol of the United States and to the National Executive Offices of the United States*. Washington, D.C.: J.C. Greer, 1854. Reprint. Woodbridge, CT: Research Publications, 1973. Microfilm.

Mitchell, Stewart, ed. *New Letters of Abigail Adams, 1788–1801*. 1947. Reprint. Westport, CT: Greenwood Press, 1973.

Mongan, Agnes. *Harvard Honors Lafayette*. Cambridge, MA: Fogg Art Museum, Harvard University, 1975.

Montgomery, Charles F. *American Furniture: The Federal Period in the Henry Francis du Pont Winterthur Museum*. NY: Bonanza Books, 1978.

Montgomery, Florence M. *Textiles in America, 1650–1870*. NY: W. W. Norton and Co., 1984.

Moss, Roger W. *Lighting for Historic Buildings*. Washington, D.C.: Preservation Press, 1988.

Moulton, Gary E., ed. *The Journals of the Lewis and Clark Expedition*. 7 vols. Lincoln: University of Nebraska Press, 1983–1992.

Mudge, Jean McClure. *Chinese Export Porcelain in North America*. NY: Clarkson N. Potter, 1986.

———. *Chinese Export Porcelain for the American Trade, 1785–1835*. 2d ed. Newark, NJ: University of Delaware Press, 1981.

Nichols, Frederick D. *Thomas Jefferson's Architectural Drawings*. 4th ed. Charlottesville, VA: Thomas Jefferson Memorial Foundation, 1978.

Nichols, Frederick D., and James A. Bear, Jr. *Monticello: A Guidebook*. Charlottesville, VA: Thomas Jefferson Memorial Foundation, 1967.

Norfleet, Fillmore. *Saint-Mémin in Virginia: Portraits and Biographies*. Richmond, VA: The Dietz Press, 1942.

O'Neal, William Bainter, comp. *Jefferson's Fine Arts Library*. Charlottesville: University Press of Virginia, 1976.

Oliver, Andrew. *The Portraits of John and Abigail Adams*. Cambridge, MA: Belknap Press of Harvard University Press, 1967.

Oliver, Andrew, Ann Millspaugh Huff, and Edward W. Hanson. *Portraits in the Massachusetts Historical Society*. Boston: Massachusetts Historical Society, 1988.

Padover, Saul K., ed. *Thomas Jefferson and the National Capitol*. Washington, D.C.: U.S. Government Printing Office, 1946.

Peale, Charles Willson. *The Selected Papers of Charles Willson Peale and his family*. Edited by Lillian B. Miller. 3 vols. in 4. New Haven, CT: Yale University Press, 1983–1991.

Peterson, Merrill D. *The Jefferson Image in the American Mind*. NY: Oxford University Press, 1962.

———. *Thomas Jefferson and the New Nation: A Biography*. NY: Oxford University Press, 1970.

Peterson, Merrill D., ed. *Thomas Jefferson: A Reference Biography*. NY: Charles Scribner's Sons, 1986.

———. *Thomas Jefferson: Writings*. NY: Library of America, 1984.

Poesch, Jessie. *The Art of the Old South*. NY: Knopf, 1983.

Prucha, Francis. *Indian Peace Medals in American History*. Lincoln: University of Nebraska Press, 1971.

Randolph, Mary. *Virginia House-Wife*. Edited by Karen Hess. 1824. Reprint. Columbia: University of South Carolina Press, 1984.

Rayner, B. L. *Life of Thomas Jefferson*. Boston: Lilly, Wait, Colman, & Holden, 1834.

Reaves, Wendy Wick, ed. *American Portrait Prints: Proceedings of the Tenth Annual American Print Conference*. Charlottesville: University Press of Virginia, 1979.

Rice, Howard C., Jr. *L'Hôtel de Langeac, Jefferson's Paris Residence, 1785–1789*. Paris: Chez Henri Lefebre; Charlottesville, VA: Thomas Jefferson Memorial Foundation, 1947.

Richardson, Edgar P., Brooke Hindle and Lillian B. Miller. *Charles Willson Peale and His World*. NY: Harry N. Abrams, 1983.

Richardson, Jonathan. *The Works, containing I. The Theory of Painting. II. Essay on the Art of Criticism, so far as it relates to painting. III. The Science of a Connoisseur*. London: B. White and Son, 1792.

Ristow, Walter W. *American Maps and Mapmakers: Commercial Cartography in the Nineteenth Century*. Detroit, MI: Wayne State University Press, 1985.

Royall, Anne. *Mrs. Royall's Southern Tour*. 3 vols. Washington, D.C., 1830–1831.

Ryan, William, and Desmond Guinness. *The White House: An Architectural History*. NY: McGraw-Hill Book Company, 1980.

Santore, Charles. *The Windsor Style in America: A Pictorial Study of the History and Regional Characteristics of the Most Popular Furniture Form of Eighteenth-Century America, 1730–1830*. Edited by Thomas M. Voss. Philadelphia: Running Press, 1981.

Savill, Rosalind. *The Wallace Collection Catalogue of Sèvres Porcelain*. 3 vols. London: The Trustees of the Wallace Collection, 1988.

Schwartz, Seymour, and Ralph Ehrenberg. *The Mapping of America*. NY: Harry N. Abrams, 1980.

Seale, William. *The President's House*. 2 vols. Washington, D.C.: White House Historical Association, 1986.

Sellers, Charles Coleman. *Benjamin Franklin in Portraiture*. New Haven: Yale University Press, 1962.

———. *Mr. Peale's Museum*. NY: W. W. Norton & Company, Inc., 1980.

Semmes, John E. *John H. B. Latrobe and His Times: 1803–1891*. Baltimore, MD: The Norman, Remington Co., 1917.

Shackleford, George Green, ed. *Collected Papers of the Monticello Association of Descendants of Thomas Jefferson*. Vol. 1. Princeton, NJ: Princeton University Press, 1965.

———. *Collected Papers of the Monticello Association of Descendants of Thomas Jefferson*. Vol. 2. Charlottesville, VA: Monticello Association, 1984.

Shadwell, Wendy. *American Printmaking: The First 150 Years*. NY: Museum of Graphic Art, 1969.

Sheraton, Thomas. *The Cabinet Dictionary*. 1803. Reprint. NY: Praeger, 1970.

———. *The Cabinet-maker's and Upholsterer's Drawing-book*. Edited by Charles F. Montgomery and Wilfred P. Cole. 1802. Reprint. NY: Praeger, 1970.

Sizer, Theodore, ed. *The Autobiography of Colonel John Trumbull, patriot-artist, 1756–1843*. New Haven, CT: Yale University Press, 1953.

Smith, Margaret Bayard. *A Winter in Washington; or Memoirs of the Seymour Family*. 3 vols. NY: E. Bliss and E. White, 1824.

Smith, William Loughton. *The Pretentions of Thomas Jefferson to Presidency Examined . . .* Philadelphia, 1796.

Spence, Joseph. *Polymetis: Or, an Enquiry concerning the agreement between the Works of the Roman Poets, and the Remains of the Antient Artists*. 1747. Reprint. NY: Garland Publishers, 1976.

Staley, Allen. *Benjamin West, American Painter at the English Court*. Baltimore, MD: Baltimore Museum of Art, 1989.

Swan, Mabel Munson. *The Athenaeum Gallery: 1827–1873*. Boston: Boston Athenaeum, 1940.

Swem, Earl G. *Maps Relating to Virginia*. 1914. Reprint. Richmond: Virginia State Library and Archives, 1989.

Ticknor, George. *Life, Letters, and Journals of George Ticknor*. 2 vols. Boston: James R. Osgood and Company, 1876.

Trumbull, John. *Autobiography, Reminiscences and Letters of John Trumbull*. NY: Wiley and Putnam, 1841.

Tucker, George. *Life of Thomas Jefferson, Third President of the United States*. 2 vols. London: C. Knight, 1837.

Verlet, Pierre. *French Furniture of the Eighteenth Century*. Translated by Penelope Hunter-Stiebel. Charlottesville: University Press of Virginia, 1991.

von Erffa, Helmut, and Allen Staley. *The Paintings of Benjamin West*. New Haven, CT: Yale University Press, 1986.

Webb, Daniel. *An Inquiry into the Beauties of Painting; and into the Merits of the most celebrated painters, ancient and modern*. London: R. and J. Dodsley, 1760.

Webster, Daniel. *The Papers of Daniel Webster: Correspondence*. 7 vols. Edited by Charles M. Wiltse and Harold D. Moser. Hanover, NH: University Press of New England, 1974–.

———. *The Private Correspondence of Daniel Webster*. Edited by Fletcher Webster. Boston: Little, Brown and Co., 1857.

Weidman, Gregory R. *Furniture in Maryland, 1740–1940*. Baltimore: Maryland Historical Society, 1984.

Weld, Isaac, Jr. *Travels through the States of North America and the provinces of Upper and Lower Canada, during the Years 1795, 1796, and 1797*. 2 vols. London: J. Stockdale, 1799.

Wick, Wendy C. *George Washington: An American Icon*. Washington, D.C.: Smithsonian Institution Traveling Exhibition Service and the National Portrait Gallery, 1982.

Wills, Garry. *Inventing America: Jefferson's Declaration of Independence*. Garden City, NY: Doubleday & Company, 1978.

Wilson, Douglas L. *Jefferson's Literary Commonplace Book*. Princeton, NJ: Princeton University Press, 1989.

Wilton-Ely, John. *Apollo of the Arts: Lord Burlington and his Circle*. Nottingham: Nottingham University Art Gallery, 1973.

Wister, Mrs. O. J., and Agnes Irwin, eds. *Worthy Women of Our First Century*. Philadelphia: Lippincott & Co., 1877.

Woods, Edgar. *Albemarle County in Virginia*. Charlottesville, VA: The Michie Company, 1901.

Unpublished Manuscripts

Bear, James A. "Curator's Annual Report." Charlottesville, VA: Thomas Jefferson Memorial Foundation, 1957–1982.

Cote, Richard C. "The Architectural Workmen of Thomas Jefferson in Virginia." Ph.D. diss., Boston University, 1986.

Granquist, Charles L., Jr. "Cabinetmaking at Monticello." Master's thesis, State University of New York College at Oneonta, 1977.

Kelso, William. "A Report on the Archaeological Excavations at Monticello, Charlottesville, Virginia, 1979–1981." Unpublished manuscript, Thomas Jefferson Memorial Foundation, 1982.

Trist, Mrs. Nicholas. "A Woman's Wilderness Journey from Philadelphia to New Orleans in 1783–84: The Diary of Mrs. Nicholas Trist." Unpublished transcription by George H. Waring, IV. Carbondale, IL, 1991.

Articles

Acomb, Evelyn M. "The Journal of Baron von Closen." *William and Mary Quarterly* 10 (April 1953): 196–236.

Alexander, Edward P. "Jefferson and Kosciuszko: Friends of Liberty and Man." *Pennsylvania Magazine of History and Biography* 92 (January 1968), 87–103.

Barton, Benjamin Smith. "A Letter to Chas. Peter Thunberg. A Botanical Description of the *Podophyllum Diphyllum*." *Transactions of the American Philosophical Society* 3 (1793): 334–347.

Batson, Barbara. "Virginia Landscapes by William Roberts." *Journal of Early Southern Decorative Arts* 10 (November 1984): 34–48.

Bear, James A., Jr. "Thomas Jefferson's Silver." *Antiques* 74 (September 1958), 233–236.

Bedini, Silvio A. "Thomas Jefferson Clock Designer." *Proceedings of the American Philosophical Society* 108 (June 1946): 163–180.

Betts, Edwin M. "Groundplans and Prints of the University of Virginia, 1822–1826." *Proceedings of the American Philosophical Society* 90 (May 1946): 81–90.

Bidwell, John. "American History in Image and Text." *Proceedings of the American Antiquarian Society* 98, pt. 2 (1989): 247–302.

Boyd, Julian P. "The Megalonyx, the Megatherium, and Thomas Jefferson's Lapse of Memory." *Proceedings of the American Philosophical Society* 102 (October 1958): 420–435.

———. "Th. J. and the Roman Askos of Nîmes." *Antiques* 104 (July 1973), 116–124.

Chambers, S. Allen. "Thomas Jefferson Takes his Granddaughters to Natural Bridge." *Lynch's Ferry* 1 (Fall 1988), 6–8.

Chinard, Gilbert. "Jefferson and the American Philosophical Society." *Proceedings of the American Philosophical Society* 87 (July 14, 1943): 263–276.

Coleman, William R. "Counting the Stone—A Census of the Stone Facsimiles of the Declaration of Independence." *Manuscripts* 42 (Spring 1991): 97–105.

Cometti, Elizabeth. "Maria Cosway's Rediscovered Miniature of Jefferson." *William and Mary Quarterly* 9 (April 1952): 152–155.

Cutright, Paul Russell. "Lewis and Clark Indian Peace Medals." *Missouri Historical Society Bulletin* 24 (January 1968): 160–167.

Daiker, Virginia. "The Capitol of Jefferson and Latrobe." *Library of Congress Quarterly* (Spring 1975): 25–32.

de Terra, Helmut. "Alexander von Humboldt's Correspondence with Jefferson, Madison and Gallatin." *Proceedings of the American Philosophical Society* 103 (December 1959): 783–806.

Ewers, John C. "'Chiefs from the Missouri and Mississippi' and Peale's Silhouettes of 1806." *Smithsonian Journal of History* 1 (Spring 1966): 1–26.

Fleming, E. McClung. "From Indian Princess to Greek Goddess: The American Image, 1783–1815." *Winterthur Portfolio III* (1967): 37–66.

Gillingam, Harold E. "An Historic Lamp Originally Owned by Thomas Jefferson." *Antiques* 13 (April 1928), 293–294.

Granquist, Charles L. "Thomas Jefferson's 'Whirligig' Chairs." *Antiques* 109 (May 1976), 1056–1060.

Hart, Charles Henry. "The life Portraits of Thomas Jefferson." *McClure's Magazine* 11 (May 1898), 47–55.

Hood, Graham. "Let Us Now Praise Famous Men—In Wax." *Colonial Williamsburg* (Summer 1990), 43–45.

Jefferson, Thomas. "A Memoir on the Discovery of Certain Bones of a Quadruped of the Clawed Kind in the Eastern Parts of Virginia." *Transactions of the American Philosophical Society* 4 (1799): 246–260.

Kane, Mary Givens. "James Westhall Ford." *Antiques* 70 (August 1956), 136–138.

Kimball, Fiske. "The Building of Bremo." *Virginia Magazine of History and Biography* 57 (January 1949): 3–13.

———. "Jefferson and Arts." *Proceedings of the American Philosophical Society* 87 (July 1943): 238–245.

———. "The Life Portraits of Thomas Jefferson and their Replicas." *Proceedings of the American Philosophical Society* 88 (December 1944): 497–534.

Kimball, Marie G. "The Original Furnishings of the White House, Part I." *Antiques* 15 (June 1929), 481–486.

Lancaster, Clay. "Jefferson's Architectural Indebtedness to Robert Morris." *Journal of the Society of Architectural Historians* 10 (March 1951): 3–10.

Lay, K. Edward. "Charlottesville's Architectural Legacy." *Magazine of Albemarle County History* 46 (May 1988): 29–95.

Meschutt, David. "The Adams-Jefferson Portrait Exchange." *American Art Journal* 14 (Spring 1982): 47–54.

———. "Gilbert Stuart's Portraits of Thomas Jefferson." *American Art Journal* 13 (Winter 1981): 2–16.

Messengale, Jean Montague. "A Franklin by Houdon Rediscovered." *Marsyas* 12 (1964/1965): 1–15.

Miles, Ellen. "Saint-Mémin's Portraits of American Indians, 1804–1807." *American Art Journal* 20 (1988): 2–23.

Montlezun, Baron de. *Voyage Fait dans les années 1816 et 1817, de New-Yorck: à la Novelle-Orleans . . .* , Edited and translated by L. G. Moffatt and J. M. Carrière. *Virginia Magazine of History and Biography* 53 (April 1945)/53 (July 1945). Reprint.

Radbill, Samuel X., ed. "The Autobiographical Ana of Robley Dunglison, M.D." *Transactions of the American Philosophical Society* n.s., 53 (1963): 1–212.

Radcliffe, Robert R. "Thomas Jefferson, Chessplayer." *Chess Life* 36 (April 1981), 24–28.

Rauschenberg, Bradford L. "William John Coffee, Sculptor-Painter: His Southern Experience." *Journal of Early Southern Decorative Arts* 4 (November 1978): 26–50.

Rice, Howard. "Jefferson's Gift of Fossils to the Museum of Natural History in Paris." *Proceedings of the American Philosophical Society* 95 (December 1951): 597–627.

———. "A 'New' Likeness of Thomas Jefferson." *The William and Mary Quarterly* 6 (January 1949): [84]–89.

———. "Saint-Mémin's Portrait of Jefferson." *Princeton University Library Chronicle* 20 (Summer 1959): 182–192.

Richard, Carl J. "A Dialogue with the Ancients: Thomas Jefferson and Classical Philosophy and History." *Journal of the Early Republic* 9 (Winter 1989): 431–455.

Simpson, George Gaylord. "The Beginnings of American Vertebrate Paleontology in North America." *Proceedings of the American Philosophical Society* 86 (September 1942): 130–188.

"Sir Augustus John Foster and 'The Wild Natives of the Woods.'" *William and Mary Quarterly* 9 (April 1952): 191–214.

Stein, Susan R. "Thomas Jefferson's Traveling Desks." *Antiques* 133 (May 1988), 1156–1159.

Verner, Coolie. "The Maps and Plates Appearing with the Several Editions of Mr. Jefferson's 'Notes on the State of Virginia.'" *Virginia Magazine of History and Biography* 59 (January 1951): 21–33.

Waddell, Gene. "The First Monticello." *Journal of the Society of Architectural Historians* 46 (March 1987): 5–29.

Wistar, Dr. Caspar. "A Description of the Bones deposited, by the President, in the Museum of the Society." *Transactions of the American Philosophical Society* 4 (1799): 526–531.

NOTES

The Worlds of Thomas Jefferson at Monticello

(pp. 11–12)

1. Marquis de Chastellux, *Travels in North America in the Years 1780, 1781, and 1782*, trans. Howard C. Rice, Jr. (Chapel Hill: University of North Carolina Press, 1963), 391.
2. See Merrill D. Peterson, ed., *Visitors to Monticello* (Charlottesville: University Press of Virginia, 1989) and James A. Bear, Jr. and Lucia C. Stanton, eds. *Jefferson's Memorandum Books: Accounts, with Legal Records and Miscellany, 1767–1826* (Princeton: Princeton University Press, forthcoming).

Setting the Stage (pp. 12–14)

1. John Wilton-Ely, *Apollo of the Arts: Lord Burlington and His Circle* (Nottingham: Nottingham University Art Gallery, 1973), 10.
2. Merrill D. Peterson, *Thomas Jefferson and the New Nation: A Biography* (New York: Oxford University Press, 1970), 47.
3. Carl J. Richard, "A Dialogue with the Ancients: Thomas Jefferson and Classical Philosophy and History," *Journal of the Early Republic*, 9 (Winter 1989): 433.
4. For an annotated description of the books in Jefferson's library, see E. Millicent Sowerby, *Catalogue of the Library of Thomas Jefferson*, 5 vols. (Charlottesville: University Press of Virginia, 1983). For a catalog of Jefferson's library as it was arranged by Jefferson, see James Gilreath and Douglas L. Wilson, *Thomas Jefferson's Library* (Washington, D.C.: Library of Congress, 1989).
5. For a full account of Jefferson's holdings on art and architecture, see William Bainter O'Neal, comp., *Jefferson's Fine Arts Library* (Charlottesville: University Press of Virginia, 1976).
6. Eileen Harris, *British Architectural Books and Writers 1556–1785* (New York: Cambridge University Press, 1990), 210.
7. Reported in a letter, Isaac Coles to John H. Cocke (owner of Bremo), 23 February 1816, cited by Fiske Kimball, "The Building of Bremo," *Virginia Magazine of History and Biography*, 57 (Jan. 1949): 8, in the introduction by Frederick D. Nichols to the facsimile edition of Kimball, *Thomas Jefferson Architect* (New York: Da Capo Press, 1968), vii, and James S. Ackerman, *The Villa: Form and Ideology of Country Houses* (Princeton: Princeton University Press, 1990), 189, 207.
8. B.L. Rayner, *Life of Thomas Jefferson* (Boston: Lilly, Wait, Colman, & Holden, 1834), 524.
9. TJ to James Ogilvie, 20 February 1771, *Papers*, 1:63.
10. William Howard Adams, *Jefferson's Monticello* (New York: Abbeville Press, 1983), 47, 49, 55.
11. Ackerman, *The Villa*, 191, summarizes Gene Waddell's analysis in "The First Monticello," *Journal of the Society of Architectural Historians* 46 (March 1987):5–29.

12. For an excellent summary of Morris's significance, see Harris, *British Architectural Books*, 317–324.
13. See Clay Lancaster, "Jefferson's Architectural Indebtedness to Robert Morris," *Journal of the Society of Architectural Historians* 10 (March 1951):3–10.
14. Evelyn M. Acomb, "The Journal of Baron von Closen," *William and Mary Quarterly* 10 (April 1953):220.
15. Chastellux, *Travels in North America*, 391.
16. Jacob Rubsamen, *Visitors*, 8.
17. Jacob Rubsamen to TJ, 1 December 1780, DLC.

Loss and Change (pp. 15–17)

1. TJ to Chastellux, 26 November 1782, *Papers*, 6:203.
2. Bear, 5.
3. For an excellent discussion of attitudes toward death, see Chapter 3, "Weep for Yourselves," in Jan Lewis, *The Pursuit of Happiness: Family and Values in Jefferson's Virginia* (New York: Cambridge University Press, 1983).
4. Noble E. Cunningham, Jr., *In Pursuit of Reason: The Life of Thomas Jefferson* (Baton Rouge: Louisiana State University Press, 1987), 87.
5. Extract from the Diary of Ezra Stiles, cited in *Papers*, 7:303.
6. Ibid.
7. TJ to Ezra Stiles, *Papers*, 7:304.

A New Horizon: Jefferson in Paris (pp. 18–40)

1. For a superbly detailed account of the Paris that Jefferson knew, consult Howard C. Rice, Jr., *Thomas Jefferson's Paris* (Princeton: Princeton University Press, 1976).
2. *Notes*, 152.
3. TJ to John Page, 4 May 1786, *Papers*, 9:445.
4. *Notes*, 153.
5. *Paris*, passim.
6. *Paris*, 15.
7. TJ to David Humphreys, 14 August 1787, *Papers*, 12:32.
8. TJ to Madame de Tessé, 20 March 1787, *Papers*, 11:226.
9. TJ to James Madison, 1 September 1785, *Papers*, 8:462.
10. See Chapter 9, "Clérisseau, Thomas Jefferson, and the Virginia Capitol: 1785–1790," in Thomas J. McCormick, *Charles-Louis Clérisseau and the Genesis of Neo-Classicism* (New York: The Architectural History Foundation; Cambridge, MA: MIT Press, 1990), 191–200.
11. *Notes*, 152.
12. *Notes*, 152.
13. The house was designed in the 1720s for Charlotte Desmares, an actress with the Comédie-Française, by the architect François Debias-Aubry, and was made available to the comte de Tessé by the king.
14. TJ to Madame de Corny, 26 October 1788, *Papers*, 14:37.
15. *Paris*, 91.
16. John Adams cited in *Paris*, 94.

17. TJ to Abigail Adams, 21 June 1785, *Papers*, 8:239.
18. TJ to Charles Thomson, 11 November 1784, *Papers*, 7:519.
19. *Anne-Paule Dominique de Noailles, Marquise de Montagu* (Paris, 1889), 108–109 cited in *Papers*, 10:158n.
20. *Paris*, 99.
21. TJ to Madame de Tessé, 20 March 1787, *Papers*, 11:226.
22. As translated in the 1854 edition of Robert Mills's *Guide to the Capitol of the United States*, and to the National Executive Offices of the United States (Washington, D.C.: J.C. Greer, 1854; reprint, Woodbridge, CT: The Research Publications, 1973, microfilm), and cited by Boyd in *Papers*, 15:364n.
23. For a full description of Jefferson's residence in Paris, see Howard C. Rice, Jr., *L'Hôtel de Langeac, Jefferson's Paris Residence, 1785–1789* Paris: Chez Henri Lefebre; Charlottesville, VA: Thomas Jefferson Memorial Foundation, 1947.
24. TJ to Abigail Adams, 4 September 1785, *Papers*, 8:473.
25. Rice, *Hôtel de Langeac*, 14.
26. TJ to Samuel Osgood, 5 October 1785, *Papers*, 8:590.
27. Jefferson's *Memorandum Books* show records of these purchases between 21 August and 6 September 1784.
28. For a richly detailed account of the packing, see *Papers*, 18:34n–39n.
29. Abigail Adams to TJ, 7 October 1785, *Papers*, 8:594.
30. For various images of these tables see, Nicole de Reyniès, *Le moblier domestique: Vocabulaire Typologique* (Paris: Imprimerie Nationale, 1987), 1:312.
31. *MB*, 30 December 1786.
32. *MB*, 26 October 1786.
33. TJ to Abigail Adams, 25 September 1785, *Papers*, 8:547.
34. Ibid., 548.
35. Ibid., 548–49.
36. TJ, "Autobiography", *Thomas Jefferson: Writings*, ed. Merrill D. Peterson (New York: Library of America, 1984), 57.
37. TJ to Rayneval, 3 March 1786, *Papers*, 9:312–13.
38. TJ to Madame de Corny, 30 June 1787, *Papers*, 11:509.
39. For a precise account of his English purchases, see *MB*, 12 March–25 April 1786.
40. Gilbert Chinard, ed., *The Letters of Lafayette and Jefferson* (Baltimore: The Johns Hopkins Press, 1929), 108.
41. TJ, "Notes of a Tour of English Gardens," [2 April] 1786, *Papers*, 9:369.
42. Ibid., 371.
43. Malone, 2:60.
44. William F. Mayor, *New Description of Blenheim*, (1793; reprint, New York: Garland Publishing, Inc., 1982).
45. TJ, "Hints to Americans Travelling in Europe," [19 June 1788], *Papers*, 13:268.
46. Ibid., 269.
47. Ibid.
48. Ibid.
49. Joseph Spence, *Polymetis: Or, an Equiry concerning the agreement between the Works of the Roman Poets, and the Remains of the Antient Artists* (1747; reprint, New York: Garland Publishers, 1976).
50. Ibid.
51. Jonathan Richardson, *The Works, Containing I. The*

Theory of Painting, II. Essay on the Art of Criticism So Far as it Relates to Painting, III. The Science of a Connoisseur. (London: B. White and Son, 1792).

52. Daniel Webb, *An Inquiry into the Beauties of Painting; and into the Merits of the most celebrated painters, ancient and modern* (London: R. and J. Dodsley, 1760), 11–12.

53. For a good brief account of the Salons, see Pierre Rosenberg, "Salons: 1785, 1787, 1789," in *The Eye of Thomas Jefferson*, ed. William Howard Adams (Charlottesville: University Press of Virginia, 1976), 152–54.

54. TJ to John Trumbull, 30 August 1787, *Papers*, 12:69.

55. John Trumbull to TJ, 17 September 1787, *Papers*, 12:138.

56. TJ to Madame de Bréhan, 19 March 1789, *Papers*, 14:656.

57. TJ to Madame de Tott, 28 February 1787, *Papers*, 11:187.

58. Michael Fried, *Absorption and Theatricality: Painting and Beholder in the Age of Diderot* (Berkeley and Los Angeles: University of California Press, 1980), 107.

59. Cited and translated in Ibid., 125.

60. For a superlative discussion of the way that eighteenth-century French painting was experienced, see ibid., passim.

61. *Paris*, 39–40.

62. *MB*, 19 October 1784.

63. *MB*, 29 October 1784.

64. TJ to Francis Hopkinson, *Papers*, 10:250.

65. TJ to Ezra Stiles, 1 September 1786, *Papers*, 10:317.

66. Theodore Sizer, ed., *The Autobiography of Colonel John Trumbull, Patriot-Artist, 1756–1843* (New Haven: Yale University Press, 1958), 92.

67. Jules David Prown, "John Trumbull as History Painter," in *John Trumbull: The Hand and Spirit of a Painter*, ed. Helen A. Cooper (New Haven: Yale University Art Gallery, 1982), 30.

68. Irma B. Jaffee, *Trumbull: The Declaration of Independence* (New York: Viking Press, 1976), 64.

69. Sizer, *Autobiography of Colonel John Trumbull*, 93.

70. John Trumbull to TJ, 11 June 1789, cited in Ibid., 159.

71. Helen A. Cooper, "John Trumbull: A Life," in *John Trumbull: The Hand and Spirit of a Painter*, 11.

72. TJ to James Barbour, 19 January 1817, cited in Sizer, *Autobiography of Colonel John Trumbull*, 310.

73. TJ to Abigail Adams, 30 August 1787, *Papers*, 12:66.

74. For a brief account of the relationship between Jefferson and Cosway, see Malone, 2:70–75. See also Helen D. Bullock, *My Head and My Heart: A Little History of Thomas Jefferson and Maria Cosway* (New York: G. P. Putnam's Sons, 1945).

75. These pictures were sold at four sales held in 1791, 1792, 1821, and 1822.

76. See Stephen Lloyd, "Richard Cosway, RA: The Artist as Collector, Connoisseur and *Virtuoso*," *Apollo* 133 (June 1991):398–405.

77. TJ to Maria Cosway, 12 October 1786, *Papers*, 10:443, 453n.

78. Ibid., 445–46.

79. Ibid., 447.

80. Ibid.

81. Ibid.

82. This information was provided by Dr. Hein-Th. Schulze Altcappenberg, Kunstmuseum Düsseldorf. See Nicolas de Pigage, *La Galerie Électorale de Düsseldorf* (Düsseldorf/Mannheim/Basel, 1778), nos. 127, 159, 160.

83. TJ to Maria Cosway, 24 April 1788, *Papers*, 13:103–104.

84. Rudolf Wittkower, *Art and Architecture in Italy, 1600 to 1750* (Baltimore: Penguin Books, 1971), 225.

85. *Compact Edition of the Oxford English Dictionary* (New York: Oxford University Press, 1971), s.v. "delicious."

86. TJ to Maria Cosway, 24 April 1788, *Papers*, 13:103–104.

87. Maria Cosway to TJ, 7 April 1819, cited in Bullock, *My Head and My Heart*, 175.

88. TJ to Maria Cosway, 27 December 1820, Ibid., 177.

89. Martha Jefferson to Eliza House Trist, [after 24 August 1785], *Papers* 8:436–39.

90. Martha Jefferson to TJ, 25 March 1787, *Family Letters*, 33.

91. Martha Jefferson to TJ, 8 March 1787, *Family Letters*, 32.

92. TJ to Martha Jefferson, 28 March 1787, *Family Letters*, 34–35.

93. Elizabeth Wayles Eppes to TJ, 13 October 1784, *Papers*, 7:441.

94. Mary Jefferson to TJ, c. 31 March 1787, *Family Letters*, 36.

95. Elizabeth Wayles Eppes to TJ, [31 March 1787], *Papers*, 11:260.

96. Abigail Adams to TJ, 27 June 1787, *Papers*, 11:503.

Return to America (pp. 40–49)

1. TJ to Nathaniel Colley, "Mem. for Capt. Colly to have made in London for Th:J." 16 November 1789, *Papers*, 15:546.

2. George Washington to TJ, 13 October 1789, *Papers*, 15:519.

3. TJ to George Washington, 15 December 1789, *Papers*, 16:35.

4. TJ to William Short, 14 December 1789, *Papers*, 16:26.

5. TJ, "An Account of the Capitol in Virginia," L and B, 17:353.

6. TJ to James Madison, 20 September 1785, *Papers*, 8:534–35.

7. Ibid., 535.

8. *Domestic Life*, 152.

9. TJ, The Response, 12 February 1790, *Papers*, 16:179.

10. TJ to James Madison, 30 July 1789, *Papers*, 15: 315–16.

11. Ross Watson, "Dr. John Morgan," in *The Eye of Thomas Jefferson*, 96–97.

12. For a fine report on the French influence in Philadelphia style during this period, see Beatrice B. Garvan, *Federal Philadelphia 1785–1825* (Philadelphia: Philadelphia Museum of Art, 1987), 54–61.

13. Deborah Norris Logan, "Biographical Sketches of the Life and Character of Dr. George Logan," MS, 19, Historical Society of Pennsylvania, quoted in Ibid., 78.

14. William Temple Franklin to TJ, 20 July 1790, *Papers*, 17:237–38.

15. Anthony N. B. Garvan, ed, "Policy Numbers 236, 237" in *The Architectural Surveys 1784–1794*, (Philadelphia: Mutual Assurance Company, 1976), 1:166.

16. TJ to Thomas Leiper, 16 December 1792, *Papers*, 24: 746–48.

17. TJ to Maria Jefferson, 7 December 1790, *Papers*, 18:142.

18. TJ to James Madison, 10 January 1791, *Papers*, 18:480.

19. William Short Papers, DLC.

20. For a summary account of the shipments to Philadelphia, the contents of the crates from France packed by Grevin, and their unpacking, see *Papers*, 18:33n–39n. For more information on the now unlocated lamp, see *MB*, 15 December 1790.

21. TJ to Martha Jefferson Randolph, 23 December 1790, *Papers*, 18:350.

22. TJ to Martha Jefferson Randolph, 20 January 1791, *Papers*, 18:579.

23. *MB*, 11 January 1791.

24. Adrien Petit's List of Packages sent to Richmond, [c. 12 May 1793], *Papers* (forthcoming) 25:872–73.

25. Jefferson recalled this meeting years later. TJ to Benjamin Rush, 16 January 1811, cited in Malone, 2:287.

26. TJ to an unknown person, 18 March 1793, cited in Malone, 3:60.

27. TJ to Martha Jefferson Randolph, 26 January 1793, *Family Letters*, 110.

28. TJ to Martha Jefferson Randolph, 10 March 1793, *Family Letters*, 113.

29. TJ to Martha Jefferson Randolph, 8 April 1793, *Family Letters*, 115.

30. TJ to John Adams, 25 April 1794, Ford, 6:505.

31. Duc de La Rochefoucauld-Liancourt, *Visitors*, 23.

32. Peterson, *Jefferson and the New Nation*, 304–12.

33. Edwin M. Betts, ed., *Thomas Jefferson's Farm Book* (Princeton, NJ: Princeton University Press, 1953).

34. Peterson, *Jefferson and the New Nation*, 543.

35. Malone, 3:295.

36. *MB*, 13 March 1797.

37. *MB*, 10 and 11 March 1797.

38. *MB*, 3 July 1797.

The Second Monticello (pp. 50–52)

1. TJ to George Wythe, 24 October 1794, as cited in Malone, 3:233.

2. TJ to John Brown, 5 April 1797, as cited in Malone, 3:227.

3. Duc de La Rochefoucauld-Liancourt, *Visitors*, 22.

4. Anna M. Thornton, 1802, from text of note on a drawing of Monticello, private collection.

5. I am much indebted to S. Allen Chambers, historian of Poplar Forest, for freely sharing so much information.

6. TJ to Elizabeth Trist, 27 April 1806, MoSHi.

7. TJ to Benjamin Rush, 17 August 1811, DLC.

The President's House (pp. 53–61)

1. Noble E. Cunningham, Jr., *Popular Images of the Presidency from Washington to Lincoln* (Columbia: University of Missouri Press, 1991), 171.

2. Jefferson to Pierre Charles L'Enfant, 10 April 1791, *Papers*, 20:86.

3. Only a scrapbook of this competition survives, preserved by Benjamin Henry Latrobe and now in the collection of the Maryland Historical Society. See William Seale, *The President's House* (Washington, D.C.: White House Historical Association, 1986), 30, and William Ryan and Desmond Guinness, *The White House; An Architectural History* (New York: McGraw-Hill Book Company, 1980), 42–47.

4. Abigail Adams to Mrs. Smith, 21 November 1800, *Letters of Mrs. Adams, the Wife of John Adams*, 2d ed. (Boston: C.C. Little and J. Brown, 1840), 241.

5. Ibid., 240.

6. Abigail Adams to Mrs. Cranch, 21 November 1800, *New Letters of Abigail Adams, 1788–1801*, ed. Stewart Mitchell, (Westport, CT: Greenwood Press, 1947), 259.

7. See Marie G. Kimball, "The Original Furnishings of the White House, Part I," *Antiques* 15 (June 1929):481–86, and George Washington, "An Inven-

tory of Goods in President's House," February 1797, #55325, National Archives and Records Service.

8. Abigail Adams to Mrs. Smith, 21 November 1800, *New Letters of Mrs. Adams*, 242.

9. Dolley Madison to Lucy Payne, 23 August 1814, copied by Dolley Payne Madison c. 1830–40, Cutts Collection, DLC, cited in Conover Hunt-Jones, *Dolley and the "great little Madison,"* (Washington, D.C.: American Institute of Architects Foundation, 1977), 45.

10. Thomas Claxton to Joseph H. Nicholson, 14 February 1805, MHi.

11. Smith, 384.

12. Generally, a multiple of ten will yield current dollars.

13. TJ to Thomas Claxton, 19 February 1809, DLC.

14. Thomas Claxton to Joseph H. Nicholson, 14 February 1805, MHi.

15. Thomas Claxton to TJ, 18 May 1801, MHi.

16. Thomas Claxton to TJ, 28 May 1801, MHi.

17. TJ to Thomas Claxton, 18 June 1802, MHi.

18. See Jefferson's White House Inventory in Kimball, "The Original Furnishings of the White House," part I, 485.

19. Ibid., 485–86.

20. Inventory of the President's House, [19 February 1809], DLC.

21. TJ, sketch of dimity window draperies, 12 January 1803, MHi.

22. Gregory R. Weidman, "The Neoclassical Style in Philadelphia and the South, 1785–1840," in *American Furniture from the Kaufman Collection*, ed. J. Michael Flanigan (Washington: National Gallery of Art, 1986), 103.

23. Smith, 387–89.

24. Ibid., 387–88.

25. Anthony Merry to Lord Hawkesbury, 6 December 1803, *Despatches of the British Ministers to the United States to the Foreign Office*, cited in Malone, 3:378.

26. William Plumer, Jr., *Life of William Plumer*, ed. Andrew P. Peabody (Boston: Phillips, Sampson and Company, 1857), 246.

The Public Monticello (pp. 61–93)

1. Sir Augustus John Foster, *Visitors*, 37.

2. For the complete account, see Isaac Weld, Jr., *Travels through the States of North America and the Provinces of Upper and Lower Canada, During the Years 1795, 1796, and 1797* (London: J. Stockdale, 1799) 1:203, 206–9.

3. TJ to James Dinsmore, 8 June 1805, transcription from Sotheby's Catalogue, *Printed and Manuscript Americana*, 26 January 1983.

4. Ibid.

5. TJ to George Rogers Clark, 26 November 1782, *Papers*, 6:204.

6. Ibid.

7. Whitfield J. Bell, Jr., *John Morgan: Continental Doctor*, (Philadelphia: University of Pennsylvania Press, 1965), 173–74.

8. William Clark to TJ, 10 November 1807, DLC.

9. Margaret Bayard Smith, *A Winter in Washington; or Memoirs of the Seymour Family*, (New York: E. Bliss and E. White, 1824), 3:226.

10. George Ticknor, "Charlottesville, 7 February 1815," *Life, Letters, and Journals of George Ticknor*, (Boston: James R. Osgood and Company, 1876), 1:34.

11. See Malone, 3:341–44, and Julian P. Boyd, "The Megalonyx, the Megatherium, and Thomas Jefferson's Lapse of Memory," *Proceedings of the American Philosophical Society*, 102:420–35.

12. Benjamin P. Richardson, "The Travel Diary of Benjamin P. Richardson," MS, private collection.

13. Ibid.

14. Charles Willson Peale to TJ, 30 August 1807, DLC.

15. TJ's Instructions to Lewis, [20 June 1803], Jackson, 1:61.

16. TJ to Charles Willson Peale, 6 October 1805, DLC.

17. TJ to Meriwether Lewis, 26 October 1806, Jackson 1:350–35.

18. Ticknor, *Life, Letters, and Journals*, 1:34.

19. *Notes*, 93–96.

20. *Richmond Enquirer*, 4 July 1808.

21. Baron de Montlezun, *Visitors*, 69.

22. E. S. Gaustad, "Religion," in *Thomas Jefferson: A Reference Biography*, ed. Merrill D. Peterson, (New York: Charles Scribner's Sons, 1986), 283.

23. Margaret Bayard Smith, "Recollections of a Visit to Monticello," *Richmond Enquirer*, 18 January 1823.

24. Chastellux, *Travels in North America*, 391.

25. Smith, "Recollections of a Visit to Monticello."

26. TJ to John Rea, 2 March 1808, DLC.

27. Catalogue.

28. Garry Wills, *Inventing America: Jefferson's Declaration of Independence* (Garden City, NY: Doubleday and Company, 1978), xv.

29. TJ to Joseph Delaplaine, 3 May 1814, L and B, 14:132.

30. TJ to Walter Jones, 2 January 1814, Ford, 11:375.

31. TJ to Samuel Smith, 22 August 1798, Ford 8:443.

32. TJ to Lafayette, 28 October 1822, Ford, 12:254–55.

33. TJ to Lafayette, 2 March 1781, *Papers*, 4:543.

34. TJ, "Autobiography," *Thomas Jefferson: Writings*, 36–37.

35. TJ to John Adams, 21 January 1812, Cappon, 291.

36. TJ to James Madison, 30 January 1787, *Papers*, 11:94–95.

37. TJ to James Madison, 20 June 1787, *Papers*, 11:482.

38. TJ to John Adams, 24 January 1814, Cappon, 425.

39. Catalogue.

40. TJ to Horatio Gates, 21 February 1798, Ford, 8:371.

41. *Paris*, 94.

42. TJ to Albert Gallatin, 16 October 1815, L and B, 14:358.

43. *Domestic Life*, 347.

44. Ellen Randolph Coolidge to Henry Randall, 16 May 1857, Ellen Coolidge Letterbook, Jefferson-Coolidge Family Collection (#9090), ViU.

45. Thomas Claxton to TJ, 27 August 1801, MHi.

46. To finance the War of 1812, various kinds of property were taxed, including land, slaves, cattle, horses, clocks, glassware, mahogany or gilded furniture, mirrors, silver, window curtains, framed pictures with glass, harpsichords, and buildings. Jefferson's "Memorandum of Taxable Property," compiled in March 1815, is in MHi (Appendix III).

47. Daniel Webster, *Visitors*, 99.

48. TJ to William Short, Jefferson's Instructions for Procuring Household Goods, 6 April 1790, *Papers*, 16:322.

49. Smith, 69.

50. Francis Calley Gray, *Visitors*, 57.

51. Martha Trist Burke, List of "Monticello Relics," 1907–1908, Trist-Burke Collection (#6696), ViU.

52. Smith, 70.

53. Daniel Webster, *Visitors*, 98.

54. Ibid.

55. Benjamin Henry Latrobe to Mrs. Latrobe, 24 November 1802, *The Papers of Benjamin Henry Latrobe: Correspondence and Miscellaneous Papers*, ed. John C. Van Horne and Lee W. Formwalt (New Haven: Yale University Press, 1984) 1:232.

56. Smith, 67–68.

57. Ticknor, *Life, Letters, and Journals*, 1:36.

58. Ibid.

59. Catalogue.

60. Ibid.

61. King wrote TJ, "Nicholas King's respects to Thomas Jefferson, and, begs his acceptance of the accompanying Drawing." Nicholas King to TJ, 12 November 1801, DLC.

62. 1815 Tax List.

63. Wallace Gusler, *Furniture of Williamsburg and Eastern Virginia 1710–1790* (Richmond: Virginia Museum of Fine Arts, 1979), 27.

64. Elisabeth D. Garrett, *At Home: The American Family, 1750–1870* (New York: Harry N. Abrams, 1990), 79; 1826 Inventory.

65. Gusler, *Furniture of Williamsburg and Eastern Virginia*, 38–39.

66. The comments of Morrison H. Heckscher and Robert Trent were helpful in comparing these chairs to other examples.

67. Francis Calley Gray, *Visitors*, 57.

68. TJ to James Madison, 17 September 1787, *Papers*, 12:138.

69. This china may be the double-bordered Nanking pattern with an armorial shield with the initial "TJ" that was found in Boston in the late nineteenth century. It was acquired then by Thomas Jefferson Coolidge, Jr.

70. Martha Jefferson Randolph to TJ, 16 January 1791, *Family Letters*, 68.

71. Martha Jefferson Randolph to TJ, 23 June 1808, MHi.

72. Joseph Coolidge to Nicholas P. Trist, 5 January 1827, DLC.

73. Martha Jefferson Randolph, silver inventory, c. 1833, ViMo. See Appendix VI.

74. Joseph Coolidge, to Nicholas P. Trist, 5 January 1827, Nicholas P. Trist Papers (#19313), DLC.

75. Randall, 3:337.

76. TJ to Ferdinand Grand, 23 April 1790, *Papers*, 16:369.

77. TJ to Reverend William Smith, 19 February 1791, *Papers*, 19:113.

78. Catalogue.

79. TJ to John Adams, 30 August 1787, Cappon, 195.

80. TJ to Dugald Stewart, 26 April 1824, *Papers*, 15:xxxiii–iv.

81. Catalogue. This medal is now in a private collection.

82. TJ to Richard Price, 17 July 1789, *Papers*, 15:280.

83. TJ to James Madison, 22 July 1789, *Papers*, 15:299–301.

84. These works are identified as 80, 81, and 82 in Sowerby.

85. Daniel Webster, "Notes of Mr. Jefferson's Conversation 1824 at Monticello," *The Papers of Daniel Webster*, ed. Charles M. Wiltse and Harold D. Moser (Hanover, NH: University Press of New England, 1974), 1:374.

86. TJ to Horatio Gates, 14 December 1781, *Papers*, 6:139.

87. TJ to Henry Dearborn, 8 January 1808, Ford, 11:4.

88. TJ to Benjamin Smith Barton, 27 February 1803, DLC.

89. TJ to William Wirt, 3 May 1811, Ford 11:200.

90. Mahlon Dickerson to Silas Dickerson, 21 April 1802, NjHi.

91. TJ to Paul Allen, 13 April 1812, DLC.

92. Susan R. Stein, "Thomas Jefferson's Traveling Desks," *Antiques* 133 (May 1988):1156–59.

93. TJ, Preliminary draft of the affidavit for the lap desk, private collection.

94. Charles L. Granquist, "Thomas Jefferson's 'Whirli-

gig' Chairs," *Antiques* 109 (May 1976): 1056–60.
95. 1826 Inventory.

The Private Monticello (pp. 94–116)

1. Bear, 136n.
2. Ibid., 84.
3. Ibid., 4.
4. TJ to Maria Jefferson Eppes, 13 April 1799, *Family Letters*, 177.
5. Martha Jefferson Randolph to TJ, 30 January 1800, *Family Letters*, 182.
6. TJ to Ellen Randolph Coolidge, 14 November 1825, *Family Letters*, 461.
7. TJ, "original Rough draught," 1776, *Papers*, 1:426.
8. Bear, 13.
9. Martha Jefferson to TJ, 3 May 1787, *Family Letters*, 39.
10. Martha Jefferson Randolph to Ellen Randolph Coolidge, 2 August 1825, Jefferson-Coolidge Family Collection (#9090), ViU.
11. Bear, 84.
12. Maria Jefferson to TJ, cited in Sarah Randolph, "Mrs. Thomas Mann Randolph," in *Worthy Women of Our First Century*, eds. Mrs. O. J. Wister and Agnes Irwin, (Philadelphia: Lippincott and Co., 1877), 25.
13. Ellen Randolph Coolidge, Diary, 1838–39, MHi.
14. TJ to N. Burwell, 14 March 1818, cited in Randall, 447.
15. Martha Randolph to TJ, 11 July 1805, *Family Letters*, 277–78.
16. TJ to Cornelia J. Randolph, *Family Letters*, 373–74.
17. Malone, 6:296.
18. TJ to Martha Randolph, 31 August 1817, *Family Letters*, 419.
19. Malone, 6:11, 218.
20. Anna Thornton, *Visitors*, 34.
21. Sir Augustus John Foster, *Visitors*, 39.
22. For an excellent account of Jefferson's library, see Douglas L. Wilson, "Jefferson's Library," in *Thomas Jefferson: A Reference Biography*, 157–79.
23. TJ to James Ogilvie, 20 February 1771, *Papers*, 1:63.
24. TJ to Samuel H. Smith, 1814, cited in Wilson, "Jefferson's Library," 165.
25. Wilson, "Jefferson's Library," 167.
26. Francis Calley Gray, *Visitors*, 59.
27. Wilson, "Jefferson's Library," 159.
28. TJ to John Adams, 10 June 1815, Cappon, 443.
29. Ellen Randolph Coolidge, cited in Wilson, "Jefferson's Library," 177.
30. *MB*, 6 April [1769].
31. Virginia Randolph Trist to Ellen Randolph Coolidge, 11 February 1827, Jefferson-Coolidge Family Collection (#9090), ViU.
32. Smith, 72.
33. TJ to Charles Willson Peale, 20 August 1811, *Thomas Jefferson's Garden Book*, ed. Edwin M. Betts (Philadelphia: The American Philosophical Society, 1944), 461.
34. Smith, 71.
35. Randall, 3:337.
36. TJ to William Short, Enclosure, 6 April 1790, *Papers*, 16:323.
37. George Tucker, *Life of Thomas Jefferson, third president of the United States* (London: C. Knight, 1837), 2:309.
38. Bear, 13.
39. TJ to John Adams, 11 January 1817, Cappon, 505.
40. TJ to John Adams, 27 June 1822, Cappon, 581.
41. For more information, see Granquist, "Thomas Jefferson's 'Whirligig' Chairs."

42. *MB*, 2 April 1798.
43. TJ to Martha Jefferson Randolph, 28 July [1819], *Family Letters*, 429.
44. TJ to James Bowdoin, 10 July 1806, cited in Silvio A. Bedini, *Thomas Jefferson and His Copying Machines* (Charlottesville: University Press of Virginia, 1984), 147.
45. Ibid.
46. TJ to Thomas Mann Randolph, Jr., 27 August 1786, *Papers*, 10:306.
47. John C. Greene, *American Science in the Age of Jefferson* (Ames: Iowa State University Press, 1984), 147.
48. TJ to Robert Patterson, 10 November 1811, cited in Bedini, 419.
49. TJ to Spencer Roane, 9 March 1821, L and B, 15:326.
50. TJ to Destutt de Tracy, 26 December 1820, Ford, 10:174.
51. TJ to William Thornton, 9 May 1817, ViU.
52. TJ to Martha Jefferson Randolph, 4 November 1815, *Family Letters*, 411.
53. Joseph Coolidge to Nicholas P. Trist, 5 January 1827, Nicholas P. Trist Papers (#19313), DLC.
54. Sir Augustus John Foster, *Visitors*, 37.
55. Daniel Webster, *Visitors*, 98.
56. Martha Jefferson Randolph to unknown, 13 February 1827, cited in Randolph, *Worthy Women*, 59.
57. TJ to John Rea, 17 October 1808, DLC.
58. Thomas Jefferson Randolph, quoted in *Domestic Life*, 426.
59. Cornelia Jefferson Randolph, Plan of the First Floor of Monticello, post July 4, 1826, ViMo. A second plan by Cornelia is in a private collection. A simplified version is published in *Domestic Life*, 334.
60. Sir Augustus John Foster, *Visitors*, 38.
61. Joseph Coolidge to Nicholas P. Trist, 5 January 1827, Nicholas P. Trist papers (#19313) DLC.
62. TJ to James Westhall Ford, 1 September 1823, cited in Mary Givens Kane, "James Westhall Ford," *Antiques* 70 (August 1956):136.
63. Ibid.
64. The definitive work is Alfred Bush, *The Life Portraits of Thomas Jefferson*, (Charlottesville: Thomas Jefferson Memorial Foundation, 1987).
65. Randall, 3:330.
66. Ibid., 331.
67. TJ to Christopher Clarke, 14 September 1811, DLC.
68. TJ to John Milledge, 22 September 1822, DLC.
69. TJ to Abbé Correia da Serra, 1 January 1816, DLC.
70. *Domestic Life*, 402.
71. TJ to John Wayles Eppes, 1814, Ford, 11:425.
72. TJ, Will, 16 and 17 March 1826, ViU.
73. TJ to James Madison, 17 February 1826, Ford, 12:458.
74. TJ to Martha Jefferson Randolph, 28 May 1801, *Family Letters*, 202.
75. Martha Jefferson Randolph to TJ, 26 October 1805, *Family Letters*, 280.
76. TJ to William Short, Jefferson's Instructions for Procuring Household Goods, 6 April 1790 *Papers*, 16:322.
77. A shadow of this paper was found on plaster in 1936 by Milton Grigg, restoration architect. Grigg traced it and accurately matched it to an identical paper found in the Lee house in Williamsburg. The existing wallpaper, hand-blocked in 1992, replicates the Lee house example in the collection of the Colonial Williamsburg Foundation.
78. Anna Thornton, *Visitors*, 34.
79. 1826 Inventory.
80. Smith, *Richmond Enquirer*, 18 January 1823.
81. Malone, 6:161.

82. Virginia J. Randolph to Nicholas P. Trist, 5 June 1823, Nicholas P. Trist papers (#19313) DLC.

Monticello Dispersed (pp. 117–120)

1. TJ to Destutt de Tracy, 26 December 1820, cited in Bernard Mayo, *Jefferson Himself*, (Charlottesville: University Press of Virginia, 1984), 327.
2. Ellen Coolidge, *Domestic Life*, 345.
3. TJ to John Adams, 1 August 1816, Cappon, 484.
4. TJ to Thomas Jefferson Randolph, 8 February 1826, *Family Letters*, 469.
5. Cornelia Randolph to Ellen Coolidge, 24 November 1825, Jefferson-Coolidge Family Collection (#9090), ViU.
6. Martha Jefferson Randolph to Thomas Jefferson Randolph, 7 February 1830, Edgehill-Randolph Papers (#1397), ViU.
7. *The Niles' Weekly Register*, 19 July 1828.
8. Virginia Trist to Virginia Cary, 2 May 1828, Nicholas P. Trist Collection (#2104), NcU.
9. Ellen Coolidge to Martha Jefferson Randolph, 28 May 1828, Jefferson-Coolidge Family Collection (#9090), ViU.
10. For a substantial account of Monticello after Jefferson's death, see James A. Bear, Jr., "Monticello," in *Thomas Jefferson: A Reference Biography*, 437–52.
11. Uriah Philips Levy to George M. Carr, 1832, Ibid., 446.
12. Malone, 6:499.

Catalogue

Paintings (pp. 122–149)

1. Agnes Mongan, *Harvard Honors Lafayette* (Cambridge: Fogg Art Museum, Harvard University, 1975), 62.
2. TJ to Barré, 3 June 1785, *Papers*, 8:176–77.
3. The portrait is now in the collection of the Fogg Art Museum. See Mongan, *Harvard Honors Lafayette*, 62–65.
4. TJ to Barré, 3 June 1785, *Papers*, 8:176–77.
5. For a full account of Wright's portraits of Washington, see Monroe H. Fabian, *Joseph Wright: American Artist, 1756–1793* (Washington, D.C.: Smithsonian Institution Press, 1985).
6. *MB*, 28 May 1784.
7. Francis Hopkinson to TJ, 30 May 1784, *Papers*, 7:295.
8. TJ to Francis Hopkinson, 6 July 1785, *Papers*, 8:263.
9. Fabian, *Joseph Wright*, 102.
10. *Papers*, 7:xxvii.
11. For a full account of this painting, see Irma B. Jaffe, *Trumbull: The Declaration of Independence* (New York: Viking Press, 1976).
12. John Trumbull to TJ, 19 December 1788, *Papers*, 14:364.
13. The miniature belonging to Mrs. Church is now in the collection of the Metropolitan Museum of Art, New York, and the portrait owned by Mrs. Cosway is in the collection of the National Portrait Gallery, Washington, D.C. For more information on it, consult Elizabeth Cometti, "Maria Cosway's Rediscovered Miniature of Jefferson," *William and Mary Quarterly* 9 (April 1952): 152–55; William Short to John Trumbull, 10 September 1788, *Papers*, 14:365n.

14. TJ to John Trumbull, 12 January 1789, *Papers*, 14:440.

15. Jack Fruchtman, Jr., "Thomas Paine," in *The Blackwell Encyclopedia of the American Revolution*, ed. Jack P. Greene and J. R. Pole (Cambridge: Basil Blackwell, 1991), 761.

16. TJ to John Trumbull, 12 January 1789, *Papers*, 14:440.

17. For detailed accounts, see David Meschutt, "The Adams-Jefferson Portrait Exchange," *American Art Journal* 9 (Spring 1982): 47–54, and Andrew Oliver, *The Portraits of John and Abigail Adams* (Cambridge: Belknap Press of Harvard University, 1967), 46–54.

18. Abigail Adams to John Quincy Adams, 4 July–11 August 1785, Adams Papers, MHi.

19. TJ to William Stephens Smith, 22 October 1786, *Papers*, 10:479.

20. Abigail Adams to TJ, 10 July 1787, *Papers*, 11:573.

21. TJ to William Stephens Smith, 2 February 1788, *Papers*, 12:558.

22. William Stephens Smith to TJ, 6 March 1788, *Papers*, 12:647.

23. Polyplasiasmos was a method of copying pictures in oil paint by a mechanical or chemical process, invented by Joseph Brook. The picture referred to here may have been a polyplasiasmos of Benjamin West's *The Prodigal Son* (1771), which was available for sale in the Polygraphic Society in the Strand in 1788. See Helmut von Erffa and Allen Staley, *The Paintings of Benjamin West* (New Haven: Yale University Press, 1986), 339.

24. John Adams to TJ, 22 May 1785, *Papers*, 8:160.

25. TJ to Benjamin Rush, 16 January 1811, Ford, 11:168.

26. TJ to John Trumbull, 18 January 1789, *Papers*, 14:467–68.

27. John Trumbull to TJ, 5 February 1789, *Papers*, 14:524–25.

28. TJ to John Trumbull, 15 February 1789, *Papers*, 14:561.

29. John Trumbull to TJ, 10 March 1789, *Papers*, 14:634–35.

30. TJ to John Trumbull, 15 March 1789, *Papers*, 14:663.

31. John Trumbull to Joseph Banks, 12 April 1789, R.S. Misc. MSS 3.25, Royal Society Archives.

32. John Trumbull to TJ, 26 May 1789, *Papers*, 15:152.

33. John Trumbull to TJ, 29 May 1789, *Papers*, 15:157.

34. Ellen Randolph Coolidge to Martha Jefferson Randolph, 21 July 1833, Jefferson-Coolidge Family Collection (#9090), ViU.

35. John Trumbull to TJ, 28 August 1787, *Papers*, 12:60.

36. John Trumbull to TJ, 17 September 1787, *Papers*, 12:139.

37. John Trumbull to Jonathan Trumbull, Jr., 6 February 1788, MHi.

38. John Trumbull to TJ, 29 May 1789, *Papers*, 15:157–58.

39. John Trumbull to TJ, 24 October 1791, *Papers*, 22:228.

40. Theodore Sizer, ed., *The Autobiography of Colonel John Trumbull, Patriot-Artist, 1756–1843* (New Haven: Yale University Press, 1953), 147.

41. For a discussion of this issue, see Irma B. Jaffe, *John Trumbull: Patriot-Artist of the American Revolution* (Boston: New York Graphic Society, 1975), 319.

42. TJ to Philip Mazzei, 17 October 1787, *Papers*, 12:245.

43. TJ to John Trumbull, 12 January 1789, *Papers*, 14:440.

44. TJ to Joseph Delaplaine, 3 May 1814, L and B, 14:132–33.

45. TJ to William Short, 6 April 1790, *Papers*, 16:318.

"Madame Le Brun" is Marie-Louise Elisabeth Vigée-Lebrun, official painter to Marie-Antoinette, known for her portraiture. She was elected to the Académie Royale in 1783. Jefferson saw her portraits in the Salon of 1787 and wrote John Trumbull that they were "much approved."

"Genl. Washington's half length picture" was the portrait by Joseph Wright. Jefferson also had a full-length likeness by Charles Willson Peale (1784).

46. William Short to TJ, 23 December 1790, *Papers*, 18:356.

47. Ibid.

48. Ibid.

49. William Short to TJ, 15 August 1790, *Papers*, 17:396.

50. TJ, speech at Charlottesville dinner, 1824, cited in John P. Foley, ed., *The Jeffersonian Cyclopedia* (New York: Funk and Wagnalls Company, 1900), 464.

51. TJ to William Stephens Smith, 22 October 1786, *Papers*, 10:479.

52. Ibid., 20 December 1786, *Papers*, 10:620.

53. Ibid., 19 February 1787, *Papers*, 11:169.

54. William Stephens Smith to TJ, 19 May 1787, *Papers*, 11:365.

55. Ibid., 22 February 1788, *Papers*, 12:620.

56. Ellis Waterhouse, *The Dictionary of British 18th Century Painters in Oils and Crayons* (Woodbridge, England: Antique Collectors' Club, 1981), 23.

57. Jean Valade to TJ, 24 August 1787, *Papers*, 12:54.

58. Charles Coleman Sellers, *Benjamin Franklin in Portraiture* (New Haven: Yale University Press, 1962), 254.

59. Joseph Coolidge to Martha Jefferson Randolph, 7 August 1828, Jefferson-Coolidge Family Collection (#9090), ViU.

60. TJ to Henry Dearborn, 5 July 1819, L and B, 19:271.

61. An art historian, however, argues that Stuart lost the second portrait and repainted it in 1821. See David Meschutt, "Gilbert Stuart's Portraits of Thomas Jefferson," *American Art Journal* 13 (Winter 1981): 2–16.

62. Henry Dearborn to TJ, 16 November 1818, DLC, cited in Fiske Kimball, "The Life Portraits of Thomas Jefferson and their Replicas," *Proceedings of the American Philosophical Society* 88 (December 1944): 514.

63. Henry Dearborn to TJ, 20 January 1820, ibid.

64. TJ to Henry Dearborn, 26 March 1820, DLC, ibid., 516.

65. TJ to Henry Dearborn, 17 August 1821, ibid.

66. Ellen Randolph Coolidge to Virginia Randolph Trist, 13 May 1828, Jefferson-Coolidge Family Collection (#9090), ViU.

67. TJ to Joseph Delaplaine, 30 May 1813, DLC.

68. TJ to Henry Dearborn, 5 July 1819, L and B, 19:271.

69. TJ to Gilbert Stuart, 18 June 1805, cited in Bush, 61.

70. Bush, 61.

71. TJ to James Westhall Ford, 1 September 1823, cited in Mary Givens Kane, "James Westhall Ford," *Antiques* 70 (August 1956), 136.

72. *MB*, 29 September 1823.

73. TJ letter of recommendation for Ford, 30 September 1823, cited in Kane, "James Westhall Ford," 136.

74. Ibid., 137.

75. Catalogue.

76. Walter L. Strauss, ed., *Hendrik Goltzius 1558–1617: The Complete Engravings and Woodcuts* (New York: Abaris Books, 1977), 616.

77. Luitpold Dussler, *Raphael* (London: Phaidon, 1971), 48.

78. Martha Trist Burke, List of "Monticello Relics," 1907–08, Trist-Burke Collection (#6696), ViU.

79. Ellen Randolph Coolidge to Martha Jefferson Randolph, 21 July 1833, Jefferson-Coolidge Family Collection (#9090), ViU.

80. Catalogue.

81. *Paris*, 40.

82. Hayot de Longpré, "Catalogue d'une belle Collection de tableaux . . . du Cabinet du Sieur Dupille de Saint-Severin" (Paris: Imprimerie de Clousier, 1785), no. 248.

83. Catalogue.

84. Benjamin West to Joseph Shippen, 1 September 1763, cited in Helmut von Erffa and Allen Staley, *The Paintings of Benjamin West* (New Haven: Yale University Press, 1986), 447.

85. Although the painting appeared in the catalogue of the Harding sale in 1833, it remained with Joseph and Ellen Coolidge and their descendants.

86. Catalogue.

87. See L. Moody Simms, Jr., "Talented Virginians: The Peticolas Family," *Virginia Magazine of History and Biography* 85 (January 1977):55–64.

88. Virginia Randolph to Nicholas P. Trist, 27 June 1822, Nicholas P. Trist Papers (#19313), DLC.

Drawings (pp. 150–161)

1. Helmut von Erffa and Allen Staley, *The Paintings of Benjamin West* (New Haven: Yale University Press, 1986), 248–49.

2. TJ to William Thornton, 14 December 1814, DLC.

3. Ellen Coolidge to Martha Jefferson Randolph, 21 July 1833, Jefferson-Coolidge Family Collection (#9090), ViU.

4. John M. Bryan, "Robert Mills," in *Master Builders*, ed. Diane Waddex (Washington, D.C.: Preservation Press, 1985), 28–31. The standard works on Mills are H. M. Pierce Gallagher, *Robert Mills, Architect of the Washington Monument* (New York: Columbia University Press, 1935) and John M. Bryan, ed., *Robert Mills, Architect* (Washington, D.C.: American Institute of Architects Press, 1989).

5. "The Architectural Works of Robert Mills," cited in Gallagher, *Robert Mills*, 168.

6. "Mills's Autobiography," cited in ibid., 159.

7. Catalogue.

8. Frederick D. Nichols, *Thomas Jefferson's Architectural Drawings*, 4th ed. (Charlottesville: Thomas Jefferson Memorial Foundation and the University Press of Virginia, 1978), no. 411.

9. "Mills's Autobiography," cited in Gallagher, *Robert Mills*, 159.

10. Fragment in Mills's handwriting, endorsed "Description of Monticello House," Mills Papers, ScHi.

11. TJ to Richard Cutts, 29 June 1804, MHi.

12. Sir Augustus John Foster, *Visitors*, 37. In September 1804 Jefferson noted in a list of work by his joiner James Dinsmore, "build the S.W. Portico", Nichols, *Architectural Drawings*, no. 147n.

13. Other inaccuracies are the number and size of panes for the portico doors and the addition of archivolt trim for the piazza arches.

14. Jefferson indicated his need for sashes for the south piazza in a letter to James Oldham, 11 October 1804, MHi.

15. "The Architectural Works of Robert Mills," cited in Gallagher, *Robert Mills*, 169.

16. Ibid., 168.

17. Fiske Kimball, *Thomas Jefferson, Architect* (New York: Da Capo Press, 1968), 68–69.

18. Ibid.

19. Nichols, *Architectural Drawings*, no. 135.

20. TJ memorandum, 11 November 1792, MHi. There is no indication the order was processed.

21. Jefferson listed the sashes to be reused from the first house. The six pair of walnut sashes from the north and south attics were for "6. windows of skyroom."

22. Gene Waddell made the same connection between the fenestration shown by Mills and first planned by Jefferson, but was willing to state, "Despite the extravagance, Jefferson did adopt a design that was similar, if not identical, to the one he later had Robert Mills draw for him, as is confirmed by the amount of glass he ordered for circular windows in 1792." Gene Waddell, "The First Monticello," *Journal of the Society of Architectural Historians* 46 (March 1987): 24–25.

23. Donald Martin, *The Architecture of New York City* (Reynolds, NY: Macmillan Publishing Co., 1984), 32–35.

24. John M. Bryan, "Robert Mills: Education and Early Drawings," in *Robert Mills, Architect*, ed. John M. Bryan, (Washington, D.C.: American Institute of Architects Press, 1989), 3–4, 15.

25. Robert Mills to TJ, 3 October 1806, DLC.

26. Ibid.

27. Cited in Charles Brownell and Jeffrey A. Cohen, *The Architectural Drawings of Benjamin Henry Latrobe*, The Papers of Benjamin Henry Latrobe, Series 2 (New Haven: Yale University Press, forthcoming).

28. Ibid.

29. Mills left the drawing with John Woodside, who then sent it to Jefferson. John Woodside to TJ, 11 October 1808, DLC; TJ to John Woodside, 14 October 1808, DLC.

30. Robert Mills to TJ, 13 June 1808, DLC.

31. *Notes*, 153.

32. For an overview of Mills's career, see Bryan, ed., *Robert Mills, Architect*.

33. Charles E. Brownell, "The United States Capitol," in *The Architectural Drawings of Benjamin Henry Latrobe*, forthcoming.

34. Robert Mills, whom Jefferson had introduced to Latrobe, drew the preparatory plan for this perspective. Latrobe hoped to do a similar perspective of Monticello, also using one of Mills's drawings, but apparently never completed that project. TJ to Latrobe, 10 October 1809, Benjamin H. Latrobe, *The Papers of Benjamin Henry Latrobe: Correspondence and Miscellaneous Papers*, ed. John C. Van Horne and Lee W. Formwalt (New Haven: Yale University Press, 1986) 2:776–77.

35. TJ to Latrobe, 26 April 1807, *Latrobe Papers*, 2:411.

36. The identity of Jefferson's "Diocletian's Portico," is enigmatic. Latrobe indicated that it was *not* the Palace at Spalatro, and described it as looking "much more like a *restoration* of a ruin by a Modern Artist." Latrobe to TJ, 7 December 1806, *Latrobe Papers* 2:321–24.

37. TJ to Latrobe, 10 October 1809, *Latrobe Papers*, 2:776–77.

38. TJ to Latrobe, 27 August 1816, *Latrobe Papers* 3:808. For details about the sundial see Silvio Bedini, *Thomas Jefferson: American Scientist*, 415–16.

39. John E. Semmes, *John H. B. Latrobe and His Times: 1803–1891* (Baltimore, MD: The Norman, Remington Co., 1917), 250–51; John H. B. Latrobe, *The Capitol and Washington at the Beginning of the Present Century* (Baltimore, 1881), 19.

40. Latrobe to TJ, 5 November 1816, DLC.

41. Latrobe to TJ, 28 October 1817, *Latrobe Papers*, 3:824n4.

42. Robert Fulton to TJ, 28 March 1810, NNP.

43. Fulton to TJ, 24 February 1810, DLC.

44. TJ to Fulton, 17 March 1810, L and B, 12:380.

45. TJ to James Oldham, 16 November 1805, MHi.

46. Michael T. Wright, Curator of Mechanical Engineering, National Museum of Science and Industry, London, to Susan R. Stein, 11 December 1991.

47. Edwin Morris Betts, ed., *Thomas Jefferson's Garden Book, 1766–1824*, (Philadelphia: The American Philosophical Society, 1944), 414, 427, 535, 541, 583–84, 586–87, 595, 600–1, 603, 630–31.

Engravings (pp. 162–197)

1. For a full account of this important work, see Irma B. Jaffe, *Trumbull: The Declaration of Independence* (New York: Viking Press, 1976). Unless otherwise noted, all dimensions given are plate size.

2. Theodore Sizer, ed., *The Autobiography of Colonel John Trumbull, patriot-artist, 1756–1843* (New Haven: Yale University Press, 1953), 92–93.

3. Reverend Henry C. Thweatt, notes on visit to Monticello before 1825, private collection.

4. Helen A. Cooper, *John Trumbull: The Hand and Spirit of a Painter* (New Haven: Yale University Press, 1982), 35.

5. John Trumbull to TJ, 29 May 1789, *Papers*, 15:158.

6. TJ to John Trumbull, 21 June 1789, *Papers*, 15:205.

7. Sizer, *The Autobiography of Colonel John Trumbull*, 88.

8. Ibid., 91.

9. Ibid., 173.

10. TJ to Barré, 11 July 1785, *Papers*, 8:282.

11. TJ to Thevenard, 13 January 1786, *Papers*, 9:173–74.

12. TJ to Martha Jefferson Randolph, 27 June 1790, *Papers*, 16:577–78.

13. Wendy C. Wick, *George Washington: An American Icon* (Washington, D.C.: Smithsonian Institution Traveling Exhibition Service and the National Portrait Gallery, 1982), 101.

14. *Paris*, 44, 96.

15. TJ to John Jay, 8 October 1787, *Papers*, 12:217.

16. TJ to James Madison, 8 October 1787, *Papers*, 12:219.

17. George Washington, 2 November 1788, *The Diaries of George Washington*, Donald Jackson and Dorothy Twohig, eds. (Charlottesville: University Press of Virginia, 1979), 5:417.

18. Ibid., 451.

19. Annual Report of the Mount Vernon Ladies' Association of the Union, 1968, 20–25.

20. Catalogue.

21. TJ "Notes of Presents Given to American Diplomats by Foreign Governments," c. 1791, *Papers*, 16:366.

22. Jefferson's Policy Concerning Presents to Foreign Diplomats, *Papers*, 16:362–63; *Paris*, 123.

23. William Short to TJ, 2 May 1791, *Papers*, 20:346; Jefferson's Policy Concerning Presents to Foreign Diplomats, *Papers*, 16:362–363.

24. William Short to TJ, 2 May 1791, *Papers*, 20:346.

25. *MB*, 19 July 1791; Jefferson's Policy Concerning Presents to Foreign Diplomats, *Papers*, 16:362–63.

26. Wendy Wick Reaves, "The Prints," *Antiques* 135 (February 1989): 502–3.

27. Catalogue.

28. TJ to Horatio Gates, 21 February 1798, L and B, 9:441–43.

29. Robert H. Wilson, *Thaddeus Kosciuszko and His Home in Philadelphia* (Philadelphia: Copernicus Society of America, 1976), 15.

30. The South Square room was used by Martha Randolph as a family sitting room. Undated memoran-

dum of Thomas Jefferson Randolph, Edgehill-Randolph Papers (#1397), ViU.

31. TJ to Isaac Coles, 29 November 1809, MHi; Isaac Coles to TJ, 29 December 1809, DLC.

32. William Thornton to TJ, July 1816, cited in Bush, 30.

33. Monica M. Gardner, *Kosciuszko: A Biography* (London: George Allen and Unwin, Ltd., 1942), 23–33.

34. Bush, 29–30.

35. Miecislaus Haiman, *Kosciuszko: Leader and Exile* (New York: Polish Institute of Arts and Sciences in America, 1946), 73ff.

36. Thaddeus Kosciuszko will, 2 April 1798, Albemarle County Will Book, 1:42.

37. The case was not settled until 1852. Edward P. Alexander, "Jefferson and Kosciuszko: Friends of Liberty and Man," *Pennsylvania Magazine of History and Biography* 92 (January 1968), 101.

38. TJ to Frantz Xavier Zeltner, 23 July 1818, MHi, cited in ibid.

39. Ellen W. Randolph to TJ, 22 March 1822, private collection.

40. TJ to James Monroe, 18 December 1786, *Papers* 10:612.

41. Highland is more commonly known as Ash Lawn–Highland, and is now owned by the College of William and Mary.

42. Jefferson also subscribed to the *Repository*. Only the Fulton engraving has been located.

43. TJ to Joseph Delaplaine, 20 May 1813, DLC.

44. Bush, 65–67; Gordon Hendricks, "A Wish to Please and a Willingness to be Pleased," *The American Art Journal* 2 (Spring 1970): 16–29.

45. Joseph Delaplaine to TJ, 27 January 1816, DLC; TJ to Joseph Delaplaine, 9 February 1816, DLC.

46. Dorinda Evans, *Benjamin West and His American Students* (Washington, D.C.: Smithsonian Institution Press, 1980), 116–20; Allen Staley, *Benjamin West, American Painter at the English Court* (Baltimore: Baltimore Museum of Art, 1989), 107–8.

47. Joel Barlow to TJ, 15 September 1801, cited in Sowerby, 1162.

48. Malone, 5:503–4.

49. TJ to Robert Fulton, 16 August 1807, cited in Sowerby, 1162.

50. TJ to Robert Fulton, 8 March 1813, L and B, 19:188.

51. David Rittenhouse to TJ, 11 January 1793, DLC.

52. Bedini, 78.

53. Catalogue. Jefferson's copy of the print is unlocated.

54. *Notes*, 64.

55. Ibid.

56. TJ to David Rittenhouse, 19 July 1778, *Papers*, 2:202–3. Rittenhouse was unable to complete the clock, and it was more than thirty years before Jefferson finally acquired one from Thomas Voight (Cat. #238).

57. Bedini, 229, 247, 374.

58. TJ to the American Philosophical Society, 28 January 1797, cited in Gilbert Chinard, "Jefferson and the American Philosophical Society," *Proceedings of the American Philosophical Society* 87 (July 14, 1943): 267.

59. Catalogue.

60. Jefferson's "original Rough draught" of the Declaration of Independence, 1776, *Papers*, 1:423.

61. John Dickinson and TJ, "Declaration of the Causes and Necessity for Taking up Arms," before July 6, 1775, *Papers*, 1:215.

62. Savage opened his gallery in February 1796. Harold E. Dickson, *John Wesley Jarvis, American Painter* (New York: New York Historical Society, 1949), 35–41; George Groce and David Wallace, *The New York*

Historical Society's Dictionary of Artists in America (New Haven: Yale University Press, 1957), 559–60.

63. E. McClung Fleming, "From Indian Princess to Greek Goddess: The American Image, 1783–1815," *Winterthur Portfolio* III (1967): 54. See also Marvin Trachtenberg, *The Statue of Liberty* (New York: Viking Press, 1976), 63–65.

64. Groce and Wallace, *Dictionary of Artists*, 559–60.

65. TJ to Maria Cosway, 12 October 1786, *Papers*, 10:446.

66. John Trumbull, *Autobiography, Reminiscences and Letters of John Trumbull* (New York: Wiley and Putnam, 1841), 118.

67. TJ to Maria Cosway, 12 October 1786, Boyd, *Papers*, 10:443–55.

68. Daphne Foskett, *A Dictionary of British Miniature Painters* (New York: Praeger Publishers, 1972), 1:220; Stephen Lloyd, "Richard Cosway, R.A.: The Artist as Collector, Connoisseur and Virtuoso," *Apollo* 133 (June 1991), 398–405.

69. John Walker, "Maria Cosway: An Undervalued Artist," *Apollo* 123 (May 1986): Appendix I, 324; George C. Williamson, *Richard Cosway, R.A.* (London: George Bell & Sons, 1897), 11.

70. James A. Bear, "Curator's Annual Report, 1963" (Charlottesville: Thomas Jefferson Memorial Foundation, 1964), 12–13.

71. Paul Lawrence Farber, Chair and Professor of History and Zoology at Oregon State University, graciously matched the print to Levaillant's work. See Jean Anker, *Bird Books and Bird Art* (Copenhagen: Levin and Munksgaard, 1938), no. 302.

72. Allan Nevins, ed., *The Diary of John Quincy Adams: 1794–1845* (New York: Longmans, Green, 1928), 26.

73. TJ, packing list, 22 June 1807, MHi.

74. TJ to Count Dugnani, 14 February 1818, L and B, 19:255. Francisco de Moncada (1586–1635) served as a general under Isabella of Spain and later as an envoy to the court of Ferdinand II. Jefferson's print of his portrait is unlocated.

75. Ibid.

76. Fiske Kimball, "Jefferson and Arts," *Proceedings of the American Philosophical Society* 87 (July 1943): 242; Harold E. Dickson, "'TH.J.' Art Collector," *Jefferson and the Arts: An Extended View*, ed. William Howard Adams (Washington, D.C.: National Gallery of Art, 1976), 110.

77. Sowerby, 4323.

78. *Paris*, 27–28. Howard Rice suggests that the source for the Louvre engraving is François Blondel's *L'architecture Française* (1756). A similar engraving of the Tuilleries is in the 1752 edition of that work.

79. Ibid., 29–30.

80. Ibid., 30–31.

81. Ibid., 32–35.

82. See also Saul Padover, ed., *Thomas Jefferson and the National Capitol* (Washington, D.C.: U.S. Government Printing Office, 1946), 58–59.

83. *Paris*, 6, 9.

84. Wend von Kalnein and Michael Levey, *Art and Architecture of the Eighteenth-Century in France* (Harmondsworth, England: Penguin Books, 1972), 281–83, 319–22; William Howard Adams, ed., *The Eye of Jefferson* (Charlottesville: University Press of Virginia, 1976), 126, 177; Alan Braham, "Drawings for Soufflot's Sainte Geneviève," *Burlington Magazine* 113 (October 1971): 583–92; *Soufflot et son temps: 1780–1980* (Paris: Caisse Nationale des Monuments Historiques et des Sites, 1980), 109–10.

85. TJ memorandum to Bernard Peyton, requesting window glass for print frames, 7 March 1826, MHi.

86. TJ to Robert Skipwith, 3 August 1771, *Papers*, 1:76–81; Randall, 3:346, 349.

87. TJ to Bernard Moore, c. 1764, enclosed in TJ to John Minor, 30 August 1814, Ford, 11:424–25.

88. TJ to John Trumbull, 18 January 1789, *Papers* 14:467–68.

89. A. E. Santaniello, ed., *The Boydell Shakespeare Prints* (New York: Benjamin Bloom, Inc., 1968), 5–9; Winifred H. Friedman, *Boydell's Shakespeare Gallery* (New York: Garland Publishing, Inc., 1976), 2–18, 223, 238, 266.

90. Jefferson recorded in his Memorandum Book paying "vales," or tips, to servants at Mount Vernon. *MB*, 15 October 1790; 12 November 1790; 16 October 1791; 1 October 1792; and 22 September 1793.

91. The date was 12 October, 1791. TJ to Thomas Mann Randolph, 25 October 1791, *Papers* 22:223.

92. TJ to Maria Eppes, 4 January 1801, *Family Letters*, 190.

93. TJ to Thomas Mann Randolph, 13 October 1792, ViU.

94. Catalogue.

95. Francis D. Klingender, *Art and the Industrial Revolution* (New York: Schocken Books, 1970), 86–93; Barrie Trinder, *The Iron Bridge* (England: Ironbridge Gorge Museum Trust, 1973), 2–8.

96. David Humphreys to TJ, 30 January 1786, *Papers*, 9:241. See also *MB*, 11 April 1786, and Catalogue. Jefferson's prints are unlocated.

97. Patrick Conner, *Michael Angelo Rooker, 1746–1801* (London: B. T. Batsford, Ltd., 1984), 24–44.

98. TJ to Benjamin Vaughan, 2 July 1787, *Papers*, 11:532–33.

99. Martin P. Snyder, *City of Independence: Views of Philadelphia Before 1800* (New York: Praeger Publishers, 1975), 226. See also Martin P. Snyder, "William Birch: His Philadelphia Views," *Pennsylvania Magazine of History and Biography* 73 (July 1949), 271–313.

100. William Birch, *The City of Philadelphia, in the State of Pennsylvania*, (Philadelphia, 1800), n.p. [introduction].

101. *MB*, 17 March and 5 May 1800; Snyder, "William Birch: His Philadelphia Views," 279. Birch's subscription book is in the collection of the Historical Society of Pennsylvania.

102. William Birch, "Autobiography," Historical Society of Pennsylvania, cited in Snyder, "William Birch: His Philadelphia Views," 281.

103. James Gilreath and Doug Wilson, eds., *Thomas Jefferson's Library*, (Washington, D.C.: The Library of Congress, 1989), 102.

104. Sowerby, 4161.

105. Wendy Shadwell, *American Printmaking: The First 150 Years* (New York: Museum of Graphic Art, 1969), 48.

106. Ibid.; Jesse Poesch, *The Art of the Old South* (New York: Knopf, 1983), 180–82.

107. Catalogue.

108. TJ to Maria Cosway, 12 October 1786, *Papers*, 10:447; TJ to Angelica Schuyler Church, 17 February 1788, *Papers*, 12:600–1; Catalogue.

109. Sowerby, 4066. Jeremy Elwell Adamson, "Nature's Grandest Scene in Art," *Niagara: Two Centuries of Changing Attitudes* (Washington, D.C.: The Corcoran Gallery of Art, 1985), 17.

110. Adamson, *Niagara*, 25–28.

111. John Davis Hatch, "John Vander Lyn's Prints of Niagara Falls," *Antiques* 138 (December 1990): 1253–55.

112. *MB*, 2 March 1803.

113. John Vanderlyn to John B. Prevost, 20 February 1804, cited in Hatch, "Vander Lyn's Prints of Niagara," 1256–57.

114. Vanderlyn to TJ, 31 December 1805, DLC.

115. *Notes*, 19–20.

116. In 1942, Mrs. Henry K. Dooley, of San Juan, Puerto Rico, reportedly owned Jefferson's painting of *The Passage of the Potomac Through the Blue Ridge*. Efforts to locate Mrs. Dooley or the painting have been unsuccessful.

117. William Roberts to TJ, 24 July 1803, MHi; William Roberts to TJ, 26 February 1808, MHi; Barbara Batson, "Virginia Landscapes by William Roberts," *Journal of Early Southern Decorative Arts* 10 (November 1984): 35–36.

118. *Notes*, 24.

119. Jefferson visited the bridge in 1815, 1817, and 1821, and possibly in 1781. The Natural Bridge tract was sold from Jefferson's estate in 1833.

120. *MB*, 1767 at the beginning of cash accounts.

121. *Notes*, 25. For a discussion of Jefferson's views of the sublime and beautiful, see Charles A. Miller, *Jefferson and Nature: An Interpretation* (Baltimore: The Johns Hopkins University Press, 1988), 102–7.

122. TJ to William Carmichael, 26 December 1786, *Papers*, 10:633. S. Allen Chambers, "Thomas Jefferson Takes His Granddaughters to Natural Bridge," *Lynch's Ferry*, 1 (Fall 1988): 6–8.

123. TJ to William Caruthers, 7 September 1809, and 15 March 1815, DLC.

124. *Notes*, 19.

125. Ibid.

126. The description comes from an unidentified visitor's account to Monticello, cited in Dumas Malone, *The Story of the Declaration of Independence* (New York: Oxford University Press, 1975), 72.

127. TJ to Henry Lee, 8 May 1825, L and B, 16:118. See Jefferson's epitaph, undated memorandum, DLC.

128. Rev. Henry C. Thweatt, D.D., manuscript diary in private collection. For a discussion of the competition between Trumbull, Binns, and Tyler, see John Bidwell, "American History in Image and Text," *Proceedings of the American Antiquarian Society* 98, pt. 2 (1989): 249, 257.

129. Malone, *Declaration of Independence*, 72, 79–80, 248, 253.

130. Bidwell, "American History," 247–303.

131. Ibid., 250–54. Tyler gave credit for his plan of reproducing the Declaration of Independence to William P. Gardner, who had corresponded with Jefferson in 1813 about the idea. See Noble E. Cunningham, *Popular Images of the Presidency from Washington to Lincoln* (Columbia: University of Missouri Press, 1991), 91–94.

132. Transcript of the 26 March 1818 letter from TJ to Benjamin Owen Tyler, as published by Tyler in the 27 April 1818 *Baltimore Patriot*, DLC.

133. Martha Jefferson Randolph to Jane Nicholas Randolph, n.d. [c. 1818–1826], Nicholas P. Trist Papers (#2104), NcU.

134. TJ to John Binns, 31 August 1819, DLC.

135. Ibid.

136. For an exhaustive examination of the distribution of copies, see William R. Coleman, "Counting the Stones—A Census of the Stone Facsimiles of the Declaration of Independence," *Manuscripts* 42 (Spring 1991): 97–105.

137. TJ to L. W. Tazewell, 5 January 1805, ViU.

138. TJ to William Thornton, 9 May 1817, ViU.

139. TJ to William Coffee, 22 November 1821; Edwin M. Betts, "Groundplans and Prints of the University of Virginia, 1822–1826," *Proceedings of the American Philosophical Society* 90 (May 1946): 81.

140. Richard Cote, "The Architectural Workmen of Thomas Jefferson in Virginia" (Ph.D. diss., Boston University, 1986), 88–89. In the past this drawing has been attributed to Jefferson.

141. Maverick sent his first proof of the work to Jefferson on November 12, 1822. Peter Maverick to TJ, 12 November 1822, MHi. When asked what type of paper to use Jefferson responded, "Perhaps you can decide what is best on my information that the prints are intended for frames." TJ to Peter Maverick, 20 November 1822, MHi.

142. *MB*, 29 March 1825.

Physiognotrace Portraits (pp. 198–207)

1. Howard Rice, "A 'New' Likeness of Thomas Jefferson," *The William and Mary Quarterly* 6 (January 1949): 84–89.

2. Howard Rice, "Saint-Mémin's Portrait of Jefferson," *Princeton University Library Chronicle* 20 (Summer 1959): 182–92.

3. Fillmore Norfleet, *Saint-Mémin in Virginia: Portraits and Biographies* (Richmond, VA: Dietz Press, 1942), 28.

4. Mary (Maria) Jefferson Eppes to TJ, 10 February 1804, *Family Letters*, 256–57.

5. Maria died on April 17, 1804. Anne Cary Randolph Bankhead to TJ, 19 December 1808, *Family Letters*, 371; Martha Jefferson Randolph to TJ, 2 March 1809, *Family Letters*, 388.

6. Cunningham, 82; Thomas Jefferson, undated list of names following sheet of paper labeled "Profiles by St. Mémin," ViU.

7. Norfleet, *Saint-Mémin*, 31. Norfleet suggests that Jefferson sat for Saint-Mémin twice, however Rice and Alfred Bush argue that there was only one sitting from which two engravings were made. See Rice, "Portrait," 183, and Bush, 51–53. The round copper-plate from the first portrait is owned by Princeton University Library, and Alderman Library at the University of Virginia owns Saint-Mémin's oval copperplate.

8. *DAB*, s.v., "Gouverneur Morris."

9. Rice, "A 'New' Likeness of Thomas Jefferson," 84–89.

10. Cited in Malone, 2:212.

11. TJ to Archibald Stuart, 14 March 1792, Ford, 6:407.

12. Anne Randolph was the sister of Thomas Mann Randolph, Jefferson's son-in-law.

13. "The Mahlon Dickerson Diary," [1802–1809], cited in Jackson, 2:677–79.

14. *DAB*, s.v. "Mahlon Dickerson."

15. TJ to Paul Allen, 18 August 1813, Jackson, 2:589–90.

16. The documentation of the expedition is copious. The most recent comprehensive works on the subject are Donald Jackson, ed., *Letters of the Lewis and Clark Expedition* 2nd ed. 2 vols. (Chicago: University of Illinois Press, 1978); and Gary E. Moulton, ed., *The Journals of the Lewis and Clark Expedition* 7 vols. (Lincoln: University of Nebraska Press, 1983–1992).

17. TJ to Paul Allen, 18 August 1813, Jackson, 2:592. For a summary of the views on Lewis's death, see Jackson, 2:573–75.

18. *DAB*, s.v. "Benjamin Smith Barton."

19. *Jeffersonia binata* is now called *Jeffersonia diphylla*, Edwin M. Betts, ed., *Thomas Jefferson's Garden Book* (Philadelphia: The American Philosophical Society, 1944), 172–73; Benjamin Smith Barton, "A Letter to Chas. Peter Thunberg. A Botanical Description of the *Podophyllum Diphyllum*," *Transactions of the American Philosophical Society* 3 (1793): 334–47.

20. TJ to Benjamin Smith Barton, 27 February 1803, Jackson, 1:17.

21. Sowerby, 3998; John C. Greene, *American Science in the Age of Jefferson* (Ames: Iowa State University, 1984), 376–85.

22. TJ to Benjamin Smith Barton, 21 September 1809, DLC.

23. Ibid.

24. TJ to Henry Dearborn, 29 December 1802, DLC, cited in Malone 4:274.

25. TJ to Henry Dearborn, 8 January 1808, Ford 11:4.

26. *DAB*, s.v. "Henry Dearborn."

27. Malone, 1:274.

28. Ibid., 5:296–97, 306.

29. Ibid., 5:302–3.

30. TJ to Caesar A. Rodney, 16 March 1815, L and B, 14:284.

31. *DAB*, s.v., "Caesar Rodney."

32. TJ to James Madison, 7 July 1793, Ford 7:436.

33. TJ to James Monroe, 28 June 1793, Ford, 7:416–17; Malone, 3:114–19.

34. TJ to Gouverneur Morris, 16 August 1793, Ford, 7:499.

35. Malone, 3:128–30.

36. William Burwell to TJ, 15 September 1805, DLC; TJ to William Burwell, 26 March 1804, DLC.

37. TJ to William Burwell, ibid.

38. William Burwell to TJ, 18 January 1805, DLC.

39. Specifically Burwell helped refute accusations surrounding the "Walker Affair." See Malone, 5:14–16. For details about the affair see Malone, 1:153–55, 1:447–51, and 4:217–18.

40. Norfleet, *Saint-Mémin* 201–2.

41. Mary Randolph to TJ, 17 March 1825, MHi; TJ to Mary Randolph, 30 March 1825, MHi.

42. Virginia Randolph Trist manuscript cookbook, ViU; Mary Randolph, *Virginia House-Wife*, ed. Karen Hess, (1825; reprint, Columbia: University of South Carolina Press, 1984) passim.

43. TJ to Mary Jefferson, 14 June 1797, *Family Letters*, 148.

44. Malone, 4:408–15. Saint-Mémin's original crayon drawing of Eppes, which descended through the family until acquired by a private collector, is on loan to TJMF.

Silhouettes (pp. 208–212)

1. [Ellen Randolph Coolidge] to Virginia Randolph Trist, 4 December 1827, Nicholas P. Trist Papers (#2104), NcU.

2. Owned by the Museum of the Society of the Cincinnatus.

3. TJMF owns three Peale silhouettes of Dr. Collin and two of these are still connected at the fold. Brooke Hindle, "Charles Willson Peale's Science and Technology," *Charles Willson Peale and His World* (New York: Harry N. Abrams, 1983), 151–53; Charles Coleman Sellers, *Mr. Peale's Museum* (New York: W. W. Norton and Co., 1980), 22, 197–9. Charles Coleman Sellers, "The Peale Silhouettes," *American Collector* 17 (May 1948): 6–8.

4. Charles Willson Peale to TJ, 28 January 1803, *The Selected Papers of Charles Willson Peale and His Family*, ed. Lillian B. Miller, (New Haven: Yale University Press, 1988), 2, pt. 2, 153; Charles Willson Peale to TJ, 15 June 1804, Miller, *Peale Papers* 2, pt. 2, 711–12. Cunningham, 123–28.

5. Sellers, "Silhouettes," 8.

6. Malone, 1:161, 393–96, 431.

7. Randall, 1:83.

8. Gerald Morgan, Jr., "Nicholas Philip and Virginia Jefferson Randolph Trist," in *Collected Papers of the Monticello Association of Descendants of Thomas Jefferson*, ed. George Green Shackelford, (Princeton: Princeton University Press for the Monticello Association, 1965), 1:100–5.

9. Eliza Trist to Nicholas P. Trist, 21 March 1820, Nicholas P. Trist Papers, (#19313) DLC. Charles Coleman Sellers attributes silhouettes stamped "Peale's Museum" to Rubens Peales's New York museum, c. 1825–1837, but Mrs. Trist's letter predates that institution.

10. Charles Willson Peale, Diary 20, Part 1: "A Journey to Washington, D.C., and Return, Including Baltimore and Annapolis, Maryland," Miller, *Peale Papers* 2, pt. 2, 699–700.

11. The identities for the above silhouettes are based upon inscriptions by Jefferson family members. The silhouette labeled "Bonpland" is puzzling because it has a different stamp than the other three and is not mentioned by Peale as one of the silhouettes he brought with him on the trip.

12. Alexander von Humboldt to TJ, 24 May 1804, cited in Helmut de Terra, "Alexander von Humboldt's Correspondence with Jefferson, Madison, and Gallatin," *Proceedings of the American Philosophical Society* 103, (December 1959): 787–88.

13. TJ to Humboldt, 28 May 1804, de Terra, "Humboldt's Correspondence," 788.

14. de Terra, "Humboldt's Correspondence," 786.

15. TJ to Meriwether Lewis, [20 June 1803], Jackson, 1:64.

16. Ibid.

17. They arrived in Washington on 11 July 1804. TJ to the Osages, [12 July 1804], Jackson, 1:199; TJ to the Osages, [16 July 1804], Jackson, 1:200–3.

18. Henry Dearborn to James Wilkinson, 5 August 1805, *Territorial Papers of the U.S.*, 13:178–79, cited in John C. Ewers, "'Chiefs from the Missouri and Mississippi' and Peale's Silhouettes of 1806," *The Smithsonian Journal of History*, 1, (Spring 1966): 10.

19. Ewers, "Chiefs," 10–12.

20. "Sir Augustus John Foster and 'The Wild Natives of the Woods,'" *William and Mary Quarterly* (April 1952): 199–200.

21. Ibid., 192.

22. Ibid., 192–93.

23. Smith, 400.

24. TJ to the Indian Delegation, [4 January 1806], Jackson, 1:280.

25. Ibid., 283.

26. Peale sent the silhouettes to Jefferson on 8 February 1806, Miller, *Peale Papers*, 2, pt. 2, 935.

27. Peale to TJ, 8 February 1806, DLC.

28. Ewers, "Chiefs," 2.

29. Peale cut silhouettes from twice-folded paper, thus creating four identical images.

Sculpture (pp. 215–239)

1. TJ to the Virginia Delegates in Congress, 12 July 1785, *Papers*, 8: 289.

2. Adrien Petit's list of packages sent to Richmond [c. 12 May 1793], *Papers* (forthcoming) 25:873.

3. Peter Carr was the son of Jefferson's boyhood friend Dabney Carr, who died prematurely and was the first to be buried in the Jefferson graveyard at Monticello. He married Jefferson's sister, Martha Jefferson Carr. TJ to Peter Carr, 10 August 1787, *Papers*, 12:19.

4. TJ to Charles Bellini, 30 September 1785, *Papers*, 8:568.

5. H.H. Arnason, *The Sculptures of Houdon* (New York: Oxford University Press, 1975), 49. For an account of the bust of Voltaire, see especially 49–53.
6. *Paris*, 70.
7. Margaret Drabble, ed., *The Oxford Companion to English Literature* (Oxford: Oxford University Press, 1985), 762.
8. TJ to James Madison, 12 January 1789, *Papers*, 14:437.
9. TJ to Thomas Mann Randolph, 30 May 1790, *Papers*, 16:449.
10. Randall, 3:336.
11. TJ to Robert R. Livingston, 6 March 1792, *Papers*, 23:229.
12. Agnes Mongan, *Harvard Honors Lafayette* (Cambridge: Fogg Art Museum, Harvard University, 1975), 66.
13. Joseph Coolidge to Thomas Jefferson Randolph, 23 July 1830, Edgehill-Randolph Papers (#1397), ViU.
14. TJ to Peter Cardelli, 4 October 1820, MHi.
15. Randall, 3:337.
16. TJ to Benjamin Harrison, 12 January 1785, *Papers*, 7:600.
17. See Arnason, *The Sculptures of Houdon*, 72–77.
18. TJ to Samuel Smith, 22 August 1798, Ford, 8:443.
19. TJ to Reverend William Smith, 19 February 1791, Ford, 6:208.
20. For a full discussion see Jean Montague Messengale, "A Franklin by Houdon Rediscovered," *Marsyas* 12 (1964/1965):1–15.
21. This account of Jones's career was drawn from J. Mark Thompson, "John Paul Jones," in *The Blackwell Encyclopedia of the American Revolution*, ed. Jack P. Greene and J. R. Pole (Cambridge: Basil Blackwell, 1991), 740–41.
22. Arnason, *The Sculptures of Houdon*, 58.
23. John Paul Jones to TJ, 28 February 1786, *Papers*, 9:305.
24. Jones to TJ, 9 September 1788, *Papers*, 13:585.
25. Jones to William Short, before 15/26 September 1788, *Papers*, 13:586.
26. TJ to J. H. Sherburne, 2 July 1825, DLC.
27. Joseph Coolidge to Nicholas P. Trist, 8 March 1827, Nicholas P. Trist Papers (#19313), DLC.
28. Mabel Munson Swan, *The Athenaeum Gallery* (Boston: Boston Athenaeum, 1940), 165–67.
29. TJ, "Autobiography," in *Thomas Jefferson: Writings*, ed. Merrill D. Peterson (New York: Library of America, 1984), 37.
30. TJ to Peter Cardelli, 4 October 1820, MHi.
31. Ellen Randolph to TJ, 12 December 1821, Private collection.
32. TJ to Ellen Randolph, 10 January 1822, Private collection.
33. TJ to Ellen Randolph, 7 February 1822, Private collection.
34. Ellen Randolph to TJ, 22 March 1822, Private collection.
35. TJ, undated memorandum, MHi.
36. TJ to John Adams, 5 July 1814, Cappon, 413.
37. TJ to the marquis de Lafayette, May 1807, Ford, 9:67, cited in John P. Foley, ed., *The Jefferson Cyclopedia* (NY: Funk and Wagnalls, 1900) 98.
38. Martha Jefferson Randolph to Thomas Jefferson Randolph, 28 July 1833, Edgehill-Randolph Papers (#1397), ViU.
39. For a fine account of Rush's busts of Jackson, see Milo M. Naeve, "William Rush's Terracotta and Plaster Busts of General Andrew Jackson," *American Art Journal* 21 (1989):19–39.
40. James Ronaldson to TJ, 1 February 1820, DLC.
41. TJ to James Ronaldson, 7 February 1820, DLC.
42. Linda Bantel et al., *William Rush, American Sculptor* (Philadelphia: Pennsylvania Academy of the Fine Arts, 1982), 156.
43. 2 June 1819, *Farmer's Repository*, Charles Town, West Virginia, cited in ibid., 157.
44. James Maury to TJ, 27 June 1820, DLC.
45. A related work in marble with similar dimensions is now in the collection of the Athenaeum Library in Liverpool.
46. TJ to William Roscoe, 27 December 1820, DLC.
47. TJ to William Roscoe, 1 July 1806.
48. Cited in Andrew Oliver, *The Portraits of John and Abigail Adams* (Cambridge: Belknap Press of Harvard University Press, 1967), 180.
49. John Adams to TJ, 29 May 1818, Cappon, 526.
50. John Adams to John B. Binon, 7 February 1819, cited in Oliver, *The Portraits of John and Abigail Adams*, 185.
51. Benjamin Gould to TJ, 14 July 1825, DLC.
52. TJ to Benjamin Gould, 5 August 1825, DLC.
53. Academie Royale de Peinture et de Sculpture, *Collection des livrets des anciennes expositions depuis 1673 jusqu'en 1800* (Paris: Liepmannsohn et Dufour, 1870), 47.
54. *MB*, 3 July 1789.
55. Very few of these terra-cotta models survive. One such example is *George Washington* in the collection of the Mount Vernon Ladies' Association.
56. Louis-Léopold Boilly, *The Studio of Houdon*, 1804, Musée Thomas Henry, Cherbourg.
57. Levett Harris to TJ, 7 August 1804, DLC.
58. TJ to Levett Harris, 18 April 1806, L and B, 11:101.
59. TJ to Joseph Priestley, 29 November 1802, DLC.
60. TJ to Dr. Thomas Cooper, 17 March 1820, ViU.
61. Ibid.
62. Bradford L. Rauschenberg, "William John Coffee, Sculptor-Painter: His Southern Experience," *Journal of Early Southern Decorative Arts* 4 (November 1978):26–27.
63. William Coffee to TJ, 4 March 1818, DLC.
64. TJ to Wilson Cary Nicholas, 5 April 1818, MHi; *MB*, 14 April 1818.
65. *MB*, 14 April 1818. Jefferson paid five dollars for each bust on 18 May 1819. Neither Coffee's original terra-cotta busts nor plaster copies of Martha Jefferson Randolph or James Madison survive.
66. Elizabeth Trist mentioned a bust of "Mr. Randolph", either Jefferson's son-in-law Thomas Mann Randolph or his grandson Thomas Jefferson Randolph, in a letter to Nicholas P. Trist, 18 April 1820, Nicholas P. Trist Papers (#19313), DLC.
67. Jefferson made no record in his Memorandum Book of payments for these particular busts.
68. Rauschenberg, "Coffee," 34. Enniscorthy is in Albemarle County.
69. TJ to James Madison, 11 April 1818, DLC.
70. Rauschenberg, "Coffee," 31.
71. *MB*, 22 March 1823; TJ to William Coffee, 10 July 1822; 4 September 1824; 19 September 1824; 5 January 1825; 29 August 1825, all MHi; William Coffee to TJ, 19 August 1825, MHi.
72. *MB*, 25 March 1822.
73. Ellen Randolph Coolidge to Virginia Randolph Trist, 13 May 1828, Jefferson-Coolidge Family Collection (#9090), ViU.
74. For Roman cement see *MB*, 15 May 1819 and 4 March 1821; TJ to William Coffee, 27 October 1818, 15 May 1819, and 5 March 1821, all MHi.
75. TJ to Ellen Randolph, 1 March 1807, *Family Letters*, 296.
76. TJ to Martha Jefferson Randolph, 31 August 1817, *Family Letters*, 418–19.
77. Cornelia Jefferson Randolph to Virginia Jefferson Randolph, 30 August 1817, Nicholas P. Trist Papers (#2104), NcU. See S. Allen Chambers, "Thomas Jefferson Takes his Granddaughters to Natural Bridge," *Lynch's Ferry* (Fall 1988): 6–8.
78. George Green Shackelford, "Unmarried Children of Martha Jefferson and Thomas Mann Randolph, Jr.," in *Collected Papers of the Monticello Association of Descendants of Thomas Jefferson*, ed. George Green Shackelford (Princeton: Princeton University Press, 1965), 1:152.
79. TJ to Anne Cary Randolph, 20 May 1803, *Family Letters*, 245–46.
80. TJ to Anne Cary Randolph, 7 June 1807, *Family Letters*, 307–8. See also Edwin M. Betts and Hazlehurst Perkins, *Thomas Jefferson's Flower Garden at Monticello*, 3rd ed., rev. and enl. by Peter J. Hatch, (Charlottesville: University Press of Virginia, 1986), 36–37.
81. TJ to Anne Cary Randolph, 7 June 1807, *Family Letters*, 307–8.
82. Olivia Taylor, "Charles Lewis and Anne Cary Bankhead," in *Collected Family Papers*, 1:71–72.
83. Ibid., 73–74; Malone, 6:159.
84. Martha Jefferson Randolph to TJ, 20 November 1816, *Family Letters*, 417. Bankhead engaged in a street fight with his brother-in-law Thomas Jefferson Randolph in Charlottesville on February 1, 1819.
85. Malone, 6:298–300.
86. Samuel X. Radbill, ed., "The Autobiographical Ana of Robley Dunglison, M.D.," *Transactions of the American Philosophical Society* n.s., 53 (1963): 34. Dunglison was the attending physician.
87. *MB*, 26 October 1784. Hercules is illustrated in Régine de Plinval de Guillebon, *Porcelain of Paris 1770–1850* (New York: Walker and Company, 1972), 60.
88. Six statuettes are mentioned on Grevin's Packing List of July 1790: four in crate number fifty-five and two in crate number fifty-six.
89. James Bowdoin to TJ, 25 March 1805, DLC.
90. TJ to James Bowdoin, 27 April 1805, DLC.
91. Ellen Coolidge to Martha Jefferson Randolph, 21 July 1833, Jefferson-Coolidge Family Collection (#9090), ViU.

Medals and Medallions (pp. 240–247)

1. Daniel Webster, "Notes of Mr. Jefferson's Conversation 1824 at Monticello," *The Papers of Daniel Webster*, ed. Charles M. Wiltse and Harold D. Moser (Hanover, NH: University Press of New England, 1974), 1:374.
2. Malone, 1:128–41. Jefferson recorded Botetourt's death in his Memorandum Book on 15 October 1770.
3. Graham Hood, "Let Us Now Praise Famous Men—In Wax," *Colonial Williamsburg* (Summer 1990) 43–44; Catalogue.
4. R. W. Julian, *Medals of the United States Mint: The First Century* (El Cajon, CA: The Token and Medal Society, Inc., 1977), xx, 77. Noble Cunningham raises the possibility that Jefferson's Indian Peace Medal was Reich's first project in the United States. See Cunningham, 73–74.
5. TJ to Martha Jefferson Randolph, 3 April 1802, *Family Letters*, 221; TJ to Maria Jefferson Eppes, 29 March 1802, *Family Letters*, 221. Elizabeth Wayles Eppes was also Maria's mother-in-law.
6. Martha Jefferson Randolph to TJ, 16 April 1802, *Family Letters*, 222.
7. Maria Jefferson Eppes to TJ, 21 April 1802, *Family Letters*, 224.

8. J. F. Loubat, *The Medallic History of the United States of America: 1776–1876* (1878; reprint, New Milford, CT: N. Flayderman & Co., Inc., 1967), 135–50.

9. TJ to the Senate and House of Representatives of the United States, 20 February 1805, cited in ibid., 136.

10. Malone, 5:37–39; *DAB*, s.v. "Edward Preble."

11. *MB*, 30 May 1805, and 12 July 1805.

12. Eccleston also included an engraving of the medal and an 1805 broadside describing the medal and Washington's qualities. David Eccleston to TJ, 20 May 1807, DLC.

13. Ibid.

14. TJ to David Eccleston, 21 November 1807, L and B, 11:396; TJ to James Maury, 21 November 1807, L and B, 11:396–97.

15. Catalogue.

16. There is disagreement among numismatics as to Reich's involvement on this medal. See Cunningham, 73–75; Julian, *Medals of the United States Mint*, 33; Francis Prucha, *Indian Peace Medals in American History* (Lincoln: University of Nebraska Press, 1971), 95.

17. TJ to William Carmichael and William Short, 30 June 1793, L and B, 9:157–58.

18. Paul Russell Cutright, "Lewis and Clark Indian Peace Medals," *Missouri Historical Society Bulletin* 24 (January 1968): 160–62; Prucha, *Indian Peace Medals*, 6.

19. William Thornton to Tench Coxe, January 1810, cited in Prucha, *Indian Peace Medals*, 95.

20. For examples of Lewis and Clark's distribution practices see Prucha, *Indian Peace Medals*, xiii–xiv, 16–24, and Cutright, "Lewis and Clark," 160–64. Prucha notes that despite attempts to present medals according to a tribe's hierarchy, peace medals sometimes bestowed rank and "made" the chiefs with whom the United States dealt.

21. Lewis and Clark to the Oto Indians, [4 August 1804], Jackson, 1:205; Cutright, "Lewis and Clark," 160–62.

22. Jackson, 1:208.

23. Ellen Miles, "Saint-Mémin's Portraits of American Indians, 1804–1807," *The American Art Journal* 20 (1988): 3–33.

24. Cited in John C. Ewers, "'Chiefs from the Missouri and Mississippi' and Peale's Silhouettes of 1806," *The Smithsonian Journal of History* 1 (Spring 1986): 15.

25. Nathaniel Pryor to William Clark, 16 October 1807, Jackson, 2:433–35; Cutright, "Lewis and Clark," 163–65.

26. TJ to George Erving, 11 April 1823, DLC. Erving also presented a set of medals, now unlocated, to the Massachusetts Historical Society in 1822.

27. The majority of their correspondence is in DLC, c. 1801–1823.

28. While in Paris Jefferson directed the execution of nine medals commissioned by Congress to commemorate the Revolutionary War. He brought to the United States tin proofs of ten medals executed in Paris and displayed them in the parlor. Jefferson's proof of the John Paul Jones medal survives in Monticello's collection. See *Papers*, 16:xxxv–xlii, 53–79; catalogue.

29. Catalogue.

30. George Erving to TJ, 9 May 1823, DLC.

31. In his letter of thanks for the medals Jefferson wrote that he intended to give the set to the University of Virginia, but he never did.

Furniture (pp. 248–272)

1. For an excellent account of the history of this table, see Gregory R. Weidman, *Furniture in Maryland 1740–1940* (Baltimore: Maryland Historical Society, 1984), 64–65.

2. See Wallace Gusler, *Furniture of Williamsburg and Eastern Virginia* (Richmond: Virginia Museum of Fine Arts, 1979), 39–40.

3. *MB*, 1772, n.d.

4. Henry Ingle to TJ, 27 May 1801, MHi.

5. Henry Ingle was paid $133.07 for furniture on May 13, 1794, "Sundries bot on account of George Washington," National Archives and Records Service, 45681.

6. 26 July 1801; 1 and 6 October 1802; 8 March 1805; 18 March and 16 April 1806; Ingle Accounts, MHi.

7. *MB*, November 1772. For a discussion of the tables, see Cat. #115.

8. For an excellent discussion of Scott, see Gusler, *Furniture of Williamsburg* 24–57.

9. *MB*, 27 April, 7 May, 6 November 1768.

10. *MB*, 6 November 1768; 13 December 1769; 4 and 5 November 1771; 6 May 1773; 29 April 1773; 18 December 1777.

11. Gusler, *Furniture of Williamsburg*, 3.

12. Ibid., 96.

13. Joseph Coolidge to Thomas Jefferson Randolph, 16 December 1826, Edgehill-Randolph Papers (#1397), ViU.

14. Joseph Coolidge to Nicholas P. Trist, 5 January 1827, Nicholas P. Trist Papers (#19313), DLC.

15. Virginia Randolph Trist to Ellen Randolph Coolidge, 11 February 1827, Jefferson-Coolidge Family Collection (#9090), ViU.

16. The note is recorded in *MB*, 1767.

17. Jefferson Randolph Kean (1860–1950) to Fiske Kimball, 19 May 1939, Accession file, TJMF.

18. Martha Jefferson Randolph to Thomas Jefferson Randolph, 7 February 1830, Edgehill-Randolph Papers (#1397), ViU.

19. For a discussion of the bureau table form, see Morrison H. Heckscher, *American Furniture in the Metropolitan Museum of Art*. Vol. 2, *Late Colonial Period: The Queen Anne and Chippendale Styles* (New York: The Metropolitan Museum of Art and Random House, 1985), 209–16.

20. Affidavit, Harry Randolph Burke, 7 May 1938, Accession file, TJMF.

21. TJ "Mem. for Capt. Colley to have made in London for Th.J," 16 November 1789, *Papers*, 15:546.

22. Nathaniel Colley to TJ, 5 September 1790, *Papers*, 17:488.

23. Bill of lading, 21 January 1791, *Papers*, 19:592n.

24. Nathaniel Colley to TJ, 22 January 1791, *Papers*, 19:591.

25. Account of Samuel Titt, 25 November 1790, *Papers*, 19:592n.

26. 1826 Inventory.

27. *MB*, 16 July 1790.

28. TJ to James Brown, 8 August 1790, *Papers*, 17:321–22.

29. TJ to Thomas Mann Randolph, 15 May 1791, *Papers*, 20:415.

30. *MB*, 6 April 1793 (12 chairs from Francis Trumble); 10 May 1800 (6 chairs from John Letchworth); 13 October 1801 (48 chairs from Adam Snyder).

31. *MB*, 10 March 1809 (36 chairs ordered from Richmond but possibly made elsewhere, shipped to Poplar Forest); TJ to George Jefferson, 10 March 1809, MHi.

32. Charles Santore, *The Windsor Style in America: A Pictorial Study of the History and Regional Characteristics of the Most Popular Furniture Form of Eighteenth-Century America, 1730–1830*, ed. Thomas M. Voss, (Philadelphia: Running Press, 1981), 256.

33. TJ to John Barnes, 24 June 1800, CSmH. John Letchworth worked at 76 and 78 South Fourth Street in Philadelphia.

34. TJ to George Jefferson, 19 July 1800, MHi.

35. Santore, *Windsor Style in America*, 132–38.

36. William MacPherson Hornor, Jr., *Bluebook of Philadelphia Furniture* (Alexandria, VA: Highland House Publishers, 1935), plate 470.

37. Snyder invoice, 31 July 1801, MHi; Santore, *Windsor Style in America*, 263.

38. An act, imposting taxes for the support of government, passed 21 December 1814, MoSHi; 1815 Tax List.

39. Monticello Dispersal Sale receipts, [1827], Thomas Jefferson Manuscripts (#5291), ViU.

40. J.R. Kane to the President of the American Philosophical Society, 20 April 1838, PPAP. Kane, who received the chair from Martha Randolph, is clearly citing her account of the chair's history.

41. Santore, *Windsor Style in America*, 199. See pages 199–200 for "The Re-creation of Thomas Jefferson's Swivel Windsor."

42. See Charles L. Granquist, "Thomas Jefferson's 'Whirligig' chairs," *Antiques* 109 (May 1976): 1059.

43. Ibid., 1060n.

44. TJ to Thomas Mann Randolph, 25 November 1800, DLC.

45. Before Burling made the revolving chair for Washington, he made an elaborate tambour writing desk that cost £74 in November 1789. He also may have made twelve chairs very much like the shield-back ones that Jefferson acquired in New York. See Cat. #134. "Sundries bot on account of George Washington," 20 November 1789–1795, National Archives and Records Service, 45681.

46. Helen Maggs Fede, *Washington Furniture at Mount Vernon* (Mount Vernon, VA: Mount Vernon Ladies' Association, 1966), 40, cited in Granquist, "Thomas Jefferson's 'Whirligig' Chairs," *Antiques* 1057.

47. William Loughton Smith, *The Pretentions of Thomas Jefferson to Presidency Examined . . .* (Philadelphia, 1796), 1:16.

48. Nicole de Reyniès, *Le mobilier domestique: Vocabulaire Typologique* (Paris: Imprimerie Nationale, 1987), 96–97, especially figure 245.

49. Ibid., 186–87.

50. For a related example, see Charles F. Montgomery, *American Furniture: The Federal Period in the Henry Francis du Pont Winterthur Museum* (New York: Bonanza Books, 1978), cat. no. 289, 324–25.

51. *MB*, 6 February 1809.

52. For related examples, see Patricia E. Kane, *Three Hundred Years of American Seating Furniture* (Boston: New York Graphic Society, 1976), 300; Montgomery, *American Furniture*, 110.

53. 1 June 1790, "Sundries bot on account of George Washington," 20 November 1789–1795, National Archives and Records Service, 45681.

54. Montgomery, *American Furniture*, 110.

55. Montgomery illustrates two (cat. no. 87 and 88) in *American Furniture*, 139–40.

56. Francis Calley Gray, *Visitors*, 57.

57. See examples published in Montgomery, *American Furniture*, 175–78.

58. Thomas Sheraton, *The Cabinet-Maker's and Upholsterer's Drawing-Book*, ed. Charles F. Montgomery and Wilfred P. Cole (1802; reprint, New York: Praeger, 1970), pl. 8.

The Joinery at Monticello (pp. 273–299)

1. This definition is paraphrased from *The Compact Edition of the Oxford English Dictionary* (New York: Oxford University Press, 1971), s.v. "joiner".
2. For an excellent account of the contributions of Jefferson's architectural workmen elsewhere in Virginia, see Richard C. Cote, *The Architectural Workmen of Thomas Jefferson in Virginia* (Ph.D diss., Boston University, 1986).
3. Insurance plat, 1796, MHi.
4. James Dinsmore "Memdm. of Carpenters tools belonging to Mr. Jefferson," 15 April 1809, MHi. (Appendix I).
5. TJ Miscellaneous Accounts, 1764–1779, CSmH, cited in Charles L. Granquist, Jr., "Cabinetmaking at Monticello" (Master's thesis, State University of New York College at Oneonta, 1977), 16.
6. TJ to Giovanni Fabbroni, 8 June 1778, *Papers*, 2:196.
7. *MB*, 3 April 1781.
8. TJ "Memorandums with respect to Watson," 25 October 1793, DLC.
9. Ibid.
10. TJ to Maria Jefferson, 15 December 1793, *Family Letters*, 127.
11. K. Edward Lay, "Charlottesville's Architectural Legacy," *Magazine of Albemarle County History* 46 (May 1988): 32–33.
12. TJ to Benjamin Henry Latrobe, 11 May 1815, DLC, cited in ibid., 33.
13. Lay, "Charlottesville's Architectural Legacy," 32–33.
14. Daniel Trump to TJ, 12 March 1801, MHi.
15. TJ to James Oldham, 11 October 1804, MHi.
16. TJ to John Harvie, 27 September 1804, MHi.
17. TJ to James Oldham, 24 December 1804, ViU.
18. TJ to James Oldham, 12 October 1807, MHi.
19. James Oldham to TJ, 24 December 1807, MHi.
20. Lay, "Charlottesville's Architectural Legacy," 37.
21. "1827 Inventory of John Neilson of Albemarle County," Albemarle County Will Book 9:269, as transcribed by K. Edward Lay, 1986.
22. Thomas Mann Randolph to TJ, 8 May 1793, MHi.
23. TJ to Daniel Trump, 21 February 1801, MHi.
24. Bear, 101–2.
25. TJ, Farm Book, MHi.
26. TJ to Francis Eppes, 17 February 1825, *Family Letters*, 451.
27. TJ to Ellen Randolph Coolidge, 14 November 1825, *Family Letters*, 461.
28. TJ, Will, 16 and 17 March 1826, ViU.
29. TJ to Thomas Mann Randolph, 23 January 1801, MHi.
30. TJ, 1 February 1818, in Edwin M. Betts, ed. *Thomas Jefferson's Farm Book* (Princeton, NJ: Princeton University Press, 1953), 114.
31. Eight chairs also descending from Joseph Cabell, but in walnut, are known today in a private collection.
32. Nicole de Reyniès, *Le mobilier domestique: vocabulaire typologique* (Paris: Imprimerie nationale, 1987), 1:48, 70.
33. TJ to Martha Jefferson Randolph, 24 August 1819, *Family Letters*, 431.
34. Ellen Randolph Coolidge to Henry S. Randall, 16 May 1857, Ellen Coolidge Letterbook, Jefferson-Coolidge Family Collection (#9090), ViU.
35. TJ to William Brown, 18 August 1818, MHi.
36. Martha Jefferson Randolph to TJ, 17 February 1809, *Family Letters*, 382.
37. TJ to Martha Jefferson Randolph, 27 February 1809, MHi.
38. Thomas B. Robertson to William Robertson, 7 June 1819, private collection.
39. Thomas B. Robertson to TJ, 2 August 1819, DLC.
40. TJ to Thomas B. Robertson, 7 November 1819, DLC.
41. Smith, 387–88.
42. William Short to TJ, 4 August 1790, *Papers*, 17:315.
43. List of furniture on verso of Jefferson's drawing of the plan of his house on the Schuylkill River (K-120/N-251), MHi.
44. TJ to Edmund Bacon, 5 December 1811, MHi.
45. Granquist, "Cabinetmaking at Monticello," pl. 14.
46. Affidavit concerning Jefferson bookcase, Virginius Randolph Shackelford, 20 September 1936, Accession file, TJMF.
47. TJ to Thomas Jefferson Randolph, 6 May 1809, *Family Letters*, 392.
48. Smith, 72.
49. Randall, 3:344–45.
50. S. Allen Chambers to Ann Lucas, 8 September 1991.
51. Object folder, Winterthur Museum, Winterthur, DE.
52. Edward H. Pinto, "Georgian Library Steps," *Antiques* 83 (January 1963): 103–4.

French Furniture (pp. 300–313)

1. 1790 Packing.
2. Comte François de Salverte, *Les Ébénistes du XVIII siècle: leurs oeuvres et leurs marques* (Paris: F. De Nobele, 1985), 322.
3. Ernest Dumonthier, *Les Sièges de Georges Jacob* (Paris: Éditions Albert Morancé, 1922). See also Jean Meuvret and Claude Frégnac, *Les Ébénistes du XVIII siècle français* (Paris: Hachette, 1963).
4. *MB*, 29 July 1789.
5. Monticello Dispersal Sale receipts, [1827], Thomas Jefferson Manuscripts (#5291), ViU.
6. Morrison H. Heckscher, *American Furniture in the Metropolitan Museum of Art*, Vol. 2, *Late Colonial Period: The Queen Anne and Chippendale Styles* (New York: Metropolitan Museum of Art and Random House, 1985), 202.
7. 1790 Packing.
8. Salverte, *Les Ébénistes du XVIII siècle*, 2.
9. *MB*, 24 July 1789.
10. Adrien Petit's List of Packages sent to Richmond, [c. 12 May 1793], *Papers* (forthcoming), 25:872.
11. 1790 Packing.
12. Adrien Petit's List of Packages sent to Richmond, [c. 12 May 1793], *Papers* (forthcoming), 25:873.
13. 1815 Tax List.
14. 1790 Packing.
15. 1815 Tax List.
16. Anne Royall, *Mrs. Royall's Southern Tour* (Washington, D.C., 1830), 1:87–91.

Silver (pp. 314–335)

1. TJ, Fee Book, 1764–1790, CSmH.
2. Arthur G. Grimwade, *London Goldsmiths, 1697–1837: Their Marks and Lives* (London: Faber and Faber, 1976), 604.
3. Martha Jefferson Randolph, housewife list, c. 1823, ViMo.
4. Martha Jefferson Randolph, silver inventory, c. 1833. ViMo.
5. George Ticknor, *Visitors*, 62.
6. TJ, canteen list, c. 1789, MHi.
7. 1826 Inventory.
8. *MB*, 21 and 23 August 1784.
9. Pierre Kjellberg, "Toute l'Argenterie du Table Louis XVI," *Connaissance des Arts* 138 (August 1963): 17.
10. TJ, canteen list, c. 1789, MHi; Martha Jefferson Randolph, housewife list, c. 1823, and silver inventory, c. 1833, ViMo.
11. George Wythe Randolph to Mary B. Randolph, 9 September 1855, Edgehill-Randolph Papers (#1397), ViU.
12. TJ to Matthew Boulton, 8 January 1787, *Papers*, 11:25–26.
13. *MB*, 17 February 1787.
14. Margaret Holland, *Phaidon Guide to Silver* (Englewood Cliffs, NJ: Prentice-Hall, Inc., 1983), 120–22.
15. 1790 Packing.
16. Martha Jefferson Randolph, housewife list, c. 1823, and silver inventory, c. 1833, ViMo.
17. Trade card of Thomas Whipham, c. 1786, TJMF collection.
18. *MB*, 16 and 17 January 1787. Jefferson and his family used the terms casserole and vegetable dish interchangeably. The word casserole comes from a French word for a cooking pan in which food was subsequently served.
19. Adrien Petit's List of Packages sent to Richmond, [c. 12 May 1793], *Papers* (forthcoming), 25:873.
20. Martha Jefferson Randolph, housewife list, c. 1823, and silver inventory, c. 1833, ViMo.
21. Martha Jefferson Randolph, will, written in Washington, D.C., by an unidentified hand, 18 April 1834, Edgehill-Randolph Papers (#1397), ViU; Thomas Jefferson Randolph, will, written 24 January 1873 and probated 6 December 1875, *Albemarle County Will Book*, 29:133. By 1873 when Randolph's will was written, the four silver plates (Cat. 180) were being used as under-plates for the vegetable dishes, even though they were not intended for that purpose originally.
22. TJ to Vine Utley, 21 March 1819, L and B, 15:187.
23. Henry Nocq, *Le Poinçon de Paris: répertoire des maîtres-orfèvres de la juridiction de Paris depuis le moyen-âge jusqu'à la fin du XVIIIe Siècle* (Paris: Léonce Laget, 1968), 3:86–87.
24. *MB*, 6 February 1789.
25. *MB*, 3 June 1789; Odiot's invoice to TJ, 3 June 1789, Vi.
26. TJ to Charles Louis Clérisseau, 7 June 1789, *Papers*, 15:172–73; for another account, see Julian P. Boyd, "Silver Coffee Urn Made by Odiot from Design by Jefferson," *Papers*, 15:xxvii–xxix.
27. Olivier Lefuel, "Les fastes de l'ère impériale," *Les Grands Orfèvres de Louis XIII à Charles X* (Paris: Hachette, 1965), 264–65.
28. Odiot's invoice to TJ, 3 June 1789, Vi. The silver cost 58 livres 10 sous per marc, or a total of 291 livres, and there was a charge of 132 livres for labor.
29. TJ, drawing of urn, c. 1789, MHi.
30. *MB*, 3 June 1789. The prices paid for the two urns are comparable. The Leguay urn weighs about 1050 grams; its price of 409 livres is roughly proportional to the sum of 423 livres paid in June for an urn weighing about 1200 grams.
31. 1790 Packing.
32. 1815 Tax List; Martha Jefferson Randolph, housewife list, c. 1823, and silver inventory, c. 1833, ViMo.
33. TJ, summary of French purchases, 1788–1789, MHi.

34. 1815 Tax List.

35. Monticello dispersal sale receipts, [1827], Thomas Jefferson Manuscripts (#5291), ViU.

36. *MB*, 3 June 1789.

37. TJ, drawing of three goblets, c. 1789, MHi.

38. Nocq, *Le Poinçon de Paris*, 1:48.

39. 1790 Packing.

40. 1815 Tax List.

41. Martha Jefferson Randolph, housewife list, c. 1823, ViMo.

42. Thomas Jefferson Randolph to Elizabeth Martin Randolph, 25 December 1837, Edgehill-Randolph Papers (#1397), ViU.

43. *Papers*, 15:xxx.

44. TJ to Charles Louis Clérisseau, 7 June 1789, *Papers*, 15:172.

45. Julian P. Boyd, "Thomas Jefferson and the Roman Askos of Nîmes," *Antiques* 103 (July 1973): 123.

46. Joseph Coolidge to Thomas Jefferson Randolph, 16 December 1826, Edgehill-Randolph Papers (#1397), ViU.

47. Martha Jefferson Randolph to TJ, 11 July 1805, *Family Letters*, 277.

48. *MB*, 2 October 1787, "Pd. for plated cream urn 18f." Summary of French purchases, 1788–1789, MHi, "60 [livres] P[lated]. 2 cream vases."

49. Partnership of Johnson and Reat described in George Barton Cutten, *The Silversmiths of Virginia* (Richmond: Dietz Press, Inc., 1952), 142–45, 155.

50. Martha Jefferson Randolph, housewife list, c. 1823, and silver inventory, c. 1833, ViMo.

51. 1826 Inventory.

52. Cutten, *The Silversmiths of Virginia*, 7–9.

53. James A. Bear, Jr., "Thomas Jefferson's Silver," *Antiques* 74 (September 1958):236. The Franzoni sugar bowl has been in the TJMF collection since 1954.

54. TJ to Martha Jefferson Randolph, 30 September 1808, *Family Letters*, 349–50.

55. Martha Jefferson Randolph to TJ, 27 October 1808, *Family Letters*, 354. The four gravy spoons and French ladle to be melted down were part of the silver Jefferson bought in Paris: two "ragout spoons" purchased in 1784 (*MB*, 23 August 1784), another ragout spoon bought in 1786 (*MB*, 24 August 1786), one of two soup ladles also bought in 1784 and 1786 (*MB*, 23 August 1784 and 9 December 1786). Four ragout spoons and two "soup spoons" (ladles) came to America with TJ's household goods (1790 packing).

56. TJ, "Prices. plate," c. 1809, MHi.

57. *MB*, 6 February 1809. The amount $39.615 reflects the balance Jefferson owed Burnett. The total cost of the pudding dish and the 18 spoons was about $80, minus just over $40 for the 39 ounces of silver that were melted down (according to Jefferson's calculations on the undated document cited above).

58. Martha Jefferson Randolph, housewife list, c. 1823, "18 dessert spoons" and "1 pudding dish"; Martha Jefferson Randolph, silver inventory, c. 1833, "18 dessert spoons" and "2 pudding dishes," ViMo.

59. William DuVal to TJ, 19 June and 12 July 1806, DLC.

60. The silver which Jefferson had melted down in 1810 included "a pair of Cans and a pair of Beakers." Jefferson had two "cans," handled mugs with rounded bottoms, at Monticello in 1790 which appear on none of the later inventories (Jefferson's list, "Silver left at Monticello," 4 March 1790, MHi), and in 1855 Jefferson's grandson, George Wythe Randolph, referred in a letter to "the beakers left him by Mr. Wythe . . ." (George Wythe Randolph to Mary B. Randolph, 9 September 1855, Edgehill-Randolph Papers [#1397], ViU).

61. G. Bernard Hughes, *Small Antique Silverware* (New York: Bramhall House, 1957), 115–17.

62. Ruthanna Hindes, "Delaware Silversmiths, 1700–1850," *Delaware History* 12 (1967):275–76.

63. *MB*, 21 April 1806, "Drew orders on the bank U.S. for the following sums & persons . . . John Letellier 22 a silver Can for Chas. Clay. Bedford a present . . ." *MB*, 6 November 1806, "Gave Joseph Daugherty ord. on bk. U.S. for 109.D. to wit . . . Letellier. Etuis case 6."

64. "John Letelier, Dentist" ran extended advertisements in the *Enquirer* (Richmond) in September and October 1806. TJ to George Jefferson, 6 October 1808, MHi.

65. TJ to John Letelier, 15 October 1808, DLC.

66. TJ to John Letelier, 27 March 1810, MoSHi.

67. *MB*, 17 February 1787. The amount paid for the cup, thirty livres, is relatively low and likely indicates a cup of silverplate rather than solid silver.

68. Francis Calley Gray, *Visitors*, 58.

69. TJ to John Letelier, 22 July 1817, MoSHi.

70. John Letelier to TJ, 11 August 1817, MoSHi.

Ceramics and Glass (pp. 336–349)

1. David N. Peters to Susan Stein, 23 September 1987.

2. *MB*, 22 October 1784. TJ purchased lamps from Daguerre on the same day.

3. Rosalind Savill, *The Wallace Collection Catalogue of Sèvres Porcelain* (London: Wallace Collection, 1988), 3:976.

4. David N. Peters to Sondy M. Sanford, 1 January 1988.

5. Savill, *The Wallace Collection Catalogue*, 3:1068.

6. The attribution to Mme. Taillandier is based on the Sèvres archives, which reveal no payments to M. Taillandier for *guirlandes de barbeaux* during this period.

7. This information was generously shared with me by Rosalind Savill.

8. H.L. Tardy, *Les Porcelaines Françaises* (Paris: Tardy, 1987), 480. Tardy cites 1787 for the jj mark, but Peters says it is 1786.

9. Peters to Sanford, 1 January 1988.

10. TJ, "Wine jellies," undated, DLC.

11. Louise Conway Belden, *The Festive Tradition: Table Decoration and Desserts in America, 1650–1900*, A Winterthur Book (New York: W. W. Norton & Company, 1983), 55, 158.

12. *MB*, 18 August 1791.

13. 1826 Inventory.

14. William M. Kelso, "A Report on the Archaeological Excavations at Monticello, Charlottesville, Virginia, 1979–1981," (Unpublished manuscript, Thomas Jefferson Memorial Foundation, 1982), 69–73.

15. Geoffrey Wills, *English and Irish Glass* (New York: Doubleday & Company, Inc., 1968), 12.

16. 1815 Tax List.

17. 1790 Packing; 1815 Tax List; 1826 Inventory.

18. *MB*, 8 February 1775.

19. TJ to M. de Neuville, 13 December 1818, L and B, 15:178.

20. For more information on the subject, see R. de Treville Lawrence, Sr., ed., *Jefferson and Wine* (The Plains, Virginia: Vinifera Wine Growers Association, c. 1976).

21. Daniel Webster, *Visitors*, 98–99.

22. 1790 Packing.

23. Martha Jefferson Randolph to TJ, 12 July 1803, *Family Letters*, 247.

24. 1826 Inventory.

25. TJ to Vine Utley, 21 March 1819, L and B, 15:187.

26. G. Bernard Hughes, *English, Scottish and Irish Table Glass: From the Sixteenth Century to 1820* (New York: Bramhall House, 1956), 333–34.

27. *MB*, 9 June 1767.

28. TJ to John Barnes, 7 August 1801, CSmH.

29. 1826 Inventory.

30. *MB*, 18 October 1772. "Glass cylinders" was the term Jefferson used for hurricane shades used to shield burning candles from drafts.

31. Helen McKearin and Kenneth M. Wilson, *American Bottles and Flasks and Their Ancestry* (New York: Crown Publishers, Inc., 1978), 224–26; TJ to Vine Utley, 21 March 1819, L and B, 15:187.

32. Virginia Jefferson Randolph to Nicholas P. Trist, Randall, 344.

33. Unless otherwise noted, these dates refer to known production dates or periods.

34. "Reconstruction" used in this manner refers to archaeological reconstruction of whole vessels from a number of shards. Some of the restored vessels shown here are also "restored," filled in and painted to match the original appearance of the ceramic.

35. "Provenience" is used in reference to archaeological objects. Like the decorative arts and art historical "provenance," this term refers to the origin of the piece, but more specifically identifies the grid location of excavation. For more discussion of archaeological methods, see Ivor Noel Hume, *Historical Archaeology* (New York: Alfred A. Knopf, 1969).

36. Jefferson made plans in 1770 to have a dry well dug "at the depth of 14 feet." Archaeologists uncovered this eighteenth-century excavation a little over two centuries later. It is clear from the nature of the deposition that the dry well was not put into permanent use. Jefferson's changing design for the house dependencies perhaps altered this project. Full reports of this excavation are located in the TJMF Archaeology Department. See also William Kelso, "A Report on the Archaeological Excavations at Monticello, Charlottesville, Virginia, 1979–1981" (unpublished manuscript, TJMF 1982).

37. This form, as well as many others produced in white saltglaze, were derived from earlier and contemporary forms first produced in silver and pewter.

38. For dating and discussion, see Ivor Noel Hume, *Guide to Colonial Artifacts* (New York: Alfred A. Knopf, 1969). There were other stonewares that were quite successful in the eighteenth century, many of them European. England produced a number of dry-bodied stonewares, too, but mostly in the form of tea services, not table services. For further reading see: Geoffrey A. Godden, *British Pottery, an Illustrated Guide* (New York: Clarkson N. Potter, Inc., 1975).

39. *Unearthing New England's Past*, Exhibition Catalogue (Lexington: Scottish Rite Museum and Library, Inc., 1984), 15–25.

40. For 1620, see Jean McClure Mudge, *Chinese Export Porcelain in North America* (New York: Clarkson N. Potter, Inc., 1986), 140; for 1791 see, Jean McClure Mudge, *Chinese Export Porcelain for the American Trade 1785–1835*, 2nd ed. (Newark: University of Delaware Press, 1981), 256–57.

41. *MB*, November 23, 1812. While Jefferson paid for these patty pans while staying at his Bedford retreat, we do not know if he intended to use them there or elsewhere, nor if they were of porcelain.

42. The archaeological deposit referred to as the Garden

Wall was uncovered in 1981, while the existing wall running south along the garden was being restored. Because records date the wall construction to 1808, this deposit is one of a particularly rare and sought-after type which archaeologists refer to as "time capsules." This deposit contains a large number of tewares. The presence of these objects together and the fact that most all the fragments could be mended suggests that they were broken all at once and deposited together. The "tray" included delft, creamware, and porcelain, offering evidence of the range of ceramic types that were used together in the early nineteenth century.

43. The variety of vessels and the population of potters producing creamware is discussed in Donald Towner, *Creamware* (London: Faber and Faber, 1978).

44. Martha Jefferson Randolph to TJ, 16 January 1791, *Family Letters*, 68. "I took account of the plate china &c. and locked up all that was not in immediate use not recollecting that there was a set of queens ware here I sent to Richmond for some, by which means the china was preserved entire except our beautiful cups which being obliged to leave out are all broke but one."

45. A further "refinement" of creamware, pearlware, had a blue-tinted glaze and became extremely popular in the late eighteenth century.

46. George L. Miller, "A Revised Set of CC Index Values for Classification and Economic Scaling of English Ceramics from 1787 to 1880," *Historical Archaeology* 25, (1991): 1.

47. Creamware, like many other eighteenth-century English ceramics, was rarely marked. Even when it was, the mark was often one used by more than one pottery. It should also be noted that the practice of "borrowing" between potters meant that virtually identical vessels might be produced by many different potteries, making stylistic attribution extremely difficult. The date of the deposit places it prior, or close to 1770. For potteries in production during this period, see Peter Walton, *Creamware and Other English Pottery at Temple Newsam House* (London: Manningham Press, 1976), 75.

48. Chinese "Imari" is used in reference to the color palette employed on this vessel. Historically this has also been called the "Japan pattern." Mudge, *Chinese Export Porcelain in North America*, 157.

49. Underglaze blue is a general term used to refer to the type of decoration applied to this type of Chinese porcelain. This particular type is often referred to as "Nanking," a historical term once thought to refer to the location where this style developed. This is misleading as Nanking was one stop along the long trip from kiln to port. It has been suggested that although eighteenth-century Americans were familiar with the term, they were not able to distinguish between "Nanking" and other wares such as "Canton" and that both terms were used loosely to refer to anything blue and white.

50. "Peony" is a pattern name employed by Monticello archaeologists solely for the purpose of recognition. Underglaze-blue patterns such as this one were not only abundant but rarely given a particular name. Unlike the more expensive overglaze patterns, which were often "special ordered," merchants usually bought stock underglaze-blue from their suppliers in China, with the knowledge that whatever they chose would find an appreciative market back home. This name is based on elements of the pattern, as seen in Christie's 1986 catalogue of *The Nanking Cargo, Sale of Chinese Export Porcelain*

and Gold, European Glass and Stoneware (Amsterdam: Christie's BV, 1986), 12–13, 162–63.

51. Paul Atterbury, ed., *The History of Porcelain* (London: Orbis Publishing, 1982), chapter five.

52. Jefferson sought to match his porcelain in 1786: TJ to William Macarty, 8 October 1786, *Papers*, 10:436; bought "cups for tea, coffee and chocolate . . ." In 1788, TJ to André Limozin, 27 March, *Papers*, 12:693, he ordered (and then returned) a set of porcelain between 1790–1793. Archaeology has recovered a number of different Chinese porcelain patterns at Monticello.

53. This pattern was popular for at least twenty to thirty years, according to D.F. Lunsingh Scheurleer, *Chinese Export Porcelain Chine de Commande* (London: Faber and Faber, 1974), 158. There is some disagreement as to whether the pattern was used first in England or China. See David Howard and John Ayers, *China for the West* (London and New York: Sotheby Parke Bernet, 1978), 364.

Scientific Instruments (pp. 350–363)

1. Peter Jefferson's will and inventory, *Albemarle County Will Book*, 2:33, 41.

2. TJ, "Autobiography," in *Thomas Jefferson: Writings*, ed. Merrill D. Peterson, (New York: Library of America, 1984), 4.

3. TJ to John Trumbull, 15 February 1789, *Papers*, 14:561.

4. TJ to Wilson Cary Nicholas, 19 April 1816, L and B, 14:484.

5. TJ to John Page, 4 May 1786, *Papers*, 9:445; List of "Mathematical Apparatus," undated, MHi, Bedini, 500–2.

6. TJ to Caspar Wistar, 10 June 1817, DLC.

7. TJ to P. S. Dupont de Nemours, 2 March 1809, Peterson, ed., *Writings*, 1203.

8. TJ to Bishop James Madison, 29 December 1811, DLC.

9. TJ to William Short, 3 January 1826, MHi.

10. TJ to David Rittenhouse, 19 July 1778, *Papers*, 2:202–3.

11. Footnote, *Papers*, 6:418–19.

12. Petit's List of Packages sent to Richmond, [c. 12 May 1793], *Papers* (forthcoming), 25:873.

13. TJ to John Jones, 26 December 1792, *Papers*, 24:790; W. and S. Jones to TJ, 9 March 1793, DLC; Patrick Hart to TJ, 1 December 1793, DLC.

14. William Small to TJ, 23 July 1807, MHi.

15. List of "Mathematical Apparatus," Bedini, 501.

16. TJ to Robert Patterson, 27 December 1812, DLC.

17. TJ to Abbé Rochon, 14 December 1813, ViW.

18. Randall, 1:337.

19. *MB*, 21 March 1786; List of "Mathematical Apparatus," Bedini, 501.

20. Alexander Donald to TJ, 10 March 1793, MHi.

21. TJ to David Rittenhouse, 12 August 1792, *Papers*, 24:287–88; *MB*, 5 January 1793; TJ to William Lambert, 29 November 1822, L and B, 14:347.

22. Bedini, 229, 344–46.

23. TJ to William Short, 3 January 1826, MHi. A second pedestal achromatic telescope made by Peter and John Dollond that is owned by the University of Virginia may have been deposited there according to Jefferson's intention. It has been on loan to TJMF since 1949.

24. *MB*, 12 January 1778.

25. TJ to Alden Partridge, 2 January 1816, DLC.

26. TJ to David Rittenhouse, 19 July 1778, *Papers*, 2:202.

27. *MB*, 15 April 1786.

28. TJ, list, undated Jefferson Papers, 42801, DLC.

29. TJ to G. C. de La Coste, 24 May 1807, L and B, 11:206.

30. Smith, 393.

31. TJ to John Adams, 11 April 1823, Cappon, 2:592.

32. TJ to William Jones, 25 October 1806, DLC.

33. List of "Mathematical Apparatus," MHi.

34. P. & J. Dollond invoice, 3 April 1786, ViU; TJ to Thomas Skidmore, 29 August 1822, DLC.

35. 1826 Inventory.

36. John Hartwell Cocke to T. J. Randolph and N. P. Trist, 20 January 1827, Nicholas P. Trist Papers (#19313), DLC.

37. *MB*, 27 March 1786 and 12 December 1805; TJ to Thomas Freeman, 16 November 1805, DLC; list of "Mathematical Apparatus," Bedini, 501.

38. *MB*, 30 May 1769, 3 November 1780, 20 March 1787, 18 March 1791.

39. TJ, list, undated Jefferson Papers, 42081, DLC.

40. Travel journal, *Papers*, 11:437.

41. TJ to John Trumbull, c. 15 February 1788, 18 May 1788, *Papers*, 12:597; 13:178.

42. *MB*, 2–12 September 1791; TJ to William Short, 1 September 1791, *Papers*, 22:118.

43. *MB*, 3 January 1794.

44. Bedini, 374.

45. TJ to James Clarke, 22 May 1807, 5 September 1820, DLC; Bedini, 374–76.

46. TJ to Thomas Cooper, 27 October 1808, L and B, 12:182.

47. *MB*, 4 July 1776; *MB*, 1776, meteorological diary; TJ to Thomas Mann Randolph, 30 May 1790, *Papers*, 14:448.

48. TJ to Lewis E. Beck, 16 July 1824, L and B, 16:72.

49. TJ to William Jones, 10 December 1788, *Papers*, 14:346; Jones to TJ, 2 January 1789, *Papers*, 14:411.

Writing and Drawing Instruments (pp. 364–373)

1. For a full account, see Silvio A. Bedini, *Declaration of Independence Desk: Relic of Revolution* (Washington, D.C.: Smithsonian Institution Press, 1981).

2. Ibid., 36.

3. TJ to Ellen Randolph Coolidge, 14 November 1825, *Family Letters*, 461–62.

4. Joseph Coolidge to TJ, 27 February 1826, DLC.

5. For information about other writing desks associated with Jefferson, see Susan R. Stein, "Thomas Jefferson's Traveling Desks," *Antiques* 133 (May 1988):1156–59.

6. TJ to Ebenezer Hazard, 18 February 1791, *Papers*, 19:287.

7. TJ to Robert Walsh, 5 April 1823, DLC.

8. TJ to Robert Morris, 15 August 1783, *Papers*, 15:608; Silvio A. Bedini, *Thomas Jefferson and His Copying Machines* (Charlottesville: University Press of Virginia, 1984), 13–16.

9. TJ to Bishop James Madison, 2 October 1785, *Papers*, 9:576.

10. TJ to William Carmichael, 26 December 1786, *Papers*, 10:634.

11. Bedini, *Copying Machines*, 28.

12. TJ to Charles Willson Peale, 5 October 1807 and 15 January 1809, *The Selected Papers of Charles Willson Peale and his Family*, ed. Lillian B. Miller (New Haven: Yale University Press, 1988), 2, Pt. 2,: 1032–33, 1168–69.

13. TJ to William A. Burwell, 26 March 1804, DLC.

14. Gilbert Chinard, *Thomas Jefferson, the Apostle of*

Americanism (Boston: Little, Brown, and Company, 1929), xvi.

15. TJ to W. S. Smith, 9 July 1786, *Papers*, 10:116; TJ to William Carmichael, 26 December 1786; *Papers*, 10:634; TJ to James Madison, 30 January 1787, *Papers*, 11:97.

16. Bedini, *Copying Machines*, 22–23.

17. TJ to James Bowdoin, 10 July 1806, L and B, 11:118. Bedini, *Copying Machines*, provides an excellent account of the development of the polygraph and Jefferson's championing of it.

18. TJ to C. W. Peale, 15 January 1809, *Peale Papers*, 2, Pt. 2, 1168–69.

19. *MB*, 11 April 1786. This machine was also included on Jefferson's list of "Mathematical Apparatus," undated, Bedini, 502.

20. *MB*, 6 November 1806. The case bears Letelier's mark.

21. Maya Hambly, *Drawing Instruments 1580–1980* (London: Sotheby's Publications, 1988), 154, 185.

22. *MB*, 29 March 1786.

23. *MB*, 18 July 1808.

24. A portable drawing board and scale are listed on William and Samuel Jones invoice to TJ, 23 July 1805, MoSHi.

25. TJ, Notes of a tour through Holland and the Rhine Valley, 1788, *Papers*, 13:8–36.

26. Charles Brownell et al., *The Making of Virginia Architecture* (Richmond: Virginia Museum of Fine Arts, 1992), 150–62.

27. Hambly, *Drawing Instruments*, 69, 84.

28. TJ to David Humphreys, 5 January [1786], *Papers*, 9:152–53.

29. Sowerby, 3718. Hambly, *Drawing Instruments*, 28–29, 48.

30. TJ to William Jones, 25 October 1806, DLC.

31. Fiske Kimball's *Thomas Jefferson, Architect* (Boston, 1916; reprint, New York: De Capo Press, 1968) remains the definitive work on Jefferson's architectural drawings. See also Frederick D. Nichols, *Thomas Jefferson's Architectural Drawings*, 4th ed. (Charlottesville, Virginia: Thomas Jefferson Memorial Foundation, 1978).

32. Malone, 1:32. Based on its early date and substantial wear, the single-handed divider may have been one of Peter Jefferson's tools. Though it was probably intended for use with nautical charts, it may have been employed with surveys and other maps.

33. Jefferson's Memorandum Books show seven purchases in the spring of 1786 from London makers.

34. TJ to William Jones, 25 October 1806, DLC.

35. Brownell et al., *The Making of Virginia Architecture*, 150–52.

36. TJ to David Rittenhouse, 19 March 1791, *Papers*, 19:584.

37. TJ to James Monroe, 10 May 1786, Ibid., 9:499.

Clocks (pp. 374–381)

1. Frederick D. Nichols, *Thomas Jefferson's Architectural Drawings*, 4th ed. (Charlottesville, VA: Thomas Jefferson Memorial Foundation, 1978), no. 56.

2. TJ, Notes of a Tour of English Gardens [2–14 April] 1786, *Papers* 9:369–75.

3. TJ to William Short, enclosure in letter of 6 April 1790, *Papers*, 16:321.

4. Ibid.

5. William Short to TJ, 14 June 1790, *Papers*, 16:501; William Short to TJ, 4 August 1790, *Papers*, 17:315; Delamotte to TJ, 12 August 1791, *Papers*, 22:31.

6. Sarah Randolph, "Mrs. Thomas Mann Randolph," in *Worthy Women of Our First Century*, ed. Mrs. O. J. Wister and Agnes Irwin (Philadelphia: Lippincott & Co., 1877), 59; Daniel Webster, "Notes of Mr. Jefferson's Conversation, 1824 at Monticello," *The Papers of Daniel Webster: Correspondence*, ed. Charles M. Wiltse and Harold D. Moser (Hanover, NH: University Press of New England, 1974), 1:370–71.

7. Webster, "Notes," *Webster Papers*, 370.

8. Martha Jefferson Randolph to unknown, 13 February 1827, as quoted in Randolph, *Worthy Women*, 59.

9. Ibid.

10. Martha Jefferson Randolph's Will, 18 April 1834, Edgehill-Randolph Papers (#1397), ViU.

11. Thomas Jefferson, "the great clock," undated manuscript, DLC.

12. TJ to Henry Remsen, Jr., 13 November 1792, DLC.

13. Franklin's gong is mentioned in Henry Remsen to TJ, 19 November 1792, DLC, after Jefferson's order, however Jefferson was likely already aware that Franklin owned a gong.

14. TJ to Robert Leslie, 12 December 1793, ViU.

15. *MB*, 27 April 1793; Silvio A. Bedini, "Thomas Jefferson Clock Designer," *Proceedings of the American Philosophical Society* 108, (June 1964): 165–70.

16. TJ to Archibald Stuart, 23 May 1795, ViU.

17. Jefferson gave a second gong to his good friend Archibald Stuart in Augusta County. *MB*, 30 October 1794, 11 December 1795; TJ to Archibald Stuart, 6 January 1797, ViHi.

18. *MB*, 9 July 1804.

19. TJ to James Dinsmore, 28 January 1804, transcription from Sotheby's catalogue, *Printed and Manuscript Americana*, 26 January 1983.

20. Thomas J. Metzgar and James B. Whisker, comps., *Pennsylvania Clockmakers and Watchmakers, Goldsmiths and Silversmiths, A Checklist* (Apollo, PA: Closson Press, 1989), 33; Brooks Palmer, *The Book of American Clocks* (New York: Macmillan and Co., 1928), 183; Margaret Berwind Schiffer, *Furniture and Its Makers of Chester County, Pennsylvania* (Philadelphia: University of Pennsylvania Press, 1966), 73; Arthur E. James, *Chester County Clocks and Their Makers*, (1947; reprint, [Chester, PA]: Schiffer Publishing Ltd., 1976), 103–7.

21. Benjamin Ferris to TJ, 20 June 1803, DLC.

22. *MB*, 8 June 1803.

23. TJ to Robert Leslie, 12 December 1793, ViU. The only other clock purchased after the Great Clock was an astronomical clock without a striking mechanism, which Jefferson kept near his cabinet for use in astronomical observations (Cat. #238).

24. Bear, 12–13.

25. *MB*, 15 February 1817.

26. 28 July 1827 entry, recorded under January 1828, Daybook of John Hartwell Cocke, John Hartwell Cocke Papers (#640), ViU.

27. Robert S. Jones to John H. Cocke, 27 January 1827, John Hartwell Cocke Papers (#640), ViU.

28. Bedini, 420–21.

29. TJ to Dr. Robert Patterson, 11 September 1811, L and B, 13:88–89.

30. Dr. Robert Patterson to TJ, 11 November 1811, MHi.

31. TJ to Dr. Robert Patterson, 10 November 1811, L and B, 13:108–9.

32. *MB*, 27 December 1815. See also Bedini, 421–22.

33. Bedini, 422.

34. Joseph Coolidge to Nicholas P. Trist, 5 January 1827, Nicholas P. Trist Papers (#19313), DLC.

35. Martha Jefferson Randolph to Septimia A. Randolph, 5 February 1827, Septimia R. Meikleham Papers (#4726A & B), ViU.

36. Samuel Radbill, ed., "The Autobiographical Ana of Robley Dunglison," *Transactions of the American Philosophical Society* n.s., 53 (1963), 34.

Maps (pp. 382–393)

1. TJ, "Autobiography," in *Thomas Jefferson: Writings*, ed. Merrill Peterson, (New York: Library of America, 1984), 3.

2. Edwin M. Betts, ed., *Thomas Jefferson's Garden Book* (Philadelphia: American Philosophical Society, 1944), 80, 84.

3. Jefferson's Hints to Americans Travelling in Europe, 1788, *Papers*, 13:264–76.

4. TJ to Pierre Charles L'Enfant, 10 April 1791, DLC.

5. Receipt from John March to TJ, 26 April 1805, MHi.

6. Smith, 385.

7. John C. Green, *American Science in the Age of Jefferson* (Ames: Iowa State University Press, 1984), 213.

8. TJ to Andrew Ellicott, 24 June 1812, L and B, 19:185.

9. John Melish to TJ, 23 November 1816, DLC; TJ to John Melish, 31 December 1816, DLC.

10. 1826 Inventory.

11. TJ, "Autobiography," *Thomas Jefferson: Writings*, 3–4.

12. Other maps that Jefferson listed as having consulted were Thomas Hutchins' map of the Western Country, and Scull's map of Pennsylvania. Dumas Malone, Introduction to *The Fry and Jefferson Map of Virginia and Maryland: Facsimiles of the 1754 and 1794 Printings* (Charlottesville: University Press of Virginia, 1966), 8. See also Coolie Verner, "The Maps and Plates Appearing with the Several Editions of Mr. Jefferson's 'Notes on the State of Virginia,'" *Virginia Magazine of History and Biography* 59 (January 1951), 21–33.

13. Malone, *Fry-Jefferson Map*, 9.

14. *Domestic Life*, 19–20.

15. Though the map was submitted in 1751, it was not acknowledged by authorities in England until March 1752. Malone, *Fry-Jefferson Map*, 11.

16. Ibid. and Malone, 1:24–27.

17. Walter W. Ristow, *American Maps and Mapmakers: Commercial Cartography in the Nineteenth Century* (Detroit, MI: Wayne State University Press, 1985), 121.

18. Earl G. Swem, *Maps Relating to Virginia* (1914; reprint, Richmond: Virginia State Library and Archives, 1989), 85.

19. *MB*, 22 June 1805 and 21 July 1807.

20. TJ to James Madison, 29 December 1811, as cited in Swem, *Maps*, 86.

21. John Wood and Herman Böÿe's 1826 Map of Virginia, which was not distributed until 1827, superceded Madison's map. Ristow, *American Maps*, 121–23. Seymour Schwartz and Ralph Ehrenberg, *The Mapping of America* (New York: Harry N. Abrams, 1980) cite 1826 as the end of the map's influence, 224.

22. See William Carmichael to TJ, 16 June 1786 for mention of a map of Mexico sent to TJ. Carmichael's description of this map's suppression by the government, and the timing of the shipment suggest that Carmichael's map of "Mexico" was actually the Cruz Cano map of South America. See *Papers*, 10:213–16 for a discussion of the details surrounding the map's reproduction.

23. TJ to William Stephen Smith, 10 August 1786, *Papers*, 10:211–17.

24. William Stephens Smith to TJ, 22 September 1786, *Papers* 10:398–99.

25. TJ to James Madison, 28 June 1791, DLC. Jefferson also asked Thomas Pinckney, then in London, to check on the map's progress. TJ to Thomas Pinckney, 24 June 1792, DLC.

26. TJ to William Tunnicliff, 25 April 1805, CSmH; W. & S. Jones bill to TJ, 3 August 1805, MoSHi.

27. *Papers*, 10:215.

28. G. R. Crone, *Maps and Their Makers: An Introduction to the History of Cartography* (London: Hutchinson, 1986), 139.

29. Schwartz and Ehrenberg, *Mapping of America*, 221.

30. Ronald Tooley, *Tooley's Dictionary of Mapmakers* (New York: Alan Liss, Inc., 1979), 24.

31. TJ to William Tunnicliff, 25 April 1805, CsMH; W. & S. Jones bill to TJ, 3 August 1805, MoSHi.

32. For a description of maps in the President's House, see Smith, 385.

33. These maps are in Monticello's collection.

34. 1826 Inventory. Next to the maps in the Entrance Hall is the following notation: "these maps we should like to have for the school, and particularly the map of South America."

35. Schwartz and Ehrenberg, *Mapping of America*, 221.

36. TJ to James Cheetham, 17 June 1803, DLC.

Natural History Specimens (pp. 394–403)

1. "John McDuffee to John Sullivan, with Answers to Queries concerning the Moose," 5 March 1784, enclosed in John Sullivan to TJ, 12 March 1784, *Papers*, 7:23.

2. For query replies see *Papers*, 7:28–30, 21–24, 317–20.

3. Sullivan to TJ, 22 June 1784, *Papers*, 7:317–20.

4. TJ to William Whipple, 7 January 1786, *Papers*, 7:161; TJ to Sullivan, 7 January 1786, *Papers*, 7:160.

5. Sullivan to TJ, 16 April 1787, *Papers*, 11:295–97; 26 April 1787, 11:320–21; 9 May 1787, 11:359; TJ to Sullivan, 5 October 1787, *Papers*, 12:208. For a summary of Sullivan's efforts, see Anna Clark Jones, "Antlers For Jefferson," *The New England Quarterly*, 12 (1939): 333–48.

6. TJ to Comte de Buffon, 1 October 1787, *Papers*, 12:194–95.

7. TJ to Sullivan, 5 October 1787, *Papers*, 12:208–9.

8. TJ to John Rutledge, Jr., 9 September 1788, *Papers*, 13:593–4.

9. Charles M. Wiltse and Harold D. Moser, eds., *The Papers of Daniel Webster: Correspondence* (Hanover, NH: University Press of New England, 1974), 1:376–77.

10. Meriwether Lewis to TJ, 7 April 1805, Jackson, 1:231–42.

11. Raymond D. Burroughs, *The Natural History of the Lewis and Clark Expedition* (East Lansing: Michigan State University Press, 1961), 133.

12. TJ Memorandum, "Sent to Monticello. Mar. 10. 06.," 10 March 1806, MHi.

13. Jackson, 1:292–98.

14. TJ's Instructions to Lewis, [20 June 1803], Jackson, 1:61.

15. Paul Russell Cutright, *Lewis and Clark: Pioneering Naturalists* (Chicago: University of Illinois Press, 1969), 29.

16. Meriwether Lewis to TJ, 7 April 1805, Jackson 1:231–42; TJ to William Claiborne, 14 July 1805,

Jackson 1:252; Etienne Lemaire to TJ, 12 August 1805, Jackson 1:253–54.

17. Etienne Lemaire to TJ, 12 August 1805, translated in Jackson, 1:253–54.

18. See Meriwether Lewis to TJ, 7 April 1805, Jackson, 1:231–42, for a full list of objects likely kept by Jefferson.

19. George Gaylord Simpson, "The Beginnings of American Vertebrate Paleontology in North America," *Proceedings of the American Philosophical Society* 86 (September 1942): 155.

20. TJ to George Rogers Clark, 19 December 1781, *Papers*, 6:139; TJ to Clark, 26 November 1782, *Papers*, 6:204. Jefferson sent similar requests to James Steptoe.

21. For a discussion of the historical use of the names mammoth and mastodon, see Simpson, "Beginnings of American Vertebrate Paleontology," n.20.

22. *Notes*, 53–54.

23. For a discussion of Jefferson's views on extinction, see Charles A. Miller, *Jefferson and Nature, An Interpretation*, (Baltimore: The Johns Hopkins University Press, 1988), 50–55. Jefferson also discussed the possibility of extinction with Ezra Stiles, President of Yale College. See *Papers*, 7:312–13; 364–65, 8:300.

24. John Stuart to TJ, 11 April 1796, cited in Julian P. Boyd, "The Megalonyx, the Megatherium, and Thomas Jefferson's Lapse of Memory," *Proceedings of the American Philosophical Society* 102 (October 1958): 421.

25. Ibid.

26. TJ to Benjamin Rush, 22 January 1797, L and B, 9:374; TJ to David Rittenhouse, 3 July 1796, DLC; TJ "A Memoir on the Discovery of Certain Bones of a Quadruped of the Clawed Kind in the Eastern Parts of Virginia," *Transactions of the American Philosophical Society* 4 (1799): 251.

27. For an exhaustive account of the circumstances surrounding Jefferson's error and the presentation of his paper, see Boyd, "Megalonyx," 420–35.

28. Dr. Caspar Wistar, "A Description of the Bones deposited, by the President, in the Museum of the Society," *Transactions of the American Philosophical Society* 4 (1799): 526–31.

29. Silvio Bedini, *Thomas Jefferson and American Vertebrate Paleontology*, Virginia Division of Mineral Resources, Publication 61 (Charlottesville, VA: Department of Mines, Minerals, and Energy, 1985), 10.

30. *Notes*, 43–44.

31. Meriwether Lewis to TJ, 3 October 1803, Jackson, 1:126–131.

32. TJ's Memorandum Book entry for 9 February 1808 records a payment of $199.66 for Clark's dig; TJ to David Ross, 24 February 1807, ViWC; Peale's Mastodon is discussed in Charles Coleman Sellers, *Mr. Peale's Museum* (New York: W. W. Norton & Co., 1980), 123–158.

33. TJ to William Clark, 19 December 1807, L and B, 11:404–5.

34. For more information see Howard Rice, "Jefferson's Gift of Fossils to the Museum of Natural History in Paris," *Proceedings of the American Philosophical Society* 95 (December 1951): 597–627.

35. Rice, "Gift," 620–21.

36. TJ to Caspar Wistar, 19 December 1807, DLC.

37. Several visitors to Monticello, such as the Baron de Montlezun and Lt. Francis Hall, mention seeing Mastodon bones in the Entrance Hall. Montlezun and Hall's visits are included in *Visitors*, 68–69, 74.

38. Richard Harlan, *Medical and Physical Researches*

(Philadelphia: Lydia R. Bailey, 1835), 409. University of Virginia Board of Visitor's Minutes, 19 July 1831, vol. 1, 260, ViU. Isaac Hayes published a paper on the Society's bones including the specimen from the University of Virginia in the 1834 volume of the Society's *Transactions*.

39. University of Virginia Board of Visitor's Minutes, vols. 1–3, ViU. A study is underway to determine which bones in the University's collection could have belonged to Jefferson.

40. Bedini, *Thomas Jefferson and American Vertebrate Paleontology*, 17.

Native American Artifacts (pp. 404–413)

1. TJ to Charles Willson Peale, 6 October 1805, DLC; TJ to Meriwether Lewis, 26 October 1806, Jackson, 2:351.

2. Meriwether Lewis to TJ, 23 September 1806, Jackson, 1:319–25; TJ to Meriwether Lewis, 26 October 1806, Jackson, 1:350–51.

3. TJ to William Clark, 12 September 1825, DLC.

4. Auguste Levasseur, *Lafayette in America in 1824 and 1825*, trans. John D. Goodman (New York: White Gallaher and White, 1829), 214.

5. Ibid.

6. TJ to John Adams, 11 June 1812, Cappon, 2:307.

7. *Notes*, 58.

8. Bernard W. Sheehan, "American Indians," in *Thomas Jefferson: A Reference Biography*, ed. Merrill Peterson (New York: Charles Scribner's Sons, 1986), 400.

9. *Notes*, 140.

10. *Notes*, 62.

11. *Notes*, 97–98, 101. His scientific approach to the excavation has been hailed as anticipating the "fundamental approach and the methods of modern archaeology by about a full century." See Karl Lehmann-Harleben, "Thomas Jefferson Archaeologist," *American Journal of Archaeology* 47 (April–June 1943), 161–63.

12. TJ to Meriwether Lewis, Jackson, 1:136–37.

13. James P. Ronda, *Lewis and Clark Among the Indians* (Lincoln: University of Nebraska Press, 1984), 1–4.

14. TJ's Instructions to Lewis, [20 June 1803], Jackson, 1:61.

15. Ibid., 1:64.

16. Meriwether Lewis to TJ, 7 April 1805, Jackson, 1:231–42; William Claiborne to the Collector at Baltimore, 23 July 1805, Jackson, 1:253; Etienne Lemaire to TJ, 12 August 1805, translated in Jackson, 1:253–54.

17. Meriwether Lewis to TJ, 7 April 1805, Jackson, 1:231–42; TJ to Charles Willson Peale, 6 October 1805, *The Selected Papers of Charles Willson Peale and His Family*, ed. Lillian B. Miller (New Haven: Yale University Press, 1988), 2, pt. 2, 893–95. TJ to Meriwether Lewis, 26 October 1806, Jackson, 1:350–51.

18. Meriwether Lewis to TJ, 7 April 1805, Jackson, 1:231–42. Jefferson's annotations denote where objects were distributed.

19. TJ to William Clark, 12 September 1825, DLC.

20. 18 June 1828 entry into Peale Museum Accession Book, Peale Papers, Historical Society of Pennsylvania.

21. Charles Coleman Sellers believed that Jefferson moved his Native American collection to his Poplar Forest retreat in Bedford County, Virginia, and that it was sold at an estate sale to Colonel Hutter. C. J. Hutter's half-brother purchased Poplar Forest in

1840. There is no evidence, however, that Jefferson moved his collection from Monticello and no record of any estate sale at Poplar Forest prior to 1828.

22. Meriwether Lewis to TJ, 7 April 1805, Jackson, 1:231–242.

23. According to one visitor, Sir Augustus John Foster, Jefferson had two buffalo hides with painted battle scenes, one in his Library and another in the Entrance Hall. Jefferson listed "An Indian painting of a battle between the Panis and Osages, on a buffalo pelt," as being on display in the Entrance Hall in his Catalogue of Paintings. It is unclear whether this robe is the same one sent by Lewis and Clark, which is now in the Peabody Museum.

24. George Ticknor, *Life, Letters, and Journals of George Ticknor* (Boston: James R. Osgood and Company, 1876), 1:34–38.

25. Louis Hue Girardin to TJ, 12 August 1820, MHi; TJ to Louis Hue Girardin, 17 August 1820, MHi.

26. As quoted by Dr. William C. Dabney to Dr. S.F. Baird, 29 April 1895, Smithsonian Institution, National Museum of Natural History.

27. Morgan Brown to TJ, 1 October 1799, DLC.

28. Catalogue.

29. A memoir of the Barclay family's time at Monticello notes that "a valuable and highly prized collection of heathen images was given Dr. Plummer of the Presbyterian Board of Missions, and were removed to the rooms of the American Board of Commissioners for Foreign Missions in Boston." Anna Mary Moon, "Sketches of the Moon and Barclay Families Including the Harris, Moorman, Johnson, Appling Families," unpublished manuscript, [1939]. Recent efforts to locate objects from this collection have been fruitless.

30. Harry Innes to TJ, 8 July 1790, *Papers* 17:20.

31. TJ to Innes, 7 March 1791, *Papers* 19:521–2.

32. *Proceedings of the American Philosophical Society*, 22, part 3 (1885), 196, as cited in *Papers*, 17:20.

33. Jay A. Levenson, ed., *Circa 1492: Art in the Age of Exploration* (Washington, D.C.: National Gallery of Art, 1991), 584; "Stone Images," *Tennessee Archaeologist* 4, no. 1 and 2, 66–67; Jefferson Chapman, Director, Frank H. McClung Museum, Knoxville, Tennessee, to Ann Lucas, 4 May 1992; Wanda Lawson, Historian, Etowah Indian Mounds, to Ann Lucas, April 1992; Kit Wesler, Director, Wickliffe Mounds Research Center, to Ann Lucas, 21 April 1992.

Lighting (pp. 414–421)

1. TJ to John Trumbull, 4 August 1789, *Papers*, 15:335.

2. John Trumbull to TJ, 18 September 1789, *Papers*, 15:453–54.

3. Seymour B. Wyler, *The Book of Sheffield Plate* (New York: Crown Publishers, 1949), 58–59.

4. Frederick Bradbury, *History of Old Sheffield Plate* (London: Macmillan and Co., Ltd., 1912), 214, 220.

5. "Thos. Jefferson Esqr. in a/c with. John Trumbull . . . ," 10 October 1789, MHi.

6. 1790 Packing.

7. Adrien Petit's list of packages sent to Richmond [c. 12 May 1793], *Papers* (forthcoming), 25:873.

8. *MB*, 27 May 1790; 11 July 1801.

9. 1815 Tax List.

10. 1826 Inventory.

11. Monticello Dispersal Sale receipts, [1827], Thomas Jefferson Manuscripts (#5291), ViU.

12. Edwin M. Betts, ed., *Thomas Jefferson's Farm Book*

(Princeton: Princeton University Press, 1953), 79–80, 83.

13. For comparable English lamps and accessories, see Winterthur Museum trade catalog #2872, [Catalog of Lighting Devices], c. 1810–1815.

14. Caldcleugh & Thomas invoice, 30 May 1805, MHi; *MB* 12 July 1805.

15. Caldcleugh & Thomas invoice, 30 May 1807, MHi; *MB*, 29 August 1807.

16. See Harold E. Gillingham, "An Historic Lamp Originally Owned by Thomas Jefferson," *Antiques* 14 (April 1928): 293–94; Auction catalog of the collection of Mr. and Mrs. Harrold E. Gillingham, April 16–20, 1945, Samuel T. Freeman & Co., Philadelphia, 56–57. For similar lamp see Frederick Bradbury, *History of Old Sheffield Plate* (London: Macmillan and Co., 1912), 395.

17. TJ to James Madison, 11 November 1784, *Papers*, 7:505; TJ to Charles Thomson, 11 November 1784, *Papers*, 7:518.

18. TJ to Thomson, 11 November 1784, *Papers*, 7:518 and TJ to Rev. William Smith, 19 February 1791, *Papers*, 19:112.

19. TJ to Richard Henry Lee, 22 April 1786, *Papers*, 9:397–98.

20. Argand fought and largely lost the battle over patent rights to the cylinder lamp in England and France. See Michael Schroder, *The Argand Burner: Its Origin and Development in France and England, 1780–1800* (Odense, Denmark: Odense University Press, 1968), especially 43–57.

21. *MB*, 27 March, 24 April, and 30 April 1786.

22. Richard Henry Lee to TJ, 29 October 1785, *Papers*, 8:685; TJ to Richard Henry Lee, 22 April 1786, *Papers*, 9:397.

23. Thomson to TJ, 8 July 1786, *Papers*, 10:102.

24. "Les Appliques Louis XV," *Connaissance des Arts* (November 1961), 87–89.

25. 1790 Packing.

26. Adrien Petit's list of packages sent to Richmond, [c. 12 May 1793], *Papers* (forthcoming), 25:872. Recent architectural investigations revealed symmetrical holes above the Parlor fireplace consistent with these sconces.

27. TJ to Thomas Jefferson Randolph, 13 October 1808, *Family Letters*, 350.

28. TJ to Thomas Jefferson Randolph, 27 October 1808, private collection; *MB*, 28 October 1808.

29. TJ to Thomas Jefferson Randolph, 6 May 1809, *Family Letters*, 392. In an undated memo, Jefferson wrote that the "alabaster vase and appendages weigh 11 lb." and would require 13 feet of suspending chain and around 5 feet of chain (3 pieces of 19″ each) "to be substituted for the 3. chains uniting the top and bottom pieces," MHi. The top piece to which Jefferson refers was most likely a shade, or "smoke bell" suspended directly over the center of the bowl at the joining of the three chains to prevent smoke from rising to the ceiling.

30. As quoted in Leroy Thwing, *Flickering Flames: A History of Domestic Lighting Through the Ages* (Rutland, VT: Charles E. Tuttle Co., 1958), 11–15. See also Roger W. Moss, *Lighting for Historic Houses* (Washington, D.C.: Preservation Press, 1988), 86.

31. TJ to Thomas Jefferson Randolph, 27 October 1808, private collection.

32. Sir Augustus John Foster, *Jeffersonian America: Notes on the United States of America Collected in the Years 1805–6–7 and 11–12*, ed. Richard Beale Davis (San Marino, CA: Huntington Library, 1954), 144ff.

Musical Instruments and Amusements (pp. 422–427)

1. Alan Kendall, *The World of Musical Instruments* (London: Hamlyn Publishing Group, Ltd., 1972), 27; Robert Spenser and Ian Harwood, "English Guitar," in *The New Grove Dictionary of Musical Instruments*, ed. Stanley Sadie (London: Macmillan Press, 1984), 706.

2. John Fesperman, "English Guitar," in *The Eye of Thomas Jefferson*, ed. William Howard Adams (Charlottesville: University Press of Virginia, 1981), 20; Kendall, *Musical Instruments*, 27.

3. *MB*, 31 August 1776.

4. *MB*, 5 September 1788 and 6 April 1789.

5. *MB*, 4 March 1816.

6. Virginia Randolph Trist to Henry S. Randall, 26 May 1839, *Domestic Life*, 348.

7. Virginia Jefferson Randolph to Nicholas P. Trist, 9 January 1824, Nicholas P. Trist Papers (2104), NcU.

8. Spenser and Harwood, "English Guitar," *The New Grove Dictionary*, 706.

9. TJ to John Paradise, 25 May 1786, *Papers*, 9:579.

10. Lucia C. Stanton, Monticello Dinner Keepsake, 12 April 1991, 4.

11. Charles Burney to TJ, 19 June 1786, *Papers*, 10:75–76.

12. Ibid., 75.

13. *Family Letters*, 4 April 1790, 51.

14. Virginia Randolph Trist to Ellen Randolph Coolidge, 3 September 1825, Edgehill-Randolph Papers (#1397), ViU.

15. For a good account of Kirckman's activity and his instruments, see Donald H. Boalch, *Makers of the Harpsichord and Clavichord 1440–1840* (Oxford: Clarendon Press, 1974), 84–95.

16. *MB*, 17 October 1769.

17. John H. Hammond, *The Camera Obscura, A Chronicle* (Bristol: Hilger, 1981), 80.

18. TJ to David Rittenhouse, 6 September 1793, PHi; *MB*, 3 January 1794.

19. TJ to Nathaniel Burwell, 14 March 1818, L and B 15:167.

20. William Jones to TJ, 22 January 1787, *Papers*, 11:61.

21. *MB*, 2 and 26 April 1786; P. & J. Dollond invoice, 3 April 1786, ViU; Alexander Pope to Edward Blount, 2 June 1725, in George Paston, *Mr. Pope: His Life and Times* (NY: G. P. Putnam's Sons, 1909), 308–9.

22. William Tatham to TJ, 15 June 1805, DLC; Learmonths & Berry invoice, 16 August 1805, DLC; TJ to Hewes & Miller, 9 November 1805, DLC.

23. TJ to John Wayles Eppes, 4 June 1808, ViU.

Personal Objects (pp. 428–433)

1. TJ to John F. Oliveira Fernandes, 28 February 1806, DLC.

2. Anne Cary Randolph to TJ, 11 July 1805, *Family Letters*, 276–77.

3. TJ to John F. Oliveira Fernandes, 28 February 1806, DLC.

4. John F. Oliveira Fernandes to TJ, 15 March 1806, DLC.

5. Ibid.

6. James Madison to Thomas Jefferson Randolph, 14 July 1826, private collection.

7. Dolley Madison to Thomas Jefferson Randolph, August, 1836, private collection.

8. Benjamin Smith Barton to TJ, 10 June 1806, DLC.

9. *DAB*, s.v., "Joseph Cabell"; Nathaniel F. Cabell,

ed., *Early History of the University of Virginia As Contained in the Letters of Thomas Jefferson and Joseph C. Cabell* (Richmond: J.W. Randolph, 1856), xxvii–xxix.

10. TJ to Joseph Cabell, 5 January 1815, Cabell, *History of the University*, 37; Malone, 6:142, 247, 267–74.

11. TJ to Joseph Cabell, 5 January 1815, Cabell, *History of the University*, 37.

12. TJ to Joseph Cabell, 21 April 1826, Ibid., 377.

13. *DAB*, s.v., "Joseph Cabell"; Cabell, *History of the University*, xxxv.

14. TJ to Vine Utley, 21 March 1819, L and B, 15:187.

15. Malone, 2:73.

16. *Domestic Life*, 382. At different times, Jefferson refers to this injury as either a dislocation or a broken bone.

17. TJ to Robert Mills, 3 March 1826, DLC.

18. Joseph Smith, *Explanation or Key, to the Various Manufactories of Sheffield, with Engravings of each Article*, ed. John S. Kebabia (Sheffield: J. Smith, 1816; reprint, South Burlington, Vermont: Early American Industries Association, 1975), figs. 253–54.

19. *MB*, 13 September 1810.

LENDERS TO THE EXHIBITION:

Academy of Natural Sciences of Philadelphia

Mary S. Allen

The American Numismatic Society, New York

The American Philosophical Society

Mrs. Cynthia K. Barlowe

The Boston Athenaeum

Allison C. and B. F. Byrd

Dr. and Mrs. Benjamin H. Caldwell, Jr.

Mr. and Mrs. Robert Carter

Carter Family, Shirley Plantation

Dr. William R. Coleman

Mr. T. Jefferson Coolidge, Jr.

Mrs. Joseph C. Cornwall (formerly Mrs. Charles B. Eddy, Jr.)

Mrs. Martina Graham Creger

Diplomatic Reception Rooms, United States Department of State

The J. Paul Getty Museum, Malibu, California

Mr. Robert E. Graham

Mr. Lawrence R. Greenough

The Historical Society of Pennsylvania

Historic Hudson Valley, Tarrytown, New York

Howard University, Moorland-Spingarn Research Center

James Monroe Museum and Memorial Library

Miss Sara Lois Jordan

Mrs. Robert H. Kean

Dr. Raymond Kimbrough, Jr.

Mrs. Lucy Buck LeGrand

The Library Company of Philadelphia

Library of Congress

Mr. John H. McMillan

The Mariners' Museum

The Maryland Historical Society, Baltimore

Massachusetts Historical Society

Mrs. James Hubard Mathewes

Maury Family

Missouri Historical Society, St. Louis

Mount Vernon Ladies' Association

Mrs. James C. Moyer

Mrs. Richard R. Mullings

Musée de Blérancourt

Museum of Early Southern Decorative Arts

Museum of Fine Arts, Boston

National Museum of American History, Smithsonian Institution

National Museum of Natural History, Smithsonian Institution

National Museum of the American Indian, Smithsonian Institution

National Portrait Gallery, Smithsonian Institution

New-York Historical Society, New York City

The New York Public Library

The Octagon Museum, The American Architectural Foundation

Mrs. John C. Parker

Peabody Museum of Archaeology and Ethnology, Harvard University

Philadelphia Museum of Art

Mrs. Rosella Trist Graham Schendel

Society of the Cincinnati

The Family of Margaret and Olivia Taylor

University of Virginia (Alderman Library, Manuscript Division, Special Collections Department; Biology Department; Environmental Sciences Department; School of Architecture; and School of Medicine)

Valentine Museum

Virginia Historical Society

Virginia Museum of Natural History, Virginia Polytechnic Institute

Mr. Houston Waring

Winterthur Museum

Worcester Art Museum, Worcester, Massachusetts

Yale University Art Gallery

PHOTOGRAPH CREDITS

The Publisher and the Thomas Jefferson Memorial Foundation thank all the lenders to the exhibition, institutions, and photographers who graciously furnished photographs for this book. All photographs were provided by lenders unless noted below. *Numbers refer to pages*.

This book was published to accompany the exhibition
The Worlds of Thomas Jefferson at Monticello,
April 13–December 31, 1993, organized by
the Thomas Jefferson Memorial Foundation.